D1598057

ENCYCLOPEDIA OF PROSTITUTION AND SEX WORK

ENCYCLOPEDIA OF PROSTITUTION AND SEX WORK

Volume 2
O–Z

Edited by
Melissa Hope Ditmore

GREENWOOD PRESS
Westport, Connecticut ◆ London

Library of Congress Cataloging-in-Publication Data

Encyclopedia of prostitution and sex work / edited by Melissa Hope Ditmore.
    p. cm.
    Includes bibliographical references and index.
    ISBN 0–313–32968–0 (set) — ISBN 0–313–32969–9 (vol. 1) — ISBN 0–313–32970–2 (vol. 2)
1. Prostitution—Encyclopedias. 2. Sex-oriented businesses—Encyclopedias.
HQ115.E53 2006
306.7403—dc22   2006010227

British Library Cataloguing in Publication Data is available.

Library of Congress Catalog Card Number: 2006010227
ISBN: 0–313–32968–0 (set)
        0–313–32969–9 (vol. 1)
        0–313–32970–2 (vol. 2)

First published in 2006

Greenwood Press, 88 Post Road West, Westport, CT 06881
An imprint of Greenwood Publishing Group, Inc.
www.greenwood.com

Printed in the United States of America

The paper used in this book complies with the
Permanent Paper Standard issued by the
National Information Standards Organization (Z39.48–1984).

10 9 8 7 6 5 4 3 2 1

Copyright Acknowledgments

The editor and publisher gratefully acknowledge permission for the use of the following material:

A more extensive version of Kerwin Kaye's entry on Male Prostitution was published in the *Journal of Homosexuality* 46, no. 1/2 (2003) under the title "Male Prostitution in the Twentieth Century: Pseudohomosexuals, Hoodlum Homosexuals, and Exploited Teens."

Alison Murray's entries on Forced Prostitution and Tourism are edited excerpts from *Pink Fits: Sex, Subcultures and Discourses in the Asia-Pacific* (Clayton, Australia: Monash Asia Institute, 2001), used with permission from the author.

Randall Platt's entry on Slang is extracted from her forthcoming *Slangmaster.*

Gail Pheterson's entry on Stigma is excerpted from "The Whore Stigma: Crimes of Unchastity," in her book *The Prostitution Prism* (Amsterdam: Amsterdam University Press, 1996, 65–89).

Stephanie Wahab's entry on Diversion Programs is an edited excerpt from "Evaluating the Usefulness of a Prostitution Diversion Project," *Qualitative Social Work*, in press, with permission from Sage Publications.

The entry on Feminism is a excerpted from Melissa Ditmore, "Trafficking and Prostitution: A Problematic Conflation" (PhD diss., City University of New York, 2002), with permission of the author.

Excerpts from *A Guide to Best Practice Occupational Health and Safety in the Australian Sex Industry*, Scarlet Alliance and the Australian Federation of AIDS Organizations, 2000. http://www.scarletalliance.org.au/pub/ are reprinted with permission from the Scarlet Alliance.

To the memory of my brother, Jonathan Levi Ditmore,
and my mentor and colleague, Paulo Longo

CONTENTS

ALPHABETICAL LIST OF ENTRIES

TOPICAL
LIST OF ENTRIES

ARTS AND CULTURE

African Literature, Postcolonial
American Literature
The Anatomie of Abuses
Ballet
Blues
British Literature
Canadian Literature
Chansons de Bilitis
Chinese Literature
Dutch Masters
Fallen Woman Trope
Fanny Hill
Fantasy and Science Fiction
Films
Films, Cult
Films, Documentary
Films, Exploitation
French Cinema
French Literature
Geisha
Gunsmoke
Hip-Hop
Imperial Chinese Theater
Intolerance
Japanese Cinema

Kama Sutra
Klute
Kuttani-mata
Latin American Cinema
Latin American Literature
Lucian's *Dialogues of the Courtesans*
Lulu
Male Prostitutes, Victorian Literature
Medieval Literature
Melas
Memoirs
Midnight Cowboy
Moll Flanders
My Secret Life
Opera
Peking Opera
Penny Dreadfuls
Poetry
Pretty Woman
Rahab
Rock Music
Romantic Literature
Sadie Thompson
Sins of the Cities
To Beg I Am Ashamed
Ukiyo-e

RELIGION

OCCUPATIONAL SAFETY AND HEALTH. Occupational safety and health refers to the standards that ensure that the well-being and safety of all workers are protected within the work environment. Many countries have occupational safety and health policies in place for those individuals who perform legal work; very few apply those standards to people who are involved in the sex industry. Two of the exceptions are **Australia and New Zealand**, which have created occupational safety and health guidelines for sex workers.

When applied to individuals involved in the sex industry, the existence of occupational safety and health standards recognizes the claim made by the sex workers' rights movement that all forms of sex work are legitimate occupations and should be viewed and treated as such. To view all sex work as an occupation draws attention to the need for the same standards of safety that are granted to workers in other industries. Policies for occupational safety and health are applicable to those who are doing legal or illegal work, as well as those who are employed by a business or who are self-employed. Also included in these policies are the managers, employers, and clients of sex workers, as well as individuals who own the businesses where sex work occurs. It is the responsibility of all who are involved in the sex industry to ensure that the work takes place in an environment where safety is guaranteed. The existence of occupational safety and health standards for sex workers recognizes the need to grant all individuals the basic **human right** of being safe and well while working (See Article 23 of the United Nations Universal Declaration of Human Rights).

Occupational safety and health standards can be applied to sex work in a variety of areas, such as health, the physical workplace environment, psychosocial factors, job performance in other venues (for example, those people who work independently), and employment rights. To address these aspects of the job, training would be developed, outreach would take place, partnerships would be established, and a commitment would be made to continually improve the levels of safety and the health of those in the sex industry. All of this would involve the participation of the sex workers because sex workers are the best sources to include when attempting to determine ways to improve their working experiences and environments.

To address sex worker health in an occupational safety and health framework, it is seen that information must be shared with all people involved. Therefore, information about safer sex would be given not only to the sex worker, but also to the client. Operational policies need to be in place for pregnant women so that the issue of reproductive health is acknowledged. Comprehensive training would be provided on the ways to safely use all equipment used during sex work (this includes items used for professional consensual sadomasochism) and advice about how to avoid repetitive strain injury. The beds provided in any facility must be in good repair and provide the proper support; massage oils and lubrication used should be nonallergenic; and the outfits worn by the workers are to be appropriate and conducive to good posture.

The workplace is also a focus of the occupational safety and health standard. The workplace facility must be clean. Included in this model of cleanliness is the provision of clean linens, sanitary facilities, and pools and spas that are routinely disinfected. At least one first aid kit must be readily available, fire safety regulations must be in place, external and internal areas must be adequately lit, and the temperature must be maintained at a comfortable level for the workers.

Among the psychosocial aspects factoring in occupational safety and health standards, **violence** is first and foremost. It must be a standard in all working situations that violence is neither accepted nor tolerated. Communication skills training would be provided, and employees, managers, and owners need to work together on developing documents and procedures to follow during potentially dangerous situations. All places are to have a strict policy that demands removing and not readmitting those people who violate the safety regulations. Furthermore, sex workers must have the ability to refuse service to anyone at any point in the transaction. If violent incidents do occur, the workers are to be supported and encouraged to do what they think best (this can include reporting the incident to the police and to fellow workers), and the management and owners need to ensure that employees receive the medical, legal, and counseling services that may be needed.

Many individuals in the sex industry work out of more than one location. For example, there are those who do outcall work. For outcall workers, specific things can be done to guarantee them safe and healthy working situations. When **clients** are booked, the name, address, and phone number of the client are to be recorded. Whoever is taking the call should then verify that the information given is correct and check the information against a "bad clients" list. When approaching the place where the transaction is to take place, the sex worker is to assess whether it is adequately lit and if the client is alone. It is in the best interest of sex workers to telephone someone to let that person know where they are. Upon meeting the client, the sex worker needs to evaluate the client for any potential dangers, such as intoxication. If everything is determined to be safe, the sex worker is to receive the money before any services are delivered, and then check the client for any visible signs of a **sexually transmitted infection**. The sex worker is to bring a kit that contains **condoms**, lubricant, dental dams, gloves, and any other tools of the trade. Additionally, a sex worker is to have in place a policy that addresses what is to be done in case of a condom slip or break.

As with other types of employment, occupational safety and health standards require the minimum level of employee rights. These rights include annual and public holidays, sick leave, bereavement leave, parental leave, minimum wage, and union membership rights. All workers are to be properly trained and supervised and granted adequate breaks between clients and shifts. In cases of employment disputes, workers are to have access to resolution processes.

Further Reading: "A Guide to Best Practice: Occupational Health and Safety in the Australian Sex Industry. 2000." Australian Federation of AIDS Organizations Web site http://www.afao.org.au/view_articles.asp?pxa = ve&pxs = 100&pxsc = &pxsgc = &id = 204; "A Guide to Occupational Health and Safety in the New Zealand Sex Industry. 2004." Department of Occupational Safety and Health of New Zealand Web site http://www.osh.dol.govt.nz/order/catalogue/235.shtml; "United Nations Universal Declaration of Human Rights." United Nations Web site http://www.un.org/Overview/rights.html.

Alexandra Lutnick

Opera

"If Berg had wanted Lulu to go down on Dr. Schön at the close of Act One, he would have said so, and written specific music for it—not left it to Thomas Adès, in *Powder Her Face,* to compose the music of opera's first fellation."

From Andrew Porter, "Lulu's Back in Town," *Times Literary Supplement,* 10 May 2002, p. 24.

OPERA. Opera has been the perfect medium for telling sentimental stories about prostitutes. Giuseppe Verdi's *La Traviata,* the best-known opera based on a prostitute's life, has become a classic, but its first performance in 1853 provoked outrage and controversy. *La Traviata* was to religious authorities in many cities what the film *Pretty Woman* was to secular American feminists in the 1990s. The opera was condemned because a prostitute, Violetta Valery, was sympathetically portrayed and central to the story—and audiences liked her.

Violetta has become the iconic prostitute in opera. Her character is an Italian adaption/version of another fictional **courtesan** with a "heart of gold": Marguerite Gautier, heroine of the Alexandre Dumas novel (and popular play) *La Dame aux Camelias.* Marguerite, in turn, was based on the well-known Paris courtesan, **Marie Duplessis**, who began working as a prostitute at the age of 12. Born in 1824, Duplessis left Normandy for Paris at 15 and died in 1847, at 23, after contracting tuberculosis. A few years before her death, she had a short love affair with Dumas.

Attacks on *La Traviata* were partly inspired by Violetta's perceived origins—her connection to a woman who had worked her way up from registered prostitute to celebrated courtesan. During negotiations with the Venetian censor, the central character's name was changed from Marguerita to Violetta. Verdi, who admired the Dumas play, reluctantly accepted the displacement of the action from current times to 1700 but complained bitterly about the further alterations imposed on later productions of the opera, which obfuscated the remaining links to Dumas's characters.

In 1937, when Alban Berg's opera **Lulu** debuted in Zurich, the opera world had grown accustomed to prostitutes as central characters, and Berg's music was more controversial than Lulu herself. A charismatic modern prostitute who marries three men in the first two acts and assumes multiple names, Lulu is the anti-Violetta. She is tried for the **murder** of her second husband but escapes imprisonment with the help of a lesbian companion, Countess Geschwitz.

Based on two plays by Frank Wedekind (*Earth Spirit* and *Pandora's Box*), the opera was incomplete when Berg died in 1935. The third act—in which Lulu becomes a streetwalker so as to elude a blackmailing sex trafficker—existed only in draft form and was suppressed by Berg's widow until 1976, when a complete version was performed at the Paris Opera.

In this thoroughly modern finale, Lulu does not die of romantic grief or consumption, and it would be unthinkable that a victim of societal hypocrisy could be saved by romantic happiness. Desperate and disoriented, Lulu picks up a **serial killer, Jack the Ripper.** Lulu, fatally wounded, expires, on a dramatic offstage scream of "No!"

Manon Lescaut, Abbé Prévost's celebrated novel (published in France in 1733) has inspired three significant operas. The beautiful, confused central character is a prostitute who tempts a besotted priest away from his vows. In 1856, Daniel Auber's opera was coy about Manon's sexual identity. Verdi's *La Traviata* was not yet established or influential. Post-*Traviata* versions of Manon Lescaut were more frank. In Jules Massenet's *Manon* (1884) and in Giacomo Puccini's *Manon Lescaut* (1893), the leading lady is imprisoned, then deported with a group of defiant prostitutes to New France (French colonial territory in the New World), where she dies of exposure in the arms of her devoted but hapless lover. Puccini, in a scene much admired for its daring realism, actually shows the embarkment of the deportees on stage.

In Jacques Offenbach's *The Tales of Hoffman* (1881), Giulietta, the courtesan, is not central but she is a memorable archetype: a temptress who ruins her customers by extracting an unbearable (and surreal) price. In exchange for intimacy, a man pays with his reflection (or his shadow). Hoffman, the central figure, kills a rival customer in a duel and loses his reflection, hoping to spend a night with Giulietta. Giulietta, who absconds with Hoffman's reflection, is both trickster and pawn. Enslaved by a diabolical procurer (Dapertutto), she is (like the other female characters in this opera) a victim of somebody else's game. She is, however, the most culpable and active of these female victims, perhaps because she is the only prostitute.

In *Peter Grimes* (1945), Benjamin Britten's first critically successful opera, two prostitutes are known as "the nieces" of Auntie, an innkeeper and madam. When the prostitute-nieces sing about the challenges of the male-female relationship, they are neither tragic nor surreal; they are joined by Auntie and a local schoolmistress. Peter Grimes himself is the tragic figure while the prostitutes, in this opera, are normal, upstanding (if saucy) citizens of the community who provide a sense of place.

La Rondine (1917) was Puccini's modern response to *La Traviata*. Magda, like Violetta, falls in love and is willing to give up her courtesan's life for romantic happiness. However, she follows a more practical path than her predecessor. When faced with social and financial difficulties, Magda renounces her only true love and returns to more profitable relationships. Violetta's 19th-century death scene is replaced with Magda's early 20th-century regret. Although this opera has been criticized for being merely sad (rather than tragic), a realistic approach to romantic loss and prostitution can also be seen as its strength. As attitudes toward prostitution continue to evolve, *La Rondine* seems more relevant and clear-eyed than *La Traviata*, yet prettier and more accessible than *Lulu*.

See also French Literature; Peking Opera.

Further Reading: Blier, Steven. "Portraits de Manon." *Opera News* 65, no. 9 (March 2001): 14; John, Nicholas, ed. *Violetta and Her Sisters: Female Responses to the "Lady of the Camellias."* New York: Faber and Faber, 1994; Perle, George. *The Operas of Alban Berg, Volume II: Lulu.* Berkeley: University of California Press, 1985; Phillips-Matz, Mary Jane. *Verdi: A Biography.* London: Oxford University Press, 1993, 1996; Porter, Andrew. "Lulu's Back in Town." *Times Literary Supplement,* 10 May 2002, p. 24; Prévost, Abbé. *Manon Lescaut.* Translated with introduction and notes by Angela Scholar. New York: Oxford University Press, 2004.

Tracy Quan

ORGANIZED CRIME. Organized **crime** owes much of its success and endurance to its co-optation of **brothel** prostitution in the late 19th and early 20th centuries. Along with gambling, boxing, and bootlegging, prostitution served as one of the mainstay vice industries, and thus sources of revenue, for organized crime in the United States. In the 19th century, brothel prostitution was widespread throughout the United States, in both major cities and on the frontier. Brothels at this time were largely owned and operated by women and were one of the few means by which women could attain wealth independently of men. In the latter half of the 19th century, control began to shift away from female brothel owners to male vice entrepreneurs, particularly ones who had strong connections to law enforcement, politicians, and other vice industries (such as gambling, rum-running, and narcotics).

There were several causes for this shift: the intensification of the Abolitionist movement and the emergence of **purity movements** such as the Women's Christian Temperance Movement and the American Purity Alliance in the major cities; a new wave of migration to the American frontier, one that also included wives and "respectable" women who were coming to create "civilization" in the now permanently settled mining towns; the invention of the telephone, and thus "**call girls**," which allowed prostitutes to establish an independent clientele; the passage of the **Mann Act** in 1910, which significantly increased the penalties for transporting women across state lines for sexual purposes and led to heavier police surveillance; and, in the post–Civil War South, the rise of Jim Crow segregation laws that required strict enforcement of racial segregation.

The destabilization of women-owned and -operated brothels translated into greater numbers of women working on the streets, out of private apartments, or in businesses owned by men. Whereas before men had largely been involved in prostitution only as clients, they were now in a position to profit from it. Neighborhood gangs with preestablished protection rackets easily extended their operations to "protect" (i.e., extort from) neighborhood prostitutes. Owners of saloons, theaters, and flophouses also quickly caught on to the economic potential of organized prostitution. As a result, prostitution became increasingly embedded in a larger, underground economy. This underground economy mirrored legitimate business in many ways in that it too was run by elites and was subject to mergers and acquisitions, hostile takeovers, and ambitious expansionism, albeit with considerably more **violence** involved. When **alcohol** was prohibited with the passage of the 18th Amendment in 1917, an all-out war emerged for control of bootlegging. Prostitution by that point was already deeply implicated and inextricably linked to this new underground industry.

La Cosa Nostra and the Syndicate are the earliest instances of truly "organized" organized crime and what is now often referred to as "the Mafia." These criminal organizations became significant players in gambling, prostitution, protection rackets, and other vice industries in the 1910s and early 1920s as a result of economic prosperity and the libertine "flapper" culture associated with it, a shift in the demographic make-up of immigrants, and ultimately the imposition of Prohibition in 1917. After a number of bloody turf wars and some strategic assassinations, Charles "Lucky" Luciano consolidated his power as the leader of the Syndicate in **New York City**. Johnnie Torrio, originally from Brooklyn, moved to **Chicago** and occupied an equivalent position there around the same time. Bootleggers from New York, Chicago, Detroit, Ohio, and elsewhere formed nationwide networks that carved up territories and parceled out industries so that everyone had his own particular piece of the pie. Control of prostitution became a central business venture in the underworld, as it was profitable and came to support the Syndicate's expansion into the heroin trade.

Luciano was the driving force behind the Mafia's widespread involvement with both prostitution and heroin. This decision was determined more by financial considerations than anything else. The predominance of the Mafia over its ethnic and regional rivals was attributable to its success in its bootlegging and bookmaking operations. With the end of Prohibition, Luciano looked to these new rackets to maintain the superiority of the Italian Mafia. Heroin and prostitution complemented one another. Luciano forced many small-time **pimps** out of business by actively introducing heroin to his prostitution labor force; heroin kept them quiescent and compliant, with a habit to support and only one way of doing so. By 1935, Luciano and his associates controlled 200 New York City brothels with 1,200 prostitutes, bringing in an estimated $10 million per year.

The sexual revolution of the 1960s and 1970s, along with the feminist movement, helped to change societal gender and sex norms. As a result, prostitution became less profitable for organized crime, at least within the U.S. domestic context. It was in the 1970s that organized crime began to redirect its operations toward the manufacture and distribution of pornography and away from prostitution. The adult film industry was dominated by organized crime until well into the 1980s, when videotape began to replace film as the primary medium.

In the 21st century, organized crime in the United States is still heavily involved in prostitution. Prostitution, pornography, sex **tourism**, and **trafficking** (whether voluntary or involuntary) remain important business activities for organized crime groups around the world, notably in Russia and other former Soviet countries, China, and many **Southeast Asian** countries.

See also Abolitionism; Appendix D, document 16; Crime.

Further Reading: Denisova, Tatyana A. "Trafficking in Women and Children for Purposes of Sexual Exploitation: The Criminological Aspect." *Trends in Organized Crime* 6 (2001): 30–36; Feder, Sid. *The Luciano Story.* New York: D. McKay, 1954; Gilfoyle, Timothy J. *City of Eros: New York City, Prostitution, and the Commercialization of Sex, 1790–1920.* New York: W. W. Norton, 1992; Hill, Marilynn Wood. *Their Sisters' Keepers: Prostitution in New York City, 1830–1870.* Berkeley: University of California Press, 1993; Hobson, Barbara Meil. *Uneasy Virtue: The Politics of Prostitution and the American Reform Tradition.* New York: Basic Books, 1987; Reppetto, Thomas A. *American Mafia: A History of Its Rise to Power.* New York: Henry Holt, 2004; Rosen, Ruth. *The Lost Sisterhood: Prostitution in America, 1900–1918.* Baltimore: Johns Hopkins University Press, 1982; Schloenhardt, Andreas. "Organized Crime and the Business of Migrant Trafficking." *Crime, Law and Social Change* 32, no. 3 (1999): 203–33.

Alexandra Gerber

P

PALERMO PROTOCOL. *See* **United Nations Trafficking Protocol.**

PALLAKE. The ancient Greek term *"pallake"* (or *"pallakis"*) refers to a concubine. Such a woman was not necessarily a prostitute, that is, a woman who offered sex for pay. A prostitute, however, whether **hetaera** or **porne,** could become a concubine. The determining factor appears to have been the expected permanence and exclusivity of the relationship. The *pallake* resided within the household, although only in the absence of a wife; her ongoing presence in a man's house distinguished her from other types of prostitutes. It could be argued that the *pallake* was not in fact a prostitute, but a common-law wife without citizen status, as she was typically of servile or foreign origins. Indeed, Plutarch referred to Aspasia, the mistress of Pericles, as a *pallake* and not a *hetaera*, probably for just this reason. Most concubines mentioned in Classical Greek literature are represented as the captives of war: they accompanied the Persian Army on its expedition into Greece and, after its defeat, were divided among the Greek soldiers. Not only were concubines typically of foreign birth, but the practice of concubinage in the mind of the Greeks conjured up the exotic and polygamous practices of foreigners. For example, all of the concubines mentioned by Xenophon were in the possession of foreign kings and leaders. Such women, however, could be Greek, as a passage from Herodotus shows, in which the concubine of a Persian man supplicates a Spartan king:

> Save me, your suppliant, O King of Sparta, from captive slavery!.... By birth I am Coan, the daughter of Hegetorides, son of Antagoras; in Cos the Persian captured me, taking me by force!

Although concubinage had foreign associations for the Greeks, its incorporation into the social fabric of Classical Athens is well attested in oratory. Such women could be slave or free, foreign or Attic. According to one oration, the law against adultery applied equally to the lawful wife and to the *pallake*.

See also Ancient World.

Further Reading: Davidson, James N. *Courtesans and Fishcakes: The Consuming Passions of Classical Athens.* New York: St. Martin's, 1998; Henry, Madeleine M. *Prisoner of History: Aspasia of Miletus and Her Biographical Tradition.* New York: Oxford University Press, 1995; Kurke, Leslie. *Coins, Bodies, Games and Gold: The Politics of Meaning in Archaic Greece.* Princeton, NJ: Princeton University Press, 1999; McClure, Laura. *Courtesans at the Table: Gender and the Greek Literary Tradition in Athenaeus.* New York: Routledge, 2003.

Laura McClure

PARAPHILIAS. Paraphilias, as defined by the *Diagnostic and Statistical Manual of Mental Disorders IV-TR (DSM-IV-TR)*, are a group of sexual activities that fall outside of the cultural norm, may cause harm if acted on, and cause the paraphiliac to experience emotional distress. The *DSM-IV-TR* has a strict set of guidelines for diagnosis of paraphilias. These guidelines include a durational component of at least six months of "recurrent, intense sexually arousing fantasies, sexual urges, or behaviors." Another component of diagnosis is that the person experiencing the paraphilia must have acted on those urges, or that "the fantasies, sexual urges, or behaviors cause clinically significant distress or impairment in social, occupational, or other important areas of functioning." One way to categorize the paraphilias is to class each into one of two categories: victimless and coercive. The coercive paraphilias assume a victim and a perpetrator, while the victimless paraphilias do not. Victimless paraphilias may still cause problems in the paraphiliac's social or occupational functioning, but no one else is being harmed by the paraphiliac's actions.

Although prostitutes may encounter clients who have paraphiliac orientations or tendencies, and may have clients who actively seek out satisfaction of paraphiliac urges, many people who indulge in alternative forms of sexual expression are not clinically considered paraphiliacs. Also, certain paraphilias currently listed may not be considered disorders in the future. For instance, homosexuality was listed in the *DSM-III*, but by 1980 it was removed. In May 2004 at the American Psychiatrist's Association's annual meeting, the idea of removing the category of paraphilias in the next revision of the *DSM* was presented.

In the case of prostitution, most paraphiliac clients who seek out a provider will be those who experience noncoercive, or victimless, paraphilias. Most of the coercive paraphilias have a component of predation that is a necessary element of the excitement of the act, therefore, planning out an encounter will not have the requisite elements for satisfaction of the coercive paraphilic urges. A planned-out scene that a client sets up with a prostitute that includes elements of consensual sadism is not likely to satisfy someone who experiences clinically defined paraphilic sadism.

Prostitutes may encounter a wide variety of unusual requests in the workplace. Most of these requests do not fall into the category of the paraphilias. For a victimless, unusual sexual desire to be diagnosed as a paraphilia, the individual must experience the desire or urge on a recurrent, ongoing basis, and this must be causing the individual distress.

See also Kink.

Further Reading: Herek, Gregory M. "Facts about Homosexuality and Mental Health." Sexual Orientation, Science, Education and Policy Web site http://psychology.ucdavis.edu/rainbow/html/facts_mental_health.html; Hucker, Stephen. "Paraphilias." PsychDirect Web site http://www.psychdirect.com/forensic/Criminology/para/paraphilia.htm; Moser, Charles, and Peggy J. Kleinplatz. "DSM-IV-TR and the Paraphilias: An Argument for Removal." Paper presented at the annual meeting of the American Psychiatric Association, San Francisco, CA, May 2004; .

LaSara Firefox

PARENT-DUCHÂTELET, ALEXANDRE-JEAN-BAPTISTE.

Alexandre-Jean-Baptiste Parent-Duchâtelet (1790–1836) was a French social commentator and researcher who made a particular study of prostitution in 19th-century France. His most influential work was *De la Prostitution dans la ville de Paris considérée sous le rapport de l'hygiène publique, de la morale et de l'administration* ("On prostitution in the city of Paris from the point of view of public hygiene, morality and administration"), published in 1836.

In addition to documenting the regulations governing prostitution in Paris and describing the outward circumstances of the women concerned, Parent-Duchâtelet devoted some space in his work to the moral and physical characteristics of prostitutes and assembling and codifying a number of stereotypes that had already obtained wide currency in society, thereby ensuring that they continued to be influential for some time to come. One such generally accepted stereotype concerned the so-called mental and emotional immaturity of the prostitute; she was seen as something of a child, who had not yet learned how to assimilate the values of society as a whole. Parent-Duchâtelet mentioned two physical stereotypes, which were to be repeated endlessly: plumpness of figure, ascribed to greed, laziness, and the taking of many warm baths, as well as to the clients' preferences, and a raucous voice, which he believed to be caused by social origin, abuse of **alcohol**, and exposure to cold.

He did not, however, agree with everything that was popularly said about prostitutes and listed some of the common beliefs so as to contradict them. He believed that the primary causes of women turning to prostitution were poverty, and, in many cases, a first incident of "seduction" (or **rape**). He considered that one of the reasons for the poverty of women was that men had been usurping jobs more suitable for women, such as waiting in restaurants and serving in shops.

Parent-Duchâtelet is most famous for having written that "Prostitutes are as inevitable in a great urban centre as are sewers, roads and rubbish dumps. The attitude of the authorities should be the same in regard to the former as to the latter."

See also France, Second Empire; Zola, Émile.

Further Reading: Parent-Duchâtelet, A.J.B. *De la Prostitution dans la ville de Paris, considérée sous le rapport de l'hygiène publique, de la morale et de l'administration.* Paris: J. B. Baillière, 1836; Ryan, M. *Prostitution in London, with a Comparative View of That of Paris and New York.* London: H. Baillière, 1839.

Virginia Rounding

PARESIS HALL.

A boy **brothel** and gay bar in **New York City** during the 1890s, Paresis Hall was located on the Bowery at 5th Street near Cooper Union. Through its own flagrancy, pulpit orations, and the crusades of various antivice groups, it was well known to the public as "a resort for male prostitutes," as one 1899 vice report phrased it.

Officially named Columbia Hall, the establishment was better known as Paresis Hall, a name taken from either a medical term for insanity or derived from the name of a patent medicine that advertised in saloons. This boy brothel was one of at least six other such resorts on the Bowery, including Little Bucks and Manilla Hall. Evidence suggests that Paresis Hall was in business from 1890–99 and beyond.

Charley Ford, age 18, a prostitute in a souvenir photo sold to his clients at Paresis Hall, a boy brothel on NYC's Bowery in the 1890s. Collection of Joe E. Jeffreys.

Functioning in a fashion similar to female brothels of the period, at Paresis Hall males as young as 14 sat for company at tables while openly offering their sexual services. Ten or more rooms or cubicles above the bar were available for private encounters. Biff Ellison, one of the principal lieutenants of the Five Pointers gang, managed the brothel. Prices reportedly started at $5 and went up from there depending on requirements, and this was split 70 percent to the house and 30 percent to the boy.

The space also functioned as a community gathering place for gay men primarily from the local immigrant and working-class populations but also hosted more affluent guests. Ralph Werther, a.k.a. Jennie June, wrote extensively of his involvement with a social group there calling themselves the Cercle Hermaphroditis. The group rented a room where they met and stored their drag items.

Paresis Hall also features in Caleb Carr's *New York Times* best-selling novel *The Alienist* (1994), most notably Chapter 11. In 2004, a series of inscribed photos of young men came up for auction that were claimed to be souvenirs that working boys in Paresis Hall sold their clients.

See also Male Prostitution.

Further Reading: Chauncey, George. *Gay New York: Gender, Urban Culture and the Making of the Gay Male World 1890–1940.* New York: Basic Books, 1994; Friedman, Mack. *Strapped for Cash: A History of American Hustler Culture.* Los Angeles: Alyson Books, 2003; Werther, Ralph, a.k.a. Jennie June. *The Female Impersonators.* New York: Medico-Legal Journal, 1922.

Joe E. Jeffreys

PATHOLOGY. Pathology in prostitutes has been a popular focus of investigation in social scientific research, usually as a potential causative or motivational factor in entering prostitution, or as an effect of involvement in prostitution. Although the "pathology as motivation" hypothesis has abated among researchers in recent years, research on pathology as an outcome of employment in prostitution continues. For some social scientists, involvement in prostitution has been assumed to be sufficient evidence of pathology, a priori of any psychiatric assessment of the prostitute. An example of this assumption may be seen in the title of one article: "Prostitution: Profession and Pathology" (Sagarin and Jolly 1997). The stereotype of the pathological prostitute often reaches outside the realm of academia into popular media; for example, books written by "experts" such as medical doctors, which portray prostitutes as desperate, deviant, and sick.

The assumption of pathology as a causative or motivational factor in entering prostitution can be see in one investigation of "deviant" male "hustlers" (Caukins and Coombs 1975). This study constructed a personality profile of the hustler as self-destructive, low in self-esteem, immature, antisocial, and lacking in personal boundaries. A similar argument arises in a study performed a decade later (Luckenbill 1986). The men sampled for these studies were assumed to be deviant a priori of any hypothesis testing. Deviancy in this sense can be assumed of male prostitutes, as evidenced by their involvement in prostitution.

For women who enter prostitution, prior traumatic life experiences are frequently investigated as factors that molded the psychology of the victim, in effect creating a "potential prostitute." Examples of this can be seen in psychodynamic literature that retrospectively investigates the prevalence of childhood sexual abuse (CSA) in prostitutes, theorizing that prostitution may be viewed as possible negative sequelae of such abuse. One commonly cited theory, termed "repetition compulsion," has been posited as an explanation for involvement in prostitution by persons with a history of CSA. According to this theory, persons working in prostitution are "re-experiencing" their original trauma through their work in prostitution, while at the same time, attempting to psychically "take control" over the situation and thus remove themselves from the position of the victim. Repetition-compulsion behaviors are frequently thought to be symptomatic of pathologies such as borderline personality disorder and **posttraumatic stress disorder** (PTSD), both of which some researchers argue act simultaneously as a cause *and* an effect of involvement in prostitution.

In the 1990s, violent experiences and PTSD in a sample of mainly street-working prostitutes in South Africa, Thailand, Turkey, the United States, and Zambia were assessed (Farley, Baral, Kiremire, and Sezgin 1998). This study found that most women (and the few men and transgendered prostitutes sampled) had experienced sexual **violence** in their work, and 67 percent met criteria for PTSD. However, there are several major limitations to this study, including the recruitment of a highly specific sample of persons who were mainly homeless and working on the street. Although the limits of generalizability of these findings are clear, the authors stated that "almost all those in prostitution are poor." Thus, poverty is seen as a finding of the research, and not an artifact of the sampling strategy (the authors argued that sampling non–street-based prostitutes proved too difficult to implement, and thus, with the exception of a small group of brothel-based prostitutes, non–street-based women were not included in the sample).

It has been theorized that when pathology does emerge in a male or female prostitute, it is the result of "the degradation involved," "the exploitation by customers," and the "struggle to maintain rationalizations" (for being a prostitute). Psychopathology has been measured in a sample of street-based, drug-using adult male prostitutes (Simon et al. 1992). Their sample was higher in symptomology than were "normal (non-prostitute) controls," but there were fewer symptoms when compared with psychiatric outpatients. These symptoms were seen to be as much attributable to the conditions of prostitution as they were to a psychological disorder that predated entry into prostitution. Regardless, these findings have been based on samples of men recruited almost entirely from the streets, then generalized to prostitutes working across all **venues**.

A more recent sample of street-based female prostitutes who use drugs assessed mental health problems such as anxiety and depression (Surratt et al. 2005). The authors found that more than one-third of the sample suffered from moderate to severe anxiety, and more than one-half were moderately to severely depressed. Approximately one-third of the sample also reported violence at the hands of a client within the previous year.

Clearly, work venue plays an important role in the emotional health of prostitutes. A ground-breaking study (Vanwesenbeeck 1994) that sampled female prostitutes in the Netherlands across all levels of the business, from the street to the highly paid independent escort, found a diversity of experiences among women working in prostitution. Approximately one-fourth of the sample were experiencing mental health problems such as anxiety, depression, and substance abuse, and another 25 percent scored higher on measures of emotional well-being than nonprostitute controls. The remaining 50 percent of women sampled scored somewhere in between.

Although the data from the Vanwesenbeeck sample clearly showed higher rates of mental disorders among samples of prostitutes than appear to exist in the general population, that venue was found to be associated with well-being in this study. Specifically, women who were working on the street were found to suffer from depression, anxiety, and substance abuse problems at higher rates than those working indoors. The findings of this study call into question the notion that prostitution is inherently traumatizing, and certainly that all prostitutes develop pathology as a result of their work. Other studies show that street-based sex workers suffer higher levels of violence than other sex workers. Following Vanwesenbeeck, many researchers call for further in-depth research that attends to contextual factors such as work venue, legal context, socioeconomic status, race/ethnicity, and other considerations that shape individual experience within sex work.

Outside of academic publications, some popular books written by "experts" such as medical doctors have reinforced stereotypes of the pathological prostitute by offering descriptions of prostitutes that are so exaggerated as to be almost cartoon-like. For example, in the classic (first published in 1969; updated and rereleased in 1999) sex manual, *Everything You Always Wanted to Know about Sex (But Were Afraid to Ask)*, psychiatrist David Reuben stated:

> All prostitutes have one thing in common. They hate men … deep underlying emotional problems drove them into the game. Basically, prostitution is an ironic form of revenge against all men…. Once a hooker, always a hooker. Sadly, unless some dramatic change like psychiatric treatment intervenes, that's usually the way it is.

Thirty years later, Reuben's opinions on the mental health of prostitutes showed little change:

> Obviously some women who choose to rent their vagina to dozens of men a week have emotional problems…. Some prostitutes have another characteristic in common—they hate men…. The full answer [to why they hate men] is a complicated one related to the underlying emotional situation that drove them into the game. Basically, prostitution is an ironic form of revenge against all men, acted out on the johns.

Reuben cited no research on prostitution to support his claim.

The stereotype of the pathological prostitute appears again more recently, this time in another sex manual authored by physicians, *The Joy of Gay Sex* (Silverstein and Picano 2003): "Think twice before hiring a hustler. While most of them are ordinary guys who may be oversexed and looking to make a few dollars, a few are angry, desperate, and even psychotic; every year gays are robbed, beaten…or killed by hustlers" (p. 133). Again, no research evidence was presented to validate the "psychosis" presumed of male prostitutes, much less any evidence of the crimes they commit. Ironically, a great deal of research has shown that it is usually the prostitute who is more vulnerable to being harmed during an encounter with a client.

In spite of the biased samples and unexamined a-priori assumptions, the findings resulting from the cited studies have been inappropriately generalized to other groups of sex workers, contributing to the labeling and marginalization of this group. The social and political consequences of this include increased **stigma**, discrimination, harassment, and violence against prostitutes.

In contrast to the theory of pathology as motivating or causative factor in entering prostitution, a consensus has emerged among most sex work researchers that economic need is usually a primary motive in entering sex work and that women, men, and transgendered individuals make the choice to enter prostitution for a variety of reasons. This view stresses the agency of the sex worker, even as it is acknowledged that most sex workers operate within a social structure that may offer limited options.

A large body of research has challenged notions of sex work as *inherently* forced and traumatizing. In a study of British indoor sex workers, it was written that

> theory that locates power and influence only with male customers or the wider structures that determine economic relations leaves female sex workers theoretically devoid of agency, responsibility and rationality (Sanders 2005, p. 336).

Following this rationale, some researchers have approached sex work as a rational choice of occupation. In a few studies, sex work has even been framed by individuals as potentially prosocial behavior. The Sex Workers Project at the Urban Justice Center of New York has approached sex work as legitimate work that is complicated by its criminalized status and marginalizing social context, a perspective that echoes that of Dutch researcher Ine Vanwesenbeeck.

For prostitutes of all genders and gender identities, recognizing that one's social status is stigmatized may lead to a reevaluation of one's personal worth. For those whose reevaluation leads to internalization of the stigma, personal well-being may be negatively impacted. The connection between social stigma attached to prostitution, internalization of such stigma, and resulting mental health problems remains a topic for future research among prostitutes.

See also Male Prostitution; Street-Based Prostitution.

Further Reading: Abramovich, E. "Childhood Sexual Abuse as a Risk Factor for Subsequent Involvement in Sex Work: A Review of Empirical Findings." *Journal of Psychology and Human Sexuality* 17 (2005): 131–46; Browne, Jan, and Victor Minichiello. "The Social and Work Context of Commercial Sex between Men: A Research Note." *Australian and New England Journal of Sociology* 32 (1996): 86–92; Caukins, S., and N. Coombs. "The Psychodynamics of Male Prostitution." *American Journal of Psychotherapy* 30 (1975): 441–52; Chapkis, Wendy. *Live Sex Acts: Women Performing Erotic Labor*. New York: Routledge, 1997; Farley, Melissa, Isin Baral, Merab Kiremire, and Ufuk Sezgin. "Prostitution in Five Countries: Violence and Posttraumatic Stress Disorder." *Feminism and Psychology* 8, no. 4 (1998): 405–26; Farley, M., and H. Barkan. "Prostitution, Violence against Women, and Posttraumatic Stress Disorder." *Women and Health* 27 (1998): 37–49; Farley, M., A. Cotton, J. Lynne et al. "Prostitution and Trafficking in Nine Countries: An Update on Violence and Posttraumatic Stress Disorder." In *Prostitution, Trafficking and Traumatic Stress*, ed. Melissa Farley Binghamton, NY: Haworth Press, 2003, pp. 33–74; Koken, Juline A., David S. Bimbi, Jeffrey T. Parsons, and Perry N. Halkitis. "The Experience of Stigma in the Lives of Male Internet Escorts." *Journal of Psychology* *and Human Sexuality* 16 (2004): 13–32; Lewis, J., and E. Maticka-Tyndale. "Methodological Challenges Conducting Research Related to Sex Work." In *Escort Services in a Border Town: Transmission Dynamics of STDs within and between Communities.* Report issued by Division of STD Prevention and Control, Laboratory Centres for Disease Control, Health Canada, Ottawa, 2000; Lewis, J., E. Maticka-Tyndale, F. Shaver, and H. Schramm. "Managing Risk and Safety on the Job: The Experiences of Canadian Sex Workers." *Journal of Psychology and Human Sexuality* 17 (2005): 147–67; Luckenbill, D. "Deviant Career Mobility: The Case of Male Prostitutes." *Social Problems* 33 (1986): 283–96; Morrison, T. G., and B. W. Whitehead. "Strategies of Stigma Resistance among Canadian Gay-Identified Sex Workers." *Journal of Psychology and Human Sexuality* 17 (2005): 169–79; Morse, E. V., P. M. Simon, H. J. Osofsky, P. M. Balson, and H. R. Gaumer. "The Male Street Prostitute: A Vector for Transmission of HIV Infection into the Heterosexual World." *Social Science and Medicine* 32 (1991): 535–39; Perkins, R., and G. Bennett. *Being a Prostitute: Prostitute Women and Prostitute Men.* 2nd ed. Sydney: George Allen and Unwin, 1997; Pheterson, Gail. "The Category 'Prostitute' in Social Scientific Inquiry." *Journal of Sex Research* 27 (August 1990): 397–407; Reuben, David. *Everything You Always Wanted to Know about Sex (But Were Afraid to Ask).* New York: Harper-Collins, 1969, 1999; Sagarin, E., and R. J. Jolly. "Prostitution: Profession and Pathology." In *Sexual Dynamics of Anti-Social Behavior,* 2nd ed., ed. L. B. Schlesinger and E. R. Revitch. Springfield, IL: Charles C. Thomas, 1997, pp. 9–30; Sanders, Teela. "It's Just Acting: Sex Workers' Strategies for Capitalizing on Sexuality." *Gender, Work and Organization* 12 (2005): 319–42; Shaver, Frances M. "Sex Work Research: Methodological and Ethical Challenges." *Journal of Interpersonal Violence* 20 (2005): 296–319; Silverstein, Charles and Felice Picano. *The Joy of Gay Sex.* New York: Harper-Collins, 2003; Simon, Patricia M., Edward V. Morse, Howard J. Osofsky, Paul M. Balson, and H. Richard Gaumier. "Psychological Characteristics of Male Street Prostitutes." *Archives of Sexual Behavior* 21, no. 1, (1992): 33–44; Simons, R. L., and L. B. Whitbeck. "Sexual Abuse as a Precursor to Prostitution and Victimization among Adolescent and Adult Homeless Women." *Journal of Family Issues* 12 (1991): 361–79; Surratt, H. L., S. P. Kurtz, J. C. Weaver, and J. A. Inciardi. "The Connections of Mental Health Problems, Violent Life Experiences, and the Social Milieu of the 'Stroll' with the HIV Risk Behaviors of Female Street Sex Workers." *Journal of Psychology and Human Sexuality* 17 (2005): 23–44; Thukral, Juhu, and Melissa Ditmore. *Revolving Door: An Analysis of Street-Based Prostitution in New York City.* New York: Urban Justice Center, 2003. http://www.sexworkersproject. org/reports/RevolvingDoor.html; Thukral, Juhu, Melissa Ditmore, and Alexandra Murphy. *Behind Closed Doors: An Analysis of Indoor Sex Work in New York City.* New York: Urban Justice Center, 2005. http://www.sexworkersproject.org/reports/BehindClosedDoors.html; Vanwesenbeeck, Ine. "Another Decade of Social Scientific Work on Sex Work: A Review of Research, 1990–2000." *Annual Review of Sex Research* 12 (2001): 242–89; Vanwesenbeeck, Ine. *Prostitutes' Well-Being and Risk.* Amsterdam: VU University Press, 1994.

Juline A. Koken

PATRIARCHY. Patriarchy is a theoretical social system in which men are dominant and women subordinate. The concept is used as a foundation for the feminist investigation of sexual relations. Within some feminist analyses, prostitution is seen as a product of a patriarchal society wherein women's primary purpose is to serve the needs and desires of men. This theory has been criticized by feminists, sex workers' advocates, and others for its one-dimensional analysis of power and failure to account for female agency.

The term "patriarchy" was first formulated by 19th-century social evolutionary theorists to describe the literal possession of family members by the male head of the household, in what many believed was the fundamental and universal structure of human society. The theory of patriarchy has since been used primarily by feminists during the late 20th and early 21st centuries to provide a historical explanation and analysis of male dominance and female subordination. In a patriarchal society, the formation of human personality is based on the interests of men, so that social and political structures serve to uphold male supremacy through techniques of control. One such technique is the male colonization of the female body through institutions such as law, **marriage**, organized **religion**, systemized **violence** against women, and the sex industry. Within this analysis, prostitution is seen as a product of a patriarchal system that defines women in terms of male desire as sexual objects to be used by men. Women who engage in prostitution are therefore understood either to have been forced into the industry or else to have internalized patriarchal values that deprive them of the human right to dignity. The conceptualization of prostitution as a product of patriarchy is particularly associated with the work of "anti-pornography" feminists **Andrea Dworkin** and **Catharine MacKinnon**.

The theory of patriarchy has been criticized by other feminists for its one-dimensional definition of power as a monolithic force, stemming from a specific source and possessed by men, and for its construction of women as powerless victims of the system. The idea that prostitutes are victims of patriarchy has also been widely criticized for ignoring the difference between free and **forced prostitution** and failing to recognize prostitutes as human beings with agency. This became a particularly contentious issue for the feminist movement during the "sex wars" of the 1980s and caused a rift between antipornography feminists and "pro-pornography" feminists, who acknowledge prostitution as a legitimate choice. Sex workers' advocates have also argued that the description of prostitution as a product of patriarchy depicts prostitutes as passive victims in need of rescuing, as opposed to adult workers capable of making their own decisions, and that such infantilization obstructs efforts to empower prostitutes.

See also Feminism.

Further Reading: Chapkis, Wendy. *Live Sex Acts: Women Performing Erotic Labor*. New York: Routledge, 1997; Duggan, Lisa, and Nan Hunter. *Sex Wars: Sexual Dissent and Political Culture*. New York: Routledge, 1995; Dworkin, Andrea. *Pornography: Men Possessing Women*. New York: Perigee, 1981; MacKinnon, Catharine. *Only Words*. Cambridge, MA: Harvard University Press, 1993.

Rachel Aimeé

PEARL, CORA. Cora Pearl (1835–86), a **courtesan** in France, was born in Plymouth, England, as Emma Elizabeth Crouch, daughter of a musician. Seduced early in life by a stranger, she began as a common prostitute but was aiming at men who would be willing to pay her bills as part of a more permanent arrangement. She made a successful career and her name came to be associated with such prominent figures as Duke de Morny and Prince Napoléon Joseph Charles Paul Bonaparte, cousin of the Emperor Napoléon. It seems that during her liaison with the Prince, Pearl had been granted access to Palais Royal so that she could visit him in his official residence. Pearl was famous for her English-style attractiveness—she was a sportswoman and loved horse-riding. In France, Pearl remained a foreigner. When in 1872 a young man, desperately in love with the courtesan, shot himself in front of Pearl, the Prefect of Police suggested that she leave the country. She did but two years later returned to France. Her popularity had diminished, and she could not afford the high style of living to which she was accustomed. In 1877, she sold her silver at an auction, but the proceeds were soon used up. In the last years of her life, she survived by collecting small sums of money from her former admirers. She died in 1886 of cancer of the intestines and was buried under her original name of Emma Elizabeth Crouch.

See also *Grandes Horizontales.*

Further Readings: Ringdal, Nils Johan. *Love for Sale: A World History of Prostitution.* Trans. Richard Daly. New York: Grove Press, 2004; Rounding, Virginia. *Grandes Horizontales: The Lives and Legends of Four Nineteenth-Century Courtesans.* New York: Bloomsbury, 2003.

Maria Mikolchak

PEER EDUCATION. Peer education describes the sharing by one or more sex workers of information, skills, techniques, and negotiation strategies with another sex worker(s). Peer education is a proven effective strategy used by sex worker organizations to engage their communities to develop responses to address issues of HIV/AIDS, **occupational safety and health**, **stigma** and marginalization, lobbying, law reform, and political representation.

However, this strategy is the replication, and formalization, of the traditional sharing of skills and information between older and younger sex workers, or between a more experienced and a new sex worker. This feature of sex work culture is acknowledged as early as the 16th century in Pietro Aretino's 1536 novel *The School of Whoredom.* Nanna explains the techniques of the **courtesan** to the much younger Pippa by comparing her talents to a haberdashery shop. "So, in her shop, a whore has sweet talk, smiles, kisses, glances—but this is nothing: in her hands and in her pussy she has rubies, pearls, diamonds, emeralds and the very melody of the world" (2003, p. 12).

Early Australian examples of peer education include self-funded provision and distribution of **condoms** in 1984 by sex workers to nearby Sydney brothels and street-based sex workers, followed by publication of a sex worker magazine in 1985. Local meetings were held at a community center to gain involvement by other sex workers. A Christmas pack, including Christmas cake and condoms, distributed to street sex–working peers on Christmas Eve was another early initiative. This was followed in 1986 by the funding of the Australian Prostitutes Collective (APC), the first-funded, peer-based sex worker organization.

Street-based sex workers in Australia were known to use condoms largely to avoid pregnancy and **sexually transmitted infections (STIs)** before the emergence of HIV, but brothel-based sex workers were slower to adopt condoms in part because of the illegality of their workplaces. Most brothels were operating under the pretense of being massage parlors and so were reluctant to have condoms on the premises in case condoms were seen as proof of prostitution.

Some brothel employees were discouraged from using condoms by brothel management for fear condom use would discourage clients. Brothel-based sex workers concealed condoms in their clothing to avoid detection and being fired. These circumstances contributed to the practice of applying condoms by mouth during oral sex—still a feature in many peer-education sessions to this day. This covert application method avoided the need for negotiation with clients and the condom was rarely noticed until after the client had ejaculated.

The successful HIV/AIDS and STI prevention work of sex worker organizations and projects in Australia can be attributed to the transformation of the historic practice of skill-sharing or imparting knowledge between sex workers into the invaluable work of current and past sex workers as peer educators. This would not have been effective without sex workers taking up the use of condoms in their workplaces. Peer education is recognized as a major contributing factor to the low rates of HIV and STIs among sex workers in Australia (National HIV/AIDS Strategy, 2005).

Peer education is supported by a community development framework using empowerment, sex-positive attitudes, and a shared interest in systemic advocacy and representation. The success of these frameworks in providing sex workers with a nonthreatening and nonjudgmental environment is illustrated by the number of sex workers who engage in peer education via their sex worker organization. A new worker entering the Australian sex industry is likely to be informed about the benefits of visiting the sex worker organization or may experience new worker training directly delivered by a sex worker organization. Sex worker organizations have a presence in sex industry workplaces via magazines, outreach visits, brochures, media activities, political representation, and public profiles. Some sex workers volunteer for their local sex worker organization. Many more become advocates for sex worker peer education and occupational safety and health rights within their workplace, ensuring that new workers are mentored and that workplace conditions are improved. These peer educators draw on information from their sex worker organization that may have been developed and added to by their peers over many years. In this way, knowledge spreads through the industry, either directly from or as a result of strong peer education strategies delivered by sex worker organizations.

Sex worker peer education is undermined when the strategy is isolated from a sex workers' rights framework or when sex worker peer educators are not housed within a sex worker community organization. Peer education cannot exist separately from a supportive sex worker community organization. Peer education that is not genuinely community-based is not only ineffective but results in a loss of support from sex workers. A community development framework requires continued participation by the sex worker community for the long term. Models that simply add a few low-paid sex workers to the bottom rungs of an organization that is otherwise driven and directed by non–sex workers do not effectively engage sex workers. Unless sex workers feel some ownership over the organization and can participate over the long term, an organization will become irrelevant.

Community development in this context involves skills building, mentoring, and/or resourcing members of a community to facilitate involvement, sharing and increasing of skills, knowledge, and capacity, and community involvement and relationships with other sex workers. Sex worker organizations around the world have deployed community development activities, including sex worker community publications, organization and participation in community events such as gay pride day, working groups and political forums addressing issues that affect sex workers, informational workshops on everything from taxation to **sadomasochism**, language classes, and performance groups (such as **Debby Doesn't Do It for Free**). All of these activities complement the usual array of safe sex, occupational safety and health, and workplace negotiation skills that are delivered through peer education by sex worker organizations.

The skills and knowledge of peer educators are captured to a high degree by modules from the **Scarlet Alliance** National Training Project *Working with Sex Workers & Community Development*. Sex worker peer educators are assessed against the identified essential skills, knowledge, and attributes of sex worker peer educators, gaining a Diploma in Community Education.

Tensions between sex worker communities and funders have often centered on the lack of acknowledgment that peer education owes its success to the fact that it is a strategy built into community development in which sex workers are engaged on a variety of levels around their workplace/space issues, and not solely on condom use.

Peer education has been challenged by sex workers who question the validity of the shared experience central to peer education when used in the context of HIV/AIDS and STI prevention education because sex workers are extremely diverse. Others believe persons who have worked as sex workers share an understanding and awareness of the stigma associated with sex work and the misconceptions of sex work and sex workers as portrayed by the mainstream media. Although the strategy that peer education describes is alive and well, even the term "peer education" can be problematic. The term has for many years been adopted by large AIDS development organizations and peer education has been divorced from community strategies in some organizations. There is also criticism of the patronizing nature of the word "education," which some believe does not reflect the emphasis on the two-way sharing of skills and techniques from which the strategy developed.

See also Appendix document 13.

Further Reading: Aretino, Pietro. *The School of Whoredom.* London: Hesperus Press, 2003; Australian Government. "National HIV/AIDS Strategy 2005–2008: Revitalising Australia's Response, 2005." http://www.health.gov.au/internet/wcms/publishing.nsf/Content/health-pubhlth-strateg-hiv_hepc-hiv-index.htm; Mawulisa S. "Principles of Peer Education with Sex Workers." Canberra, Australia: Scarlet Alliance, 2001; Murray, Alison. *Pink Fits: Sex, Subcultures and Discourses in the Asia-Pacific.* Clayton, Australia: Monash Asia Institute, Monash University Press.

Janelle Fawkes

PEKING OPERA. Peking Opera is regarded by many as the national **opera** of China. It integrates music, singing, speech, gesture, dance, acrobatics, makeup, costume, and stagecraft in a comprehensive art. The history of Peking Opera is also associated with sex and prostitution, especially during the early stages of its development.

The evolution of Peking Opera was influenced by *Clapper Opera, Kunqu, Xipi,* and *Erhuang,* and its origin could be traced back to the reign of Qianlong (1735–96) in the Qing Dynasty (1644–1911), when the Emperor's 80th birthday was celebrated and regional theaters were invited to the capital for performances. Following the Confucian social ethics of gender segregation, the Qing rulers at that time prohibited female performance on stage. Two actors who impersonated female roles, Wei Changsheng and Chen Yinguan, were quickly known for lewdness on stage and their love affairs with prominent men of the city, as their performances "captivated the minds" of both ordinary people and the aristocracy. Concerned with the moral corruption, the Imperial Court banned men from performing in Beijing.

Major themes of Peking Opera have dealt with love, **marriage, religion,** and injustice. The *Story of Sue San (Yu Tang Chun)* is a typical example of traditional Chinese drama. It recounted the tale of a poor girl named Su San who was sold as a prostitute because of family hardship. At the brothel, she fell in love with a young scholar named Wang Jinlong. Wang did not have sufficient funds to free Su San, so he decided to work hard at the civil service examination so that he could secure a high-ranking position in the Imperial Court and eventually marry her. At the same time, Su San was sold as a concubine by the brothel to a rich merchant named Shen Yanlin. Shen's wife was so jealous of Su San's beauty that she plotted to poison her. However, Shen accidentally drank the fatal drug, and Su San was subsequently accused of poisoning him and sentenced to death. Unwilling to give up, Su appealed to a higher court where her case eventually arrived before the presiding judge who turned out to be the scholar Wang Jinlong. He had lost contact with his first love in the intervening years. Wang examined the case carefully to reveal the truth, and the couple finally reunited.

Wang Fang, a veteran Kun Opera actress, second left, performs in her role as Yang Yuhuan, a concubine to a Qing dynasty emperor for the opera "The Palace of Eternal Youth" at a theater in Beijing, China, 2004. Courtesy of AP / Wide World Photos.

In spite of various genres and a fan base from all classes and ages, a main premise of the early Peking Operas was to entertain male audiences, and the role of women on stage was to serve men. For instance a classical play, *Longing for Worldly Pleasure* (*Si Fan*), told the story of a novice in a nunnery who escaped down the mountain in search of love. Another showpiece, *Intoxicated Concubine* ("*Drunken Beauty*," *Gui Fei Zui Jiu*), portrayed the life of Lady Yang Yuhuan (719–756), who was favored by Emperor Li Longji (685–762) of the Tang Dynasty (618–906). One day, Lady Yang prepared a banquet in the Imperial garden and waited for the Emperor to favor her with a visit. However, the Emperor unexpectedly went to the palace of Lady Mei, another concubine. Lady Yang was so disappointed that she indulged in drinking to drown her sorrow.

Although female performance was officially banned, the order was repeatedly violated in cheap amusement centers such as Tianqiao in Beijing, where the hoi polloi viewed the presence of women as intimate and enjoyable entertainment. Tailoring to the taste of the urban audiences, **actresses** commonly staged seductive performances with exaggerated love scenes, flirty glances, and enticing gestures. Women's theaters were therefore regarded by social conservatives as even more dangerous than **brothels**. They claimed that prostitutes could not easily seduce decent citizens. Despite the fact that such public performances were condemned by the defenders of traditional values, some of the male fans among the elite became ardent supporters of Peking Opera; they would write glowing reviews in the press and shower their adored artists with money and gifts. In return for male patronage, actresses usually had to pay in the form of companionship or sexual favors. Some of the performers became concubines of rich customers. The prevalent custom of *xiadan* (dallying with actresses or female impersonators) implied the improper intimate relationships between performers and their powerful patrons.

In ancient China, acting was considered a despicable trade, and actors and actresses were generally regarded as immoral people, in the same rank of beggars and prostitutes. Because of their lowly social status, various decrees were issued forbidding actors or members of their families from participating in the civil service examinations. In fact, some Chinese theaters in the early days were associated with brothels, and performers were inevitably linked with prostitutes. For instance, Lin Fenxian was a prostitute before shifting to a stage career. Even after she became a Peking Opera star in the early 20th century, she was still involved in her previous profession for extra income and protection. In her novel *Farewell to My Concubine*, (1992) Lillian Lee vividly depicted a prostitute who sold her son to an opera school. As he grew up, he had to bear the sexual harassment of Mandarin nobles and suffer his on-stage partner falling in love with another prostitute. The story was made by Chen Kaige into a feature film, starring Gong Li and Leslie Cheung; it instantly became an international sensation during the Cannes Film Festival in 1993.

Further Reading: Cheng, Weikun. "The Challenge of the Actresses: Female Performers and Cultural Alternatives in Early Twentieth Century Beijing and Tianjin." *Modern China* 22, no. 2 (April 1996): 197–233; Cheng, Weikun. "The Use of 'Public' Women: Commercialized Performance, Nation-Building, and Actresses' Strategies in Early Twentieth-Century Beijing." *Working Papers on Women and International Development* 275. June 2002. http://www.isp.msu.edu/wid/papers/pdf/WP275.pdf; Mackerras, Colin. "Peking Opera before the Twentieth Century." *Comparative Drama* 28, no. 1 (Spring 1994): 19–42; Tian, Min. "Male Dan: The Paradox of Sex, Acting, and Perception of Female Impersonation in Traditional Chinese Theatre." *Asian Theatre Journal* 17, no. 1 (Spring 2000): 78–97.

Wenxian Zhang

PELAGIA. Saint Pelagia, one of the **Desert Harlots**, was an actress in the city of Antioch. Although she may not have technically been a prostitute, she was, nevertheless, part of a group considered to be immoral and promiscuous. She was both beautiful and wealthy. In fact, the people of Antioch renamed her Margaret (which means "pearl") because of the gems that she had acquired through her sins.

One day, the young woman and her retinue happened by a group of Christian bishops. Fearful of their own lust, all the bishops but one, Nonnus, hid their faces at the sight of the scantily clad beauty. Nonnus, however, admired Pelagia as a beautiful creature of God. From his experience, he formulated a sermon comparing the prostitute who cultivates her beauty for her clients with the halfhearted Christian who fails to beautify his or her soul for God. Then he proceeded to pray fervently for the source of his inspiration, Pelagia. Pelagia, on hearing his sermon, was so moved that she begged Nonnus to baptize her. At first, he refused, but Pelagia persisted so doggedly that he eventually relented.

After her baptism, Pelagia donned male clothing and fled into the desert. Several years later, Nonnus sent his deacon, James, into the desert to visit the hermit Pelagius. James, finding the hermit almost completely enclosed in his cell, mentioned that he had been sent by Nonnus. The hermit requested that the bishop pray for him, and he closed up his cell and James left. However, before James returned to Antioch, he made one more attempt to visit the holy hermit. On his arrival, James found the cell quiet and the occupant deceased. It was at this point that he learned that the hermit Pelagius was really Pelagia, the former actress.

This hagiography has sometimes been described as a "love story" between Nonnus and Pelagia, despite the fact that they never acted on it. More important, Pelagia's story served as a rebuke for weak Church officials, who prostituted themselves to the world and did not repent. Finally, her story marked the beginning of the "transvestite saint" legend, which became somewhat common in the early desert tradition.

See also Actresses; Mary Magdalene; Mary of Egypt; Religion.

Further Reading: Cloke, Gillian. "*This Female Man of God*": *Women and Spiritual Power in the Patristic Age*, A.D. *350–450*. New York: Routledge, 1995; Pavlovskis, Zoja. "The Life of St. Pelagia the Harlot: Hagiographic Adaptation of Pagan Romance." *Classical Folio* 30 (1976): 138–49.

Michelle M. Sauer

PENAL COLONIES. Prostitution has been closely associated with the transportation of women convicts to British penal colonies. Convict labor was used to found a number of British colonies including Barbados, Jamaica, Maryland, Virginia, Singapore, New South Wales, Tasmania, and Western Australia. Between 1607 and 1939, Britain transported approximately 400,000 convicts, 162,000 of whom came to Australia and about 50,000 to North America. Significant numbers of women were among those transported to the Australian and North American colonies, although their numbers were relatively small in comparison to male convicts. Transportation was typically reserved for the most recalcitrant of female offenders. Most women transported came from working-class populations, resided in metropolitan centers, and were single at the time of their offense. Although few of these women were actually sentenced for activities associated with prostitution, large numbers had a history of involvement with prostitution. Transportation was considered to offer prostitutes a chance at redemption, with colonial commentators drawing contrasts between the Old World and its vice-ridden sensuality and the colonies, which offered opportunities for redemption through religious devotion and hard work.

Many women transported to the Australian colonies were described by officials as being "on the town" at their time of apprehension and were collectively considered to be "damned whores, possessed of neither virtue nor honesty." Recently, historians have argued that these assessments were emblematic of middle-class prejudices toward the open and aggressive sexuality of working-class women. The number of convict women involved in prostitution may have been higher than recorded crimes, typically involving "larceny," suggest. A number of women were charged with theft from men who had paid them (or, in some instances, refused to pay them) for sex. Historians have estimated that one in five convict women were part-time or full-time prostitutes before transportation. Many continued in prostitution after transportation, with prostitution becoming an important element in the social and economic life of the Australian colonies, where, between 1788–1830, men outnumbered women six to one. Officially, prostitution was tolerated to dissuade men from vice. For women, prostitution presented a means of securing physical protection and accommodation at a time when general amenities and employment opportunities were restricted.

The possibilities of redemption for "abandoned women" in the colonies were fictionalized in Daniel Defoe's popular novel ***Moll Flanders*** (1722). This book, which has been likened to a conversion narrative, tells the story of a country girl who travels to London and descends into a life of **crime**. Moll becomes a prostitute following the deaths of her four husbands, with whom she had previously traded sex for economic entitlements. In the 1800s, English law did not allow women to inherit anything when their husbands died, and Moll chooses prostitution to survive. Moll views sex as an economic ends and children as a byproduct of having sex, who are to be given away or sold upon birth. At the age of 48, when she can no longer profit from prostitution, Moll turns to other criminal activity, is caught, and imprisoned. While imprisoned, she is convinced by a priest to repent for her life of sin and the priest arranges for her to be transported to Virginia. Here, she is joined by her husband, with whom she establishes a happy and prosperous middle-class life. Defoe, a Puritan and advocate of transportation, contrasts the pains associated with a life of sensual pleasures with the rewards offered by industry.

See also Religion.

Further Reading: Robinson, Portia. *The Women of Botany Bay: A Reinterpretation of the Role of Women in the Origins of Australian Society*. Sydney: Macquarie Library, 1988.

John Scott

PENNY DREADFULS. Also called penny novels, bloods, and (in the United States) dime novels, penny dreadfuls circulated melodramatic tales of **crime** and adventure to a large audience during much of the 19th century. Because many of the stories shared an urban setting and an interest in crime, prostitutes and prostitution were commonly depicted in penny dreadfuls. Some publications, such as Renton Nicholson's *The Town* (1837–40), pushed the boundaries between melodrama and pornography through stories of **brothels** and public houses. Other issues described the sexual exploits of the aristocracy and reprinted erotic 18th-century narratives. Deemed "dreadful" because of their disregard for Victorian sexual and moral etiquette, penny dreadfuls were nonetheless extremely popular among working-class individuals, who for a penny, enjoyed the thrilling tales of romance, gore, and intrigue.

The *Young Ladies of London; or, The Mysteries of Midnight* (1867–68) captured both the melodrama and the raciness that distinguished many dreadfuls of the 1850s and 1860s aimed at an adult audience. Inspired by the rise of sensation fiction, newspaper accounts of crime and scandal, and a widespread interest in prostitution, *The Young Ladies* told the story of the wicked Count Lewiski who used his "Ghastly Gaskill" to drug innocent women and sexually exploit them in his Haymarket (**London**) brothel, which was vividly depicted on the frontispiece of the serial. *The Work Girls of London* (1865) also played on formulaic stories of victimized women, often from the middle class, who through misfortune found they must do needlework, and sometimes turn to prostitution, to survive. Many other dreadfuls such as G.W.M. Reynolds's *The Mysteries of London* (1844–46), which boasted sales of almost 40,000 a week, depicted London "low" life and frequently capitalized on stereotypes of prostitutes and their work. Depictions of prostitutes in penny dreadfuls often played with Victorian categorizations of women as either angels or whores, and while responding to male fantasies that envisioned sexual playmates who were intrinsically "pure," succeeded to some extent in collapsing the boundaries dividing good and bad women.

The penny dreadfuls, however, are difficult to categorize, because the term refers to several types of cheaply printed stories that evolved over the course of the century. In the 1830s, penny dreadfuls often followed the gothic theme of the late 18th century, and by the 1880s, penny dreadfuls were marketed toward young, primarily male, readers. With inferior-quality paper, illustrations, and writing, penny dreadfuls responded to a growing urban working class who was increasingly literate but unable to afford more expensive sources of literary entertainment. Published serially, initially in weekly numbers of eight pages that could later be bound together, the dreadfuls thrived among the urban poor, who found in them cheap, plagiarized versions of novelist **Charles Dickens**'s more expensive serial novels, as well as lurid tales that would have offended middle-class mores.

See also Stead, William, and "The Maiden Tribute of Modern Babylon"; Victorian Literature.

Further Reading: "Dime Novels and Penny Dreadfuls" http://www.sul.stanford.edu/depts/dp/pennies/home.html; Dunae, Patrick. "Penny Dreadfuls: Late Nineteenth-Century Boys' Literature and Crime." *Victorian Studies* 22 (1979):133–50; James, Louis. *Fiction for the Working Man 1830–50.* London: Oxford University Press, 1963; Springhall, John. "A Life Story for the People'? Edwin J. Brett and the London 'Low-Life' Penny Dreadfuls of the 1860s." *Victorian Studies* 33, no. 2 (1990): 223–46.

Esther Godfrey

PERVERSION. *See* **Kink; Paraphilias.**

PHRYNE (CA. 371 B.C.E.–330 B.C.E.). Phryne ("toad") is the nickname of one of the most frequently mentioned Greek **courtesans** in Classical literature. Her trial, as well as her love affair with the 4th-century Greek sculptor Praxiteles, contributed to her notoriety, which is said to have extended from Athens to all of Greece. The nickname "Phryne" referred to the paleness of the courtesan's complexion. She was also known by the name Saperdion ("little fish"). Phryne was probably born around 371 B.C.E., in Boeotian Thespia, and was the daughter of Epicles. Her real name was apparently Mnesarete. Phryne escaped her early poverty—the comic poets represent her as picking capers for her keep—to become one of the wealthiest women in the Hellenic world. She is best known for her impiety trial around 350 B.C.E., in which the orator Hyperides, possibly also one of her lovers, defended her. Moreover, she is said to have served as the model for Praxiteles' sculpture *Cnidian Aphrodite*, as well as for Apelles' painting *Aphrodite Rising from the Sea*, during the 340s B.C.E. She outlived the reconstruction of Thebes after 316 B.C.E. and even offered to finance the rebuilding of its city walls.

Phryne's legendary beauty explains her pervasive association with art works, rhetoric, and stories of **voyeurism** and display. At one religious festival, Phryne is said to have taken off her cloak in sight of all the Greeks, and, after letting down her hair, to have stepped into the sea. A central trope contrasts her genuine beauty with the spurious attractions of other courtesans. One anecdote recounts a party game in which Phryne required the women at the table, presumably all courtesans, to wash the makeup—alkanet, white lead, and red paint—off their faces. Full of blemishes, they looked like monsters, while Phryne appeared even more beautiful.

Phryne was also considered skillful at witticisms, as evidenced by some of her surviving jokes. In one, she responds to a client's complaint about her high price by stating that she will accept a lower amount when she, not he, wants to have sex. Others involve a man who smelled like a goat, the stinting amount of wine sent by an admirer, sympotic wreaths (used at drinking parties or banquets), and the mockery and flattery of her lovers. A popular story about her unsuccessful attempt to seduce a celibate philosopher gives the *hetaera* the last laugh. Although he had offered to share his only couch with her when she sought refuge inside his house, he refused to have intercourse with her. On her departure, she joked that she had left not a man but a statue.

Phryne is perhaps most famous for her public display of nudity in the law court. Charged with engaging in illicit activities under the pretext of **religion**, the courtesan hired the orator Hyperides to defend her. Desperate to win the case, the orator paraded Phryne into the courtroom and pulled off her clothes. Hyperides "delivered an epilogue made piteous at the sight of her and caused the jurors to fear as a deity this prophetess and servant of Aphrodite, and indulging in pity, they did not put her to death." The remarkable afterlife of this story is largely owing to its popularity among the late rhetorical writers and commentators, for whom it served as the supreme example of the pity schema, in addition to being a fine example of oratory.

See also Ancient World.

Further Reading: Davidson, James N. *Courtesans and Fishcakes: The Consuming Passions of Classical Athens.* New York: St. Martin's Press, 1998; Kurke, Laura. *Coins, Bodies, Games and Gold.* Princeton, N J: Princeton University Press, 1999; McClure, Laura. *Courtesans at Table: Gender and the Greek Literary Tradition in Athenaeus.* New York: Routledge, 2003.

Laura McClure

PIMPMOBILES. Pimps in the United States have been stereotyped as wearing flashy clothing and jewelry and for driving souped-up cars, such as Cadillacs, sometimes called "pimpmobiles," in the inner city. This stereotype was most visible in 1970s exploitation **films** and more people saw them on the big screen than on the streets. However, in at least one instance, a pimpmobile was lent to filmmakers by a pimp.

The pimpmobile's aesthetic heritage predates the motor car and the moving picture. In his well-researched historical novel, *I, Stagolee* (2004), Cecil Brown establishes his narrator's credentials by describing his flourishing livery station and his "bay of horses trimmed in yellow to match the dress of the coachman" (p. 9). Stagolee, a 19th-century pimp, boasts about a St. Louis **madam** who hires "five surreys to drive her sporting women for a ride in Forest Park" every Thursday afternoon, while "hundreds of men watch from the street cheering," and points out that "Miss Larkin's Young Ladies Academy hires the same surreys" to transport its "puritan girls" to and from their prosperous homes (p. 9). A 1927 ballad about this mythic figure recalls: "The horses and carriages/Stretched out for about a mile./Everybody whore and pimp had gone in hock/To put Old Stackerlee away in style" (Brown 2003, 57).

Ostentatious displays of high style were also a defining feature of the Paris demimonde, before the **World War I**, and have sometimes been described more evocatively in fictional accounts of the era. In *Gigi* (1952), "fashionable automobiles were being built with a slightly higher body and a rather wider top, to accommodate the exaggerated hats" being worn by the most conspicuous courtesans of 1899, one of whom "gadded about" in a "coupé upholstered in mauve satin" (Colette 1987, 15, 16).

Stereotypical pimps and pimpmobiles are passé outside **hip-hop** representations while custom cars have become a mainstream interest, most visible in the television show "Pimp My Ride." Despite the eye-catching title, this show is about cars and not pimps.

See Also Films, Exploitation.

Further Reading: Adelman, Bob and Susan Hall. *Gentleman of Leisure: A Year in the Life of a Pimp.* 1972. Reprint, New York: Powerhouse Books, 2006; Brown, Cecil. *Stagolee Shot Billy.* Cambridge, MA: Harvard University Press, 2003; Brown, Cecil. *I, Stagolee.* Xlibris Corporation,

2004; Colette. *Gigi, Julie de Carneilhan, Chance Acquaintances.* 1952. Reprint, New York: Farrar, Straus and Giroux, 1987.

Tracy Quan

PIMPS. Stereotypically, "pimps" are associated with street prostitution, where those who participate in the exchange of sex for money or drugs are more vulnerable to arrest and assault. The pimp is usually identified as a man who forces, to various degrees, a worker who is male, female, or transgender to exchange sex for money and then requires that the worker bring a portion of the money back to him. In exchange for this money, the pimp offers some protection for the worker from police and potential assaults and may provide security, housing, foods, and drugs. And yet the relationships between pimps and those who participate in these exchanges are often far more complicated. The power relationships between pimps and workers vary dramatically.

Because prostitution is illegal in many countries and therefore leaves those who exchange sex for drugs or money vulnerable to arrest and **violence** from potential clients, many people who participate in these exchanges do have what is commonly referred to as a pimp. Many women have a husband or boyfriend who works as a lookout against police and/or violence. The illegality of the profession often requires that a worker surrender some control over the working conditions. In addition to legal harassment by the police, the illegal status of the work undermines workers' abilities to protect themselves from dangerous clients and then dissuades them from filing charges if such violence does occur. The illegality of the work also requires that negotiations and transactions are speedy and occur in vulnerable locations such as cars, parks, or alleys. This so-called lookout "pimp" status can also be more organized. In many countries, people referred to as "pimps" organize and run bars, **brothels**, or houses where people can come to have sex with gay or straight workers. This situation often places the organizers at risk and serves to protect the workers from arrest, as they are not responsible for directly contacting their clients.

The social **stigma** and criminal status of exchanging sex for drugs or money causes many people who participate in these exchanges to be afraid to reach out for help or information. Pimps/protectors/organizers/managers often further isolate some workers because they do not allow them to talk with other workers. Although many workers do not identify as members of a profession and view their involvement in the sex trade as a temporary activity, the business is often more organized and structured than outsiders realize. This organization is further complicated by the existence of pimps in myriad capacities that can serve to protect and further isolate the workers.

See also Films, Exploitation; Hip-Hop; Venues.

Further Reading: Weitzer, Ronald John, ed. *Sex for Sale: Prostitution, Pornography, and the Sex Industry.* New York: Routledge, 2000.

Jill McCracken

PINZER, MAIMIE (1885–1940). May "Maimie" Pinzer, born in Philadelphia to Russian Jewish immigrants, turned to prostitution after her father was brutally murdered, and her mother and an uncle who had molested her as a child had her arrested for waywardness. She established her clientele through men she met while working at a department store and continued as a prostitute until she lost an eye, possibly because of a syphilitic infection. While ill, she met Herbert Welsh, a Philadelphia social worker, who encouraged her to go straight, often providing financial support, and who introduced her to Fanny Quincy Howe, an upper-class Boston woman, with whom she corresponded from 1910–22. Pinzer's extant letters to Howe reveal the details of her life: her unhappy **marriage** to Albert Jones and their separation, her friendship with and eventual marriage to Ira Benjamin, her conflicts with her family who treated her as an outcast, and her efforts at achieving respectability. After leaving Philadelphia, Pinzer worked as a stenographer in New York, later moving to the firm's Montreal office where Benjamin joined her. In Montreal, she successfully ran a letter-writing and duplication service until the wartime economy forced her to close her business. Pinzer's genuine interest in helping others led her to found a halfway house to assist young prostitutes by providing a comfortable place where these girls could find companionship, encouragement, and a cup of tea, as well as a cheerful place to spend holidays. When the mission closed because of financial problems, Pinzer returned with Benjamin to Philadelphia, where she adopted her brother James's son and daughter after their mother died of influenza. Pinzer then relocated to **Chicago**, later to **Los Angeles**, and finally to Germantown, Pennsylvania. The details of these final years of her life are unknown.

Further Reading: Pinzer, Maimie. *The Maimie Papers: Letters from an Ex-Prostitute.* Edited by Ruth Rosen and Sue Davidson. New York: Feminist Press, 1977.

Deborah Israel

POETRY. The status of prostitutes in society has always been mirrored in the poetic utterances of the age. The early matriarchal societies in the Middle East worshipped the fertility goddess Ishtar and sacred prostitution was a focal point of the holy ritual in the temples of Mesopotamia. One of the world's first recorded poems, the *Epic of Gilgamesh* (written down around 2000 B.C.), shows the crucial role of prostitutes in the process of civilization. A form of religious prostitution survived well into the Classical Greek era, with temples dedicated to Aphrodite and staffed with sacred prostitutes. Famous *betaerae* (**courtesans**) such as **Phryne** and Aspasia set an example for the educated, "emancipated," and self-subsistent prostitute, and **Sappho**'s erotic poetry celebrated heterosexual and lesbian love. Sappho was to become the first victim of the prejudice that deemed that writing women are whores, and only 5 percent of her poems have survived destruction by those who stigmatized her as a nymphomaniac. In **ancient Rome**, prostitution was an accepted profession with no shame attached to it, and prostitutes were often well-educated professional **actresses** and dancers. The poet Horace eulogized the virtues of prostitution in contrast to the disadvantages of adultery. Ovid in his *Ars amatoria* advised men to look for whores at the theater. Many of Rome's most famous poets—Horace, Catullus, Ovid, Propertius, and Tibullus—frequented courtesans and celebrated them in their verses.

Negation of the body and idealization of chastity in the dark Middle Ages did not eradicate the **brothels** in the cities and the immorality of kings and bishops. The French poet François Villon, student of theology, vagabond, and criminal, exemplified the sexual excesses that extended from the student to the upper reaches of the clergy. In his "Ballad of Fat Margot," he celebrated his life as a student and a pimp. Although the **Renaissance** brought prostitutes more freedom, the Reformation instigated a new wave of persecution. Under Queen Elizabeth I, prostitutes were flogged, shaved, and imprisoned at Bridewell; the brothels, beer-gardens, and theaters in London were removed to the fringe of the city at Southwark, where playwright

William Shakespeare might have met the mysterious "Dark Lady" of his sonnets going about her profession. The English Restoration ended the Puritan Commonwealth and its moral austerity under Oliver Cromwell, and the English aristocracy set the tone for sexual indulgence as a compensation for their loss of real power. King Charles II and his court became notorious for licentiousness and debauchery, and sexual affairs took up more time than the affairs of state: "And love he loves, for he loves fucking much," as **John Wilmot, Earl of Rochester**, characterized the king. Rochester (1647–80), rake, wit, and poet, belonged to the king's circle, and his poetry about the "aristocratic" way of life was quite outspoken: "I send for my whore, when for fear of a clap, / I spend in her hand, and I spew in her lap." The obscene realism included such details as that the prostitute might be diseased, that she stole his purse, and that in her absence he molested his servant: "And missing my whore, I bugger my page." Rochester represents the contradictions of his age: having been a debauched rake in the city, he was a caring husband and father in the country. In his poem "A Letter Fancied from Artemisia in the Town to Chloe in the Country," he adopted a female voice to express the dangers for female writers, since "whore is scarce a more reproachful name than poetess."

That women authors were prostitutes was a prejudice from which Aphra Behn (1640–89), the first professional English woman writer, who wrote about a woman's illicit sexual desires ("The Willing Mistress"), also suffered. She was denigrated by Robert Gould's well-known couplet: "For Punk and Poesie agree so pat, / You cannot well be this and not be that," an equation that poets such as Mary Robinson or Elizabeth Barrett Browning also had to grapple with.

The Romantics developed an increasing social conscience, and William Blake (1757–1827) in his poem "London" expressed concern about the suffering wretches of the city, such as underage chimney sweeps, pressed soldiers, and prostitutes. Being a prostitute is not a moral state, but a social condition created by the repressive forces of marriage: the "marriage hearse," a deathbed of love and desire, has to be compensated for by prostitution. The curse of the harlot can be read as the beginning of social change through the rebellious voice of the suppressed.

The Victorians were obsessed with the theme of the "fallen woman," her stigmatization under the **Contagious Diseases Act** (passed in 1864) and her humanity. Thomas Hardy (1840–1928) satirized in his poem "The Ruined Maid," written in 1866, the Victorian view of prostitutes as doomed and "ruined" women and suggested that they may in fact be happy, educated, and much freer than chaste housewives. The commonplace expression of the ruined woman was turned upside down in her transformation from a beggarly country girl into a prosperous and refined prostitute: "'And now you've gay bracelets and bright feathers three!' — / 'Yes: that's how we dress when we're ruined,' said she."

Robert Browning (1812–89) used the dramatic monologue to delve into the male (or female) mind, and in his poem "Porphyria's Lover" (1836), he showed the male objectification of a female (whore) and its fatal result for the woman. The aggressive, pathological male speaker is afraid of his mistress' power, she clearly is socially superior to her lover, and he kills her to possess her absolutely in death.

Christina Rossetti (1830–94), who worked with the prostitutes who were confined to the Highgate Penitentiary, warned against seductive males in her poem "Goblin Market" (1859). Her female character Laura is tempted by the forbidden fruits the goblin men offer her: "She never tasted such before … / She sucked until her lips were sore." Laura is seized by an immense craving for the forbidden fruit and can only be saved through her sister Lizzie's sacrifice, when Lizzie undergoes the torments of the Goblin men. A world of sisterly (lesbian) and motherly love is given as an alternative to male seduction, and yet the moralistic message clashes with the sensuality of the poem itself: "Hug me, kiss me, suck my juices" is the remedy for Laura's obsession with male fruit. Other women writers dealing with fallen women and the plight of prostitutes in their poems are Mathilde Blind in "The Russian Student's Tale," Augusta Webster in "A Castaway," Amy Levy in "Magdalen," and May Probyn in "The Model."

Rossetti's brother, the Pre-Raphaelite poet and painter Dante Gabriel Rossetti (1828–82), used the dramatic monologue in his poem "Jenny," to expose the thoughts and prejudices of a male (the scholar John) confronted with the humanity of his whore Jenny, who has fallen asleep on his knee instead of pleasing him sexually. The student watches her voyeuristically and comes to doubt the clear-cut differentiation between the Madonna (his innocent fiancée) and the Magdalene (the sinful whore Jenny), yet his middle-class narrowmindedness does not allow him really to grasp Jenny as a human being, but merely as a mythical character such as Eve: "A cipher of man's changeless sum of lust, past, present, and to come." An even more realistic view of prostitution is given in his poem "Found" and the accompanying painting, depicting a farmer who is trying to raise a woman (with conspicuously red, "sinful" hair) from the street where she has sunk in shame, while a calf on his cart is struggling to break free from the net. His former girlfriend who has become a prostitute does not want to be "saved"; she cries in the poem: "Leave me—I do not know you—go away!," leaving it open to interpretation, where a woman's real freedom lies.

In the United States, poetry about prostitution has been written by Walt Whitman ("To a Common Prostitute," 1900) and Damon Runyon ("The Funeral of Madame Chase"). In France, it was Charles Baudelaire (1821–67), the *poète maudit*, who not only compared poetry to prostitution, but also depicted prostitutes frequently in his poems about the Parisian underworld. In his 1857 poem *"Le Crépuscule du Soir"* ("Evening Twilight"), he compared prostitution in Paris to the worm in an apple, but also saw the many possibilities for prostitution as an invitation to the imagination: "Prostitution kindles in the streets;/ Like an anthill, opens up her gates/ And everywhere she makes her secret way/ Like an enemy who tries his master stroke;/ Like an enemy who tries his master stroke."

The 20th century has brought a breaking of almost all taboos, and prostitution has become a common theme in poetry. The modernist poetess Mina Loy wrote poems on prostitution, George Orwell, in his "Ironic Poem about Prostitution," wrote about the exoticism and sentimentality of sex with young girls in Burma. The poetic jargon "her skin was gold, her hair was jet / Her teeth were ivory" clashes with the realism of the financial transaction: "And in her lisping, virgin voice, stood out for twenty-five."

See also Romantic Literature; Appendix documents 5–8.

Further Reading: Auerbach, Nina. *Woman and the Demon: The Life of a Victorian Myth*. Cambridge, MA: Harvard University Press, 1982; Lipking, Lawrence. *Abandoned Women and Poetic Tradition*. Chicago: University of Chicago Press, 1988; Roberts, Nickie. *Whores in History: Prostitution in Western Society*. New York: Harper Collins, 1992; Trudgill, Eric. *Madonnas and Magdalenes*. London: Heineman, 1975.

Heike Grundmann

PORNE. The term *"porne,"* from the ancient Greek verb *pernêmi* ("to sell"), denoted a **brothel** slave. The male equivalent is the *pornos*, a man who sold his body to others for sexual use. The *porne* was often distinguished from the *hetaera* by the number and anonymity of her partners, as well as by the fact that she could not choose them; she was said to sell herself to "anyone who wished her." As with the term *"hetaera,"* however, the word *"porne"* admits of considerable semantic ambiguity. In a 4th-century contractual dispute, for instance, a *porne* is described by the opposing parties both as a freed woman and as co-owned property put to torture for legal evidence, like a slave. Conversely, the idea of the acceptance of all customers applies to *hetaeras* in two other court speeches.

In contrast to the *hetaera* or concubine, the *porne* inhabits a public place that men patronized. She sat in a brothel or openly offered herself for hire on city streets, pacing the dark alleys near the marketplace or by the city walls. The example of a slave girl in one Attic court speech confirms this distinction: a concubine (*pallake*) while resident in her master's house, she was to be placed in a brothel as a *porne* unless she regained his affections. Fragments from Greek comedy represent brothel prostitutes as readily available and easy to spot in ancient Athens; they stood before the brothel either fully naked or scantily clad in transparent draperies. Some are depicted as aggressively grabbing potential clients and pulling them inside; others seduced men with their voices. The *porne* was also known for her ability to perform a variety of sexual positions. She received cash for her services and expected no ongoing commitment from her partner, as one fragment from a comic play explains:

> One obol. Hop in. There is no coyness,
> no idle talk, nor does she snatch herself away.
> But straight away, as you wish, in whatever way you wish.
> You come out. Tell her to go to hell. She is a stranger to you.

See also Ancient World.

Further Reading: Davidson, James N. *Courtesans and Fishcakes. The Consuming Passions of Classical Athens.* New York: St. Martin's Press, 1998; Kurke, Leslie. *Coins, Bodies, Games and Gold: The Politics of Meaning in Archaic Greece.* Princeton, NJ: Princeton University Press, 1999; McClure, Laura K. *Courtesans at Table: Gender and the Greek Literary Tradition in Athenaeus.* New York: Routledge, 2003.

Laura McClure

PORTS. Traditionally, the presence of large numbers of merchant marines, dock workers, tourists, and military in port cities has ensured the existence of robust red light districts near the docking areas of ships. Yet busy ports have not always developed adjacent red light districts. In **New York City** in the 19th century, the urban geography of commercial sex passed through various stages—from the segregation of commercial sex in specific streets and taverns near the seaport, to its dispersion to residential areas from 1820 to 1830, then concentrated into what is today the Soho area of lower Manhattan. Today, moral geographies of seaports are in a process of dispersion because of the high value of seaside real estate associated with traditional dockside red light locations. For example, in San Diego, California, where a naval base and fishing and tourist industries have created a market for prostitution, old waterfront establishments, such as topless bars and massage parlors, are being demolished and replaced with sleek office towers and new condominiums. Street-based prostitutes in San Diego may work in several communities throughout the city, depending on the police enforcement patterns or the time of day.

This pattern is allowing prostitutes in many U.S. cities to resist police harassment and go more unnoticed, even though prostitution is legally prohibited in most parts of the country.

In other parts of the world, the geopolitical climate of the post–Cold War era, as well as vast economic changes associated with **globalization**, have combined to create a situation where new port cities have materialized seemingly overnight and engendered paid sex economies sometimes run by **organized crime** and often involved in the human **trafficking** in a situation not unlike the purported white slave trade of the late 19th and early 20th centuries. For example, the port of Shenzhen, China, now the hub of the vast Pearl River Delta across the Shenzhen River from **Hong Kong** (the busiest seaport of the world, where most prostitution is illegal), in two decades has been transformed into the sixth busiest port city of the world, where prostitution is open and attracts much of the business prohibited in Hong Kong. Before 1990, picturesque fishing villages and Chinese junks dominated the region. Local officials are apparently lax in monitoring the trafficking of women and children from China's interior, as well as neighboring Asian countries, to centers of commercial sex such as Shenzhen. Designated by Chinese leader Deng Xiaoping in the early 1980s as a "special economic zone," Shenzhen is described by Westerners as a Wild West. In the downtown area, Las Vegas–like hotels promote prostitution alongside a gritty red light district catering to the business created by the maze of dockyards that dominate its shores, a steel and concrete testament to the velocity of China's emergence as a free-trade titan. The case of Shenzhen shows how prostitution in China has been transformed from a condemned economic activity to an exploited one.

Santos, Brazil, the largest port city of South America, offers another example of how problems associated with prostitution—in this case **child prostitution**—have been amplified by local poverty combined with the greater market for sexual services made possible by globalization. Estimates of numbers of children in prostitution in Brazil by 1990 were half a million with a good percentage of this number in Santos. In the past, the great seaport of Rio de Janeiro was often romanticized by merchant marines as the site for exotic encounters with beautiful prostitutes. Today, no one dares to characterize commercial sex in the port of Santos as anything but sad and typical of prostitution in ports throughout the world of the 21st century.

Further Reading: Gilfoyle, Timothy J. *City of Eros: New York City, Prostitution, and the Commercialization of Sex, 1790–1920.* New York: W. W. Norton, 1992; Riccio, Rita. "Strolling the Strip: Prostitution in a North American City." In *Geographical Snapshots of North America*, ed. Donald G. Janelle. New York: Gilford Press, 1992, pp. 114–16.

Anne Hayes

POSTTRAUMATIC STRESS DISORDER (PTSD). Individuals who have been victimized in the sex industry may experience biologically based reactions such as posttraumatic stress disorder (PTSD) or other trauma-related symptoms. "Posttraumatic stress disorder" refers to a group of symptoms that some individuals experience after overwhelming, frightening, or horrifying life experiences. The *Diagnostic and Statistical Manual of Mental Disorders- IV (DSM-IV)* describes three symptom clusters occurring in PTSD, including: Reexperiencing the trauma through intrusive memories, dreams, and flashbacks; physical and mental distress in response to reminders of the event; avoidance of thoughts, feelings, and reminders of the trauma; loss of interest in activities; a general numbing of feeling; feelings of estrangement from others, and persistent symptoms of increased bodily arousal manifested in sleep problems, irritability, and anger, concentration problems, hypervigilance, and exaggerated startle responses.

Exposure to Violence and Trauma within the Sex Industry

Individuals working in prostitution who develop PTSD have been exposed to one or more extreme traumatic stressors, including threats of harm, physical assaults, sexual assaults, witnessing harm to someone else, or hearing about serious harm to someone close to them. Physical abuse and sexual abuse are common occurrences in the sex industry, as is psychological abuse. Individuals working in the sex industry report experiencing brutality from a range of sources, including customers, organizers of prostitution such as "**pimps**" and "**madams**," gang members, and the police. Because prostitution is an illegal activity in the United States, individuals involved in the sex industry may think that they have no recourse for the **violence** perpetrated against them. This perceived lack of control is a risk factor for the later development of disorders such as PTSD and depression.

Posttraumatic Stress Disorder (PTSD)

"Victims of trafficking often endure brutal conditions that result in physical, sexual and psychological trauma. Sexually transmitted infections, pelvic inflammatory disease, and HIV/AIDS are often the result of forced prostitution. Anxiety, insomnia, depression, and post-traumatic stress disorder are common psychological manifestations among trafficked victims. Unsanitary and crowded living conditions, coupled with poor nutrition, foster a host of adverse health conditions such as scabies, tuberculosis, and other communicable diseases. Children suffer growth and development problems and develop complex psychological and neurological consequences from deprivation and trauma."

From U.S. Department of State, *Assessment of U.S. Government Activities to Combat Trafficking in Persons* (Washington, DC: U.S. Department of State, June 2004).

Traumatic Stress in Sex Trafficking

In situations of human sex **trafficking**, individuals are forced to work in the sex industry through **violence**, fraud, or coercion. These individuals are essentially victims of modern-day slavery and may be physically assaulted and raped repeatedly over the course of months or even years. Traffickers often physically and psychologically brutalize their victims to gain total control over them. Victims of human trafficking are typically exposed to multiple traumatic experiences, including verbal and psychological abuse, enforced physical and emotional isolation, lack of basic human necessities, threats, forced abortions, physical assaults and violence, and sexual violence. Women are often forced to continue prostituting even when they are menstruating, pregnant, or sick. They may witness others being assaulted, and their family members may be threatened or hurt as a way of pressuring them into continuing to prostitute.

The Cadena Case

In a landmark case of sex trafficking in the late 1990s, members of the Cadena family lured Mexican women and girls as young as 14 years old to Florida and the Carolinas with promises of employment as waitresses and domestic workers. In the United States, the traffickers repeatedly raped their victims to "initiate" them into the sex industry; they then forced the women to work as prostitutes servicing migrant workers in remote farm locations. Many of the customers had weapons and regularly threatened and beat the women. Several of the women became pregnant and were forced to have abortions. In one instance, one of the traffickers kicked a pregnant woman in the stomach, leading to a miscarriage. The women were beaten if they attempted to escape; in one case, a young woman was locked in a closet for 15 days after attempting to escape. Forced **prostitution**, sexual abuse, and physical abuse were daily occurrences for these young women.

The Biological Basis of PTSD

Exposure to this sort of severe violence triggers an innate survival response that allows a rapid, instinctive response to danger. During a physical or sexual assault, physiological changes in the body prepare the victim to deal with the threat by fighting, fleeing, or freezing. The autonomic nervous system triggers a neurohormonal release of chemicals, activating survival responses. All of the body's resources are directed toward dealing with the threat, while functions less important for survival are shut down. For many individuals, when the danger passes, the survival mode eventually turns off and the body settles back into its normal or steady-state level, called "homeostasis"; however, for some people, the survival response remains activated. With ongoing exposure to trauma, such as often occurs in situations of human trafficking and sexual exploitation, the same physiological responses that are initially protective become maladaptive and may lead to illness such as PTSD.

Complex Posttraumatic Stress Reactions

Individuals working in prostitution who have been exposed to chronic interpersonal victimization may experience more extensive reactions than are explained by PTSD alone. Their ability to self-regulate may be impacted, with resulting emotional mood swings and problems with impulse control. Some individuals develop substance abuse problems as a coping mechanism, to avoid intrusive memories or to regulate their emotional states. For instance, in the Cadena case, a number of the victims used drugs and **alcohol** as a way of coping with what was happening to them. Victims may dissociate or "space out" as a way of coping with overwhelming stress. They may experience physical manifestations of stress, including compromised immune system functioning and somatic symptoms such as gastrointestinal discomfort, headaches, and muscular tension. Because trafficking victims are treated as commodities to be sold over and over, they may lack a positive sense of self and view themselves as property. Shame is a widespread emotional reaction in victims of sex trafficking; in many cases, shame about being seen as a prostitute or a criminal prevents victims from reconnecting with their families or from seeking help. In addition, the chronic interpersonal victimization that often occurs within the sex industry causes many of these individuals to have difficulties with interpersonal relationships, including issues with trust and boundaries.

Trauma-Related Symptoms in Individuals Working in the Sex Industry.

There is a paucity of information regarding trauma-related symptoms in individuals who have been trafficked or victimized in the sex industry. Despite this fact, initial investigations indicate that individuals who have been victimized in the sex industry report a range of emotional, behavioral, and psychological difficulties. Preliminary studies have found that the most trafficked and sexually exploited women have reported symptoms such as depression or sadness, guilt and self-blame, anger and rage, and sleep disturbances. Clinical experience indicates that depression and PTSD are primary problems for victims of sex trafficking. There is clearly a link between exposure to violence within the sex industry, biologically based survival responses, and trauma-related symptoms in individuals who have been victimized within the sex industry.

See also Pathology; Rape.

Further Reading: Free the Slaves and Human Rights Law Center. *Hidden Slaves: Forced Labor in the United States.* Washington, DC: Free the Slaves and Human Rights Law Center, 2004. http:// www.freetheslaves.net/resources/whitepapers/; Herman, J. L. *Trauma and Recovery.* New York: Basic Books, 1997; *United States v. Cadena.* 1998. Case number 98–14015-CR-RYSKAMP, U.S.

District Court, Southern District of Florida; van der kolk, B. A., A.C. McFarlan, and L. Weisaeith, eds. *Traumatic Stress: The Effects of Overwhelming Experience on Mind, Body, and Society*. New York: Guilford Press, 1996; Yehuda, R., ed. *Psychological Trauma*. Washington, DC: American Psychiatric Press, 1998.

Elizabeth K. Hopper and Jose A. Hidalgo

PRETTY WOMAN. *Pretty Woman*, a film about a streetwalker and a corporate raider who fall in love, was one of the highest-grossing Hollywood releases of 1990. Critics have panned it as a fairy tale with the hooker as Cinderella; others have been pleased to see a sexy, capable, health-conscious prostitute featured in a popular romantic comedy. The film has endured as a cultural reference point and marks a change in Hollywood's portrayal of sex workers.

Vivian Ward, a drug-free "hooker with a heart of gold," is luckier than her roommate, who is depicted as dysfunctional, drug-addicted, and incorrigible. In earlier iconic Hollywood movies about prostitutes, such as *BUtterfield 8* (1960), **Klute** (1971), and *Taxi Driver* (1976), a prostitute was typically rescued by the male lead or "killed off" by the screenwriter. In *Pretty Woman*, the male lead is rehabilitated by a streetwalker. Attractive and malleable, Vivian is rescued from the streets, but her evolution is a prelude to her savior's transformation, for she helps him to see that his business practices are morally bankrupt. Her roommate continues to work as a street-walker—and lives.

See also Films, Opera.

Tracy Quan and Melissa Hope Ditmore

PRISON. Under the present system of criminalization in the United States, spending time in jail or prison is a common occurrence for many prostitutes. Prostitution, both soliciting and procuring, is a misdemeanor offense in most states, with certain parts of Nevada being a notable exception. Many states have provisions to bring felony prostitution charges against "repeat offenders" or those who are HIV-positive and continue to engage in prostitution. Felony conviction typically results in a prison, as opposed to a jail, sentence. Forty-eight of the fifty states do not permit incarcerated felons to vote, and in fourteen states, there are laws that prevent even those who have completed their sentences from voting.

In prison, however, most of those engaged in prostitution had no previous experience with it on the outside. Despite the prevalence of prostitution in prison, there is very little written on the topic; the push and pull factors of prostitution in prison differ in crucial ways from those in society at large. Among male prisoners, prostitution within the institution is primarily between inmates and is an important component of both the internal black-market economy and the ongoing power struggle among inmates. In women's prisons, prostitution is more likely to occur between guards and prisoners, where the latter will exchange sex for contraband items or additional privileges from the former.

Prostitution in prison is often a result of limited access to conventional expressions of sexuality, or the need or want to participate in the prison black-market economy. Frequently, prison prostitution is far from voluntary and is linked to the prevalent phenomena of prison **rape** and gang **violence**. Prisoners perceived as weak or vulnerable—often young, nonviolent, homosexual or transsexual, first-time offenders—are "claimed" by an older or stronger prisoner or a guard. In exchange for protection, or through coercion, the dominant prisoner, sometimes called a "daddy" or "bandit," will force his dependent "punk" into prison prostitution. Transgender prisoners, for example, engage in prostitution both as a mechanism of self-protection and as a means of coming by hard-to-get items such as makeup, jewelry, drugs, and cigarettes. Making themselves available as sex partners, rather than objects to be taken, is often the only means of escaping the brutality of prison rape.

Further Reading: Donaldson, Stephen "Donny." *A Million Jockers, Punks, and Queens: Sex among American Male Prisoners and Its Implications for Concepts of Sexual Orientation.* New York: Stop Prisoner Rape, 1993. Stop Prisoner Rape Web site http://www.spr.org; Fellner, Jamie, and Marc Mauer. *Losing the Vote: The Impact of Felony Disenfranchisement Laws in the United States.* New York: Human Rights Watch, the Sentencing Project, 1998; May, Glenn. "Jail Assaults Described." *Pittsburgh Tribune-Review,* 25 March 2004; Posner, Richard, and Katharine Silbaugh. *A Guide to America's Sex Laws.* Chicago: University of Chicago Press, 1996; Wasserman, Joanne. "Prison Rapes 'Routine.'" *New York Daily News,* 28 January 2003; Wistrom, Brent. "Elusive Evidence in Rape Cases; Allred Investigation Not Accurate, ACLU Says." *Times Record News,* 27 February 2004.

Alexandra Gerber

PROFUMO AFFAIR. The Profumo Affair was one of the biggest scandals ever to hit British politics. It incorporated all the essential ingredients of a "Cold War" thriller, including a Government War Minister, a Russian spy, aristocratic sexual frolics with high-class prostitutes, and a gangland shooting. It culminated with the Minister's resignation, a high-profile court case, suicide, and an alleged "cover up."

John Profumo (1915–2006) was a talented "middle-ranking" member of the 1959 Conservative Government, who served as a War Minister under Prime Minister Harold Macmillan. In July 1961, he went to a party held by Lord Astor, where he met **Christine Keeler**, a beautiful young woman with whom he had a short affair. He ended it abruptly after he was warned of a security risk. Unfortunately for Profumo, Keeler shared an apartment with the osteopath Steven Ward (who attended many well-known personalities, including Winston Churchill). Ward amused himself by grooming young women for high society and dabbling in security matters for danger and excitement.

The connection that brought ruin and disgrace to the hapless Minister was through Yevgeny Ivanov, a Russian naval attaché at the Soviet Embassy, who also had a brief liaison with Keeler. He was suspected of spying and consequently was being monitored by MI5, the British intelligence agency. The details of these connections were leaked to the press, and Profumo was forced to resign, not so much because of his "immoral" behavior, or any security risk that it might have posed, but because he lied to Parliament about the nature of his affair. In the meantime, one of Keeler's gangland boyfriends tried to shoot Ward. During the subsequent trial, Keeler disappeared from the country, it was believed, to prevent her from making embarrassing revelations in the anonymity of the court.

After a Parliamentary debate into the affair, the Government set up an enquiry headed by Lord Denning, which was later condemned as a "cover-up." The drama concluded with the high-profile trial of Ward for "living off the earnings of prostitution." Ward committed suicide while the jury was considering its verdict.

Keeler herself was interesting because she mixed easily with both high and low society. Significantly, this included the raffish black nightlife of Notting Hill, with its music, drinking, drugs, and dubious collection of resident convicts, **pimps**, and prostitutes. However, it heralded the dawn of a new liberal British society during which many of the old social barriers were broken down.

Perhaps the most memorable phrase to come out of the affair was uttered during the Ward trial by Keeler friend, Mandy Rice-Davies, "He would, wouldn't he," meaning that in some circumstances, any man was likely to lie.

Further Reading: Baston, Lewis. *Sleaze: The State of Britain.* London: Macmillan, 2000; Denning, Lord Alfred. *John Profumo and Christine Keeler 1963.* London: H. M. Stationery Office, 1963; Keeler, Christine, with Douglas Thompson. *The Truth at Last: My Story.* London: Sidgwick and Jackson, 2001; Kennedy, Ludovic. *The Trial of Stephen Ward.* London: Victor Gollancz, 1964.

Helen J. Self

PROHIBITION. All countries have legal systems that regulate prostitution. These approaches may be addressed at the federal, state/province, or local level. Prohibition, related to criminalization, is the system in which prostitution itself and all activities that surround it are criminalized and prohibited by law. Most states in the United States, excluding some counties in Nevada, use this system. Other countries that use this system include China and Saudi Arabia.

Where prostitution is prohibited, every aspect of the business of prostitution is criminalized. This includes prostitution itself, management or promotion of prostitution, and soliciting sexual services in exchange for money as a client or a prostitute. The legal impact extends beyond the criminal justice system. For example, in the United States, evidence of involvement in prostitution can cause "immigrants" to be removed from the country. This system leaves low-income prostitutes and those from minority ethnic communities more susceptible to arrest, because of increased police presence in these neighborhoods. Prostitutes who are working on the street are more visible and therefore are more likely to be arrested. The most vulnerable prostitutes are usually working on the street because they cannot coordinate working indoors, which might shield them from visibility.

Prohibition also exacerbates the potential for sex workers to experience **violence**, and, at the same time, makes them less likely to approach the police for assistance, because of their unlawful behavior. Because criminalization dehumanizes those who work in prostitution and stigmatizes them, police and others are more readily able to abuse prostitutes with impunity. Furthermore, this **stigma** makes the provision of services and assistance for prostitutes a low priority in the public arena.

Proponents of prohibition argue that by criminalizing prostitution, society is combating the deterioration of neighborhoods, supporting moral behaviors, and closing off opportunities to sexually exploit people who might be trafficked into prostitution.

See also Abolitionism; Appendix documents 16, 17 and 19; Criminalization of Clients; Decriminalization; Legal Approaches.

Further Reading: Thukral, Juhu and Melissa Ditmore. *Revolving Door: An Analysis of Street-Based Prostitution in New York City.* New York: Urban Justice Center, 2003 http://www.sexworkersproject.org/reports/RevolvingDoor.html; Thukral, Juhu, Melissa Ditmore, and Alexandra Murphy. *Behind Closed Doors: An Analysis of Indoor Sex Work in New York City.* New York: Urban Justice Center, 2005. http://www.sexworkersproject.org/reports/BehindClosedDoors.html.

Juhu Thukral

PROSTITUTES' RIGHTS. *See* **HIV/AIDS and the Prostitutes' Rights Movement.**

PROTESTANT REFORMATION. In 1517, a German Catholic monk named Martin Luther posted a series of reforms on the church door in Wittenberg, Germany. In what became known as the Protestant Reformation (1517–1700), the Catholic Church, as well as European society, underwent a substantial change. Luther's Reformation was a far-reaching social movement that sought to return to the original foundations of Christianity. It challenged the Catholic idea that divine authority should be mediated through institutions or hierarchies, and it denied the value of tradition. Instead, it offered radical new notions of the supremacy of written texts (that is, the books of the **Bible**), interpreted by individual consciences. Moreover, it offered a reinterpretation of social and gender relations within patriarchal Europe. Women and their place in European society also underwent a serious transformation after the Reformation, as did the role of prostitution.

The major thinkers of the Reformation continued to view women as subordinate to males. The social order bordered on the patriarchal. Thus an assertive and aggressive woman was a woman who did not understand her social role as mother and wife. French theologian John Calvin noted that motherhood was a sign, even a precondition, of a woman's moral and physical health. A woman could be a good Christian solely through **marriage** and motherhood. Essentially, marriage was a microcosm of a larger social order.

Luther was a leading defender of the rights of women and the foundational importance of marriage. Luther placed the home "at the centre of the universe." In a radical reinterpretation of the household economy, Luther assigns more independence to the women in the Lutheran home. His teachings on the institution of marriage and the family were indeed considered radical. Before the Reformation, under the Catholic Church, it was a generally accepted idea that sex was a procreative act, not meant for pleasure. This argument was based on biblical scripture as well as the Church writings of **Saint Augustine**. Luther and the first generation of Protestant Reformers rejected this tradition—in both their beliefs and their daily lives. They rejected the celibate ideal of the Middle Ages. Luther vigorously urged fathers to remove their daughters from convents. Many Protestant towns closed the Catholic cloisters and nunneries, thus freeing many women from sexual repression, cultural depravity, dominance by male clergy, and Catholic practices. Moreover, where the Reformation had succeeded, Catholic monks and nuns who wished to marry received automatic permission to do so.

Despite his claim that women were independent in the household economy, Luther also taught that women were physiologically inferior to men and were created to be ruled by men. As proof, he cited the shape of a woman's hips; their broad base indicated that God meant for them to sit at home. He further believed that women had stronger sexual urges than men, and that if a man was impotent (or could not satisfy his partner), he should actively supply a sex partner for his wife.

Luther's ideas on divorce also changed the social environment. The Reformers endorsed, for the first time in Western Christendom, legitimate divorce and remarriage. Protestants, in contrast to Catholics, generally allowed for divorce and remarriage on five grounds: adultery, willful abandonment, chronic impotence, willful deceit, and life-threatening hostility. In other aspects as well, the Reformation opened the door for a more liberalized acceptance of what were previously "misbehaviors." Throughout the Middle Ages, prostitution was generally confined to "streetwalkers" and **brothels**. Essentially, municipal governments regulated these municipal areas. It was acknowledged that young men would seek out sexual relations regardless of their options, and thus prostitution served to protect "respectable" townswomen from seduction and even **rape**. Moreover, prostitution allowed men to seek recreational sex outside of the confines of marriage. To a certain degree, the Reformation altered this behavior. As the fathers of the Reformation accepted the tenet of a liberalized marriage and social system, Europeans became more accepting of prostitutes.

During Luther's time, official brothels existed in many German towns, sometimes even owned by the municipality, and the brothel keeper was frequently a salaried public official. Civic brothels were a civic possession, an amenity: thus in the 15th century, when the Emperor Sigismund and his retinue visited several towns of the Empire, they were feasted and entertained in the brothels as part of their civic welcome. In Ulm, there were reports of boys aged 12 spending time in the brothel, and though the city council thought this a little too young, it considered boys of 15 quite old enough to visit prostitutes. Brothels evolved into centers of amusement, not just of the sexual trade, where dice, cards, and other games were played. City authorities sometimes set the fees prostitutes could charge, deliberately restricting the women's earnings so that journeymen could afford to pay their prices. For the parties of young men who went there, visits to the brothel were part of the progress to male adulthood. Essentially, society sanctioned and legitimated the male sexual drive as energy, which could and should be allowed expression: sexual experience was part of growing up.

In the aftermath of the Reformation, the Catholic Church responded by holding a series of councils to address the calls for reform. The result of these meetings was a direct pressure on Catholics to suppress any sexual urges, especially outside of marriage. A more direct result of the Reformation on sexual attitudes was an increase in the role of women in political affairs. Despite Luther's, Calvin's, and other reformists' claims to a minimal amount of gender equality, women at a political level prospered. Over the course of the 17th century, women acquired more political legitimacy in the reigns of Elizabeth I, Mary I, and other women rulers who dominated the political scene. The Reformation would transform not just the political and household arenas, it also changed the traditional social aspects of European society, including prostitution.

See also Rites of Passage.

Further Reading: McClendon, Muriel C., Joseph P. Ward, and Michael Macdonald. *Protestant Identities: Religion, Society, and Self-Fashioning in Post-Reformation England.* Stanford, CA: Stanford University Press, 1999; Weisner-Hanks, Mary. *Convents Confront the Reformation: Catholic and Protestant Nuns in Germany.* Milwaukee, WI: Marquette University Press, 1996.

Jaime Ramon Olivares

PROTOCOL TO PREVENT, SUPPRESS AND PUNISH TRAFFICKING IN PERSONS, ESPECIALLY WOMEN AND CHILDREN. *See* **United Nations Trafficking Protocol.**

PURITY CAMPAIGNS.

Purity campaigns (also often called *social purity campaigns* or *purity crusades*) refer to collective attempts to eliminate activities that are perceived to be sinful, detrimental to human betterment, or likely to promote destructive behavior. Groups and individuals involved in such campaigns typically push for greater public awareness of, and increased social control over, prostitution, extramarital or premarital sexual relations, pornography, and the use of **alcohol** and illicit drugs. Reformers and activists attempt to influence important decision makers, especially legislators, in implementing specific policies and practices that are aimed at disrupting, punishing, or suppressing such activities. The main opposition that such campaign-ers face in the political arena are "regulationists" or those who believe that such activities cannot be eradicated and are better "controlled" by government agencies and health providers. Those who either engage in such activities or profit from them form another kind of resistance to the ambitions of reformers. Prostitutes have often found themselves resisting the power of both reformers and regulationists.

Social Purity Reform in the United States and England

Social historians have extensively studied the period 1860–1915 in the United States and England. This era's purity campaigns begin with an almost exclusive focus on prostitution and the desire to eliminate what they termed "the Social Evil." Purity campaigners also launched a parallel campaign to strengthen chastity among youth.

Many of them saw prostitution as a form of slavery and did not believe that any girl or woman would choose to engage in it. Along with early feminists and religious activists, these reformers claimed that they were against prostitution, but not the prostitute, whom they saw as a victim. Her pathway into the sex trade was attributed to either economic desperation, previous seduc-tion by men down a path of moral deregulation, or physical abduction by procurers.

The latter claim would come to be called "**white slavery**," a term later applied to prostitution in general. Although historians of prostitution differ on how common coercive practices were, all agree that it represented a small minority of cases. Crusaders represented instances of coercion, and of **child prostitution**, as representative of the industry as a whole. Social purity campaigners were, however, largely responsible for scandalizing the public on these matters.

In the United States, "white slavery" invoked the specter of sex between white women and nonwhite, usually immigrant men, whom reformers claimed were **trafficking** in young girls. As the idea of "white slave traffic" gained ground, it represented the whole of prostitution as a coer-cive conspiracy.

Political Advancement of the Reformers

Purity campaigners defeated nearly every "regulationist" alternative that appeared in major cities, such as red light districts. (These were districts, mostly in cities, where prostitution, pandering, and brothel keeping were decriminalized.) By the turn of the 20th century, their political clout was formidable, even causing medical associations (previously strong supporters of regulation) to abandon such proposals.

Regulationism offended reformers in several ways. First, it was seen as too complacent about the inevitable existence of prostitution, which reformers did not accept. Many believed instead that modern men should learn to be as chaste as they believed most women "naturally" were. Regulationism facilitated a sexual outlet for men that enabled two negative outcomes, accord-ing to reformers: it would cause them to have no incentive to become more chaste, and, as the famed reformer **Josephine Butler** suggested, it maintained a "double standard" of morality for men and women that perpetuated inequality. Additionally, regulationist practices, particularly in England, implied forced gynecological examinations, which purity campaigners thought was itself a kind of **rape**.

Reformers operated with a different understanding of prostitution's causes than did pros-titutes themselves. Many women who worked in prostitution in fact had economic motives. However, even this conclusion, where sometimes recognized by reformers, was oversimplified: she had no choice, lest she starve. Although some women and girls engaged in prostitution to meet bare survival needs, others selected prostitution as a course that they thought was the least problematic among a number of other poorly paid, exploitative, drudging, even boring income options. Many working-class women pursued this line of work for its comparative advantage over other employment available to them, such as industrial, retail, or domestic work. Still others maintained "legitimate" jobs while supplementing their income with prostitution. Many simply desired a means to live with some amount of leisure, comfort, independence, and small luxuries.

This complexity underscored the reformers' social distance from those they wished to save. Reformers attempted to develop programs to steer prostitutes into alternative, albeit unskilled, employment. The reformers saw this as offering honest work to a "lost" girl, but the girls themselves often saw it otherwise: as a return to low-wage exploitation without the nicer clothes and entertainments that went along with their previous lives in the sex trade.

Prostitution continued to grow despite the many tangible political victories won by the movement. Yet the aims of the purity campaigns were broader. Reformers identified prostitution as "the social evil" for reasons beyond sexual propriety. For the middle class, prostitution came to symbolize a thorough commercialization of all aspects of intimate life, which was widely sentimentalized in the Victorian period. Nonmarital sex also implied the loss of virginity, which middle-class commentators associated with a loss of social status and marriageability. This view of virginity does not appear to have been widely shared by working-class girls.

The Decline of the Social Purity Movements

By the turn of the 20th century, reformers in the United States refocused their energies toward **abstinence** from alcohol. Also, a number of city governments by the 1910s had convened vice commissions to do research, publish reports, and develop recommendations on prostitution. The social science–trained fieldworkers hired to examine the problem developed the consensus opinion that, while present, coercion into the sex trade was largely anecdotal. Concluding that entry into prostitution was mainly voluntary, municipal leaders returned to an older tone of moral condemnation of the prostitute. The previous elimination of licensed **brothels** and red light districts put "the social evil" more out of sight, and continued attempts to suppress prostitution focused on the arrest, incarceration, and "rehabilitation" of prostitutes. The era of "rescue" was over.

See also Abolitionism; Marriage; Purity Movements.

Further Reading: Butler, Josephine. "The Double-Standard of Morality." *Philanthropist*, October 1886; Grittner, Frederick K. *White Slavery: Myth, Ideology, and American Law.* New York: Garland, 1990; Pivar, David J. *Purity Crusade: Sexual Morality and Social Control, 1868–1900.* Westport, CT: Greenwood Press, 1973; Rosen, Ruth. *The Lost Sisterhood: Prostitution in America, 1900–1918.* Baltimore: Johns Hopkins University Press, 1982; Vice Commission of Chicago. *The Social Evil in Chicago: A Study of Existing Conditions.* Chicago: Gunthorp-Warren Printing Company, 1911; Walkowitz, Judith R. *City of Dreadful Delight: Narratives of Sexual Danger in Late-Victorian London.* Chicago: University of Chicago Press, 1992.

Pamela Donovan

PURITY MOVEMENTS. Social **purity campaigns** in the United States and Britain addressed prostitution and other issues of sexuality (such as age of consent, **white slavery**, and birth control), usually taking the position that unregulated sexuality caused widespread social damage. Although many organizations worked alongside the police, they had no legal authority and were generally independent "vigilante" movements. People who founded and joined social purity movements often did so for religious reasons, although medical, political, and economic reasons for regulating or abolishing prostitution were commonly invoked. One of the most striking elements of these organizations was that prostitutes themselves were rarely consulted about policies that affected their lives and livelihoods. Instead, prostitutes appear to have been invoked as examples of martyred womanhood, social disease, or other ideological symbolism; even organizations that worked to rescue prostitutes, rather than punish them, had little interest in addressing prostitutes as individuals or exploring the reasons why prostitution may have been a practical or desired choice of profession.

Between the 1690s and 1730s, London **societies for the reformation of manners** brought about the closure of brothels and "Molly Houses" (homosexual **brothels**). The prostitutes risked being flogged, sentenced to beating with hemp, or even—for convictions of sodomy—executed. The next major wave of organized social purity campaigns came in the late 18th century and led to the formation of the Society for the Suppression of Vice (known simply as the Vice Society) in 1802. An evangelical movement, this society campaigned against a variety of social ills, including brothels, before coming to focus almost exclusively on obscenity. The mid-19th century saw the rise of organizations dedicated to rescue work; as a result, many prostitutes entered **Magdalen Homes**, where they were required to demonstrate penitence and rehabilitation, although the efficacy of such methods was doubtful.

The most significant British social purity campaign resulted from activism dedicated to repealing the **Contagious Diseases Acts. Josephine Butler**, who learned of the Acts during her rescue work with prostitutes in Liverpool, founded the Ladies' National Association for the Repeal of the Contagious Diseases Acts (LNA). By 1877, there were more than 800 regional and local chapters throughout Britain. Drawing on her religious beliefs, as well as lessons learned from her abolitionist father, Butler emphasized that repeal of the Acts was an issue that affected all women, regardless of class. She directly opposed the belief that prostitutes (who were mostly of the working class) should be exploited by middle-class men so as to protect their wives from male sexuality. The irony was that, in many cases, "innocent" wives became infected with their husbands' venereal disease. It was unfair, claimed Butler, that women should be not only the victims of male vice, but punished for it. The women of the LNA were not the only ones working for repeal—Quakers, working men, and physicians were among those who formed organizations and took active roles—but this marked the first time that women had spoken publicly about venereal disease, and it was a significant turning point in the perception of prostitution as an issue that was relevant to all women.

Ellice Hopkins, an influential but now largely forgotten campaigner, played a large role in encouraging the active participation of women in rescue movements, in spite of her personal revulsion of such work. She also worked to establish the White Cross League, a society within the Church of England that urged men to vow personal chastity. Such an approach highlights one of the fundamental beliefs of purity movements, that both genders must strive for sexual purity. A more dramatic attempt at gaining the support of the public came from the reformer **William T. Stead**, editor of the *Pall Mall Gazette*, who decided to use his newspaper as a mouthpiece to promote purity and the dangers of the prostitution industry. In 1885, Stead arranged for a madam to buy an underage virgin from her parents, with the proclaimed intent of selling the girl to a continental brothel. "The Maiden Tribute of Modern Babylon" earned Stead three months in prison, but the outrage it stirred in both Britain and the United States led to a far greater public awareness and abhorrence of the issue of the white slave trade and **forced prostitution**.

American social purity movements shared much of the ideological foundations of their British counterparts, such as a religious impetus that emphasized the redemption of fallen women and a rejection of the sexual double standard. However, although American feminists had worked both politically and personally with prostitutes since the 1830s, through groups such as the Female Moral Reform Society, there was no American counterpart to the LNA. Legislation similar to the Contagious Diseases Acts was proposed only on very limited and local scales in the United States, most notably in St. Louis between 1870 and 1874, so there was no overarching issue that required activism.

In the late 19th and early 20th centuries, U.S. groups such as the Women's Christian Temperance Union, which created a Social Purity Department in 1885, argued against prostitution on the grounds that it reduced women to second-class citizens. This tied into contemporary debates about women's suffrage: not only should women be equal to men in possessing the right to vote, but once women were able to vote, they might use their political clout to protect other women from being exploited by men.

See also Abolition; Fallen Woman Trope; Marriage; Religion.

Further Reading: Bolt, Christine. *The Women's Movements in the United States and Britain from the 1790s to the 1920s.* Amherst: University of Massachusetts Press, 1993; Bristow, Edward J. *Vice and Vigilance: Purity Movements in Britain since 1700.* Totowa, NJ: Rowman and Littlefield, 1977; Hobson, Barbara Meil. *Uneasy Virtue: The Politics of Prostitution and the American Reform Tradition.* New York: Basic Books, 1987; Pivar, David J. *Purity Crusade: Sexual Morality and Social Control, 1868–1900.* Westport, CT: Greenwood Press, 1973; Walkowitz, Judith. *Prostitution and Victorian Society: Women, Class, and the State.* Cambridge: Cambridge University Press, 1980.

Tracey S. Rosenberg

R

R&R. R&R is an abbreviation for "rest and relaxation," a phrase promoted first by the military. English sailors in the 18th and 19th centuries under captains Benjamin Wallis, William Bligh, and James Cook in Polynesia and elsewhere, along with scientists and writers such as Scottish writer and poet Robert Louis Stevenson, enjoyed exotic and seemingly easily erotic stays among "other people" in lands of good climates. During World War II, in Hawaii, naïve young servicemen paid $3 for three minutes of R&R, of morale uplift in the face of tedium and lengthy sea voyages. The Spanish had built two military installations in the Philippines that were later ceded to invading Americans and that eventually became Subic Bay naval base and Clark Air Force base. Tens of thousands of American servicemen enjoyed their first exotic port of call, too, this time at Olongapo City. The 20 or so R&R sites in the late 1950s had swelled to 1,567 in Olongapo and another 615 in Angeles city by the late 1980s.

Hawaii and the Philippines were only two of the many places where military sexism found its logical expression. Soldiers viewed the girls and women there through lenses of compliant Asian femininity but referred to them derogatorily as "slant eyes." The "little brown sex machines" referred to on T-shirts in Okinawa, Japan, morphed quickly into "little brown fucking machines powered by rice" in displays of militarized **misogyny**. Following six months of service, soldiers tired of drinking and playing billiards and video games could fly cheaply to Thailand, Hong Kong, Okinawa, or South Korea for more of the same, where structurally similar R&R venues had been set up for them. The 500,000 American soldiers in and near Saigon during the Vietnam War were matched in number by women and girls in prostitution, many in a kind of licensing system approved by the U.S. military.

At least four historical developments enabled the growth of R&R. By name and institution, it originated in the Mutual Defense Treaty signed in the late 1950s by U.S. and Korean authorities that granted American servicemen sexual access to Korean females at a 3-to-1 ratio. Second, the Japanese occupation of Manchuria, Korea, and Okinawa included the sexual enslavement, to the Japanese Imperial Army, of 200,000 women and girls (**comfort women**) in state-sponsored

brothels known as Comfort Stations. Third, near the end of World War II, the Battle of Okinawa occurred, during which far more civilians died than soldiers. Surviving Okinawan women were given by retreating or surrendering Japanese soldiers to the American occupation forces. Fourth, sex tourism got a huge boost in **Bangkok** and Pattaya, Thailand, during the1960s and 1970s because of the Vietnam War, when American participants were flown to R&R sites not formally attached to military bases. In 1966, the Thai government passed the Entertainment Places Act, which codified the practice of police tolerance of military prostitution. The following year, an agreement allowing American soldiers to travel to Pattaya for R&R was signed, and spending in Pattaya grew from US$5 million in 1967 to US$20 million in 1970. **Venues** created to cater to American GIs expanded and today accommodate international tourists.

As in Hawaii, Okinawa, and Olongapo, Bangkok's central role in military prostitution promoted severe abuse of women, distortion of local economies, flaunting of traditional values, abandonment of biracial children, and penicillin-resistant strains of gonorrhea. At the end of the first Persian Gulf War in Iraq, the U.S. military once again sent troops on sex vacations to Thailand.

Further Reading: Bailey, Beth, and David Farber. *The First Strange Place: The Alchemy of Race and Sex in World War Two Hawaii.* New York: Free Press, 1992; Enloe, Cynthia. *Bananas, Beaches and Bases: Making Feminist Sense of International Politics.* Berkeley: University of California Press, 1989; Jeffrey, Leslie Ann. *Sex and Borders: Gender, National Identity, and Prostitution Policy in Thailand.* Honolulu: University of Hawaii Press, 2003; Moon, Katherine. *Sex Among Allies: Military Prostitution in U.S.-Korea Relations.* New York: Columbia University Press, 1997; Sturdevant, Saundra, and Brenda Stoltzfus, eds. *Let the Good Times Roll: Prostitution and the U.S. Military in Asia.* New York: New Press, 1992.

Lawrence Hammar

RACE AND ETHNICITY. Race and ethnicity are aspects of identity by which people categorize others, and different races and ethnicities predominate in various places and communities. These categories play out in the sex industry as well as in general culture. For example, race and ethnicity are key components in how women are structurally positioned within the sex industry, especially in prostitution. The categories used to classify race and gender are reflected and reinforced with hierarchies within the sex industry, which are reflected in working conditions and earnings. The sex industry is an extension of various niche markets in the service sector that also reflect racial and ethnic social construction and stereotypes. Racial categories shift according to historical era, individual and group definition, and geography. This is true within the sex industry across geographic spaces and cultural epochs.

Race is a key variable in stratification among sex workers (mainly women, though men are also workers as well as consumers in the sex industry). The history of prostitution and race within the United States offers insight to the racial positioning of ethnic minorities. Cultural and economic production of sexual images throughout the sex industry reproduces racial categories of the society in which they are situated. Racialized desire is a form of desire influenced by racial and ethnic ideologies regarding sexuality and degrees of attractiveness as grounds for racial and ethnic status.

Origins of Racial Sexual Stereotypes in the United States

Sex slavery is part of America's history. In spite of white men's sexual and economic domination of slave women, some slave women engaged in sexual relationships with elite white

Categories in the New York listings of "female escorts."

vip escorts
all escorts
blonde
brunette
redhead
gfe
independent
agency
xxx stars
centerfolds
super busty
mature ladies
full figured
European
verified photo listings
visiting
incall
outcall
Asian
ebony
latina
women for women
women for couples
manhattan
long island
new jersey
staten island

From http://www.eros.com (2005).

men to avoid field work or obtain special treatment. In rare cases among free slave women, **marriage** occurred. Slave women may have prostituted their bodies in exchange for amenities or special treatment, but they were owned rather than employed, and many were raped. Thus, there is a distinction between free and paid sexual labor, which underscores the current situation in which many minorities find themselves positioned in the sex industry vis-à-vis the dominant ethnic group.

Sex and the Reproduction of Race

In Louisiana the positioning of mulattos stemmed from Catholic French culture. Similar to the situation in South Carolina, in Louisiana mulattos enjoyed a certain level of privilege vis-à-vis unmixed blacks. Some mulattos "rose to elite status in the Louisiana sugar economy and then with cotton … became wealthy, cultivated the arts of education, bought freedom from slavery … and owned slaves. The mulatto elites avoided identification and marriage with both blacks and whites … carefully arranging marriages with other mulattos" (Davis 2001, 36).

Louisiana, unlike other southern states, had a three-tiered racial classification. The Louisiana Civil Code of 1808 outlawed free people of color from marrying unmixed blacks or whites. The term "Creole" in Louisiana refers to U.S-born whites with French or Spanish origin. The term "Creole of color" means mixed black persons with French or Spanish origin. The sexual economy of prostitutes evolved around elite white men having mulatta concubines for sexual pleasure, during and post-slavery. Concubines and prostitutes were "sold as 'fancy girls' in the internal slave market, and **New Orleans** and Frankfort, Kentucky, became the largest market for pretty quadroons and octoroons" (Davis 2001, 37). In New Orleans mulattas were brought in from plantations, and mulattas became lighter with each generation.

Miscegenation was tolerated because the "one-drop" rule, which held that any trace of black blood classified a person as "black," was rejected in this part of the South. Miscegenation was central to the slave system on Southern plantations. The ownership of black women slaves by white men was an extension of their economic power over slaves, especially women slaves. The closing of the slave trade in the early 19th century "did not weaken the institution of slavery … it had a reverse effect. It increased the financial commitment of slavery … in addition to the increased financial commitment of slavery, the slave-trade ban increase the reliance of natural reproduction for replenishing the slave population" (Wilson 1978, 31). F. James Davis avers that control of black women under the institution of slavery meant control of her sex life as well. This was common in places with slavery, and Kempadoo (2004) describes similar control of slaves' sexuality used for profit in the **Caribbean.**

Thus, miscegenation was tolerated as long as sexual contact took place between white men and black women, but not vice versa. Davis (2001, 39) states that the reasoning was that "a mixed child in a white household violated and threatened the whole slave system. A mixed child in the slave quarters was not only no threat to the system, but … a valuable economic asset, another slave."

Social opprobrium directed at interracial carnality was not limited to the South. Gilfoyle (1992) describes clustering that led to **brothels** featuring particular racial and ethnic groups in specific areas of **New York City.** "Most black-run establishments operated with little fanfare or opposition, except for the interracial 'black and tans.' By ignoring many of the conventions of racial segregation, these establishments drew criticism from many who normally tolerated commercial sex" (Gilfoyle 1992, 209). **Five Points** was known for its ethnic variety, including in prostitution. The most reviled prostitutes were white women who sold sex to men of color, especially Chinese men (Gilfoyle 1992, 232).

Native Populations in the United States

Native women also have been sexually commodified historically and were often forced into prostitution during the years of European conquest and the extraction of Native land in the United States. According to sociologist Joanne Nagel (2003), Native women were often coerced into prostitution with European men as the latter's way to assert control and dominance over a land and people. Similar to the example of racial sexual boundaries being crossed by black and white, racial boundaries were crossed between Native women and white men, but often as a result of **rape.**

Upon first contact, European men were fascinated by what they perceived in the behavior of Native people as an uninhibited sexuality wherein the women were scantily dressed and participated in sexual promiscuous sexual behavior (Nagel 2003). Like the ideology of African slave women in the United States as lustful and sexually seducing white men, ideology that white men used to justify the systematic raping of black women within the institution of slavery, Native women were viewed as prostituting their bodies to white men, whereas white settler men were seen as indulging in desires with these women.

However, the sexual exchange between Native women and white men was also a consequence of increasing poverty as a result of the relocation of Native people. As Nagel points out, "many white sexual advances were not welcomed by Native people, but were accepted in acts of desperation. The poverty resulting from forced Indian removals from homelands and the destruction of indigenous economics left many Native communities destitute" (70). Hence, the relocation of Native peoples to remote, impoverished reservations also rendered prostitution an act of economic desperation among Native women and men. In an interview conducted by Brooks in 1998, an HIV-positive Native man, Chata, described the social circumstances and his life on a reservation as a prostitute.

> I was born on the Indian reservation outside of El Paso, Texas. I have been HIV positive for fifteen years. Sex work for me was a situation that just kind of happened… it was a survival issue. There's very little running water and electricity on the rez; there's a lot of bars and liquor. Being born on the rez and being oppressed as people, as well as having lack of facilities—I

used to spend a lot of time on the strip in hotels and bars, while selling corn, tamales. I did sex work for survival. The guys used to play guard for the girls inside the hotels. When you're out on the streets, cleaning houses, picking cotton, and selling food—again, it was about survival. I've been doing AIDS work for the last twelve years, and I do HIV prevention policy… when it comes to equal access to information and drugs there's not equality while our communities of color continue to be affected with HIV and AIDS. (Brooks 2000)

Ethnic Marketing

The sex industry offers examples in support of the argument put forth by various race scholars that race is socially and biologically constructed and has real-life consequences. Sex workers who are members of a dominant racial or ethnic group generally earn more than those who are members of ethnic and racial minorities. It has been noted that "women of color are disproportionately clustered in the least well-paid and most stigmatized sectors of the sex industry such as street prostitution" (Chapkis 2000, 187).

There is a clientele for racial and ethnic minorities in the sex industry, but their working conditions often reflect their racially stratified position and their typically lower wages in all fields. Sex workers from racial and ethnic minorities frequently are seen as worth less than white colleagues. This corresponds to their clients: venues that cater to an ethnically mixed clientele are more likely to feature a wider variety of ethnicities among dancers, prostitutes, and other sex workers. In the United States these venues typically cater to working-class clientele, whereas more upscale venues cater to white-collar workers and may employ a token African American or Latina, as well as Asians and whites. In East Asia, some brothels post signs listing prices and services offered: In a **Hong Kong** brothel, the girls who work there are priced by ethnic group, with Malaysian and Philippine sex workers listed lowest" (Louie 2003, 8). **COYOTE** member Gloria Lockett, a black former prostitute stated,

> Race played a very big part in how much money you made. Fortunately or unfortunately, I hung around a bunch of sisters who were white. We all helped each other out. If one of the girls would catch a date, we had an apartment or checked out the pad that we were working out of. The two or three Black women would wait until they got to the apartment and we would double date. So, if you were standing out on the corner, they would definitely pick up the white girl first. No matter how big, ugly, or old she looked—it didn't matter: The white girl went first, then the black girls. (Brooks 2000)

However, the eroticization of ethnicity also creates a "niche market" in the sex industry based on race. Ethnic enclaves in prostitution both cater to minority communities and provide "exotic" sex workers in niche markets in the United States and elsewhere. For example, in India, Nepalis are stereotyped as sexy and sexual, in ways similar to how African Americans are eroticized. "In India's red-light districts, the demand for Nepali girls, especially virgins with fair skin and Mongolian features, continues to increase" (Human Rights Watch 1995). Ethnic enclaves within the practice of prostitution may also feature **trafficking**.

In an ethnic niche, prostitution often becomes another example of a job in the expanding service sector and a way many people contribute to supporting their families. Many people do sex work to supplement their income from other types of jobs in the service sector.

Ethnic markets include sex **tourism** with sex workers of all genders. In the Caribbean, stereotypes of the hypersexual Caribbean man and the hot Latina who enjoys sex combine with the Caribbean stereotypes of white women as sexually greedy and the reality that foreigners of a certain age generally have financial and other resources to offer to create an unequal sexual economy. In **Bangkok**, the sex industry entertainers who are successful with Western, usually white tourists have dark skin, a feature of the peasants and ethnic minorities, whereas those deemed most desirable by local standards of beauty have fair skin.

Race and Performance

The consequences of racial preference are evident in the racial stratification of sex workers. Racial performances in the sex industry are often performed via stereotypes of what each group is supposed to be like sexually. It has been argued that black and Latina women are stereotypically viewed not only as hypersexual, but also as hyper-heterosexual as a way to equate them with animals.

> Depicting people of African descent as symbols of embodied, natural sexuality that "fucked" like animals and produced babies installed Black people as the essence of nature. Moreover, the concern with Black fertility linked perceptions of promiscuity to assumptions of heterosexuality. Within this logic, homosexuality was assumed to be impossible among Black people because same-sex sexual practices did not result in reproduction. (Hill-Collins 2004, 105)

Stereotypes of black and Latina women, including women from the Caribbean, are that they are "hot" and sexually aggressive, vis-à-vis white women, who are viewed as pure "real" women, and Asian women are often portrayed as being submissive. This is evident in **Internet** advertisements for phone sex and online sex sites where these adjectives are used to describe the sexuality of various women of color.

Categories from the New York listings of "female escorts" at the Web site http://www.eros.com refer to characteristics such as body shape, hair color, or age. Four categories refer to race or ethnicity: "Asian," "Latina," "Ebony," and "European." Some may assume that the categories of "blonde, brunette, and redhead" could also refer to women of European descent; however, a quick perusal of these pages shows that women of a diverse variety of racial and ethnic backgrounds list their profiles here. Most of the women do not list their fees on this site, so it is difficult to know if there are significant differences in the amount women of color are able to command as opposed to white women.

Some advertisement text seems to play on racial stereotypes of "exotic" beauty and the hypersexuality of such women. For example, one ad in the "ebony" category reads in part, "Almost Nothing is Taboo, but it is Sweet! Hey guys my name is Sade, and I am an exotic and passionate escort." Another listing in the ebony section plays with racial stereotypes but also incorporates symbols of the upper middle class: "How about a little death by chocolate? Guaranteed to satisfy your sweet tooth. I stand 5'3", 123 lbs., solid, short n' sweet and good enough to eat! With the hottest backside this side and that side of the Mississippi, and baby soft skin to boot! I am a college educated, articulate, and cultured young lady." However, it should be stated that many of the ad texts do not play on such stereotypes and are not overly racialized. For example, emphasizing such personal qualities as "caring," "fun," and "intelligent" were common across ads of all racial and ethnic categories.

Race and Trafficking

The "**comfort women**"—sexual slaves of the Japanese military during World War II—represent the most notorious case of sex **trafficking**. That Japanese women were not conscripted and mostly Korean women were highlights the ethnic aspect of trafficking. However, most trafficking cases involve people known to and trusted by the people who are trafficked. The element of **migration** brings in concepts of race and ethnicity in another way—given that trafficking often involves movement from one cultural and linguistic area to another and may be complicated by ethnic ties.

Race is also played out in efforts to "rescue" people in the sex industry, in what has been labeled "White women saving Brown women from Brown men" (Spivak 1994, 93) Rescuing women from prostitution in the 19th century initially focused on class and was used to professionalize social work as a career for women. Now rescues and raids are conducted in Asia by international organizations that intend to save women and children from prostitution. Problems begin when organizations conducting these raids do not find out if women want to be rescued or what would be helpful for them to change careers. Organizations that seek to rescue children have forcibly removed adult women, particularly those who look young to their would-be rescuers, from their workplaces. Some women have no other source of support and do not want to be rescued, especially if rescue organizations have not provided for livable wages in another line of work. Many women removed from **brothels** in raids return to brothels with greater debts than before they were rescued.

See also Stigma.

Further Reading: Agustín, Laura. "Helping Women Who Sell Sex: The Construction of Benevolent Identities." *Rhizomes* 10 (Spring 2005), http://www.rhizomes.net/issue10/agustin.htm; Brooks, Siobhan. "Working the Streets: Gloria Lockett's Story." *Spectator.net interviews* (2000), http://www.spectator.net/1155/pages/1155_lockett.html; Bulmer, Martin, and Solomos, John. *Racism.* New York: Oxford University Press, 1999; Chapkis, Wendy. "Power and Control in the Commercial Sex Trade." In *Sex for Sale,* ed. R. Weitzer. New York: Routledge, 2000, pp. 181–201; Davis, Angela. *Women, Race, and Class.* New York: Vintage, 1983; Davis, F. James. *Who Is Black?: One Nation's Definition.* University Park: Pennsylvania State University Press, 2001; Dominguez, Virginia R. *White by Definition: Social Classification in Creole Louisiana.* New Brunswick, NJ: Rutgers University Press, 1986; Gilfoyle, Timothy J. *City of Eros: New York City, Prostitution, and the Commercialization of Sex, 1790–1920.* New York: W.W. Norton, 1992; Hill-Collins, Patricia. *Black Sexual Politics.* New York: Routledge, 2004; Human Rights Watch. *Rape For Profit: Trafficking of Nepali Girls and Women to India's Brothels.* New York: Human Rights Watch, 2005. http://www.hrw.org/reports/1995/India.htm; Kempadoo, Kamala, and Jo Doezema. *Global Sex Workers: Rights, Resistance, and Redefinition.* New York: Routledge, 1998; Kemapadoo, Kamala. *Sexing the Caribbean.* New York: Routledge, 2004; Lerner, Gerda. *Black Women in White America.* New York: Vintage, 1973; Louie, Reagan. *Orientalia: Sex in Asia.* New York: Powerhouse Books, 2003; McClintock, Anne. *Imperial Leather: Race, Gender and Sexuality in the Colonial Contest.* New York: Routledge, 1995; Model, Suzanne. "The Ethnic Niche and the Structure of Opportunity: Immigrants and Minorities in New York City." In *The Underclass Debate: Views from History,* ed. Michael B. Katz. Princeton, NJ: Princeton University Press, 1993; Nagel, Joanne. *Race, Ethnicity, and Sexuality: Intimate Intersections, Forbidden Frontiers.* New York: Oxford University Press, 2003;Roberts, Dorothy. *Killing the Black Body.* New York: Vintage 1997; Spivak, Gayatri Chakravorty. "Can the Subaltern Speak?" In *Colonial Discourse and Post Colonial Theory,* ed. Patrick Williams and Laura Chrisman. New York: Columbia University Press, 1994, pp. 66–111; Thukral, Juhu, Melissa Ditmore, and Alexandra Murphy. *Behind Closed Doors: An Analysis of Indoor Sex Work in New York City.* New York: Urban Justice Center, 2005. http://www.sexworkersproject.org/reports/BehindClosedDoors.html; Wilson, William Julius. *The Declining Significance of Race: Black and Changing American Institutions.* Chicago: Chicago University Press, 1978.

Siobhan Brooks, Melissa Hope Ditmore, and Juline A. Koken

RAHAB. Rahab the prostitute (Hebrew *zônâ*) appears in the biblical account of the conquest of Jericho (Joshua 2 and 6). She shows herself to be resourceful and shrewd. Judging the invaders the stronger, she hides the two spies sent to assess her city's strength, lies to thwart the king who asks her for them, and, using a crimson cord, aids their escape over the town wall. The cord also marks her house for safety during the invasion. She and her family settle with the people of Israel.

Later Jewish sources are divided on whether to stress her unsavory origin. Based on an Aramaic translation, Rashi and other early rabbis rendered *zônâ* as "innkeeper" rather than "prostitute." This saves the spies' reputation and makes plausible legends of her marriage to Joshua and presence in a line of prophets, including Jeremiah and Huldah. Other rabbis called Rahab a prostitute and began to idealize her as one of the world's most beautiful women. It was claimed she was a harlot from age 10 through the 40-year Israelite sojourn in the desert and that repeating "Rahab, Rahab" caused a seminal discharge.

Like the Hebrew **Bible**, the New Testament only begins to develop an idealized portrait. One text names her as a prostitute saved by faith (Hebrews 11:31); another declares her a prostitute justified by works (James 2:25). Matthew simply listed her in the genealogy of Jesus (1:5).

Medieval and modern artists have represented Rahab in poses based on the Bible. Writers did not often tell her story until the 18th century, and then they were able to conceive her freely, as in Frank G. Slaughter's *The Scarlet Cord* (1956). Or they idealized her, as in sermons and retellings for children.

Further Reading: Kramer, Phyllis Silverman. "Rahab from Peshat to Pedagogy, or: The Many Faces of a Heroine." In *Culture, Entertainment and the Bible*, ed. George Aichele. *Journal for the Study of the Old Testament*, Supplement Series 309. Sheffield, England: Sheffield Academic, 2000; Nelson, Richard D. *Joshua: A Commentary*. Louisville, KY: Westminster/John Knox Press, 1997; Sölle, Dorothée. *Great Women of the Bible in Art and Literature*. Macon, GA: Mercer University Press, 1994, pp. 104–13.

Robert P. Dunn

RAPE. As a result of the **stigma** and often-unlawful nature of prostitution, prostitutes and sex workers are frequent victims of **crime**, including rape. Police, customers, and others who commit **violence** against, threaten, or rob prostitutes know that police and society do not take these crimes seriously and that they, rather than addressing the violent crimes committed against sex workers, often blame the prostitute/crime victim for engaging in unlawful or immoral behavior. In fact, in addition to fearing violence from customers, prostitutes all over the world also legitimately fear police violence, and they complain about police indifference to violence committed against them, including rape. This indifference is often compounded by the myth that sex workers or prostitutes cannot be raped, a view that is especially pernicious when held by the medical community. Prostitutes who have been victims of rape deserve the same attention and care as any other victim of crime. Rape is often considered a crime against women—most women are taught to fear rape and anticipate situations in which it might occur, even though there may be little one can do to prevent it in some situations. However, any person can be raped. Transgender persons are vulnerable to rape, as are men, particularly those in vulnerable situations or those who do not conform to societal stereotypes of masculinity.

Many prostitutes have been raped or have experienced other sexual assault by customers. A 2004 study conducted by sex workers in Cambodia, who interviewed approximately 1,000 sex workers, found that 97 percent reported being raped by someone in the past year (Jenkins 2005). Of 50 sex workers interviewed in one U.S. city in 1997 and 1998, 32 percent had a customer attempt to rape them, and 26 percent had been actually raped (Norton-Hawk 2001). Although most prostitutes fear the prospect of being raped, most relate this concern to the lack of attention paid by police and society to this problem and the particular neglect of rape and other violence committed against sex workers. Therefore, it is not that men who are customers of prostitutes are predisposed to rape, but that anyone who might want to engage in this violence knows that he is likely to act with impunity against sex workers or other sexually marginalized people.

In addition to being subjected to officials' indifference to prostitutes' being raped by customers, many prostitutes have been raped by police. Prostitutes are also victimized by police who extract sex acts from them in exchange for not arresting them, and such a situation is unambiguously coercive. Although a prostitute may at that point make a decision as to which is the lesser of two evils—the sex act or the arrest—many people would also construe this coercion as rape.

During times of war or military occupation, societies often see an increase in rape and prostitution. The most notorious examples of the confluence of rape and prostitution are the **comfort women** forced into prostitution by the Japanese military during World War II. Conflict areas and war zones may not offer many income-generating opportunities for most women, and with many young men in the area, an environment develops in which rape in general, including rape of sex workers, may generally increase. This is particularly so when rape is systematically used as a weapon of war.

Human Rights Watch (2003) documented abuse of sex workers by army personnel in Dhaka, Bangladesh, when the city was occupied by the military. A sex worker interviewed by Human Rights Watch in Dhaka said, "I have been beaten by the army twice. Once the day before yesterday [December 15, 2002] and once the day before that [December 14, 2002].... When they beat me, the soldiers asked me, 'Why are you doing this kind of work. Why aren't you doing a good job?' But at the same time they also want sex. Twice, soldiers on duty raped me. [One of these times] [t]here were five or six soldiers altogether. Two raped me and the others raped other sex workers nearby."

Rape can lead to **posttraumatic stress disorder (PTSD)**, which has been noted as an effect of involvement in the sex industry. However, it is more accurate to view PTSD as a side effect of violence, further compounded by the difficulty for sex workers in most locations to address violence committed against them. Furthermore, sex workers in conflict areas, like everyone in war zones, may have higher rates of PTSD as opposed to general members of civil society, including prostitutes, outside war zones.

Substance abuse is another factor to consider. Some women with a personal history of rape or other sexual abuse may use drugs to deal with the pain of past violence, which can lead to prostitution when she needs to make quick money to feed an **addiction**. Additionally, some women with a history of sexual abuse enter into new sexual encounters with a desire to control their sexual experiences, thus possibly leading to prostitution, which allows them to control the activity. These links between prostitution and history of violence are difficult to ascertain with any kind of specificity because many studies of sex workers and history of sexual abuse or rape occur in settings where rape victims are more likely to be found, such as rape treatment centers or conflict zones.

Finally, rape is often used as a tool against women who are trafficked, forced, or coerced into prostitution. Rape has been used in these settings to control and "prepare" women for prostitution and to break their will to ensure a fear of escaping or otherwise crossing the traffickers. This, of course, is another area in which the correlation between prostitution and PTSD is high.

See also Forced Prostitution; Trafficking.

Further Reading: Human Rights Watch. *"Making Their Own Rules": Police Beatings, Rape, and Torture of Children in Papua New Guinea.* New York: Human Rights Watch, 2004. http://hrw.org/reports/2005/png0905/; Human Rights Watch. *Policy Paralysis: A Call for Action on HIV/AIDS-Related Human Rights Abuses Against Women and Girls in Africa.* New York: Human Rights Watch, 2003. http://www.hrw.org/reports/2003/africa1203; Human Rights Watch. *Ravaging the Vulnerable: Abuses Against Persons at High Risk of HIV in Bangladesh.* New York: Human Rights Watch, 2003. http://www.hrw.org/reports/2003/bangladesh0803/; Jenkins, Carol. "Cambodian Sex Workers Conduct Their Own Research." *Research for Sex Work* 8 (2005), http://www.researchforsexwork.org; Norton-Hawk, Maureen. "The Counterproductivity of Incarcerating Female Street Prostitutes." *Deviant Behavior* 22, no. 5 (Sept–Oct 2001): 403–417; NSW Rape Crisis Center. "I Am a Sex Worker." http://www.nswrapecrisis.com.au/Information%20Sheets/I-am-a-sex-worker.htm; Weitzer, Ronald. "Flawed Theory and Method in Studies of Prostitution." *Violence Against Women* 11, no. 7 (July 2005).

Juhu Thukral

RAPE, STATUTORY. The legal concept of statutory rape is related to age-gap distinctions. If an adult is having sex with a person below the age of majority and charges are pressed against him or her, then this act is penalized either as a misdemeanor or as a felony. Statutory rape charges have been leveled in instances of prostitution involving children and adolescents. The legal definition, if namely this sexual act will be punished as a misdemeanor or as a felony, depends on the age of the involved persons and the age-gap between them. The laws on statutory rape are not homogenous, but they differ from state to state and from country to country. Persons at the age of 13 to 16 years are usually regarded as minors and persons at the age of 16 to 18 years are usually considered to be at the age of consent. If the person having sex with a minor is 2 to 5 years older than the minor, charges can be pressed against him or her. If two minors are the same age, however, having sex is not necessarily considered statutory rape. The sentence can be increased if the adult is more than 5 years older than the minor. These age definitions, however, vary from state to state.

Statutory rape laws are meant to have several functions. Basically, they tend to protect vulnerable ages groups from being coerced to having sex with adults and guard them from sexual exploitation. Statutory rape laws raise moral issues about seduction of minors and they criminalize sexual **violence** against them. At the same time, statutory rape laws aim to prevent problems caused by adolescent pregnancy. In cases of pregnancy by adults at a minor age, mediation measures are hard to implement if fathers refuse to provide the needed financial support. These costs then have to be undertaken by the state. In this sense, the latent function of statutory rape laws is the reduction of public expenditures for the provision of welfare and health care benefits. Social issues are also very important in cases of adolescent pregnancy. Victims of statutory rape, who were forced to become mothers at a minor age, do not only face a number of serious emotional and psychological consequences, but they are also socially excluded from the education and labor system. The possibility of being able to work, of finding a regular job, and raising the child is in the case of the minor very limited. Failing financial support through family and state networks has often driven young mothers to prostitution, especially those from unprivileged families and those with low social end economical status. The minor violently passes from adolescence to adulthood and is expected to fulfill the new role of mother. The rapid change of life style caused by the increased duties and the new responsibilities, the social stigmatization of the abused young mother, and the marginalization and the isolation from the teenager's community are some of the problems that the victim of statutory rape has to deal with.

Maria Makantonatou

RECHY, JOHN (1934–). John Rechy is an American writer best known for his novels based on his experiences as a gay hustler. Born in El Paso, Texas, to Mexican parents, Rechy began drifting and hustling his way around the United States after a stint in the U.S. Army. In his autobiographical first novel, *City of Night* (1963), a nameless narrator recounts his adventures, the street life, and people and johns he encounters as he wanders and hustles himself from **New Orleans** to **New York City**, **Chicago**, San Francisco, and **Los Angeles**. The novel also recounts a childhood in El Paso. *City of Night* was an international literary sensation, creating such a strong demand for copies that the book landed on several best-seller lists before it was even published. It is considered a classic of modern American literature for its subject matter, style, and structure.

Rechy eventually settled in Los Angeles where he hustled until he was 55 years old. He claims he stopped counting after 7,000 sexual partners. A landscape of rough-trade gay hustling provides the backdrop for most of his novels. *Numbers* (1967), *This Day's Death* (1969), *Rushes* (1979), and *The Coming of the Night* (1999) all deal with some aspect of hustling or the changing gay scene. *The Sexual Outlaw: A Documentary* (1977) is his nonfiction take on the subjects.

The author of more than a dozen novels to date, he has also written several that include a gay character but do not feature hustling at their core. These include *Marilyn's Daughter* (1988) and *The Miraculous Day of Amalia Gomez* (1991) and reveal his interest in Hollywood's mystique and his Chicano roots. Rechy disparages the label "gay writer."

Rechy has taught writing at UCLA and USC and is the recipient of two Lifetime Achievement awards: one from PEN USA West and another from the Publishing Triangle. Rechy lives in Hollywood with his partner of many years, film producer Michael Snyder.

Further Reading: Casillo, Charles. *Outlaw: The Lives and Careers of John Rechy*. Los Angeles: Advocate Books, 2002; Reys, Jeff. "LA Outlaw." *Blue* 46 (September 2003): 40–43.

Joe E. Jeffreys

RED THREAD. *See Rode Draad.*

REFORM. Efforts to reform prostitutes, especially female prostitutes, seem to be nearly as ubiquitous as sex work itself. The **Renaissance** and the **Protestant Reformation** marked a turn from the widespread tolerance of prostitution during the Middle Ages. In modern history European women suspected of loose morals have been institutionalized in **Magdalen homes** and asylums or lock hospitals, reform schools, and **prisons**. Contemporary reform efforts in Cuba, China, and Vietnam include internment and "reeducation" of prostitutes.

Reform efforts have never been free of sexism or classism. Female sex workers have been the targets of reformers far more frequently than male or **transgender sex workers** have been. Attempts to prevent or regulate prostitution have punished some women, usually working-class and poor women, for behavior that would be entirely innocent when engaged in by others. Prostitute advocacy was one way wealthy women professionalized social work and made a career out of the reform of "wayward" women. This phenomenon generally took the form of upper-class and middle-class women attempting to change the way poor people lived.

Historically, the two "occupations" of respectable women were domestic work and **marriage**, and most women in prisons and Magdalen homes for prostitution had been domestic servants. Domestic service meant labor with low wages and often sexual harassment, seduction, and **rape**. Drudgery could well motivate a person to accept money for what may not have actually been more distasteful service. Considering available options, it becomes easier to see why some women would engage in sexual transactions on a professional and overt level or an "amateur" and unspoken level, as with "charity girls," and so become the object of reform efforts.

Moral panics promote greater attention to prostitution and have often been accompanied by reform efforts. These efforts to reform women have often been resisted by prostitutes. Reform efforts have been used to restrict female autonomy, as illustrated in Victorian **London**, with the mob response to both William Stead's **"Maiden Tribute of Modern Babylon"** and **Jack the Ripper**'s violence against women. In both cases, women and girls were expected to stay close to home rather than society being expected to respond to **violence** against women.

Women who reject or disobey reform efforts have been deemed fair game for exposure, punishment, and imprisonment. Reformers and social workers can be great allies against violence, but can also create difficulties for sex workers who, for example, are viewed as unfit parents solely because of their occupation. Despite this, a "whore **stigma**" extends from prostitutes and other sex workers even to social workers and other advocates for the **human rights** of sex workers. Advocates for the human rights of sex workers, including the Nobel Peace Prize recipient Doctors Without Borders, have been misconstrued as being "pro-prostitution," a term like "pro-abortion."

Industry- and law-reform efforts include attempts to promote better working conditions in the sex industry, with the introduction of **occupational safety and health** standards, attempts to prevent **trafficking** of persons into the sex industry, and different efforts to change **legal approaches** to sex work, from **decriminalization** to legalization to criminalization and **abolition**.

Further Reading: Agustín, Laura. "Helping Women Who Sell Sex: The Construction of Benevolent Identities." *Rhizomes* 10 (2005), http://www.rhizomes.net/issue10/agustin.htm; Coalition Against Trafficking in Women. "CATW Debates Pro-Prostitution NGOS." *Coalition Report* 5–6 (1998–2000): 8–9; Hughes, Donna. "The 2002 *Trafficking In Persons Report*: Lost Opportunity For Progress: 'Foreign Government Complicity in Human Trafficking: A Review of the State Department's 2002 Trafficking in Persons Report.'" Oral presentation to the House Committee on International Relations, June 19, 2002; Pheterson, Gail. *The Prostitution Prism*. Amsterdam: Amsterdam University Press, 1996; Self, Helen J. *Prostitution, Women and Misuse of the Law The Fallen Daughters of Eve*. London: Frank Cass, 2003.

Melissa Hope Ditmore

REGULATION. *See* **Legal Approaches.**

RELIGION. The relationship between religion and prostitution has varied immensely through history. Prostitution has been an integral part of some religions, tolerated by others, and opposed by still others, though with varying degrees of vigor.

Sacred Prostitution

Sacred prostitution, also known by the Greek term *hierodouleia,* may have occurred among pagan peoples of the ancient Middle East, and still persists today. A number of its ancient versions sought to ensure agricultural fertility because of associations generally believed to exist between human sexual activity and the general fecundity of nature.

Apffel-Marglin has shown that contemporary Indian sacred prostitution and religious prostitution in the ancient Middle East share important characteristics. In both, sacred prostitutes are often identified as the living embodiment of a goddess or are considered married to a deity. Both also feature a strict separation between secular and religious prostitution. In the *Epic of Gilgamesh*, a prostitute teaches the wild Enkidu how to be human before Enkidu himself tames the tyrannical ruler Gilgamesh. In an analogous story in Indian mythology, Rsyasrnga, a deer-human hybrid, is able to save a kingdom from drought after being civilized by a **courtesan.**

In pre-Columbian northwestern Mexico, transvestite and female prostitutes played important religious roles. In Borneo both priests and priestesses served as prostitutes. Fertility-oriented temple prostitution has existed in recent times in West Africa, among the Ewe, the Ibo, and the coastal tribes of Ghana. Upon reaching puberty, women of the North African Awlad Na'il tribe have traditionally engaged in temporary prostitution to raise funds for their dowries. French colonial efforts to discourage the practice were resisted by the populace, which associated the practice with good harvests.

Today, religious prostitution is rare outside of India but plays a role in some new religions, such as the California-based Children of God. Neo-pagans and goddess-worship advocates have promoted the practice in recently published volumes.

Hinduism

According to a Vedic tale, prostitution originated when a holy blind man introduced the concept of selling sex. References to secular prostitution abound in the Vedas and other Hindu scriptures, such as the *Ramayana* and *Mahabharata*. In the centuries before the beginning of the Common Era, Sanskrit contained more than 300 words for prostitutes, referring to sacred prostitutes, high-class courtesans, and many other varieties.

Hindu temples have long hosted sacred prostitutes. Since the 19th century, some Indians have campaigned against the institution; Gandhi denounced it in the strongest possible terms. Sacred prostitution has been completely abolished in some areas, but still flourishes in several regions, particularly in the South, where its prevalence has historically been higher. These prostitutes, who frequently serve as dancers and servants as well, can be born into their trade, sold by their parents, or simply donated by the parents as an alternative to infanticide and to encourage the gods to bless the parents with a male child. Although most sacred prostitutes are women (*devadasis*), some are men (*devadasas*), and others are *hijras*, transvestite eunuchs understood as a third gender.

Christianity

Jesus is described in the Christian scriptures as associating with prostitutes and other marginalized characters. In one scene, he declared to a crowd that tax collectors and prostitutes would go to heaven before the members of the crowd would because these other groups were the first to accept his teachings.

According to the canonical gospels, **Mary Magdalene** was a disciple of Jesus and the first to witness his resurrection. Early church fathers discussed her favorably, and several noncanonical gospels and related writings (including the Gospel of Mary, which survives in fragments) describe her as a spiritual leader and the most important apostle. However, by the 4th century, church leaders in the Latin West had begun to depict her as inferior to the other disciples, and Gregory the Great (who became pope in 590) sealed her identity as a repentant prostitute. He also thought it necessary to declare that she was never sexually involved with Jesus (which was a prevalent rumor, then as now). The Eastern Orthodox Church has never associated her with prostitution, revering her simply as the first disciple to witness the resurrection. Modern scholars uniformly reject her depiction as a prostitute, which is not biblical in origin.

Early Christianity featured numerous tales of repentant prostitutes. Several of the Church's early female saints, including **Thaïs**, were former prostitutes. After repenting, Thaïs, it is said, spent three years imprisoned by a monk, praying for forgiveness in a pool of her bodily waste. She subsequently died, having been purified of sin.

Roman Catholicism

Saint Augustine, a church father from the 4th and 5th centuries, argued that prostitution was a necessary evil, without which sexual immorality would destroy society. Saint **Thomas Aquinas** repeated this view in the 13th century, holding that prostitution prevented the far more serious sin of adultery with married women and that prostitution could prevent a rise in homosexuality (considered a worse sin than heterosexual premarital sex.)

The Catholic Church from 904 to 963 has been described as a "pornocracy" (rule by prostitutes) because of the influence that Theodora and her daughter Marozia, the mistresses and biological progenitors of several popes during this period, held over the papacy. Theodora and Marozia, who are properly understood as concubines, not prostitutes, wielded enormous power over Rome's secular and papal affairs.

In the 14th and especially 15th centuries, city governments in Western Europe commonly owned **brothels**. Prostitutes belonged to guilds, were forced to cease work on Easter and Christmas, and in some places were required to wear a scarlet cord or red armband or other specific **clothing**, recalling the biblical harlot **Rahab**. Prostitutes were among the only literate women; for this reason, Mary Magdalene is frequently depicted with a book in medieval artwork. On Mary Magdalene's feast day in the 15th century, municipalities sponsored races and other sporting events between teams of prostitutes. In this era, the Bishop of Strasbourg opened his own brothel, which clergy attended openly. An English bishop, Saint Swithin of Winchester, built an entire district for brothels in Southwark, the proceeds of which went to the bishopric, per **Henry II**'s decree in 1161. This practice lasted nearly 500 years and financed the construction of numerous churches.

Though tolerant of prostitution as an institution, the Church encouraged individual prostitutes to repent. Pope Innocent III, in an 1198 decree, declared marrying an ex-prostitute a morally commendable act. Pope Gregory IX, in 1227, founded an order of nuns for repentant prostitutes and named the order for Mary Magdalene.

Even if its existence was accepted, prostitution was sometimes regarded as a threat. In late medieval Italy, gangs of young men calling themselves "monastic brotherhoods" perpetrated group **rape** against women found walking alone, ostensibly to protect society from prostitutes. These groups were completely accepted and sometimes included members of governing councils. Also in the late medieval period, the plague was often interpreted as divine punishment for fornication, leading to the repression of prostitution.

Magdalen homes, begun by the **Sisters of the Good Shepherd** in 19th-century Ireland, originally served as a home for ex-prostitutes and other "fallen" women but eventually began to include women accused of minor sexual improprieties. Until very recent times, these institutions imprisoned women for life without trial, forcing them to work in the infamous Magdalen Laundries.

Catholics in the late 20th century have sometimes analyzed prostitution in terms of social justice. *Pastoral da Mulher Marginalizada*, a Brazilian ecclesiastical movement, has existed for two decades. Influenced by liberation theology, the group understands prostitutes as victims of sexism, racism, and police brutality and corruption, and it stresses education and community awareness. Sister Mary Soledad Perpinan, a Philipina nun in the Sisters of the Good Shepherd, founded the Campaign Against Military Prostitution in the early 1980s. An international activist and expert on prostitution, she coordinates the Third World Network Against the Exploitation of Women. Pope John Paul II depicted prostitution as a symptom of the mentality that considers human beings only as things to be traded and used for selfish interests, the same mindset that led to slavery. South Korea's Minjung theology, a mainly Protestant movement that also incorporates traditional shamanistic practices, has also addressed prostitution as a social justice issue.

Protestantism

German theologian Martin Luther argued against both the celibacy of clergy and the toleration of fornication among laity, establishing a universal norm of moderate sexuality within the confines of marriage in the 1500s. Jean Calvin's views on fornication were even more severe, leading to the prosecution of sexually active fiancées. He attempted to force all prostitutes to either repent or leave Geneva.

Protestants succeeded in closing numerous brothels. The Catholic Counter-Reformation, particularly through the Jesuits, also fought against officially sanctioned prostitution. During an episode in the Wars of Religion, Protestant soldiers beat prostitutes and severed their ears.

Nineteenth-century moral-reform societies, originally begun by male Protestant ministers, were later dominated by lay Protestant women. These groups appear largely responsible for the turn against state-regulated prostitution in English-speaking countries. In Britain, feminist campaigns against the 1864 law mandating medical treatment for prostitutes addressed for the first time the sexual double standard of Victorian society, in which male promiscuity was expected and tolerated as instinctual, whereas prostitutes were derided as fallen temptresses to blame for betraying their inherently chaste nature. These campaigners sought a single standard of purity for both sexes, endeavoring both to save prostitutes' souls and to protect all women from the evils caused by male lustfulness. The resultant radicalization of many women contributed to the mobilization for female suffrage in Britain.

Mormonism

Early Mormons were widely reviled for their polygamy, which they claimed eliminated prostitution. Antipolygamy campaigners responded by calling polygamy itself a form of prostitution.

Once the federal government had come to the aid of antipolygamy forces, some Mormons attempted to entrap federal officials in a prostitution scandal, in order to prove that the officials, not the Mormons, were the ones guilty of sexual immorality. After Mormons decided to end polygamy in the late 19th century, Mormons and non-Mormons campaigned together against prostitution, in the fashion of the age.

Judaism

The Jewish Bible contains numerous references to prostitutes and prostitution, many of them relating to the religious prostitution of neighboring peoples. Such prostitution was sometimes incorporated into Hebrew religious practices, including during Solomon's reign. The Bible expressly forbids temple prostitution, a prohibition that was later interpreted by the Talmud as referring to all prostitution (though Talmudic views differ). The prophets employ prostitution as a metaphor of spiritual decline or apostasy.

Although prostitution is generally treated negatively, two Biblical women engaged in prostitution, Tamar and **Rahab**, are regarded as heroines in rabbinic literature. In Genesis, Tamar, an ancestor of King David, was impregnated by her father-in-law Judah after posing as a prostitute; she had been left childless because of the death of two husbands. One Midrashic tale explains this action by the well-regarded Judah as caused by an angel, who knew that the encounter was necessary because Tamar's offspring would become the progenitors of kings (including David). Another traditional commentary has said that because the Torah had not yet been given, prostitution was not yet forbidden.

In the book of Joshua, the gentile prostitute Rahab housed Hebrew spies before the siege of Jericho, saving their lives. Both this act and her eventual conversion were prompted by tales of Jewish military victories, which she saw as divinely ordained. She is regarded as an especially pious, ideal convert in the Talmud, according to which she married Joshua and became the ancestor of several prophets, Jeremiah and Ezekiel among them.

Romans forced Jewish women and sometimes men into prostitution. Some escaped, even to become respected rabbis, and some committed suicide. According to the Talmud, the famous Rabbi Meir rescued his sister-in-law from a Roman brothel, where she had been imprisoned after her parents were executed by the Roman authorities for their religious activities. In Talmudic times, commercial prostitution was understood as a greater threat than religious prostitution, and it was the subject of many warnings and anecdotes. The Talmud tells of a rabbinical student whose tzitzit (ritual fringes) slapped him in the face and pulled him back from the brink of sin with a well-known prostitute. She was so impressed by his piety that she converted to Judaism and married him. Another passage describes a rabbi who spent large sums on prostitutes but eventually repented in response to one prostitute's wise remark.

From Talmudic times onward, all sex outside marriage has been considered to fall under the category of prostitution. Jewish prostitution was occasionally tolerated by medieval Jewish authorities because it was thought to prevent adultery with married women and because Jews found to have visited Christian prostitutes were often executed or mutilated by Christian governments. More generally, however, Jewish communities vigorously opposed prostitution whenever it appeared, and it seems to have been rare.

In 19th-century Eastern Europe, traditional religious and social structures in Jewish life began to erode in some areas as a consequence of forced urbanization, pogroms, and the emergence of the Jewish Enlightenment movement. Commercial prostitution thrived in this environment. Jewish involvement in an international trade in prostitutes, some of whom were coerced or misled, encouraged anti-Semitism, which was often expressed in the movement against this "**white slavery.**" A young Adolf Hitler was especially influenced by the accusation that Jewish pimps were trading in Christian women, as he described in *Mein Kampf.* In reality, Jewish **pimps** dealt nearly exclusively with Jewish prostitutes. In both Eastern Europe and Argentina, pimps and prostitutes constructed separate synagogues and cemeteries after being rejected by the larger Jewish community. In May 1905, Russian Jews rioted against Jewish pimps and prostitutes, whom most Jews resented for their collaboration with the tsarist secret police and for their use of **violence** and blackmail.

Jewish women participated in late 19th and early 20th-century antiprostitution campaigns in the United States, Britain, and Germany. Bertha Pappenheim, a leader of the Jewish women's movement in Germany, was the most well-known of these activists. Like her Christian contemporaries, she campaigned against "white slavery" and built institutions for former prostitutes and unwed mothers.

Israel, like many other countries, hosts large numbers of prostitutes procured by Eastern European criminal gangs, which secular and religious authorities have done relatively little to abate. As in Islam, sex with prostitutes outside the faith appears to be considered a less serious sin. All religious authorities in both religions, however, vigorously condemn prostitution.

Islam

The Koran instructs believers not to sell their slaves into prostitution against their will and states that Allah is forgiving to those who are forced into prostitution. Although the Koran does not specifically condemn paying for sex with a willing woman, Islam has generally discouraged prostitution. However, both male prostitution and female prostitution have existed throughout most of Islamic history.

The Koranic institution of **temporary marriage**—which allows men to take wives for any allotted amount of time, at the end of which time the **marriage** automatically ends—existed among Arab tribes before the rise of Islam and was originally thought to counteract prostitution. Temporary wives would often provide companionship for traders and soldiers away from their families, lessening the demand for prostitutes. Temporary marriage survives among the Shi'ite Muslim community. Its abolition among the Sunnis is attributed to Umar, who reportedly viewed it as fornication. Iran's Ayatollah khomeini publicly praised the practice, and some Muslims have exalted it as something holy that all Muslim men should experience. Today, it is generally understood as a cover for prostitution, which is otherwise punished harshly, including by stoning.

Despite official disapproval, prostitution exists in all Muslim countries. After Saudi Arabia outlawed slavery in 1962, many former slaves turned to prostitution. In Pakistan, a shari'a law in 1991 diminished the position of women and enforced strict sexual morality, but left intact the widespread system of dancing-girl prostitutes, apparently adapted from the Hindu custom of the temple prostitute and dancer. Most of these girls are born into the profession or sold into it at a young age. With extremely high rates of HIV and other diseases and little medical treatment, many die in early adulthood. Political and religious authorities appear to tolerate the industry. Under the Taliban in Afghanistan, the traffic in women for prostitution thrived. In the wake of the Iranian Revolution in 1979, some prostitutes were publicly stoned, and Iranian women known to have engaged in premarital sex are sometimes forced into prostitution by their families. Prostitutes have recently been sentenced to death under shari'a law in Sudan, and Muslim authorities in Northern Nigeria have banned prostitution and paid prostitutes to abandon their trade.

Buddhism

Gautama Buddha welcomed prostitutes as disciples, and Buddhist legends tell of prostitutes whose enlightened compassion shamed monks and other high-status men. Partly because Buddhism has no explicit sexual code, Buddhist countries have been comparatively tolerant toward prostitution.

Traditional Japanese folk religions emphasized sexuality, and there are numerous tales about sexually active Buddhist monks. It was once common for monks to visit prostitutes and be prostitutes, whose clients also included Samurai. Prostitution is ubiquitous in contemporary Japan.

Thailand, whose dominant religion is Theravada Buddhism, has hosted prostitution at least since the 1400s and is today home to one of the world's largest prostitution industries. Some attribute the high rates of prostitution of women and girls in Thailand to the lack of a convent system with the same prestige and resources as monasteries, which provide education for many boys. Some young female prostitutes interviewed by researchers have expressed a hope that they would eventually escape prostitution by becoming a traditional healer or spirit medium, within the animistic beliefs still held by many Thais.

Buddhists in Thailand have occasionally expressed the opinion that engaging in prostitution purely for helping others can be a source of karmic merit. The desire to help their families, in accord with the belief that one gains merit through gratitude to one's parents, indeed motivates many prostitutes. Some Thai Buddhist monks recommend that the negative karma resulting from prostitution be atoned for through offerings and gifts to Buddhist temples, resulting in lavishly decorated temples in some parts of the country. The Thai Buddhist hierarchy is silent on prostitution.

See also Ancient World; Protestant Reformation; Reform; Renaissance; Sacred Prostitution in the Ancient World; Sacred Prostitution, Contemporary.

Further Reading: Apffel-Marglin, Frederique. *Wives of the God-King.* Oxford: Oxford University Press, 1985; Bristow, Edward J. *Prostitution and Prejudice: The Jewish Fight against White Slavery, 1870–1939.* Oxford: Clarendon Press, 1982; Brock, Rita N., and Susan B. Thistlewaite. *Casting Stones: Prostitution and Liberation in Asia and the United States.* Minneapolis: Fortress Press, 1996; Montgomery, Heather. *Modern Babylon: Prostituting Children in Thailand.* New York: Berghahn Books, 2001; Nichols, Jeffrey. *Prostitution, Polygamy and Power: Salt Lake City, 1947–1918.* Urbana: University of Illinois Press, 2002; Otis, Leah Lydia. *Prostitution in Medieval Society: The History of an Urban Institution in Languedoc.* Chicago: University of Chicago Press, 1995; Phillips, Melanie. *The Ascent of Women: A History of the Suffragette Movement and the Ideas Behind It.* London: Abacus, 2004; Ringdal, Nils J. *Love for Sale: A World History of Prostitution.* New York: Grove Press, 1997, 2004; Rossiaud, Jacques. *Medieval Prostitution,* trans. Lydia G. Cochrane. Oxford: Basil Blackwell, 1988; Singh, Nagendra. *Divine Prostitution.* New Delhi: A.P.H. Publishing Corporation, 1997.

Jesse Norris

RENAISSANCE. The European Renaissance (1450–1600) ushered in a period of harsh and repressive measures against prostitutes. Between 1450 and 1600, attitudes toward prostitution changed from toleration and regulation to **prohibition** and criminalization. The most visible sign of this new order was the closing of the official **brothels**. These publicly owned, municipally

Courtesan and old man, panel painting by Lucas the elder Cranach: 1472–1553. The Art Archive / Musée des Beaux Arts Besançon / Dagli Orti.

regulated houses had provided venal sex for more than 300 years. But beginning around 1520, cities closed them. East of the Rhine, Augsburg (1523), Basel (1534), Nordlingen (1536), Ulm (1537), and Regensberg (1553) eliminated their official brothels. In southern France, Toulouse, Arles, and Beaucaire shut the doors of their houses between 1520 and 1540. In England, Southampton expelled prostitutes in 1540, and the authorities in London's Southwark issued ordinances limiting the operation of the area's notorious bathhouses or "stewes." Similarly in Florence and **Venice**, existing red light districts were never entirely closed but were more closely monitored. In Rome, Pope Puis VI banished prostitutes from the holy city several times during his pontificate (1566–1572). Spain too adopted a harsher attitude toward venal sex: in the late 16th century, most Spanish cities closed their houses. Seville shut the doors of its official brothel in 1620. The Renaissance monarchies followed suit. In France, the ordinance of Orleans in 1560 made owning and operating a bordello illegal in Paris. In 1623, Philip IV of Spain officially banned brothels throughout his domains.

What caused this sea change in attitudes? An obvious explanation would be the appearance of **syphilis** in Europe in 1494. The brothel closings seem to have coincided with the advent of this horrific disease. But a closer look reveals that the closings occurred several decades after the first and most lethal attacks of the disease. The most deadly phase of the syphilis epidemic—1492 to 1510—did not coincide with brothel closings or the appearance of a more punitive attitude toward prostitution. In fact, ordinances stigmatizing and punishing prostitutes began to appear in the early –15th century, long before syphilis arrived in Europe.

As early as the 1480s, officials began to punish prostitutes—in particular, clandestine or unofficial prostitutes. These women flouted the regulations: they serviced **clients** on religious holidays, consorted with priests and Jews, and (worst of all) maintained close, lasting relationships with some men. In the 1480s, the cities of southeastern France issued dozens of edicts condemning such women to banishment and fines. Similarly in Venice, **courtesans** who solicited outside the red light district were subject to incarceration or expulsion from the city.

The threat of the unlicensed prostitute was not just a figment of the authorities' imagination. Signs abounded that clients preferred the unregulated side streets to the official brothel. As early as 1501, Augsburg was unable to find a manager for its municipal brothel: the institution was no longer profitable. The official brothels closed not because of syphilis but because of a shift in client taste.

Because few men of letters admitted to frequenting prostitutes, there are no written records of these new tastes for clandestine sexual relations. The advent of syphilis probably did play some role, as did the growth of armies. The Renaissance witnessed an increase in the powers of the state and the frequency of warfare. The new monarchies of the Renaissance put much larger armies into the field, which swelled the ranks of **camp followers**, that is, prostitutes who serviced soldiers. Officials in Strasbourg, Frankfurt, and Nuremberg complained of the hordes of prostitutes who accompanied Imperial armies and camped out in the forests near the city. When the Spanish army moved in the −16th century, it dragged behind it a rag-tag assembly of prostitutes, soldiers'"wives," and female peddlers almost half as large as the army itself. Soldiers probably invaded the official brothels and made them places of danger, sites of **violence** and robbery. Theft in a brothel incurred unusually high penalties, indicating that it was both common and greatly feared. Similarly, municipal ordinances repeatedly banned weapons in brothels, suggesting that assault was common. With the growth of armies, brothels became dangerous, and many clients took their business elsewhere.

New social distinctions and a desire for intimacy also caused men to seek sexual satisfaction in the side streets. The Renaissance saw the multiplication of social distinctions, and many men may have felt uneasy sharing a woman with a common solider. They preferred more refined company, equal to their status or self-image, and they found such company among higher-paid, unregulated prostitutes, that is, courtesans. The Renaissance witnessed the birth of the European courtesan, the highly paid, high-toned prostitute. She flattered the client's sense of his own superiority and promised a more exclusive, intimate relationship. Of course, exclusivity brought with it some protection from syphilis. But it also entailed a more intimate sexual relationship and (most important of all) secrecy.

In the Middle Ages, men went to the brothel publicly. From the Renaissance forward, they went secretly and in shame. Prostitution was no longer an approved activity for unmarried men. In the 1480s, priests in Italy, southeastern France, and Seville railed against prostitutes and condemned all forms—including official forms—of mercenary sex. They rejected medieval notions of the"good life" in favor of a more rigorous morality that prohibited consorting with prostitutes. Eventually this religious ferment took the form of the **Protestant Reformation**, but Catholics too condemned prostitutes. In Rome itself, the papacy sought to drive prostitutes out of the holy city by banishing them. Throughout Europe, the religious revival, be it Protestant or Catholic, condemned mercenary sex and made it a crime. The Renaissance brought to an end 300 years of medieval toleration and ushered in an equally long period of criminalization, prosecution, and even persecution of prostitutes.

See also Medieval Prostitution.

Further Reading: Roper, Lyndal. *Holy Household: Women and Morals in Reformation Augsburg.* Oxford: Oxford University Press, 1991; Rossiaud, Jacques. *Medieval Prostitution.* London: Blackwell Publishers, 1988.

Kathryn Norberg

RESEARCH ETHICS. A great deal of research has been carried out using the bodies of sex workers, but very little of this research has been responsive to issues that are a priority to sex workers. Consequently, the research has been of negligible benefit to them. Indeed, much of the research has had foreseeable adverse consequences.

Behavioral research on sex workers tends to focus on individual relationships, in particular those between sex worker and client, as well as those between sex worker and private partners.

Such research commonly includes an examination of the frequency of condom use and factors determining it. At the present time epidemiological studies generally address HIV-infection rates and the rates of other sexually transmitted diseases. HIV/AIDS-related clinical trials using sex-worker cohorts test **microbicides**, vaccines, and treatments. Researchers often seek out sex-worker populations, attempting to take advantage of their vulnerability to disease in order to produce reliable results in the shortest amount of time.

In addition, in an environment in which significant interest has arisen in transnational **crime** and terrorism, there has been an upsurge of interest in research on **trafficking** of women and children. Much trafficking research has confused issues pertinent to **migration** and employment with the imagery of the 19th-century white slave trade.

One of the earliest systematic responses to research misconduct arose as a direct outcome of research conducted on sex workers. Albert Neisser is known today for his pioneering work in the area of sexually transmitted diseases, and *Neisseria gonorrhoeae* and *Neisseria meningitidis* are named after him. However, less well-taught in medical schools is the content of the scandal that exploded in Prussia during 1898. Neisser had injected serum from patients with **syphilis** into other patients, mostly prostitutes, some of whom were minors. This was done without the prostitutes' knowledge, and a number of the them contracted syphilis. Although his research drew support from the medical community, no similar support was forthcoming from the public. Neisser was tried and convicted of the crime of inflicting unlawful physical injury. He was ordered to pay a significant fine. In addition, an inquiry resulted in legislation in 1900 prohibiting the conduct of nontherapeutic research without informed consent. This is particularly significant given the behavior of many German medical professionals during World War II.

More recently, other studies worthy of examination have demonstrated different facets of failures and successes in the application of research ethics to sex-worker research. Three prominent examples are cited here. The first example relates to a microbicide trial, the results of which were published in 2002. It was a randomized, placebo-controlled trial of a vaginal gel containing a chemical known as **nonoxynol-9**. The trial involved 892 female sex workers in Benin, Cote d'Ivoire, South Africa and Thailand. A total of 449 women were provided with nonoxynol-9 gel, and 443 other women received a placebo gel. The study found that those sex workers using nonoxynol-9 were *more* likely to become HIV-positive and were also at an increased risk for gonococcal and chlamydial infections.

Particularly significant was the finding that the risk of infection was especially high in women who used the gel more than 3.5 times per day. At low-frequency use, nonoxynol-9 had no effect, either positive or negative, on HIV infection. The research team ignored that sex workers had earlier reported independently that they found nonoxynol-9 to be an irritant to skin lining of the anus and vagina. Sex workers themselves had discouraged its use. Nonetheless, sex workers included in the trial used the gel before each instance of sexual intercourse. The gel's use would thus have been more frequent among sex workers than among other groups in the community who might otherwise have been targeted for the trial. Had the researchers chosen to pay attention to what sex workers were saying, HIV infections attributable to the trial might have been avoided.

Another example is that of a proposed trial among 960 sex workers in Cambodia to test **tenofovir**, a drug developed to prevent infection with HIV. This was another instance of researcher-established priorities and a failure to understand and work with the trial population or with those who have the ability to influence their welfare. Sex workers were asked to take tenofovir for one year and were offered free medical services, counseling, and $3 per month. Although tenofovir had been used as a treatment for those already infected with HIV, sex workers were concerned that it would have adverse effects in healthy human beings. They were also unsatisfied with the commitment of the researchers to provide treatment for only the duration of the trial. Authentic negotiation between trial sponsors, researchers, and potential participants did not take place. Sex workers saw themselves as being asked to take risks not in their own long-term interests but for those in the industrialized world who would ultimately have access to medical services and be able to afford treatment.

Ultimately, in a unique and historic turn of events, sex workers refused to agree to participate. Trials were scheduled to begin in Botswana, Cameroon, Malawi, Nigeria, and Thailand, but the trial in Cameroon was put on hold, and the trial in Nigeria was canceled because researchers determined the trial site was not adequate. As a result of these unprecedented events, trial sponsors met with community members and advocates to discuss what would give these populations enough confidence to participate in the trials.

In contrast, another case is illustrative of a sound ethical approach to research among sex workers. Once again Cambodian sex workers were approached. However, instead of being presented with a fait accompli, they were advised by the principal researcher that funds were available for research and advocacy. Sex workers were informed that they could prioritize an area for study, and they would then be trained so that they could carry out the research. They would also be assisted in disseminating results. Sex workers identified the issue of **violence**, including sexual violence. Three trusted ex-policemen were also identified by the sex workers and recruited to assist with the study.

In 2004, 1,000 sex workers were interviewed as well as 58 police and 2 gangsters over a period of two months. Refusal rates were about 5 percent, which is quite low. Most sex workers were frank about their experiences. This is in contrast to many other studies in which sex workers, who do not trust the researchers, say what they believe the researchers expect to hear. Again, unlike most other studies dealing with violence, studies in which the incidence of violence is notoriously underreported, in this study 97 percent of sex workers reported being raped by someone in the past year, somewhat more often by **clients** and gangsters than by police. Independent data from police corroborated information provided by sex workers.

In research that is driven by sex workers and rigorously conducted, it is far more likely that the outcome will benefit sex workers. This benefit to the research's subjects is a fundamental ethical requirement of research and in the instance of sex workers tends to remain unfulfilled. A benefit may be the formation of a basis for advocacy with respect to a better working environment or provision of services where none or poor services exist. A benefit may also be strengthening the support networks among sex workers.

A further basic ethical requirement is that the participants should not be placed at risk. Participants must not be sacrificed for the benefit of the research or the greater good. When the knowledge and views of sex workers are not taken into account, it is likely that avoidable risks will occur as amply demonstrated by the nonoxynol-9 trials.

In relation to HIV infection and sex workers, a body of research literature has been amassed that creates a discourse that is often moralizing, categorizing, unifying, and stigmatizing. Underlying much of the research and many interventions is the concern that sex workers are a potential hazard for society and a vector of the disease. Concern is not for the health of the sex worker but rather for the risks the sex worker might pose for the community (the community, therefore, excluding sex workers as citizens for whom attention and care should be demonstrated). As such, sex workers are the first group in many nations to be targeted as vectors of HIV and sexually transmitted disease rather than as people whose employment conditions and lack of **human rights** placed them in a highly vulnerable situation for acquiring HIV.

Sex-worker research is often misdirected. Because sex workers are commonly seen as the vectors of disease, other potential avenues for fruitful health research are often ignored. For example, it has been observed that in places where **condoms** are used consistently, there have been effective health-promotion campaigns that are not addressed solely or even mainly to sex workers, and these campaigns have created client demand for condom use. In addition, discriminatory paths of research may be adopted. Once sex workers are in their homes engaging in intimate relations with their partners in an environment of "trust," where they may wish to have children, it is difficult and indeed improper to demand that they use condoms. Nonetheless, research is undertaken to explore the behavior of sex workers in the private sphere for reasons that are often unclear.

The problems with sex work are often attributed to the nature of the work itself instead of to the **stigma** attached to it or to specific negative circumstances, for example violence and lack of protection and exploitation by authorities. Sex workers are often represented as a homogeneous population, even though stark differences may be seen in gender, race, and class as well as in labor conditions. Also left unaddressed is the stance adopted by most governments to this most economically significant population. Unsurprisingly this creates significant difficulties when attempting to produce research that is both a reflection of reality and of any use.

Concepts such as informed consent and confidentiality are often understood as underpinning themes of ethical research. However, debates confined to how an individual researcher might deal with an individual participant fail to constitute an adequate ethical framework for research. Sex-worker advocates believe that ethical research must address issues of value to the participant community, that the research must be sound scientifically, and that it must respect and promote the standards and norms of human rights. Most research focused on sex workers has failed to meet these standards.

See also HIV/AIDS and the Prostitution Rights Movement; Rape; Sexually Transmitted Infections; White Slavery.

Further Reading: Jenkins, Carol. "Cambodian Sex Workers Conduct Their Own Research." *Research for Sex Work* 8 (2005): 3–4, http://www.researchforsexwork.org; Longo, Paulo. "From Subjects to Partners: Experience of a Project in Rio de Janeiro, Brazil." *Research for Sex Work* 7 (2004): 9–10, http://www.nswp.org/r4sw/; *Research for Sex Work.* http://www.researchforsexwork.org; Van Damme, Lut, Gita Ramjee, Michel Alary, Bea Vuylsteke, Verapol Chandeying, Helen Rees, Pachara Sirivongrangson, Lonard Mukenge-Tshibaka, Virginie Ettigne-Traore, Charn Uaheowitchai, Salim S. Abdool Karim, Benot Msse, Jos Perrins, and Marie Laga on behalf of the COL-1492 study group. "Effectiveness of COL-1492, a Nonoxynol-9 Vaginal Gel, on HIV-1 Transmission in Female Sex Workers: A Randomised Controlled Trial." *Lancet* 360; no. 9338, 28 September 2002, pp. 971–977; Vanwesenbeeck, Ine. "Another Decade of Social Scientific Work on Sex Work: A Review of Research 1990–2000." *Annual Review of Sex Research* 12 (2001): 242–289.

Bebe Loff

RESIDENT ACTIVISM. Although almost no public debate or protest occurs at national levels regarding prostitution, resident activism at local levels has grown through neighborhood antiprostitution groups. Street prostitution, as compared with exchanges of sex for money that occur –through in-call and outcall services and in massage parlors, **brothels**, or other locations that are not as open to public scrutiny, affects the communities in which it occurs in direct ways. Street prostitution is more visible than other types of exchanges, and many consider it to be disruptive to the peace. These types of exchanges of sex for drugs or money are therefore the subject of heightened public awareness. This awareness leads not only to the **stigma** about sex workers, but also to some people's active work to remove street prostitution from their neighborhoods.

As reasons for these activities to be criminalized, many neighborhood groups cite disorderly conduct, noise, declining property values, loss of business to local merchants, increase in crime, dangerous environments for children and women, and the public health risk of the spread of AIDS and other **sexually transmitted infections** that is evidenced by used **condoms** and drug paraphernalia that litter streets and sidewalks. Criminalization, in turn, allows for the removal of those who participate in these acts from the neighborhoods and society in general, at least for a short time. Rather than focusing on moral concerns, many studies find that people believe prostitution threatens their quality of life as well as a neighborhood's image and reputation.

In his 1994 article "Community Groups vs. Prostitutes," Ronald John Weitzer outlined the grievances and concerns of neighborhood groups and what they are willing to do to "fight back" and "reclaim" their neighborhoods. Rather than referring to these activities as immoral, the residents and activists point to the negative environmental factors and the immediate consequences of prostitution in a neighborhood. Weitzer argued that it "would be a mistake to simply dismiss these community groups as fanatics who are **scapegoating** prostitutes for problems not of their making. These groups may sometimes exaggerate the problem, but for the most part they appear to be reacting to real problems resulting from illegal street prostitution—problems that some prostitutes acknowledge as well" (1994, 124).

In addition to enlisting support from local authorities, these groups also use tactics to intimidate both prostitutes and their clients, in an effort to remove them from their neighborhoods. For example, groups often follow prostitutes up and down the streets carrying signs displaying such messages as "You're Hooking, We're Looking" and "Whores and **Pimps** are Wimps" (Weitzer 123). Groups also photograph and videotape customers, hold up signs about the risk of AIDS and venereal infections, and write down license plate numbers in hopes of contacting "the woman of the house." These tactics directly affect street prostitutes and their ability to control their own workspace and working conditions.

Street prostitutes are some of the most marginalized and victimized people in society and in the sex industry. Their work involves real time and proximal contact with their customers, which implies varying levels of danger and risk. Of all sex workers, street prostitutes have the fewest resources, work in the most dangerous circumstances, and face the most harassment from the police and those who are commonly referred to as pimps. They make less money than higher-end prostitutes, and they are often beaten, victimized, robbed, and raped—crimes that they have virtually no means to prosecute. They also have an increased risk of contracting drug-related illnesses, especially HIV/AIDS. Their low social status within the hierarchy of prostitution and within their communities as a whole, along with their lack of access to social and medical services, makes it difficult for them to leave prostitution for areas of work that are deemed more "legitimate" and less risky than their current position.

See also Attitudes toward Prostitution, Sociopsychological.

Further Reading: Chapkis, Wendy. *Live Sex Acts: Women Performing Erotic Labor.* New York: Routledge, 1997; Chapkis, Wendy. "Power and Control in the Commercial Sex Trade." In *Sex for Sale: Prostitution, Pornography, and the Sex Industry,* ed. Ronald John Weitzer. New York: Routledge, 2000, pp. 181–201; Leigh, Carol. "Prostitution in the United States: The Statistics." *Gauntlet* 1, no. 7 (1994): 17–18; Weitzer, Ronald John. "Community Groups vs. Prostitutes." *Gauntlet* 1, no. 7 (1994): 121–124; Weitzer, Ronald John. "The Politics of Prostitution in America." In *Sex for Sale: Prostitution, Pornography, and the Sex Industry,* ed. Ronald John Weitzer. New York: Routledge, 2000, pp. 159–80.

Jill McCracken

RESORTS. *See* **R&R; Sex Tourism; Venues and Labor Forms.**

RETROGRESSIVE DYNAMIC. Many factors affect the economic well-being of the women and men who work in the sex industry—legal status, police harassment, discrimination by both society at large and individual clients, and various occupational risks, such as **sexually transmitted infections** (STI), HIV, and drug use—but the retrogressive dynamic is one of the most significant economic factors affecting the careers of sex workers.

"One interesting thing about this business," porn director Kristen Bjorn observed of the retrogressive dynamic, "is that the longer you are in it, the less money you are paid. Once you are an old face, and an old body, forget it. You're through as far as your popularity goes." Sociologist Paul Cressey was one of the first scholars to identify this distinctive socioeconomic pattern. In his 1932 ethnographic study of "dime-a-dance" girls, *The Taxi-Dance Hall: A Sociological Study of Commercialized Recreation and City Life*, he explored an occupation that employed young women to dance and socialize with young single men for a fee and that was widely seen as a step on the road to prostitution.

Cressey found that the social and economic prospects of these young women followed a distinctive pattern that has been recognized by many of those working in prostitution, the adult entertainment industry, and other forms of sex work. The pattern was essentially one in which the longer an individual worked in the industry, the less money that individual made—for the same work—over time. Cressey formulated his hypothesis as the "theory of retrogressive life cycle."

In the *Taxi-Dance Hall*, Cressey explained the theory of retrogressive life cycles primarily in terms of social status and racial stratification. But the "regressive" stages of the taxi-dancer's career that Cressey identified translated directly into economic consequences. Many young women who entered the world of commercialized dance entertainment found that after an initial success as a "novelty" in the taxi-dance hall, they ceased to be "the new girl" and experienced a loss of favor and status, which soon resulted in an exit from the dance hall: "Finding herself losing favor in one social world, the taxi-dancer 'moves on' ... from taxi-dance hall to another, perhaps one of lower standing" (Cressey 1932, 87). This cycle continues in the young woman's life as long as she continues work in the taxi-dance hall: "Her decline ... may be rapid or slow, depending upon the personality, ingenuity, and character of the individual girl. But ... a decline in status seems almost inevitable."

Many of those who engage in sex work of one kind or another probably first began to engage in sex work either as a temporary source of income during periods of unemployment or as a way of supplementing their regular income. Few enter the workforce of the sex industry as part of a long-planned career move, although once engaged, many will continue to work in the industry over a period of several years.

In economic terms, the retrogressive dynamic has two significant results: "careers" in sex work are frequently fairly short (between two and four years in many types of sex work), and earnings may increase sharply over the first year as a sex worker, stripper, porn star, and so on, but earnings (for the same type of work) rapidly decline in the next few years.

The typical pattern of earnings over time for people in the sex industry differs sharply from the standard profile of earnings over time widely observed in many conventional forms of employment. The standard earnings profile shows as an upward sloping curve over several decades. This pattern reflects increases in productivity from on-the-job learning, training and education, and other human-capital improvements. Of course, in the long run, after a career peaks, earnings decline with age. The steepness of the curve and the peak time period vary according to gender, race, education, and other factors. In contrast, the standard career in sex work is fairly short, the peak earning period occurs early, and earnings drop off quickly after the peak year(s).

Prostitutes, **call girls**, and escorts may undergo a period of apprenticeship during which they learn how to successfully manage their customers or **clients** in the context of the sexual exchange. Such an apprenticeship is a form of on-the-job training during which time the sex worker earns less than in her or his peak years.

Although, ultimately, the retrogressive dynamic, as Cressey suggested, may be an inevitable process, it is possible for sex workers to slow down its impact and stretch out their careers. Cressey cited "the personality, ingenuity, and character of the individual girl," but there are also a number of common work-based strategies that help to prolong a sex worker's career.

This usually involves integrating new and different activities into the sexual encounter with the customer. Whereas some customers want the same thing every time, many want their sexual encounters to change and have variety so that they can avoid experiencing boredom. Different types of sex work incorporate the fantasy component in unique and distinctive ways. Most prostitutes or sex workers who have direct contact with customers seek to identify their customers' favorite sexual activities, fantasies, and social interactions as a matter of course. Changes in appearance, clothes, hair color, weight, and physical fitness also contribute to enhancing the sex worker's erotic appeal.

Another means by which sex workers renew their appeal and put off the debilitating effects of the retrogressive dynamic is by moving into different sexual markets (either geographically or socially), and yet another is working in complementary forms of sex work. Thus, for example, in the latter case, a person working initially as a stripper (who performs a "fantasy") may at some point decide to work also as escort, which involves direct sexual contact—with each form of sex work contributing to a heightened erotic appeal of the person who engages in both activities. Those sex workers who establish long-term relationships with regulars—to some extent by shifting from an emphasis on sex to one on intimacy—engage similarly in a commercial activity that complements or includes sex.

See also Stripping.

Further Reading: Bernstein, Elizabeth. "The Meaning of the Purchase: Desire, Demand and the Commerce of Sex." *Ethnography* 2, no. 3 (2001): 389–420; Cressey, Paul. *The Taxi Hall Dance.*

Chicago: University of Chicago Press, 1932; Escoffier, Jeffrey. "Porn Star/Stripper/Escort: Economic and Sexual Dynamics in a Sex Work Career." In *Male Sex Workers*, ed. Todd Morrison. Binghampton, NY: Haworth Press, in press; Frank, Katherine. *G-Strings and Sympathy: Strip Club Regulars and Male Desire*. Durham, NC: Duke University Press, 2002.

Jeffrey Escoffier

REVIEWS. *See* **Blue Books; Directories; Guidebooks; Internet.**

RICHARD, MARTHE (1889–1980). In 1946, the French government passed a law closing **brothels** throughout the country. The law was the result of a press campaign and bore the name of the instigator of the campaign, Marthe Richard.

Richard was a complex figure. Born Marthe Betenfeld at Blamont in 1889, she is known to have worked as a prostitute in Nancy at age 16. She married a wealthy local official, Henri Richer, who purchased the Manoir de Beaumont at Joué-en-Charnie in the Loire region for his bride. In 1913, she became one of the first women in France to qualify as a pilot.

After her husband's death, she spied for France during World War I, using the code names "l'Alouette" ("The Lark") and "S-32." The name by which she is now known was invented by her handler, Captain Ladoux, in his memoirs. Ladoux sent her to Stockholm and Madrid to gather information by seducing German officers. She is credited with having unmasked a number of German agents and methods, but a car accident in Spain attracted unwelcome attention and cut short her career as a spy. The 1937 film *Marthe Richard au service de la France* is a fictionalized account of her exploits.

After the war, she married an Englishman, Thomas Crompton, who died in 1928. Using her former nom de guerre as a pen name, she then entered politics and became a municipal councilor in Paris. In 1945, she submitted a proposal to close the brothels in the region. The proposal was accepted, and she began a wider campaign to implement the measure nationally. Ironically, she was living with a **pimp** at the time, and some commentators suggest that she may have been partly motivated by conflicts with her lover.

Her efforts bore fruit with the passage of the law bearing her name on April 13, 1946. Some 1,400 brothels were closed, including nearly 200 in Paris. The law also made soliciting an offense and imposed heavier penalties for pimping.

Richard's book *Appel des sexes* (1951) hinted at a later softening of her position on prostitution. She died in 1980.

Further Reading: Lacassin, Francis. "Mata Hari, ou le romance interrompue." *Le Magazine Litteraire*, no. 43 (August 1970), http://www.magazine-litteraire.com/archives/ar_378.htm; Richard, Marthe. *Appel des sexes*. Paris: Editions du Scorpion, 1951.

Angus McIntyre

RIEHL, REGINE. The trial of 46-year-old Regine Riehl and two others charged with crimes associated with the operation of Riehl's tolerated bordello, opened in Vienna, Austria, on November 2, 1906. Not only that city's residents but other people throughout the **Habsburg Monarchy** and even beyond avidly read about the proceedings. The trial transfixed the public and reignited public interest in prostitution in the Monarchy, which was governed by police rather than statutory criteria. With the alleged connivance of the Viennese morals police, whom she had reputedly bribed, Riehl had pursued her position with the "relentless rigor of a jailer." Because some of the very officials who were meant to be enforcing regulations were those accused of helping Riehl evade them, a review of the trial also highlights some of the contradictions inherent in the regulation of illegal behavior and opens up a unique window into the attitudes of local police and other officials toward regulation of prostitution.

Unbeknownst to her bookkeeper-clerk husband, Riehl had become involved in pandering almost 30 years earlier, initially because she had accrued financial obligations. Following three arrests and convictions in the mid-1890s for undertaking her activities in secret, she had opened a tolerated house in the late 1890s. Business had gone well, so she had rented an entire house for the up-to-20 prostitutes she employed.

In the summer of 1906, following earlier complaints about the Riehl establishment from the Liga zur Bekämpfung Mädchenhandels and the city sanitation department, journalist Emil Bader published an expose that brought goings-on in the Riehl bordello, which was camouflaged as a clothing store, to the attention of the public. During the subsequent trial, witnesses contrasted the spacious, comfortable reception area for clients with the small, unsanitary, locked and barred rooms upstairs where girls slept two to a bed. Witnesses testified that girls as young as 14, their mail censored and their movements limited, had been employed there. They also testified that the prostitutes in Riehl's employ were meant to encourage guests to drink cognac and champagne by drinking themselves. In the Riehl establishment, hunger, beatings, and imprisonment allegedly alternated with champagne orgies. Thus, many prostitutes soon wanted to leave her employ, which she allegedly prohibited. In the rare cases that she did permit someone to leave, that person was required to leave the city immediately.

On the evening of November 7, 1906, the criminal court judge sentenced the defendants. Riehl, found guilty of a variety of crimes, including limiting the personal freedom of others, embezzlement, fraud, suborning testimony, and procuring, was sentenced to three-and-a-half years of hard labor. The two codefendants, her maid, Antoinie Pollack, and the plumber's helper, Friedrich König, who forced his daughter to remain in Riehl's employ, were convicted of complicity in limiting the personal freedom of others. They were also sentenced to hard labor. Seven prostitutes, all of whom were convicted of lying under oath, received sentences ranging from 14 days to 4 weeks. Riehl began serving her sentence in February of 1907.

Involving, as it did, parents who profited from their daughters' employment in the bordello, the testimony of prostitutes who spoke little German, and public concern over the morals of these young women, the Riehl trial stood at the intersection of issues of class, nation, and gender. The scandal generated widespread demands for reform. Thus, the Viennese police, who were responsible for the regulation of prostitution throughout Austria, issued a series of decrees beginning in late 1906 concerning the regulation of prostitution and obliged police in Cisleithania to provide detailed descriptions of their practices. Although there were subsequent accusations that the Prague police were also involved with organized prostitution, a local official in Aussig/Ústí nad Labem (northern Bohemia) asserted that the situation that occurred in Salon Riehl could not have happened in his city. In contrast to Viennese practice, that medium-sized town compelled prostitutes to register and unregister personally with the local police, who made them aware of their rights and responsibilities as prostitutes.

The Riehl trial was the subject of discussion in the imperial Parliament, where on November 6, 1906, deputies demanded that Interior Minister Richard von Bienerth explain what measures his ministry was taking in response to the criminal proceedings. The minister acknowledged that the government had been made aware of the need for sweeping reform in the area of police surveillance of prostitution in connection with the Riehl trial. Indeed, the police headquarters and the governor's office had already taken the necessary steps within their area of influence to subject the regulations concerning prostitution to a thorough review and make the necessary changes. Moreover, Biennerth planned to ask other political agencies to propose modifications for the regulation of prostitution.

Further Reading: Kraus, Karl. "Die Prozeß Riehl." *Die Fackel*, 13 November1906, 8; Mayreder, Rosa. "Die Frauen und der Prozess Riehl." *Neues Frauenleben* 18, no. 11 (1906); Vyleta, Daniel. *Crime, Jews and News, Vienna 1895–1914*. New York: Bergahn Books, in press.

Nancy M. Wingfield

RITES OF PASSAGE. In some societies, a visit to a prostitute is a rite of passage for an adolescent male. The term "rites of passage" (*rites de passage*) was coined by Arnold Van Gennep (1873–1957), a German-born French ethnographer and folklorist. He observed that all cultures had designated celebrations or ceremonies that marked movements or changes in status of an individual's life from birth to death. These stages were usually crisis-provoking. Societies assuaged the emotional trauma and anxiety by creating ceremonies with prescribed costume, food, and ritual, usually elaborate. The person undergoing change, the initiate, was given membership, and that membership was made visible in ways specific to every culture. Often a modification was added to the initiate's body to demonstrate that he or she had achieved the new status.

Van Gennep divided the activities associated with the ceremonies into three phases: separation, transition, and incorporation. Each society differs in the amount of elaboration they give to these three that is, they are not developed to the same extent or apparent in every set of ceremonies. A funeral is a rite of separation; an engagement, a transition; and a marriage, an incorporation. A particular type of transition is an initiation: a rite of passage from one phase of status in a society to another. In preliterate societies, physical puberty was marked with social puberty in a ceremony that may have included hair being cut, tattoos put on the body, scarification performed, tortures inflicted to test endurance, or isolation enforced for a period of time. The initiate went into the ceremony a child and came out an adolescent. During transition, the initiate experienced a state of insecurity because he or she was neither in one category nor the other. This state of emotional turmoil is known as liminality, akin to "being in limbo," neither here nor there. The ceremonies practiced are known as coming-of-age ceremonies. Margaret Mead, a 20th-century anthropologist, researched Samoan and Balinese rites of passage to compare the problems experienced during transition with those of American teens. In societies with state formation in which complex social structures are based on political hierarchies rather than kinship, events such as confirmations, Bar Mitzvahs, and Quinceaños (la fiesta Quinceañera) are examples of rites of passage, transition ceremonies, or initiations into a new stage of life. Although they are occasions for both family and community to celebrate, the preparation and awareness generate anxiety.

In 19th- and early 20th-century European and American societies, a rite of passage from boy to man was sometimes marked by his first visit to a prostitute, who initiated him into the sexual world. On the chosen day he would be separated from other members of his family, perhaps dressed in a respectable way, and taken to a house of prostitution by his father or other male relative. He would experience anxiety and fear because he did not know what awaited him. He would be encouraged and assured that this would be an enjoyable event during this liminal phase. Afterward, he was incorporated into the world of his father and all adult males who had sexual knowledge and experience.

If ancient literature can inform social science, there is evidence that sexual-initiation ceremonies in Rome and Greece were performed by sacred prostitutes. The goddess cult offered its worshipers the opportunity to experience divine power through the vehicle of sexual pleasure. The association of prostitution with profanity came after monotheism and **patriarchy** began dominating belief systems, relegating it to low rather than high status and making it illegal in most societies. Until the sexual revolution of the 1960s, a double standard existed regarding morality. Female prostitutes were arrested and jailed, whereas their male customers were released and chastised. Yet prostitutes retained a unique and important place in society because some fathers chose to send their sons to them for their first sexual experience. In Thailand, 46 percent of never-married males and 34 percent of married males sampled reported that their first sexual intercourse was with a prostitute.

Pretty Baby (1978), a Louis Malle film, showed a fictional house of prostitution in **New Orleans** and a rite of passage celebrating the transition of a prostitute's young daughter into the ranks of her mother's house. A more recent and realistic film, *Born into Brothels* (2004), written and directed by Ross Kauffman and Zana Briski, documented the conditions of children of prostitutes in Kolkata and how they were being prepared for a similar life.

Further Reading: Brundage, James. *Law, Sex, and Christian Society in Medieval Europe*. Chicago: University of Chicago Press, 1987; Mead, Margaret. *Coming of Age in Samoa: A Psychological Study of Primitive Youth for Western Civilisation*. 1973. Reprint, New York: Harper Perennial, 2001; "Sexual Behaviour of Young People." *Progress in Reproductive Health Research* 41 (1997). Website of the World Health Organization. http://www.who.int/reproductive-health/hrp/progress/41/news41_1.en. html; Van Gennep, Arnold. *The Rites of Passage*. Chicago: University of Chicago Press, 1960.

Lana Thompson

ROCHESTER, JOHN WILMOT, EARL OF (1647–1680).

Rochester was a Restoration poet and, for some, the quintessential libertine. His father was named the first Earl of Rochester for his role in King Charles II's escape following the disastrous Battle of Worcester in 1651. Rochester was educated at Oxford. As a sign of aristocratic disdain, little of his verse was published in his lifetime—circulating only in manuscript among court figures—and up until 1968, his work was heavily censored.

Rochester's verse often relies on representations of prostitutes within the sexual and political contexts of Charles II's court. As libertinism—a gender ideology comprising hard drinking, sexually promiscuity, and wit—became the dominant form of masculinity in the Restoration, the prostitute came to occupy a specifically ambivalent position. Not only was she necessary for sexual "conquest" and the public acknowledgment of masculine, libertine virility, but she also became a troubling symbol of Charles II's negligent political behavior. Literary wit was intimately tied with sexual performance, and this association exacerbated the sexual and political anxieties relating to prostitutes. In Rochester's work, however, this equation takes on a unique critical valence, as sexual impotence comes increasingly to be a marker of political impotence.

The figure of the "whore," then, operates on four key sociopolitical levels in Rochester's verse. First, the prostitute's accessibility enables the maintenance of male virility, often, however, in an ironically self-reflexive, satirical manner whereby the libertine speaker becomes "a common fucking post" ("The Imperfect Enjoyment" 63). Second, she is a sign of Charles II's hedonism, as he restlessly rolls "about from whore to whore / A merry monarch, scandalous and poor" ("Satyr on Charles II" 20–21). Third, the prostitute is a liminal figure, marking the transgressive crossing of class and status boundaries—"A passive pot for fools to spend in!" ("A Ramble in St. James' Park" 102). And, finally, the prostitute provides a troubling analogy for the court wit, or perhaps, Rochester himself: "For wits are treated just like common whores, / First they're enjoyed, and then kicked out of doors" ("Satire on Reason and Mankind" 37–38).

Rochester's critical view of libertinism enacts the futility of a masculinity dependent on sexual "conquest." Although Rochester was not particularly attuned to recognition of the exploitation of prostitutes in Restoration London, the prostitute functioned as a key symbol for the breaking down of sociopolitical bonds in a debauched age.

See also Poetry.

Further Reading: Thormalen, Marianne. *Rochester: The Poems in Context*. New York: Cambridge University Press, 1993; Turner, James Grantham. *Libertines and Radicals in Early Modern London: Sexuality, Politics, and Literary Culture, 1630–1685*. New York: Cambridge University Press, 2002; Wilmot, John, second Earl of Rochester. *The Complete Poems*, ed. David M. Vieth. New Haven, CT: Yale University Press, 1968.

Jim Daems

ROCK MUSIC. "Rock and roll," like "jazz," is a term that refers not only to the performance of music, but also to the act of sex. Because of the influence of the **blues**, country and western music, rhythm 'n' blues, and other music genres (jazz, hillbilly music), from early on rock relied on similar lyrical themes. Many songs in these other genres referred to loose women and sexual activity, and so several early rock and roll songs celebrated the loose sexual mores of prostitutes, hookers, and "queens."

Most early hit rock and roll records were based on sexual themes: "Good Golly Miss Molly," recorded in 1958 by Little Richard, describes a woman who "sure like to ball." "Rock Around the Clock," released in 1955 by Bill Haley and the Comets, one of the earliest hits, has been interpreted to mean playing music all night, but many teenagers in the 1950s assumed it referred to the alternate definition of "rock."

Few of the initial rock and roll records specifically referred to prostitution, but the sexual liberation implied in the lyrics would have a profound influence as time passed. Hank Ballard and The Midnighters (a.k.a The Royals) recorded the raunchiest and most sexual early rock and roll songs, beginning with "Get It" in 1953 and "Work with Me Annie" in 1954, which featured lyrics such as "Give me all my meat, ooo!" and "Annie had a Baby." Billy Ward & the Dominoes also had a hit record with sexual lyrics with "Sixty Minute Man."

Once the initial rock and roll revolution of the 1950s had passed (and after the radio payola scandal disgraced the music business), the recording industry promoted clean-cut, white teenagers singing harmless love songs, and the music business went back to the "June/Moon/Swoon" school of love song lyrics. This all changed in 1963, when the phenomenal success of the Beatles ushered in the British Invasion. The Beatles were followed by several bands that took musical and lyrical inspiration from blues musicians. The Animals, led By Eric Burdon, became the first British group after the Beatles to chart a number-one single in America with "House of the Rising Sun," the first number-one single explicitly written about a whorehouse.

According to folklorist Alan Lomax in his book *Our Singing Country* (1941), the melody of "The House of the Rising Run" is a traditional English ballad, though the lyrics were written by Georgia Turner and Bert Martin, both from Kentucky. The song was first recorded in the 1920s by black bluesman Texas Alexander and later covered by such diverse musicians as Leadbelly, Charlie Byrd, Roy Acuff, Woody Guthrie, the Weavers, Henry Mancini, Dolly Parton, and Peter, Paul & Mary, as well as many others. But the Animals' version became the most famous recording of this musical standard and opened the door for many more rock songs about prostitutes.

Jimi Hendrix (who was discovered and managed by Chas Chandler of the Animals) recorded another famous song about a house of ill repute, "Red House," which appeared on his first album (*Are You Experienced*), released in 1967. The song also shows up in many of his live concert recordings and became his tribute to blues music. The song tells the story of how a man (after serving 99 1/2 days in jail) tries to visit his girlfriend who lives in a "red house." Upon finding out that she has left him, he decides it is not all that problematic because if she does not love him anymore, "her sister will."

In 1968 The Beatles recorded a song that, according to many interpretations, is about a prostitute: "Lady Madonna." Although some people interpret it as referring only to the difficulties of single motherhood, its lyrics about a woman who has difficulty paying the rent and supporting her children and who "creeps in like a nun" on Sunday mornings indicate that Lady Madonna is selling her body to feed her children.

By the late 1960s, the theme of prostitution had become sufficiently mainstream that Simon and Garfunkel, a folk/rock duo, had a top-10 hit called "The Boxer," with lyrics describing the tough life of a "poor boy" who could not find a job. The young man finds "just a come-on from the whores on Seventh Avenue," and he admits that he "took some comfort" with them.

In August 1969 The Rolling Stones released "Honky Tonk Woman," a blues-influenced number-one hit and certified as a gold record. It is probably the most celebrated song about a sex worker in recent history. A honky tonk was a type of bar common throughout the South. Honky tonks were rough establishments that served alcoholic beverages to working-class clientele and that sometimes also offered dancing to music by piano players or small bands; they sometimes were also centers of prostitution. In some rougher tonks the prostitutes and their customers would have sex standing up clothed on the dance floor while the music played.

"Honky Tonk Woman" describes a "gin soaked, bar-room queen in Memphis" who gives the songwriter the "honky tonk blues (i.e., "the clap"). The term "queen" subsequently became a code word for loose women who were easy with their sexual favors, and as a result, several successful songs with the word "queen" in the lyrics or title referred to loose women (or men in drag) who performed sexual favors, often at a price. "Mississippi Queen" by Mountain is allegedly about a real woman who is a well-known stripper and groupie. "Rock 'N' Roll Queen" by Mott the Hoople also refers to a loose woman who performs sexual favors.

The sexual revolution in the 1960s was formed by popular songs that treated the subject of prostitution as less of a taboo and more like a part of sexual liberation. "Groupies" became common in rock and roll culture, and they were known for freely offering sex to members of rock 'n' roll bands. As the 1960s culture ended, it was natural that sex of all kinds was being glamorized and celebrated.

When forms of societal censorship began to loosen in the 1970s and social protest gained ground, rock and roll performers began to produce more overtly sexual music. In 1970, as rock and roll entered its third decade, the glitter rock phenomenon (also known as glam rock) was emerging. This type of rock music, which celebrated sexualities of many kinds, prostitution, and drugs, was made famous by such performers as David Bowie, T. Rex, and KISS. The flamboyant, theatrical, and sexually ambiguous Alice Cooper Band released their first albums in 1970 and 1971, but both were commercial failures. T. Rex, led by Marc Bolan, released "Hot Love" and "Bang a Gong," which became hit records in England, a year later. Glitter became a full-fledged phenomenon later that year when David Bowie (who had worked with Bolan as a mime performer), announced that he was bisexual and expressed his fear that he would be the first rock star to be assassinated onstage, boosting sales of his 1971 album *Hunky Dory*. That album included the song "Queen Bitch," with lyrics referring to the protagonist's sexual jealousy of a transgender hooker who picks up a man he or she is interested in. Bowie (who played a male prostitute in a Berlin brothel in the 1979 film *Just a Gigolo*) was infatuated with **New York City**'s Andy Warhol and the Velvet Underground (a 1960s band whose song lyrics referenced everything from shooting drugs to sexual orgies to homosexuality and transsexuals). Although no Velvet Underground songs referred directly to prostitution, their masterwork "Sister Ray" (written by singer/songwriter Lou Reed) vividly describes a sex-and-drugs orgy attended by drag queens and a sailor (**slang** for "john"). This infatuation with New York City's gay scene led Bowie to produce Lou Reed's first commercially successful album (*Transformer*) in December 1972. "Walk on the Wild Side," a top-10 hit from that album, refers to various New York/Warhol superstars—notably "Little Joe," a male hustler who "never once gave it away," and several drag queens.

Angie and David Bowie pose in all of their glam glory. Courtesy of Photofest.

Rock music was in line with the gay liberation movement, which was gaining in attention and popularity as the anti–Vietnam War movement began to wane. Glam rock bands promoted openly homosexual behavior in order to ally with the burgeoning gay liberation movement, and band members dressed in effeminate attire to shock audiences, but most of these glam bands featured heterosexual males in search of a hit record. Cross-dressing rock performers soon became the norm. Edgar Winter, a blues rocker, dressed in drag on the cover of his album *They Only Come Out at Night* (a reference to prostitutes as well as flamboyant gays). Another early 1970s New York glam/punk band, inspired by the New York Dolls, called themselves the "Harlots of 42nd Street." The band Queen Elizabeth starred transsexual performer Wayne County (who changed his name and sexual orientation to Jayne County in 1980). His next band, Wayne County and the Back Street Boys, performed songs such as "(If You Don't Wanna Fuck Me Baby) Fuck Off," "Toilet Love," and "Stick It in Me."

The trend set by the Rolling Stones' 1969 hit "Honky Tonk Woman," about a "barroom queen" and seemingly inspiring a multitude of songs about "queens," reached its peak as a band calling itself Queen, a slang term for a gay man, released their first records. One of their first major chart successes was "Killer Queen" (from their third album, *Sheer Heart Attack*, in 1973), which refers to a high-class call girl who is "recommended at the price."

Kiss, arguably the most successful glam act from the 1970s (rivaled only by Queen and David Bowie), recorded "Ladies in Waiting" for their third album *Dressed to Kill* in 1975. Gene Simmons's lyrics describe a visit to a typical **brothel**, where women line up to offer themselves to the client.

Meanwhile, mainstream rock tended to avoid the subject. Tom Waits recorded "I'm Your Late Evening Prostitute" in 1971 for a demo tape, but the song was not released until 1993. It is not the case that there were no mainstream songs about prostitution during this time. Black Oak Arkansas recorded a song called "Happy Hooker" (about a woman who enjoys her work) on their 1973 album *High on the Hog*. "He's A Whore," from Cheap Trick's 1977 self-titled debut album (which is itself a sex work reference), is indeed about a gigolo (male prostitute), but the lyrics seem to be more about greed than about sex work.

Glam rock represented the extreme limit of sexual liberation that resulted from the political movements of the 1960s. Once glam rock began to decline in 1974, songs that used "whore" or "prostitute" in their lyrics tended to take on a less favorable definition. Patti Smith's provocative lyrics "Rock 'n' Roll Nigger" (on the 1978 album *Easter*; the song was later covered by Marilyn Manson) included the lyrics "baby was a whore" and used the word for its shock value. In fact, as glam rock faded into memory, prostitution was rarely discussed anywhere in a positive way, which probably had to do with the prevalence of AIDS and other **sexually transmitted infections** in the 1980s.

Sex work was rarely referred to in the 1980s, but there were some instances. Iron Maiden recorded "Charlotte the Harlot" for their self-titled debut album in 1980, which describes a woman who charges a "fiver" for "starters" and "ten for the main course." Frank Zappa released "Teenage Prostitute" on his 1982 album *Ship Arriving Too Late to Save a Drowning Witch*, and the lyrics of this song describe the rather bleak existence of a runaway teenage girl who works as a streetwalker. The biggest hit in the 1980s about prostitution was The Police's "Roxanne," in which the singer discourages the title character from working as a prostitute.

David Lee Roth left Van Halen and recorded an immensely popular song and video cover of Louis Prima's "Just a Gigolo" for his 1985 EP *Crazy From the Heat*. Unlike most songs about sex work, "Just a Gigolo" is a light and entertaining romp, which reflects the double standard society has toward men who perform sex for money.

Jane's Addiction recorded a song called "Whores" for their first album. It was reportedly written about the band's first manager Bianca, who was a prostitute and financed a good portion of the bands earlier shows.

"My Michelle" by Guns 'n' Roses (from their *Appetite For Destruction* album, released in 1987) was written about a friend of the band named Michelle who was a prostitute and drug addict.

The Pixies, one of the most influential alternative rock bands, recorded a couple of songs featuring prostitutes. On their debut EP *Come on Pilgrim*, the song "I've Been Tired" refers to the singer's biggest fear as "losing my penis to a whore with disease." On *Doolittle*, their second album, the song "Hey" repeatedly invokes "whores."

As the 1990s geared up and alternative rock became more popular, prostitution became a popular topic for songwriters. Courtney Love wrote and recorded "Teenage Whore" for Hole's debut album *Pretty on the Inside* (1991). The song refers to the negative image the protagonist has from seeing herself, and from her mother referring to her, as a teenage whore, although it is unclear whether she is one or whether she is the victim of parental verbal abuse that makes her feel like one.

Bon Jovi recorded "Prostitute," released as a demo recording in 1995, with lyrics that referred to the male protagonist's willingness to do anything required for the woman he loves.

Canadian musician Lisa Dal Bello, who received her first recording contract in 1977 when she was 19 years old, recorded an album called *Whore* (with a song by the same name) in 1995. The somewhat obscure lyrics feature a chorus that equates the face of an angel with that of a "whore."

The thrash metal band GWAR (an acronym for God What an Awful Racket) used shock value and humor for their song "Preschool Prostitute" on their *Carnival of Chaos* album, released in 1997.

Finland's Impaled Nazarene, a satanic death metal band, also used humor and shock value for their song "Whore," recorded for their 1996 album *Motorpenis*. The lyrics refer to the protagonist's penchant for sex with "your mother" (a "fucking whore") and his subsequent boredom with the act, which leads to his decision to use her as a human sacrifice to Satan. The song also describes a four-year-old girl who is used for sex. The infamous, and more serious, black metal band Mayhem, whose members have actually participated in **murder**, suicide, cannibalism, satanic rituals, and church-burning, recorded "Whore" on their 2004 album *Chimera*. The lyrics are difficult to decipher but appear to refer to the Whore of Babylon and describe a multitude of obscene acts.

The all-female metal band Kittie recorded "Do You Think I'm a Whore?" on their debut album *Spit* in 1999. Although the protagonist admits in the song, "I'm a whore," the statement is obviously meant to be ironic.

Punk Rock

The relationship between punk rock and prostitution is compelling because the earliest meaning for the word "punk" is "prostitute" and an often-cited modern definition is "young man used as a homosexual partner in prison." It also of course refers to rebellious and immature young people. The term "punk rock" came about in the early 1970s, when rock writer Greg Shaw used it to refer to "garage rock" groups such as Count Five, The Troggs and The Standells. Later, Nick Tosches, Lester Bangs and Richard Meltzer used "punk" to label those bands, as well as the Velvet Underground, the MC5 and The Stooges, in Detroit's *Creem* magazine, and the term "punk rock" described hard rock bands such as the New York Dolls and The Sweet as well as English "pub rock" bands such as Eddie and the Hot Rods. *Creem* featured Alice Cooper on the magazine's cover for winning their "Punk of the Year" award in 1974.

The first punk rock band that enjoyed commercial success was Alice Cooper, with a hit record "I'm Eighteen" in 1971. The only song the band recorded that made a direct reference to prostitution was "Never Been Sold Before," which appeared on their last album *Muscle of Love*, and the lyrics seem to be a bout a woman who refuses to become a whore. Released in 1973, the record's interior photographs feature the band in before-and-after poses, first dressed in sailor suits and carrying lots money before they enter the "Institute of Nude Wrestling," which the band obviously believes is a brothel. The "after" pose features the band in battered and bloody poses with a gorilla dressed in drag with its arms raised in victory.

The New York Dolls, a prominent New York City punk rock band whose flair for attracting publicity inspired many imitators, posed in female attire and wrote songs with ambiguous, overtly sexual song lyrics and titles that suggested male or female prostitution such as "Babylon," "Trash," and "Bad Girl." Their lack of commercial success helped to bring an end to the glam rock movement around 1974, and soon afterward, "punk rock" shifted meaning to refer to a new wave of rock bands such as The Ramones, Suicide, Television, The Patti Smith Group, and The Dictators, who performed at clubs such as CBGB and Max's Kansas City in New York City. The fashion sense of these early punks was not as sexually suggestive as the glam rockers, but the lyrical content was more shocking, violent, and humorous.

It seemed that it was an unwritten rule for 1970s punk rock bands to write one song about prostitutes. One of the Ramones' earliest songs, "53rd & 3rd," is written from the point of view of a male prostitute who works on a well-known New York street corner where young men were picked up, and the protagonist of the song stabs a client to prove that he is "no sissy." Dee Dee Ramone, the songwriter, refused to provide specifics about whether the song was autobiographical, but it was often rumored that he wrote it from personal experience.

Janie Jones, whose name was the title of a song by England's The Clash, was a famous madam of the 1970s, and the song lyrics describe a man who hates his job, does drugs, listens to rock and roll, and visits Janie Jones (to represent a prostitute or escort service) after work to relieve all his stress and tensions.

The Dictators penned "Minnesota Strip" for their third album, *Bloodbrothers*. It describes the area near the Port Authority bus station, where newcomers to New York City were sometimes recruited by **pimps**.

X-Ray Spex recorded "I Live Off You" for their first (and only) album *Germ Free Adolescents*. The song makes the case that everyone is exploited by someone else and includes lyrics about a pimp beating a prostitute.

Coincidentally, women who worked in the sex industry as strippers or prostitutes sometimes supported individual punk rock band members. Nancy Spungeon, the infamous girlfriend of Sid Vicious (born John Ritchie) of the English punk band The Sex Pistols, was known for **stripping** and turning tricks when she lived in New York City. She was known to many members of the early punk rock bands as "Nauseating Nancy" (because of her tendency to have sex with musicians who already had girlfriends). The Dead Boys "Caught with the Meat in Your Mouth," which appeared on their debut album *Young Loud and Snotty*, describes this lifestyle.

The only Sex Pistols song that referred to prostitution is "Friggin' in the Rigging" (which was recorded after the core group broke up). The song describes a wooden ship *Venus* with a figurehead that was a "whore in bed," and the rest of the lyrics describe various onboard sexual perversions.

The Misfits, a New York City hardcore band who kept the punk rock tradition alive in the early 1980s, recorded "Hollywood Babylon" about the most famous whore of all. They also recorded a song titled "Devil's Whorehouse."

In the 1980s, as punk rock became influenced by the anti-Reagan politics of West Coast hardcore punk bands such as the Dead Kennedys, references to sex declined in popularity, and most punk bands wrote politically inspired lyrics. When a reference to "whore" appeared, it was more likely to be a negative political reference, such as the hardcore punk band Millions of Dead Cops' 1981 7-inch single "John Wayne Was a Nazi," which referred to Wayne as "just another pawn for the capitalist whore."

There were exceptions. The Germs' "Let's Pretend" (from *Germicide: Live at the Whisky, 1977*) marked one of the first, but hardly the last, times a punk song used a reference to a prostitute as a personal smear. The list of punk rock songs that do so numbers in the thousands, and virtually every punk band in the 1980s and 1990s—the Angry Samoans, Anti-Flag, Bad Brains, Bad Religion, Bikini Kill, Black Flag, Blink 182, The Business, Butthole Surfers, The Circle Jerks, Crass, The Damned, Descendents, Dropkick Murphys, The Dwarves, The Exploited, G. B. H., Guttermouth, Husker Dü, Leftover Crack, the Lunachicks, NOFX, Stiff Little Fingers, Sublime, Social Distortion, The Queers, and U.S. Bombs—use "whore" in a song lyric. However, there are some punk rock songs that stand out because of to their unusual content.

In 1985, Johnny Thunders (of New York Dolls and Heartbreakers) took this to its limit with his song titled "(There's a Little Bit of) Whore in Every Little Girl," which appeared on his album *Que Sera Sera*.

GG Allin, a New York rocker who represented the extreme of both shock and punk rock (he was notorious for flinging his own feces at audiences), recorded "Be My Fucking Whore" in 1988 for his album *Freaks, Faggots, Drunks & Junkies*. The song describes a variety of perverted sexual acts ("sit on my face," "I'll piss in your mouth," "suck it") that are underlined by his insistence that his partner "be my fucking whore." Allin made many more references to "whore" in his song lyrics, such as "Needle Up My Cock" (which refers to how the protagonist of the song caught a social disease from a prostitute or "whore"), "I Wanna Fuck Myself," and "Bite It You Scum," to name just a few.

Recent punk rock bands have recorded any number of songs that mention or refer to prostitution, whores, hustlers, and the like. One that deserves mention is Fifteen, who released "Prostitute" on their 2002 album *Survivor*. This is perhaps the most sympathetic portrayal of a streetwalker's life to be found in any punk rock song. It is told from the point of view of a social worker who works with streetwalkers and refers to the child abuse and drug use that sometimes accompanies the work. It also expresses the opinion that social workers themselves are in business to keep sex workers where they are. Fifteen also recorded "Hello My Name Is Whore," a song that questions why people are often sexualized.

The most famous punk rock band of the 1990s to the present, Green Day, wrote "Misery" for their best-selling Grammy Award–winning 2004 album *American Idiot*. The first verse describes a girl named Virginia who was a "lot lizard," a term that describes prostitutes, some of whom are underage, who offer sex for money to truck drivers at interstate highway truck stops. Virginia and the other characters in the song meet unhappy ends.

See also Appendix document 10, Hip-Hop.

Further Reading: Gendron, Bernard. *From Montmarte to the Mudd Club*. Chicago: University of Chicago Press, 2002.

John Holmstrom

RODE DRAAD. The Rode Draad ("Red Thread") is an organization that serves the interests and fights for the rights of sex workers in the Netherlands. The Rode Draad was founded in 1985, just before the first World Whore Conference was held in **Amsterdam.**

The organization works with both paid staff and volunteers who do outreach work. They visit the **brothels**, shop windows and official streetwalking zones to monitor the working conditions, gather information, and inform sex workers about their rights. Sex workers can contact the organization if they have questions about the business or if they want to exchange thoughts and ideas with colleagues or—anonymously—lodge a complaint about a club, private brothel, or window proprietor.

The Rode Draad has consistently supported the legalization of the sex industry as an instrument to improve the working conditions of sex workers and their access to protection through labor laws. The organization is still critical of several aspects of the new legislation and of the way it is being implemented.

The Rode Draad negotiates on behalf of sex workers with brothels owners about working conditions and labor relations in the sex industry. The foundation also acts as an interlocutor in the legislations processes for (local) government and governmental divisions such as the taxation, social services, and labor inspection departments.

In the late 1990s the Rode Draad became a member of the FNV, the largest labor **union** in the Netherlands. The FNV fully supports the Rode Draad's work on behalf of both individuals and groups of sex workers in labor conflict cases within the sex industry. The union is also an important support for the Rode Draad's political action, given that the FNV has long been recognized by the government as a valuable social partner. The relationship between the Rode Draad and the FNV allows individual sex workers, who may be hesitant to join a sex workers union, to still have their labor rights protected. The Rode Draad has resisted traditional ideas of "employment" in sex work in favor of a worker status as independent entrepreneur or self-employed contractor. More recently, the organization has recognized that employment in a sex business with a labor contract may be a desirable option for some sex workers. On a national level the FNV may draw up collective labor agreements for those sex workers who wish to enter into an employer–employee relationship. In addition, because the FNV decided some years ago to create a division specifically concerned with labor issues of entrepreneurs without personnel, they are able to serve the interests of sex workers who prefer self-employment.

The Netherlands lifted the ban on brothels in 2000, formally recognizing the sex industry. Since these changes, the Rode Draad has allocated its organizational tasks to two organizations: the Foundation Rode Draad and Vakwerk. The foundation continues its important work of drawing public and political attention to the social, economic, and legal position of sex workers in the Netherlands and informing women and men involved in sex work of their rights. Vakwerk (which means "skilled or professional work") functions as a union representing the individual and collective interests of sex workers in the Netherlands.

See also Window Prostitution.

Further Reading: Rode Draad Web site. http://www.rodedraad.nl

Marieke van Doorninck

ROMANTIC LITERATURE. The prostitute in Romantic Literature is certainly not as prominent a figure as she was in later 19th-century Victorian literature, but she is often present in a variety of revealing roles. For the Romantics, a woman could signify pleasure, domestic bliss, death, or nature. When she was a prostitute, however, a woman could also signify moral decay as well as deep injustice. On the one hand, the prostitute represented the corruption and degradation of urban life. On the other, hers could be a marginalized voice added to the other anguished cries of the city. Further, because the Romantic poet indulged a suspicion that the act of writing for an audience was a form of artistic prostitution, he could identify with the prostitute, complicating her symbolic value all the more.

Most literary histories date the Romantic Movement as the period between 1785 and 1830, a turbulent time in European history. The years following the storming of the Bastille in Paris in 1789 were ones in which the long-intact class system was challenged while, at the same time, the growing importance of business and commerce solidified the status of the burgeoning middle class.

Mary Wollstonecraft, an 18th-century feminist and early Romantic, clearly saw the prostitute as victim, not transgressor. In her essays and fiction, she identified gender inequities, often focusing on the particular problems of class for women, and laid these problems at the feet of the laws and customs of society. Wollstonecraft saw the prostitute's case as one of desperate economic need rather than moral weakness. She further recognized that a woman's virtue was the only valuable commodity that she possessed, and when this was compromised, she was ruined, morally, economically, and emotionally.

Although Wollstonecraft approached the prostitute with sympathetic feminist sensibilities, the major figures of the Romantic Movement were all male poets whose primary concerns were the imagination and liberating effects of fully engaging one's creative faculties. William Wordsworth, William Blake, Samuel Taylor Coleridge, Byron, Percy Bysshe Shelley, and John Keats lived in a time of dramatic political, social, and literary change and were vitally engaged in every aspect of their culture.

Politically liberal, they were inclined to idealize the rural landscape and abhor the soul-deadening grime and bustle of the city. Although in many ways radical literary theorists who advocated a central role for common people and common language in **poetry**, they also lamented the decline in public taste that accompanied the rise of popular culture and the novel. They were sympathetic to poor and marginalized victims of urban life even as they celebrated the rural sage. Yet, for all their compatible views, these poets were rarely of one voice. All used the trope of the prostitute to different ends, and if the sage occupied the countryside, the prostitute occupied the city.

The older Romantics witnessed the French Revolution, and the younger ones saw the beginning of the Industrial Revolution and the rise of the middle class. Coleridge wrote a number of essays that addressed the popular taste for the new form of the novel and, to his mind, the corresponding divide of literature into two categories—literature and popular fiction. The influences of urbanization and industrialization further developed the tastes and habits of the new middle class, but, at least for the Romantics, the city was the site of society's greatest ills; the prostitute proved a useful symbol, both of moral degradation and of the corrupt society that brought her to this state. Further, because the cash nexus and commodification became the basis for most human interaction, the very fact of prostitution provided a wealth of metaphoric possibilities.

Perhaps reflecting their own marginal status as artists, many Romantics seemed to simultaneously sympathize with and revile the figure of the prostitute. In Wordsworth's "The Reverie of Poor Susan," the prostitute is a country girl who, foolishly perhaps, has left the country for the city, only to find that the morning song of a bird she hears in Cheapside as she returns from the streets is a bittersweet reminder of the wholesome life she left. Similarly, in the autobiographical *Confessions of an Opium Eater*, Romantic Thomas de Quincey tells of a 15-year-old prostitute named Ann who befriends him when he is 17, alone and on the streets. He credits her kindness with saving his life and refuses to pass judgment on the lives of the "street-walkers."

A more complex, less idealized portrayal of the prostitute as both victim and transgressor is suggested in Blake's "London" from *Songs of Experience*. In this poem, a dark and dirty London is home to a prostitute who curses the marriage bed, presumably with venereal disease acquired by the husband as he visited the streets. The harlot, however, is described as "youthful," implying a prematurely lost innocence.

The image of the prostitute as a figure to be feared is present in Coleridge's "Rime of the Ancient Mariner," Byron's "Childe Harolde," and Keats' "Lamia." In the first example, the nightmarish figure Life-in-Death is described by the Mariner as a woman whose lips are red and looks are free—symbols of wantonness often associated with prostitution. For Byron and Keats, the presence of lewd women signals a depraved urban sensuality that indicates real danger to their protagonists. For all of these artists, the act of commodifying one's body, and the subsequent social and moral fall it implied, signified deeper ills, both in the literary marketplace and in the sociopolitical structure of the early 19th century.

Further Reading: Goodwin, Sarah Webster. "Wordsworth and Romantic Voice: The Poet's Song and the Prostitute's Cry." In *Embodied Voices: Representing Female Vocality in Western Culture*, ed. Leslie C. Dunn and Nancy A. Jones. Cambridge: Cambridge University Press, 1994, pp. 65–79; Mellor, Anne K. *Romanticism and Feminism*. Bloomington: Indiana University Press, 1988; Mudge, Bradford K. *The Whore's Story: Women, Pornography, and the British Novel, 1684–1830*. New York: Oxford University Press, 2000.

Anita R. Rose

RUSSIA. *See* **Imperial Russia.**

S

SABATIER, APPOLONIE (1822–1890). French **courtesan** Appolonie Sabatier was born April 7, 1822, to a washerwoman and a sergeant named Savatier. Aglaé-Joséphine, as she was christened, had a talent for music and the beauty of a model, both of which she used to make her way into bohemian life, which was paid for by her short liaisons. In 1846 she accepted as her protector Alfred Mosselman, who rented her an apartment, and celebrated the next step on the social ladder by changing her first name to Appolonie and slightly altering her last name— to disassociate herself from her family. It was Mosselman who commissioned a sculpture of Appolonie that immortalized her. In 1847 Auguste Clesinger exhibited his sculpture *La Femme piquée par un serpent*, which represented a naked woman bitten by a snake but was read by the public as a woman in sexual ecstasy (the sculpture is on permanent display in the Musée d'Orsay in Paris). Charles Baudelaire wrote a series of poems for Appolonie, some of the most beautiful masterpieces of French poetry. She also inspired Théophile Gautier's hymns to female beauty and sexuality. Appolonie's Sunday evenings attracted the intellectual elite of Paris. Among her guests were the writers Gustave Flaubert, Victor Hugo, and Ernest Feydeau; the artists Eugène Delacroix and Paul Joseph Chenavard; the poets Gérard de Nerval and Théophile Gautier; and the critic Sainte-Beuve. Appolonie became the female president of the evenings and became known as "La Presidente." When in 1860 Mosselman, Appolonie's protector of many years, left her for a younger woman, she refused the money he offered her and decided to support herself through painting and repairing miniatures. She still entertained, but not lavishly, and she never again had a permanent relationship of the type she had had with Mosselman. However, at the age of 48, she prudently accepted an annual income from an admirer, Richard Wallace. She was now at the age when it became increasingly difficult for her to find protectors. Appolonie died of influenza in 1890 and was buried in the cemetery at Neuilly.

See also Grandes Horizontales.

Further Reading: Hickman, Katie. *Courtesans: Money, Sex and Fame in the Nineteenth Century*. New York: William Morrow, 2003; Ringdal, Nils Johan. *Love for Sale: A World History of Prostitution*, trans. Richard Daly. New York: Grove Press, 2004; Rounding, Virginia. *Grandes Horizontales*. New York: Bloomsbury, 2003.

Maria Mikolchak

SACRED PROSTITUTION IN THE ANCIENT WORLD. Sacred prostitution is the temporary sale of a person's body for sexual purposes in which either all or some portion of the money received for this transaction belongs to a deity. In the ancient Near East, this deity was usually understood as Ishtar or Astarte; in ancient Greece, it was Aphrodite.

At least three separate types of sacred prostitution have been distinguished. In some examples, such as argued by Herodotos for Babylon and Cyprus, once in life every woman must prostitute herself, often to a foreign man, and give the money to the relevant deity.

> The most shameful of the customs among the Babylonians is this: It is necessary for every local woman to sit in the sanctuary of Aphrodite once in life to "mingle" with a foreign man … in the sanctuary of Aphrodite many women sit wearing a garland of string about their heads. Some come forward, others remain in the background. They have straight passages in all directions through the women, by which the foreigners passing through might make their selection. Once a woman sits there, she may not return home before someone of the foreigners tossing money into her lap should mingle with her outside the sanctuary. And in tossing he must say thus: "I summon you by the goddess Mylitta." The Assyrians call Aphrodite Mylitta. The money is of any amount, for it may not be rejected: This is not their sacred custom, for the money is sacred. The woman follows the first man who tossed her money, nor may she reject anyone. When she should have mingled, having discharged her obligation to the goddess, she leaves for home. (Herodotus 1.199)

A second type of sacred prostitution involves women and men who are professional prostitutes and who are owned by a deity or a deity's sanctuary, as described by Strabo:

> Eryx, a lofty mountain, is also inhabited and has a sanctuary of Aphrodite which is very much esteemed; in former times it was filled with women hierodules, whom the inhabitants of Sicily, and also many others, dedicated through vows. But now the neighborhood is much less inhabited, and the sanctuary not so well supplied with sacred bodies. (6.2.6)

There are also references to a temporary type of sacred prostitution, in which the women and possibly men only prostitute themselves during certain rituals. One such example is presented in Lucian's *Syrian Goddess*(6):

> The women of Byblos shave their heads, as do the Egyptians when Apis dies. The women who refuse to shave pay this penalty: For a single day they stand offering their beauty for sale. The market, however, is open to foreigners only and the payment becomes an offering to Aphrodite.

In the first and third examples, sacred prostitutes do not appear to belong to any specific profession or subgroup within society but presumably come from all walks of life. In the second category, sacred prostitutes belong to a clearly delineated profession.

The textual evidence for sacred prostitution can be divided into two distinct categories—direct references to the institution in the works of the ancient Greeks, Romans, and early Church Fathers and implied references in the Near Eastern corpus. The direct, Classical references are apparently unambiguous in that they refer to women who sell their bodies for sex, who are either "sacred" or who hand over the money they earn to a deity. The words used to describe them are *hetairai* (**courtesans**), *hierodouloi* (sacred slaves), and *sômata hiera* (sacred bodies).

The implied references in the Near Eastern corpus are more difficult to analyze, given that the identity of sacred prostitutes depends on the translation of words that are not as blatant as "hetaira." The individuals most commonly referred to as sacred prostitutes are the *qedesh* (male) and *qedeshah* (female) of the **Bible** and, in the Mesopotamian cuneiform corpus, the *entum, naditum, qadishtum, ishtaritum, kulmashitum*, and the *kezertum* for women and the *kalbu* (literally meaning "dog"), *assinnu, kurgarru*, and *kulu'u* for men (Hooks 1985, 3). The biblical qedeshah seem to be the most obvious sacred prostitutes in the Near East. The radicals (*qdš*) generally refer to holiness or sacredness in Semitic languages. The use of the words in Genesis 38 leaves little doubt that it refers to a prostitute. Here, Judah inadvertently solicited his daughter-in-law Tamara, taking her to be a prostitute (*zonah* in the text). Later, when he sent his servant to pay for her services, the servant claimed to be looking for the "*qedeshah* who was at Enaim by the wayside." Prostitution is clearly at issue. The radicals refer to holiness. Thus, sacred prostitution seems to be intended. Another usage though of as referring both to male and female prostitutes, appears in Deuteronomy:

> You shall not bring the hire of a whore [zonah] or the wages of a dog [*keleb*, Hebrew for *kalbu*] into the house of the Lord your God in payment for any vow; for both of these are an abomination to the Lord your God. There shall be no *qedeshah* of the daughters of Israel, neither shall there be a *qedesh* of the sons of Israel. (23:18–19)

The Mesopotamian terminology is more difficult. Many of the cult functionaries deemed to be prostitutes are thought to have had strict limitations placed on their sexuality. The naditum, for example, was not allowed to bear children, although she was allowed to adopt, suggesting that she was not allowed to reproduce sexually. The same was true for the qadishtum, who was, however, allowed to marry, as was the kezertum. In short, it seems that the early Assyriologists were not sufficiently rigorous in their translations, applying the definition "sacred prostitute" too freely.

Such "freedom" has recently come under considerable scrutiny, as has the undeniable fact that most references to sacred prostitution occur as invective, condemning "other" societies, usually far away and long ago. Furthermore, there is, to date, no evidence of the sacred prostitution practices mentioned in the Classical texts: there is no Babylonian evidence, for example, that Babylonian women prostituted themselves once in life for Mylitta. This has suggested that sacred prostitution never actually existed, but was a literary device or an accusation used to denigrate others. Herodotus used it poetically to describe the conquered status of Babylon. The Church Fathers used it to impugn pagans: "In times past women displayed themselves in front of idols in Phoenicia, offering the price of their bodies to the local gods, and believing that by prostitution they conciliated their goddess and incurred her favor through these practices," wrote the 4th-century Athenasius in his *Against the Nations* (Oden 2000, 143). New studies based on this perspective that cite the lack of any corroborating evidence for Herodotos's and Strabo's accounts are slowly chipping away at the sacred prostitution myth. The Mesopotamian vocabulary is being redefined with a view toward functions as described in the cuneiform texts, not based on the accusations of later Classical and Christian authors. The Biblical qedeshah is being seen more as non-Yahwistic priestesses, a holdover from Canaanite times, which was redefined in insulting fashion to refer to common whores. Sacred prostitution is now being studied as a long-term aspect of propaganda and rhetoric.

See also Ancient World; Child Prostitution, Cultural and Religious; *Devadasi; Hetaera.*

Further Reading: Beard, Mary, and John Henderson. "With This Body I Thee Worship: Sacred Prostitution in Antiquity." In *Gender and the Body in the Ancient Mediterranean,* ed. M. Wyke. Oxford: Blackwell Publishers, 1998, pp. 56–79; Bird, Phyllis. "'To Play the Harlot': An Inquiry into an Old Testament Metaphor." In *Gender and Difference in Ancient Israel,* ed. P. Day. Minneapolis, MN: Fortress Press, 1989, pp. 75–94; Budin, Stephanie L. "*Pallakai,* Prostitutes, and Prophetesses." *Classical Philology* 98 (2003): 148–159; Budin, Stephanie L. "Sacred Prostitution in the First Person." In *Prostitutes and Courtesans in the Ancient World,* ed. Laura McClure and Christopher Faraone. Madison: University of Wisconsin Press, in press; Hooks, Stephen M. "Sacred Prostitution in Israel and the Ancient Near East." Ph.D. dissertation, Hebrew Union College, 1985; Oden, Robert A., Jr. *The Bible without Theology.* Chicago: University of Illinois Press, 2000; Westenholz, Joan G. "Tamar, Qedeša, Qadištu, and Sacred Prostitution in Mesopotamia." *Harvard Theological Review* 82:3 (1989): 245–265.

Stephanie Lynn Budin

SACRED PROSTITUTION, CONTEMPORARY. Modern sacred prostitutes, also called sacred harlots, sacred whores, or *Qadesh(im),* are people (mostly women) who interact sexually with strangers for the purpose of offering healing or an experience of divinity. This is based on ancient polytheistic traditions in which men would come to a temple to worship a Goddess (such as Astarte or Shakti) by making love to her priestesses. The vast majority of the clients/worshippers are male (and probably were even in ancient times), even when one takes into account the male and transgender sacred prostitutes.

Modern sacred prostitutes fall into two overlapping categories. Some are primarily spiritually motivated, and these people act as sexual therapists or surrogates or teach Tantra or similar techniques. Some simply feel they have a calling to be sexually available to all and are less formal about it. Sometimes they accept money, and sometimes they do not. Another category of modern sacred prostitutes are people who identify primarily as sex workers and who bring an element of spirituality or healing to their work. Generally, these people are earning a living from their sex work, so money is almost always exchanged. During the course of the individual's career and path, she may go from one type to the other or may function in both ways simultaneously.

Sacred harlots differ in their spiritual paths. Some are *Tantrikas,* who embody the Goddess Shakti and follow a Hindu-based path. Others are NeoPagan priestesses, who may identify with a Goddess from an ancient European pantheon. Still others may not be focused on any deities, but proceed from the belief that sexuality is a sacred force and something to be enjoyed. The notion of the sacred embodied in the physical (pantheism) is a common idea.

Activities may include touch and sensual massage; hand jobs; oral, vaginal, or anal sex, bondage and **sadomasochism** (BDSM), and role-play. Sacred prostitutes may even interact with clients over the phone, practicing in an astral temple. Not all are "full service"; each harlot sets her own limits.

Modern sacred prostitution has an element of therapy to it. Female sacred prostitutes who receive male clients/worshippers say that men have been wounded by our society by being taught that their sexual desire is bad or wrong, either in its focus (such as a fetish) or its intensity. In this way, they may provide acceptance, encouragement, and understanding for the client. They may also help the men become more comfortable with women and women's bodies, including offering instruction on techniques (energetic and physical), birth control, and safer sex. With spiritually or energetically experienced clients/worshippers, they may be able to take things further and create a Great Rite or *hieros gamos* (a ritualized coupling between God and Goddess) or assist them in raising energy for magical purposes.

The issue of money is hotly charged for people in this area. Some believe that to charge for the service is to strip it of its sacredness or demean the priest or priestess. Others see it as precisely the opposite situation: people value that which they have to pay for, and the harlot should be compensated for her time and hard work. Prostitution is illegal in most places, so sacred prostitutes who are compensated are sometimes paid as therapists, escorts, or performers.

The client who visits a sex worker is generally looking merely for pleasure and entertainment, not a spiritual experience; some sacred prostitutes stay on a physical level with such clients, and others try to bring them a little further into the realm of worship and communion. Regardless, the sacred prostitute provides pleasure and release, which increases the amount of pleasure and joy in the world.

Some well-known modern sacred prostitutes include Pat Califia, **Carol Leigh** (a.k.a Scarlot Harlot), Magdalene Meretrix, and **Annie Sprinkle**.

See also Religion; Sacred Prostitution in the Ancient World.

Further Reading Fabian, Cosi. "The Holy Whore: A Woman's Gateway to Power." In *Whores and Other Feminists*, ed. Jill Nagle. New York: Routledge, 1997, pp. 44–54; Stubbs, Kenneth K. *Women of the Light: The New Sacred Prostitute.* Tucson, AZ: Secret Garden Publishing, 1995.

Jennifer Hunter

SADE, MARQUIS DE (1740–1814).

Donatien Alphonse, the Marquis de Sade, was an 18th-century French poet and writer. Sade was involved in a number of sexual scandals and personified the excesses of –18th-century French aristocracy. Sexual themes and overindulgence permeate Sade's literary works, which are still considered controversial in modern society. He employed the services of prostitutes to satisfy his own desires, and the theme of prostitution pervades his works.

Sade's first criminal conviction came in 1763, after an encounter with a French prostitute, Jeanne Testard, whom, during the course of their encounter, Sade threatened to torture for the purpose of sexual gratification. Testard was able to talk her way out of the situation with the promise that she would later indulge Sade. She reported the events to the police the next day. At the time of the incident, the young Sade had been married for six months. He was sentenced to death in 1772 after being convicted of sodomy and poisoning two prostitutes, but he managed to avoid execution.

Sade's first completed novel was *The Misfortunes of Virtue*, which was written in 1787 during the last of his imprisonments. His most well-known works were to follow: *The 120 Days of Sodom* (written in 1785; date of first publication unknown), *Juliette* (1797; a revised version of *The Misfortunes*), and *Philosophy in the Boudoir* (1795). Throughout these narratives, sexuality and violence are entwined in shocking plots.

The works of Sade are still considered controversial, depicting rape, theft, prostitution, and degradation. However, in the latter part of the 20th century, Sade's work received critical and theoretical attention, which allowed it to slowly become more available.

See also Masoch, Leopold von Sacher; Sadomasochism.

Further Reading: Lynott, Douglas B. "The Marquis de Sade." *Court TV's Crime Library*. http://www.crimelibrary.com/classics/marquis/; Thomas, Donald. *The Marquis de Sade: A New Biography*. Secaucus, NJ: Citadel Press, 1992.

Shannon Schedlich-Day

SADIE THOMPSON. The famous fictional prostitute Sadie Thompson was created by W. Somerset Maugham. His short story "Rain," published in 1921, tells of Thompson's encounter with a zealous missionary on a Pacific island. Several successful adaptations of the story have spread Thompson's fame. Maugham's story centers on a clash between the pleasure-loving Thompson and the judgmental Christian, Mr. Davidson. Davidson strives to ensure that Thompson will fail to reach her hoped-for destination, Sydney, and will instead return to San Francisco to face impris-

Gloria Swanson (as Sadie Thompson) in Raoul Walsh's 1928 film *Sadie Thompson*. Courtesy of Photofest.

onment for prostitution offences. This punishment is necessary for Thompson's moral reform, Davidson insists. The story ends with the discovery of Davidson's corpse; although Maugham provides scant details, Davidson has shot himself after a sexual encounter with Thompson.

Instantly renowned, the story was adapted into a play by John Colton and Clemence Randolph in 1922. The play was performed and revived several times on Broadway and elsewhere. Gloria Swanson starred in the 1928 Raoul Walsh–directed film adaptation, *Sadie Thompson*, and Lewis Thompson's *Rain* (1932) featured Joan Crawford in the Thompson role. The 1946 film *Dirty Gertie from Harlem U.S.A.* twists the Sadie Thompson myth: a black showgirl is cast as the troubled woman in a very similar plot. John Mackenzie directed a 1970 TV version. The best-known adaptation of "Rain," the 1953 Curtis Bernhardt–directed film, *Miss Sadie Thompson*, differs from the original story in important ways. The action is moved from the 1920s to the postwar era, where Rita Hayworth's vivacious Thompson enraptures bored, ill-disciplined American soldiers. A sergeant falls in love with Thompson, and she reciprocates with equal affection—Thompson, possibly, will not engage in prostitution again. Also, Davidson's hypocrisy is more ferocious, because he forces himself sexually upon a shocked, unwilling Thompson. In Maugham's story, the reader is not told whether if Davidson or Thompson initiated the fatal sexual act.

Further Reading: Colton, John, and Clemence Randolph. *Rain: A Play in Three Acts*. New York: Boni and Liveright, 1925; Maugham, W. Somerset. "Rain." In *The Exotic Novels and Short Stories of Somerset Maugham*. New York: Carroll & Graf Publishers, 2001, pp. 342.

Kevin De Ornellas

A French dominatrix flexes her whip in anticipation, circa 1920. Sean Sexton/Getty Images.

SADOMASOCHISM. As a form of prostitution, sadomasochism, abbreviated as S/M, typically describes the domination of a man by a woman, usually known as a dominatrix or mistress, for payment. More rarely does it describe the domination of a woman by a man, though dominatrices often receive female clients. Sadomasochism combines sexual dominance (sadism, derived from **Marquis de Sade**'s name) and submission (masochism, derived from **Leopold von Sacher Masoch**'s name). It is fundamentally an expression of power over another human being in which the dominatrix "tops" or dominates and the client "bottoms" or submits, whether through bondage, wrestling, whipping, body-piercing, and so on. Most often, this kind of prostitution does not involve sexual penetration, and it usually involves no nudity on the part of the dominatrix. For this reason, this form of prostitution enjoys a certain immunity from law enforcement in some parts of the United States.

In the dominatrix's "dungeon," the session takes place with the client, in a submissive role, seeking some form of humiliation, typically through receiving pain or being rendered immobile. A dominatrix may cause pain by whipping, spanking, caning, or verbally abusing her client. Some clients seek the experience of being bound or tightly wrapped through, for example, rope bondage, mummification (being wrapped or fitted in latex or leather), entombment, or suspension. A client may also desire to be humiliated through receiving "golden showers" (being urinated on), depersonalization fantasies (being treated like an object, such as a footstool, or an animal, most often a pony) or infantilism (being treated like a baby, wearing a diaper and sucking on a bottle). Other forms of pleasurable humiliation include cross-dressing (especially being forced to do so), body worship (foot fetishism is common), enemas, branding, and scarification.

The paid session is in many ways a mutually created role-playing or theatrical event with the dominatrix and the client enacting a fantasy of dominance and submission. Great attention may be paid to setting, dialogue, and costume. The dungeon, for example, may recreate a medieval torture chamber with its instruments of pain such as a rack, cage, or hooks. An elaborate drama may unfold in which the client is being tortured for some imaginary crime and begs for his mercy. What makes any session work, no matter how basic or how elaborate, is the contract between the dominatrix and the client. This usually formalized agreement may involve something as simple as a "safe word," a word uttered by the client when the pain becomes unbearable or the scenario too threatening or debasing. It may also involve something elaborate such as a detailed contract of servitude in which the client agrees to do certain tasks for the dominatrix such as cleaning her bathroom or floors with a small brush.

Currently, thousands of dominatrices and mistresses advertise their services on the **Internet**. Some even offer more technologically advanced forms of sadomasochism such as email or phone domination. A live session may range in price from $100 to more than $1,000 an hour. Nick Broomfield's documentary *Fetishes* (1996) takes the viewer inside Pandora's Box, an upscale dungeon where investment bankers, lawyers, executives, and other **New York City** powerbrokers go to be humiliated by professional dominatrices. A thriving part of the sex industry, sadomasochistic prostitution holds special appeal for well-to-do urbanites who seek a combination of physical and imaginative stimulation.

See also Kink.

Further Reading: Brame, William, Gloria Brame, and Jon Jacobs. *Different Loving: The World of Sexual Domination and Submission.* New York: Random House, 1993; Stoller, Robert J. *Pain and Passion: A Psychoanalyst Explores the World of S&M.* New York: Plenum, 1991; Theroux, Paul. *Nurse Wolf and Dr. Sacks.* London: Faber & Faber, 2001.

Michael Uebel

SAI, JINHUA (1872–1936). Originally from Yancheng, Jiangsu Province, Chinese concubine Sai Jinhua spent her childhood in Suzhou, China. When her father died and the family faced hard times, Sai became a prostitute at age 13, with the professional name Fu Caiyun. In 1887 she was taken as a concubine by Hong Jun (1839–1893), a high-ranking official who was visiting Suzhou. When Hong was appointed by Empress Dowager Cixi (1835–1908) as the Chinese envoy to Europe, Sai accompanied him on his diplomatic mission touring Russia, Austria, Holland, and Germany. In Berlin she reportedly made the acquaintance of a high-ranking officer in the German army named Alfred von Waldersee (1832–1904). Hong died shortly after returning to Beijing, and his relatives refused to support Sai, who was forced back into prostitution in 1894, now known by the name Cao Menglan. A few years later she organized a courtesan theater company called Golden Flower Troupe (Jinhua Ban), which became widely known in Beijing and Tianjin. In 1900 when the antiforeign Boxer Rebellion was crushed down by the allied forces of the Western powers, Sai renewed her acquaintance with Waldsee, who was then the chief commander of the occupation army. With her German connection, Sai was credited with influencing Waldsee to moderate the harsh treatment of Beijing residents. When the dust settled, the imperial Qing government was not grateful to her, and so Sai returned to her old business. In 1903 she was jailed for mistreatment of one of her courtesans, who committed suicide because of Sai's abuse. Banished to her hometown, Sai first entered into a brief marriage to a railroad official and then married a member of the National Assembly. In 1936 she died penniless and was buried in Beijing. Her life became the subject of Zeng Pu's novel *Nie Hai Hua* (meaning "Flower in a Sea of Evil"). It has been repeatedly adapted into plays, films and TV series, and she was regarded by some as a cross-cultural courtesan.

Further Reading: Wan, Xianchu. *Famous Prostitutes of Ancient China (Zhong Guo Ming Ji)*. Taibei, China: Xiapu Press, 1994.

Wenxian Zhang

SALVATION ARMY. The Salvation Army, a British-based worldwide Evangelical Christian organization, provides social services for prostitutes. It began as the Christian Mission in 1865. In 1878, founder William Booth changed the organization's name to the Salvation Army and adopted a martial structure.

The Salvation Army formed groups of people who had been conspicuous sinners. The groups, which included former prostitutes, went from place to place attracting attention with colorful antics, brass bands, and parades. Women, led by William's wife Catherine Booth, were particularly drawn to the movement because they were treated as the equals of men. They had the chance to preach and to serve as leaders.

By 1883, the Salvation Army had begun to turn from a focus on proselytizing to social concern for fallen women, drunkards, and released prisoners. In 1885, it joined the efforts to pass the Criminal Law Amendment in Britain to raise the age at which a girl could consent to be a prostitute. Both William and Catherine Booth promoted women's suffrage to give women a voice in choosing the lawmakers who made prostitution laws.

The Booths recognized that poor economic circumstances prevented many people from hearing a spiritual message. In his 1890 book *In Darkest England and the Way Out*, William proposed that social services be combined with religious outreach. American Salvationists were also moving in this direction. The Salvation Army established national networks of shelters, cheap hotels, and rescue homes for fallen women. The modern Salvation Army includes homes for families with AIDS, adult rehabilitation centers for substance abusers, and after-school centers for children.

See also Fallen Woman Trope; Religion.

Further Reading: McKinley, Edward H. *Marching to Glory: The History of the Salvation Army in the United States, 1880–1992*. Grand Rapids, MI: William B. Eerdmans, 1995; Murdoch, Norman H. *Origins of the Salvation Army*. Knoxville: University of Tennessee Press, 1994.

Caryn E. Neumann

SAN FRANCISCO. *See* **American West, 19th Century**.

SANGER, WILLIAM WALLACE (1819–1872). William Wallace Sanger was the first resident physician at the Houses of Correction on Blackwell's Island, New York. In 1853, with the public increasingly alarmed by the visibility of growing numbers of female prostitutes on **New York City** streets, the city's aldermen commissioned Sanger to investigate the factors causing women to turn to prostitution. Under Sanger's direction, police interviewed 2,000 women incarcerated at Blackwell's venereal disease hospital. Police asked the women questions about their ethnic and social backgrounds and their reasons for entering the profession, and the result was an 1858 groundbreaking statistical study, *The History of Prostitution*, similar one conducted in 1830s Paris by French physician **Alexandre-Jean-Baptiste Parent-Duchâtelet**. Like Parent-Duchâtelet's,

Sanger's findings challenged popular preconceptions. Nearly 47 percent of the women were very young (median age of 15), foreign-born (mostly recent Irish or German immigrants), and unskilled, though 38 percent were native-born. Although most came from unskilled backgrounds, more than half were daughters of skilled workers or came from elite artisanal families. Male desertion, widowhood, single motherhood, and especially death of a male wage-earner made prostitution a viable choice for many. Economic factors, low wages, and the monotony of mill life for many young working women clearly led to prostitution. Casual prostitution became a relatively easy way to supplement low-wage employment. Disconcerting to the public and reformers alike, who saw these women as victims of circumstance and destitution, was that one-fourth of the women cited attraction or an easy life as a reason for entering the profession, thus revealing some element of personal choice on the part of these young women.

Further Reading: Gilfoyle, Timothy. *City of Eros: New York City, Prostitution, and the Commercialization of Sex, 1790–1920.* New York: W.W. Norton, 1992; Stansell, Christine. *City of Women: Sex and Class in New York, 1789–1860.* Chicago: University of Illinois Press, 1987.

Melissa Ellis Martin

SAPPHO OF LESBOS (c. 630 B.C.E.–?). Sappho, a poet born in either Mytilene or Eresus on Lesbos, was claimed by some ancient, apocryphal sources to have been a courtesan. She composed wedding hymns and ritual mourning songs, and ancient sources also claimed that she composed epigrams, elegiac poems, and iambics, although none survive. Most of her **poetry**, in fact, is no longer extant: one complete poem and numerous fragments survive from an ancient edition that probably comprised eight books and was arranged according to meter and genre several centuries after her death. Her poetry dealt with erotic and homoerotic themes, the goddess Aphrodite, and her relationship to the Muses. Her poetry was particularly influential to the Roman poets Catullus, Horace, and Ovid and remains canonical despite its fragmentary state.

The apocryphal claim that Sappho had been a courtesan was probably influenced by representations of her in Attic drama: numerous comedies entitled *Sappho* were produced in Athens during the 4th century., and although none of them survive, at least one by the comic poet Diphilus represented Sappho as the object of erotic pursuit by the male poets Hipponax and Archilochus. Hermesianax's *Leontium*, a poem that was influenced by comic representations of Sappho, depicts a rivalry between the lyric poets Alcaeus and Anacreon for the erotic attention of Sappho, who spurns them both. Erotic pursuits featuring agonistic rivalries between lovers for the attentions of beautiful and accomplished **courtesans** were typical scenarios in Attic comedy. The fact that courtesans in antiquity, particularly in Classical Athens, were well educated in music, political and philosophical discourse, and drama may have reinforced the association between Sappho and mercantile sexuality.

See also Hetaera.

Further Reading: Hunter, Richard. *The New Comedy of Greece and Rome.* Oxford: Oxford University Press, 1985.

Angela Gosetti-Murrayjohn

SCAPEGOATING. The scapegoating of prostitutes has a long history. Attacks on prostitutes as threats to public space, morality, and health are a long-term fixture of discourses on prostitution. These moralistic views of sex for monetary transactions typify and transform the public response from one of tolerance for a victimless crime toward more punitive approaches. Most prostitu-

HIV/AIDS poster warning against sex with prostitutes, Hanoi, Vietnam. The text reads, "Prostituting yourself: the quickest way to HIV/AIDS." Courtesy of Angus McIntyre.

tion law is framed as a conflict between a "sex monster" and the innocent victims he or she is polluting, damaging, or contaminating; the patriarchal state steps in to punish, regulate, and preserve the nuclear family. The following highlights a number of flashpoints in this age-old conflict.

Competing Discourses and World War

"A German bullet is cleaner than a whore," stated American hygiene propaganda during **World War I**. During the **syphilis** outbreak of the period, public health publications and announcements suggested that prostitutes were "pools of contagion," "reservoirs of infection," and "vectors of transmission"; they were thought to sell "death" to "pure" victims. Most important, prostitutes were thought to reduce the will to fight among the young. Thus, their presence increased anxiety about the preparedness of U.S. soldiers, whose leaders thought they needed to focus on war instead of sex. As the war proceeded, some 30,000 accused or suspected prostitutes were incarcerated and quarantined in response to increasing syphilis cases (yet the government failed to distribute **condoms** to its servicemen). Those women under suspicion were forced to submit to mandatory tests harking back to the "inspections" required with the **Contagious Diseases Act of 1864**. And in the end, syphilis rates never decreased; instead, the basic civil rights and human dignity of a group of women were sacrificed under the auspices of protecting the public at large. Concurrently, many of the jurisdictions that had quietly tolerated prostitution in their red light districts shut them down. As syphilis rates continued to increase, one state after another passed legislation outlawing prostitution. Many states used feminists' concerns about a **white slavery** trade of white women (which few historians seem to think ever existed) to justify criminalization. Others suggested that shutting the **brothels** had more to do with military concerns about mobilizing men to fight than with a feminist agenda.

Contemporary Panics

As the prostitute quarantines during World War I clearly demonstrated, treating prostitutes as the source of infection for **sexually transmitted infections** is rarely an effective tool of public health. Yet, as the AIDS epidemic spread in the 1980s, prostitution was once again defined as a social problem of "disease" and "disorder." During the AIDS panic, prostitutes were thought to be responsible for spreading the disease. In 1988, California passed a law mandating HIV tests for prostitutes. The results of the tests would be permanently placed on their record. In addition to the violation of basic rights to privacy and confidentiality, criminal charges for prostitution in relation to AIDS shifted from the usual misdemeanor charge to that of a felony offense, once again with mandatory jail time. The result was a radical escalation in the punitive treatment of prostitutes. However, the Centers for Disease Control has never demonstrated that prostitutes are more likely to have HIV/AIDS than the general public. To the contrary, studies suggest that prostitutes use condoms at higher rates than the general population does. Panics influence the way prostitution has been understood, defined and enforced as a social problem. Here, accusations of prostitutes and their patrons as "disease carriers" are closely linked with the redefinition of prostitution as a criminal offense in relation to transmission of HIV.

Narratives that defined prostitutes as carriers of disease fit within a plotline that has a powerful cultural resonance. These "carrier narratives" build on the suspicion that certain groups function as pathogens. These cultural tales function much like epidemiological detective novels, recounting how professionals track the spread of a disease to its culprit and source. Those who promote these narratives are generally professionals, such as judges, juries, doctors, psychiatrists, and other representatives of law enforcement, who label prostitutes as "disease carriers" or "threats to moral order." They make use of the narrative to make visible the dangerous carriers in an effort to justify their containment and control. Central to the "carrier narrative" is a contagious disease—such as syphilis or AIDS—that presents a threat to the population and social order at large. To propel the stories, their narrators use different types of scientific research—such as the study of bacteria—to invent social theories; all the while, scientific terminology transforms social biases against outsiders into social truths. The results are often the "get tough" policies that turn prostitutes into social scapegoats.

Others describe these stories as panic scripts. "During a sex panic, a wide array of free-floating cultural fears are mapped onto specific populations who are then ostracized, victimized, and punished," notes Eric Rofes (1998). Historian Allan Bérubé defines a sex panic as "a moral crusade that leads to crackdowns on sexual outsiders" such as those who engage in sex for money transactions (Wockner 1997). Those entrusted with protecting the public good, who may not be able to control larger social forces, have often resorted to using the panic script to target and label prostitutes as threats to the public good. The Fritz Lang silent film *M* presented an instructive example of the treatment of the prostitute as emblem of social decay.

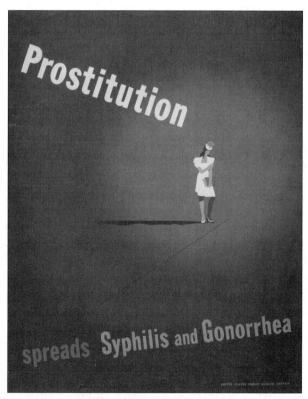

Prostitution spreads syphilis and gonorrhea/Karsakov. Courtesy of the Library of Congress.

By the 1990s in **New York City**, prostitution was defined as a "quality of life crime" dangerous to public health and morality. The subtext of this part panic, part social **purity campaign**, part real estate land grab was to clean up the city so that it would be more attractive for business and investment. Getting prostitutes and other displays of public sexual culture off the streets was a core factor in the Disney Company's agreement to move to Times Square. So Mayor Rudolph Giuliani and his pro-growth governing coalition generated a social purity campaign against prostitutes. To a great degree, the process worked. In the weeks after September 11, 2001, many New Yorkers started getting nervous. Although the overall **crime** in New York City declined by 7 percent during the first four months of 2002, compared with a year earlier, sustaining a long-term trend, residents remained anxious, particularly as the news reported that budget cuts were reducing the number of police on the street. And statistics showed that overall crime in the Sixth Precinct, covering Greenwich Village where prostitutes generally worked, was down nearly 10 percent compared with the same months of the previous year. Nonetheless, fears of a return to the rotten-apple days of the mid 1970s through the early 1990s persisted. Early in March 2002 an engineer was murdered in a way that harked back to that earlier era. As a sign of negative turn, residents noted an increased presence of prostitutes in the streets. In response to such concerns, a small group of village residents, calling themselves Residents in Distress (RID), began organizing against the presence of prostitutes and youth of color in their neighborhoods. As a goal, RID organized to get more police to target the runaways and prostitutes whom they argued had taken over their neighborhood. Opponents suggested that inequalities in class, race, and gender determined who was attacked and who was left alone. Deviance among the poor is generally harder to disguise without the privacy provided by middle-class homes. Low-income, gender-deviant, poorer prostitutes in the streets faced inordinate attention and harassment as the New York Police Department followed RID's lead. Prostitutes who catered to more affluent clientele with ads in expensive papers and who charged higher fees fared better. Even the *New York Times* suggested the New York Police Department "may also be inadvertently feeding the syndrome with high-profile measures, like the recent sweep for prostitutes in Times Square" (Murphy 2002). Prostitutes become easy targets in periods of social anxiety.

Moral Panic as the Study of Deviance

Many of the first attacks on prostitutes in the United States occurred during the Temperance Movement, which led to Prohibition. . Thirty years later, Joseph Gusfield (1963) described the period as a symbolic or moral crusade, and in the 1970s, sociologist Stanley Cohen borrowed from this idea to frame his theory of moral panic, another useful framework for considering the scapegoating of prostitutes. For Cohen, the process begins when cultural institutions draw parameters around deviance. As the process escalates, "groups of persons emerge to become defined as a threat to societal values and interests; its nature is presented as a threat to societal values and interests; its nature presented in a stylized and stereotypical fashion" (1972, 9). The crusade is mounted with the publicity and mobilization of interest groups, resulting in a moral enterprise and creating a new moral constitution of a society. These moral constituencies are the stakeholders who tend to define prostitution as a social problem.

Moral panic can be understood as part of the school of labeling theory that first emerged in the 1950s and 1960s as a branch of research on deviance. Labeling theory views the act of labeling as deviant. Without objective criteria for what is and is not deviant, it becomes impossible to discern appropriate occasions for the arbitrary deployment of the label. Moral entrepreneurs use this void to exploit the panic script, using the media and other discourses to label one group, such as prostitutes, as a scapegoat or folk devil and threat to the public at large while framing different groups as protectors of the public at large. All too often, those entrusted with protecting the public good have used the panic script to scapegoat socially vulnerable groups, such as prostitutes, as social threats.

Theories of Moral Panic

Moral panics about prostitution generally conform to well-established patterns. Indicators of collective behavior that form moral panic generally include the following: (1) volatility—a sudden anxiety about the social threat presented by a group of cultural outsiders or moral deviants; (2) hostility—the group is faced with an angry public because the group is perceived to be a threat to social order. They are viewed as part of a stereotype of evil; (3) measurable concern—anxiety about the threat can be measured by public polls or surveys; (4) consensus—there is widespread agreement about the threat by this group; and (5) disproportionality—the perceived threat presented by the deviant group is far greater than can be verified with measurements of harm. The targeted group's numbers are often small and their threat objectively non-existent. Cultural anxieties generally propel hysteria over the social threats, and the hysteria is translated into calls for absolutist positions, moral barricades, and quick fixes. As noted with the AIDS panic regarding prostitutes, prostitutes were no more likely to carry HIV than the general population, yet prostitutes had their basic civil rights to privacy and confidentiality denied them. Inappropriate or unrealistic solutions often are put forward. Quarantines, the closings of brothels, or the incarceration of prostitutes have never solved problems in their respective eras.

Elite-Engineered Moral Panics

One of the most significant models of moral panic is that of the elite-engineered model offered by Hall et al.'s 1978 book *Policing the Crisis: Mugging, the State, and Law and Order*. Functioning as a Marxist "mass-manipulative" model, this elite-engineered theory assumes that crime stories divert attention away from the real problems of capitalist society, which, if solved, could shift power arrangements out of the favor of the elites. Thus, elites use state institutions to promote campaigns to generate and sustain public anxiety over perceived threats from specific, targeted population groups—often prostitutes, youth, people of color, and sexual minorities. The aim is to legitimate greater social control measures during crises of capitalism. Within this engineered frame, moral panics serve as ideological distortions of reality, created as political tools used to deploy ideas and control reality and, by extension, control other people including prostitutes. According to Hall, panic was used to justify forms of discreet and overt ideological oppression during the 1970s mugging panic. Law and order policies and structures were initiated, including preemptive control cultures of those who worked in public space, such as low-income prostitutes. Instead of the interest group model's gradual escalations, sequences of control radically accelerated, creating a frenzy. From **World War I** to post–September 11, 2001, the state routinely stepped in to stir such panic when things got bleak. In terms of prostitution policy, the linkage of ideologies of crime control to a theory of the state presented in *Policing the Crisis* offers a useful framework for understanding the ideology of police strategies toward the social problem of prostitution.

In the last 100 years, the definitions of prostitution have shifted, as prostitution has been defined as both a social necessity and a problem of vagrancy, later as a problem of morality, public health, inequality between the sexes, workers rights, HIV transmission, and full circle again a problem of public visibility. As suggested by the view of prostitution as a public emblem of urban decay in New York, prostitutes are still easy targets and scapegoats. The fear or concern driving panics generally has a social foundation that explains the inner workings of the culture in which it takes place. In the case of the panic regarding prostitutes as indicators of decay, the social foundation at hand is post-9/11 anxiety; in the case of AIDS panic, the social foundation is a fear of a disease; in the case of the World War I syphilis quarantine, the foundation is an anxiety about the preparedness of U.S. soldiers whose leaders thought they needed to focus on war instead of sex; and so on. Theories of deviance, moral panic, and labeling help explain the scapegoat script.

Further Reading: Bastow, Karen. "Prostitution and HIV/AIDS." *HIV/AIDS Policy & Law Newsletter* 2, no. 2 (1995), http://www.walnet.org/csis/papers/bastow-aidslaw.html; Bernstein, Elizabeth. "What's Wrong with Prostitution? What's Right with Sex Work? Comparing Markets in Female Sexual Labor." Symposium Issue: Economic Justice for Sex Workers. *Hastings Women's Law Journal* 10, no. 1 (Winter 1999); Bernstein, Elizabeth. "The Meaning of the Purchase: Desire, Demand, and the Commerce of Sex." *Ethnography* 2, no. 3 (2001); Bland, Lucy "'Purifying' the Public World: Feminist Vigilantes in Late Victorian England." *Women's History Review* 1, no. 3 (Oct 1992): 397–412; Brock, Debi. "Prostitutes Are Scapegoats in the AIDS Panic." *Resources for Feminist Research* 18, no. 2 (June 1989): 13–17; Bromberg, Sara. "Feminist Issues in Prostitution." In *Prostitution: On Whores, Hustlers, and Johns*, ed. by James Elias, Vern L. Bullough, and Veronica Elias. New York: Prometheus Books, 1999; Cohen, Stanley. *Folk Devils and Moral Panics: The Creation of the Mods and Rockers*. London: Martin Robinson, 1972; Fine, Bob. "Labelling Theory: An Investigation into the Sociological *Critique of Deviance*." *Economy and Society* 6, no. 2 (May 1977): 166–193; Gilfoyle, Timothy J. *City of Eros: New York City, Prostitution, and the Commercialization of Sex, 1790–1920*. New York: W.W. Norton, 1992; Goode, Erich, and Nachman Ben-Yehuda. *Moral Panics: The Social Construction of Deviance*. Cambridge, MA: Blackwell, 1994; Gusfield, Joseph. *Symbolic Crusade: Status Politics and the American Temperance Movement*. Champaign: University of Illinois Press, 1963; Hall, Stuart, Chas Critcher, Tony Jefferson, John Clarke, and Brian Roberts. *Policing the Crisis: Mugging, the State, and Law and Order*. New York: Holmes & Meier Publishers, 1978; Hobson, Barbara. *Uneasy Virtue: The Politics of Prostitution and the American Reform Tradition*. Chicago: University of Chicago Press, 1990; Jenness, Valerie. "From Sex as Sin to Sex as Work: Coyote and the Reorganization of Prostitution as a Social Problem." *Social Problems* 37, no. 3 (August 1990): 403–17; Lee, Danny. "Street Fight." *New York Times*, 31 March 2002, C1; Leonard, Zoe, and Polly Thistlethwaite. "Prostitutes and AIDS." In *Women, AIDS, & Activism*, ed. The ACT UP/NY Women & AIDS Book Group. Boston, MA: South End Press, 1990; Rofes, Eric. *Dry Bones Breathe: Gay Men Creating Post-AIDS Identities and Subcultures*. Birmingham, NY: Harrington Park Press, 1998; Rosen, Ruth. *The Lost Sisterhood: Prostitution in America, 1900–1918*. Baltimore, MD: Johns Hopkins Press, 1982; Rubin, Gayle. "Thinking Sex: Notes for a Radical Theory of the Politics of Sexuality." In *Social Perspectives in Lesbian and Gay Studies: A Reader*, ed. Peter M. Nardi and Beth E. Schneider. New York: Routledge, 1984; Shepard, Benjamin. "Culture Jamming a SexPanic!" In *From ACT UP to the WTO: Urban Protest and Community-Building in the Era of Globalization*, ed. Benjamin Shepard and Ron Hayduk. New York: Verso Press, 2002; Wagner, D. "The Universalization of Social Problems." *Critical Sociology* 23, no. 1 (1997): 3–23; Walkowitz, Judith. "Male Vice and Female Virtue: Feminism and the Politics of Prostitution in 19th Century Britain." In *Powers and Desire: The Politics of Sexuality*, ed. Ann Snitow, Christine Stansell, & Sharon Thompson. New York: Monthly Review Press, 1983; Ward, Prescilla. "Cultures and Carriers: 'Typhoid Mary' and the Social Science of Control." *Social Text* 52–53 (1997): 181–214; Wockner, Rex. "Sex-lib activists confront 'SexPanic!'" *Gaywave*, 2 December 1997. http://gaytoday.badpuppy.com/garchive/events/111797ev.htm/; Worth, Robert. "Tolerance in Village Wears Thin Drug Dealing and Prostitution Are Becoming a Hazard in a Normally Quiet West Village Area." *New York Times*, 19 January 2002.

Benjamin Shepard

SCARLET ALLIANCE. The Scarlet Alliance, Australian Sex Workers' Association Incorporated, is an Australian organization formed in 1989 after the AIDS Debate 88 conference in Melbourne, Victoria. At that time Queensland and Northern Territory sex workers were trying to set up their own state-based organizations, and it was decided that forming a national sex worker rights body could assist them and others around Australia to establish local sex-worker political advocacy for the purpose of sex worker rights work. The national body was formed and called Scarlet Alliance. Founding members included sex-worker activists from a variety of Australian sex worker groups: Prostitutes Association of South Australia (PASA), Prostitutes Collective of Victoria (PCV), Australian Prostitutes Collective (New South Wales), and the Self Information Education Referral Association (Western Australia). Early years of the organization saw a focus on HIV-positive sex workers, including consultation, research, rights protection, and information. Organizational support for state and territory sex-worker groups was also a priority, including training and skills recognition for **peer education** staff and sex-worker volunteers. In 1995 Scarlet Alliance participated in the International Womens' Conference in Beijing, and this saw the beginning of major international work carried out by elected Scarlet Alliance representatives. The issue of migrant sex workers and the impact of anti-**trafficking** discourses was pursued by a Human Rights Caucus at the United Nations, in which the Scarlet Alliance (though not holding official UN nongovernmental organization status) was heavily involved, working with the Network of Sex Work Projects. Successful anti-licensing campaigns in Western Australia and Tasmania marked the early years of the 21st century. Leading the campaign to defend migrant sex workers' rights in Australia and strengthening links in the Asia-Pacific Region, Scarlet Alliance is a recognized expert in Australia on the issues of migrant sex work and sex-worker peer education, and members are assisting Papua New Guinea sex workers to develop an autonomous and peer-driven response to HIV/AIDS. Scarlet Alliance holds an annual National Forum for members and sex workers, in a different Australian state or territory each year. They have an affirmative action policy that ensures that delegates and elected officers of Scarlet Alliance are sex workers. The National Forum is not open to members of the public or sex-industry operators. National objectives, policy directions, and funding priorities are determined at the sex worker–only National Forum. In 2005 Scarlet Alliance was honored with the National Australia Bank Volunteer Award.

See also Migration and Mobility; Occupational Safety and Health; Sex Worker–Only Communication Tools; Appendix document 15.

Further Reading: Banach, Linda, and Metzenrath, Sue. "Model Principles for Sex Industry Law Reform." Sydney, Australia: Scarlet Alliance/AFAO, 2000; Scarlet Alliance Web site. http://www.scarletalliance.org.au

Scarlet Alliance

SCIENCE FICTION. *See* **Fantasy and Science Fiction**.

SEAMSTRESSES. "Seamstress" was a euphemism for "prostitute" in census records and other documents of the 19th century in the United States. Historical documentation showing several "seamstresses" sharing common living quarters may generally be assumed to represent a brothel. Whether this occupation was reported by prostitutes or supplied by census enumerators and other officials remains speculative, although potential reasons for both are easily understood.

Legitimate uses of the term should not be confused with the codified use. Other historical and modern euphemisms exist, including **laundresses** and **actresses**.

Karen K. Swope

SERIAL KILLERS. Street prostitutes are often the victims of choice for predatory serial killers, who are usually white middle-aged men. Prostitutes are some of the most vulnerable victims of serial killers because of their availability, and for many serial killers, prostitutes are the representative group for their rage against women.

One of the earliest documented and most famous serial killers who targeted prostitutes was England's **Jack the Ripper**, who, beginning on August 31, 1888, with the **murder** of prostitute Polly Nichols, began a series of viciously brutal attacks on prostitutes in London's Whitechapel, a poverty-stricken neighborhood. Jack the Ripper sadistically dismembered six prostitutes between August and November 1888, a crime spree that was never solved. The Ripper murders shocked London, even though the victims were prostitutes. Though elite London society did not approve of prostitution, the general attitude toward prostitutes was less moral condemnation than age-old attitudes concerning the lower classes in general. The crimes were shocking because of their brutality against vulnerable women, who just happened to be prostitutes.

Most in American society do not view prostitutes as vulnerable women, but rather as social castoffs, women who represent moral deficiency and are therefore of less value. Many crimes against prostitutes go virtually unnoticed and are considered a natural part of harsh street life. In the case of prostitute murders, however, many times links between the murders will go unnoticed by authorities for whom prostitute murders are not surprising and sometimes even common, particularly in major metropolitan areas. Usually, links between individual murders of prostitutes are only made when a significant number of prostitutes are murdered, which then signals a possible serial killer. In 1983 in Vancouver, British Columbia, prostitutes began to vanish. The authorities did not begin searching for the missing women until 1998 and only after a written demand from an advocate group for prostitutes. Fifty-four women went missing from Vancouver's Downtown Eastside between 1983 and 2001. The case was finally solved with the arrest and later conviction of pig farmer Robert Pickton. In August 1987 a hunter in Oregon's Molalla Forest stumbled on the scattered remains of seven prostitutes. Dayton Leroy Rogers was later convicted of the 1987 murder of prostitute Jenny Smith, and in 1988 Rogers was convicted of the Molalla Forest killings. The police were unaware there had been a serial killer in their midst for years.

The most notorious and prolific serial killer in the United States is Gary Leon Ridgway, the Green River Killer in Seattle, Washington. Ridgway admitted to killing 48 women, mostly street prostitutes, many of them teenagers, between 1982 and 1984. No one knows exactly how many prostitutes Ridgway killed over the years; some estimates are in the hundreds. Ridgway was spared the death penalty by a plea agreement for life in **prison**. Ridgway stated that he chose prostitutes because he figured he could kill as many prostitutes as he wanted without getting caught. He was almost right.

See also Violence.

Further Reading: Egger, Steven A. *The Need to Kill: Inside the World of the Serial Killer*. Upper Saddle River, NJ: Prentice Hall, 2003; Leyton, Elliott. *Hunting Humans: The Rise of the Modern Multiple Murderer*. New York: Carroll & Graf, 2003; Newton, Michael. *The Encyclopedia of Serial Killers*. New York: Facts on File, 2000.

Debbie Clare Olson

SEX WORK. *Sex Work: Writings by Women in the Sex Industry* (1987), edited by Frédérique Delacoste and Priscilla Alexander, is a highly influential book that was foundational to feminist literature on the lives, choices, experiences, and activism of prostitutes. The text was one of the first to use the now widely used term "sex work," originally coined by sex worker **Carol Leigh**, aka Scarlot Harlot. *Sex Work* highlights the many facets of prostitution as fundamentally about labor. Part 1 of the book emphasizes the editors' interest in centering the voices of sex workers "in the life," providing a range of moving and personal essays, **poetry**, and interviews by street prostitutes, **call girls**, exotic dancers, and porn **actresses**. The next part turns to theoretical considerations of sex work, power, and **feminism**. Here influential essays by Priscilla Alexander, Gail Pheterson, and Joan Nestle posit sex work as a socially marginalized and misunderstood form of labor that is informed by gender, class, race, sexuality, and national differences. Part 3 situates as a central concern activism for sex workers' rights and unity among sex workers and allies internationally. Articles by the leaders of such national and international organizations as US PROStitutes Collective, **COYOTE**, The English Collective of Prostitutes, Holland's **Rode Draad**, and the International Committee for Prostitutes' Rights provide important accounts of the groups' organizational histories and perspectives on movements toward legalization and **decriminalization** of prostitution. Although the book describes a wide range of experiences and opinions about sex work, an overall belief in the agency and rights of sex workers to be protected from criminalization, abuse, and **stigma** runs through all the pieces. The second edition (1998) of *Sex Work* features an expanded bibliography and resource list that now includes Web sites and search engines for research on the subject.

Further Reading:; Delacoste, Frédérique, and Priscilla Alexander, eds. *Sex Work: Writings by Women in the Sex Industry.* San Francisco: Cleis Press, 1987; 2nd ed., 1998; Nagle, Jill, ed. *Whores and Other Feminists.* New York: Routledge, 1997; Pheterson, Gail, ed. *A Vindication of the Rights of Whores.* Seattle, WA: Seal Press, 1989.

Mireille Miller-Young

SEX WORKER–ONLY COMMUNICATION TOOLS.
Sex workers share information among themselves that is only accessible to those in the sex-work community. This insider-only communication in Australia has formalized into publications, Web sites, performance groups, and political meetings on a local and national level and has successfully impacted the life, health, and cultural expression of the Australian sex-worker community. It also forms the basis of Australian understandings and practical application of "**peer education**" in service delivery, policy development, and funding.

The importance of sex worker–only communication tools is recognized in Australia by Government Health policy and funding, articulated through the National HIV Strategies. Sex worker–only communication tools implemented through peer education are identified as vital to inform, educate, and create common knowledge and best practice within the sex industry, in a nonjudgmental environment.

In the early 1980s the success of sex-worker communication in Australia was acutely identifiable in sex workers' adoption of prophylactic technology in response to the HIV virus. By 1986 in some states and territories of Australia, sex workers reported close to 100 percent condom use for penetrative sex at work. In the early 1990s sex-worker condom use was compared with condom use among sexually active women of the same age who were not sex workers, and surprising discrepancies were found. Sixty-six percent of the sex workers interviewed used condoms

"We are living in a cultural moment in which representations of the sex trade abound. If the figure of 'the prostitute' has been so compelling in this era, it may be precisely because she (almost always, she) has stood-in for broader cultural anxieties: globalization, changes in gender roles and kin networks, the specters of social disorder and crime. The (art of sex workers) make these linkages explicit, transforming sex-workers from empty stereotypes into complex, contradictory, and historically-rooted beings."

Elizabeth Bernstein, from *Re-Presenting Sex Work, Readings in Sex Worker Sinema,* San Francisco Sex Worker Film and Video Festival, May 2001.

in their private lives; however, among sexually active women of the same age in Australia who were not sex workers, condom use was only 24 percent (Perkins 1991). Higher condom use has resulted in sex workers' having lower rates of **sexually transmitted infections** (STIs) than non–sex workers of the same demographic. Throughout the history of the HIV epidemic in Australia, there have been no documented cases of transmission through commercial sex. Sex-worker communication in Australia has prevented HIV and STIs among the sex-worker community.

Sex workers in Australia share information about **clients** who have displayed offensive behavior, from bouncing checks to committing sexual assault and **violence**. These clients are known as "ugly mugs." Sex workers have traditionally been able to report ugly mugs to sex-worker organizations who then compile a regular broadsheet and distribute it back to sex workers. The Prostitutes Collective of Victoria won the Australian National Violence Prevention Award in 1995 for their Ugly Mugs project after publishing the list for more than eight years. More recently sex workers have shared this information through sex worker–only sections of sex-industry Web sites, outside the formal structure of sex-worker organizations. Sex workers also use mobile phone text messages to communicate about ugly mugs to watch out for.

Scarlet Alliance is the Australian Sex Workers' Association, and its members are Australian sex workers. Potential members are required to demonstrate the value that is placed on communication tools for sex workers only and promotion of sex workers within the organization. Scarlet Alliance also hosts an electronic mailing list for sex workers. The annual sex-worker meeting is called the National Forum and is organized by Scarlet Alliance and funded by the Commonwealth Health Department. Members of Scarlet Alliance share written reports and the executive members are elected. Constitutional changes, policy direction, and the year's finances are approved at the National Forum. This sex worker–only political space is a vehicle of accountability and transparency among sex worker networks in Australia and is attended by 50 or more sex workers each year.

Sex worker–only publications in Australia have included *The Professional* (New South Wales, with more than 55 issues and a distribution of 3,000 per quarter), *Working for a Living* (western Australia, published for more than 10 years but currently not printed, with a distribution of 2,000 every four months), *SIN* (south Australia, with a distribution of 700, three quarterly issues), *WISENEWS* (ACT, currently not printed, with a regular distribution of 300 at time of publication), and a Northern Territory Newsletter (distribution of 150 to Darwin and remote areas, including Alice Springs). These publications are available to the industry only and as such are "unclassified." Sex workers contribute content and often will use a pseudonym or work name to protect their identity. The magazines list sex worker–friendly services, tips about work, information for new workers, questions and answers about STIs, and media clippings.

Sex-worker groups in Australia have a growing tradition of hosting their own "sex workers and friends" parties. "Hookers Night Out" in Adelaide, South Australia, celebrates International

Whores Day each year. "Red Light Disco" (formerly known as the Hookers and Strippers Ball) is the annual industry-only event in Sydney. "Whoretown" was a one-time sex worker–only event in western Australia held at the Blue Room, Northbridge, in 2002.

In Australia, as funding for community–based projects becomes deprioritized and the "pox clinic" pathologization of sex-worker health services emerges, independent sex worker–only communication tools are more important than ever. Sex worker–only performance groups such as **Debby Doesn't Do It for Free** and autonomous sex-worker organizations are taking up the mandate of sex worker–only communication and using it to strengthen peer networks. The **Internet** is also playing a large role; the Australian Babe Web site, based in Queensland, is run by sex workers and also has an active sex worker–only chat area.

Further Reading: Commonwealth Department of Health and Aging. "5th National HIV Strategy; Revitalising Australia's Response." Commonwealth of Australia, 2005; Metzenrath, Sue. "To Test or Not to Test." Website of the Scarlet Alliance. http://www.scarletalliance.org.au/library/metrenrath-testdonttest/file_view; Murray, Alison. "Pink Fits: Sex, Subcultures and Discourses in the Asia-Pacific." Melbourne, Australia: Centre of South East Asian Studies, Monash University, 2001; Perkins, Roberta. "Sexual Health and Safety among a Group of Prostitutes." *Sex Industry and Public Policy* (1991): 147–153.

Elena Jeffreys

SEXUALLY TRANSMITTED INFECTIONS. Sex workers, along with soldiers and sailors, have been on the forefront among history's participants in the acquisition and transmission of sexually transmitted infections (STIs).

STIs, which can be bacterial or virological in nature, can be present in human semen, vaginal fluid, blood, and sometimes saliva.

Although sexually transmitted disease (STD) is the most frequently used term to describe a range of clinical manifestations, STI is a more medically appropriate descriptor given that most of the ailments under the general rubric of these infections are not diseases per se. The term STI encompasses all the physical maladies that can be transmitted sexually, including infections that may not be clinically manifest.

Sexually transmitted infections also have been described as venereal diseases (VD), derived from "Venus," the name of the Goddess of Love. Whether labeled "STIs," "STDs," or "VD," these infections are and always have been acquired mainly through sexual contact. Their presence can be traced back millennia to ancient Chinese, Indian, Hebrew, Greek, and Roman writings.

Today, in **brothels** and sex **venues**, in streets and temples, and on the highways and byways all over the world, men and women and those who defy gender stereotypes engage in prostitution. They do so in a climate in which the risks associated with the 21st century's array of STIs are, though serious, not necessarily a death sentence.

The potential transmission of STIs from sex workers to their clientele or vice versa is often considered by public health officials to justify both outreach and research initiatives—many of which have been initiated largely as a result of the appearance of HIV.

In the late 1880s the germ theory, regarding the causal relationship of bacteria and viruses to disease, led to public health's moral panic in regard to sex work and STIs (that is, until the 1940s, when penicillin proved invaluable as a treatment for a host of STDs experienced by sex workers and their clients). For the global sex-work industry, as for others, it was not until the appearance of HIV and AIDS in the mid-1980s that the prevalence and incidence of STIs within sex-working populations began to be taken seriously as an international public health issue.

Regardless of laws or regulatory frameworks, STIs are usually present within the social environment in which sex workers work. Therefore, many have suggested that a measure of **occupational safety and health** should be provided. Although STIs are frequently an occupational hazard of sex work, there are highly effective mechanisms to prevent the infection and transmission of such.

Generally, both female and male sex workers and male and female clients are susceptible to STIs within the prostitution workplace, although the infections to which male and female prostitutes are susceptible may vary.

There is some understanding in the broad literature that there are fewer risks associated with the exchange of sex for money than with sex in personal relationships. However, this tends to differ between the Northern and Southern hemispheres and between developed- and developing-country contexts.

Historically, rates of STIs have varied both within and across communities and periods of time. Prevalence (cumulative infections) and incidence (new infections) can be understood in part by the availability of preventive (such as prophylactics or **condoms**) and/or curative measures, and these measures can act as barometers to help understand prevalence and incidence.

In general, when faced with the choice of treating STIs once they have appeared or preventing infections in the first place, modern public health's goal is to choose the latter option: prevention and education. Yet within the context of sex work, this does not necessarily need to signify "no glove, no love." Some countries have instigated 100 percent condom-use programs as a means to address local HIV and AIDS epidemics, but such programs are not the only—or necessarily the preferable—option, in part because they are not always pragmatic, desired, enforceable, or community-based. Other options include techniques for harm reduction that enable sex workers and their clients to negotiate safer sex within the context of individual sexual history, STI testing, sexual activity, and experience.

Current understandings of the intersection between prostitution and STIs suggest that the professionalism of sex workers and their ability to engage in and promote safer sex activities with clients and partners relies not only on the availability of tools and techniques to lower risk, but also on their ability to provide and interact within a peer-education model in which others within the industry take some responsibility for disseminating information about and teaching how to reduce risks associated with sexual activity. One example of such activities is the document *Making Sex Work Safe*, produced by the Network of Sex Work Projects (NSWP).

Yet from the 12th century (when it was illegal for brothels in Europe to employ sex workers known to be infected with STIs) until the very present, the world's peoples have managed to live side by side with these infections, largely because beyond the social construction of sex work—be it influenced by public opinion, editorial stance, or governmental policy—such sexual exchanges are biological. They are the biological acts of two or more people. Within that context, sexually transmitted infections are a normal and known correlate of intimate interaction, be it financially motivated or otherwise.

Sexually transmitted infections are a fact of nature among all sexually reproducing species, including plant and nonhuman animals species. The existence and transmission of STIs is considered by many people to be a moral issue. It is this moralist stance that has helped facilitate a powerful social **stigma** that can prevent open discussion of prostitution and its related issues.

Further Reading: Eadie, Jo, ed. *Sexuality: The Essential Glossary*. London: Hodder Arnold Publishers, 2004; Nettleton, Sarah. *The Sociology of Health and Illness*. Cambridge, England: Polity Press, 1995; Public Health Agency of Canada. *What You Need to Know About Sexually Transmitted Infections.* Minister of Public Works and Government Services, Canada, 2002. http://www.phac-aspc.gc.ca/publicat/std-mts/

Dan Allman

SHAKESPEARE, WILLIAM (1564–1616).

William Shakespeare is acclaimed as English literature's greatest dramatist. His most significant portrayal of prostitution occurs in *Measure for Measure*, in which Angelo, ruling in the Duke's absence, has begun ruthlessly enforcing laws against fornication and prostitution. **Brothels** are pulled down, including one run by the comic character Mistress Overdone and her servant Pompey, and Angelo condemns a young man, Claudio, to death for impregnating his fiancée. The play ultimately suggests that the moral assumptions behind such laws run counter to human nature. The Duke returns to a more tolerant and compassionate administration of the law, and characters like Angelo and Claudio's sister Isabella come to accept their previously repressed sexuality.

Whores or bawds appear in several other plays. In *The Comedy of Errors,* Antipholus of Ephesus dines with a **courtesan** and promises her a gold chain because he is angry with his wife. In *Timon of Athens,* Alcibiades's mistresses Phrynia and Timandra accept Timon's verbal abuse in exchange for gold. In *Henry IV,* part II, Doll Tearsheet, a prostitute, appears with Falstaff at the Boar's Head Tavern. In *Pericles,* Pander, Bawd, and Bolt purchase Mariana for their brothel, although her eloquence preserves her virginity. In *Othello,* the *dramatis personae* lists Bianca as a courtesan, and she is commonly depicted as one although this means accepting that Iago uncharacteristically speaks truthfully about her. In several other plays, women are denigrated by falsely being called whores or other insulting terms that suggest they lack sexual virtue. For example, Hamlet questions Ophelia's "honesty," Othello berates Desdemona as a whore, and Claudio in *Much Ado About Nothing* accuses Hero of unchastity.

Further Reading: Dollimore, Jonathan. "Shakespeare Understudies: The Sodomite, the Prostitute, the Transvestite and Their Critics." In *Political Shakespeare: Essays in Cultural Materialism,* 2nd ed., ed. Jonathan Dollimore and Alan Sinfield. Ithaca, NY: Cornell University Press, 1994, pp. 129–152; Pechter, Edward. "Why Should We Call Her Whore? Bianca in *Othello.*" In *Shakespeare and the Twentieth Century: The Selected Proceedings of the International Shakespeare Association World Congress, Los Angeles, 1996,* ed. Jonathan Bate, Jill L. Levenson, and Dieter Mehl. Newark: University of Delaware

Measure for Measure, Act 1 Scene 2

POMPEY. Yonder man is carried to prison.
MISTRESS OVERDONE. Well; what has he done?
POMPEY. A woman.
MISTRESS OVERDONE. But what's his offence?
POMPEY. Groping for trouts in a peculiar river.
MISTRESS OVERDONE. What, is there a maid with child by him?
POMPEY. No, but there's a woman with maid by him. You have not heard of the proclamation, have you?
MISTRESS OVERDONE. What proclamation, man?
POMPEY. All houses in the suburbs of Vienna must be plucked down.
MISTRESS OVERDONE. And what shall become of those in the city?
POMPEY. They shall stand for seed: they had gone down too, but that a wise burgher put in for them.
MISTRESS OVERDONE. But shall all our houses of resort in the suburbs be pulled down?
POMPEY. To the ground, mistress.
MISTRESS OVERDONE. Why, here's a change indeed in the commonwealth! What shall become of me?
POMPEY. Come; fear you not: good counsellors lack no clients: though you change your place, you need not change your trade; I'll be your tapster still. Courage! there will be pity taken on you: you that have worn your eyes almost out in the service, you will be considered.
MISTRESS OVERDONE. What's to do here, Thomas tapster? Let's withdraw.

Press, 1998, pp. 364–377; Stanton, Kay. "'Made to Write "Whore" Upon': Male and Female Use of the Word 'Whore' in Shakespeare's Canon." In *A Feminist Companion to Shakespeare*, ed. Dympna Callaghan. Oxford: Blackwell, 2000, pp. 80–102.

Bruce E. Brandt

SHANGHAI. Shanghai was a small town before the Western intrusion in the mid-19th century but grew to be the largest and most cosmopolitan city in China and became known, among other things, as "the brothel of the Orient." This dubious reputation was derived from the fact that prostitution in its varied forms was thriving and, at times, even omnipresent in the city in the first half of the 20th century. The number of prostitutes has been estimated at between 50,000 to 100,000 shortly before the Communist take-over in 1949 (Henriot 2001, 119).

Evolution of Prostitution in Shanghai

Prostitution in Shanghai underwent a dramatic change both in scale and in character in the past century and a half. "The world of flowers" in the late Qing dynasty (1644–1911) was dominated by a group of high-class **courtesans**, whose primary function was artistic entertainment rather than sexual service and who were patronized by members of the traditional elite of gentry, officials, and merchants. This elite-oriented system of entertainment was eroded by the rapid modernization of the city around the turn of the 20th century. By 1920s, a more commercialized and popularized sex market emerged to meet the demand of a bigger clientele from the new middle and working classes. The expansion of prostitution with its accompanying social ills aroused concerns and debate first in the Western communities and the authorities of the foreign concessions and then in the Chinese ones. The Western efforts to regulate or abolish prostitution from the late 19th century to the 1940s were not very effective, which contrasted sharply with the successful campaign by the Communist regime in the 1950s. Yet, the revival of the sex market since the 1980s after China's economic reform and opening up belied the success of the Communist government to eradicate prostitution as short-lived.

The early Qing government banned prostitution and punished scholars and officials for visiting prostitutes. As the administrative control relaxed in the last years of the Qianglong era (1736–1799), prostitution first revived in the south of the Yangtze River. In the early 19th century when Shanghai was a small town, prostitution was carried on the "the flower boats," which cruised along the merchant ships moored in the Huangpu River to solicit the merchants customers. After the 1820s, courtesan houses were set up on the bank in the walled Chinese city. The early 1860s was a turning point, as a large refugee population displaced by the Taiping upheaval poured into the city and boosted its economy, including the business in the pleasure quarters. Also at this time, many courtesan houses moved into the foreign concessions for security and business opportunities (the International Settlement was established in 1845, the French Concessions in 1849). For the next eight decades until the Communist takeover in 1949, prostitution in Shanghai saw a tenfold growth from more than 5,500 prostitutes in the 1860s to over 50,000.

The women in "the world of flowers" in the late Qing Shanghai were highly varied, from high-class courtesans to common and low-class prostitutes and streetwalkers. A hierarchy was formed among them according to such factors as artistic skills, age, beauty, and elegance. Such a hierarchy, to a considerable extent, corresponded to the social backgrounds of the women's patrons. On the top resided a group of elite courtesans known as *shuyu*, who were young and pretty, and good at singing, storytelling, and playing musical instruments. They were considered artists and professional entertainers rather than prostitutes, providing entertainment, companionship, prestige, and status. Shuyu distinguished themselves from not only common prostitutes but also courtesans of a lower rank. To obtain sex from a shuyu, a complex etiquette of courtship had to be followed and a trusting relationship established besides the monetary transactions. With no more than 400 in number by the end of the 19th century, this was a small and exclusive group, but the group's economic, social, and cultural influence was strong.

Below the shuyu was a group called *changsan*, whose artistic skills, beauty, and elegance were considered of lesser quality. Their fees were lower as well. Even though a ritual of courtship was also necessary, they were more available for sex service. Next on the hierarchy were two groups known as *ersan* and *yao er*. Yao er courtesans would entertain both regular customers and strangers as long as a set fee was paid. Below these groups of courtesans were various types of common and low-class prostitutes working in brothels or soliciting customers on the street and in public places. Along with the growth of foreign communities in the foreign concessions, there were growing numbers of foreign brothels and prostitutes including Europeans, Americans, Russians, Koreans, and Japanese. A hierarchy was also formed among them with the Euro-Americans on the top, and Russians, the most numerous and the least expensive, at the bottom. Foreign prostitutes numbered about 10,000 in the 1930s, 80 percent of whom were Russians.

By the early 20th century, industrialization, urbanization, commercialization, and migration made Shanghai into a world metropolis. A new and larger clientele from the emerging middle and working classes demanded immediate sex satisfaction for their money. By 1920s, Shanghai's prostitution scene had undergone three important changes: First was the decline of the high-class courtesans and the luxury market they used to serve. Shuyu were absorbed into changsan, who themselves underwent a downward transformation. For example in the 1940s, changsan courtesans exchanged sex for money just like common prostitutes. Second was the emergence of various new agencies and institutions of the entertainment and service industry, including dance halls, massage parlors, restaurants, tea and coffee houses, and guide agencies, whose employees worked as ancillary prostitutes, even though their official job description was different. Third was the expansion of the ranks of common and low-class prostitutes, in particular, the street-walkers known as *yeji* (pheasants). As a result, prostitution in Shanghai became more accessible, more varied, and more pervasive. A mass sex market was formed.

In the Republican era (1911–1949), most prostitutes came from the two provinces of the lower Yangtze—Jiangsu and Zhejiag. Another source was Shanghai. They were a very young group, especially the courtesans. A 1923 study showed that 90 percent of 77 courtesans were between the ages of 16 to 20. The trend afterward showed an increase in age for those in the profession. Most were poorly educated single women of the lower classes from towns and cities rather than from the countryside. In the 1940s, 86 to 90.5 percent of them were illiterate. Most prostitutes surveyed gave "poverty," whether as a typical status or caused by a sudden change of fortune, as the reason for their entry into the trade. Their life and working conditions varied. Those of the higher ranks seemed to have more control over their life and labor, and they probably enjoyed more freedom and material comfort than most working women and wives. Those working in low-class brothels had little freedom and comfort, especially those who were sold or pawned. The length of time as a prostitute varied from some months to some years. A major way of existing and reintegrating into society was marriage. About one-third became concubines and wives.

Social and Governmental Interventions

The early attempt to regulate prostitution in Shanghai can be traced to 1868, when the French ambassador in Peking wrote to the authorities in the French Concession, urging them to establish a system similar to the one in Europe to check and treat the Chinese prostitutes catering to Western customers. A lock hospital jointly financed by the authorities of the International Settlement and the French Concession was set up in 1877. But throughout the existence of the hospital until 1899, the Chinese prostitutes who registered for regular checkups were consistently fewer than half of the population working in **brothels**. The increasing visibility of prostitution caused growing concerns among the Western and the Chinese reformers for its effect on public health and social and moral order. They carried out a continuous debate as to its causes and solutions from the late 19th century onward. During **World War I**, a dozen religious associations in the International Settlement began to mobilize public opinion for abolishing prostitution. With their high moral ground, the abolitionists won the support of the ratepayers in the debate with the authorities who urged a strengthening of regulations. Prostitution was banned in 1920 in the International Settlement, and all the brothels were to be closed by annual lot-drawing in five years. The movement, however, eventually failed for at least two reasons: the government lacked the will and resources to enforce the elimination plan, and the Chinese and the French authorities did not cooperate. As a result, prostitutes either moved out to the French Concession or continued to do business underground. The re-legalization of the courtesan houses in 1924 marked the end of the **abolition** movement.

After coming to power in 1928, the Nationalist government banned prostitution in the three provinces of the lower Yangtze River effectively under its control. Yet prostitution either continued to operate illegally or moved to Shanghai, in particular, to the International Settlement. The Chinese authorities of the city requested, to no avail, that their counterparts in the foreign concessions regulate prostitution. Probably for economic reasons, the Nationalist government eventually lifted the ban on prostitution in mid-1930s, despite the protest of women's organizations. When its full authority was restored in Shanghai at the end of the World War II, the Nationalist city government began to regulate prostitution, including registration, physical examination and treatment, zoning, and crackdown on the illegal prostitution with the final aim to end prostitution. Yet, a variety of factors—including the government's lack of will and resources and poor coordination between agencies and official corruption—made the regulation effort ineffective. The downfall of the Nationalist government on the mainland after three years of civil war left the task to eliminate prostitution to the Communist regime.

The People's Republic of China under Mao Zedong, especially in its early years, proved to be an effective totalitarian revolutionary regime capable of mobilizing the masses and transforming society. Not surprisingly, its campaign to eradicate prostitution throughout China in the 1950s was a success. The revolutionary regime adopted a totalitarian approach with a uniform policy of abolition, a coordinated program of reintegration, determined enforcement, propaganda and media control, mobilization of activists, and establishment of a grassroots monitoring system. Unlike previous Western and Chinese authorities in Shanghai, the Communist government did not hesitate to close down brothels, to arrest madams, to severely punish traffickers of women, and to detain and **reform** prostitutes. A key component in the campaign was the rehabilitation program in which prostitutes were subject to medical treatment, thought reform, job training, and family reintegration. Under Mao, it seemed that prostitution had indeed been eliminated.

Since the economic reform in 1979, prostitution along with other social vices have revived in Shanghai as in other parts of China. Prostitution is still illegal, so hardly any open brothels can be seen. Yet, with the rapid growth of the entertainment and service industry, the underground sex market and ancillary prostitution in its varied forms are thriving. The large number of women in the increasing flow of **migration** from the countryside to the cities and in the growing rank of laid-off workers from state-owned enterprises has conspired with limited employment opportunities for women who lack education and skills to induce women to seek alternative opportunities in casual or full-time prostitution. Despite periodic campaigns by the government and repeated crackdowns by law enforcement officers, the rank of the prostitutes in China today is 4 million strong and growing.

Further Reading: Henriot, Christian. *Prostitution and Sexuality in Shanghai: A Social History, 1849–1949.* Cambridge, England: University of Cambridge Press, 1997; Hershatter, Gail. *Dangerous Pleasure: Prostitution and Modernity in Twentieth-Century Shanghai.* Berkeley: University of California Press, 1997.

Yusheng Yao

SHOES. Shoes have been associated with prostitutes since antiquity. Today, shoes probably account for the biggest professional expense sex workers have and are sometimes the only piece of **clothing** worn throughout the engagement.

Throughout history sumptuary laws have attempted to restrict clothing according to social status and occupation. In most societies respectable women were to dress modestly, and where prostitution was tolerated, dress codes were enforced as a **stigma**. Shoe styles often featured in sumptuary laws that regulated what prostitutes could wear.

Walking on high heels elongates the legs, causing the bosom to protrude and the buttocks to tighten. The resulting gluteal limp increases pelvic floor tone, emulates the precoital position, and appeals equally to the romantic and the predator.

In ancient Egypt, working girls' sandals left the message "follow me" in the sand. During the Middle Ages, German prostitutes were prevented by law from wearing heeled shoes. Chinese **courtesans** (and others) had their feet bound and wore lotus-shaped shoes to excite and pleasure men. By the 17th century, high platform shoes (*chopines*) had been made popular by Italian courtesans. From the French Revolution to the American Civil War, respectable women wore heelless pumps. During La Belle Époque, heeled boots were synonymous with French prostitutes. Historians believe the popularity of hookers in heels was the main reason for the introduction of the shoe-fashion industry to the United States.

In the United States, the bad-girl image included the wearing of high-heeled shoes. Hollywood used the psychosexual association with shoes as a means to portray characters. Stereotypically, screen Jezebels wore high heels.

The outrageously high platform shoe has been iconic of the prostitute since the 1970s. Shoe fetishes and the role of the shoe in **sadomasochism** also figure in prostitution.

Further Reading: Kippen, Cameron. "The History of Footwear." Web site of the Curtin University Department of Podiatry. http://podiatry.curtin.edu.au/history.html

Cameron Kippen

SHORE, JANE (c. 1450–1527). Born Elizabeth Lambert, sometime in the mid-15th century in England, Elizabeth "Jane" Shore was twice married, was the mistress of King Edward IV, and was linked to numerous other powerful men during a dangerous, troubled period of English history. Although already infamous during her lifetime, Shore's notoriety expanded after her death, when she became famed as the quintessential fallen woman. She is consistently referred to as "Jane Shore" in the many literary characterizations of her that have been produced from the 16th century onward.

In 1476, Shore successfully divorced her first husband, the London mercer William Shore, because of his impotence. Shore's affecting looks and personality attracted Edward IV, who rewarded her with much attention and gifts. A possibly contemporary portrait, traditionally thought to be a likeness of Shore, hangs at Eton College. The painting explains Shore's appeal to 15th-century statesmen: she appears bare breasted, expensively jeweled, clear skinned, and of confident disposition. Many later portraits similarity exploit and perpetuate rumors of Shore's enthusiastic sexuality.

Edward IV died in April 1483; Shore then became involved with a number of influential men, although it is difficult to separate fact from mere accusations. Shore was linked with a follower of William, Lord Hastings, a supporter of Edward IV, but it is certain that she became the mistress of Thomas Grey, Marquess of Dorset. This angered the new King, Richard III, whose coronation had been opposed by Grey. Suggestions that Shore was a go-between in elaborate plots against Richard are plausible but unproven. Shore's infamous immorality was cited by Richard's regime to smear Grey, and Shore was coerced into making a public penance. She was also imprisoned at Ludgate for her many alleged transgressions but was released to controversially marry a royal secretary, Thomas Lynom.

Settling down after the coming-to-power of the Tudors in 1485, Shore survived into obscure widowhood, finally dying in or around 1527. That decade, Thomas More, in a prose history of Richard III's reign, immortalized her as a great harlot who faced penitence with impeccable patience. Her legend flourished. Thomas Churchyard wrote a stirring monologue for Shore's ghost in the mid-16th–century poetic compendium, *A Mirror for Magistrates*. Three plays of the 1590s alone feature Shore prominently: she has a role in an anonymous drama about Richard's rise and fall; she is referred to several times in Shakespeare's *Richard III* (although Shakespeare gives her character no lines, Shore's character often enlivens filmed and staged versions of the play with colorful, silent, walk-on appearances); and Shore is a crucial character in Thomas Heywood's two-part play, *Edward IV*.

Mythologized both as a vivacious temptress and as an overpunished, sincere penitent, Shore's legend has persisted. Nicholas Rowe's *Tragedy of Jane Shore* (1714) is the most famous play to feature Shore as the actual protagonist. In the 19th and 20th centuries, Shore continued to inspire ballad singers, playwrights, poets, writers, and historians.

Further Reading: Beith-Halahmi, Esther Yael. *Angell Fayre or Strumpet Lewd: Jane Shore as an Example of Erring Beauty in Sixteenth-Century Literature*. 2 vols. Salzburg, Austria: Universität Salzburg, 1974; Horrox, Rosemary. "Elizabeth Shore." In *The Oxford Dictionary of National Biography*. Vol. 50. New York: Oxford University Press, 2004, pp. 216–17; Scott, Maria M. *Re-presenting Jane Shore: Harlot and Heroine*. Aldershot, England: Ashgate, 2005.

Kevin De Ornellas

SINS OF THE CITIES. Homosexual erotic literature was rare in Victorian England, and *Sins of the Cities*, an erotic memoir, was especially unique. Published in London in 1881 by the mysterious William Lazenby, it purported to be in great part the autobiography of Jack Saul, a male prostitute, as told to "Mr. Cambon," who narrates the story. Saul, or "Dublin Jack" as he was known, was a real character who, at the age of about 20 in 1871, was acquainted with the defendants in the celebrated Boulton and Park case involving a pair of transvestites. In 1889 he was interviewed by the police in connection with the much more serious Cleveland Street affair, which concerned a homosexual brothel with titled clientele.

There is good circumstantial evidence that Saul sold his fragmentary memoirs to Pre-Raphaelite artist Simeon Solomon, who in turn suggested to James Campbell Reddie that they edit the manuscript together and have it published. Both Solomon and Reddie were homosexual, and Solomon also moved in the same circle as those implicated in the Boulton and Park case, which suggests he knew Saul. Reddie had connections in the erotica publishing business and could have arranged the printing; he was himself the author and translator of many erotic texts and was an intimate friend of Henry Spencer Ashbee, who was the possible author of *My Secret Life.*

Further Reading: Hyde, H. Montgomery. *The Cleveland Street Scandal.* New York: Coward, McCann and Geoghegan, 1976; Mendes, Peter. *Clandestine Erotic Fiction in English 1800–1930: A Bibliographical Study.* Aldershot, England: Scolar Press, 1993; Simpson, Colin, Lewis Chester, and David Leitch. *The Cleveland Street Affair.* Boston: Little, Brown, 1976.

Patrick J. Kearney

SISTERS OF THE GOOD SHEPHERD.

"Sisters of the Good Shepherd" is the popular name for the Roman Catholic order of the Congregation of the Sisters of Our Lady of Charity of the Good Shepherd, founded in 1641 in France and still existing today. In addition to the common vows of poverty, chastity, and obedience, the Sisters in this order take a fourth vow of charity, dedicating their lives to saving delinquent girls and prostitutes. To this end, the Sisters established houses of refuge, known as Good Shepherd Homes, in many countries, mostly in Europe in the 19th century. The Sisters continue to work to reform prostitutes and keep wayward girls from further acts of criminality through a program of religious instruction and training for domestic service. Some prostitutes voluntarily sought out the homes, whereas other young women are committed by their families. From the 1850s to the 1920s in the United States, many prostitutes were sent to the Good Shepherd Homes by court order because communities lacked other facilities for incarcerating women or reforming juveniles. During this period, the Sisters' method of isolating their charges was a qualified success; although some prostitutes rejected **religion** and the strict regimen of the homes and returned to the streets, others converted and either married or found respectable employment when they left. A few chose to remain with the Sisters and join their order. In the United States, the Sisters established the first Home of the Good Shepherd in 1855 in Buffalo, New York; homes in St. Paul, Denver, and other large cities followed. Today the Sisters number fewer than 200 in North America.

See also Magdalen Homes.

Further Reading: Butler, Anne M. *Daughters of Joy, Sisters of Mercy: Prostitutes in the American West 1865–90.* Urbana: University of Illinois Press, 1985; Lebrun, Charles. "Our Lady of Charity of the Good Shepherd." The Catholic Encyclopedia Web site. http://www.newadvent.org/cathen

Rachel Hays Williams

SLANG. If it is true that prostitution is the world's oldest profession, then it only stands to reason that brothels are the oldest stores, madams and pimps are the oldest managers, and johns are the oldest customers. And given this, it further stands to reason that the slang of whoredom is also the world's oldest "professional" discourse. It can be assumed that there were words to describe the sex profession long before there were literate societies. The basic words of the trade are hundreds, if not thousands, of years old. "Whore" and "meretrix" came into the lexicon in the 12th century, whereas harlot, first meaning a "low, common person," only appears to have begun defining a "whore" in 1432. The more professional-sounding "prostitute" didn't appear until the early 1600s, even though "working girl" had been known to refer to a "slut" since 1450. A "brothel" first meant a "whore" in 1493 but 100 years later became the common term for the house in which whores plied their trade.

In more modern times, a woman may be considered a borderline whore if she is known as a beddy, bimbette, bimbo, biscuit, hank, hoser, jump, party girl, slag, skag, skanky box, skeezer, slut, strawberry, swinger, tart, tramp, trollop, or whoopee mama.

Prostitution slang reflects a certain caste within its ranks. A young and fresh whore can be called green goods, kid leather, "something," fresh meat, or young stuff. Slang treats the opposite end of the age spectrum more brutally with words such as harridan, nag, cow, artichoke, blowser, tank, garbage can, Tom, zook, zucke, and the generic "old timer."

If a whore is considered of a higher class, she might be called a miss, prima donna, courtesan, flash dona, incognita, purest pure, Kate, pro, boulevard woman, or the more elegant "thoroughbred."

Language does not, generally, treat the lowest of whores very kindly. This lower class of whore has been called a dress lodger (so-called because she does not even own her own clothes), flag-about, jack, mawk, screw, quiff, burlap sister (with a reference to a "bag"), mud-kicker, two-bit hustler, Hershey Bar (indicating she would turn a trick for a 5 cent candy bar), skank, slouch, and, some of the worst names, blisterine (a cross between a blister and Listerine, which means the woman is uncouthly unclean), glue neck, and carrion.

On the other hand, there are kinder, gentler words from different cultures and eras to describe a prostitute, some seeming almost benign. No doubt proper folks could not issue the word "whore," so along came clever synonyms such as bona roba, Cyprian, woman about town, fille de joie, puta, unfortunate woman, camp follower, scarlet woman, cousin Betty, fancy woman, dollymop, nymph du prairie, nymph of darkness, warm 'un, warm member, fallen woman, working girl, calico queen, sporting lady, lady of infinite leisure, pavement nymph, perfect lady, lorette, chippie, saleslady, scarlet sister, call girl, hostess, behavior problem, clever girl, heart hostess, pro skirt, pavement princess, model, bar girl, inmate of ill-fame, chere amie, demirep, tommy, sex worker, prosty, molly, actress, or any number of sisters, such as frail, erring, red, scarlet, street, or sister-in-law.

Then there are the animal references; allusions to cats, birds, and fish are the most prominent. A whore therefore can be one of the following creatures: mutton, hobbyhorse, minx, shrimp, cat, cattle, laced mutton, quail, game, mackerel, squirrel, wag tail, hen, flashtail, tail, goat-milker, nightingale, owl, cow, painted cat, soiled dove, guinea hen, roach, sardine, pig, bat, moose, alley cat, and nag.

As with all slang, humor and irony have a place. These terms might have brought a bit of a knowing smile to the face: natural, occupant, spinster (female prisoners were required to spin wool while in prison), convenient, Dutch widow, Madam Van Harlot, nanny, abbess, dasher, public ledger, receiver general, cooler, disorderly, early door, ceiling expert, twofer, trading girl, hotsy, painted lady, cocktail, two-by-four or forty-four (rhymes with "whore"), sailor's bait, cat house cutie, tail-peddler, soldier moll, split mechanic, star-gazer, trickster, tricking broad, roundheel (her heels are round because she falls backward so frequently), kite, trick babe, curfloozie, virtue after ("sin first, virtue after"), field worker, lobby lizzie, pure, Q.T. cutie (Q.T. meaning "on the quiet"), and saleslady. The English have such slang as Picadilly commando and Thatcher girl, so-named because of the economic woes forcing British women into prostitution during the Margaret Thatcher administration.

A whore has also been called a treadle, trug, wapping dell, white meat, tackle, wanton, baggage, piece of trade, scab, market-dame, blow, blower, frow, bitch, bangster, gook, nockstress, bag, flesh-peddler, stew bum, hip peddler, hay bag, hat rack, whisker, notch moll, whore bitch, blimp, leg worker, sex-job, ass peddler, butt peddler, mat, piece of goods, middle-britch worker (stealing while applying one's trade), dead meat, blister, flat tire, town bike, punchboard, and town pump.

The more generic, yet descriptive, British terms include hackney, puttock, tweak, fen, belter, Judy, fly-by-night, **Jane Shore**, shake, pinch-prick, hay-tit, mollisher, and scupper. Universally, a whore is also a strumpet, cyprian, doxy, tib, streetwalker, punk, moll, brim, white slave, hooker, trip, jilt, cross girl, cocotte, flash moll, hop picker, jintoe, tart, beat moll, cruiser, bimmy, walker, red-lighter, rip, or roller. "Ladies of the evening" are also night poachers, night shades, night traders, and night pieces.

Equally interesting are the words describing a prostitute's workplace. In addition to "whorehouse," "bordel," and "brothel," other names were seemingly coined to introduce elements of sin, humor, or secrecy. Some, simply and brutally, tell it like it is and most were likely coined by the working women themselves. Humorous terms include academy, ladies' college, girlery, window-tappery, finishing academy, hotel-de-loose, hot pillow shop, resort, heifer den, man trap, service station, school of Venus, old ladies' home, vaulting school (where a gentleman might spend time "improving" himself), and steer joint (as in "one is steered in").

Other words that when preceding the word "house" denote a whorehouse include occupying, bawdy, accommodation, nanny, coupling, disorderly, fancy, fofaraw, flop, panel, dress, goat, grinding, assignation, sporting, parlor, dipping, hot, fast, bilking, call, notch, joy, cat, can, nugging, slaughter, and trugging.

Other places where prostitution is practiced are quaintly noted: flesh factory or market; gooseberry, goosing, hog, or chicken ranch; hook, cat, whore, girl, or warm shop; house of ill repute or ill fag; ice-palace; sporting place or stable; or the more genteel massage or beauty parlor.

On the sleazier side, the brothel might be called stew, lift-skirts, goosing slum, snoozing ken, panel crib, catwagon, drum, nautch joint, dead fall, cab joint, creep joint, lay joint, dirty spot, cap, cat's nest, hot hole, zoo, cowbay, shake joint, rib joint, lupanar, hooch, melina, vrow case, kip, cab, bagnio, or smugging ken.

Randall Platt

SLAVERY. *See* **Forced Prostitution; Trafficking; White Slavery.**

SOCIETIES FOR THE REFORMATION OF MANNERS.
Reacting to the dissipation and immorality introduced in the reign of King Charles II of England (1660–1685) and not trusting the Church of England to deal effectively with the nation's sinners, groups of lay persons formed societies dedicated to enforcing a stricter, more puritanical code of conduct. The nation's criminal justice system dealt with such common **crimes** as theft, fraud, coining, **rape**, and **murder**, but many sins or vices including drunkenness, gambling, swearing, blasphemy,

lewdness, profaning the Lord's day, and whoring were left to the ecclesiastical courts. These new societies, dedicated to stamping out vice or sinful conduct primarily among the common folk, first appeared in the London area in the1690s and spread to other cities in England. The societies reached their peak of power and influence in the mid-1720s and operated until about 1740, by which time the public had lost confidence in their methods and in their claims to have reformed the vicious. The members of these voluntary associations were not officially appointed or elected and they did not wear uniforms. Their primary activity was to report any sinful behavior to constables so as to initiate the process of apprehending, charging, and sentencing those whom they named. They initiated this process by acting as informers. Although they were motivated by religious values, they ignored the ecclesiastical courts that had existed for centuries and turned instead to the nation's secular courts of law to secure swifter prosecutions of those charged. Women arrested for prostitution might have come off with a fine, but sometimes the punishments were whipping and carting or incarceration for a limited period in Bridewell. Generally these women belonged to the lowest levels of society, but a number of the middle-class males who patronized them were also arrested and charged—a sign, perhaps, that these societies were also targeting male customers to reform them as well. By the middle of the 18th century, attitudes toward the culpability of prostitutes were changing, and new groups supported the **Magdalen Homes** that were being erected to house and support former prostitutes.

See also Mandeville, Bernard; Medieval Prostitution; Syphilis.

Further Reading: Burtt, Shelley. "The Societies for the Reformation of Manners: Between John Locke and the Devil in Augustan England." In *The Margins of Orthodoxy: Heterodox Writing and Cultural Response, 1660–1750*, ed. Roger D. Lund. Cambridge, England: Cambridge University Press, 1995, pp. 149–69; Curtis, T. C., & W. A. Speck. "The Societies for the Reformation of Manners: A Case Study of the Theory and Practice of Moral Reform." *Literature and History* 3 (1976): 45–64; Isaacs, Tina. "The Anglican Hierarchy and the Reformation of Manners, 1688–1738." *Journal of Ecclesiastical History* 33, no. 3 (1982): 391–411; Shoemaker, Robert B. "Reforming the City: The Reformation of Manners Campaign in London, 1690–1738." In *Stilling the Grumbling Hive*, ed. Lee Davison. New York: St. Martin's Press, 1992, pp. 99–120.

Irwin Primer

SOILED DOVES. Soiled doves were prostitutes of the **American West** working in bordellos, tents, houses, cribs, and hog ranches in the red light districts. In the 1800s, there were approximately two women for every 100 men, and thus the services of painted ladies were in high demand and paid better wages than domestic work, and the job was thrilling. In the old West, becoming a prostitute was a logical solution for a woman to make money if she was not married, and soiled doves were good for the economy and community. These ladies of easy virtue wore elaborate gowns, black silk stockings, or scanty costumes while entertained in their houses by a professor playing the piano. Most prostitutes were of the ages 16 to 35. Once a prostitute lost her looks, she could find work in cheaper houses, or she could become a madam. Some famous **madams** of the time were Mattie Silks in Illinois, Lil Lovell in Colorado, Rowdy Kate and Big Nose Kate in Arizona, **Chicago** Joe in Montana, and Pearl Starr in Arkansas. Well-known prostitutes were **Ah Toy** in San Francisco, Julia Bullette in Nevada, Lottie Johl in California, and Molly b' Dam in Idaho. Some soiled doves worked in hurdy-gurdies (*dance halls*) where they

Two Mexican prostitutes, referred to as soiled doves, entertain clients in front of a saloon. New Mexico, c. 1880–95. The Art Archive / Bill Manns.

danced, served drinks, and often provided sexual favors for a price. By the mid-1850s, respectable women began to arrive in the old West and the dichotomy between good and bad women was enforced by a new morality. Though many women enjoyed being a prostitute, they often could not improve their reputation despite **marriage**, charity work, or donations to the town.

See also Clothing; Dance Hall Girls; Organized Crime.

Further Reading: Leaton, Anne. *Pearl.* New York: Alfred. A. Knopf, 1985; Seagraves, Anne. *Soiled Doves: Prostitution in the Early West.* Hayden, ID: Wesanne Publications, 1994; Traywick, Ben T. *Hell's Belles of Tombstone.* Tombstone, AZ: Red Marie's, 1993.

Laura Madeline Wiseman

SONAGACHI PROJECT. A sex workers' collective in Kolkata, India, the Durbar Mahila Samanwaya Committee (DMSC) was formed by women who were brought together by the state-sponsored STD and HIV Intervention Project (SHIP) in 1992. This project, tremendously influential and implemented by Smarajit Jana, later came to be known as the Sonagachi Sexual Health Project. A central principle of the program was to help sex workers on their own terms, without attempting rehabilitation, asserting external expectations or moral judgments, or dismissing the emotional and material complexity of the women's lives.

Early in 2004, Subrata Mukherjee, the mayor of Kolkata, offered to legalize sex work in the city if prostitutes would consent to mandatory HIV testing. The DMSC refused this offer on the grounds that only sex workers can effectively and rightfully regulate themselves. The DMSC states in its "Sex Workers' Manifesto" that it seeks **decriminalization** of sex work in India rather than legalization. Its members want for sex workers to have more influence in the administration of their industry and to face no threat of arrest for doing their work and for the local police to turn their attention from harassing prostitutes to prosecuting those who commit **crimes** against them.

The principles of the DMSC closely parallel those supporting the **harm reduction** movement begun in England in the 1980s, which seeks to make dangerous actions less damaging, given that it may not be possible or even desirable to simply eliminate such behaviors. Other dangerous circumstances in an individual's life (poverty, abuse, and so on) may pose the greater threat to her or his well-being, so sex workers need protection as professionals rather than rehabilitation. The DMSC members have used these ideas to successfully lobby for their increased legitimization as workers, citizens, and mothers with civil rights and human needs.

Sex-worker organizing in Kolkata and Dhaka overlaps with other social welfare movements in the cities. The DMSC structured itself as a labor union and, within a few years of its formation, began including male and **transgender sex workers**, incorporating a response to homophobia and transgenderphobia into its feminist analysis.

In addition to conducting HIV/STD-prevention work and lobbying for civil rights as laborers, the DMSC has set up sexual health clinics throughout the state for testing and care, more than 30 literacy and legal literacy centers throughout the red light districts of Kolkata for themselves and their children, and a microcredit cooperative (the Usha Multipurpose Cooperative Society) to foster economic security. The organization also has a cultural wing called Komal Gandhar in which workers and their children perform dances, plays, and music to educate others about their work.

The DMSC has hosted a series of *melas*, festivals-cum-conventions, for sex workers from throughout India and from other countries, with the first of these held in Kolkata in March 1998. The conferences have been organized annually since then and have taken place in other cities as well. The Millennium Milan Mela, held in March 2001, was particularly large, with thousands of attendees from several different countries and a broad agenda, including the declaration of March 3 as "International Day for Sex Workers' Rights." However, the conference was threatened by a coalition of Indian women's groups that influenced the local government to ban the conference just days before it was planned to begin. This coalition argued that the meeting would promote the use of the city for sex **tourism** and sex **trafficking** and that the legalization of prostitution would exacerbate the abuses ongoing within the trade. DMSC members countered that they sought decriminalization rather than legalization, which would allow for better prosecution of crimes of force and **violence**, and that the meeting was meant to further legitimize sex workers as laborers and citizens rather than to contribute to their exploitation. In the end, the DMSC won back their permit to hold the conference, which was very successful and a key event in putting the organization's struggles into the mainstream of West Bengali and Indian media and political conversations.

Organizing work in Kolkata has received a great deal of international attention. The World Bank/UNAIDS program recognizes the Sonagachi Sexual Health Project and the DMSC as providing models for effective community-based prevention work, and the Bill and Melinda Gates Foundation has also supported their efforts, offering publicity and partial funding. Perhaps most important, the sex workers in Kolkata have formed close and productive international alliances with the Network of Sex Work Projects and other sex workers' groups and with prominent women's rights groups in other countries, hosting many of them at a variety of conferences. They have achieved impressive gains toward improving their own working and living conditions and determining their own choices and have done so in a poor city in politically conservative times.

See also Feminism; South Asia; Unions.

Further Reading: DMSC. "Manifesto for Sex Workers' Rights." 1997 BAYSWAN Web site. http://www.bayswan.org/manifest.html; "The Sonagachi Project: A Global Model for Community Development." *Horizons Report* (May 2002), http://www.comminit.com

Ananya Mukherjea

SOUTH ASIA. Sex work has had a long and visible place in the history of South Asia, with red light districts established in certain Indian, Bangladeshi, and Pakistani cities centuries ago during the Raj, meant to be mainly patronized by British officers and Indian administrators. In the form of services ritually performed by temple dancers, young male craftsman apprentices, and *hijras* (a highly defined transgender community), sex work has been integrated into South Asian culture for even longer. Since the early 1990s, however, ongoing conversations about prostitution in the region have shifted to focus on the matters of sex-worker mobilizing, HIV prevention, and the **trafficking** of women and children. The bulk of public, international discussion regarding prostitution and Nepal focuses on increasing concerns that Nepali girls are being coerced by economic and political circumstances or by physical force into migrating to India and Pakistan to work as prostitutes. Other South Asian countries, however, present more transparent and complex scenarios with respect to sex work.

India

Sex work in India has changed and has gained an international focus through the highly effective organizing work done by prostitutes in Kolkata, Chennai, in Falkland Road in Bombay, and elsewhere in the country. Kolkata sex workers have been cooperatively organizing themselves since 1992, growing out of the state-sponsored STD and HIV Intervention Program (SHIP) known as the **Sonagachi Project** that placed sex workers and their self-determined needs at the center of their planning and implementation. These women and men have gone from doing safer-sex peer education to organizing for better fees, developing literacy and legal advocacy centers for themselves, establishing a microcredit organization for their own use, producing a cultural wing that puts on educational plays and performances, and hosting conferences for sex workers from all over India and other countries. They have been tremendously effective at increasing their visibility and agency, thereby improving the overall wellness of their constituency. Other sex workers' groups in India have followed similar courses, also hosting conferences and mobilizing for better healthcare, prevention of **sexually transmitted infections** (STIs) and HIV, and greater economic security. In Bombay, for example, the Saheli Project in Falkland Road works with principles and goals similar to those of the Kolkata SHIP.

In August 2000, however, the national government sought to tighten antiprostitution laws, focusing on **brothel** owners and **pimps**. Sumitra Mahajan, the junior human resources minister, intended to give more force to the existing 1956 Immoral Traffic Prevention Act in the interest of rescuing and rehabilitating women being exploited by brothel owners. Although illegal, sex work in India is often overlooked by authorities who recognize its place in the economies of Indian cities. Raids and arrests are generally motivated by current morality campaigns or by police seeking to be paid bribes by prostitutes who want to avoid jail time. In 2004, the mayor of Kolkata, Subrata Mukherjee, offered to make sex work in the city legal if local prostitutes would submit to mandatory HIV tests. The Kolkata sex workers' union (the DMSC) refused, however, on the grounds that only the sex workers could rightfully and properly regulate themselves. Although concerns about the national AIDS epidemic and growing concerns about trafficking prompt much of the legal attention given to prostitution, the social gains and increased visibility achieved by organized sex workers in the country have promoted tolerance and leniency in the legal treatment of sex workers themselves. These organizations have also made slow but certain gains in terms of improved health care and housing options and, more generally, gains toward ensuring that prostitutes are treated as citizens, with protected civil rights.

Bangladesh

In October of 1996, the independent nonprofit group UBINIG (a Bengali acronym that stands for Policy Research for Development Alternatives) held the "South Asian Workshop on Trafficking in Women and Children" in Bangladesh. As the group describes the problem of trafficking, five of the seven South Asian countries have a close relationship with respect to trafficking in the region. Bangladesh, Sri Lanka, and Nepal are often the countries from which women and children are trafficked, and India and Pakistan are the countries that receive these people or act as transit centers that ship trafficked persons to the Middle East, Europe, and North America. UBINIG estimates that 4,000 to 5,000 women and children are trafficked to Pakistan each year, most of these from Bangladesh or Nepal, to work there as prostitutes or to be shipped to the Middle East. This is one major aspect of policy discussion and organizing work regarding sex work in Bangladesh.

The other is the sort of work done by brothel-based prostitutes at **Tan Bazar** and elsewhere in the country. Prostitution is legal in Bangladesh, but legal conflicts arise with respect to the morality of sex work and its influence on local communities and with regard to trafficking, particularly of children. The largest of such conflicts in recent years occurred when police began monitoring and harassing women working at Tan Bazar, the oldest and largest brothel in Bangladesh, following the **murder** there of a prostitute named Jesmin in 1994. In 1999, police raided and closed the brothel on grounds of immorality, forcing its workers into ill-paid "rehabilitative" programs, unemployment, or unprotected sex work. Some Tan Bazar workers created the collective organization Shonghoti, which fought a legal case for the reopening of their brothel. Although they won the case in the courts, Tan Bazar has never been reopened.

Pakistan

There is relatively little information available outside the country about the state of sex work and sex workers' organizing in Pakistan. A significant proportion of women prostitutes in Pakistan are Bangladeshi, and although some section of this population may well have been trafficked over the border, others seem to come of their own volition to work in Pakistani brothels or to provide services to businessmen and travelers to Karachi, Lahore, and other larger cities. There are also many women from Nepal and Burma, and several organizations such as the Bangladeshi, UBINIG, and the International Human Rights Monitoring Group claim that most of these women are kidnapped and trafficked. Much of the sex work in Pakistan, though, is done by Pakistani women and men who work more informally, as street prostitutes sometimes or in exchange for goods and services from employers or landlords. Erratically applied but severe legal and social strictures against homosexuality, promiscuity, adultery, and prostitution make it all the more important to maintain discretion in sex work and for individuals not to identify themselves too strongly as prostitutes. Those who are arrested are most often convicted of crimes against the state and can serve long sentences in **prison**. A prostitute who is also an illegal immigrant, whether that immigration was forced or not, has four years automatically added to her or his sentence. Nevertheless, red light districts flourish in every city, including the historically famous Heera Mandi in Lahore. In 2003, the International Human Rights Monitoring Group estimated that there are almost 800,000 prostitutes working in Pakistan. The National AIDS Control Organisation sometimes attempts rehabilitation programs in these districts, although they show low levels of efficacy. Local women's groups seem more effective in helping prostitutes gain access to health care, housing, and other basic resources.

A Pakistani woman, who runs a prostitution service and did not want to be identified, looks out from home in Quetta, Pakistan, 2001. Courtesy of AP / Wide World Photos.

Sri Lanka

As in India, the organizing of sex workers in Sri Lanka has been closely interlinked with HIV-prevention efforts. As with the Kolkata SHIP, the objective of a program advanced by the Community Front for the Prevention of AIDS (CFPA) focuses on helping sex workers to do their current job more safely, securely, and lucratively rather than on persuading them to give up prostitution in favor of work that requires different types of physical exertion and does not pay nearly as well. This program adopted a social–psychological approach, focused on improving self-esteem and self-image. With partial funding from the World Health Organization, the CFPA launched a number of initiatives aimed at facilitating safer sex, better financial management, and increased access to medical and legal services for sex workers in Sri Lanka. They organized workshops on antihomophobia training, cooperative banking, and how best to negotiate for higher fees and invest one's income. They also hired and trained sex workers as peer educators to counsel each other about condom usage and self-defense. The CFPA backs the sex workers in their bids against mandatory testing for drug use and STIs and for full-scale legalization of the adult sex trade in the country.

The type of Sri Lankan sex work that receives international media coverage is prostitution that caters exclusively to tourists. Sri Lanka gained a reputation, through the 1990s, as an appealing Asian **sex tourism** destination, although this reputation has been compromised at times by escalations in conflict and terrorism in the country. The "beach boys" who frequent the shore resorts have received a great deal of international attention because many of these workers are children—boys in their late preteen or early teen years. Young women work these resorts as well, but they are usually at least into their teen years. Local police report a increase since 2000 in the number of Sri Lankan women working as high-end "**call girls**" for the new influx of businessmen with ready cash. Women sex workers from other parts of Asia and from Eastern Europe also travel to work in Sri Lanka, although they tend to work in the major cities, away from the coastline. There seem, however, to be fewer reports of forced trafficking to and from Sri Lanka for the purposes of prostitution. Some women sex workers from the country have attended the *melas* in India as well as the International AIDS Conferences, but it is difficult for these "beach boys" to formally organize themselves because they are so young, they see their participation in the sex trade as transient, and their groupings are strongly governed by the informal organization of their social relationships and attachments with each other. These young male prostitutes also struggle with homophobia in their communities and with the conflicts of social identity they themselves face because many do not identify as homosexual except in their work behavior. Sex work in the country has been receiving more international attention over the past few years because the rate of HIV infection in Sri Lanka is still very low and because prostitutes working with tourists present some of the highest concentrations of HIV infection in the country. Therefore, the work of the CFPA has been particularly significant.

See also Child Prostitution; Forced Prostitution; HIV Interventions in India; Southeast Asia.

Further Reading: Bay Area Sex Worker Advocacy Network. Prostitute Rights Demonstration in South Asia. http://www.bayswan.org/seasian.html; Gansinghe, Mallika. "No Stray Dogs: Sex Worker Empowerment in Sri Lanka." *Research for Sex Work* 3 (2000): 21–22. http://www.nswp. org/r4sw; Russell, Sabin. "The Role of Prostitution in South Asia's Epidemic: Push for Safe Sex in Red-light Districts." *San Francisco Chronicle*, 5 July 2004.

Ananya Mukherjea

SOUTHEAST ASIA. Sex work in Southeast Asia has varied with economic conditions throughout history. References to upper-class sex workers in Thailand date from at least the 13th century. The King of Vajjshe created the class of *sopaynee*, in which a small number of high-class women were available at an extremely high price to nobles and to men of considerable wealth passing through the village. Traditions existed among the foreign merchant class of an unregistered **temporary marriage** with a local woman. The lack of population concentrations and of disposable income among the poor during these times likely limited the ability of most women to seek payment for sexual services, though gifts, as in dating, were likely common. The middle class was limited in size. Royals and other men of wealth had slaves and multiple wives and thus no need for paid sex workers. References exist to Thai nobles threatening disobedient daughters with banishment to a brothel, but the nature, prices, and clientele of such places are unknown. Some Thai kings had many hundreds of wives, a practice that began to decline with Rama IV and Rama V in the later 19th century. A King's new wife might visit him only once, but she was forever his wife from that point and thus unavailable to other men.

In the early 1800s, green lanterns were suggested as the color to be hung in the doorway of **Bangkok brothels** to keep away those not wishing to encounter such a business, creating green-light districts. By the mid-1800s, the canals in Bangkok were insufficient to carry commercial traffic and new roads were needed. Although various taxes on opium were sufficient for upkeep of the canals, a tax on brothels was instituted to pay for the new and expanded roads and their upkeep, and the brothel tax was sufficient to do so. Thus, brothels were a profitable operation in Bangkok by the mid-19th century.

The 20th Century

During the 20th century, sex work expanded with the economy and population, with the increase of disposable income among the middle and lower classes, and with concentrations of males. With the **abolition** of most acknowledged slavery in Thailand by the early 20th century, large numbers of freed slave women no longer had support or domicile, and the existing brothels were flooded with new workers. The form taken by sex work varied according to cultures, economies, and cultural expectations. An increase in the Thai rice trade with China may have accounted for some increase in customers, but Chinese merchants preferred Chinese-style brothels with Chinese workers, not Southeast Asian women. Relationships with freed slaves began to replace temporary marriage among Western foreigners. Higher-priced services were available in more expensive hotels, restaurants, and bars. Lower-priced services were often delivered from the cover of a part-time job, such as selling vegetables or merchandise on the street, or from a brothel. Streetwalking has always been discouraged throughout Southeast Asia because of a desire to keep what is improper out of sight. It exists nonetheless.

Although the Napoleonic Code outlawed prostitution in the early 19th century, the French were never enthusiastic about enforcing this provision, and certainly not within their colonies. French women often found better prices and working conditions as sex workers in Saigon than in Paris. The protection of French law was extended to French women in the colonies but not to native women engaged in sex work, making such work more dangerous and much more low-paying for local women.

Late in the 19th century, the Dutch Colonial Administration in the East Indies introduced female laborers to work in the fields alongside men, to entice male workers to labor for less pay. The British in India had done the same. The women were paid even less than the men, ensuring that male wages would be spent in part on making up this differential, forcing women to engage in sex work so as not to starve and keeping both men and women bound to their field labor.

The Vietnam War

Sex work depends on a sizable population of males with disposable income and few social sanctions controlling their behavior, and as such Cambodia had relatively little sex work before the late 1960s compared with its neighbors, Vietnam and Thailand, with their larger populations and better economies. Following Richard Nixon's 1969 to 1973 extension of the Vietnam War into Cambodia through supposedly secret bombings, together with secret invasion missions in 1970, the Khmer Rouge with the complicity of King Norodom Sihanouk convinced significant portions of the Khmer population that the United States was the enemy. The Lon Nol regime in Phnom Penh, set up and then abandoned by the United States, was overthrown by the Khmer Rouge in 1975. The disaster that followed from 1975 to the rescue by Vietnamese forces in 1979 destroyed almost all Cambodian society and culture, aside from that remembered in the minds of the starved and enslaved populace.

Tu Do Street in Saigon became a street of bars catering to American GIs during the Vietnam War period, but it was only the most infamous of many smaller such areas spread around the city. Sex work and public nudity were first outlawed in Thailand in 1960, following pressures from the United Nations and Western countries. The need for a two-week period of **R&R** (rest and recuperation; the GIs called it I&I: Intoxication and Intercourse) for U.S. troops in Vietnam led to the passage of the Thai Entertainment Places Act of 1966, which kept sex work illegal but legalized places of entertainment where sex work could occur. Persons caught in the act by police—a highly unlikely event because many entertainment places had police connections or paid off the police—could simply claim to be in love as a defense.

Two locations in Vietnam and 12 outside were available for R&R. Bangkok was closest, soldiers had more out-of-country ground time there, and it took only three months to qualify to go there. A Thai Air Force General negotiated the Bangkok R&R. Working with his wife as a travel agent, they booked thousands of GIs on R&R into newly constructed hotels on an extension of Petchburi Road in Bangkok between Soi Nana Tai and Soi Ekamai, with bars and massage parlors scattered among the hotels.

After the Vietnam War

Neither the infrastructure nor the management skills from the R&R period translated into increased levels of sex work in Thailand following the end of R&R in the early 1970s. Grants in the 1970s from the World Bank to transform the sleepy fishing village of Pattaya into a tourist attraction did increase sex work, together with the knowledge gained from the R&R period that foreigners with money would pay more for sex than would locals if it were packaged in a way acceptable to their culture. Although most sex work—about 90 percent—in Southeast Asia continues to cater primarily to local customers, beginning in the mid 1970s, Pattaya became a mecca for German tourists and other Westerners. By the 1990s Pattaya had

Detail of a karaoke bar in Mae Hong Son, Thailand. Courtesy of Angus McIntyre.

supplanted Chiang Mai as the second largest city in Thailand, principally as a tourist haven and primarily based on sex work. A 1996 revision of the Thai prostitution laws in theory tightened controls on sex work and increased penalties, but in fact exceptionally few prosecutions resulted.

In communist countries such as Vietnam, where sex work is classified as bourgeois, not proletariat, and thus is strongly opposed by the government, brothels and other fixed sex-work locations are often attacked by the police. Although streetwalking is dangerous in such countries, it is perceived by many workers as safer than fixed-location work. Today, such attacks drive Vietnamese sex workers into more accepting capitalist climates such as present-day Cambodia.

The 1975 communist victory in Vietnam led to the immediate dissolution of the foreign-oriented portion of the sex industry in Vietnam and the incarceration of those former workers who could be located, for "reeducation." While local sex work remained, foreign-oriented sex work in Vietnam slowly reemerged in the 1980s as a hidden and highly illegal industry. More expensive "hugee bars," public dances at hotels and small, discreet restaurants and bars were the main competition for the furtive cheap sex work occurring in the parks and on darkened Saigon streets.

As Cambodia reinvented itself in the early 1980s, sex work together with other old institutions reemerged as a new and stronger economic force. Driven by money from UNTAC troops and other United Nations nongovernmental organizations and foreign aid operations, as well as by business forces from Asia and rampant poverty, sex work locations increased in the cities and larger towns of Cambodia wherever such economic forces were present. Infighting within the government, preoccupation with eliminating the remnants of the Khmer Rouge, and a general lack of law and order allowed large sex-work areas to form in Phnom Penh and other cities. These areas operated freely until the mid-1990s, when Tuol Kork, Street 63, Steg Menchey, Street 154, and other large brothel areas in Phnom Penh faced increasing harassment from various police agencies.

By the later 1990s, Vietnamese sex workers in Phnom Penh no longer engaged in friendly "attacks" on potential customers, attempting to drag them into the brothel as they passed by on the street. Brothels were segregated by mutual choice according to worker ethnicity into those with Vietnamese or with Khmer workers. Khmer brothels were somewhat more discreet. Vietnamese brothels frequently have operated behind locked doors and have quickly opened for a motorcycle and its passengers to speed into the front room, then closing and locking again. As the police began to own more of the brothels, these restrictions eased somewhat. Sadistic practices were never in vogue, but underage workers were available. Most such workers were 15 or older, but certain brothels, especially in Toul Kork and in Svay Pak, north of the city, featured a number of younger workers.

By early in the 21st century, workers under 18 had largely disappeared in Toul Kork but continued to be available in Svay Pak. One tightly guarded brothel featured only girls under 15. The economic impact of customer traffic in Svay Pak encouraged a few local children to become available, sometimes inside and sometimes outside of the brothels. According to two different U.S. government sponsored investigations, one child outside of the brothels who offered oral sex only was well under 10. Although most of the women in Svay Pak were of age, the existence of about 50 underage sex workers in one location led to international concern and consternation. Police raids against Svay Pak continued intermittently until one led by the International Justice Mission, funded by the U.S. Department of Labor, shut it down relatively permanently in November 2004. Although a few younger workers were apprehended, most escaped capture and continued to work in new locations in Phnom Penh and other Cambodian cities.

See also Child Prostitution.

Further Reading: Lewis, M., S. Bamber, & M. Waugh, ed. *Sex, Disease and Society: A Comparative History of Sexually Transmitted Diseases and HIV/AIDS in Asia and the Pacific*. Contributions in Medical Studies 43. Westport, CT: Greenwood Press, 1997; Steinfatt, T. *Working at the Bar: Sex Work and Health Communication in Thailand*. Westport, CT: Greenwood Press, 2002; Steinfatt, T. M. *Measuring the Number of Trafficked Women and Children in Cambodia. Part I of a Series*. Phnom Penh, Cambodia: USAID, Embassy of the United States of America, 2002. http://slate.msn.com/Features/pdf/Trfcamf3.pdf; Steinfatt, T. M. *Measuring the Number of Trafficked Women and Children in Cambodia: A Direct Observation Field Study. Part III of a Series*. Phnom Penh, Cambodia: USAID, Embassy of the United States of America, 2003. http://slate.msn.com/Features/pdf/Trfciif.pdf.

Thomas M. Steinfatt

SPECULUM. The speculum, a device used to dilate the vagina in order to view the cervix, vaginal walls, and other tissues, was used in antiquity by Galen, and Soranus and was known to Paul of Aegina. Their writings were not available in Europe in translation until the 19th century.

In 1801, Joseph Recamier (1774–1852) tried to reintroduce the speculum use in France. His instrument was a thin tube, but despite its ability to visualize diseased tissues, it was met with criticism and controversy. Two problems associated with the use of the speculum involved social mores at the time. One was the fact that men were looking at women's bodies and, in particular, their genitals. The other was that any instrument or device inserted in the vagina was allegedly indecent and compromising of a woman's honor. This particularly was significant if the woman was a virgin. The belief was that when the speculum was introduced, erotic feelings would be awakened and uncontrollable urges would dominate the woman's life from then on. She might crave repeated insertions of the speculum and become addicted.

During the Napoleonic wars, venereal disease caused more morbidity than battle injuries. Female prostitutes were the first group to be targeted for checking its spread. Although prostitutes were already allegedly indecent, they too suffered from the insults of this gynecological technology. The use of the speculum on these prostitutes became a political issue, so much so that the speculum was referred to as an "instrument of **rape**."

"Morals" were stronger than science in the verbiage of many medical professionals. In the mid-19th century, Charles Meigs, a professor of medicine at the Jefferson Medical College in Philadelphia, urged "restraint" in the use of the speculum. According to Meigs, the physician's major responsibility was to preserve the moral fabric of society. There was to be strict limitation in the speculum's use, as if it would cause some kind of disease itself. Apocryphal stories arose in which physicians were accused of leaping into bed with the women they examined or making the vagina into a "Chinese top shop." A genre of humor regarding "speculumizers" arose, with public theatrics mimicking the use of the speculum.

By 1830 the vaginal speculum had gained popularity in France, and prostitutes were examined for venereal infection and treated accordingly. There was no penicillin yet, and prostitutes had been douching with irritating chemicals and damaging a large surface area of the vagina. To see the venereal lesions, a speculum was necessary. An English physician, Fleetwood Churchill gave brief mention to the speculum in his 1835 edition of a text but, in 1844, stated that although it was a valuable instrument, he thought it had been used improperly and unnecessarily.

J. Marion Sims (1813–1883) is the American physician most often associated with the use of the speculum for obstetric and gynecological surgery. When he began his obstetrics practice in Alabama, there were strong beliefs about male physicians attending women. Those who did were taught not to look at a woman's genitals but to use touch: a good physician need only have a reassuring manner and know the body by touch. There was already controversy regarding obstetrical forceps, a new technology not used by, or acceptable to, midwives, who were the traditional health care providers for women. Sims believed in using forceps and had recently assisted in a birth in which the woman was in labor for 72 hours and the baby's head became wedged in her pelvis. Sims delivered the child, but the woman developed an infection and urinary and fecal incontinence. Sometimes, particularly after a difficult birth, a tear between the anterior vaginal wall and surrounding tissues developed, resulting in a vesicovaginal fistula. These complications were both painful and embarrassing for the woman. Once they occurred, they were incurable. Sims was called back to see the new mother and, upon examination, was unable to see far into the birth canal. He reached for a spoon and bent it, pulling down on the posterior portion of the vaginal canal. He bent another spoon and pulled up, revealing the entire canal up to the cervix. He was able to see the fistula and, using what he referred to as "silver sutures," sewed the injured tears closed. Both the knee-chest position used to position the woman and the speculum were named after him. This first case in 1846, although complicated, paved the way for acceptance of the speculum in gynecologic surgery.

When **William Acton** (1813–1875) tried to introduce the speculum into general gynecological practice in England in the 1850s, he was severely criticized by his colleagues. The speculum examination was perceived by patients and doctors as a voyeuristic and degrading act, one that inflicted mental and physical pain on the female. Marshall Hall, a physiologist, wrote an article in *Lancet* cautioning the readers that a speculum could damage the delicacy and purity of a woman and dull the edge of virgin modesty.

In 1864, the first **Contagious Disease Act** was passed. It attempted to legislate the spread of **syphilis** by allowing a plainclothes law enforcement officer to detain and arrest a woman, keep her overnight, and subject her to a speculum examination. Two more laws were enacted in 1866 and 1869. Outrage was not expressed publicly until the 1870s when emotional meetings were held to demonstrate the ramifications on the general population. Speakers would display the vaginal speculum, waving it, gesticulating to a rapt audience.

Josephine Butler (1828–1906) was the feminist who raised consciousness about the inequity of the Contagious Diseases Acts. She organized the Ladies National Association for the repeal of the Acts. Although the government was desperate to stop the spread of syphilis, women, not men, were subjected to examinations by law enforcement officers. Any woman could be detained and subjected to a speculum examination. When too many non-prostitutes were arrested and forced to undergo the internal examination, reformers acted, and the Acts were repealed in 1886.

Speculum use and the Contagious Disease Acts had an incidental beneficial aspect. As women's health care became more medicalized and less traditional and folk-oriented, women lost the self-knowledge that their ancestors had passed from generation to generation. With attention directed to this new technology or "instrument of rape," women could not ignore the need to know about their own bodies and could not leave everything to the doctor. Although physicians bemoaned the fact that patients spoke about the womb and uterine organs with a familiarity that was formerly unknown, a certain amount of self-awareness gave many women agency that they sorely needed.

Further Reading: Dally, Ann. *Women Under the Knife*. New York: Routledge, 1992; Drachman, Virginia. "The Loomis Trial: Social Mores and Obstetrics in the Mid-Nineteenth Century." In *Women and Health in America*, ed. Judith Waltzer Leavitt. Madison: University of Wisconsin Press, 1984, pp.156–165; Fissell, Mary E. "Speculations on the Speculum." *Women's Health in Primary Care* 3 (2000): 298; Groneman, Carol. "Nymphomania: The Historical Construction of Female Sexuality." *Signs* 19 (1994): 337–367; Wertz, Robert, and Dorothy Wertz. *Brought to Bed*. New Haven, CT: Yale. University Press, 1989; Walkowitz, Judith. *Prostitution and Victorian Society Women, Class and the State*. Melbourne: Cambridge University Press, 2001.

Lana Thompson

SPRINKLE, ANNIE (1954–). Porn actress, pinup model and photographer, author, sex film director and producer, college lecturer, sex-oriented performance artist, and sex-worker activist, Sprinkle began her career as a prostitute in 1973. She worked in Manhattan massage parlors for 20 years and starred in close to 100 feature XXX porn **films** and 508-mm loops. She became the second best-selling video star in 1982 in the United States for the film *Deep Inside Annie Sprinkle*, which she wrote and directed. Frustrated by the industry's lack of response to her pro-condom campaigning in the time of the emerging AIDS crisis, she left the world of mainstream pornography shortly thereafter.

Sprinkle was perhaps the first-known porn actress to advertise openly for prostitution. A member of the organization **COYOTE** and Prostitutes of New York (PONY) since 1975, she continued to be an active advocate of sex workers and their rights but phased out her own work in prostitution by 1993.

Annie Sprinkle during one of her performances. Courtesy of Annie Sprinkle.

Sprinkle began to see her work as a porn star and prostitute as a foundation for her creative self and made the shift from prostitution to art, with innovative theater performances such as "Post-Porn Modernist" (1989–95) which featured her infamous Public Cervix Announcement, in which she showed her cervix to her audiences, and The Legend of the Sacred Prostitute, during which she performed a sexual-healing masturbation ritual and the theater piece. Annie Sprinkle's Herstory of Porn (1998–2004) centered around her life in porn. She toured internationally to great acclaim. Today her performance art is studied in colleges and universities. Her unique "postmodern sex films" include Linda/Les & Annie: The First Female-to-Male Transsexual Love Story (1989), The Sluts and Goddesses Video Workshop (1992), and Annie Sprinkle's Amazing World of Orgasm (2004).

In 2002, Sprinkle became the first porn star to earn a doctoral degree, making her a certified sexologist. She served on the board of the **St. James Infirmary**, a free clinic for sex workers in San Francisco, for five years. She is the author of several books, including Hardcore from the Heart: The Pleasures, Profits and Politics of Sex in Performance (2001), Post-Porn Modernist: My 25 Years as a Multi-media Whore (1998), and Dr. Sprinkle's Spectacular Sex—Make Over Your Love Life (2005).

Further Reading: Annie Sprinkle's website. http://www.anniesprinkle.org; Sprinkle, Annie. Post-Porn Modernist: My 25 Years as a Multi-media Whore. San Francisco: Last Gasp Books, 1998.

Tom Garretson

ST. JAMES, MARGO (1937–).

Margo St. James, a former prostitute in the United States, has spent more than 30 years advocating for the rights of sex workers. Her many years of sex work activism started in 1962 when a judge labeled her a prostitute because she used the word "trick" in pleading not guilty. She said, "I've never turned a trick in my life." Labeled by that ruling, she then became a prostitute for four years. In 1972, St. James founded the group Whores, Housewives, and Others (WHO), with "Others" referring to lesbians. This group resulted in the establishment of **COYOTE** (Call Off Your Old Tired Ethics) in 1973 to provide services to sex workers and to draw attention to the abuses sex workers experience.

Shortly after the creation of COYOTE, St. James began organizing at the international level. She cofounded the National Task Force on Prostitution as well as the International Committee for Prostitutes' Rights. In the mid-1980s St. James moved to France to escape the shifting political climate in the United States. She returned to San Francisco in 1993, and in 1996 she ran a close race for a seat on the San Francisco Board of Supervisors and ultimately lost by a small number of votes. In 1999, St. James and COYOTE cofounded **St. James Infirmary** in San Francisco,. The St. James Infirmary is a peer-led **occupational safety and health** clinic that offers free, confidential, nonjudgmental medical and social services for sex workers of all genders.

Alexandra Lutnick

ST. JAMES INFIRMARY.

St. James Infirmary (SJI), founded on June 2, 1999, is a multiservice, peer-led **occupational safety and health** clinic located in San Francisco, California, for current, former, and transitioning sex workers of all genders. This unique organization is the result of the collaboration between Call Off Your Old Tired Ethics (**COYOTE**), founded by **Margo St. James** in 1973, the Exotic Dancers' Alliance (EDA), cofounded by Johanna Breyer and Dawn Passar in 1993, and the San Francisco Department of Public Health, specifically the STD Prevention and

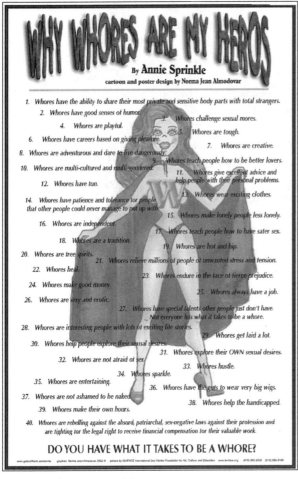

Courtesy of Annie Sprinkle.

Control Department headed by Jeffrey Klausner. All services at SJI are delivered in a nonjudgmental, **harm reduction** fashion by staff and volunteers made up largely of former, current, or transitioning sex workers.

SJI provides all its services free of charge to its participants. Currently SJI has four clinics during the week that offer sexual health care inclusive of testing and treatment for HIV, sexually transmitted infections. (STIs), tuberculosis, and hepatitis, primary medical care, immunizations, acupuncture, chiropractic care, massage therapy, Reiki, food, **clothing**, harm-reduction groups and supplies, syringe exchange, social service and legal referrals, mental health counseling, substance use counseling and treatment, smoking-cessation groups, support groups, career counseling and training, child care assistance, individual peer-counseling sessions, and apprenticeship programs. On a monthly basis, harm-reduction counselors offer testing for HIV/STIs at local venues, and the outreach program provides referrals, harm-reduction supplies, and support to those individuals who work on the street and in strip clubs, massage parlors, and single-room occupancy hotels. SJI also offers a pretrial **diversion program** for those charged with prostitution-related crimes.

SJI provides education to the community and other organizations about sex workers, facilitates a medical student elective about the health care needs of sex workers, and collaborates with other agencies.

Alexandra Lutnick

STATUTORY RAPE. *See* **Rape, Statutory.**

STEAD, WILLIAM. *See* **"The Maiden Tribute of Modern Babylon."**

STEEN, JAN (1626–1679). Steen was a Dutch painter best known for his moralizing scenes of everyday life. Steen's genre paintings depict busy interiors that simultaneously celebrate and warn about the dangers of overindulgence in sex and drink. In the paintings, playful pairings and subtle suggestions of monetary exchange make reference to prostitution in both humorous and admonishing ways.

Although Steen is most remembered for his genre scenes, during his life he experimented with a wide variety of subjects, ranging from biblical subjects to portraiture. Steen moved frequently between Dutch cities and emulated the work of many **Dutch masters**, perhaps in hopes of finding the success that continually eluded him. By the 18th century, however, Steen's genre scenes had garnered significant attention in popular culture, even generating a new Dutch saying, "a Jan Steen household," referring to a crowded home in disarray. The attraction of Steen's genre paintings lies in their dual role as moral instruction and low-life entertainment. The populated interiors are an intricate web of exchanged glances and suggested misbehavior. Several of Steen's paintings are set in taverns, which appear to double as **brothels**, and the characters of such scenes always convey a jovial nature. However, Steen often appended moralizing proverbs to his paintings, continuing a 16th-century tradition that admonished decadent or immoral behavior. In witnessing these realms of temptation and misconduct, the viewers of Steen's painting are invited to both laugh at and reprimand the sexual mischief.

Further Reading: Chapman, H. Perry. *Jan Steen: Painter and Storyteller.* Washington, DC: National Gallery of Art, 1996; Westermann, Mariët. *The Amusements of Jan Steen: Comic Painting in the Seventeenth Century.* Zwolle, the Netherlands: Waanders, 1997.

Rachel Epp Buller

STIGMA. The prostitute is the prototype of the stigmatized woman. She is both named and dishonored by the word *whore*. "Whore" does not, however, refer only to prostitutes. The label can be applied to any woman. A whore is "unchaste," defined as "indulging in unlawful or immoral sexual intercourse; lacking in purity, virginity, decency (of speech), restraint, and simplicity; defiled (i.e., polluted, corrupted)" (Pheterson 1996). Significantly, charges of unchastity do not make a man a whore, although they may stigmatize him according to color, ethnic, sexuality, or class discriminations. The word "whore" is specifically a female gender stigma. Given that "stigma" is defined as "a brand marked on a slave or criminal, a stain on one's character, a mark of shame or discredit and/or a definite characteristic of some disease" (Pheterson 1996), the whore stigma is then a mark of shame or disease on an unchaste woman or female slave or criminal.

The lack of chastity that dishonors women is not an exceptional or avoidable state. Sexuality, racial or ethnic status, class position, history of abuse, disease, manner, appearance, or independence can all be used as evidence of female unchastity. Prostitutes reappear on every dimension of dishonor as the prototypical whore. They are perceived as the personification of (adulterous) sex, (dark) race, (dirty) money, (deserved) abuse, (sexually transmitted) disease, and (taboo) knowledge. Other women are threatened with a loss of honor when accused of unchastity; whorish women are shamed for sexuality, blamed for **violence** and disease, and punished for financial, sexual, or intellectual initiative.

Not every woman may feel equally controlled and judged. But every woman, like every man, has learned the social criteria of female chastity within her culture. The verb "to chasten" or "to chastise" means "to punish (as by whipping)," "to censure severely," and also "to purify" (Pheterson 1996). The concept and practice of "purifying" women is thus linguistically as well as socially synonymous with punishment through control and battering. The menace of the whore stigma acts as a whip holding females in a state of subordination. Until that whip loses its sting, the liberation of women will be in check.

Further Reading: Pheterson, Gail. "The Whore Stigma: Crimes of Unchastity." In *The Prostitution Prism*, by Gail Pheterson. Amsterdam: Amsterdam University Press, 1996, pp. 65–89.

Gail Pheterson

STORYVILLE. Storyville was the famous turn-of-the-century red light district of **New Orleans,** Louisiana. It opened in 1897 under special ordinance of the city government and closed in 1917 under orders of the federal government. It occupied 18 square blocks bounded by North Basin, Customhouse (now Iberville), North Robertson, and St. Louis streets. The district was famous for its extravagant bordellos, its jazz music, and its promotion of interracial sex and octoroon prostitutes at the beginning of the Jim Crow era.

The author of the ordinance was council member Sidney Story, hence the name "Storyville." The government that created Storyville was dominated by reformers and businessmen and represented a brief interruption in the decades of machine rule of the city. The creation of a red light district was their attempt to curtail the spread of prostitution and to limit commercial sex to a small, discrete neighborhood on the outskirts of town. However, Storyville became one of the most visibly flamboyant legal red light districts in history.

The neighborhood the City Council chose for the new commercial sex district was on the margins of both the French Quarter and the rapidly developing business district, known as the American section. At the time of the ordinance, the area was inhabited by a mix of people, both in terms of race and respectability. There were small businesses and working-class families. There was one church, the Methodist Episcopal Church for "colored" parishioners; one school (for "colored" children); and three "Negro Dance Halls," in the predominately residential neighborhood. There were prostitutes, but they did not dominate the area. The largest business in the neighborhood was the lumber company owned by George L'Hote. L'Hote also lived in the neighborhood with his wife and their eight children. L'Hote sued the city to prevent passage of the ordinance after an amendment to the original ordinance, passed in July 1897, extended the district's boundaries to allow prostitution on St. Louis Street. The original ordinance stipulated that St. Louis would serve as boundary only, with no houses of prostitution allowed on it. The same amendment created another, smaller red light district above Canal Street, in "uptown" New Orleans. Its borders were Perdido, Gravier, Franklin, and Locust streets. This four-block area was never associated with the downtown Storyville. It was a poor black neighborhood known for drugs, **violence,** and commercial sex. L'Hote's case went all the way to the U.S. Supreme Court, but the city prevailed and Storyville gained the sanction of the judicial branch. Technically, while L'Hote's case was pending, the opening of the district was held in abeyance, but construction of bordellos began as early as 1897.

The most spectacular bordello was Mahogany Hall. Built especially for Lulu White, the self-styled "Diamond Queen of the Demi-monde," Mahogany Hall reportedly cost more than $40,000 to build and decorate. It had an imposing marble staircase, four floors, two parlors, including a parlor in which the walls and ceiling were covered with mirrors, 15 bedrooms with water closets attached to each, and an elevator. Sometimes called "The Octoroon Club," Mahogany Hall featured octoroon prostitutes for an exclusively white clientele. Other bordellos were Willie Piazza's, which also featured octoroons, Emma Johnson's "House of All Nations,"

Street scene of Storyville, the famed jazz, blues, and red light district of New Orleans, early 1900s. Frank Driggs Collection/Getty Images.

which put on elaborate sex circuses under the direction of Johnson, a black woman, and Josie Arlington's business, which billed itself as the "most costly fitted-out sporting palace" in the country. Arlington was white.

Entrepreneurs, **madams**, and property owners created a guidebook to Storyville that was published every year from 1898 until 1915. Known as the "**Blue Books**," these **guidebooks** listed the brothels and the prostitutes according to race: "W" for white, "C" for colored, and "Oct." for octoroon—the district's specialty. Some editions listed "French" prostitutes or "French 69" bordellos. "Jews" were included in several editions, and one Blue Book featured a "Jew Colony."

Storyville is often called the birthplace of jazz, and it did provide venues for the new musical style developing in New Orleans at the time. Jelly Roll Morton, Bunk Johnson, Manuel Manetta, Tony Jackson, King Oliver, and a young Louis Armstrong, among others, all played in Storyville. Spencer Williams, who wrote "Basin Street Blues" in the 1920s, lived for a while in Mahogany Hall.

Storyville intersected the two most trafficked areas of the city: the French Quarter and the American section. The business district developed adjacent to Storyville and provided much of its clientele. In 1908 the train terminus at Canal and Basin streets, only one block from Storyville's border, was completed. As the trains entered the station, they went past the Basin Street bordellos, where the prostitutes waved to passengers from windows and balconies, often naked. The increased visibility of Storyville, its flagrant violation of Jim Crow, and its flouting of bourgeois morality spurred local reformers to take action against the district. They objected most strenuously to the district's promotion of interracial sex. In 1917 the city attempted to force all nonwhite prostitutes to relocate to the "uptown" neighborhood, but several octoroon and "colored" prostitutes and madams successfully fought the measure. Later that year, the Woodrow Wilson administration forced Mayor Martin Behrman to close the district because it violated a law designed to protect American sailors and soldiers as they prepared for war.

Storyville has lived on in memory and memorial throughout New Orleans. Numerous clubs, bars, and music venues use its name to evoke a kind of golden age of New Orleans' transgressive culture of pleasure. Recent scholarly work on Storyville promises to bring the women of Storyville, from the ostentatious Lulu White and Willie Piazza to the crib girls and street walkers, back into the center of the story.

See also Bellocq, Ernest J.

Further Reading: Landau, Emily Epstein. "'Spectacular Wickedness': New Orleans, Prostitution, and the Politics of Sex, 1897–1917." Ph.D. dissertation, Yale University, forthcoming; Long, Alecia P. *The Great Southern Babylon: Sex, Race, Respectability in New Orleans, 1865–1920.* Baton Rouge: Louisiana State University Press, 2004; Roach, Joseph. *Cities of the Dead: Circum-Atlantic Performance.* New York: Columbia University Press, 1996; Rose, Al. *Storyville: Being an Authentic, Illustrated History of the Notorious Red-Light District.* Tuscaloosa : University of Alabama Press, 1974; Shapiro, Nat, and Nat Hentoff, comps. *Hear Me Talkin' To Ya.* New York City: Rinehart & Co., 1955; Dover, 1966.

Emily Epstein Landau

STREET OFFENCES ACT OF 1959. This statute (7 & 8 Eliz. 2. c 57), passed by the British Government, embodied the recommendations of the 1957 **Wolfenden Report**. It applied to England and Wales (Scotland and Northern Ireland had their own legislation). The original purpose of the act was to eradicate the nuisance caused by prostitutes soliciting on the streets of **London**. The act was underpinned by a nonstatutory "cautioning system" that provided for two cautions before a woman was taken to a police station and officially registered as a "common prostitute." She was entitled to appeal within 14 days if she felt wrongly accused. The caution was intended to forge a link between the prostitute and social worker in the hope of persuading her to change her lifestyle, a tactic that proved ineffective. However, it also provided a presupposition of guilt, given that a women would be presented to the court as a "common prostitute" seen "loitering or soliciting for the purpose of prostitution," leaving her with no defense. Escalating fines were introduced with a three-month **prison** sentence on third conviction (repealed by the Criminal Justice Act in 1982).

Initially, the act worked well, and the women vanished from the streets, reappearing in striptease clubs, bars, and private flats. From a policing point of view, it was deceptively simple because there was no longer any need to provide evidence that a citizen had been annoyed when harassed residents might call them in to "clean up" their area. However, this led to displacement of the problem from one district to another, which relieved one group of residents while infuriating another. And because the street prostitute became less visible, curb crawling intensified, so that by 1985 additional legislation was introduced to deal with a new situation.

The nature of the trade also adjusted as women adopted a peripatetic lifestyle, disguising their appearance, giving false addresses to police officers, moving from place to place, or working in one area and living in another. Thus, a problem that had been largely London-based spread rapidly around the country. Additionally, the old accommodation among prostitute, police officer, and voluntary social worker broke down as the women became distrustful. Eventually, however, they regained their confidence and the street scene recovered, so that prostitution became more complex and difficult to police.

During the 1960s, reaction to the perceived injustice of the act was intense, and a campaign to repeal or reform it was led by the **Josephine Butler** Society, previously known as the Association of Moral and Social Hygiene, in cooperation with some members of the House of Lords. Three private Members bills were introduced but failed, principally because the Members of Parliament who had originally pushed the act through the Commons had been elevated to the Lords and were in a position to oppose them. The legislation continues to generate resentment.

Further Reading: Self, Helen J. *Prostitution, Women and Misuse of the Law: The Fallen Daughters of Eve*. London: Frank Cass, 2003.

Helen J. Self

STREET-BASED PROSTITUTION. Street-based prostitution involves someone who solicits or negotiates sex outdoors—for example, on the street or in some other outdoor venue, such as a boardwalk, pier, or parking lot. Outdoor prostitution is more common in warmer than in colder climates.

Street-based prostitution is stereotyped as the province of drug addicts, and many street areas include drug sellers and users. However, sex workers on the street are not always involved with drugs. In some places, sex workers of many economic strata are represented on the street. For example, in Germany, where prostitution is legal, men and women who engage in prostitution on the street do so by choice and can move easily between indoor and outdoor prostitution. For them, the difference is not between inside and outside but between addicted or not addicted or, more often, EU citizen and noncitizen.

Street-based prostitutes may be entirely independent and work only when they choose to do so, but their work can also be surprisingly structured. **Tippelzones** were outdoor prostitution zones with specific hours, regulations, and services in the Netherlands. Some street-based sex workers are part of structured networks including coworkers and **pimps** or other people who are expected to assist in cases of assault or arrest. Such relationships vary and can be mutually beneficial, altruistic, or exploitative. In some cases, street-based sex work can appear to be safer than other sex work **venues**. For example, Jenkins (2005) describes the way Cambodian brothel workers were victimized when they left the brothel for work on an "out-call," whereas other sex workers, particularly those on the street, were not. The ratio of on-street prostitution to off-street venues (such as saunas, massage parlors, or incall/outcall escort services) varies in cities depending on local law, policy, and custom.

Prostitution on the street, because of its visibility, often receives the most attention from the press, communities, police, and researchers. This research is problematic for some scholars because they think it calls too much attention to street work at the risk of making other sex work invisible. Community concerns about nuisance crimes such as loitering and littering mean police aggressively target street prostitution. **Resident activism** against street prostitution is often a response to increased traffic, litter, and gentrification of areas where prostitution and other activities take place. In some cities, even though police are aware of street-based prostitution, they will only act on it and make arrests if prompted by local residents. As a result, street prostitutes tend to move within a city or travel from one city to another in an attempt to avoid being arrested.

Street-based prostitution often involves women, transgender women, and men for whom few other options exist. They may face more problems with substance dependency, poverty, and unstable housing and may lack opportunities for mainstream employment of any kind, even sub–living wage jobs. These vulnerabilities, coupled with these individuals' higher visibility, create an environment in which street-based prostitutes are more likely to face problems such as **violence**, police harassment, and false arrest. A number of factors keep people on the street, even when they would like to leave. Because both drugs and prostitution are illegal in most of the United States, street-based prostitutes are often pulled into the criminal justice system. Once arrested, they may spend time in jail or, less commonly, in drug treatment. As a result of the collateral consequences of incarceration, such as being barred from certain jobs and housing, in addition to the lack of comprehensive and targeted drug treatment, the street prostitute often leaves jail with even fewer options or sources for support than before.

See also Addiction.

Further Reading: Jenkins, Carol. "Cambodian Sex Workers Conduct Their Own Research." *Research for Sex Work* 8 (2005). http://www.researchforsexwork.org; Sterk, Claire E. *Tricking and Tripping: Prostitution in the Era of AIDS*. New York: Social Change Press, 1999; Thukral, Juhu and Melissa Ditmore. *Revolving Door: An Analysis of Street-Based Prostitution in New York City*. Web site of the Sex Workers Project of the Urban Justice Center. http://www.sexworkersproject.org/ reports/ RevolvingDoor.html; Weitzer, Ronald. "Prostitution Control in America: Rethinking Public Policy." *Crime, Law & Social Change* 32 (1999): 83–102; Wotton, Rachel. "The Relationship Between Street-based Sex Workers and the Police in the Effectiveness of HIV Prevention Strategies." *Research for Sex Work* 8 (2005). http://www.researchforsexwork.org

Jill McCracken, Juhu Thukral, and Eden C. Savino

STRIPPING. Stripping (also known as striptease or exotic dance) is a continually evolving art form in the contemporary United States. Strippers, or male or female entertainers who disrobe and perform in varying stages of nudity for money, have appeared in many different kinds of entertainment **venues** historically. In 19th-century U.S. cities, striptease shows were indeed often part of an encounter with a prostitute in a **brothel**. But stripping performances were also being given in venues that did not allow contact between the audiences and the performers, including model artist shows, burlesque performances, and "cooch dance" performances, which were first seen at the **Chicago** World's Colombian Exposition in 1893, and in upscale cabarets such as the celebrated Ziegfeld's *Follies*. Some strippers, such as Gypsy Rose Lee, Lilly St. Cyr, Blaze Starr, Maggie Hart and Ann Corio, became well-known celebrities.

Contemporary stripping is also to be distinguished from prostitution because the two occupations are not always synonymous. In its current form, striptease is a specialized service because it is not necessarily coupled with sexual activity: when it occurs in strip clubs, it is a legal form of gendered spectacle and an opportunity for public **voyeurism**—a form of (usually male) sexualized "entertainment." Despite popular beliefs to the contrary, strippers are generally not selling sex to their customers—although they are indeed selling sexualized and gendered services. Regulations regarding contact and the amount of nudity vary around the United States, and thus one finds different kinds of performances being offered in different locales. Dancers may be allowed to strip down to bikinis, to perform topless or with pasties, or to dance completely nude, sometimes depending on whether the club serves alcoholic beverages. Though occasionally only stage performances are allowed, most clubs also allow the dancers to circulate among the customers and offer personal or "private" dances as well as companionship and conversation. Many of these venues may restrict contact but allow table dances offered to the customers at their seats, either on a raised platform or table or while the woman stands on the ground between the man's knees. Some cities allow lap dancing, or friction dancing, a practice that involves varying amounts of contact between the dancer and the patron and can lead to sexual release for the customer, who may even wear a condom underneath his clothes. Such services may blur the line between performance and prostitution, depending on one's definition of each. Strippers who perform outcall services for bachelor parties and other private engagements, as well as porn stars who travel and perform in strip clubs as feature entertainers, may also blur these boundaries.

Significantly, however, some studies of the male customers of female dancers have found that the men's visits to strip clubs are desirable to them precisely because they do not involve actual sex or prostitution (Frank 1998, 2002). Instead, customers may be purchasing the conversation and attention of young women just as much as they are paying for an opportunity to see their bodies. Further, most entertainers who perform in strip clubs explicitly understand their jobs to be about the creation of a fantasy of access rather than as the provision of actual sex.

Sophisticated arguments have been made for a perspective of stripping as a form of expressive conduct that should be protected under the First Amendment.

See also Gentlemen's Clubs; Male Stripping.

Further Reading: Allen, Robert C. *Horrible Prettiness: Burlesque and American Culture*. Chapel Hill: The University of North Carolina Press, 1991; Erenberg, Lewis A. *Steppin' Out: New York Nightlife and the Transformation of American Culture*. Westport, CT: Greenwood Press, 1984; Foley, Brenda. "Naked Politics: Erie, PA v the Kandyland Club." *NWSA Journal* 14, no. 2 (2002): 1–17; Frank, Katherine. "The Production of Identity and the Negotiation of Intimacy in a 'Gentleman's Club.'" *Sexualities* 1, no. 2 (1998): 175–202; Frank, Katherine. *G-Strings and Sympathy: Strip Club Regulars and Male Desire*. Durham, NC: Duke University Press, 2002; Gilfoyle, Timothy J. *City of Eros: New York City, Prostitution, and the Commercialization of Sex, 1790–1920*. New York: W. W. Norton, 1992; Hanna, Judith Lynne. "Undressing the First Amendment and Corsetting the Striptease Dancer." *The Drama Review* 42, no. 2 (1998): 38–69.

Katherine Frank

STROZZI, BARBARA (1619–1677).

An extraordinary composer and singer, Barbara Strozzi published eight collections of songs, containing 125 pieces of vocal music that were printed during her lifetime, more than some of her male contemporaries. Her work displays a full range of the musical forms used in 17th-century **Venice**. She was the first female composer to publish significantly and was often referred to as *la virtuosissima cantatrice*, the most virtuosic singer. Born in Venice and raised in a literary and musical household, Strozzi was the adopted daughter of poet Giulio Strozzi, whose family was second in wealth only to the Medici family. Some believe that Barbara was actually the illegitimate daughter of Strozzi and his long-term servant, Isabella Garzoni, herself rumored to have been a **courtesan**. Barbara received formal musical instruction, and by age 16 had already made a name for herself. She is believed to have created the Italian Secular Cantata, a musical form for a chorus or soloist based on a religious text, and one that developed a new way of expression in music. Though her first informal vocal performance was at the Accademia degli Incogniti, Strozzi sang in many important academies of her day. Her presence was considered scandalous because women generally did not attend. It caused such great interest that her chastity was questioned and it was rumored that she was a courtesan. She never married, but gave birth to four children, three of whom she had with her father's colleague and friend, Giovanni Paola Vidman.

Further Reading: Bowers, Jane, and Judith Tick, eds. *Women Making Music: The Western Art Tradition, 1150–1950.* Urbana: University of Illinois Press, 1987; Jezic, Diane Peacock, and Elizabeth Wood, eds. *Women Composers: The Lost Tradition Found,* 2nd ed. New York: Feminist Press, 1993; Magner, C. *Barbara Strozzi: la Virtuosissima Cantatrice.* http://www.home.earthlink. net/~barbarastrozzi/index.htm

Anne Marie Fowler

SURVIVAL SEX. *See* **Transactional Sex**

SYPHILIS. Syphilis is a congenital or **sexually transmitted infection** that has prompted the regulation of prostitution for nearly 500 years. The historiography of syphilis has been greatly influenced in recent years by social and cultural studies in the history of medicine. Although syphilis has traditionally been associated with the early modern affliction called the "French Pox" or the "French Disease," historians have been increasingly reluctant to conflate the two in recent scholarship. Despite its etymological origins from Girolamo Fracastoro's 16th-century pastoral poem about the affliction of an eponymous shepherd, this reluctance to use retrospectively the term "syphilis" recognizes that the epidemiology and symptomatology of the two may not be identical, whether because they were in fact different maladies or a single disease that may have mutated over time.

The French Disease

Traditionally identified as syphilis, that which was most commonly known as the French Disease *(morbus gallicus)* or Pox was, according to most accounts, first recorded in 1493 and 1494 among the French troops laying siege to Naples at the onset of the Italian Wars. (The French rejected this aspersion in favor of an alternative name like the "Italian disease.") Its seemingly sudden appearance in epidemic form at the end of the 15th century encouraged a search for its origin; in fact, a 1524 medical treatise listed more than 200 possible names for the affliction, each citing another geographical source. Symptoms of the Pox (French or otherwise) included fever, achy limbs, and pervasive skin ulcers. Although its etiology was not fully understood, the association of sexual intercourse with the diffusion of the ailment was quickly observed. Venetian chronicler Marin Sanudo noted in one of the first accounts of the affliction in 1496 that the disease began at the genitals before and during intercourse but was not otherwise contagious (except perhaps congenitally, he seems to have interestingly observed, given that he reported that children were also rumored to suffer from it). Traditional historiography has cited the advent of the French Disease as one of the key factors in the subsequent crackdowns on European prostitution beginning in the 16th century, although it is unclear whether the new reform-minded, sexually conservative mentality of the time had a greater influence.

Beyond Europe, the epidemic seems to have arrived in Japan by 1512, carried by Chinese sailors to Nagasaki. Called the "T'ang sore" or the "Chinese ulcer," within a few decades its venereal character was likewise recognized by the name *karakasa,* or the "Chinese pleasure disease." Although the illness was still clearly associated with an "Other," a Jesuit missionary writing in 1585 interestingly recounted that the Japanese did not, however, regard the ailment as a social **stigma**, but rather as a disease like any other.

Treatment

This new malady was supposed to be very difficult to cure, but it was rarely fatal. Early treatments involved oil baths and various unguents but soon veered toward the use of mercury, which contemporaries believed would encourage the purgation of the pollution. Though highly toxic, mercury apparently could retard the spread of the disease and thus persisted in antisyphilis salves and draughts into the 20th century. In addition, the discovery in the Antilles of *guaiacum*—also known as "holy wood"—for syphilis treatments encouraged Europeans finally to designate the New World as the original source of the infection because many believed it was only natural that a cure would originate in the same location as the disease itself. (The debate about the American origins of syphilis continues to this day.)

> ## Syphilis
>
> Shakespeare, in Henry IV, Part 2 Act 2 Scene IV, wrote this salty and punning exchange about venereal disease between Falstaff and Doll Tearsheet, a prostitute.
>
> FALSTAFF (...) How now, Mistress Doll!
> MISTRESS QUICKLY Sick of a calm; yea, good faith.
> FALSTAFF So is all her sect; an they be once in a calm, they are sick.
> DOLL TEARSHEET You muddy rascal, is that all the comfort you give me?
> FALSTAFF You make fat rascals, Mistress Doll.
> DOLL TEARSHEET I make them! gluttony and diseases make them; I make them not.
> FALSTAFF If the cook help to make the gluttony, you help to make the diseases, Doll: we catch of you, Doll, we catch of you; grant that, my poor virtue grant that.
> DOLL TEARSHEET Yea, joy, our chains and our jewels.
> FALSTAFF 'Your broaches, pearls, and ouches:' for to serve bravely is to come halting off, you know: to come off the breach with his pike bent bravely, and to surgery bravely; to venture upon the charged chambers bravely,—
> DOLL TEARSHEET Hang yourself, you muddy conger, hang yourself!

Modern Syphilis

"Syphilis" did not appear as a frequent medical term until the 18th century, and only in 1905 was its cause discovered to be a spirochete, *Treponema pallidum*, that enters the body usually through the mucus membranes, where it incubates for between two to four weeks before producing a chancre near the infection site. After this first phase, about one-third of modern-day subjects develop multiple sores on the skin and internal organs during the second stage, and in the rarer late or third phase, the lesions may destroy tissues throughout the body, causing neurological or cardiological damage should they attack the nervous or cardiovascular systems. Only the development of commercially available penicillin in the 1940s finally permitted a consistent, effective treatment regimen.

Contagious Disease Acts

Fears of syphilis in the 19th and 20th centuries tended to encourage a demonization of the women thought to be carriers, more often than condemnation of sexually promiscuous men. When, for example, the British military estimated a syphilis infection rate of around 369 per 1,000, the British government responded with the **Contagious Disease Acts** of **1864**, **1866**, **and 1869**. As a result, prostitutes in certain military garrison towns throughout Britain and the Empire were required to register with the police and undergo a medical examination for venereal disease. If they were found to be infected, they were incarcerated in a quarantine (or "lock") hospital until cured. Likewise, any woman even suspected of soliciting (no probable cause was required), if she refused to submit to a genital (**speculum**) exam (accepting the examination was tantamount to a confession of prostitution), could be arrested. Increasing popular dissent over the next two decades, spearheaded by activist **Josephine Butler**, eventually led to the repeal of registration and to legalized prostitution in Britain in 1885 (although the Contagious Disease Acts continued to be enforced elsewhere in the Empire until the early 20th century).

Syphilis Today

In 1972, the U.S. Public Health Service admitted to having conducted human experiments for 40 years, not on the effectiveness of various cures, but rather on the progression of untreated syphilis in nearly 400 African American men in Macon County, Alabama. Perhaps 100 individuals may have died as a consequence of what subsequently became known as the infamous "Tuskegee Experiment." As a result of this public disclosure, a class action lawsuit awarded more than nine million dollars to the study's subjects, as well as free medical and funeral services. The Centers for Disease Control was given the responsibility of administering these health services, not only for surviving participants, but also for wives, widows, and children who had been infected in the course of the experiment. In addition, new regulatory norms were imposed on the ethical treatment of human subjects, and in 1997, President Bill Clinton extended a formal apology on behalf of the country to the survivors.

Syphilis cases in developed nations seemed to be on the decline in the late 20th century. The rate of primary and secondary syphilis in the United States, for example, dropped by nearly 90 percent between 1990 and 2000, to the lowest levels in nearly six decades. But the U.S. Centers for Disease Control and Prevention have reported that cases have slightly increased annually in the early 21st century, inspiring the additional concern that syphilis may increase from two to five times the risk of transmitting and contracting HIV. Although syphilis among women seems to have instead dropped, more than two-thirds of the new syphilis patients in 2001 were men. Debate continues regarding the significance of this increase in infection rates. Some experts fear that present diagnostics could be inadequate, suggesting that standard syphilis tests may give not only false-positives but false-negatives as well. On the other hand, it appears from U.S. urban public health data that syphilis rates also seem to increase and decrease in regular cycles, perhaps as those previously infected develop a temporary immunity, and thus worries that the disease is spreading rapidly in the United States and Europe mainly as a result of greater complacency about safer sex practices may be unfounded.

See also Research Ethics; Scapegoating.

Further Reading: Beck, Stephen V. "Syphilis: The Great Pox." In *Plague, Pox and Pestilence: Disease in History*, ed. Kenneth F. Kiple. New York: Barnes & Noble, 1997, pp. 110–15; Centers for Disease Control. "The CDC Tuskegee Syphilis Study Page." http://www.cdc.gov/nchstp/od/tuskegee/index.html; Foa, Anna. "The New and the Old: The Spread of Syphilis (1494–1530)." In *Sex and Gender in Historical Perspective*, ed. Edward Muir and Guido Ruggiero. Baltimore, MD: Johns Hopkins University Press, 1990, pp. 26–45; Gould, Stephen Jay. "Syphilis and the Shepherd of Atlantis (Renaissance Poem about Syphilis Attempts to Explain Its Origins; Genetic Map Revealed in 1998)." *Natural History* 109 (October 2000): 38–42, 74–82; Jones, James H. *Bad Blood: The Tuskegee Syphilis Experiment*. New York: Free Press, 1981; Kohn, George Childs, ed. *Encyclopedia of Plague and Pestilence*. New York: Checkmark Books, 2001; Laughran, Michelle A. In "The Body, Public Health and Social Control in Sixteenth-Century Venice." Ph.D. dissertation, University of

Connecticut, 1998, pp. 57–104; National Library of Medicine, "Visual Culture and Public Health Posters: Veneral Disease" http://www.nlm.nih.gov/exhibition/visualculture/venereal.html; Quétel, Claude. *The History of Syphilis.* Baltimore, MD: Johns Hopkins University Press, 1986; Watts, heldon. *Epidemics and History: Disease, Power and Imperialism.* New Haven, CT: Yale University Press, 1997, pp. 121–66.

Michelle A. Laughran

T

TAN BAZAR. The Bangladesh Women's Health Coalition, in collaboration with Smarajit Jana, formerly of the **Sonagachi Project**, began a sexual health initiative in 1994 at Dhaka's Tan Bazar, the largest and oldest brothel in Bangladesh. However, after a sex worker named Jesmin was murdered at the brothel in 1999, local authorities began pressing for its closure. Later that year, a police raid permanently closed the facility and evicted all workers, for the purpose of their social rehabilitation. The Sonagachi Project organized sympathy demonstrations, and Tan Bazar sex workers organized a union called Shonghoti ("collaboration"), which successfully won a court case to reopen the brothel. Tan Bazar, however, remains closed.

See also South Asia; Unions.

Further Reading: Ahmed, Julia. "Health Impacts of Prostitution: Experience of Bangladesh Women's Health Coalition." *Research for Sex Work* 4 (2001): 8–9. http://www.med.vu.nl/hcc/artikelen/ahmed.htm

Ananya Mukherjea

TEA HOUSES. *See* **Geisha; Venues and Labor Forms.**

TEL AVIV. Prostitution and **trafficking** in women in Israel predates the establishment of the state in 1948. In Jerusalem, prostitution increased under the rule of the Turkish Empire during **World War I**, with the number of women who worked as prostitutes growing in subsequent years. On one hand, large numbers of British troops were stationed in Palestine, and on the other, waves of migrants, including a few thousand widows, divorcees, and single women, some of them with children, were flowing into the area. Many women were not able to find work, and those who did were not able to support themselves and their children on their pay. During the same period, prostitution in Tel Aviv was concentrated around the seashore and the boardwalk alongside it. In the 1990s the phenomenon of trafficking in women for the purpose of prostitution began in Israel.

Currently, while there are some Israeli sex workers, many women who are victims of trafficking are involved in commercial sex in Israel, with an estimated (by police) 98 percent of them being foreign women. They are primarily trafficked from Uzbekistan, Moldova, the Ukraine, and Russia. Today there are a few thousand prostitutes. (The population of Israel is approximately seven million.) Estimates of the number of women who are trafficked into Israel every year range between 1,000 and 3,000. The women are primarily located in Tel Aviv, Haifa, Eilat, and Beer Sheva, with the largest number located in Tel Aviv. Their presence is felt most strongly in south Tel Aviv where one can find brothels open for business 24 hours a day. Victims of trafficking suffer from **violence**, threats, and **rape** by traffickers, smugglers and clients.

The penal code in Israel specifically prohibits pimping, solicitation for the purpose of prostitution, the managing of **brothels**, and trafficking. However, social norms carry more weight than the law, use of the services of a prostitute enjoys widespread legitimacy in Israel, and a strong distinction remains between prostitution and trafficking, including a misunderstanding of the concept of trafficking. Most people and most law enforcement agencies believe that if a woman agrees to work in prostitution, she is not a victim of trafficking, regardless of abuse or intolerable working conditions. As a prostitute, she is not deemed to be deserving of protection. According to estimates, one million visits a month are made to brothels. In Tel Aviv, although prohibited by law, dozens of brothels are open to the public in the vicinity of two major police stations. Tel Aviv, as the largest center of flesh trade in Israel, is sometimes considered "the brothel of the Middle East." In the Middle East, Tel Aviv is the only city that displays the sex trade publicly, with no religious, legal, or moral holdbacks.

See also Migration and Mobility.

Further Reading: Amnesty International. "Israeli Government Must Stop Human Rights Abuses Against Trafficked Women." http://web.amnesty.org/library/Index/engMDE150242000; Kantorowicz, Liad. "Discrimination and Sex Work in Israel-Palestine." *$pread* (Spring 2005): 20–21; Specter, Michael. "Traffickers' New Cargo: Naive Slavic Women," *New York Times*, 11 January 1998; Vandenberg, Martina. *St. Petersburg Times*, 13 October 1997.

Nomi Levenkron

TEMPLE PROSTITUTION. *See* **Ancient World**; *Devadasi*; **Sacred Prostitution in the Ancient World**; **Sacred Prostitution, Contemporary**.

TEMPORARY MARRIAGE. Temporary **marriage** is a contractual relationship entered into by a man and a woman for an agreed period of time. It is often considered a form of prostitution because the women in these arrangements receive money on dissolution of the union. Temporary marriage was a common feature of many premodern societies in Europe, Africa, and Asia, and the institution remains operational in some countries today.

Temporary marriage was known to the peoples of the Middle East well before the advent of Islam. The practice, known as *mut'a* in Islamic texts, was so common that the prophet Muhammad did not at first prohibit it, deeming it a preferable alternative to more illicit sexual relations for pilgrims, soldiers, and other men enduring extended separations from their wives. Men, married or unmarried, could enter into mut'a unions with unmarried, divorced, or widowed women. The only stipulation was that a woman could not be married, temporarily or permanently, to more than one man at once, whereas men could simultaneously maintain four permanent wives and an unlimited number of temporary wives. Witnesses were not necessary to solemnize temporary marriages, but the duration of the union and the amount of money owed to the woman concerned were required to be fixed before the marriage could be consummated. Furthermore, although mut'a marriages differed from permanent marriage (*nikah*) in that the purpose of the former was expressly reserved for sexual enjoyment and the latter for procreation, the children of both types of marriage were perceived as equal in social standing and inheritance rights. The Sunni sect of Islam later outlawed mut'a on the grounds that the specific circumstances under which Muhammad had allowed the practice were no longer extant, whereas Shiite law has continued to recognize temporary marriages.

The practice of temporary marriage was also prevalent throughout **Southeast Asia** in the premodern period. Local elites would incorporate foreign traders, usually Chinese, into existing socioeconomic networks largely based on familial relationships through temporary marriages with their female relatives, clients, or slaves. Women were responsible for day-to-day marketplace transactions; they were usually related to persons in remote areas with access to a greater selection of raw materials or specialized goods, and their connections to powerful local men enabled them to facilitate trade. In the 16th, 17th and 18th centuries, European traders also engaged in temporary marriages, lasting from a single rainy season to five years in duration, with local women in Southeast Asian **ports**. The women would have their everyday expenses met, learn new languages and customs, and receive cash settlements on the dissolution of the marriage, thus increasing their repertoire of skills to offer their next liaison. Some women in Southeast Asia arranged their own temporary marriages.

Europeans accepted the institution of temporary marriage in Southeast Asia with such ease because of precedent in their own cultures. The Celtic peoples of Scotland, Ireland, and Wales practiced a form of temporary marriage known as "hand-fasting" until the 18th century. According to this custom, men would choose female companions at local fairs with whom they would cohabit for one year and one day. At the end of this period, during which both parties were perceived as a legitimate couple, they could either marry in earnest or separate without reprisal. Until the 18th century, there was no **stigma** attached to a woman who had been a temporary wife in Southeast Asia. Status was actually increased as a result of temporary marriage with Europeans. Multiple sexual partners did not immediately impact the status of women in the premodern period, although this certainly contributed to their construction as exotic and licentious in later periods.

European men came to prefer slave women as temporary marriage partners in Southeast Asia because they were more likely to be obedient, were used to fulfilling sexual and domestic roles without exerting their rights as wives, and were less likely to have recourse to family in the event of mistreatment. Women living as slaves in the households of powerful local men contributed to the incomes of their masters by manufacturing textiles or preparing food later sold in markets. They were also sometimes used as sexual currency, offered to their masters' guests as gestures of hospitality and goodwill. In the 18th and 19th centuries, the association with slavery, perceived as a dishonorable, and the confusion of temporary marriages with prostitution lowered the status of the temporary wife in Southeast Asian societies.

The institution of temporary marriage has been almost universally devalued since the 19th century. *Mut'a* has become synonymous with legalized prostitution in many Islamic countries. Sex workers claim to be Shiite practitioners of mut'a so as to avoid prosecution during the frequent crackdowns on prostitution in Pakistan. Elsewhere in **South Asia** and the Middle East, young girls are tricked into consenting to a mut'a union with a rich man, only to discover that their marriage certificate was falsified and their "marriage" lasted only as long as the consummation. Women who voluntarily enter into mut'a marriages are perceived as advertising that they are no longer virgins and as therefore bringing shame on their families. Temporary marriages continue to be contracted in Southeast Asia between local women and foreign men living in the region. Often, the women who engage in these marriages are perceived as prostituting themselves in return for having their expenses and those of their children met regardless of whether there is genuine affection between the parties.

Some Islamic commentators have heralded the existence of mut'a as an alternative to perceived Western promiscuity. In Iran, temporary marriage (known as *sigheh*) has been advocated as a form of Islamic modernization—a reconciling of tradition with the pressures of the younger generation in the face of changing global attitudes toward sexuality.

See also Religion.

Further Reading: Andaya, Barbara Watson. "From Temporary Wife to Prostitute: Sexuality and Economic Change in Early Modern Southeast Asia." *Journal of Women's History* 9, no. 4 (Winter 1998): 11–35; Haeri, Shahla. "Temporary Marriage and the State in Iran: An Islamic Discourse on Female Sexuality." *Social Research* 59, no. 1 (Spring 1992): 201–24; Nagar, Richa. "Religion, Race, and the Debate over *Mut'a* in Dar es Salaam." *Feminist Studies* 26, no. 3 (Fall 2000): 661–90.

Trudy Jacobsen

TENDERLOIN DISTRICTS. "Tenderloin," a late-19th-century term, refers to an urban vice district characterized by visible **brothels**, gambling salons, saloons, dance halls, entertainment palaces, vaudeville halls, and illicit theatres. In **New York City**, areas such as Bottle Alley, the Bowery, **Five Points**, and Mulberry Bend were identifiably tenderloin districts. The more popular a tenderloin district, the more prime the assignment for corrupt police who would, for a price, provide official protection for prostitutes and toleration of prostitution. By 1916, there were 47 fewer cities with operating vice districts according to an American Social Hygiene Association publication. Whenever one vice district shut down, its occupants migrated to another city, to another Tenderloin.

Further Reading: Rosen, Ruth. *The Lost Sisterhood: Prostitution in America, 1900–1918.* Baltimore, MD: Johns Hopkins University Press, 1982.

Kate Kramer

TENOFOVIR. Tenofovir is a drug used to treat HIV, and it is being tested for efficacy as a preventative for HIV infection. Sex workers in Asia and Africa have been approached about participating in the tenofovir trials. Sex workers in Cambodia who had been approached about participating in the trial held two press conferences and a demonstration at the 2004 International Conference on HIV/AIDS because they received conflicting and inaccurate information about participation and because no provisions for long-term care for HIV infection or side effects of tenofovir were made for trial participants. In an unprecedented historic moment, a tenofovir trial involving sex workers in Cambodia was canceled by the Cambodian Prime Minister Hun Sen for **human rights** reasons. Sex workers have participated in many clinical trials, most recently for drugs intended for use in combating HIV. A number of drug trials have not lived up to ethical standards, but this is the first time a trial has been stopped by a protest by sex workers.

See also Research Ethics.

Further Reading: Kao Tha, Chuon Srey Net, Sou Sotheavy, Pick Sokchea, and Chan Sopheak. "The Tenofovir Trial Controversy in Cambodia." *Research for Sex Work* 7 (2004): 10–11; Loff, Bebe, Carol

Jenkins, Melissa Ditmore, Cheryl Overs, and Rosanna Barbero. "Unethical Clinical Trials in Thailand: A Community Response." *The Lancet* 365, 6 May 2005, 1618–1619.

Melissa Hope Ditmore

TERMINOLOGY. The terminology of prostitution is contested and complicated and often serves to reinforce the **stigma** associated with the profession. Some of the terms most often used in the field (both academically and socially) are *prostitution, sex work,* and *exchanging sex for drugs or money.* These terms refer to commercial sexual services performed in exchange for material compensation. It is called "the world's oldest profession," and some scholars argue that the concept of prostitution is a relatively modern social construction created as an identifiable concept only within the last 200 years. Laura Agustín (2005), for example, argues that the term and identification of the prostitute was invented to create a pathetic victim who required "saving." Before the late 18th and early 19th centuries, Agustín argues, "the buying and selling of sex was treated as one of an array of social offences ... [and] there was no word or concept which signified *exclusively* the sale of sexual services." During this time period, Agustín asserts, middle-class women created the classifications of prostitution and prostitute in order to have someone to "help"—which not only provided employment for these rescuers, but also provided an activity that made these women feel good about themselves. This construction also created a governmental avenue through which these women were able to pass "down" their own values, which were the middle-class values of the family, to those whom *they* identified as prostitutes. By not questioning the "invention" and construction of the term, those who use it continue to reinforce the stigma associated with this term, which in turn can ultimately hurt the lives of the women and men who participate in commercial sex.

Perhaps, then, these "acts" should be defined as commercial sexual services provided for material compensation. And yet even that definition needs to be questioned. Commercial sexual services, and many other types of services, are exchanged for all types of material compensation. The term *prostitution* makes it easy for the reader to categorize the object of the identification. The terms *prostitute, sex worker,* and *victim of sexual exploitation,* among others, in addition to the definition of prostitution (commercial sexual services provided for material compensation), make it easy to identify and categorize certain activities in specific ways. And yet the women, men, and transgendered people who are the objects of this discourse do not easily fall into one category or another. Agustín argues that this category of prostitute, as imposed on a whole person, was never separated out in this way prior to the late 18th and early 19th centuries. Before this, prostitution was one "act" among others in which people participated. At this point in history, the act of exchanging sex for material gain became the identifying mark of these people. And yet there are many other aspects in and of their lives. So even to focus on the word—the identification of *an* act—serves to reinforce the stigma and the identification of people who perform this act, among others, in certain ways.

These terms are also contested in discourses within the framework of **feminism**. Although the term *prostitution* is well known and even used by most people, the term *sex work,* initially coined by **Carol Leigh**, is not used as often in laypersons' conversations. Leigh created this term in an attempt to reconcile the reality of her life and the lives of other women she knew with her feminist goals. Ultimately, she was working to "create an atmosphere of tolerance within and outside the women's movement for women working in the sex industry." Words or phrases such as *prostitute, sex worker,* or *victim of sexual exploitation* are used within these debates, and the choice of words reflects the viewpoint of the speaker. But each "choice" ultimately places the object, based on the definitions and assumptions embedded in the terms, within the dichotomy of victim and agent. The actor either is a victim of others' actions or is his or her own agent of commercial enterprise. Although complicated by many scholars, this victim-versus-agent dichotomy holds fast in many debates. The language positions the speaker on one side or the other of the debate while also positioning the object of the discourse as one who is acting or being acted on. Neither "victim" nor "agent" does justice to the person who is the subject of the discourse.

And yet currently, there are men, women, and transgender persons who are identified as prostitutes, sex workers, or other similar terms. The fact that these words and the transactions these words signify—and do not signify—have been so widely discussed and debated implies that there is a lot still to learn—not only about the transactions and the people who participate in these transactions, but also about the words and their power to define and reinforce these concepts that are so thoroughly contested.

One solution is to continue to talk to the people who are participating in these transactions to better understand how they identify themselves, their actions, and their lives. Rather than being identified by outside groups who have their own political purposes, the people about whom these outsiders speak should be able to identify themselves. And yet simply asking people how they wish to be identified is also political. However, continuing the conversation can encourage a transition from the overtly politicized words of *prostitute* and *sex worker* to new terminology.

International sex "**trafficking**" is also a highly contested term. According to the **Victims of Trafficking and Violence Protection Act of 2000**, international sex trafficking is defined as a commercial sex act that is induced by force, fraud, or coercion or in which the person who is induced to perform such acts has not reached 18 years of age. Based on this concept of trafficking, the sexual acts being exchanged for drugs or money are not consensual. And yet the distinction of offering or withholding consent is not always clear when related to acts of prostitution or sex work. The situations are complicated at best. There are situations in which migrants are tricked into joining the sexual trade but then decide that this is their best option. Others may be aware of the terms of their work but then may find the conditions in which they work unacceptable and are no longer free to leave. Are these cases of trafficking or prostitution? These questions are controversial and complicated, especially as they relate to transnational issues.

Although sex acts exchanged for money have been performed for thousands of years, during the past 10 years within a global, transnational, capitalist context, governments, the media, nongovernmental organizations (NGOs), and individuals have increasingly brought this terminology to the world's attention. The terms are contested because, like the people who supposedly "choose" to perform sexual acts for drugs or money, these people are often defined by only one side of the debate and are often not asked how they wish to be identified or how they understand the situation in which they are participating. Although the definitions of sex trafficking and exchanging sex for drugs or money by choice are very different, various political and academic groups, on the basis of their own moral and political agendas, often conflate the two. And at times, the two are not easily separated. Women and men who are trafficked and forced to perform sexual acts are not free to choose their work and therefore are not identified as sex workers or women and men who trade sex for drugs or money, but as slaves or victims. And women and men who choose to perform sexual acts for any kind of economic gain or security are defined as sex workers.

The language used to identify people who exchange sex for drugs or money is not the language often used by those who are in these positions. The terms ultimately place individuals into predetermined positions, which then allows outsiders to feel more comfortable in that they can know how to better "act on" the situation. Agustín (2002) argues for a framework of migration studies to think about those who work in sex, domestic, and "caring" services and also advocates identifying these women as migrants, which then "allows consideration of all conceivable aspects of people's lives and travels, locates them in periods of personal growth and risk-taking and does not force them to *identify* themselves as sex workers (or as maids, or 'carers,' for that matter)." The language used to talk about these issues is powerful because it represents people's lives and actions while also reaffirming ideologies and belief systems about this work that have existed for hundreds, if not thousands, of years. Exploring underlying roots and ideologies of these terms encourages a deeper understanding, not only of the language itself, but also of the people who participate in these exchanges.

See also Male Prostitution; Migration and Mobility; Slang; Street-Based Prostitution; Venues and Labor Forms.

Further Reading: Agustín, Laura. "The (Crying) Need for Different Kinds of Research." *Research for Sex Work* 5 (2002): 30–32; Agustín, Laura. "Helping Women Who Sell Sex: The Construction of Benevolent Identities." *Rhizomes Neo-Liberal Governmentality: Technologies of the Self and Governmental Conduct* 10 (2005); Agustín, Laura. "Migrants in the Mistress's House: Other Voices in the 'Trafficking' Debate." *Social Politics: International Studies in Gender, State and Society* 12, no. 1 (2005): 96–117; Chapkis, Wendy. *Live Sex Acts: Women Performing Erotic Labor.* New York: Routledge, 1997; Ehrenreich, Barbara, and Arlie Russell Hochschild, eds. *Global Women: Nannies, Maids, and Sex Workers in the New Economy.* New York: Henry Holt, 2002; Leigh, Carol. "Inventing Sex Work." In *Whores and Other Feminists*, ed. Jill Nagle. New York: Routledge, 1997, pp. 225–31; Thorbek, Susanne. "Introduction: Prostitution in a Global Context: Changing Patterns." In *Transnational Prostitution: Changing Global Patterns*, ed. Susanne Thorbek and Bandana Pattanaik. New York: Zed Books, 2002, pp. 1–9.

Jill McCracken

THAÏS. Three famous **courtesans** in the ancient Classical world were named Thaïs. In literature, Thaïs is the name of a main character in the Greek comedy *Eunuchus* (The Eunuch) by Menander (340–290 B.C.E.). She is the prototype of the "hooker with a heart of gold," and she genuinely cares for one of her young admirers and decides do take him under her wing. Only fragments of Menander's play are extant, but a Latin language adaptation by Terentius (who died in 159 B.C.E.) has survived.

According to some ancient historians, including Plutarch (*Life of Alexander*, 38), Thaïs was also the name of an Athenian *hetaira* who accompanied Alexander the Great on his expedition against the Persian empire. In a famous episode, set during a lively banquet in the Persian capital of Persepolis, Thaïs is said to have convinced an inebriated Alexander to burn down the palatial complex, so as to avenge the destruction of her hometown by the Persian king Xerxes, in 490 B.C.E. In 1697, the event was celebrated in English verses (the lovely Thais by his side / Sate like a blooming eastern bride) by John Dryden (1631–1700) in *Alexander's Feast*, an ode for St. Cecilia's Day that was eventually (1736) reset to music by Georg Frideric Handel (1685–1759). In later life, Thaïs became the mistress and possibly one of the wives of Alexander's general Ptolemy, son of Lagos (King of Egypt, as Ptolemy I Soter, from 304 on), with whom she had three children.

Thaïs was also the name of a Christian saint venerated in the East (Feast Day: October 8), but not in the Latin West. According to her legend, Saint Thaïs lived in Alexandria, in Egypt, in the 4th century C.E., where she was feted as one of the most admired courtesans and female entertainers of her day. Her whole life changed, however, the day she met with a Christian hermit, whose name, depending on the source, is given as Paphnutius, Bessarion, or Sarapion, and who converted her to Christianity. Suddenly turning her back on her past life, she withdrew to a monastery in the desert. There, she had herself walled up in a cell, where she subsisted on bread and water and atoned for her sins by spending her waking hours endlessly repeating the same short prayer: "You who created me have mercy on me!" After three years, she was freed from her living tomb and took the veil, but she died within a fortnight.

The traditional story of Thaïs became known in the West through various channels, including *Paphnutius,* a morality play by the 10th-century German Benedictine nun Hrotswitha of Gandersheim, as well as the *Legenda Aurea,* an authoritative collection of lives of saints by Jacopo de Voragine (13th century), in which she is called Thaide.

In 1890, the French anticlerical writer and pamphleteer Anatole France (1844–1924) published his best-seller novella *Thaïs,* which immediately became controversial. In it, Thaïs's path to salvation becomes her spiritual mentor's path to eternal damnation, as he progressively succumbs to her earthly charms, until, in the end, he surrenders to the demon of the flesh, loses all faith, and irretrievably sinks into utter despair. France's version was soon turned into a successful **opera,** *Thaïs,* with a libretto in blank verse by Louis Gallet (1835–1898), set to music by Jules Massenet (1842–1912). It premiered at the Paris Opera, on March 16, 1894. The work remains on the fringes of the repertory: infrequently staged, it has, however, been recorded several times, and one of its set pieces, the "Méditation" for violin, remains a concert favorite.

See also Ancient World; Desert Harlots; *Hetaera.*

Further Reading: Ward, Benedicta. *Harlots of the Desert: A Study of Repentance in Early; Monastic Sources.* Kalamazoo, MI: Cistercian Publications, 1987.

Pierre Marc Bellemare

THEODORA, EMPRESS OF BYZANTIUM (497–548 A.D.).

Wife of Emperor Justinian, Theodora was the daughter of a bear trainer in Constantinople (present-day Istanbul, Turkey). When he died, she became an actress, the equivalent of a prostitute during that time. At 16, she accompanied an official named Hecebolus to Africa and lived there for four years. She later converted to monophysitism, the belief that Jesus was solely a divine being, rather than both human and divine. She left her profession and returned to Constantinople. Theodora married Justinian after his uncle, Emperor Justin I, repealed an old Roman law that forbade government officials from marrying **actresses.** During the Nike revolt, Theodora proved her leadership ability. Justinian and his advisers had prepared to leave the city, but Theodora addressed the government council saying it would be better to die as a ruler than to run and lose everything. She convinced them to fight and helped save the crown. She and Justinian rebuilt the city and their reconstruction of Constantinople included the architecturally outstanding *Hagia Sophia,* the Church of the Holy Wisdom. Though she did not serve as a joint monarch, under her influence **forced prostitution** became illegal, and women gained more rights in divorce cases. She had homes for prostitutes built as well.

See also Ancient World.

Further Reading: Cesaretti, Paolo. *Theodora: Empress of Byzantium.* New York: Vendome Press, 2004; Evans, James Allen. *The Empress Theodora: Partner of Justinian.* Austin: University of Texas Press,

Sarah Bernhardt, as Theodora on throne. Courtesy of the Library of Congress.

2003; Prioleau, Betsy. *Seductress: Women Who Ravished the World and Their Lost Art of Love.* New York: Penguin, 2003.

Anne Marie Fowler

TIPPELZONES. In the late 1980s and 1990s, eight official zones for **street-based prostitution** were designated in the Netherlands. Distinct from the famous windows and **brothels**, these areas were called Tippelzones (*tippelen* is the Dutch word for soliciting on the street). Before the designation of the zones, city governments repressed street sex work. Other prostitution, such as **window prostitution**, has been legal for a long time, whereas **brothels** were only recently decriminalized for European Union residents. For the sake of public order, the police regularly arrested street prostitutes. As a result, women left the original beat and started soliciting in other parts of town. Inevitably, more residential areas were affected by street prostitution and more importantly by the associated impacts, such as drug-related nuisances and associated **crime** and antisocial behavior such as noise and littering.

This repression caused a lot of tension on the street. In periods of frequent police raids, the women were robbed, raped, and assaulted more often. The police force was not altogether happy with their difficult and unsatisfying task. On the one hand they had to arrest the women, and on the other they had to protect them from **violence**. Also, workers from health and welfare services found it difficult to make contact with the women, to build trust and offer services and interventions to them. These circumstances led to social, health, and drug problems as well as to pleading by police officials for the designation of an area where soliciting would be tolerated or even legalized.

Some of these zones had started as tolerance zones; others were official streetwalking zones from the start. The difference between the two is that a tolerance zone is designated by the city council but not formalized in the city bylaws, whereas the streetwalking zones are. In every single case the designation was the result of a complicated, sensitive, and sometimes long process. The most difficult part in each case was to choose a location.

The main criteria for a location for a zone are that it is in a nonresidential area that can provide a reasonable degree of safety for sex workers and that is easy to access by car and by public transport.

Every zone has a shelter, called a "living room," where sex workers can have a break, drink a cup of coffee, eat something, talk with their colleagues (for instance, exchange the features of the cars of dangerous clients), talk to the staff, and buy or get **condoms** for free. On a number of nights, a medical doctor can be consulted regarding **sexually transmitted infections** and general health issues. Drug use is prohibited in the living rooms.

All the zones had a working area, parking boxes where the sexual services can be provided, either in the zone itself or in the direct environment. There is also space to receive clients who come on foot or bicycle. The working area has proven to be very important for both the safety of the women, given that they do not have to leave the surroundings of the zone for desolate places, and the protection of the public—because sex workers and their clients do not go to residential areas for sexual contact.

The police have a key role in the functioning of the zone. In most cities a special and stable "tippelteam" is formed. This is a small group of policemen and women who control the zone and know the area and the workers. The team checks the zone a few times a night, and team members are on call if the project or sex workers need them. They can visit the living room as guests according to the rules of the living room. The presence of the police in the zone is a strong signal to the clients but also to **pimps** and drug dealers. Outside the zone, the police warn and fine sex workers who solicit.

The zones are managed by the municipalities, which means that the city is responsible for the environment of the zone, the (in some cases daily) cleaning and financing of the parking boxes, for example, and the employment of the police team dedicated to the area. The results from the first scientific evaluation of the Tippelzone showed a decrease in violence against sex workers and an enormous decrease in women in police custody and in other legal measures taken against sex workers. Sex workers reported that the zone and the project resources had a stabilizing effect on their lives and were happy that the zone was far from the drug scene because they did not like working next to their competition.

The earliest established zones (in Utrecht, Den Haag en Nijmegen) have encountered fewer problems than the other zones. The first zones were situated in areas where sex work already took place, whereas the others were especially built for the purpose of streetwalking. All but one of the latter were fenced-off areas, only open during the evening and night hours. The areas where the first zones are located function as normal streets during the day. In a sense the first zones are more integrated in society whereas the others are placed outside "normal" life. This major difference in approach had an impact on the functioning of the zone.

The Tippelzones in the Netherlands have been slated to close between 2002 and 2006 for moral, political, and legislative reasons. Factors leading to the closure of the zones include the visibility of drug addicts who work in the zones. Another factor that has contributed to the criticism of the zones is the changed political climate: there is now less sympathy for marginalized groups of people. In addition, brothels have been legalized. Now that brothels are a legal business, people who are working in the European Union illegally are no longer able to work in the brothels, so many migrants have moved to working in the street zones. Critics of the zones have accused the city governments of running an open-air brothel for illegal workers. This has led to greater vigilance about work permits, repression of the sale of hard drugs, and even the closing of some of the Tippelzones. Some cities have responded to the presence of migrants in the Tippelzones by officially or unofficially changing the accepted rule that women were not asked to show identification to enter the zones. This was made official policy in Groningen and Utrecht. Migrants soon learned where they were still able to work, but this was also known to traffickers and other criminals. More and more signs indicated that a large number of women in the zones could be defined as victims of **trafficking** and that criminal activities were taking place in some of the zones and their surroundings.

The zoning discussion since 2003 has conflated the zones themselves with complex social problems that predate the zones, including failed drug policies and migration issues. The successful functioning of a zone is dependent on the policies of police law enforcement. Too much police control and too strict enforcement will make the zone unattractive for a large group (especially drug-using sex workers) to work in. Too little law enforcement will create a "free state" or a "lawless area" where criminal activities such as drug dealing and trafficking can occur. So a balance of clear rules for the sex workers with a show of police restraint needs to be achieved. A stable police team that is committed to the zone and the members of which know the women and their situation can provide this balance.

Although street prostitution policies are a local affair, sex work is not. Developments in one city impact other zones. Therefore, a degree of coordination or at least communication between cities that have a zone is necessary.

The experiences in the Netherlands have shown that public order and the safety and health of street workers as well as public health benefit from zoning. Zones are a good solution to the problems associated with street prostitution, but they are also fragile. Political involvement and commitment cannot stop once the zones are established. Social economic changes in society can have immediate and sometimes drastic effects on street prostitution, and the zones should be in the position to respond to these changes. Ongoing involvement and commitment, not from the local government alone but from all parties, are necessary to have and maintain a well-functioning zone.

See also Addiction; Legal Approaches; Migration and Mobility.

Further Reading: Bernstein, Elizabeth. *Economies of Desire: Sexual Commerce and Post-Industrial Culture*. Chicago: University of Chicago Press, 2006; Molina, Fanny Polanía, and Marie-Louise Janssen. *I Never Thought This Would Happen to Me: Prostitution and Traffic in Latin American Women in The Netherlands*. Rotterdam: Foundation Esperanza, 1998; Vanwesenbeeck, Ina. "Another Decade of Social Scientific Work on Sex Work: A Review of Research, 1990–2000." *Annual Review of Sex Research* (2001); Vanwesenbeeck, Ina. *Prostitutes' Well Being and Risk*. Amsterdam: VU University Press, 1994.

Marieke van Doorninck

TO BEG I AM ASHAMED. *To Beg I Am Ashamed*, the alleged autobiography of a **London** prostitute, "Sheila Cousins," was published in 1938 in London. Review copies sent out to the newspapers were followed by hostile reactions from the *Daily Mirror*, the *Spectator*, and the *Daily Mail*, all of whom were suspicious of its socially redeeming qualities. A purity watchdog group called the Public Morality Council sent a copy to the Director of Public Prosecutions, resulting in the publishers (Routledge and sons) being visited by the police, who threatened them with "serious consequences" if the book was not withdrawn, a demand with which the publishers quickly complied. In 1939, the book was reprinted in Paris by Jack Kahane's Obelisk Press, where it sold briskly to the tourist trade. Richards Press successfully published the book at London in 1953 with no further trouble.

The authorship of *To Beg I Am Ashamed* remained a mystery until quite recently, when an examination of the original publisher's records revealed that it was mostly written by Ronald Matthews, "a failed poet," with the assistance of his friend, novelist Graham Greene. Both men were much addicted to the services of prostitutes, and their shared knowledge and experience of "the life" doubtless contributed to the authenticity that the book portrayed.

See also Memoirs.

Further Reading: Craig, Alec. *The Banned Books of England*. London: Allen & Unwin, 1962; Sheldon, Michael. *The Enemy Within*. London: William Heinemann, 1994.

Patrick J. Kearney

TOKYO. Since World War II, Japan has experienced rapid industrialization, the 1980s bubble economy, subsequent economic contraction, and radical accompanying shifts in demographics, lifestyle, social organization, and popular culture. Technological developments and the postwar affluent worldviews held by many young Japanese have contributed to, among other things, new types of social and sexual relationships, most conspicuously in the capital of Tokyo, one the world's largest metropolitan areas. In dealing with prostitution, Japanese law has struggled to keep up with transforming social realities while framing policy appropriate to Japan's status as a developed nation and leading Asian democracy.

Contemporary Japan's sex and entertainment businesses are collectively known as the *mizu shobai* (literally "water business," a linguistic descendant of feudal Japan's "floating world"). Taking advantage of Japan's legal definition of "sex" as penetration, soft-core "pink salons" (*pinku saron*) feature scantily clad waitresses serving drinks and offering massages, with the options of oral sex or assisted masturbation. "Soaplands" (*So-pu*), in contrast, are a full-service combination of massage parlor, bathhouse, and brothel, at which women perform full-body "assisted baths." Previously called *toruko* (for "Turkish baths"), until growing political correctness motivated a name change, soaplands are located throughout Tokyo (and Japan) with high concentrations in Kabukicho and Yoshiwara (Senzoku 4-chome, the city's former pleasure quarter). For many years, soaplands were the mainstay of full-service prostitution, although since the mid-1990s, increased competition has emerged, particularly from budget-price "fashion health" and *este* ("aesthetic salon") massage emporiums and *deriheru* ("delivery health"), outcall massage services.

At hostess bars women earn excellent wages to chat and sing karaoke with men while lighting their cigarettes and topping off their drinks. Hostessing does not necessarily include sex, though at the hostess's discretion, and with the permission of her boss, she may go on shopping trips and dates with a patron, possibly leading to a more intimate relationship. Bars staffed by male hosts also exist, with clients including professional women, housewives, and female hostesses looking to relax. Many hostess bars feature foreign staff, cashing in on the perceived glamour of women from Western Europe, North America, and Australia. Though even the seedier areas of Japan are generally considered safe, a number of foreign hostesses have been raped, and several have disappeared or been murdered. Because most hostesses work illegally on tourist visas, they generally do not turn to the Japanese government when mistreated by their employers.

Neon signs of "pink salons" that promise sexual massage, "image clubs" for role-play and "soapland" bathhouses are seen among bars and restaurants in Tokyo's Kabuki-cho entertainment district, 2002. Courtesy of AP / Wide World Photos.

Japan's foreign hostesses received international attention in 2001 when a British hostess in a Roppongi club disappeared and was later found dead. The trial prosecuting her death has continued for several years and includes links to the 1992 death of an Australian hostess and a large cache of **rape** videos. Despite this, conditions for Western women are better than the conditions faced by sex workers imported from **Southeast Asia**, Eastern Europe, and Latin America, and hostessing remains a sizable industry, a popular employment option, and a much-discussed cultural feature. Japan's brisk traffic in women from a range of locations and across varying strata of the *mizu shobai* has come under increased attention from **human rights** organizations and advocacy groups in recent years.

Japan has also garnered international attention for restaurants with racy gimmicks, such as *no-pan* (for "No panties") coffeehouses, featuring short-skirted waitresses with no underwear, and specially arranged *nyotai-mori* service in restaurants in which patrons eat sushi off the bodies of naked women. International attention has also centered on novel enterprises catering to fetishists. At image clubs (*imekura*), a variation on the fashion health shops, customers can role-play fantasies in private cubicles with women in costumes such as maid, police, and schoolgirl uniforms in thematically decorated rooms. *Bura-sera* ("bloomer seller") stores sell schoolgirls' worn underpants (for around 5,000 to 8,000 yen per pair). Buru-sera shops (and for a brief period, vending machines) have operated since the early 1990s, but because the Tokyo municipal government banned such stores in 2004 (though underage sellers remain immune from prosecution), many have gone either under or underground. Some commentators have also expressed concern that for teenage girls selling underwear, this may be a first step toward deeper involvement with prostitution.

Enjo Kosai

Teen prostitution, under the name of *enjo kosai* ("compensated dating"), has stirred up domestic and international debate. In this arrangement, high school–age girls date older men in return for gifts, shopping sprees, or cash. *Enjo kosai* (often abbreviated as "enko") emerged with the widespread availability of pagers, cellular phones, and **Internet** access. In the 1980s teenage girls began to meet men through *Tere-kurabu* ("telephone club"), party-line chat rooms, and telephone message services. In the 1990s these were joined (and partially displaced) by online matchmaking (*deai-kei*) sites on which girls can post their cell phone numbers and by the increasing use of mobile messaging and Internet technology. Japan's national police agency affirms that 97 percent of its **child prostitution** cases involve some form of phone dating services.

Surveys conducted by the Japanese Ministry of Health, Labor, and Welfare and by newspapers, university researchers (notably Mamoru Fukutomi of Tokyo Gakugei University), and advocacy groups suggest that *enjo kosai* does exist, though its pervasiveness may often be exaggerated. Estimates of how many Japanese girls have used a telephone service for compensated dating range from 5 percent to as high as 40 percent. Of those engaging in enjo kosai, about 25 percent report having sex with their dates, with 25 percent engaging in other sexual contact.

Although debates over enjo kosai are part of a larger moral panic concerning the erosion of traditional values (in an early 2005 Internet poll, 84 percent of respondents cited a decline sexual morals among Japanese), interpretations vary widely. Some argue that enjo kosai is driven by a craze among young women for luxury brand goods (most famously Louis Vuitton), which can be had by dating older men. In this sense, enjo kosai is an alternative to a low-paying part-time job and a way to support the lifestyle many grew accustomed to during Japan's bubble years. Others cite survey responses that evidence a desire to live adventurous teen years before settling into perceived lackluster adulthoods as housewives. Still others describe enjo kosai as a reasonable rite of passage through which young woman are socialized, through contact with older men, into the conventions of adult romantic relationships. Fukutomi has observed that some teenage girls perceive their schoolgirl image as itself a kind of brand-name glamour, akin to that of high-end merchandise, that can exploited. In this sense, enjo kosai is one element of the widespread sexualization of young women in Japan, reflected by the slang term *loli-kon*, a truncation of "Lolita complex."

Teen prostitution and promiscuity have fed into broader public health issues, such as sexually transmitted infections (STIs) and birth control. Gynecologist Tsuneo Akaeda, who has operated a clinic in Roppongi since 1977 and a free counseling booth since 1999, notes high rates of pregnancy (birth control pills only became available in 1999 and remain difficult to obtain) and STIs (primarily chlamydia) among his patients. HIV/AIDS has also become a greater concern, linked to greater promiscuity and the popularity of Southeast Asian sex tours among men. Legal responses to this include a 1999 law making paid sex with someone under 18 illegal, followed by broader legislation forbidding sex with someone under 18 altogether. Since then, there have been several public scandals involving prominent individuals (including athletes, police, and politicians) who have paid for sex with underage women. Despite legislative efforts, *enjo kosai* shows no signs of slowing down. Additionally, recent studies conducted by universities, law enforcement agencies, and ECPAT, an international advocacy group, suggest that it has taken root in other countries, notably South Korea and Thailand.

Kabukicho and Roppongi

Kabukicho and Roppongi represent two prominent but distinct areas in Tokyo's sex trade. Kabukicho, located to the east of the Shinjuku station (Japan's largest train station), features numerous bars, hostess clubs, pornography retailers, peep shows, **sadomasochism** clubs, and street walkers. After the area was leveled by American bombing raids during World War II, a kabuki theater was planned. It was never built, but the name Kabukicho stuck and the area's ambitions as a modern entertainment quarter took off in other directions. After the passage of laws outlawing prostitution in 1956, previously regulated red light districts went under, and Kabukicho became a haven for officially illegal but tolerated prostitution. Clustered around the northern edge of Kabukicho are "love hotels" (with anonymous check-in, rooms with extensive theme décor, and hourly rates). Also nearby is Shinjuku 2-chome, the center of Tokyo's gay nightlife, and Okubo, a Korean immigrant enclave.

The Yakuza, Japan's **crime** syndicate, have always been well represented in Kabukicho, though recent years have seen increasingly public clashes between Japanese and foreign (particularly Japan-born Korean and Chinese) crime organizations, making it one of the more dangerous precincts in a famously safe city. Increasingly visible crime since the mid-1990s has attracted cleanup efforts from the government and law enforcement. Kabukicho's high percentage of listed foreign residents (around 40 percent) and the high incidence of visa violations has led to the establishment in Kabukicho of a local branch of the Immigration Bureau. Another Kabukicho institution that has received official attention is the formerly ubiquitous group of *kyakubiki* ("customer pullers"), young men who cajole and lure pedestrians into bars (often for surprisingly overpriced drinks they are forced to pay for); police crackdowns since 2003 have thinned their ranks. Although a combination of increased police measures, the installation of extensive street surveillance cameras, and talk of commercial development has made Kabukicho's future seem uncertain, it remains Japan's largest and most renowned pleasure district.

Roppongi ("six trees") is a dense district of approximately two square miles in Tokyo's Minato ward. As far back as the Edo Era (1603–1868), when it served as quarters for samurai, Roppongi has been a barracks area devoted to housing and training soldiers. This continued through postwar occupation, when the district housed American forces, which contributed to the area's international atmosphere and demand for nightlife. Roppongi, sometimes called "foreigners' Kabukicho," features many nightclubs and hostess bars, centering around the neon-lit Roppongi crossing, the intersection of Roppongi Dori ("street") and Gaien-Higashi Dori. Some of the more prominent and longer-lived clubs include Lexington Queen, Disco and Night Club, and Gaspanic, impishly named after the 1995 sarin gas incident in the Tokyo subway. Roppongi's cosmopolitanism also includes more upscale areas, which feature several foreign embassies, the 333-meter-tall Tokyo Tower built in 1959, and, since 2003, the 54-story Roppongi Hills Mori Tower complex. Besides Kabukicho and Roppongi, sex-trade businesses can be found near most major railway stations, many of them enjoying lower rent and less rigorous law enforcement in Tokyo suburbs, such as Machida, and the neighboring prefectures of Kanagawa, Chiba, and Saitama.

Recruitment for sex-industry workers is conducted on the street by aggressive male "scouts" and is also carried out through a number of specialty magazines (some running to hundreds of pages) that attract women with offers of "high-income part-time work." In addition to generous remuneration, the advertisements often offer such perks as "alibi services," which provide women employed in the sex trade with spurious employment documents and other forms of assistance to conceal their activities.

See also Tourism, Yoshiwara.

Further Reading: Allison, Anne. *Nightwork: Sexuality, Pleasure, and Corporate Masculinity in a Tokyo Hostess Club.* Chicago: University of Chicago Press, 1994; Bornoff, Nicholas. *Pink Samurai: Love, Marriage, and Sex in Contemporary Japan.* New York: Pocket Books, 1991; Louis, Lisa. *Butterflies of the Night: Mama-sans, Geisha, Strippers, and the Japanese Men They Serve.* New York: Tengu Books, 1992; Schreiber, Mark, ed. *Tabloid Tokyo.* Tokyo: Kodansha International, 2005;

Schreiber, Mark, ed. *Tokyo Confidential: Titillating Tales from Japan's Wild Weeklies.* Tokyo: The East Publications, 2001.

Alex Feerst

TOUCHING BASE. Touching Base is a grassroots Australian community organization that has been bringing together people with disabilities, sex workers, caregivers, advocates, and service providers since 2000. The first event held by Touching Base was a forum in 2001, cohosted by People with Disabilities New South Wales and the Sydney Sex Worker Outreach Project. Touching Base addresses myths, **stigma**, and discrimination that affect the rights of disabled people to access the sex industry or that marginalize sex workers and their work. Touching Base has developed innovative training programs for sex workers to develop specialized skills to work with clients with disabilities and for service providers to gain increased awareness of the sex industry and access issues.

Touching Base has contributed to a cultural shift in Australian disability organizations by highlighting the sexuality of people with disabilities and the professional ethics applied by sex workers in this field. In February 2004, the Governor of New South Wales launched the Web site http://www.touchingbase.org. As leaders in a developing field, Touching Base trainers and presenters are sought after to provide stimulating workshops and presentations at local and international conferences.

Saul Isbister and Elena Jeffreys

TOULOUSE-LAUTREC, HENRI DE (1864–1901). Henri Marie Raymond Montfa, Vicomte de Toulouse-Lautrec, eldest son and heir of Count Alphonse-Charles de Toulouse, was born to one of the oldest aristocratic families in France. His parents were first cousins, and he inherited most of the infirmities running in the family and was sickly and physically weak. Having broken both his legs at the age of 12, Toulouse-Lautrec remained crippled for the rest of his life. His legs were disproportionately short and he was only four-and-a-half feet tall. Deprived of participation in typical aristocratic physical pursuits such as hunting and horse-riding, Toulouse-Lautrec overcompensated by passionately studying art. He lived in the center of Parisian bohemia, Montmartre, and painted portraits of the common people as well as social outcasts around him: **laundresses**, prostitutes, singers, and dancers. Toulouse-Lautrec frequented **brothels** as a client, which inspired his series of brothel paintings. His paintings demystify the eroticism of the prostitutes and oftentimes focus on the ugliness where others might find beauty or eroticism. His images of women show them as objects, with elements of perversion or degradation, caricatured in anatomically impossible poses, which psychologically might be linked to his own deformity. Another of his interests was lesbian love. He was known to frequent lesbian bars, observing and painting scenes of lesbian affection, which, unlike his images of heterosexual relationships, lack the usual cynicism. Among these paintings are images of prostitutes sleeping together, kissing, embracing, and enjoying each other's bodies. Lautrec's bohemian life and his heavy drinking led to an early death at the age of 36.

The 1952 *Moulin Rouge* movie depicts the life of Toulouse-Lautrec (played by Jose Ferrer) and features many characters from Lautrec's life. The movie emphasizes the discrepancy between the painter's exquisite art and the misery of Lautrec's life as a crippled alcoholic painter unable to find female company except in brothels.

An illustration of Au Moulin Rouge. Courtesy of the Library of Congress.

Further Reading: Cooper, Douglas. *Masters of Art: Toulouse-Lautrec.* New York: Harry N. Abrams, 1983; Frey, Julia. *Toulouse-Lautrec: A Life.* New York: Viking Penguin, 1994; Heller, Reinhold. *Toulouse-Lautrec: The Soul of Montmartre.* New York: Prestel, 1997.

Maria Mikolchak

TOURISM. The stereotypical sex tourist is a white Western man in Asia procuring the services of a very young girl. However, Western women also can afford to pay for sex. An example is the phenomenon of gigolos or "tour guides"—young men who go to tourist destinations, such as Bali's Kuta Beach and now many other places as well, including in the Caribbean and Africa, to pick up Western and Japanese women.

It is clearly easier for both Western and Asian feminists to focus on, and blame, Western "sex tourists" than to acknowledge the local client base (i.e., middle-class husbands, fathers, and so on) and institutional support of most sex industries. Prostitution is thereby placed outside middle-class feminists' own families and surroundings. Sex workers themselves are unable to translate financial independence into political power because of the **stigma** of prostitution and their low status. If the commercialization of sexual desire and pleasure is constructed as sordid and deviant, then these qualities are attached by implication to anyone who "chooses" the occupation.

Many otherwise-staid journals have followed the trend of almost hysterical writing on Asian prostitution. Their articles invariably open with a profile of an extremely young sex worker and a male Western sex tourist. The worker's story involves being coerced into prostitution when underage and ends with the prostitute becoming HIV-positive:

> Sam Nang is not sure how old he is. He thinks he's nine or ten, but he could be younger with his skinny physique.... Sam Nang has one clear memory. He recalls the night last year when a "rich" foreign man approached him outside a nightclub. (Baker 1995, 15)
>
> Twenty-two year old Chantana has the dark circles under the eyes of a drug user. . . . $20 and she is yours. She tells the English man inquiring as to her price that he can also bring the Australian on the next stool. There are no rules. All three leave for her room. (Williams 1991, 73)
>
> At ten, Bo was tricked into prostitution.... Bo endured countless Thai and Western men, including many Australians, whom the brothel owner called "kangaroos." (*Sunday Age*, 18 April 1993 [apparently at 17 Bo was HIV-positive])

Marlon, 12, started his life in Manila as an urchin … Soon [a man] was sending Marlon
to five star hotels where he was sexually abused by foreign tourists. For each encounter he
received gifts and some $20. Most of the money went to the pimp. There are an estimated
60,000 to 100,000 Marlons in the Philippines. (*Asiaweek*, 25 August 1995)
Fourteen year old Mat Srey Mon got her first economics lesson [in] a brothel, and she
says her mother sold her there two months ago for $200. (*Far Eastern Economic Review*,
14 December 1995)

One *Time* special report offers a classic example of such writing, with its "typical" story of a
14-year-old Thai girl sold by her impoverished parents:

When she reached Phuket, a centre for sex tourism, she was forced into prostitution in
conditions of virtual slavery until she was rescued last December by Thai police. But they arrived
too late; Armine has tested HIV-positive and will die of AIDS. (Hornblower 1993)

And the punch line:

Souls do not count, only bodies, debased over and over, unmindful of social cost or disease. Few corners of the world are immune to the burgeoning sex trade. (Hornblower
1993, 28)

In their analyses, these reports usually blame poverty and North–South inequalities as the
cause of oppression and prostitution, typically focusing on Thailand, but recently also crossing
borders as Thailand has become a newly industrialized country that imports as well as exports
sexual labor. The movement of prostitutes within Asia indicates the effects of the patchy economic boom in creating inequalities within Asia "with Indochina as Ground Zero" (*Far Eastern
Economic Review*, 14 December 1995). Elsewhere, Cambodia is described as "the new frontier
for international paedophiles" (Baker 1995, 15).

These news media reports claim that American GI dollars have encouraged the boom
in Southeast Asian sex industries since the late 1960s. Prostitution has spread through the
region as rapacious clients travel to ever more areas for cheap sex. The underlying premises are
that the United States is at fault, that the wealth brought home to the villages is somehow not
real, and that the villagers should not want televisions and videos. Prostitution has brought
devastation, not wealth. For instance, Long et al. (1993: 5–21) report whole regions empty of
children and a generation destroyed either by AIDS or by tourists' passion for maiming and
torturing.

Western literature has focused on Western-oriented bars, so that this small part of the sex
industry has been exaggerated. There are significant differences between the foreign-oriented
business and the indigenous; for one thing female sex workers are often older (rather than young
"virgins") and may have already left a marriage or have some other reason to question or reject
the sexism inherent in their own culture.

The bar work environment can form a supportive subculture for these workers, but the foreign customers need not be seen as purely tourists or "sexploiters." Often, they are long-term expatriates or repeat business visitors. The women are explicitly looking for more than short-time
sex for payment and will seek out older, wealthier men for extended relationships (e.g., contract
wives or *mia chaaw*) and possibly **marriage**. The women speak of these partners in terms of love
and affection, although this has to be seen in the context of cultures of patronage and the material expectations attached to marriage (as in northern and northeastern Thailand). Gigolo, gay,
and street-kid sex-work subcultures also involve seeking older patrons.

Frequent repetition has created a popular "truth" about sex tourism, which mounting evidence about the vast predominance of local clients in Asian sex industries is finally starting to displace. It is quicker to refute such myths in the age of instant communication than in the time of the white slave trade.

See also Child Prostitution; Male Prostitution; Migration and Mobility; R&R; South Asia.

Further Reading: Baker, M. "Guilty or innocents?" *Sydney Morning Herald*, 16 November 1995; Brennan, Denise. *What's Love Got to Do with It?: Transnational Desires and Sex Tourism in the Dominican Republic*. Durham, NC: Duke University Press, 2004; Hicks, R. "Women in Tourism: A Case Study of Bukit Lawang." Honors thesis, Murdoch University, Perth, Australia, 1994; Hornblower, M. "Special Report: The Skin Trade." *Time* 8, no. 25 (1993): 18–19; Law, Lisa. "A Matter of 'Choice': Discourses on Prostitution in the Philippines." In *Sites of Desire, Economies of Pleasure*, ed. Lenore Manderson and Margaret Jolly. Chicago: University of Chicago Press, 1997, pp. 233–261; Long, F., M. Horsburgh, M. Rodgers, and R. Roberts. *Pleasure in Paradise?: Sex Tourism in Asia*. Sydney, Australia: General Synod Office, 1993; Manderson, L. "Public Sex Performances in Patpong and Explorations of the Edges of Imagination." *Journal of Sex Research* 29, no. 4 (1992); Murray, Alison J. *No Money, No Honey: A Study of Street Traders and Prostitutes in Jakarta*. Singapore: Oxford University Press, 1991; Murray, Alison. *Pink Fits: Sex, Subcultures and Discourses in the Asia-Pacific*. Clayton, Australia: Monash Asia Institute, 2001; Odzer, Cleo, *Patpong Sisters: An American Woman's View of the Bangkok Sex World*. New York: Blue Moon Books/Arcade Publishing, 1994; Sancho, N., and M. Layador, eds. "Traffic in Women: Violation of Women's Dignity and Fundamental Human Rights." Manila, The Philippines: Asian Women's Human Rights Council, 1993; Williams, L. "Harlots and Heroin: A holiday in Hell." *Sydney Morning Herald*, 17 March 1991.

Alison Murray

TRAFFICKING. Trafficking involves the movement of persons to exploit their labor. Trafficking in persons is a form of slavery and encompasses debt bondage, peonage, and involuntary servitude. Historically, trafficking of women and children was associated with the capture of young women and girls for **forced prostitution**. Trafficking was originally referred to as "**white slavery**" in the late 1800s when the phenomenon was distinguished from the African slave trade as the sale of women and girls of European descent for sexual servitude. Because of this early definitional connection, many still conflate trafficking and prostitution. The definition of trafficking in persons is still disputed. Some groups, notably a section of the feminist movement, define trafficking as the buying and selling of women and children for sexual exploitation. This definition includes all forms of prostitution, pornography, and any labor in the sex industry and does not require a lack of consent by the women or children involved. This definition assumes that no woman would ever choose to engage in such activity without some form of economic or social coercion. The current international legal definition of trafficking in persons looks not to the industry in which a person works, but to the elements of force or coercion involved in the labor. This definition is much broader, in that it includes forced labor in any industry. However, voluntary consensual labor in the sex industry is not included in this definition of trafficking, given that the element of coercion is central to the current understanding of trafficking.

Trafficking in persons is also often conflated with the smuggling of migrants. Smuggling generally involves one person paying a fee to another person to bring him or her safely across an international border. In this way, smuggling of people is akin to smuggling of drugs or arms. Trafficking of persons may involve the elements of smuggling, but trafficked persons are transported for the purpose of subjection to labor against their will. The relationship between the trafficker and the victim continues far beyond the act of transportation. Smuggling and smuggling debts are often used by traffickers to gain control over their victims, but in a case of smuggling, the relationship between the parties ends once the smuggled person has reached the agreed destination.

Mobility is a common feature of the sex industry, which can cause confusion between trafficking and smuggling and between trafficking and legitimate forms of labor. Work opportunities in the sex industry often require moving between the mainstream economy in the form of porn work, **stripping**, or lap dancing to criminalized activities of prostitution. Prostitutes may also change their locations frequently, often on a circuit between cities or countries.

Trafficking

"Trafficking in persons (refers to) the recruitment, transportation, transfer, harboring or receipt of a person by means of the threat or use of force or other means of coercion, or by abduction, fraud, deception, abuse of power or of a position of vulnerability, or by the giving or receiving of payments or benefits to achieve the consent of a person, having control over another person, for the purpose of exploitation."

Office to Monitor and Combat Trafficking in Persons, U.S. Department of State, Model Law to Combat Trafficking in Persons, Article One, *§100* (2003).

"In situations of captivity" like cases of human trafficking, "the perpetrator becomes the most important person in the life of the victim, and the psychology of the victim is shaped by the actions and beliefs of the perpetrator."

—Judith Herman

J. Herman, *Trauma and Recovery: The Aftermath of Violence- From Domestic Violence to Political Terror* (New York: Basic Books, 1992), 77.

As a result, a prostitute who decides to move to another country to increase her or his ability to find work may be considered by some to be trafficked, even if no or coercion was involved.

Actual figures of the numbers of people trafficked vary widely. According to the United Nations, trafficking in persons involves anywhere from 700,000 to 4 million people worldwide and at least 1.2 million children. The U.S. State Department estimates that 800,000 to 900,000 people are trafficked across international borders every year and that 18,000 to 20,000 of those enter the United States (State Department Trafficking in Persons Report 2003). Most of these trafficked persons are women and children. Many of the figures do not distinguish between trafficking of persons for consensual or nonconsensual sexual services or between the sex industry and other forms of labor.

Trafficked people come from almost every country and from almost every background. However, trafficked persons tend to be from more vulnerable populations within a country, such as ethnic or religious minorities, women, children, disabled persons, the poor, or new migrants to urban areas. Newly uprooted populations, such as persons displaced by armed conflict, natural disasters, or political uprisings, are also particularly vulnerable to trafficking. Social or cultural practices that discriminate against women often lead to an increase in trafficking of women from those areas.

Trafficking occurs into all categories of labor. Besides for sex work, people are trafficked for domestic service, agricultural labor, factory or sweatshop work, restaurant work, construction labor, professional services, and more. Trafficked persons may have legitimate work authorization in that country, or they may be undocumented.

Traffickers may work alone or as a family, or they may be part of large criminal organizations. Trafficking may also occur within loose networks of people, and legitimate businesses or agencies may unwittingly play a part in trafficking. The United Nations estimates that trafficking in persons is the third most lucrative international criminal enterprise, after smuggling of drugs and arms.

Traffickers gain control over their victims through a wide variety of methods. Some people are kidnapped or physically forced to follow the orders of their traffickers. Some are recruited through agencies in their home country that deceive them by promising them good jobs in a more prosperous country and by arranging for their travel, only to force them to work against their will on their arrival. Others are recruited more informally by someone familiar to them. This person may have experience living and working in another country and may be a family member, a boyfriend, or a person from the same town or village as the victim. Some people fall prey to unscrupulous smugglers who force their victims to work to pay off a smuggling debt after they have entered that country. Some people agree to servitude for a certain period of time to pay for a debt incurred by facilitated transportation and entry into another country. Some children are given to traffickers by their parents or guardians in exchange for money, goods, or promises of education, jobs, and a better life for that child.

Trafficked persons are held in servitude to their traffickers by a variety of methods. Often, the traffickers will confiscate the passports or other documentation from their victims to make it difficult or impossible for that person to leave their situation. Traffickers will often use physical **violence**, such as physical or sexual assault, to gain compliance from their victims. Psychological coercion in the form of threats against the victim or the victim's family are often effective. Threats to turn the person in to police or immigration authorities are common. Coercive debt practices also proliferate. Usually the debt is incurred for the transportation of the person to the promised country or promised work, and the victim is then held in the position by an inability to repay the loan immediately. In some cases, the loans may be paid off and the person freed once the debt is completed. In most cases, the traffickers will use excessively high interest rates, deductions from the victims' pay for inflated room and board charges, or unreasonably high payments to ensure that they will be unable to repay that debt.

Trafficking is a phenomenon found throughout the world, but trafficking routes tend to follow certain patterns. Poorer regions that have a net outflow of trafficked persons are known as countries of origin or sending countries, and wealthier regions that have a net inflow of trafficked persons are countries of destination or receiving countries. These areas may be within the same country or in two different countries. Certain countries are also countries of transit, where people are trafficked through, but not trafficked to or from. Some countries, such as Thailand or Mexico, are a combination of all three regions; their own citizens are trafficked to wealthier neighboring countries or wealthier regions within the country, and citizens of poorer neighboring countries are trafficked to their economies and through their lands. Conflict areas often have increased trafficking for the sex industry into and out of the region. Women are often made more vulnerable to trafficking in conflict areas, and military bases are often magnets for voluntary prostitution and trafficked women and children.

Because trafficking is an international problem, countries have developed multilateral treaties and agreements to deal with trafficking. These agreements have taken the form of international treaties such as the 1949 Convention on Sexual Exploitation and the **United Nations Trafficking Protocol**. Methods to combat trafficking have also been agreed on in bilateral agreements between individual countries.

Countries have attempted to prevent trafficking through national laws in a number of ways. One is to place restrictions on the travel of certain classes of their citizens, such as young women. In the United States, this took the form of the **Mann Act**, which criminalized the movement of women across state lines for illicit purposes. In Romania, this took the form of restrictions on international travel of young women. Another prevention attempt is the development of laws that specify a criminal offense of trafficking and the subsequent prosecution and punishment of offenders. A third response is the creation of better economic opportunities for people who are vulnerable to trafficking and the launching of public educational campaigns informing people of the problem. Others have required increased documentation from employers in receiving countries before granting exit visas to their citizens, to verify that the employment opportunity is legitimate.

In most countries, few if any protections exist for trafficked persons. Countries often view trafficked persons simply as undesired illegal migrants, or as criminals, particularly if the trafficked person has been working in the sex industry. Most trafficked persons are summarily deported if discovered by law enforcement as illegal migrants; some countries detain them in prison or jails and may charge them criminally for activities such as working without permission or engaging in prostitution. Trafficked persons may also be subject to discriminatory practices on their return home. They may be imprisoned for having been deported from another country, for leaving the country without proper exit visas or permissions, or for having violated the laws of another country. Trafficked persons may also not have sufficient protections from being retrafficked or from suffering reprisals from the traffickers.

A relatively new development in trafficking that reflects the more recent focus on **human rights** protections for trafficked persons is reporting on the phenomenon worldwide by governmental and nongovernmental organizations. Many human rights organizations such as Human Rights Watch have researchers dedicated to reporting on trafficking in persons in certain regions of the world. Intergovernmental organizations such as the European Union and OSCE have

Women rescued from brothels in Indian cities line up to identify an alleged trafficker at the Maiti Nepal shelter in Katmandu, Nepal, 2003. Courtesy of AP / Wide World Photos.

investigated trafficking within their regions. Governmental entities have also begun to create such reports. Signatories to the U.N. Trafficking Protocol are required to report on their country's efforts to maintain compliance with that agreement. The United States, through the **Victims of Trafficking and Violence Prevention Act of 2000**, is now publishing reports on how every country is responding to trafficking in persons. The countries are ranked into three tiers as to the effectiveness of criminal and human rights laws and enforcement of those statutes, and the countries in the third tier are subject to economic sanctions until they meet certain minimum standards for the prevention of trafficking and the protection of trafficked persons.

See also Migration and Mobility; Trafficking, Politics and Propaganda; Appendix documents 17, 18, 19, and 20.

Further Reading: Global Alliance Against Trafficking in Women Web site. http://www.gaatw.org/; IHRLG Annotated Guide to the Complete United Nations Trafficking Protocol (PDF). http://www.hrlawgroup.org/initiatives/trafficking_persons/default.asp; Skrobanek, Siriporn, Nattaya Boonpakdi, Chutima Janthakeero. *The Traffic in Women*. New York: Zed Books, 1997; Trafficked Persons Rights Project. Introduction to the VTVPA. http://www.tprp.org/resources/index.html; United States Victims of Trafficking and Violence Protection Act of 2000: Trafficking in Persons Report. http://www.state.gov/g/tip/rls/tiprpt/2004/; Wijers, Marjan, and Lin Lap Chew. Trafficking in Women: Forced Labour and Slavery-like Practices in Marriage Domestic Labour and Prostitution. Utrecht, the Netherlands: Foundation Against Trafficking in Women (STV), 1997.

Melynda Barnhart

TRAFFICKING, POLITICS AND PROPAGANDA.

Propaganda is a one-sided, fear based, campaign, and the messages within that campaign attempt to subvert both rational processes and the available reasoning and evidence. It is often based in the negative emotions of hate and fear. For propaganda with a negative message, the arousal and creation of fear in the target audience is a necessary but not sufficient part of propaganda. Additional elements are often attempts to subvert rational processes through discouraging thinking about opposing ideas and evidence, attempts to control whom is accepted as a valid source, attempts to hide evidence from public scrutiny, and the biased selection of information.

In the United States and places subject to its jurisdiction, forced labor except as a punishment for a duly convicted crime has been outlawed since 1865 when the Thirteenth Amendment concerning slavery and involuntary servitude was ratified, adding constitutional status to President Abraham Lincoln's freeing of the slaves in 1863. The Thirteenth Amendment prohibits individuals from selling themselves into bondage. Peonage was defined by the U.S. Supreme Court in 1903 as a condition of enforced servitude by which the servitor is compelled to labor against his or her will to pay off a debt or obligation, real or pretended. In a 1988 ruling on the Slaughterhouse Cases of 1873, the Court held that involuntary servitude occurs when the victim is forced to work by the use or threat of physical restraint or physical injury, including threat of coercion through the legal process, but that psychological coercion is not prohibited.

Trafficking in persons is a form of slavery. The U.S. definition of sex trafficking is "the recruitment, harboring, transportation, provision, or obtaining of a person for the purpose of a commercial sex act," with severe forms of such trafficking taken to be sex trafficking in which a commercial sex act is induced by force, fraud, or coercion or in which the person induced to perform such an act has not reached 18 years of age (U.S. Public Law 106–386 Sec. 103 [8] and

[9]). Thus, sex trafficking involves sexual work that occurs through force, fraud, coercion, or with persons under 18. Minors are forced by definition because they are legally incapable of consent.

Trafficking Allegations as Propaganda

Child prostitution and trafficking in persons arouses great emotional intensity among the public. The intense emotions arising from the discovery of such abuse can and often do lead to a strong desire to rectify the situation and punish the guilty. The strength of these emotions often produces a diminished reliance on cognitive processes and factual evidence among persons immersed in an actual situation of trafficking or child abuse, and consequently leads to a rush to judgment concerning the guilt or innocence of other persons involved. It creates the necessary initial conditions of fear and uncertainty for effective propaganda.

The mere allegation of the existence of child abuse can be and has been used to smear reputations. Such allegations have also served as a propaganda tool to attack political programs, occupational categories, and research results, as well as individuals. Many child care centers, owners, and their employees across the United States were prosecuted for sexual child abuse in the 1980s without credible evidence that such abuse had actually occurred. Many lives and businesses of innocent persons were ruined, and false confessions were obtained from some witnesses. The propagandistic bases of unfounded allegations of child sexual abuse bear similarities to the religious witch hunts in 17th-century Salem and the communist witch hunts of the post–World

Anti-prostitution poster, Ho Chi Minh City, Vietnam. The text reads, "It is necessary to be vigilant (and determined) to check the scourge of trafficking in women and young girls." Courtesy of Angus McIntyre.

War II period in which known Communist spies such as Ted Hall were not prosecuted, but many innocent Americans were hounded and vilified. Cases of sex workers being branded and killed as witches in some countries have been alleged by the United Nations.

Prostitution and other forms of sex work provide remuneration to women for acts they often perform voluntarily without pay. Conservative elements in many cultures have fought against the concept that sexual work is work, arguing that the only acceptable form of sexual activity occurs within **marriage**. Sexual activity occurring outside marriage, as in dating, is frowned on but allowed to exist. Because dating often involves giving items of value, and the likelihood of sex in the relationship is affected by such gifts, less conservative societal elements may see the exchange of something of value for sex as normal. The political attack by conservative moral forces on prostitution as a social evil that must be eliminated is encumbered by this less conservative view, requiring conservative forces to allege a greater evil to attack sex work successfully. Some conservatives believe that the evils of child prostitution and **forced prostitution** do not have to exist. It is sufficient for propaganda purposes to allege their existence in a given instance. The concepts of prostitution as the source of **sexually transmitted infection** (STIs) and of abuse of sex workers by **pimps** are used in a similar fashion.

Although each of the common bases for political attacks on the concept of sex work—child abuse, force, abuse of women, and disease—do occur in specific instances and often with tragic consequences, some conservative forces see the public's perception of the frequency of such occurrences as related to the level of the public outcry against sex work that can be produced. If the perceived frequency of such evils increases in the public mind over and above the actual frequency, the public outcry can be increased and then used to attack what the propagandists want to attack. Thus, as a form of this propaganda, some antiprostitution activists charge that the concept of "voluntary prostitution" is empty, that prostitution is always forced or coerced. Other such activists invent statistics that have no factual empirical basis, suggesting the existence of large numbers and proportions of sex workers who are children or who are forced into sex work. Abuse of sex workers by pimps is presented as standard operating procedure. Data indicating that abuse of wives by husbands occurs more commonly and with greater intensity than abuse of sex workers by pimps are neither presented nor discussed.

Propaganda through equivocation also occurs, wherein the persons involved in sex work are in fact 17, but the implication of the propaganda offensive is that they are far younger children, in addition to there being greater in number. Western audiences do not perceive Chris as a child molester in *Miss Saigon*, though Kim is only 17. But if an audience could be made to believe her to be far younger then Chris would be so perceived, and the goal of the propaganda would be achieved. Thus, although "child prostitutes" usually means older teenagers, the term is presented and used in propaganda as though it refers to small children. The extent to which the transmission of sexual disease is related to the paid-versus-free status of a sexual encounter is overstated in such offensives, and the "relational bond effect"—the strong tendency of persons to use **condoms** with unfamiliar sexual partners and to avoid them as the relationship progresses—is ignored.

Silencing as Propaganda

In addition to media campaigns based on claims of large numbers of trafficked women and children engaged in sex work, propagandistic tactics have included the use or attempted use of political influence to remove speakers who have an opposing view from the list of those scheduled to testify before Congress and at scientific meetings. Other silencing tactics have included drowning out and shouting down those opponents who do appear and alleging ethical violations and incompetence by experts with a different point of view.

One form of silencing works through regulations that either outlaw or severely penalize disagreement with the propagandists' stance. Although the First Amendment makes this unconstitutional in America, the second Bush Administration issued regulations requiring all organizations receiving U.S. funding to take an overt stance against all forms of prostitution in order to receive any financial support from the U.S. government. Every group aiding the poor must agree with a particular government policy or face losing its funding. Similar regulations require agreement with the current U.S. government position on **abortion** and needle exchanges.

The propaganda of silencing opposing views prevents scientific evidence on sex work from being presented and diverts attention from empirical studies of trafficking and from well-designed campaigns against trafficking. This leads to a diminished focus on rational means of reducing and eliminating trafficking in women and children and finding actual child victims, thus allowing actual trafficking to escape undetected or go unpunished. The case of Cambodia provides an example.

Beginning in 1998, publications of the Cambodian government, the United Nations, nongovernmental organizations (NGOs), and foreign organizations discussing the number of sex workers in Cambodia and the number of children involved in this sex work began vastly overstating the numbers involved, reporting 80,000 to 100,000 trafficked sex workers in Cambodia, some 15,000 of whom were said to be children. In 2000, an intelligence monograph published by Center for the Study of Intelligence, an office of the Central Intelligence Agency (CIA), cited a briefing held by the CIA in April 1999 as providing a preliminary estimate, on an unstated basis, of at least 700,000 cross border women and children trafficking victims worldwide each year. This number was later modified to 400,000 women and children, out of 800,000 trafficking victims worldwide. The Cambodian Government and United Nations numbers, when considered with the CIA numbers, would mean that potentially 14 to 25 percent of the world's trafficking occurs in Cambodia, which has only 00.02 percent of the world's population. A similar situation occurred in Thailand in 1988, when a worker for one nongovernmental organization issued an estimate of two million sex workers in Thailand, 800,000 of whom were said to be children. These Thai numbers are still cited by Western print and electronic media as accurate although they have been thoroughly discredited by a Thai government investigation of the time as an urban myth. (Steinfatt, 2002a, pp. 108–9)

The publicizing of these numbers diluted the focus on child workers as they actually existed in small numbers in specific places and created an impression of a society gone berserk with paid child sexual abuse. U.S. Agency for International Development (USAID)–sponsored research (Steinfatt 2002b, 2003) found between 2,000 to 2,500 actual sexual trafficking victims in Cambodia in the early 21st century and 18,000 to 21,000 sex workers, in agreement with AIDS researchers' estimates. When the USAID research was released in 2003, a group of nongovernmental organizations beseeched the British Ambassador in Phnom Penh to intervene with the U.S. Ambassador to quash the USAID research findings. Though a 2004 Asia Foundation International Roundtable on the issue supported the U.S. findings, one nongovernmental organization sponsored a non–research-based paper attacking the USAID results by misstating the methods employed in the research. The NGO then sent a representative to Bangkok, demanding that a scheduled paper identifying and analyzing their own misstatements be removed from the program of the International AIDS Conference of 2004.

Thus the conditions of propaganda that incorporates fear of sex work and sex workers, subversion of rational processes, and attempts to control who is accepted as a valid source and the nature of what constitutes accepted message content are present in many campaigns against sex work.

See also Abstinence; Appendix document 20; Southeast Asia; Trafficking.

Further Reading: Steinfatt, T. *Working at the Bar: Sex Work and Health Communication in Thailand.* Westport, CT: Greenwood Press, 2002a; Steinfatt, T. M. *Measuring the Number of Trafficked Women and Children in Cambodia. Part I of a Series.* Phnom Penh, Cambodia: USAID, Embassy of the United States of America, 2002b. http://slate.msn.com/Features/pdf/Trfcamf3.pdf; Steinfatt, T. M. *Measuring the Number of Trafficked Women and Children in Cambodia: A Direct Observation Field Study. Part III of a Series.* Phnom Penh, Cambodia: USAID, Embassy of the United States of America, 2003. http://slate.msn.com/Features/pdf/Trfciif.pdf; U.S. Senate Committee on Foreign Relations Subcommittee on East Asian and Pacific Affairs. (2003). *Trafficking in Women and Children in East Asia and Beyond: A Review of U.S. Policy.* Washington, DC: Supt. of Docs., Congressional Sales Office.

Thomas M. Steinfatt

TRANSACTIONAL SEX. Transactional sex occurs when something is given in exchange for sexual services. This term is particularly useful to refer to sexual exchanges that are not necessarily between a professional sex worker and a client. Unlike survival sex, in which people with extremely few resources trade sex for food, shelter, and other necessities, transactional sex can encompass less desperate situations. Relationships that are generally referred to as transactional sex include informally compensated sexual exchanges. For example, transactional sex has been used to refer to some "sugar daddy" relationships in which a woman is supported or given presents by a man with whom she has sex. Participants in such exchanges may not identify as prostitutes or sex workers.

In the late 19th and early 20th centuries, the term "charity girls" referred to young women who engaged in sexual relationships in dating situations so as to be taken to places and do things that would otherwise be outside their means. Although practitioners of transactional sex may be viewed as mercenary **gold-diggers**, they may also use transactional sex as a way to move ahead. This is demonstrated in accounts of sex given in return for school tuition or in some cases leading to long-term relationships, **marriage**, and in some cases **migration**.

Transactional sex is a particularly useful to describe situations involving women who offer gifts or payment to male prostitutes. The term "romance tourism" has been used to describe this phenomenon. Female **clients** seem willing to participate in this exchange but may be less likely to conceptualize it as prostitution, whereas the men they pay are clear about their motivations.

Heather Montgomery (1999) described **child prostitution** in Thailand and pointed out that the children very rarely identified as prostitutes but did acknowledge their transactions and relationships. Nancy Luke and Kathleen Kurz (2002) wrote about transactional sex between girls and older men in sub-Saharan Africa. They noted that gifts such as soap, perfume, dresses, meals out, and jewelry have become symbolic of a girl's worth and a man's interest, and girls who do not receive gifts in exchange for sexual relations are humiliated."

See also Male Prostitution; Terminology.

Further Reading: Luke, Nancy, and Kathleen M. Kurz. *Cross-generational and Transactional Sexual Relations in Sub-Saharan Africa: Prevalence of Behavior and Implications for Negotiating Safer Sexual Practices.* Washington, DC: International Center for Research on Women, 2002. http://www.eldis.org/static/DOC11364.htm; Montgomery, Heather. "Children, Prostitution, and Identity: A Case Study from a Tourist Resort in Thailand." In *Sun, Sex and Gold: Tourism and Sex Work in the Caribbean,* ed. Kamala Kempadoo. Lanham, MD: Rowman & Littlefield, 1999, pp. 139–150; Peiss, Kathy. "'Charity Girls' and City Pleasures: Historical Notes on Working-Class Sexuality, 1880–1920." In *Powers of Desire: The Politics of Sexuality,* ed. Ann Snitow, Christine Stansell, and Sharon Thompson. New York: Monthly Review Press, 1983, pp. 74–87; Phillips, Joan L. "Tourist-Oriented Prostitution in Barbados: The Case of the Beach Boy and the White Female Tourist." In *Sun, Sex and Gold: Tourism and Sex Work in the Caribbean,* ed. Kamala Kempadoo. Lanham, MD: Rowman & Littlefield, 1999, pp. 183–200.

Melissa Hope Ditmore

TRANSGENDER SEX WORKERS. Transgender people are disproportionately represented in the sex industry because of employment discrimination that severely limits the economic options of many people who do not conform to standard ideas of male and female gender. "Transgender" is an umbrella term used to refer to identities, expressions, and behaviors that challenge traditional notions of gender and sexuality. Transgender individuals may cross, blur, violate, or transcend the socially constructed division of the world into discrete male/female, masculine/feminine dichotomies. Transgender people do not identify, in varying degrees, with the sex and gender assigned to them at birth. The identity categories that fall under the transgender umbrella include cross-dressers, transgenderists, drag queens, drag kings, transsexuals, genderqueers, and others. Members of the transgender community may or may not seek contra-gender hormonal therapy, sex reassignment surgery, or other cosmetic surgery procedures in an attempt to live in congruence with their preferred gender role. Here are definitions of some of the more common terms.

Cross-dressers, sometimes referred to as "transvestites," are individuals who dress, on a part-time or occasional basis, as members of a gender that does not match their assigned birth sex. Usage of "transvestite" has fallen out of favor because of its excessive clinical, fetishistic, and psychiatric connotations. Reasons for cross-dressing vary widely. Most cross-dressers are heterosexual men, many married with children. Reasons for cross-dressing include sexual release, expression of an alternate gender role, relaxation, and enjoyment of femininity.

Transgenderists are individuals who live full-time in their preferred gender role and may pursue hormonal therapy but do not want or need sex reassignment surgery (SRS). Transgenderism is another point along the gender continuum whereby people live as a gender other than the one assigned at birth but still retain elements of that original gender designation.

Transsexuals are people who desire not only to live full-time in their preferred gender role, but also to have their bodies changed via surgery to make their gender identities and bodies congruent. There are both female-to-male (FTM) and male-to-female (MTF) transsexuals. Transsexuals are often said to be suffering from "gender dysphoria" because there is a fundamental and persistent incongruence between their sex and their gender identity. Transsexuals often do everything possible to live comfortably in congruence with their gender identity. "Gender dysphoria" may change to "gender euphoria" as individuals are able to outwardly express the person inside that they have had to hide for decades because of shame and bigotry. Although some trans people may seek hormones or SRS to become a woman or a man, other trans folks may identify as neither male nor female, or as both.

The genderqueer movement seeks to destabilize traditional roles of male and female and open up space for gender fluidity and multiplicity. *Genderqueer* refers to individuals or groups who "queer" or problematize the dominant notions of sex, gender, and desire in a given society. Genderqueers possess identities that fall outside of the widely accepted sexual binary. *Genderqueer* may also refer to people who identify as both transgender and queer (i.e., individuals who both challenge gender and sexuality regimes and see gender identity and sexual orientation as overlapping and interconnected). Authors such as Kate Bornstein and Leslie Feinberg have both criticized the enforcement of a strict gender binary and endorsed the need for acknowledgement and celebration of the rich tapestry of gender expression found in society.

Transgender Life Experiences

The period during which people change their gender from male to female or from female to male is known as "transition." Although going through transition can be an exhilarating time because the individuals are finally living in harmony with their internal self, it also can be very difficult. Those who break the mold of traditional gender face a variety of serious life challenges.

Transphobia is the irrational fear and hatred of all individuals who transgress, violate, or blur the dominant gender categories in a given society. Transphobia is intimately related to **misogyny** and heterosexism. The hatred of women and the hatred of lesbians, gays, and bisexuals, are forms of gender oppression that may be found under male supremacist patriarchal societies. Transphobic attitudes (such as sexism and homophobia) lead to massive institutional discrimination against gender-variant persons. Such discrimination may manifest itself in the following ways:

1. Employment discrimination. Transitioning on the job can be very challenging for trans people. Often, employers are ill-equipped to correctly deal with a transitioning employee. Trans people report discrimination on the job, and many are fired or demoted after they transition. In addition, finding gainful employment is still a serious concern for trans people. Many employers do not want trans individuals working with their clients, customers, students, or other business acquaintances.

2. Familial rejection. Trans people may be rejected by family members. Trans youth who come out may be rejected by their families and even ejected from the home. This can cause them to wind up on the streets and to become homeless. Although some spouses or partners of trans people stay in the relationship, others leave. The loss of a partner's love and support after many years can be devastating to a trans individual.

3. Housing discrimination. Trans people may have difficulty finding housing as a result of unfounded assumptions by landlords. It is often assumed that trans people are criminals or that they work in the sex industry. **Stigma** against sex workers coexists with transphobia. Trans people may be seen as a "negative" element, the presence of whom will bring down property values or cause a neighborhood to gain a negative image.

4. Police brutality. Although some police departments have received sensitivity training and are better equipped to deal with transgender people, harassment and brutality directed against the trans community by police officers continues. Harassment of trans sex workers can include physical and sexual assault. Transgender people whose gender expression does not match their state-issued identification may be singled out for harassment as well. There is a history of police harassing, baiting, and accosting of transgender

people. Transgender people historically were treated horribly by police when gay and lesbian bars were raided before the 1969 Stonewall Rebellion, the watershed event that sparked the queer liberation movement. Trans women were often sexually assaulted by police and humiliated by entire departments. In addition, they were, and still are, often placed in men's facilities, exposing them to abuse and **rape**.

5. Religious persecution. A transitioning person faces a range of potential treatment from his or her church, synagogue, or mosque. This could range from receiving warm and wholehearted acceptance to being asked to leave and never return. Transgender people face harassment from religious institutions for similar reasons that gays and lesbians do. Some religious doctrines state that cross-dressing or changing one's sex is sinful or evil. Such doctrines state that trans people have no right to change their god-given gender. This type of attitude can take a toll on trans people and cause them to question their religious and ethical beliefs.

6. **Violence** (sexual assault, hate crimes, verbal abuse, physical threats, intimidation). It is estimated that approximately one trans person per month is murdered in a hate-motivated attack. The Web site of the Remembering Our Dead project lists transgender people who have died because of antitransgender hatred and prejudice. Many victims of transphobic violence are MTF, young, and people of color. Some are workers in the sex industry. Some cases involve men having sexual relations with MTFs. Many such perpetrators claim that they discovered the person's biological maleness during or after the sex act and that this caused them to go "berserk." This "gay panic" defense is used by defense attorneys attempting to exonerate their clients. Transgender people are often brutally killed—stabbed multiple times or shot execution style. Trans people also face sexual assault and domestic violence.

7. Culturally incompetent medical and psychological care. Many trans people, especially in rural areas, receive inadequate medical and psychological care. Providers may be unfamiliar with the unique needs of trans clients and, even worse, may discriminate against them. FTM Robert Eads, whose story is told in the poignant documentary *Southern Comfort* (2001), developed uterine cancer and was unable to find doctors willing to treat him because he was a transsexual. Psychologists may also serve as gatekeepers and refuse individuals the authorization needed to access hormonal therapy or sex reassignment surgery.

All of these serious issues can compound the challenge of living as a transgender individual, and each problem can contribute to isolation and be a factor in an individual's entry into the sex industry. A middle-aged MTF transsexual, for example, can face multiple losses during gender transition. She may lose her job, her spouse may leave her, a custody battle may ensue, economic hardships may become serious, and so on. This loss of family and economic stability, coupled with social stigma and bigotry, can lead to a variety of physical, mental, and psychological health issues. Some possible examples include depression; social isolation (loss of friends, spouse, children, parents); substance abuse; suicidal ideation or attempts; use of "black-market" hormones; use of industrial-grade silicone, including dangerous "pumping parties"; self-injury (cutting, for example); and unsafe sex or promiscuity (which could expose the individual to AIDS and other **sexually transmitted infections**).

Further, because of rampant employment discrimination, some trans people may find their job options extremely limited. One way to survive is through participation in the sex industry.

Teens ejected from their homes by transphobic parents, for instance, may find themselves on the street and engaging in survival sex. However, the situations faced by trans people are diverse. Although some may opt for participation in the sex industry out of sheer financial need or desperation, others have more agency in their choices and emerge as empowered sex workers.

The Sex-Industry Worker

The term "sex worker" refers to an individual who earns money by providing sexual services. Like "transgender," the term is an umbrella term to refer to a broad range of sex-industry work, including the work of prostitutes, porn performers, nude models, strippers, peep-show dancers, professional dominatrices, erotic massage providers, phone sex workers, and more.

Carol Leigh, also known as Scarlet Harlot, coined the term "sex work" to avoid some of the negative connotations of words such as "prostitute." To Leigh, the term "sex worker" is "a feminist contribution to the language. The concept of sex work unites women in the industry—prostitutes, porn **actresses**, and dancers—who are enjoined by both legal and social needs to disavow common ground with women in other facets of the business.... The usage of the term 'sex work' marks the beginning of a movement. It acknowledges the work we do rather than defines us by our status" (230). The term "transgender" emerged from within the gender-variant community. Unlike "transvestite" and "transsexual," which are hegemonic, psychiatric terms of reference, transgender is a grassroots term of empowerment and community pride. Similarly, "sex worker" emerged from someone working in the field, and it promotes unity among and between sex workers and functions to destigmatize those engaged in sex for pay.

In our erotophobic and sex-negative culture, individuals working in the sex industry have been stigmatized, discriminated against, and seen as social outcasts and deviants. The terms "slut" and "whore" speak of the pejorative ways that sex industry workers are seen in U.S. society. Because of a patriarchal social structure, women are expected to be chaste, virtuous, and virginal. Expressions of bold, assertive, and "promiscuous" sexuality are condemned by religious and cultural institutions. Many forms of sex-industry work, including prostitution, are illegal in most of the United States. Prostitutes are often arrested, humiliated, and physically and sexually abused by police.

As a result of this persecution, sex workers have organized to demand liberation and empowerment for their community. These efforts have included attempts to decriminalize prostitution and to improve the image of sex workers in the media and in society. Although others countries such as The Netherlands and Germany already have legal recognition for prostitutes, the United States has remained steadfast in its opposition to commercial sex work.

Transgender Sex-Industry Workers

Transgender sex workers engage in many different areas of the sex trade, including being escorts, **call girls** and street-based prostitutes, phone sex operators, strip show performers, and actors in pornographic adult **films**. Trans street prostitutes may work alongside their genetically female counterparts, or there may be a specific section of the city that is known for having trans women offering sex. Trans exotic dancers may "pass" as female and work along side genetic female strippers, or they may work in venues or shows that cater to customers who seek trans dancers. Transsexual woman Rosalyne Blumenstein detailed her experiences working as a peep show dancer at Les Gals in **New York City**: "In the Peeps, anything went as long as there was money to be made on it. 'Changes' [transsexuals] were allowed to work with the other women but I still didn't want to be identified as a 'Change.' There was also a peep show specifically for women with penises. They were marketed as 'she-males.' The adult industry used that term even though many of the women didn't identify with that negative idiom" (139).

Pornography is a multibillion dollar a year industry in America. In any pornography outlet, there is a wide variety of different categories of pornography available for purchase. These different genres, both print publications and videos, include heterosexual, gay male, and "girl-girl" porn, **sadomasochism** porn, and porn featuring a host of different fetishes. One genre of pornography that is a mainstay in many pornography stores is known as "she-male." This pornography is also known as "chicks with dicks," "dolls with balls," "TV/TS," and even "transgendered performances." Although seemingly a small segment of the overall pornography market, this "she-male" pornography is available across the country and globe in pornography retail stores, and it is also widely obtainable online. Both print publications and videos and DVDs are available for purchase and feature transgender women engaging in various sexual acts; the target consumer is almost exclusively nontransgender, heterosexual men. Very little has been written about this subgenre of pornography, and it seems to both intersect with and part company from gay male and heterosexual pornography. The term "she-male" is an invention of the sex industry, and most trans women find the term abhorrent.

Although the vast majority of trans porn features male-to-females, there is a growing body of sex films featuring FTMs. *Linda/Les and Annie: The First Female-to-Male Transsexual Love Story* (1990) is a 32-minute "docu-drama" created by Al Jaccoma, Johnny Armstrong, and **Annie Sprinkle**. It tells the story of a relationship between performance artist and former porn star Annie Sprinkle and FTM transsexual Les Nichols, nee Linda Nichols. There is also a full-length porn film by Asian American transman Christopher Lee entitled *Alley of the Tranny Boys* that puts the graphic sexuality of transmen center stage, as does the recent film *Tranny Fags* by FTM Morty Diamond. *Enough Man* by FTM Luke Woodward features nine FTMs being interviewed about their sexuality and engaging in explicit sex acts for the camera. Buck Angel is one of the most visible FTM porn stars and a successful entrepreneur who runs a Web site (transsexual-man.com) and produces his own videos (*Buck's Beaver*, for example).

Representational strategies are based on different political, social, and cultural ideals. Some believe that promoting pleasurable trans sex in films is an absolute priority in making people see and appreciate trans bodies and trans pleasure. The idea is to make people expand their limited paradigms regarding sex, gender, and sexuality by forcing them to leave their comfort zone and see transgressively gendered bodies engaged in subversive sexual acts.

Most "she-male" porn is directed by non-trans men and produced for the enjoyment of straight-identified men with a particular "fetish" interest. Gia Darling, a MTF porn veteran, is trying to create sexually explicit films that are more respectful of trans women: "Behind most portrayals in tranny porn are men, and there's a lot of 'you dirty-ass-whore' this, 'you-cum-eating slut' that. When I direct a tranny girl porno, I am representing transsexual women, I am representing myself. I take that seriously" (Taormino). Even newer is a groundbreaking porn film featuring sex between an MTF and an FTM. Directed by Gia Darling and starring Buck Angel and MTF star Allanah Starr, it promises to be a cutting-edge sexual representation.

Transgender sex industry workers face many of the things that their non-trans counterparts do: police harassment and brutality, arrests and possible imprisonment, violence from unstable johns, and physical or mental health issues resulting from societal stigmatization. However, transgender sex-industry workers also face specific challenges and issues:

+ Dealing with disclosure of one's gender status to potential clients
+ Transphobic bashings and hate crimes when the birth sex is discovered
+ Brutal harassment from police, including expectation of "sexual favors," sexual assault, and humiliation
+ Stigmatization from the middle-class, or bourgeois, trans and gay community who share cultural disdain for sex industry workers
+ Social service agencies that are unaware of trans issues, identities, and communities
+ Gender segregation in homeless shelters, domestic violence shelters, prison holding cells, public restrooms, juvenile detention centers, and so on
+ Refusals by gender-identity clinics and other "gate-keepers" to assist trans sex workers in their transition, thus withholding much-needed hormones and surgery and forcing sex-industry workers to go to "underground" sources
+ Predominance of black-market hormones and industrial-grade silicone used by MTF sex workers to make their appearance more feminine and marketable
+ Lack of health insurance, job protection, and other benefits
+ Being seen as sexual fetishes by some clients who engage trans prostitutes or use "she-male" pornography
+ Lack of trans-specific outreach for HIV/AIDS education and treatment
+ Dealing simultaneously with the double stigma of being trans and a sex-industry worker in a transphobic, sex-negative culture

Although these challenges are real and often difficult, trans sex industry workers also report many positive aspects to their work. These positive features can include the following:

+ They can gain access to other trans community members through their work.
+ Individuals may be able to earn good money, especially if they are struggling; to find employment in the "straight" world due to transphobia.
+ Individuals have a sense of autonomy and of running their own business.
+ Individuals have access to a diverse range of sexual experiences.
+ Trans women may feel validation for their appearance or beauty from clients in a culture that regularly invalidates them as "fake," "ugly," or "unnatural."
+ Trans men may enjoy interaction with gay and bisexual male clients who find them attractive and validate their masculinity.
+ Trans people value their work, and some find it fun and enjoyable.
+ Non-trans people get to interact with trans people in an intimate encounter and see their humanity up-close and personal, thus breaking down barriers.
+ Trans sex-industry workers may unite with non-trans sex workers and allies in a fight for the **decriminalization** of sex work and civil rights for all gender and sexual minorities.

Global Trans Sex Work

Trans people are engaged in sex work all over the globe for several reasons. Everywhere, there is a market of individuals who wish to purchase sexual services. In particular, there is a subcategory of (mostly) heterosexual-identified men who wish to sexually engage with MTF trans women. These men often find trans women powerfully sexy, alluring, and "exotic." Secondly, trans people across the globe continue to face massive discrimination and oppression. The situation in some Latin American countries, for instance, is particularly serious. Trans prostitutes are regularly murdered, assassinated by police, illegally held in police custody, tortured, and mutilated. Because of prejudice and discrimination, the only professions open to trans women in some countries are in sex work, hairdressing, and female impersonation.

Transphobia also combines with economic impoverishment, which is a result of **globalization** and (post)colonization. Many transgenders in Brazil, known as *travestis*, move temporarily or permanently to European cities such as Milan or Paris to engage in the sex industry there. They can make more money there than in their home country, and there is a class of European men who desire sex with MTF Brazilian transsexuals. In **South Asia**, the transgendered and intersex persons known as *hijras* frequently engage in prostitution for economic survival. Sex **tourism** is an international phenomenon and often contributes profoundly to the local economy.

As in the United States, all over the globe, trans people are demanding their right to a dignified life free of discrimination. Transnationally, transgenders work together for their **human rights** and freedom from violence, harassment, and oppression. Trans women have been known to play active leadership roles in sex-worker activism in the United States and abroad. Sex work is not "the problem" faced by trans people; rather, the problems are pervasive discrimination, impoverishment, and unsafe working conditions.

Some social workers, researchers, and activists have allied themselves with trans sex workers in creating nondiscrimination policies that ban discrimination on the basis of gender identity and expression at the local, state, and national levels as well as in supporting efforts to decriminalize or legalize prostitution at the local and national levels. This is intended to increase job and housing options for transgender people and to reduce the violence faced by transgender people, especially transgender sex workers. There is still a great need to educate social workers and social service providers about the specific needs and experiences of trans and sex-working clients. Trans sex workers continue to be underserved and marginalized by social services, including life-saving HIV/AIDS education programs.

As mentioned, transgender sex workers have produced and performed in films that depict their situations. The best of these include *Yapping Out Loud: Contagious Thoughts from an Unrepentant Whore* (2002), a performance by Mirha Soleil Ross, and historians Susan Stryker and Victor Silverman's *Screaming Queens: The Riots at Compton's Cafeteria* (2005). These cultural productions serve to educate the mainstream society about the realities of trans people and sex workers and demystify their experiences and counter distortions and stereotypes.

See also Migration and Mobility; Murder; Patriarchy.

Further Reading: Amnesty International. *Stonewalled: Police Abuse and Misconduct against Lesbian, Gay, Bisexual and Transgender People in the US*. New York: Amnesty International, 2005. http://www. amnestyusa.org/news/document.do?id = ENGUS20050922002; Blumenstein, Rosalyne. *Branded T*. 1st Books Library, 2003; Bockting, Walter, and Sheila Kirk, eds. *Transgender and HIV: Risks, Prevention, and Care*. Binghampton, NY: Haworth, 2001; Boles, J., and K. W. Elifson. "The Social organization of Transvestite Prostitution and AIDS." *Social Science and Medicine* 39 (1994): 89–93; Bornstein, Kate. *Gender Outlaw: On Men, Women and the Rest of Us*. New York: Vintage Books, 1995; Cullen, J. "Transgenderism and Social Work: An Experiential Journey." *The Social Worker* 65, no. 3 (Fall 1997): 46–54; Feinberg, Leslie. *Stone Butch Blues: A Novel*. Ithaca, NY: Firebrand Books, 1993; Feinberg, Leslie. *Transgender Warriors: Making History from Joan of Arc to RuPaul*. Boston: Beacon Press, 1996; 519 Church Street Community Center. "The Happy Transsexual Hooker." Toronto: 519 Church Street Community Center. http://www.the519.org/programs/trans/index.shtml; Gender Identity

Project Web site. http://www.gaycenter.org/program_folders/gip/index_html/program_view; High Risk Project Society Web site. http://mypage.direct.ca/h/hrp/; Israel, Gianna, and Donald Tarver, eds. *Transgender Care: Recommended Guidelines, Practical Information, and Personal Accounts.* Philadelphia: Temple University Press, 1998; Kulick, Don. *Travesti: Sex, Gender and Culture Among Brazilian Transgendered Prostitutes.* Chicago: University of Chicago Press, 1998; Leichtentritt, R. D., and B. D. Arad. "Adolescent and Young Adult Male-to-Female Transsexuals: Pathways to Prostitution." *The British Journal of Social Work* 34, no. 3 (April 2004): 349–374; Leigh, Carol, aka Scarlot Harlot. "Inventing Sex Work." In *Whores and Other Feminists,* ed. Jill Nagle. New York: Routledge, 1997; Nemoto, T., et al. "Social Context of HIV Risk Behaviors Among Male-to-Female Transgenders of Color." *AIDS Care* (August 2004): 724–735; Network of Sex Work Projects Web site. http://www.nswp.org/; Pettiway, Leon E. *Honey, Honey, Miss Thang: Being Black, Gay and on the Streets.* Philadelphia: Temple University Press, 1996; Prieur, Annick. *Mema's House, Mexico City: On Transvestites, Queens, and Machos.* Chicago: University of Chicago Press, 1998; Remembering Our Dead Web site http://www.gender.org/remember/; Schifter, Jacobo. *From Toads to Queens: Transvestism in a Latin American Setting.* Binghampton, NY: Haworth Press, 1999; Sycamore, Matt Bernstein. *Tricks and Treats: Sex Workers Write About Their Clients.* Binghampton, NY: Haworth Press, 2000; Taormino, Tristan. "Havin' Buck for Breakfast: On the Set of the Groundbreaking Transwoman-Fucks-Transman Porno." *The Village Voice,* 1 September 2005; Wilchins, Riki, Joan Nestle, and Clare Howell, eds. *Gender Queer: Voices from Beyond the Sexual Binary.* Los Angeles: Alyson Publications, 2002.

Films: Aparicio, Carlos, and Susana Aiken. *The Salt Mines.* Frameline, 1990, 47 minutes; Aparicio, Carlos, and Susana Aiken. *The Transformation.* Frameline, 1995, 58 minutes; Davidson, John Paul. *Boys from Brazil.* 1993, 69 minutes; Finch, Nigel, director. *Stonewall.* Fox Lorber, 1999, 99 minutes; Gibson, Alex, and Kirk Streb, directors. *Transgender Teens.* Discovery Health Network, 2003; Goldman, Henrique. *Princesa.* Strand Releasing, 2002, 96 minutes; Goldson, Annie, and Peter Wells, producers. *Georgie Girl.* Women Make Movies, 2001, 69 minutes; Lifshitz, Sébastien, director. *Wild Side.* 2005, 93 minutes; Livingston, Jennie. *Paris is Burning.* Buena Vista Home Video, 1990, 78 minutes; Owens, Brent, director. *Downtown Girls: The Hookers of Honolulu.* A Home Box Office (HBO) Production, 2005, 53 Minutes; Patton, Parris, director. *Creature.* Seventh Art Releasing, 2001, 76 minutes; Stamp, Nicole, director. *Yapping Out Loud: Contagious Thoughts from an Unrepentant Whore.* V-Tape Distribution, 2002, 74 minutes; Stryker, Susan, and Victor Silverman. *Screaming Queens: The Riots at Compton's Cafeteria.* KQED Television, 2005, 57 minutes.

Joelle Ruby Ryan

TRANSSEXUAL. *See* **Transgender Sex Workers.**
TRANSVESTITE. *See* **Transgender Sex Workers.**
TVPA. *See* **Victims of Trafficking and Violence Protection Act of 2000 (VTVPA).**

U

UKIYO-E. Japanese late medieval (Edo period, 17–19th centuries) color woodblock prints called "pictures of the floating world" (*ukiyo-e*) have never been as highly esteemed in Japan as they have been in the West. During the 18th and 19th centuries, ukiyo-e was popular among low- and middle-class people; it was a part of the hedonistic culture of entertainment that flourished in the capital city of Edo (now **Tokyo**) and, to a lesser degree, in Osaka and Kyoto. As Asai Ryoi wrote in *Tales of the Floating World* (*Ukiyo-monogatari*, 1661), "Living for the moment … drinking wine, caring not of poverty, drifting like a gourd along the stream—this is what we call the floating world." The images of this world were of leisurely lighthearted entertainment: picnicking, travels, and Sumo wrestling, but most of all, of Kabuki theater and beautiful women (*bijinga*). The latter became the most popular genre of ukiyo-e prints, and with few exceptions, these women were **courtesans**—from exquisite **geishas** to low-class streetwalkers. Bijinga (literally "pictures of beautiful people") included a certain proportion of male prostitutes shown as young boys or transvestites. Ukiyo-e is rather unique in the history of art in that the women portrayed are mainly prostitutes.

A combination of socioeconomic, political, and religious reasons led to the eminence of the prostitutes' images in ukiyo-e. City dwellers, often well-to-do middlebrow folks of humble origin, were politically deprived and restricted in the rigid society with limited opportunities for social, class, and geographic mobility. Often they had to channel their time and money to a rather narrow range of spare-time activity, such as theater and pleasure quarters. Also, there was a chronic shortage of women in Edo (in some periods the ratio of men to women was 10:1), and sex never had serious connotations of sin. So catching the fleeting pleasures of life basically meant having fun with the fleeting beauty of prostitutes. Prostitutes were considered the very embodiment of the transient world in its Buddhist sense. On a certain level they were closer to the real understanding of the impermanence of life than the major population was because they had less attachment to worldly things—no family, no property, and no permanent relationships, but a succession of transient guests. All this made prostitutes in the traditional Japanese society

Japanese Ukiyo-e print. Courtesy of the Library of Congress.

a counterpart of monks or even the incarnation of religious deities, like bodhisattva Fugen. Often prostitutes were called *Daruma*—after a semi-legendary founder of Zen Buddhism, who was a popular subject in erotic prints ("A Prostitute as Daruma" and "Daruma Crossing the River to Visit Yoshiwara Pleasure Quarters," for example).

Pictures of beautiful women served several purposes in Edo society. They were first seen as illustrations in erotic books (in the fiction genre [*ukiyo-zoshi*], in books on prostitutes and **brothels** [*keisei-mono*], or in sex manuals known as "pillow-books") at the end of the 17th century. Later they were compiled in albums and series of loose leaves (often 12 pictures in a series). They served as promotional pictures of prostitutes in description of **Yoshiwara** brothels and critical catalogs with price lists. Another important use of images of courtesans was as a sexual aid. Men who could not afford to go to the Yoshiwara district frequently would buy a cheap print of a famous geisha and masturbate in front of it. (Women also used prints with portraits of actors for similar purposes). A number of prints bear these "human stains" left by sloppy or ecstatic users. All in all, the cultural atmosphere in Edo Japan made prostitutes, or at least the upper ranks of them, the glamorous objects of desire.

Images of prostitutes and other erotic pictures were called *shunga* ("spring pictures"), *makura-e* ("pillow pictures"), *higa-e* ("secret pictures"), or *abuna-e* ("dangerous pictures").

Most prominent artists of ukiyo-e dedicated themselves to depicting prostitutes and erotic scenes. The father of ukiyo-e, Hisikawa Moronobu (1618/25–1694), left black and white prints with entertainments in Yoshiwara. In the early period (up to the 1760s), prominent artists were the Kaigetsudo family; Nishikawa Sukenobu (1671–1750/1), who illustrated numerous *keisei-mono* books; and Ishikawa Toyonobu. Around 1765, Suzuki Harunobu (1725–1770) invented polychrome "brocade" prints (*nishiki-e*) and depicted extremely young, slender prostitutes, female and male, often distinguishable only by some minor details of their dress or hairstyle. (Around that time young prostitute boys [*yaro*] who worked in special *kodomo-ya* ["boys' houses"] outside of Yoshiwara, were fashionable.)

The end of the 18th and the beginning of the 19th centuries was the best period for ukiyo-e on the whole and for the *bijinga* genre in particular. Many artists, of whom **Utamaro** was the most important, worked at that time. Not so gifted artistically but influential as a writer, Kitao Masanobu (aka Santo Kyoden, 1761–1816) wrote and illustrated about 15 books on brothels and depicted many famous prostitutes with remarkable psychological introspection. That he found each of his wives, O-Kiku and O-Yuri, in brothels perhaps contributed to his intimate knowledge of the subject. Kikugawa Eizan (1787–1867), who was recently attributed with a famous book, *Niku Buton* ("The Mattress of Flesh," c. 1820), his pupil Keisai Eisen (1790–1848), an extremely prolific author of erotic prints, and Hokusai (1760–1849) left their important marks too.

There are numerous and varied iconographic types of depiction of prostitutes and scenes in pleasure quarters, from innocent outdoor views with geishas' processions on Nakanomachi (the main street in Yoshiwara) to coital scenes with greatly emphasized and oversized private parts. Often many seemingly innocent details bear hidden symbolism, such as bare feet with slightly bent toes showing a little from underneath the hem of a kimono, which was considered highly suggestive. A girl walking along the street and biting a corner of her headscarf was advertising her passionate temperament—during sex she had to bite something to keep from moaning and groaning too loudly. A wad of tissues tucked at her sash

Japanese Ukiyo-e print. Courtesy of the Library of Congress.

represented the readiness for sex—by being prepared to wipe her partner and herself after the job. Numerous crumpled tissues scattered on the floor implied a long, steamy orgy. A rolled straw mat under the arm of a street beauty identified her as in the lowest rank of streetwalkers, unaffiliated with any bordellos, who had to perform under the sky, always ready to unroll her portable mattress. There is an extensive floral symbolism; for example, very often in the background of sexual scenes, a branch of plum blossom, associated with sex, is present, or a willow tree at the background demonstrates a submissive role of a woman under it.

Prostitutes and the culture of mercenary carnal pleasure found their ultimate artistic image in the phenomenon of ukiyo-e, and such representation is unparallel in art history. Many celebrated Japanese artists can only be properly understood through consideration of their involvement with *bijinga* and *shunga*.

Further Reading: Hickey, Gary. *Beauty and Desire in Edo Period Japan*. Canberra: National Gallery of Australia, 1998; Screech, Timon. *Sex and the Floating World*. Honolulu: University of Hawaii Press,

Japanese Ukiyo-e print. Courtesy of the Library of Congress.

1999; Swinton, Elizabeth de Sabato, ed. *The Women of the Pleasure Quarter: Japanese Paintings and Prints of the Floating World*. New York: Hudson Hill Press in association with the Worcester Art Museum, Massachusetts, 1996.

Evgeny Steiner

UNIONS. Sex workers all over the world have organized in order to establish civil, human, and labor rights. Around the world, sex workers have less autonomy and control in their work than many other workers do. Most sex-worker organizations believe that for autonomy and control to be established, sex work must be seen as a labor issue and must be established as legitimate work.

Thus, some actors in the global movement for sex workers' rights have used the strategy of aligning themselves with the workers' movements or trades unions' movement. Labor rights are at the center of these organizations' demands. They demand the regulation of the sex industry in a way that ensures that sex workers have occupational conditions enjoyed by workers in other industries. That is, they demand labor rights, sick pay, accident compensation, **occupational safety and health** regulations, and protection from exploitation.

Most sex-worker organizations work in much the same way as unions, even if they do not call themselves unions or are not recognized by the national or international labor movements. They do so by bringing sex workers together and mobilizing and campaigning for rights. For example, The Durbar Mahila Samanwaya Committee (Committee for Co-ordination of Women; DMSC) in India is perhaps the strongest and best-known sex-worker organization. It is better known as **Sonagachi.** The DMSC organizes sex workers and campaigns and negotiates on behalf of its members in much the same way a union would do. It also operates a credit union for its members.

It is difficult to ascertain when the first sex-worker union was established. The tradition may go back to the early 20th century, with attempts in Spain during the nation's civil war.

In the United States, the first successful move toward official unionization came with the establishment of a closed-shop union in a peep show strip club in San Francisco. After repeatedly complaining to management about the lack of security, which allowed clients to photograph and film dancers without their knowledge or consent, some of the dancers at the Lusty Lady requested support from the Erotic Dancers' Alliance (EDA), a sex-worker advocacy group based in San Francisco that put them in touch with the local branch of the Service Employees International Union. As soon as plans for unionization were announced, management removed the one-way glass that caused the filming and photographing problem. But other problems remained: favoritism toward certain dancers, no sick pay, and dismissal of workers based on ambiguous reasons, to name a few. In 1996 the Exotic Dancers Union was formed, and soon after, its members started negotiating a contract with the company. This proved a tiresome, frustrating, and long task. Some months later, they staged a job action to protest against the slow pace at the bargaining table. "No Pink" consisted of a day during which dancers continued to dance nude but kept their legs "demurely closed." The management responded by firing one of the dancers who took part in the action. The dancers retaliated by picketing the club for two days. After that, the company rehired the dancer it had fired and began to cooperate at the bargaining table—discourse about the need to fire long-term dancers was replaced by an offer of a pay increase.

In Argentina, the association of female sex workers AMMAR (Associacion de Mujeres Meretrices Argentinas) has since 1995 been affiliated with the National Workers' Union CTA (Central de Trabajadores Argentinos). This national union counts 1.5 million members. AMMAR has five branches and offices around Argentina, and it is led by sex workers, although it counts on the help and work of technical and professional consultants. Most of AMMAR's members work in **street-based prostitution.** AMMAR has also established a primary school for its members' children. They now demand government recognition as an official union.

In the United Kingdom, sex workers have entered the mainstream union movement through the affiliation of the collective IUSW with the official general union, the GMB. The IUSW was formed in 2000 and started as a small coalition of sex workers from several sectors of the industry and sex-worker rights advocates who came together to plan a demonstration through Soho, **London**'s red light district, on International Women's Day. The group organized to support a strike in protest against a so-called cleanup by Westminster Council, which was seeking to evict local sex workers. The success of the event encouraged the group to continue its campaigning. The IUSW published a bulletin entitled "RESPECT" (Rights and Equality for Sex Professionals and Employees in Connected Trades). After approaching several existing workers' unions and the Trades Union Congress with no positive results, the group was finally successful in March 2002. By affiliating with the GMB, the British general union and one of the main unions in the United Kingdom, the group automatically became recognized officially as part of the mainstream trades union movement. Thus, sex workers based in the United Kingdom have the right to join an official branch of the GMB, the Sex and Fantasy Workers Branch. All genders and sectors of the sex industry are represented in the branch.

Now sex workers are unionized in other countries such as Australia, the Netherlands, Greece, and Sweden.

Further Reading and Viewing: The International Union of Sex Workers Web site. http://www.iusw.org/; *Live Nude Girls Unite!* Documentary, 2000.

Ana Lopes

UNITED NATIONS OPTIONAL PROTOCOL. *See* United Nations Trafficking Protocol.

UNITED NATIONS PROTOCOL TO PREVENT, SUPPRESS AND PUNISH TRAFFICKING IN PERSONS, ESPECIALLY WOMEN AND CHILDREN. *See* United Nations Trafficking Protocol.

UNITED NATIONS TRAFFICKING PROTOCOL. The United Nations Protocol to Prevent, Suppress and Punish Trafficking in Persons, Especially Women and Children (hereinafter, the UN Trafficking Protocol), also commonly referred to as the United Nations Optional Protocol or UNOP), is the primary international agreement addressing the issue of **trafficking**—the transport and trade in human beings for the purpose of exploitation. It is one of three supplementary protocols to the United Nations Convention Against Transnational Organized Crime, along with protocols on the smuggling of migrants and the illicit manufacturing and trafficking in firearms. The Protocol on Trafficking and the main convention were adopted by the General Assembly of the United Nations in November 2000 and opened for signature in Palermo, Italy, the following month (the protocol is sometimes referred to as the Palermo Protocol). The protocol entered into force in December 2003, after reaching the necessary forty-state ratifications.

The convention and supplementary protocols were negotiated in response to intense international concern about the threat posed to national security by transnational **organized crime,** including the **crime** of trafficking in persons. During the 1990s, trafficking in persons—and particularly the traffic in women and children for sexual purposes—attracted growing attention from governments and civil society worldwide, resulting in numerous national, bilateral, and regional antitrafficking policies and programs. The UN Protocol on Trafficking represents the first major international agreement on the actions states should take to combat this problem.

Negotiated at the headquarters of the United Nations Office on Drugs and Crime, the Convention Against Transnational Organized Crime and the Protocol on Trafficking are primarily law enforcement documents. State parties are obligated to take a number of steps in areas such as cross-state information-sharing, measures to combat money-laundering and corruption, the criminalization of organized crime groups, and the confiscation of the proceeds from crime. In addition, the protocol and convention include provisions related to assisting and protecting victims and ensuring them access to justice and compensation. These provisions offer a framework for establishing an appropriate state response to the rights and needs of trafficked persons, though the language in such paragraphs is generally vague and nonbinding.

Another important function of the UN Protocol on Trafficking is providing an authoritative international definition of trafficking in persons. Earlier international conventions, such as the 1949 Convention for the Suppression of the Traffic in Persons and of the Exploitation of the Prostitution of Others and the 1979 Convention on the Elimination of All Forms of Discrimination against Women, condemn trafficking, but without explicitly defining the term. Renewed attention to the issue of trafficking was accompanied by significant definitional debates, and the Protocol on Trafficking responds to some of these disputes.

According to paragraph 3(a),

"Trafficking in persons" shall mean the recruitment, transportation, transfer, harboring or receipt of persons, by means of the threat or use of force or other forms of coercion, of abduction, of fraud, of deception, of the abuse of power or of a position of vulnerability or of the giving or receiving of payments or benefits to achieve the consent of a person having control over another person, for the purpose of exploitation. Exploitation shall include, at a minimum, the exploitation of the prostitution of others or other forms of sexual exploitation, forced labor or services, slavery or practices similar to slavery, servitude, or the removal of organs. (A/RES/55/25, annex II)

The protocol thus makes it clear that for an act to qualify as trafficking, persons engaged in the facilitation of **migration** must use some kind of coercive or deceptive tactic. (An exception is made for children, who are presumed to be trafficked if transported for the purpose of exploitation, regardless of the tactics used.) The protocol goes on to emphasize that if such a tactic is used, the initial "consent" of the victim to the act of migration is irrelevant. And the definition confirms that despite the common emphasis on "sex trafficking," persons can be trafficked into slavery-like conditions in any labor sector.

However, the protocol does not resolve the most contentious definitional issue—the question of what constitutes "the exploitation of the prostitution of others or other forms of sexual exploitation." The legal status of prostitution and of other commercial sexual activities varies significantly between, and often within, countries. Where prostitution is legal, it may be treated like other labor sectors or subject to additional regulations, such as compulsory medical checks. Where illegal, there may be penalties on all participants and all actions or only, for example, on persons who profit from another's prostitution or from the act of soliciting clients. Similarly, women's groups and other nongovernmental organizations hold widely divergent positions on the proper legal treatment of prostitution, and these disagreements have resulted in a sharp divide among those engaged in antitrafficking efforts.

During the drafting of the UN Protocol on Trafficking, state delegates on one side of the debate held that for the purpose of defining trafficking, the term "exploitation" should be reserved for situations in which coercion is used to extract a person's labor, sexual or not. In this view, migrant women who voluntarily engage in prostitution should not be considered victims of trafficking. (Note that this argument was applied only to adults; there is wide agreement that a child cannot consent to sex work or other types of work understood to be injurious to a child's health or development.) Other delegates held that all prostitution should qualify as exploitation because it is inherently abusive, and a woman cannot legitimately "consent" to engage in it. The compromise reached between these two positions is described in the protocol's official interpretative notes (*travaux préparatoires*). According to the notes, "the exploitation of the prostitution of others" and "sexual exploitation" are not defined, and the protocol is "without prejudice to how States Parties address prostitution in their respective domestic laws" (A/55/383/Add.1, note 64).

See also Appendix D, documents 17, 18, and 20; Trafficking, Politics and Propaganda.

Further Reading: Dinan, Kinsey Alden. "Establishing an International Standard for States' Treatment of Trafficked Persons: The UN Anti-Trafficking Protocol and the UN Convention Against Transnational Organized Crime." In "*To Prevent, Suppress and Punish*": *Ideology, Globalization and the Politics of Human Trafficking*, ed. Nancie Caraway. New York: Routledge, in press; Ditmore, Melissa Hope. "Trafficking in Lives: How Ideology Shapes Policy." In. *Trafficking and Prostitution Reconsidered*, ed. Kamala Kempadoo. Boulder, CO: Paradigm, 2005; Jordan, Ann D. *The Annotated Guide to the Complete UN Trafficking Protocol*. Washington, DC: International Human Rights Law Group, 2002. http://www.globalrights.org/site/PageServer?pagename = wwd_index_49; United Nations Office on Drugs and Crime. The United Nations Convention against Transnational Organized Crime and Its Protocols. United Nations Office on Drugs and Crime Web site http://www.unodc.org/unodc/en/crime_cicp_convention.html

Kinsey Alden Dinan

UTAMARO (1753–1806). The Japanese artist, most important master of "pictures of beautiful women" (*bijinga*) on woodblock prints (**ukiyo-e**) was born Kitagawa Yuusuke and adopted the name Utamaro in 1782. He worked for the prominent publisher Tsutaya Juuzaburoo and lived in Juuzaburoo's house opposite the main gate of the **Yoshiwara** pleasure quarters. The images of Yoshiwara women became the major subject of Utamaro's art. Portraits of prostitutes and **geisha** were one of the most popular genres of ukiyo-e for several decades before Utamaro began creating such work, but he perfected the genre. He found in prostitutes the paragon of eternal femininity and immortalized them as highly artistic creatures. In late 1780s he revolutionized bijinga by developing his style of tall and elegant female figures and paying much attention to psychological characteristics of his models. He often depicted only the upper part of the figure ("big heads" type) with an almost empty background and very few details. He did not try to glamorize prostitutes, but rather preferred to show them in various mundane occupations (making themselves up, brushing their hair, taking a bath, drinking, writing letters) and psychological states ("Ten Studies in Female Physiognomy," 1792–93). In "A Collection of Portraits of Reigning Beauties" (1794–95), he showed the most celebrated **courtesans:** Hanaoogi and Takigawa of the ögiya brothel, Komurasaki of the Tamaya, Hanazuma of the Hyoogoya, and so on. In the series "Five Shades of Ink of the Northern Land" (1794–95), Utamaro depicted five ranks of prostitutes of Yoshiwara (situated at the northern outskirts of the capital, it was frequently called the "Northern Country") from the highest *oiran* to the lowest *teppoo*. The latter is the strikingly expressive portrait of a girl, most probably in the moment of her professional activity: with disheveled hair, exposed breast, and absent gaze and biting a handkerchief (to demonstrate her passionate nature). Utamaro also left numerous erotic works of extremely explicit nature ("Ehon Utamakura" [1788], an illustrated pillow book, and about 90 more).

Further Reading: Goncourt, Edmond de. *Outamaro—le peintre des maisons vertes*. Paris: Bibliotheque-Charpentier, 1891; Kobayashi, Tadashi. *Utamaro*. New York: Kodansha International, 1993.

Evgeny Steiner

V

VENICE. Venice, Italy, was an early center of sexual **tourism**. Initially, however, prostitution there was like prostitution in other contemporary medieval urban centers. Prostitution was considered the lesser of sexual evils, and around the 14th century, prostitutes were permitted to practice their trade in municipal **brothels**, such as the "Castelletto" or the "Carampane" near the city's primary commercial district surrounding the Rialto Bridge. Prostitutes also worked at other sites through-out the city, leaving a legacy of landmarks, from the *Ponte delle tette* ("Bridge of Tits") to the *Calle della donna onesta* ("Alley of the Honest Woman"). By the turn of the 16th century, the perception had developed that prostitution was particularly prevalent in Venice; though almost certainly an exaggeration, in 1509, prolific Venetian diarist Marin Sanudo reported that the city's prostitutes numbered in excess of 11,000 (or approximately 10 percent of the estimated population).

The perception, if not the reality, that prostitution had exceeded acceptable limits in the city encouraged waves of governmental legislation and repression throughout the 16th century. In 1539, the city's public health magistracy, the Provveditori alla Sanità (meaning the "Overseers of Health"), was granted jurisdiction over the city's prostitutes in addition to the magistracy's author-ity over the poor and over urban disease-control measures. By order of these public health officials, all prostitutes who had arrived within the last two years were required to depart the city, and those who remained were forbidden from living too close to churches or entering them at those hours when they were also frequented by women of "good and honest condition"; they were also forbid-den from keeping female domestic servants under the age of 30 in their homes. Although the extant mid-16th century documentation indicates that prostitutes were indeed prosecuted for in-fractions of these regulations, the success of the regulations' enforcement is certainly questionable, considering that, beginning in this period, Venice became more famous—not less—for its sexual tourism. According to the anonymous, satirical 1535 poem "Price List of the Whores of Venice" ("La tariffa delle puttane di Vinegia"), a foreigner claims to have come to the city to assuage his "famine of fornication" with the great variety of prostitutes who reside there, "some of whom live in grand houses and some of whom live in whorehouses." Indeed, a social hierarchy of prostitution was already evident, from the city's famously cultured high-class **courtesans** to public prostitutes registered in the municipal brothels to those operating illegally in neighborhoods all over the city to the lowest ranks of streetwalkers. Throughout the early modern period, the Venetian Republic periodically attempted to eliminate these distinctions, together with any temptation courtesans' luxuries might present to "honest" women, through extensive sumptuary legislation. Starting in at least 1416 with the injunction that prostitutes and procurers should wear yellow scarves to identify themselves, sporadic laws throughout the 16th and 17th centuries also attempted to limit their wearing of silk, gold, silver, lace, and pearls.

Although earlier 16th-century Venetian literary sources already extolled the city's sex trade, the first major recorded instance of sexual tourism in Venice was French King Henri III's 1574 visit to the city, at least in part to meet the famous Venetian courtesan-poet **Veronica Franco** (whose fictionalized biography was brought to the big screen as *Dangerous Beauty* in 1998). In 1608, in his travel memoir *Crudities*, Englishman Thomas Coryat claimed that "so infinite are the allurements of these amorous Calypsoes, that the fame of them hath drawn many to Venice from the remotest parts of Christendom." Even as the republic's status as a major political and economic power was on the wane, the city's continued role both as an obligatory stop on the Grand Tour and as a major seaport ensured the persistence of a vigorous sex trade beyond the 18th century until well into the 20th. As Alexandre Saint Disdier insisted in his late–17th-century **guidebook**, it was unclear whether Venice or else Rome boasted the most courtesans, but sometime after 1728, Baron de Montesquieu lamented that a great number of Venetian women lived and dressed like princesses, without any other source of income other than "this traffic." Throughout the 18th century, until the fall of the Republic to Napoleon in 1797, prostitutes were still forbidden in legislation to promenade through Saint Mark's Square, to attend plays or casinos without a mask, to live on or else travel in procession by gondola on the Grand Canal, to wear jewelry, or to otherwise demonstrate their wealth with expensive apartments or possessions, such as opulent furniture.

Although the profession of courtesan seemed to disappear after the fall of the Venetian Republic (because courtesans could no longer depend on the patronage and protection of powerful local noblemen to mediate the city's regulations), from Italian Unification in 1860 until 1958, Venice's brothels nevertheless remained open and legal under Italian law. When, on September 20, 1958, the Italian Republic officially outlawed brothels under the "Merlin law" (named after Lina Merlin

Sixteenth-century painting of a courtesan, by Vittore Carpaccio. The Art Archive / Galleria Borghese Rome / Dagli Orti.

[1889–1979], the socialist senator who sponsored the legislation), around ten "closed houses" (*case chiuse*) or "houses of tolerance" (*case di tolleranza*) were still operating in the city, handling clientele ranging from students, military draftees, and sailors to the elite. After 1958, some of these sex workers transferred to a handful of clandestine brothels throughout the city, whereas others decided to move to an area near Saint Mark's Square called Corte Contarina, which had been associated with Venetian prostitution since at least the 16th century and where they continued to work publicly as streetwalkers until the 1970s. Today, the local sex trade is practiced primarily by non-Italians and occurs principally on the mainland, facilitated there by the availability of automobiles.

See also Clothing; *Grandes Horizontales.*

Further Reading: Barzaghi, Antonio. *Donne o cortigiane? La prostituzione a Venezia. Documenti di costume dal XVK al XVIII secolo.* Verona: Bertani Editore, 1980; Canosa, Romano, and Isabella Colonnello. *Storia della prostituzione in Italia dal quattrocento alla fine del settecento.* Rome: Sapere 1989, 2000; Davanzo Poli, Doretta, et al. *Il gioco dell'amore: Le cortegiane di Venezia dal trecento al settecento.* Milan: Berenice, 1990; Dell'Orso, Claudio. *Venezia erotica.* Florence: Glittering Images, 1995; Dell'Orso, Claudio. *Venezia libertina: I luoghi della memoria erotica.* Venice: Arsenale, 1999; Laughran, Michelle A. "Regulating Bodies: Prostitution and the *Provveditori alla Sanità.*" In "The Body, Public Health and Social Control in Sixteenth-Century Venice." Ph.D. dissertation, University of Connecticut, 1998, pp. 57–104; Pajalich, Armando. "Come nelle fiabe. Per Adele, l'ultima 'battona' veneziana." *Insula Quaderni: Stranieri e foresti a Venezia* 6 (2004): 101–102; Rosenthal, Margaret F. *The Honest Courtesan: Veronica Franco, Citizen and Writer in Sixteenth-Century Venice.* Chicago: University of Chicago Press, 1992; Ruggiero, Guido. *Binding Passions: Tales of Magic, Marriage and Power at the End of the Renaissance.* New York: Oxford University Press, 1993; Ruggiero, Guido, ed. *Storia dossier: La storia della prostituzione.* Florence: Giunti, 1988.

Michelle A. Laughran

VENUES AND LABOR FORMS. Commercialized sexual activities occur at bus stops and on beaches, in **brothels** and bushes, and in barrooms and military barracks, but few researchers have explored the influence of venue on price, safety, meaning, or public health consequences. When prostitution occurs in bush locales, alleyways, or squalid compounds, the absence of safety, soap and clean water, light, or privacy promotes poor sexual hygiene and stigmatization of both the sex and the people who purchase and sell it. Even fewer researchers have considered the ways in which prostitution's many labor forms (for example, streetwalking, brothel, window display, outcall, or **stripping**) are shaped by political, cultural, economic, and technological developments. Even when different types of prostitution are recognized, similarity between the women toiling in them is often assumed rather than demonstrated. Stereotypes and myths abound, such as in the trope in films about streetwalking such as **Pretty Woman,** *Taxi Driver, Miami Blue,* and *Leaving Las Vegas,* that **marriage** will somehow take women out of prostitution.

Prostitution helps to maintain gender, ethnic, colonial, racial, and other relations. In Peruvian brothels, a sort of theater of *machismo,* a broad-ranging culture complex, is enacted. Not all men can fulfill all its requirements, such as to own property, marry well, be respected intellectually, and command a household. However, by patronizing a brothel, a man can demonstrate his masculinity by drinking, engaging in salacious talk, and enjoying styles of intercourse otherwise prohibited, such as *la secretaria,* in which the woman sits "side-saddle" in the man's lap. In the brothels of San José, Costa Rica, by contrast, masculine and (seemingly) heterosexually identified *cacheros*, or men who are paid to have sex with other men, exhibit a dynamic cultural tension between machismo and cacherismo.

Brothels have spatial and temporal parameters that shape and make sex meaningful. For example in Peru, the sexual acts negotiated in nearby alleyways *(callejon)* between roughly 6:00 P.M. and 10:00 P.M. are cheaper, quicker, and less intimate and appeal to lower-class Peruvian males arriving primarily by bus, given that brothels must legally be located outside of town. Sex that occurs in the higher-class *salon* after 10:00 P.M., by contrast, is negotiated by means of alternative conversational styles and involves different entrances, clientele, prices, durations, and frequencies. Women in the streetwalking form of prostitution in Dakar, Senegal, cater to the sexual needs of students, mostly on the spot, atop cars or in the open air, whereas those frequenting Dakar's hotels cater mostly to civil servants, foreigner contract workers, and tourists. Assignations that occur in dismal, poorly lit, and often unsafe brothel compounds, however, are usually anonymous and distinctly unhygienic. Sexual repertoire is limited to vaginal intercourse only (often unprotected by **condoms**), which has been timed by researchers to average about four minutes in duration. Because of dismal working conditions, low pay, and severe police harassment, the turnover of women in this kind of venue is swift.

Whereas the brothels of Cuzco, Peru, are located and regulated so as to keep prostitution away from the public eye and to confirm the general rural/urban divide, brothels in the Nevada counties that permit them are purposely located along major and minor roadways. Geographic location determines both the size of brothels (in terms of the number of employees housed there) and the kinds and variety of sexual and other services that can be provided there—for example, pornography, hot tubs, sex toys, multiple women, and **alcohol**. Historically, locale has shaped the relationship between buyer and seller in Nevada's brothels, too, by upholding racist county laws that allowed black women to sell, but not black men to buy, sexual services.

The Political Economy of Sex Industries

Prostitution's venues and labor forms can reveal much about the time, place, and culture under consideration. "Freelance" prostitution is common wherever resource extraction, migrant agricultural laborers, and military installations (such as in border zones) can be found. "Streetwalkers" and the "hand-whores" in "jack-shacks" and "rub-n-tugs" (massage parlors) are just as common in Costa Rica and St. Louis as they are in **London** and Port Moresby insofar as women who are cut "free" from access to land and the ties of tradition attempt to uphold kinship obligations and failing family fortunes by engaging in prostitution, as during the colonial period in Nairobi, Kenya. The so-called *femme libre* ("free women") of French-speaking Africa who have been operating since the 1960s in slums, canteens, roadside diners and stops, marketplaces, and truck stops generally cater to extremely mobile, distressed, culturally dislocated, often war-torn populations. The state-sponsored and municipally controlled brothels of Argentina and England were common before the AIDS era and were justified by appeal to the alleged social benefits of separating "good" women and sex from "bad," but they are increasingly common nowadays in Thailand, Laos, and Indonesia and justified more in terms of alleged ability to decrease overall HIV transmissions. Bar-style prostitution is common at and near military installations and tourist destinations in the form of "go-go" bars, coffee shops, and teahouses.

Intra- and international sex tourism is increasingly promoted on the **Internet** and aided by developments in digital photography, video conferencing, and e-mail. One Australian company has designed computer software to help brothel owners manage bookings and banking and payment details. For a set fee, some American companies take small groups of men on package tours from New York to Costa Rica, Tijuana, and Nevada to visit sex venues, sometimes under the guise of instructional endeavors or research opportunities for scholars of legal prostitution. Some states function as **pimps** insofar as they sponsor, regulate, and tax brothels, as in Thailand and Indonesia.

The Labor Forms of Prostitution

Sex industries always involve multiple venues and labor forms. Prostitution in pre-revolutionary China was organized by locale, clientele, physical attributes of the women, type and price of sexual activities, and other nonsexual attributes. The most prestigious brothels, or "sing-song houses," housed **courtesans**, the "elite of the profession," who dressed and displayed themselves elegantly, with feet bound, but who were also highly skilled in the entertainment arts. Wine-house, restaurant, and tavern brothels also featured female entertainers, but who were not as lavishly outfitted or displayed. Women in the inexpensive brothels were little trained in the entertainment arts and occupied barely furnished rooms. Flower boats (floating brothels) were anchored along the waterways and equipped with compartments for eating, having sex, and smoking opium. Streetwalking women, usually the poorest of the poor, solicited openly on the street without legal or physical protection.

Particular labor forms spring not just from culture or tradition, but also from the dictates of militarization, capitalism, **globalization**, **religion**, and colonial administration. In colonial Nairobi, the *watembezi* form involved streetwalking women, mostly homeless and runaway, who solicited men in public places and engaged in cheap, anonymous sex nearby. *Malaya* women waited in their own rooms for men to come to them. Because British colonial and capitalist labor demands prohibited the construction of family housing equipped with kitchens, women practicing the malaya form were able to charge for nonsexual items and services, too, such as food, tea, laundry, bathwater, and conversation. *Wazi-wazi* women waited outside the rooms of returning workmen and provided brief sexual encounters at fixed prices. Throughout the American Southwest and along the border between the United States and Mexico, by contrast, Latino and Anglo women follow Latino male migrant laborers from bars and barracks and service them sexually, but without performing further domestic labors. These Latino laborers bond by all having intercourse with the same woman. This is similar to the practice of gang **rape** of prostitutes in Cambodia and Papua New Guinea as a form of male bonding and, some have said, ethnic-boundary maintenance.

The Sex Industry on Daru

The sex industry in Daru, the capital of Papua New Guinea's Western Province, illustrates some of these social and behavioral processes and principles. Since 1893, sailors, missionaries, patrol officers, soldiers, collectors and traders of sea cucumbers and pearl shells, seafood workers, and mining workers and representatives have traveled to and from Daru. Thirty different tribes have migrated to Daru, some having once engaged in sexual networking forms that later became commercialized and exploitative. Economic downturns, cultural dislocations, the flight of expatriates following independence (1975), and worsening access to health and educational services have slowly produced four different, somewhat overlapping labor forms of prostitution.

The "family" form is that in which fathers, brothers, husbands, boyfriends, and male friends of the family, typically members of the Kiwai and Bamu tribes, find generally older, married, wage-earning sexual partners for their daughters, sisters, wives, and girlfriends age 15 to 45. The women engage clients sexually in their own homes, in nearby bush areas, and at guesthouses.

The "freelance" form is engaged in by mostly unmarried, somewhat older Daruan females who exchange sex more or less on their own for money (or promise thereof), alcohol, food, **clothing**, and other material goods and services. They count public servants, businessmen, sailors, and crocodile-skin and sea-cucumber buyers among their customers and hope that customers turn into at least boyfriends if not husbands. The "women with sex broker" form involves some of the same Kiwai, Gogodala, Bamu, and Suki women who work freelance, but on whose behalf well-known brokers solicit businessmen, villagers who have come to Daru to sell marine, riverine, and garden produce, and especially government workers. In addition to free alcohol, food, tobacco, and betel-nut, the broker receives roughly 20 percent of the woman's earnings to provide condoms and protection and to carry beer and food.

The most stigmatizing and brutalizing form of prostitution on Daru is located at and called *sagapari* ("small, mangrove garden"), the Daruan equivalent of a form known throughout Papua New Guinea as *tu kina bus*, or "two-dollar bush prostitution." *Sagapari* is starkly patterned in terms of tribe (until very recently, only Bamu women were involved), locale (a particular bush area), price ($2 by day, $1 by night), and customer (non-Bamu villagers and laborers). Its former location west of the wharf was a mangrove scrub area bordered by tidal creeks and the sandy foreshore strewn with glass and bottle tops. It functioned also as a rubbish dump and outdoor toilet. Sagapari has since been relocated to the other side of the island, between cemetery and swamp.

Daru's sex industry persists in part because of a distressed political economy; male privilege in kinship, marriage, production, and sexuality; and shame and fear about sexual expression.

See also R&R; Street-Based Prostitution.

Further Reading: Do Espirito Santo, Maria Eugeñia G., and Gina Etheredge. "And Then I Became a Prostitute ... Some Aspects of Prostitution and Brothel Prostitutes in Dakar, Senegal." *The Social Science Journal* 41(2004): 137–146; Gronewold, Sue. "Beautiful Merchandise." *Women and History* 4 no.1 (1982): 3–102; Hammar, Lawrence. "Caught Between Structure and Agency: Gendered Violence and Prostitution in Papua New Guinea." *Transforming Anthropology* 8, no. 1–2 (1998): 77–96; Primov, George, and Carolynne Kieffer. "The Peruvian Brothel as Sexual Dispensary and Social Arena." *Archives of Sexual Behavior* 6, no. 3 (1977): 245–53; PSI. "Sweetheart Relationships in Cambodia Love, Sex & Condoms in the Time of HIV." December 2002. http://www.psi.org/resources/pubs/cambodia; Schifter, Jacobo. *Lila's House: Male Prostitution in Latin America*. New York: Harrington Press, 1998; White, Luise. *The Comforts of Home: Prostitution in Colonial Nairobi*. Chicago: University of Chicago Press, 1990; Wilkinson, David, and Gillian Fletcher. "Sex Talk—Peer Ethnographic Research with Male Students and Waitresses in Phnom Penh." Phnom Penh: PSI, 2002.

Lawrence Hammar

VERMEER, JOHANNES (1632–1675).

Johannes Vermeer was a prominent Dutch painter, and several of his paintings depict sexual liaisons and prostitution. One painting, *The Procuress*, of 1657, specifically addresses the monetary sexual exchange, but several other paintings by Vermeer establish sexual tensions between the male–female pairings and hint at sexual impropriety.

Vermeer produced only 35 paintings, the best known of which feature solitary young women in interior settings and contemplative atmospheres. Similar in mood and composition are a handful of paintings that center on the quiet interactions of a young male and female couple, such as *The Music Lesson* or *Officer and a Laughing Girl*. The subjects of these paintings toe the line between decorum and dubious behavior, raising the possibility of sexual relations. Vermeer only subtly hints at these sexual suggestions, through such devices as a smirk, a knowing look, a raised wineglass, or simply the questionable situation of an unmarried woman and man alone together. In Vermeer's genre paintings, or scenes of daily life, the viewer must infer whether the compromised decorum will indeed lead to debauchery.

In an isolated work from early in his career, Vermeer provided a clearer reference to sexuality and prostitution. The main action of *The Procuress* involves a man fondling a young woman's breast as he simultaneously places a coin into her outstretched palm. Also integral to the scene is the procuress, the old woman who establishes and observes the transaction. A smiling fourth figure, possibly Vermeer himself, raises a glass to the viewer and reinforces the licentious nature of the scene.

See also Dutch Masters.

Further Reading: Liedtke, Walter A. *Vermeer and the Delft School.* New York: Metropolitan Museum of Art, 2001; Wheelock, Arthur K., and Ben Broos. *Johannes Vermeer.* New Haven, CT: Yale University Press, 1995.

Rachel Epp Buller

VICTIMS OF TRAFFICKING AND VIOLENCE PROTECTION ACT OF 2000 (VTVPA).

The Victims of Trafficking and Violence Protection Act of 2000 was passed by the U.S. Congress in October of 2000. The purpose of the act was threefold: to prevent **trafficking** in persons via public awareness and economic development programs in other countries, to protect the **human rights** of trafficked persons in the United States, and to prosecute traffickers through new criminal laws. One of the main focuses of this law was trafficking into the "international sex trade" (sec.102 [b][2]). The Trafficking Victims Protection Reauthorization Act was passed by the U.S. Congress in January of 2004 and amended several of the original provisions.

The VTVPA defines a commercial sex act as "any sex act on account of which anything of value is given to or received by any person" (sec.103[3]). Sex trafficking is considered the recruitment, harboring, transportation, provision, or obtaining of a person for the purpose of a commercial sex act (sec.103 [9]). For a person who has been trafficked for sexual activity to be considered for immigration or other federal benefits, the person must also meet the definition of a victim of a severe form of trafficking. "Severe form of trafficking" is defined in two parts: "(A) sex trafficking in which a commercial sex act is induced by force, fraud or coercion, or in which the person induced to perform such act has not attained 18 years of age; or (B) the recruitment, harboring, transportation, provision, or obtaining of a person for labor or services, through the use of force, fraud or coercion for the purpose of subjection to involuntary servitude, peonage, debt bondage, or slavery" (sec.103[8]). A person who is trafficked for commercial sexual activity could possibly meet either part of this definition; however, there is no clear distinction made and certified victims of trafficking are eligible for the same services regardless of which part of the severe forms of trafficking definition is met. A victim of a severe form of trafficking is defined as a person who meets the definitions under sec.103(8), and a victim of trafficking is defined as a person who meets the definitions under either sec.103(8) or (9) (sec.103[13][14]). Thus, the definition of sex trafficking is much broader and does not require the use of force, fraud, or coercion. Sex trafficking under the law only requires the movement of a person for commercial sexual activity.

Under the section dealing with prevention of trafficking, the act sets out the details for Annual Country Reports on trafficking in persons. Countries that do not meet certain standards of combating trafficking are subject to economic sanctions. Some critics describe political use of the annual reports and sanctions. The act created an interagency task force to monitor and combat trafficking in persons and also created an office to monitor and combat trafficking within the State Department. Under the TVPRA, the chair of this office is now a member of the president's cabinet. Finally, the President is required to create initiatives in collaboration with non-governmental organizations to increase economic opportunities for potential trafficking victims in their home countries and to increase public awareness of the problem.

The victim protection section of the act looked first at protection of trafficked persons in other countries and required the State Department and the U.S. Agency for International Development to create programs to assist victims of trafficking in other countries. The act created an entirely new federal program for trafficked persons in the United States, focusing on immigration relief and access to federal benefits for trafficked persons who have been "certified" as such by the Department of Health and Human Services Office of Refugee Resettlement (ORR).

Federal assistance is offered to certified victims of a severe form of trafficking. When a person has received the status of "continued presence," the immigration authorities send a request to ORR for certification of that person for benefits. Another method of certification is a request made by Citizenship and Immigration Services based on a bona fide application for a T visa. The third method, added by the TVPRA, involves a local or state law enforcement agent requesting certification on behalf of a person who is cooperating in a reasonable way in the investigation or prosecution of state or local crimes relating to a situation of trafficking.

The act requires that such certified victims of trafficking be given certain benefits from the federal government, including appropriate shelter and care, access to legal assistance and translation services, and all other federal benefits available to incoming refugees. Therefore, certified trafficking victims may access social services through currently established refugee-resettlement service providers. Grants were established for both local governments and nonprofit organizations to expand their services to include trafficked persons.

Finally, the prosecution of traffickers was enhanced by the creation of a new federal crime of trafficking, following the definition of severe forms of trafficking. The act also enhanced penalties for existing federal **crimes** relating to trafficking, such as peonage and slavery. The maximum penalties for these crimes is now 20 years, with life imprisonment for violations that result in death or involve kidnapping, aggravated sexual abuse, sex trafficking involving force, fraud or coercion of children under the age of 14, or attempted homicide. The act also criminalized the possession or destruction of identification or immigration documents of individuals in order to restrict their movement. The offense of trafficking was added to federal racketeering statutes, and the law allows the federal court to order full restitution for victims.

Aside from the changes noted, the TVPRA also created the possibility for trafficked persons to sue their traffickers in federal court for the damage caused them by the trafficking. Thus, trafficked persons may now seek compensation for personal or monetary injuries done to them by their traffickers.

See also Legal Approaches.

Further Reading: Trafficked Persons Rights Project. "Introduction to the VTVPA." http://www.tprp.org/resources/index.html

Melynda Barnhart

VICTORIAN NOVELS. Although Victorian fiction offers numerous portrayals of fallen women, few novels directly address the problem of prostitution, which was considered unseemly subject matter for a morally proper, impressionable reading public. Novels of the period that discuss the issue share several characteristics. All of them present sympathetic and sanitized depictions of lower-class prostitutes, never directly stating the physical or practical details of the sex trade. To counter the widespread belief that women chose to become prostitutes, writers represented them as victims of socioeconomic circumstance rather than as innately depraved and vicious. Novelists hoped to rouse readers' sympathy for lower-class prostitutes and, in turn, encourage audience participation in reclamation and reform efforts. The novels fall into two categories, the social problem novels of the 1830s and 1840s and the more direct accounts of the 1860s onward. The prostitutes featured in the social problem novels are Nancy in Charles Dickens's *Oliver Twist* (1839), Alice Marwood from Dickens's *Dombey and Son* (1848), and Esther from Elizabeth Gaskell's *Mary Barton* (1848). These characters are constructed as virtuous, humanized variations on the traditional prostitute stereotype. In keeping with the stereotype, each woman succumbs to a violent or disease-induced death, despite attempts made for her rescue and rehabilitation. Although the women are only minor characters, their noble efforts on behalf of the works' major protagonists are crucial to the positive resolution of the primary plots. Novels from the second half of the century likewise incorporate certain traditional, stereotypical elements in their depictions, but they ultimately present a more realistic view of the women's lives and potential futures. Unlike in representations from the social problem genre, in these works prostitutes are the central characters. In Henry Jebb's *Out of the Depths* (1860), the prostitute Mary Smith is the novel's protagonist, as are Mercy Merrick in Wilkie Collins's *The New Magdalen* (1873) and Ida Starr in George Gissing's *The Unclassed* (1884). In these novels, reformed prostitutes do not die violent deaths. In keeping with the social reality of the period, they are reformed and, in the cases of Mercy and Ida, embark on respectable futures.

Early Novels

Early Victorian novelists tailored their subject matter and method of presentation to suit the demands of social propriety and middle-class Christian values. The Victorians looked to their fiction for behavioral guidance; improper subject matter that glamorized vice and **violence** was not considered acceptable for consumption in most middle-class households. The social problem novel provided the perfect vehicle for safely presenting the topic of prostitution in popular fiction. On the surface, these were not novels about prostitution: *Oliver Twist* critiqued the New Poor Law, *Dombey and Son* derided middle-class **marriage** and business practices, and *Mary Barton* addressed the Chartist movement and condition of the poor in industrial Manchester. A prostitute's narrative, however, is embedded in each text. The portrayals of lower-class prostitutes in these works remain true to the social problem genre by offering highly detailed descriptions of the women's wretched living conditions. The causes given for prostitution are likewise true to the social reality of the period, for it is made clear that socioeconomic necessity led these characters to the sex trade. Nancy is born to a life of poverty and is forced into thievery and prostitution by Fagin and Bill Sikes. Esther resorts to prostitution after her lover abandons both her and their illegitimate child. Like Nancy, Alice is born into poverty and is sold into the sex trade as a kept woman by her own greedy mother. Dickens and Gaskell also showed that prostitutes were social victims, not social plagues, by highlighting their extant virtues. Nancy pays with her life for trying to get Oliver away from Fagin and Sikes. Both Jem and John Barton's lives are saved because of the pistol wadding Esther finds and brings to Mary. These displays of virtue induce other characters to attempt rescue efforts. Rose Maylie tries to persuade Nancy to leave Sikes and begin a new life. Similarly, Jem attempts to convince Esther to leave her life of prostitution; at the novel's conclusion, Mary nurses Esther in her final hours. Harriet Carker likewise offers aid to Alice and nurses her as she dies. These relationships between prostitutes and their virtuous counterparts encourage readers to pursue rescue and reclamation efforts of their own accord, illustrating textually that such efforts would be physically and morally safe.

Whereas Dickens's and Gaskell's novels were progressive in their descriptions of prostitutes' lives and called for reform efforts, their method of constructing these characters perpetuated certain stereotypical views. For example, Nancy and Esther paint their faces, mimic fancy dress with their shabby attire, and manifest a love of **alcohol**. Nancy, Esther, and Alice also suffer the traditional prostitute's death. Nancy is beaten to death by Sikes, and Esther dies from illness, as does Alice. Despite their redeeming qualities, Dickens and Gaskell ultimately could not conceive of narratives in which these women survive.

Later Novels

Subsequent renditions of lower-class prostitutes still manifest a certain degree of stereotype. However, these works offer prostitutes as their protagonists. Additionally, these authors resolve the women's fates in a more realistic fashion. In *Out of the Depths*, the prostitute Mary Smith repents, is saved by a clergyman, and receives a marriage proposal, only to die from the pox. Like Dickens and Gaskell, Jebb could not construct an outcome in which Mary survives the effects of her life as a prostitute. Yet the novel is progressive, for it suggests that repentant prostitutes can be found worthy of marriage. Collins elaborated on this idea in *The New Magdalen*, in which the reformed prostitute Mercy Merrick actually marries. She and her husband must immigrate to America, however, because English society deems their union unrespectable. At the conclusion of *The Unclassed*, former prostitute Ida Starr is likewise given hope for future happiness. Although it is uncertain whether she and Osmond Waymark will choose to marry, it is clear that they are both hopeful for a future that they will pursue together.

See also Fallen Woman Trope.

Further Reading: Anderson, Amanda. *Tainted Souls and Painted Faces: The Rhetoric of Fallenness in Victorian Culture*. Ithaca, NY: Cornell University Press, 1993; Basch, Francoise. *Relative Creatures: Victorian Women in Society and the Novel*. New York: Schocken, 1974; Hess, Marcy A. "Discursive Decontamination: Domesticating the Great Social Evil in Early Victorian Novels." Ph.D. dissertation, University of Alabama, 2001; Nord, Deborah Epstein. *Walking the Victorian Streets: Women, Representation, and the City*. Ithaca, NY: Cornell University Press, 1995.

Marcy A. Hess

VIE D'UNE PROSTITUÉE. *Vie d'une Prostituée* by "Marie-Thérèse" is a remarkable short memoir of a French prostitute during the German occupation of World War II. It first appeared in an abridged form in issue 27 (December 1947) of Jean-Paul Sartre's periodical *Les Temps Modernes*. It formed part of a series of existential documents with titles such as *Vie d'un juif* and *Vie d'un Légionnaire*. The following year, the complete text was issued sub rosa in an edition of 1,550 copies, with, as a frontispiece, a facsimile of a page of the original handwritten manuscript. The Olympia Press of Paris published an English translation, which dropped the name "Marie-Thérèse," in April 1955, with the title *I'm for Hire*. The translation is anonymous, but the translation work has been credited to Robert Nurenberg.

For a number of years following the book's publication, there was much speculation as to who the author may have been on the presumed understanding that the name "Marie-Thérèse" concealed the identity of some well-known author with a sense of mischief. Simone de Beauvoir was most often mentioned in this respect, but she made an elegantly phrased denial of the attribution in *La Force de l'âge* (1960). Oddly, the first official American edition of *Vie d'une Prostituée*, published in 1966 as *Memoirs of a Prostitute*, expanded the author's name to "Marie-Thérèse Cointre" and carried a foreword by de Beauvoir.

See also Memoirs.

Patrick J. Kearney

VIOLENCE. Violence against sex workers is pervasive around the world and is a common theme in academic literature and popular fiction and in political debates about prostitution, but the hidden and criminalized nature of prostitution means that reliable statistics are hard to come by. Examples are given here from many parts of the world, but local experience varies with social policy, police practice, and the structure of the sex industry.

Sex workers experience violence from those they encounter while working, such as clients, robbers, and vigilantes; from those who organize or control sex work, such as brothel managers, traffickers, and police; and from other sex workers, drug dealers, acquaintances, and partners. However, sex workers' risk of violence is variable and depends greatly on the individuals' method of work (e.g., whether indoors or outdoors, whether alone or with others). It also depends on the response of police and courts to these crimes, on the extent to which legislation exposes sex workers to violence, and on societal attitudes toward them.

Most research focuses on female sex workers, but violence, including serial killings, against male and **transgender sex workers** has also been documented.

Legal Frameworks

To avoid police attention, street-based sex workers make hurried deals with clients, leaving little time to negotiate prices and services (disagreements later can lead to violence) or to assess whether the client is likely to turn violent. If they have nowhere else to take **clients** for sex, they are forced into dark, isolated places where they can be attacked with impunity. A recent survey of street workers in **New York City** found that 80 percent had experienced either violence or threats in the course of their work (Thukral and Ditmore). More than 80 percent of Ugandan sex workers said clients had used violence to force them into unsafe sex (S. Sentumbwe, D. S. Nakkazi, N. Nantege), and similarly high rates have been found in many other places. Indoor work is usually safer, especially if there are other people close by to help if there is trouble. But antibrothel legislation criminalizes group working, and receptionists and "minders" can be prosecuted for controlling or profiting from prostitution. Consequently many sex workers operate alone. Thus, laws aimed at eliminating or controlling prostitution promote sex workers' vulnerability by forcing them to operate in risky ways and in dangerous places. Such laws also inhibit them from reporting violence to the police, allowing for repeat victimization and escalation of attacks.

Laws that relate to sexual violence can also fail to offer sex workers protection or redress. Most legal codes define a sexual assault in terms of the victim's lack of consent to a sexual act. When a sex worker alleges sexual assault against a client, the assailant will claim consent was given. Police, courts, and jurors may believe that, by offering sex for sale, the victim has forfeited the right to refuse any partner or any sexual practice. Although such beliefs are not reflected in modern legal principles, they frequently underlie acquittals or lenient sentences when the victim is a sex worker.

Law Enforcement Tactics

Antiprostitution drives, even when intended to tackle abuse within the sex industry, frequently increase sex workers' vulnerability to violence. Sex workers often change their place or style of working in response to crackdowns, so that the benefits of experience in identifying dangerous people or situations are lost. Sex workers may also be forced into environments that are intrinsically more dangerous. For example, in 2003, reports of widespread gang rapes of sex workers in Cambodia were linked to a government campaign to close **brothels**, forcing many more sex workers onto the streets.

In some countries, police target clients instead of (or as well as) sex workers, but when client numbers are reduced, sex workers have to take more risks, working longer hours and in more dangerous places, to make up for loss of earnings; clients may commit revenge attacks on sex workers whom they blame because they have been arrested or because they have been robbed by sex workers made desperate by the reduction in numbers of clients.

Social Attitudes: Impact on Vulnerability

Those who attack or kill sex workers often rationalize their violence with beliefs that sex workers are worthless human beings and deserving of punishment. Sometimes these beliefs are linked to **religion**; for example, in Iran in 2001, Saeed Hanaie, later hanged for killing 16 sex workers, said he "killed the women for the sake of God, and for the protection of my religion because they were prostitutes and were corrupting other people."

Fear of AIDS, often fueled by anti-vice and "educational" campaigns that blame sex workers for HIV transmission, can also lead to violence against sex workers. In Nepal, researchers found that fear-based messages, emphasizing links between **trafficking**, prostitution, and HIV, resulted in condemnation of trafficked women and girls for bringing HIV/AIDS into their communities on their return, to the extent that "94.0% of adolescent girls report that communities regard returnees with hate" (Sharma Mahendra 2002).

The common antiprostitution rhetoric of "respectable citizens" may also promote a climate of hate toward sex workers, making attacks more likely. Lowman (2000) described this "discourse of disposal," such as the demands to "clean up the streets" used by Canadian media and action groups opposed to street prostitution. He found associations between the intensity of such rhetoric and the incidence of sex-worker murders, suggesting that the social acceptability of using language that equates sex workers with rubbish, polluting the rest of society, legitimizes the actions of those who attack and kill them.

Attackers who claim to be on a mission to "cleanse society" can be highly dangerous, as can those who derive sexual satisfaction from hurting another person. However, aggression from clients during sexual encounters is more commonly related to disputes about sexual practice, money, or condom use, all of which suggest that the attacker resents the commercial nature of the transaction, refusing to accept the sex worker's rules on what she or he will do, for how long, and for how much. Clients' **alcohol** or drug use, often leading to inability get an erection or ejaculate, may also trigger attacks.

Despite these rationalizations, many attacks happen for no apparent reason. The strong associations between violence and sex workers' isolated situations when working suggests that those who attack sex workers do so because there is no one to stop them and the environment allows it; they do it because they can.

Murders of Sex Workers

American research has found that sex workers are far more likely to be murdered than other people (Potterat et al. 2003). (Potterat et al. may underestimate total numbers of sex workers, making the homicide rate seem very high. They assume that all sex workers will have been identified by police or health departments.) Not all are killed by clients: in both Canada and Britain, more than 40 percent of sex-worker homicides have been attributed to acquaintances, partners, robbers, and the like. Even those classified as clients may never have paid for sex, although they may have approached their victims in this role, taking advantage of sex workers' vulnerability and criminalized situations.

Serial killings of sex workers have occurred in many countries, including the United States, the United Kingdom, China, Canada, Kazakhstan, Ghana, Iran, and South Africa. These cases grab headlines and lead to common assumptions that most sex-worker murders are committed by serial killers and that such killers do not target other people.

British research (Kinnell 2004) indicates that both these assumptions are incorrect. Of those convicted of killing sex workers, 63 percent had also attacked other people, including men and children. Only 25 percent had other convictions for homicide, and half of the other victims were not sex workers. Only one man was convicted of more than two sex-worker murders in 15 years. This may reflect relatively vigorous investigations following sex-worker murders in Britain, reducing the likelihood of serial killings by interrupting offenders' "criminal careers" at an early stage. However, even in Britain more sex-worker murders remain unsolved than any other category of victim.

Police Abuse and Violence

Sex workers in many countries report victimization by police, from demands for unpaid sexual services to sexual abuse and humiliation, **rape**, physical violence, and extortion. This behavior is not confined to police who abuse their power while off duty, but is reported as happening during arrests and in police custody. It is evident that, even where police abuse is rare and complaints against police are taken seriously, any such experience will deter sex workers from reporting attacks or expecting any help from police.

Responses to Violence

Sex workers have many strategies for defending themselves: working collectively, watching out for each other on the street, noting car registration numbers, sharing safety tips, carrying personal alarms or whistles, taking self-defense classes, and sharing information about attackers.

Sex workers know that someone who attacks one sex worker is likely to attack another, so they have developed many verbal and other warning systems. Descriptions of attackers are distributed through "bad trick sheets" (printed flyers), newsletters, and multiple text messaging and through the **Internet**.

However, attacks are rarely reported to police: victims may be unwilling to identify themselves or their work place, and they may fear arrest and prosecution for prostitution or other offenses or deportation if they are in the country illegally. Many sex workers do not expect prosecution of violent clients, and in areas where police abuse of sex workers is common, victims may fear the police more than they fear repeat victimization by other attackers. Even when sex workers do report attacks, investigations may be halfhearted, courts may not regard sex workers as credible witnesses, and even a guilty verdict may bring a more lenient sentence than if the victim had not been a sex worker.

Violence against sex workers is intimately related to hostile legislation, law enforcement, and public attitudes. Society's abhorrence of commercial sex, even when voiced by those who regard all sex workers as victims, results in laws and law enforcement strategies that prevent neither violence nor exploitation or even public nuisance. Instead, the legal framework makes all forms of sex work more dangerous, and proposals for making sex work safer are rejected lest they "encourage prostitution," indicating that many view violence against sex workers as an important deterrent to discourage the sale of sex and a punishment for those who do sell it.

See also Murder.

Further Reading: BBC News. "More Iranian Prostitutes Murdered," 30 July 2001. http://news.bbc.co.uk/1/hi/world/middle_east/1464990.stm; Kinnell, Hilary. "Murder Made Easy: The Final Solution to Prostitution?" In *Prostitution Now*, ed. Rosie Campbell and Roger Matthews. Devon, England: Willan Publishers, in press; Lowman, John. "Violence and the Outlaw Status of (Street) Prostitution in Canada." *Violence Against Women* 6, no 9 (September 2000); Potterat, J. J., D. D. Brewer, et al. "Mortality in a Long-term Open cohort of Prostitute Women." *American Journal of Epidemiology* 159, no. 8 (2004); Sentumbwe, S., D. S. Nakkazi, and N. Nantege. "Legislation and Vulnerability to HIV/AIDS among Commercial Sex Workers in Kampala city." International Conference on HIV/AIDS, 2002, abstract TuOrE1202; Sharma Mahendra, V., et al. "Over-emphasizing HIV/AIDS Risk in Anti-trafficking Programs Can Contribute to Increasing Stigma and Discrimination—Lessons from Nepal." International Conference on HIV/AIDS, 2002, abstract ThPeE7910; Thukral, Juhu and Melissa Ditmore. *Revolving Door: An Analysis of Street-Based Prostitution in New York City*. New York: Sex Workers Project at the Urban Justice Center, 2003. http://www.sexworkersproject.org/reports/RevolvingDoor.html.

Hilary Kinnell

VOYEURISM. Voyeurism or "peeping tomism" is a form of paraphilia (a love beyond "'normality") or scopophilia (love of gazing). The voyeur obtains sexual arousal and gratification by observing individuals' sex acts or sexual organs without their knowledge or consent. On a general level, human beings tend to be voyeuristic and are sexually aroused by the naked body, and visual seduction precedes most sexual activities. Prostitutes and other sex workers, perhaps especially strippers, may encounter voyeurs in their professional lives, people who want to watch women disrobe or masturbate. Clinical voyeurism can manifest itself in exhibitionist behaviour (e.g., masturbation at beaches while watching naked bathers). To be considered diagnosable, the fantasies, urges, or behaviors must cause significant distress in the individual or be disruptive to his or her everyday functioning. Diagnostic criteria for voyeurism are recurrent sexual urges, fantasies, and behaviors involving the observation of an unknowing and nonconsenting person who is naked, in the process of disrobing, or engaged in sexual activity. The etiology of this sexual disorder has been variously explained by psychoanalysts as resulting from childhood trauma (e.g., sexual abuse) or other childhood experiences. Treatment typically involves psychotherapy aimed at uncovering and working through the underlying cause of the behavior.

The term "'peeping Tom'" is derived from the story of Lady Godiva's ride in the nude through Coventry, England, in 1040 to protest against a tax imposed by her husband. The people of Coventry were instructed to stay indoors with windows closed; one man, however, defied the order, and as punishment he was blinded and branded with the nickname "Peeping Tom." The act of window peeping was prosecuted historically as a crime of disorderly conduct or breach of the peace. Today, the criminalization of privacy intrusion is firmly established in many state penal codes, which include it under a wide variety of crimes: trespass, secret peeping, eavesdropping, indecent or unlawful viewing or photography, and violation of privacy, as well as unauthorized videotaping.

The male gaze at a female (or male) body has always been the driving moment in prostitution if not in all kinds of sexual activity; it was, for example, key in the story of Susanna and the Elders and in the Old Testament story of King David, who was driven to adultery and murder after watching Bathsheba in her bath. Peep shows and striptease exploit the desire of (predominantly male) customers to subject the (female) body to their sexual fantasies by the power of their gaze. Voyeurism in the sex industry extends beyond the gaze in strip clubs, and prostitutes are sometimes hired not for sex but for other services, including being looked at by voyeurs. In such an instance, the voyeur may like to watch the sex worker undress or masturbate. Voyeurism is becoming more and more widespread through the technological revolution: mobile phones with inbuilt cameras have been used to spy on women disrobing in department stores or swimming, and cameras can be hidden everywhere, from sunglasses to locker rooms. Video surveillance in

Lady Godiva riding nude on a horse through town, by Jules Lefebvre. Courtesy of the Library of Congress.

public spaces (parking lots, stores, schools) is becoming more and more widespread, and privacy experts and legislators have only recently begun to debate the issue.

Films such as *Mr. Hire* (1989) and *Sliver* (1993) have addressed the issue of voyeurism, heating up the debate about privacy in the media age, and spying on neighbors via cameras has only recently been outlawed. The movie *Peeping Tom* (1962) lays bare the voyeuristic underside of cinema, exploring the uneasy connections between violence, sex, and the urge to gaze. Pornography websites, erotic paintings, and magazines exploit the common human drive to be aroused by watching others engaged in sexual activity, thus contributing to the commodification of the (female) body through the (male) gaze.

See also Internet; Stripping.

Further Reading: Öhlschläger, Claudia. *Unsägliche Lust des Schauens. Die Konstruktion der Geschlechter im voyeuristischen Text.* Freiburg, Germany: Rombach, 1996; PsychNet-UK Web site. http://www.psychnet-uk.com/dsm_iv/voyerism_disorder.htm; Rose, Jacqueline. *Sexuality in the Field of Vision.* New York: Verso, 1986; Sex Education Links Web site. http://www.bigeye.com/sexeducation/voyeurism.html.

Heike Grundmann

WEIMAR REPUBLIC. During the progressive period of the Weimar Republic (1919–1933) in Germany, social reform campaigns resulted in the end of "regulationism" (*Reglementierung*) there. The new Law for Combating Venereal Diseases in 1927 outlawed state-regulated **brothels** and decriminalized prostitution in general. This brief period of legality was characterized by significant improvements in prostitutes' legal status and increasing mobilization. However, the reform was met with strong resistance by religious conservatives and municipal authorities, eventually resulting in the reintroduction of state- controlled brothels in **Nazi Germany**.

Until 1927, prostitution had been illegal in Germany. However, registered prostitutes were tolerated in strictly state-regulated brothels in restricted locales assigned by the police. All prostitutes had to undergo regular compulsory medical examinations for venereal infections, were banned from most public spaces, and needed special permission to travel. A specifically assigned force of "morals police" (*Sittenpolizei*) was responsible for their supervision as well as the general enforcement of the law.

From the end of the 19th century, social reform movements that originated in both religious circles and the women's movement included a critique of regulation in their campaigns. Especially after the introduction of suffrage for women in 1919, feminists attacked the law's misogynistic double standard: whereas female prostitutes were regimented and controlled, their male **clients'** use of commercial sex remained condoned. Social reform efforts combined with growing public concerns about the spread of **sexually transmitted infections** (STIs) led to a general political discussion about the purpose and legitimacy of state-regulated prostitution. Consequently, the government passed several decrees during the first quarter of the 20th century that, for example, dictated mandatory tests and eventually forced medical treatment on all individuals suspected of having STIs. Although these new regulations were intended to be a neutral basis for the protection of society from perceived moral or hygienic threats, their practical enforcement by the police was often restricted to prostitutes.

The objectives of the various divisions of the reform movement pointed to different ends. "Moralists" aimed for the expansion of the existing criminalization of prostitution to include

male clients. In contrast, more radical fractions advocated the **abolition** of regulation by pointing to the law's inability to confine the rise of STIs and its implicit recognition of prostitution as
a profession. Many public health professionals, hoping that legalization would result in voluntary testing and treatment of STIs among prostitutes, also supported the efforts of abolitionists
to decriminalize prostitution. Key to the emerging alliance between social movements and radical professionals were associations such as the Society for Sexual Reform (*Gesellschaft für Sexual-
reform*), founded in 1913, that became central players to Weimar welfare reform. Other critiques
of regulationism, particularly from Social Democratic and Liberal circles, pointed to the "morals
police" as an institution irreconcilable with the new Weimar constitution.

Responding to demands for social reform, the Reichstag passed a new Law for Combating Venereal Diseases (*Reichsgesetz zur Bekämpfung der Geschlechtskrankheiten*) on February
18, 1927, which handed over to medical authorities what had previously been a police function
in the treatment and prevention of STIs. The law abrogated the institution of state-regulated
brothels, decriminalized prostitution in general, and abolished the "morals police." Nevertheless,
the vigorous resistance of conservatives resulted in significant concessions to the reform's actual
scope. For instance, clause 16/4 of the new law—the so-called church tower paragraph (*kirch-
turmparagraph*)—prohibited street soliciting in areas adjacent to schools and churches as well as
in towns with fewer than 15,000 inhabitants.

Although the enactment of the Law for Combating Venereal Diseases was based more on
health and welfare considerations than on concerns about prostitutes' social standing, the nationwide abolition of state-regulated prostitution led to considerable improvements in prostitutes' legal and civil status. Previous municipal regulations that restricted prostitutes to special
streets or buildings (*kasernierung*) were repealed and authorities' power to control the public
appearance of streetwalkers became limited. Revised penal code 361/6, which was identical to
clause 16/3 of the Law for Combating Venereal Diseases, allowed police intervention only if
prostitutes solicited publicly "in a manner that violates morals and decency or harasses others."
As a result, the number of arrested prostitutes declined sharply. **Decriminalization** also allowed
prostitutes to successfully defy violations and encouraged their political mobilization against infringements on their civil rights. In many cities, prostitutes increasingly challenged illegal forms
of police repression such as unauthorized imprisonment or grievous bodily harm. For example,
prostitutes in Leipzig and Bremen founded organizations that employed legal counsel to defend
their members against violations of their rights by the police.

Despite its decriminalized status in the Weimar Republic, prostitution remained in a legal
vacuum. It still lacked official recognition as a profession; for example, prostitutes were not subjected to the same tax and income regulations as other workers. In most cities brothels continued
to exist, often leading to problematic situations for prostitutes working there. On the one hand,
brothels offered some safety, but on the other hand, owners often demanded compliance with
(now illegal) police orders and regulations to protect their business. In fact, authorities frequently
controlled the trade by regulations and restrictions in a fashion similar to "regulationism."

The 1927 law reform was met with much resistance from different parts of society. Within
the state, police and other municipal authorities repeatedly complained about their inability
to protect respectable citizens, control crimes associated with commercial sex, and intervene
against the growing "shamelessness and excesses" of streetwalkers under the new law. Thus, in
1931 several police presidents filed a mutual claim demanding the revision of clause 361/6
of the penal code to outlaw all forms of street soliciting. Religious and morality associations
raised similar demands. The perceived increase in prostitution, owing to an increased visibility

of streetwalkers, led to a popular opposition to the law as well as the mobilization of conservative and Catholic politicians who demanded the return to criminalization of prostitution. Yet, representatives of the Lutheran church and various women's associations, though disagreeing with the existence of prostitution for moral reasons, opposed its total criminalization for fear of a renaissance of state-controlled brothels.

The controversies surrounding social and welfare reforms came to an abrupt end with the demise of the Weimar Republic. The intense economic and social crisis of the late 1920s resulted in a coup against Prussia's Social Democratic government in July 1932 and the installation of Fritz von Papen as *Reichskommissar* ("Papen Putsch"), thereby bringing to power the most prominent opponents of the Weimar social welfare experiment. The conservative backlash against the 1927 reform was then used by Adolf Hitler to advance his own political agenda. Nazi propaganda continually blamed Weimar's Social Democrat government for its inability to maintain law and order and its failure to combat immorality. After the National Socialist triumph in 1933, many Weimar achievements were abolished, resulting, for example, in the ban of street soliciting and the reestablishment of state-regulated brothels in Nazi Germany.

See also Criminalization of Clients.

Further Reading: Bleuel, Hans Peter. *Sex and Society in Nazi Germany*. Philadelphia: Lippincott, 1973; Gleß, Sabine. *Die Reglementierung von Prostitution in Deutschland*. Berlin: Duncker & Humblot, 1999; Grossmann, Atina. *Reforming Sex: The German Movement for Birth Control and Abortion Reform*. New York: Oxford University Press, 1995; Herzog, Dagmar. "Hubris and Hypocrisy, Incitement and Disavowal: Sexuality and German Fascism." *Journal of the History of Sexuality* 11, no. 1–2 (January–April 2002): 3–21; Roos, Julia. "Backlash against Prostitutes' Rights: Origins and Dynamics of Nazi Prostitution Policies." *Journal of the History of Sexuality* 11, no. 1–2 (January–April 2002): 67–94.

Antonia Levy

WEST AFRICA. In West Africa, women are involved in four main types of prostitution: rural or village prostitution, junction town or truck park prostitution, urban or city prostitution, and international prostitution. The prostitute often lives a nomadic existence—moving from place to place to earn a living. She can be described as "running with the wind"—an apt Guinean expression for prostitutes, which captures the West African sex worker's tendency to migrate from rural to urban areas and when feasible, across the seas, in search of "the good life." This propensity to "run with the wind" is captured on a Benin City, Nigeria, billboard in the following way: "Have you been offered a trip abroad? Be careful. Don't throw your future away"—this challenge written in sharp admonition of the young Edo (Nigerian) woman who might otherwise be snared by the lures of international prostitution.

Rural or Village Prostitution

There are essentially two types of rural or village prostitutes in West Africa. The first operates within the bounds of her rural village, servicing her clientele from the comforts of her home. This kind of prostitute can be found tucked away in rural West African villages as far east as Nigeria and Benin and west as Ivory Coast and Senegal. She often sets up business in her primary residence, providing her male customers with services that range from sex to conversation to food. Sometimes, prostitutes form long-term reciprocal relationships with their clients, and other encounters are short-term and casual. The rural West African prostitute controls her own affairs and as such never answers to a male or female pimp or **madam**. She is in total control of her body and decides when, where, and how much. Payment is often made in money or in kind. In most parts of rural West Africa, the village prostitute is considered a vital member of her community and is believed to perform services that are deemed useful to that community. She is therefore often viewed with a degree of deference.

The second type of rural prostitute in West Africa lives as a *nomada* (nomad), journeying from her rural village to the major population centers and busy crossroads in search of work. Prostitutes from the Guinea Bissau village of Caio regularly move eastward to the capital city of Bissau or settle in the northern city of Ziguinchor, and some of them work as far north as Banjul, Casamance, and Dakar, Senegal. In Ghana, most prostitutes are also rural/urban migrants. These girls and women go as far as Abidjan, Pikine-Dakar, and Brazzaville to trade sex for money.

Junction-Town or Truck-Park Prostitution

Junction-town prostitutes are sex workers who work on and along major West African highways. These sex workers either work full-time or part-time. The school-age girls among them often supply sex to fund their education. These young junction-town prostitutes get more action because of the truck drivers' misconceived ideas that HIV is more prevalent among populations 20 years and older.

Trucks parks—truck stops situated in junction towns where drivers can spend the night—are often adjacent to West African day-and-night markets. Itinerant female hawkers and solitary market women are known to offer sexual services to these drivers. Prostitution tends to be most prevalent in major junction towns of transport commerce, such as the Nigerian towns of Lagos, Ibadan, Calabar, and Maiduguri.

West African long-distance truck drivers stop for the night in designated areas—usually where the road widens or where they can park off the road. They then frequent popular roadside eating houses and bars called "Mama Puts," as well as other buildings that serve as places to sleep and find sexual partners. Sexual activity between drivers and prostitutes is often high, not because the men earn substantial salaries as drivers, but because many of them perform additional services on the side for which they are handsomely remunerated.

The young sex workers who service these drivers live for the most part in shantytowns near these stops. Truck drivers who work the same route for long periods cultivate relationships with these junction-town or truck-park prostitutes much like in the rural areas where the sex workers provide home-cooked meals, familiar surroundings, friendships, conversation, and sex. Many of these relationships thus established become long-term.

Urban or City Prostitution

The vast majority of city or urban prostitutes in West Africa come from elsewhere. In the Ivory Coast, for instance, most city prostitutes come from Ghana, Nigeria, Togo, Mali, Senegal, and other West African states. In Bamako, Mali, there is noticeable flux of young students from various parts of West Africa between July and August; these students spend their summer vacation working as prostitutes and then return home when school resumes in September.

There are many types of urban or city prostitutes in West Africa. In the Ivory Coast, the women in one group of prostitutes are known as "Dioula women" or "women of Dyato-Mouso." Malian (mainly Bambara and Peul) in origin, these are usually young girls who after brief stints as prostitutes become vendors in the local markets. Another category of prostitutes is the

"Karoua women." These Zerma or Hausa prostitutes are mainly divorced women from Niger. A third group are the "Westernized or évolue prostitutes." These sex workers, mainly operating in French West Africa, hang out at bars and dance halls and service European and African clientele. "Toutou" prostitutes can be found all over West Africa. Originating primarily from British West Africa, they belong chiefly to the following ethnic groups: the Fante and Asante of Ghana; the Ewe of Ghana, Togo, and Benin; and the Igbos, Ijaws, and Calabaris of Nigeria. The name "Toutou" derives from "2 shillings, 2 pence," and the women are so called because they charge low rates for sex. In Cote d'Ivoire, Toutou prostitutes have no general quarters and are mainly street prostitutes who cluster on the side streets of main avenues. This migratory pattern also lends credence to the other name by which they are known—"Walk About Women." In Accra, Ghana, they live in a separate red light area and position themselves on their respective doorsteps in clear view of potential clients. When engaged, they lower a curtain in front of their doorways. An Accra Toutou may visit a client in his own home and spend the night with him there, but it would be rare for an Ivory Coast Toutou to do so. Nigerian "Toutous" en route to Abidjan make an initial stop in Ghana, where they offer sex for money on the major city streets. The "Karvas or Karuwai" prostitutes are Hausa, Fulani, and Zerma (Nigeria), and they rent small houses in the *zongo* (strangers') quarters of the respective West African city to which they migrate. Their clients visit them for up to a week to talk, play music, and have sex. The city name for the modern-day Igbo prostitute is *akwunakwuna* or *okada*—the ubiquitous motorcycle that has taken the place of taxi cabs in Nigeria.

The urban prostitutes who frequent the hotels and bars are known as "door knockers" in Nigeria. They are so called because they frequent four-and five-star hotels, knocking on the doors of potential clients. Door knockers often stay the length of their client's stop in the hotel, serving their sexual needs. In Lagos, Nigeria, high-price prostitutes work along the busy Allen Avenue in Ikeja. In a country where traditional religion and beliefs still hold sway, traditional medicines are said to be used by these prostitutes to procure clients.

Many city prostitutes in West Africa have organized associations that protect their interests as commercial sex workers. One such organization is The Nigerian Union of Prostitutes. In the Ivory Coast, city prostitutes have organized a number of large, highly formalized associations that are founded along ethnic lines. Each association is headed by a president, who is in turn aided by several elected officers. These officers are older prostitutes who are deemed wiser and are therefore trusted. They look after the interests of their group and act as spokeswomen for their members, especially in dialogues with the often-antagonistic police.

International Prostitution

There have been two types of international prostitution in West Africa. The first, which was especially common during the early days of independence in the 1960s, involved the importation of European prostitutes into French West Africa for sex. In the Ivory Coast, 90 percent of these European prostitutes lived in the capital city, Abidjan. These European prostitutes were predominantly barmaids attached to one of the city's numerous nightclubs or bars. Most of them were between the ages of 25 and 40. Generally from Paris or Marseille, these prostitutes were sent from France to Africa expressly for the purpose of becoming sex workers. Like their African counterparts, they moved around quite a bit. They rarely spent more than six months in a particular bar and would often spend two to three years in one French West African country and then move to another. European prostitutes charged high fees. Consequently, they were frequented mainly by fellow Europeans and a select group of Africans who could afford their services. In the late 1960s Ivory Coast's European prostitutes charged an average of 6,000 African francs (CFA) ($24) and as much as 10,000 francs ($40) per visit. They were said to make between 250,000 and 300,000 francs ($1,000–$1,200) per month, but were obliged to pay a per-client "air-conditioning" commission of 1,000 francs ($4) to the proprietor of the bar in which they were stationed. Many European prostitutes were able to make enough money to return to France at the end of their three-year prostitution stints.

The influx of West African prostitutes into Europe is a more recent phenomenon. For nearly 20 years, women from Benin City, Nigeria, as well as from other West African cities, have been going to Italy and other European countries (e.g., Spain, Denmark, Germany, Holland) to work as sex workers. Called "Italos," many of these women are single, but some are married and seek work abroad with the blessings of their husbands. They build lavish homes in their hometowns, sink private boreholes to supply water, and buy four-wheel-drive luxury cars that they drive on the oftentimes unpaved West African country roads. The Italos often seem to be engaged in a never-ending cycle, as successful prostitutes recruit younger ones to join them in Europe. These younger recruits are encouraged by the success stories of the Italos before them who have purchased expensive cars and built mansions and estates for their families. The popular Nigerian singer, Ohenhen, in a hit song played the country over, recently celebrated the enormous wealth of a prominent Italo called Dupay who was said to sponsor younger women to follow her lucrative example. This apparent adulation of the international West African prostitute is not limited to the music world. The Nigerian Film Industry, Nollywood, seems also to have put a positive spin on prostitution in Nigeria and abroad. A number of popular low-cost videos that glorify prostitution have saturated the market. One such film, *Glamour Girls*, appeared in two volumes.

Many factors influence the young West African woman's decision to become a prostitute, but the most prevalent by far is the fact that prostitution is lucrative. In situations in which West African currencies have been devalued by more than 800 percent, in which countries have been broken down by corruption, and in which still other countries have been ravaged by war, it is not surprising that young West African women take what appears to be the easy way out. When these West African girls come of age, they think only of survival—of how to put food on the table—and to many of these young women, survival in what has become a dry and unforgiving land often involves trading sexual favors for money. With limited education, West African prostitutes earn much more money than they ordinarily would in other modes of "legitimate" commerce. They are moved to enter prostitution because they see sex work as a temporary vice—a period of intense saving—that will allow many to marry and will allow still others to engage in "lawful" business.

See also Migration and Mobility; Unions.

Further Reading: Achebe, Nwando. "The Road to Italy: Nigerian Sex Workers at Home and Abroad." In *Women's Labors, Special Issue of Journal of Women's History* 15, no. 4 (Winter 2004): 177–184; Anarfi, John K. *Female Migration and Prostitution in West Africa: The Case of Ghanaian Women in Côte d'Ivoire.* Accra, Ghana: GTZ Regional AIDS Programme for West and Central Africa, 1995; Buckner, Margaret. "Village Women as Town Prostitutes: Cultural Factors Relevant to Prostitution and HIV Epidemiology in Guinea Bissau." In *Social Sciences and AIDS in Africa: Review and Prospects; Experiencing and Understanding AIDS in Africa.* Paris: Karthala, 1999, pp. 389–404; FaSanto, Maria Eugenia, G. Do Espirito, and Gina D. Etheredge. "And Then I Became a Prostitute ... Some Aspects of Prostitution and Brothel Prostitutes in Dakar, Senegal." *The Social Science Journal* 41 (2004): 137–

46; Fagbohungbe, Tunde, ed. *The Rape of the Innocents: Evolving an African Initiative Against Human Trafficking*. Proceedings of the First Pan African Conference on Human Trafficking, Abuja, Nigeria, February 19–23, 2001; ICWAD International Council for Women of African Descent, Trafficking of African Women Fact Sheet. http://www.npcbw.org/newweb/icwad_04_trafficking_facts.htm; Loconto, Allison. "The Trafficking of Nigerian Women Into Italy." *TED Case Studies* 656 (January 2002): 1–15, http://www.american.edu/TED/italian-trafficking.htm.

Nwando Achebe

WESTERN EUROPE. Prostitution in Western Europe is documented in Ancient Greece, with kept women or brothel slaves known as hetaerae, **porne**, and auletrides. The city of Pompeii offers the most relics of prostitution in Ancient Rome, when freeborn Romans were prohibited from marrying prostitutes and **pimps**. Laws from the 11th to 14th centuries document the state's approach to prostitution in the Medieval Era, including widespread regulation and taxation of **brothels**. Sumptuary laws regulating prostitutes' **clothing** indicated both what clues were worn to mark a woman a prostitute, such as a particular color scarf, and what she could not wear, usually expensive materials such as silk and fur that might be deemed above her status. **Magdalen homes** and orders were first established by a directive approved by the church in 1227.

Renaissance prostitutes faced harsher treatment than their predecessors as prostitution was gradually criminalized in much of Europe. This shift seems to have coincided with a growing prevalence of independent, unregulated prostitution, which rendered the municipal houses unprofitable, and brothels were closed in many cities. Religious fervor was not limited to the Catholic Renaissance. The **Protestant Reformation** promoted procreative sex and condemned recreational sex, especially sex with prostitutes.

Syphilis was first recorded in Europe in the late 15th century, and prostitutes were scapegoated for its spread. The **Contagious Diseases Acts** (CDA) in Britain in the 1860s stipulated that women suspected of prostitution be examined and held in a locked hospital if they showed symptoms of **sexually transmitted infections**. Victorian-era abolitionists including **Josephine Butler**, William Coote, and William Stead sought to eliminate prostitution, **white slavery**, and **trafficking** as well as to repeal the CDA.

Sex work in contemporary Western Europe takes many forms. In most places, sex work is not illegal; however, ancillary activities, such as managing the sex business of another, are generally criminalized. In Sweden, only the male buyer, and not the female prostitute, is committing a crime. **Street-based prostitution** is found almost everywhere, with supervised **tippelzones** in the Netherlands.

The low countries—the Netherlands, Belgium, and Luxembourg—are known for prostitutes working in the windows. The windows are essentially shop fronts for prostitution: women stand in the window of a small room facing the street, clients negotiate at the door and then the curtains are drawn while services are provided.

Brothels were widely closed after the 1949 Convention for the Suppression of the Traffic in Persons and of the Exploitation of the Prostitution of Others, which addressed only prostitution (as opposed to trafficking for work in other fields) and more specifically, living off the earnings of a prostitute. This meant that in Italy and France, the only legal venue for prostitution was the street, until the Sarkozy laws passed in France in 2002 made soliciting a crime. The Netherlands has allowed brothels to reopen in 2000. In Germany, large "Eros Centers" are state-supervised venues in which services including prostitution and **sadomasochism** are provided.

Despite the fact that antipimping laws prohibit them, **escort agencies** persist and, in Denmark, may even be patronized at government expense to secure sexual services for the elderly or disabled.

The International **Union** of Sex Workers is based in **London** and is affiliated with Britain's largest general union. Sex workers in Europe held a summit, attended by 120 people, in October 2005, echoing the original World Whores Congress held in 1985 during which the International Charter for Prostitutes' Rights was written.

See also Amsterdam; Appendix item 14; Hapsburg Empire; Medieval Prostitution; Syphilis; Unions; Window Prostitution.

Further Reading: Brussa, Licia, ed. *Health, Migration and Sex Work: The Experience of TAMPEP.* Amsterdam, the Netherlands: TAMPEP, 1999; Cabiria. *Women and Migration in Europe.* Lyons, France: Le Dragon Lune, 2004; Pheterson, Gail. *A Vindication of the Rights of Whores.* Seattle, WA: Seal Press, 1989; Roberts, Nickie. *Whores in History.* London: Grafton, 1989.

Melissa Hope Ditmore

WESTWARD EXPANSION. In the 19th century, prostitutes were frequently among the first civilians to settle an area in the American West after the army arrived. They also had close relationships with military personnel and law enforcement officials and contributed to town coffers through fines and licensures (though often unwillingly). Towns that grew by catering to the needs and desires of soldiers stationed at frontier posts often gained a reputation as dangerous centers of debauchery. During the 19th century, prostitution in the West offered a form of employment in a society in which many job opportunities were closed to women. With clerk and secretarial positions in the West dominated by men, women had very few options for earning a living. Although prostitution sometimes seemed to be the only answer in a dire economic situation, by making that choice, many of these women became trapped in a lifetime of dwindling economic prospects in light of the **retrogressive dynamic** of prostitution and possible exposure to dreadful and (at the time) incurable venereal infections.

Most full-time prostitutes on the frontier found themselves placed in one of four categories within the occupation. These categories included brothel dwellers, saloon or **dance hall girls**, crib women, and streetwalkers. The earning potential was highest with brothel dwellers (as were economic liabilities), and earning potential descended in the order the categories were previously listed. Brothel girls were usually younger, more attractive, and able to demand higher prices for their services. Likewise, renting a room in a brothel was quite expensive. Although a building rented for legitimate purposes could $25, the same building as a brothel could be rented out for nearly $200 a month. As brothel workers got older, they either became dance hall girls or rented cribs (small shacks in which the prostitutes lived and saw clients). These were steps down and also reduced the earning potential and living conditions of the women. The lowest step on the ladder was that of the streetwalker. Frequently these women did not earn enough to rent a crib and usually depended on clients to provide shelter for the night or squatted in an abandoned building.

Career prostitutes in the American West usually began working as early as age 15 and were often forced into "retirement" by age 30 because of younger competition. Some former prostitutes then began managing younger women in **brothels**, operating saloons, or working as abortionists. Prostitutes sometimes had their children living with them, and often, daughters followed in their mothers' footsteps. The presence of the industry and lack of education and marketable skills frequently left these young women with little hope for a different life.

Prostitution and Frontier Military

Whereas many prostitutes chose to locate within growing towns, others found their way to rural brothels, called hog ranches, located near military posts. Other prostitutes found lodgings in sutlers' stores (merchants who catered to the military), posing as domestic help. These often proved to be lucrative operations because military expeditions to the **American West** after the Civil War called for large garrisons of soldiers, providing a steady supply of customers. Although there was no official policy regarding prostitution near military posts, officers had diverse opinions regarding the institution. Post commanders rarely sought to banish prostitutes from the post, usually being content to allow brothels to exist nearby as long as they did not disrupt operations. If they were forced to act, commanders usually ordered such women away from the post. However, the women frequently ignored the orders.

Laundresses

Although some prostitutes pursued their careers full-time, others turned to prostitution to supplement their meager, and often unreliable, earnings as **laundresses** for the frontier army. In 1885, laundresses typically earned 37.5 cents per soldier per week and were paid by the soldiers after the soldiers were paid by the federal paymaster. Although the paymaster was supposed to make his circuit at least every two months, at times the soldiers, and in turn the laundresses, were not paid for six months at a time. The period after payday took on a near-carnival atmosphere. Soldiers gorged themselves on delicacies and **alcohol**, and some went directly to the brothels. Although post laundresses received rations from the military until they were withdrawn in 1883, between pay periods they were forced to incur debts for other necessities. After paying their debts, laundresses quickly found themselves destitute once more and in need of income. As a result, some laundresses seemingly had no choice but to supplement their income through occasional prostitution.

Laundresses also sometimes became common-law wives of various soldiers. Although some soldiers and frontier women found love in the West, for many soldiers the situation was a way to adapt the institution of **marriage** to meet their needs. At times, married soldiers were allowed to live outside of the barracks, and their "wives" frequented the post, drew rations, and found work as laundresses in a legitimate light. As evidence of the weakness of some such marital bonds, when a laundress's husband was transferred to another post, she often simply married another soldier.

Frontier soldiers sought out the company of laundresses and prostitutes for other reasons as well. Army regulations forbade married men from enlisting (with the exception of officers). Furthermore, enlisted men were forced to gain permission from their superior officer if they wanted to marry after they had entered the army. In addition, after 1883, laundresses and other women at the post had to be married to a soldier in order to draw rations. Thus, because of suspicion of marriages of convenience, marriage applications were closely scrutinized.

Venereal Disease on the Frontier

The loose morals and questionable arrangements embraced by soldiers and laundresses on the frontier often had bitter consequences. Although most post commanders frequently ignored the immoral behavior displayed by their men as long as they created few problems, post surgeons often argued against the mixing of soldiers and the undesirable elements of frontier towns. Consequently, commanders and surgeons commonly disagreed on allowing soldiers to venture into town and carouse with laundresses. The animosity between commanders and surgeons could also likely explain why orders for prostitutes to leave the area were rarely enforced.

The need to address the problems with prostitutes mainly arose from the transmission of infection. Medical records from posts in West Texas and the rest of the frontier often show several new cases of **syphilis** and gonorrhea each month. The young soldiers who contracted syphilis (which was incurable during the period) were discharged to endure the disease on their own. At Fort Griffin, Assistant Surgeon Henry McElderry discharged three soldiers in May 1871 for syphilis. Enlisted men were not the only soldiers who visited prostitutes on the lonely frontier. Brigidier General Ranald Slidell MacKinzie died in 1889, having retired from the army in 1884 during the late stages of syphilis.

Often the treatment of venereal disease by doctors during the 19th century was dangerous in itself. Syphilis was frequently treated by imbibing mercury, which not only did not cure the disease, but also poisoned the body while the disease ravaged it. The accepted medical treatment for gonorrhea involved a urethral injection of lead nitrate with a large syringe (which was also ineffective).

Although soldiers received treatment for their venereal diseases (ineffective though the treatment was) before they were discharged, prostitutes had to obtain their own treatment from local doctors. Furthermore, because they were often on the verge of economic collapse, prostitutes rarely received treatment for their medical conditions. Ironically, in this situation their desperate economic state probably saved them from the poor treatment at the time. Subsequently, both infected prostitutes and soldiers who sought their company commonly suffered with their diseases for the rest of their lives.

Suicide

Unable to endure their situations, many prostitutes sought solace in suicide. Newspapers of the period often documented the deaths of prostitutes by drug overdoses. "Red-Headed Mabel" Pratt of Salt Lake City attempted suicide by taking strychnine but was revived by a Dr. Witcher in June 1887. Three days later, Edna Scott, who had married a soldier in 1880 and was later abandoned, overdosed on morphine, ending her life in her crib on Commerce Street in the heart of the red light district.

Further Reading: Butler, Anne M. *Daughters of Joy, Sisters of Misery*. Urbana: University of Illinois Press, 1985; Green, Bill. *The Dancing Was Lively: Fort Concho Texas: A Social History, 1867 to 1882*. San Angelo, TX: Author, 1974; Seagraves, Anne. *Soiled Doves: Prostitution in the Early West*. Hayden, Idaho: Wesanne Publications, 1994; Wooster, Robert. *Soldiers, Sutlers, & Settlers: Garrison Life on the Texas Frontier*. College Station: Texas A&M University Press, 1987.

John J. Gaines

WHITE SLAVERY. The term "white slavery" has, at least since the middle of the 19th century, referred to an international traffic in white women and girls who have been sold or trapped into forced prostitution that usually involves transportation abroad, or out of the home nation. The traffic is sometimes referred to as the "white slave trade," a term that suggests both a coherent, organized system of exchange and a concomitant systemic representation of the white female body as sexual commodity within an international economy of masculine desire in which race and nation, along with gender, are indices of particular values. Although the term "white slavery" is occasionally used as if it were synonymous with prostitution, it represents rather a somewhat specialized category of sexual commerce that depends both on the racial visibility of the women and girls as white and on the widespread entrapment and transportation of white women and girls against their will into a condition of sexual enslavement for money. It is extremely difficult to ascertain the extent or even the existence of a white slave trade, historically or in the present. White slaves "disappear," and in the absence of compelling documentary evidence, the history of such a traffic remains obscure, despite the large body of anti–white-slave rhetoric produced in many nations from the late 1880s into the present and despite the widespread legislation in many nations and internationally to protect women and girls from **forced prostitution** and exchange across borders. Noteworthy legislation includes the Criminal Law Amendment Bill in England in 1885 and 1912; the White Slave Traffic Act, or **Mann Act**, in the United States in 1910; and the **League of Nations** International Agreement for the Suppression of the White Slave Traffic in 1904 and 1949. Application of anti–white-slave legislation has been fairly limited.

Concern about white slavery has nonetheless been apparent in many national contexts over a period of at least 200 years, at least, that is, from the time that the term began to circulate in the English language, in the late 18th century. From the late 19th century until the aftermath of **World War I**, and especially in the years just before the war, fears about white slavery coalesced into a moral panic, a widespread, anxious conviction that white women and girls were being abducted in large numbers into an international sexual traffic, and a flurry of attempts to simultaneously make visible the existence of white slavery and stem the putative tide of white women and girls into foreign brothels or other locations for controlled, forced sexual labor.

In the British imperial context, the first blast against white slavery is usually attributed to *Pall Mall Gazette* editor William T. Stead, who, in the summer of 1885, published **"The Maiden Tribute of Modern Babylon,"** an exposé of a trade in white women and girls based in London and leading to conditions of sexual entrapment abroad. After Stead's report, information about the **trafficking** began increasingly to appear in commentary and social reform rhetoric as well as in cautionary tales—white slave narratives—in print and, in the early 20th century, in **films**. These white slave narratives were produced in a range of genres, from didactic fiction to what purported to be firsthand accounts of enslavement or the witnessing of enslavement. White slave narratives of this period are characterized by the representation of women and girls in what are shown to be situations of vulnerability, notably through traveling alone or more generally moving through public space. Emphasized in these narratives and in the reports of the time was a conviction about the existence of the commerce and a sense of the concomitant danger for all white women and girls who might be caught by the snares of white slavers if they did not observe due care in their movement and conduct outside of the home.

The late 19th- and early 20th-century moral panic around white slavery had the effect less of protecting than of policing women and girls through efforts to restrict and control their movements as potential sexual subjects; it worked secondarily to demonize male lust as the basis for a commerce in white female bodies. Social reform activists and particularly feminists took up the cause of white slavery on these terms within and in relation to a broad range of problems, or "social evils," seen to be affecting the strength and quality of the white races that were then engaged in competition for imperial power. Anxiety about population rates was rife, as were fears that the imperial races were not producing adequate numbers of people to fill the new territories into which the imperial nations were rapidly expanding through various acts of acquisition and colonization. The disappearance of white women and the apparent decline in white male moral behavior—as procurers and traders, as purchasers of women and girls—were taken as alarming signs of racial "degeneration."

The existence of white slavery continues to be debated in historical analysis, as well as in contemporary discussions of sexual enslavement at the present time. Facts and statistics remain elusive in the documenting of a sexual traffic in white women and girls, but the conditions that would lead to an exchange of white female bodies as sexual commodities remain intact in ideological structures of gender and race in many national and international contexts.

Although white slavery is now generally understood in relation to an international commerce in forced prostitution, the term was also used from the late 18th century and throughout the 19gh to refer to white-skinned people exchanged in the African slave trade, to descendents of white and black parentage held as slaves in the United States during the period of slavery, and, at a metaphorical level, to exploited industrial workers in Britain.

Further Reading: Cordasco, Francesco, and Thomas Monroe Pitkin. *The White Slave Trade and the Immigrants: A Chapter in American Social History*. Detroit, MI: Blaine Ethridge, 1981; Devereux, Cecily. "'The Maiden Tribute' and the Rise of the White Slave in the Nineteenth Century: The Making of an Imperial Construct." *Victorian Review* 26.2 (2001): 1–23; Doezema, Jo. "The Re-emergence of the Myth of 'White Slavery' in Contemporary Discourses of 'Trafficking in Women.'" International Studies Convention, Washington, DC, February 16–20, 1999. *Gender Issues* 18.1 (2000): 23–50, http://www.walnet.org/csis/papers/doezema-loose.html; Irwin, Mary Ann. "White Slavery as Metaphor: Anatomy of a Moral Panic." *Ex Post Facto: The History Journal* 5 (1996), http://www.sfsu.edu/~hsa/ex-post-facto/wslavery.html; Stamp, Shelley Lindsey. "Is Any Girl Safe?: Female Spectators at the White Slave Films." *Screen* 37, no. 1 (1996): 1–15.

Cecily Devereux

WHOREHOUSE MUSICIANS. *See* **New Orleans; Storyville.**

WHORES' CONGRESS. *See* **Appendix A, document 2.**

WILDE, OSCAR (1854–1900). Anglo-Irish author Oscar Wilde was known as an author, playwright, poet, aesthete, and wit and infamously as a decadent "sodomite" convicted of "gross indecency." Son of an eminent Irish surgeon and a literary mother, Wilde embraced the Aesthetic Movement while at Oxford University, which heralded "art for art's sake," an ethos that later contributed to his tragic downfall for excluding moral considerations from the production of "art." Although Wilde married and had two children with his wife, Constance, the grand passion of his life was Lord Alfred "Bosie" Douglas, whose father, the Marquis of Queensbury, accused Wilde of "posing [as a] Somdomite [*sic*]" (Ellman 1987, 438)and corrupting his son, 16 years Wilde's junior. Encouraged by Bosie, Wilde foolishly brought a charge of libel against his lover's despised father for false allegation. Queensbury was not convicted, but Wilde was. Queensbury's evidence against Wilde resulted in his being charged with gross indecency. Wilde was cross-examined about his literary associations and his controversial homoerotic novel *The Picture of Dorian Gray* (1891), which was brought in to prove Wilde's "sodomitical" tendencies, which Wilde denied. Wilde's conviction was secured because of his actual relations with a host of younger men, although he insisted his dinners, hotel stays, and trips abroad with them were mere platonic "friendships" and he neither had sex with them nor paid them for sexual favors. The depositions by these men—at least one of whom had blackmailed Wilde over his passionate letters to Bosie—and the testimonies of various hotels' staff who asserted they witnessed many of Wilde's assignations were more convincing than Wilde's vehement denials. Ironically, it was Bosie who had introduced Wilde to the other young men who were already "corrupted" and who would prostitute themselves for a small amount of money and an excellent meal. Wilde spent

Oscar Wilde. Courtesy of the Library of Congress.

two years in jail, and with his reputation destroyed, he subsequently died a broken, impoverished exile in Paris. This anxiety about older aristocratic men corrupting lower-class youths had gained momentum in 1889, with the so-called Cleveland Street Scandal, which is considered to have fueled the prosecution of Wilde. The scandal surrounded the exposure of a West End male brothel that was filled with "rent-boys" or "painted boys" and patronized by many prominent aristocrats and titled men, allegedly including Prince Albert Victor, second in line to the throne.

See also Male Prostitution.

Further Reading: Ellman, Richard. *Oscar Wilde.* New York: Alfred A. Knopf, 1984; repr. 1987; Holland, Merlin. *The Real Trial of Oscar Wilde.* New York: 4th Estate/HarperCollins, 2003; Hyde, H. Montgomery. *The Cleveland Street Scandal.* London: W. H. Allen, 1976.

Janet Tanke

WINDOW PROSTITUTION. Window prostitution is a form of soliciting **clients** that is found mainly in Dutch, Belgium, and German cities. **Amsterdam** is most famous for its red light district with more than 400 shop windows from which female and **transgender sex workers** conduct their business.

Window prostitution is an independent way of working. The sex worker rents the window and working room (and some facilities such as clean sheets and towels) per day or per shift from the window brothel owner, who is not a boss but a landlord. The sex worker is an independent entrepreneur. She negotiates with the clients, sets her own fees, and decides for herself what services she will or will not provide and to whom.

Historically, in red light areas, sex workers who worked in bars and **brothels** would stand in the doorway to attract clients and seduce them to come in. In the early 20th century, just after brothels were banned in the Netherlands, women started to work from their own homes or rooms they rented from **madams** (often former sex workers) in the red light district. To protect public order and public decency, they were not allowed to stand in the doorway. Most women had their rooms upstairs and picked up their clients on the streets or in the bars. Some women, however, rented the room downstairs and could sit behind the window. From behind closed curtains they lured their customers with a tap on the window. The police decided to turn a blind eye to this "hidden" form of soliciting. With these conditions this form of home prostitution gradually expanded in Amsterdam's red light district and gave the area the character that still makes it famous today. The women behind the windows often worked "at a half" with the owner of the room. This meant that half of her earnings were paid to the madam, who usually had three or four women renting rooms from her.

As the years passed, the curtains were allowed to be opened further. In the 1950s the women sat in elegant dress in their living room behind the windows. With the gradual opening of the curtains came changes to the dress and behavior codes of sex workers, from wearing dresses to wearing lingerie and from tapping on the windows to standing visibly illuminated by red or black lights. Now, if the curtain is closed, it means that the sex worker is doing business. From the 1970s onward the character of the red light districts has changed. The sex industry has become more commercialized. Businessmen bought the prostitution houses from the landladies. They expanded the commercial business within their buildings by increasing the number of windows spaces and building small working rooms directly behind the windows. Sex workers no longer lived in the window brothels, and the owners started to introduce shifts. Most brothels now have two shifts and some of them even three.

Since the legalization of the Dutch sex industry, the window brothels are required to meet various **occupational safety and health** standards, such as standards regarding fire, safety, and public health, in order to obtain or retain a license to operate. Although the owners of the window brothels are not considered to be bosses, they are responsible for checking the passports of sex workers renting from them to make certain that they satisfy legal residency and age restrictions. Although sex workers in the Netherlands are not required to have a license or to register with local authorities, migrants from countries outside of the European Union do need a work permit.

Marieke van Doorninck

WOLFENDEN REPORT. The Wolfenden Report, officially entitled the "Report of the Committee on Homosexual Offences and Prostitution 1957," was a 1957 British government study on sexual morality, especially prostitution and homosexuality, as they related to public issues. It led to the **Street Offences Act of 1959**, a law that proposed to stop the nuisance caused by prostitutes soliciting on the streets of London.

Sir John Wolfenden (1906–85) was the chairman of the study. Born in Halifax, Yorkshire, he was a fellow and tutor in philosophy at Magdalen College, Oxford (1929–34); headmaster of Uppingham (1934–44) and Shrewsbury (1944–50); and vice-chancellor of Reading University starting in 1950. He was made a life peer in 1974.

Wolfenden was a man who believed in the efficacy of corporal punishment and rose to prominence in British society during the late 1950s after the publication of the report named after him. His appointment as chairman of this committee followed a chance meeting with the Home Secretary, Sir David Maxwell Fyfe, on an overnight sleeper train traveling from Liverpool to London in 1954.

Maxwell Fyfe had been concerned for some years over the "shameless display" of prostitutes "flaunting" themselves in the West End of London and "pestering" passersby. This activity had attracted attention in the press and complaints from leaders of the churches. He considered it a particularly deplorable example of London's immorality, likely to shock the increasing number of foreign visitors coming to Britain during an era of post-war celebration.

Wolfenden

"There were precious few occasions of light relief. One occurred when a highly respectable society of lawyers arranged for a party of girls from the street to come and expound their point of view. My colleagues were looking forward with naughty expectation to my conduct of this particular interview, and were more than usually fertile in their suggestions about questions which might be asked. A few hours before it was due the visit was called off by the girls themselves. They had not realised they would have to come to the Home Office, and they were not going to be seen dead entering or leaving the place. Besides, they thought it would be bad for trade.... So that piece of firsthand experience was denied us."

John Wolfenden, *Turning Points; The Memoirs of Lord Wolfenden* (London: The Bodley, 1976).

ON PUBLICATION OF THE REPORT

"We were accused by some highly respectable women's organisations of discriminating against the prostitute and doing nothing against her wicked client. Indeed, one very distinguished ecclesiastic charged me with this in conversation. 'Surely', he said, 'you would agree that the man who goes with a prostitute is just as guilty as she is.' To which I replied, 'My dear Archbishop, he may be just as guilty as she is of what you and I might call the sin of fornication: He is not a guilty as she is of cluttering up the streets of London.'"

John Wolfenden, *Turning Points; The Memoirs of Lord Wolfenden* (London: The Bodley, 1976).

The legal system regulating prostitution at the time was believed to be unsatisfactory. Prostitutes were rounded up by the police on the basis of a rota system, and they were then taken to a magistrates' court, where they were fined a trivial amount that they swiftly recouped by returning to the street. It was suggested that this system brought the law into disrepute.

Maxwell Fyfe had prepared the ground in 1951 when a senior civil servant, Philip Allan, was dispatched to the United States to investigate the American method of regulation. Although prostitution was illegal in the States, a discreet equilibrium was maintained through a call-girl system. In response to Allan's report, Maxwell Fyfe formulated a plan that he set out in a confidential Home Office memorandum (to which the final report of the Wolfenden committee bore a remarkable resemblance). The legislative formula was a combination of steeply increased, incremental fines accompanied by a prison sentence for repeat offenders and, crucially, the withdrawal of the need for the police to provide evidence in court that a citizen had been annoyed. To achieve the desired end and override any antagonism from women's organizations, Maxwell Fyfe considered it necessary to appoint a group of impartial, unbiased professional men and women who would command the respect of the public. This committee would then investigate the subject in detail and suggest a legal remedy.

Once committee members were appointed (three women and thirteen men), one of the committee's earliest decisions was to meet in private, purportedly to limit sensational reporting in the press, which it feared might influence public perceptions of the problems. This turned out to be an astute move: official secrecy has prevented historians from examining the committee documents for 40 years. Moreover, this policy meant that the feared "women's organizations" (principally the Association of Moral and Social Hygiene, later to become the **Josephine Butler** Society) could be ignored and lampooned behind closed doors while the chief of police and other high-status officials were treated with obsequious respect.

A number of things are now clear, most significantly that the committee was appointed primarily to deal with prostitution. Homosexuality was included as an afterthought (possibly a camouflage) by Maxwell Fyfe in an effort to avoid criticism because that topic had also received attention in the press. He was a notorious homophobe, and it is unlikely that he would have conflated the two issues if he had suspected that the final recommendations would include liberalizing measures. Thus, although the harsh and repressive measures with regard to prostitution can be seen as a forgone conclusion, they were eclipsed by the public impact of the recommendations concerning homosexuality. However, what took the country by storm was the famous liberal assertion that "unless a deliberate attempt is to be made by society, acting through the agency of the law, to equate the sphere of crime with that of sin, there must remain a realm of private morality and immorality which is, in brief and crude terms, not the law's business."

The impact of this statement on law and on public perceptions of homosexual behavior has been profound, but with regard to prostitution exceedingly devious. To justify the Home Office aims for harsher penalties, Wolfenden and his committee argued that they were not concerned with morality but with public order. As Wolfenden put it in his **memoirs**, "questions of morality apart," something had to be done to protect "the right of the ordinary citizen to have free and uninterrupted passage along the streets of London." This denial of any moral component neatly sidestepped the responsibility of the client (who merely accepted an offer and annoyed nobody) and the inappropriateness of a prison sentence for "loitering or soliciting," an activity described by the committee's secretary, W. C. Roberts, as "hanging around."

The subtleties of this argument were forgotten when it came to legislation, and the recommendations of the Wolfenden Committee were embodied in the Street Offences Act of 1959. It became an offence for a "common prostitute" to loiter or solicit in a street or a public place for the purpose of prostitution. This was underpinned by a nonstatutory cautioning system that provided for two cautions before a woman was officially registered in police files as a "common prostitute," a label that could not be expunged.

In effect, this provided a presupposition of guilt, given that the subsequent presentation of a woman before the court as a "common prostitute" left her with no defense. Repeated attempts to repeal or reform this law have ended in failure.

Further Reading: Self, Helen J. *Prostitution, Women and Misuse of the Law: The Fallen Daughters of Eve*. London: Head, Frank Cass, 2003; Wolfenden, John. *Turning Points: The Memoirs of Lord Wolfenden*. London: The Bodley, 1976.

Helen J. Self

WOODHULL, VICTORIA (1838–1927). Victoria Woodhull was a fearless feminist activist who spoke against the hypocrisy of 19th-century attitudes toward sexuality. Born in frontier Ohio, Victoria rarely attended school, traveling with her family to hawk questionable medicines. At age 15, she married an alcoholic physician, Canning Woodhull; later, her daughter Zula became her lifelong companion. Victoria reunited with her sister, Tennessee Celeste (1845–1923) when Canning abandoned his family, creating a female-headed household that scandalized the Midwest. Woodhull's new lover, Colonel J. H. Blood, introduced the sisters to the century's many intellectual crazes. The family moved to Manhattan, where Woodhull and "Tennie C." persuaded a millionaire to finance their Wall Street brokerage firm. In April 1870, Woodhull announced her candidacy for President of the United States, even though women did not have the right to vote. Woodhull's denunciation of the sexual double standard that penalized women, but not men, for taking multiple lovers cemented her notoriety when Canning joined her possibly polygamous household. In *Woodhull & Claflin's Weekly*, published from 1870 to 1876, the sisters advocated **free love**, legalized prostitution, spiritualism, and dress reform, especially the abandoning of corsets. When a famous Brooklyn minister dismissed them as "two prostitutes,"

Victoria Woodhull

"Yes, I am a Free Lover. I have an inalienable, constitutional and natural right to love whom I may, to love as long or as short a period as I can; to change that love every day if I please, and with that right neither you nor any law you can frame have any right to interfere."

Victoria Woodhull, Steinway Hall, May 9, 1872. "Official Report of the Equal Rights Convention, New York City."

the *Weekly* retaliated, publishing a detailed account of his adulterous affair with a parishioner. The federal government invoked the new Comstock law, jailing Victoria Woodhull for distributing "obscene" material. Defended by a leading Congressman, the sisters won their free speech case. Woodhull and Tennessee Caflin immigrated to England in 1877, each marrying wealthy society men. Victoria Woodhull and Zula Woodhull were later advocates for birth control.

Further Reading: Victoria Woodhull & Company Web site. http://www.victoria-woodhull.com; Goldsmith, Barbara. *Other Powers: The Age of Suffrage, Spiritualism and the Scandalous Victoria Woodhull.* New York: Alfred A Knopf, 1998; Horowitz, Helen Lefkowitz. *Rereading Sex: Battles over Sexual Knowledge and Suppression in Nineteenth-Century America.* New York: Alfred A. Knopf, 2002.

Melinda Chateauvert

WORLD CHARTER. *See* **Appendix C, document 11: World Charter for Prostitutes' Rights, 1985.**

WORLD HEALTH ORGANIZATION. The World Health Organization (WHO) is a branch of the United Nations, and it addresses sex work as part of its effort to address problems with **sexually transmitted infections** and HIV. When AIDS was identified as a

Victoria Woodhull reading her argument in favor of woman's voting, in front of the Judiciary Committee of the House of Representatives, 1870. Courtesy of the Library of Congress.

significant threat to public health, WHO formed a department, the Global Programme on AIDS (GPA), under the leadership of Jonathan Mann. In 1989, Mann recruited Priscilla Alexander to review the experiences of projects that worked with sex workers in developing countries and to develop guidelines on how to organize HIV-prevention programs in the context of sex work. It was GPA's position that the people most affected by the epidemic had a crucial role to play in developing an effective response. Perhaps because of the urgency of the AIDS epidemic, GPA was given a freer hand than is typical of WHO departments, which traditionally are required to function within a formal bureaucracy that gives member states a leading role. As a result, GPA was able to bypass national governments in some cases. GPA's approach to prostitution used a labor perspective by which HIV was addressed as a workplace issue for sex workers. The GPA promoted the growth of nongovernmental organizations, which continue to play a crucial role in prevention of HIV in developing countries. A large number of nongovernmental organizations addressing HIV work with prostitutes. This program later became UNAIDS.

Priscilla Alexander

THE WORLD OF SUZIE WONG. Richard Mason's 1957 novel, *The World of Suzie Wong*, is narrated in the first person by a British artist, Robert Lomax. Starting a new life in **Hong Kong**, the initially naïve Lomax is both appalled and compelled by the rampant prostitution in the British colony. Living in a seedy hotel in the Wanchai district, where Chinese women can solicit sailors through a legal loophole, he befriends many of the women; however, Lomax becomes fixated on one particular prostitute: Suzie Wong. Their relationship is at first chaste, but after many dramatic ups and downs—convincingly narrated through Mason's matter-of-fact and sober prose—the couple marry in Macau and plan a new life together in Japan.

The couple face many obstacles to their union, including drink-sodden rivals and Wong's tuberculosis, her short prison spell for attacking a rival prostitute, and the death of her baby and the baby's *amah* (wet-nurse). Perhaps the biggest obstacle to contentment is Wong's low self-esteem: after being raped by an uncle as a teenager and sleeping with thousands of men for money since, she sees herself only as a "dirty little yum-yum girl." On one level a love story between an unlikely couple, the novel also contains a range of comment on social ills. Prostitution, Lomax insists, is a minor ill compared with the overcrowding and lack of hygiene in refugee-packed Hong Kong and compared with the racism shown toward mixed-race children of Western and Chinese parents. The novel is notable for its vivid depiction of Hong Kong's humidity-wracked nightlife, its gambling, drinking, and eating cultures, and its cast of colorful cameos of frustrated businessmen, irritable English wives, nervous officials, and harassed hotel staff. But it is also notable for its frank depictions of sexual activity and miscegenation and—above all—for its defense of the women who sell their bodies and even of the lonely men who resort to seeking out prostitutes.

The novel was quickly adapted for stage and screen. The dramatist, Paul Osborn, crafted a play based on Mason's novel, also called *The World of Suzie Wong*. Although Osborn's script has never been published, the play has been performed on Broadway and in Britain. The film version of 1960, which also retained the novel's title, was directed by Richard Quine and was a breakthrough film for Nancy Kwan, whose depiction of the Hong Kong prostitute established her as one of the leading Asian stars in the West.

France Nuyen and William Shatner in Joshua Logan's 1958 play *The World of Susie Wong*. Courtesy of Photofest.

Further Reading: Ho, Elaine Yee Lin. "Connecting Cultures: Hong Kong Literature in English, the 1950s." *New Zealand Journal of Asian Studies* 5, no. 2 (2003): 5–25; Mason, Richard. *The World of Suzie Wong*. London: Collins, 1957.

Kevin De Ornellas

WORLD WAR I REGULATION. During the World War I, the appearance of **syphilis** and gonorrhea among Allied and German troops produced heightened worries about the dangers of prostitution and **sexually transmitted infections**. From 1914 to 1918, European governments increased police surveillance of prostitutes to halt the spread of disease, yet prostitution as an economic force grew. Thousands of soldiers visited brothels to dance, drink, and forget the war. In turn, many women ran successful businesses catering to soldiers, only to retire from prostitution after the war.

During the 19th century, Britain and France introduced systems of medically regulated prostitution, seeking to ensure the health of prostitutes for customers. Regulation required prostitutes to register with police and receive medical examinations from police physicians. Doctors examined prostitutes monthly or bimonthly, giving them pelvic and visual screenings for chancres or pox, both signs of syphilis. If deemed healthy, prostitutes received an official document to certify their health and could continue to work. If symptomatic, prostitutes were isolated in **brothels** or sent to a women's prison-hospital to recover. Regulation, however, did not stop the spread of disease; by 1917, Paul Faivre, a physician, complained that medical examinations infected women with venereal disease. Police doctors, he said, did not clean their instruments between exams, often using the same **speculum** dipped in a jar of grease. In this way, they transmitted infection from woman to woman.

Germany also had a system of regulation and police that kept prostitutes under surveillance. During the war, however, German authorities also suspected women who engaged in sexual activities outside of **marriage** to be prostitutes, identifying them as amateur prostitutes (*heimliche Prostitutierte*). To curtail prostitution and disease, German officials increased police surveillance and closed public bars.

When healthy, prostitutes did not have to work hard to attract soldiers to their services; prostitution as sex work increased during the war. In France, British officer Robert Graves witnessed long lines in front of brothels, up to 150 strong. With such demand, the women working as prostitutes learned to make use of men's eagerness; they passed rapidly from one client to the next without spending much time on any individual. Stories circulated among soldiers and officials that a single prostitute could service a battalion of men a week, or upward of 60 to 80 men a day, for as long as she was able. French police doctor Léon Bizard reported that, near the front lines, women found ample if disagreeable work in the sexual economy. "There," Bizard wrote, "it was a pressing crowd, a hard, dangerous and sickening 'business': fifty, sixty, even one hundred men of all colors and races, 'to do' per day, under the continual threat from planes, bombardments." The prostitutes who had worked on the front lines explained to Bizard that "the profession was so laborious—eighteen hours of 'slaving at it' per day!—that every month, even every two weeks, [the women] had to go to Paris to regain their strength." But by that time, Bizard said, they had earned nearly a fortune and could begin life anew (Bizard 1925, 197).

Not all prostitutes left the business quickly or stayed near the front lines to work; some made use of the war to turn small brothels into larger businesses, sometimes selling them later. Aline Zink worked as an unregistered prostitute in Paris and, just before the war started in 1914, purchased a small brothel. On the first floor, the brothel included a bar, sitting room, and kitchen. She rented many of the second-floor bedrooms to *pensionnaires* (women who rented rooms to work as prostitutes). From eight in the morning until midnight, Zink allowed four women to dress in street clothes and solicit **clients** downstairs. A client could be expected to pay two or three francs for his visit, at a time when the exchange rate was nearly six francs per dollar.

Aline Zink ran her business carefully. She did not allow the women to cause problems and developed a solid working relationship with the police; they closed her brothel only once, for a minor infraction. She made certain that her house had a doctor and that all women received medical exams to continue working. On several occasions Zink acted as informant to the police, providing them with useful information on customers and troublemakers. After the Armistice in 1918, Zink and her husband (then a war veteran) sold the brothel for a tidy profit and began a new life. She never appeared in the police records again.

Regulated prostitution did not slow the spread of disease during the World War I. This slowing happened only at the end of the war, when soldiers returned home and resumed a normal life. Throughout the conflict, each of the warring nations took steps to increase surveillance of prostitutes. In spite of increased police attention and regulation of prostitution, sex work increased from 1914 to 1918. Many women, such as Aline Zink, created profitable businesses, running them strictly and working within the confines of police regulation.

See also Scapegoating.

Further Reading: Bizard, Léon. *Souvenirs d'un Médecin de la Préfecture de Police et des Prisons de Paris (1914–1918)*. Paris: Bernard Grasset, 1925; Grayzel, Susan. *Women's Identities at War*. Chapel Hill: University of North Carolina Press, 1999; Rhoades, Michelle K. "'No Safe Women': Prostitution, Masculinity, and Disease in France during the Great War." Ph.D. dissertation, University of Iowa, 2001; Rhoades, Michelle K. "'There Are No Safe Women': Prostitution in France During the Great War." *Proceedings of the Western Society for French History* 27 (2001): 43–50; Sauertig, Lutz D. H. "Sex Medicine and Morality During the First World War." In *War, Medicine and Modernity*, ed. Roger Cooter, Mark Harrison, and Steve Sturdy. Phoenix Mill, Stroud, England: Sutton Publishing, 1998, pp. 167–188.

Michelle K. Rhoades

WUORNOS, AILEEN (1959–2002). Dubbed the "Damsel of Death," Aileen Wuornos was accused of killing seven men while she worked as a prostitute in 1989 and 1990. She is known

Convicted serial killer Aileen Wuornos waits to testify in the Volusia County courthouse in Florida, 2001. Courtesy of AP / Wide World Photos.

as one of the first female **serial killers** in the United States. Of the seven murders that she was suspected of committing, Wuornos was convicted and sentenced to death for six. Her initial defense revolved around the premise that she was acting in self-defense, protecting herself from being raped and sodomized. She later recanted. According to Wuornos, devotion to her lesbian lover Tyria Moore drove her to kill to earn money so that they could continue to live. Aileen, also known as Lee, began life in Michigan abandoned by her mother and left in the care of her grandparents. Her father was a convicted child molester who committed suicide while in prison. Pregnant at 14, Wuornos gave her child up and started her career as a prostitute. It was believed that Wuornos suffered from borderline personality disorder as a result of the neglect and abuse she faced as a child at the hands of her grandparents and the townspeople. During her trial, Arlene Pralle adopted Wuornos, claiming that she had received a message from God.

Wuornos's story was made into three movies. The first, *Aileen Wuornos—The Selling of a Serial Killer*, details her appeals process and features interviews conducted by documentarian Nick Broomfield, who also made a second film about her. These were followed by a Hollywood version titled *Monster* (2003), featuring Charlize Theron as Wuornos, a role for which Theron won an Academy Award.

See also Films; Violence.

Further Reading: Kennedy, Dolores, with Robert Nolin. *On a Killing Day: The Bizarre Story of Convicted Murderer Aileen "Lee" Wuornos.* Chicago: Bonus Books, 1992; Russell, Sue. *Lethal Intent.* New York: Pinnacle Books, 2002.

Anne Marie Fowler

Y

YOSHIWARA. Yoshiwara, the Edo, Japan, pleasure quarter, was for more than three centuries a center of prostitution, theater, and art. From 1617, Yoshiwara was located to the northeast of the city and, in 1657, was moved to a larger plot further from the city center. Originally named for the "field of reeds" it was built on, the initial character, "*yoshi*," was later altered to signify "good fortune." Yoshiwara's geographical separation from the rest of the city (by distance, walls, and a moat) made it a social space distinct from that of strictly regimented Edo society. The fluid social relations of the Yoshiwara "floating world" (**ukiyo-e**) provided respite from the rigid hierarchies of everyday life in Edo. Once inside the Yoshiwara walls, which were locked at night, people hid visible signs of their social status, mixed with other classes, and, for a price, took pleasure where they could find it.

The Edo Era of Japan (1603–1868), also known as the Tokugawa Era, began with the nation's unification under the Shogun Ieyasu, who settled in Edo, previously a small fishing village, thus making it the nation's political and military seat. Over the next century, the city of Edo (current-day **Tokyo**) swelled to more than a million residents, of which around two-thirds were male, most of them samurai, merchants, and laborers. Populated by sojourners separated from family life, Edo grew into a "bachelor city" with great demands for diversion. To manage this social reality, a group of Edo brothel owners led by Shoji Jin'emon petitioned the Shogun to allow prostitution within a contained pleasure quarter. In 1617, the Shogun licensed the operation of **brothels**, set aside a section of land, and ordered the construction and settlement of a pleasure quarter.

With the Shogun's concession came a number of rules: people entering and leaving the quarter by its single gate were to be monitored, with suspicious strangers being reported to the authorities; **courtesans** were not allowed to work in other parts of the city or leave the quarter without permission; courtesans were not allowed to wear ostentatious **clothing**; buildings in the quarter were to be kept modest in size and plain in style; and the amount of time a guest could stay in the quarter was limited to one day and night. Ways to bend these rules were found soon enough, and periods of relative laxity and renewed enforcement would come and go. During periods of increased government vigilance, prostitutes found in other parts of the city were sent to the Yoshiwara. Confined to its set area by law and walls, the Yoshiwara's density increased greatly as the number of inhabitants and courtesans increased, housing at its height around 3,000 courtesans.

Though its location was marginal, the Yoshiwara (often referred to as *fuyajo*, the "nightless city") developed into a thriving cultural center packed with teahouses, restaurants, and theaters featuring kabuki and *bunraku* (puppet) drama. Artists and musicians recognized the Yoshiwara's potential as both a venue for their work and a source of material, reflected in visual art such as woodblock prints depicting the floating world (ukiyo-e) and erotic scenes (*shunga*, literally "spring pictures"). The quarter's internal folkways gave rise to distinct styles, behaviors, and speech patterns. Yoshiwara courtesans became known, in comparison to those of Kyoto or Osaka, for their self-possession and panache, known as *hari*. Frequent male visitors to the Yoshiwara strove for recognition as *tsu*, sophisticated dandies versed in style, the arts, and the workings of the pleasure quarter.

In many ways, the Yoshiwara was effectively exempt from common social restrictions, but a sophisticated hierarchy nevertheless resulted among its courtesans. From the early years of the Yoshiwara, the highest level of courtesan was the *tayo*, possessed of exceptional beauty and accomplished in traditional arts, followed by *koshi, tsubone, kirimise*, and the lowest class, *hashi*. The state of Yoshiwara's internal order was advertised through *saiken* (literally "**directories**"), which listed the names and locations of various courtesans and **guidebooks**, called *yujo hyobanki*, which considered at greater length the courtesans' respective merits and flaws. The prestige level of a given brothel rested significantly on the number, quality, and renown of its *tayo*.

"Morning at the Yoshiwara." A man looking out windows at snow falling while courtesans prepare tea and perform other domestic duties. Courtesy of the Library of Congress.

Throughout the 17th, 18th, and 19th centuries, courtesans faced competition from several directions, and the taxonomy continued to evolve and consolidate in response to internal and external pressures. Unlicensed prostitutes in other areas, such as Fukagawa, drove down prices. **Geisha** ("artist") emerged as a distinct profession whose practitioners specialized in high arts. Although geisha were not considered courtesans and were even prohibited from directly competing with courtesans, they filled the elevated cultural niche formerly occupied by elite courtesans. Former teahouse waitresses who had been relegated to the Yoshiwara in the late 17th century became known as *sancha*, displacing prior groups. Tayo and Koshi deteriorated in number, level of accomplishment, and price, causing the terms to fall into disuse and be replaced by other classes, such as *oiran*.

By the beginning of the Meiji Era (1868), when Edo became Tokyo, many Kabuki theaters had already moved to nearby Asakusa, and although many courtesans remained in Yoshiwara, it no longer was the city's cultural center. A number of trends and events contributed to the Yoshiwara's decline. Yoshiwara, since the blaze that had uprooted it in 1657, had always been vulnerable to fire. Blazes in the 1850s and 1860s, followed by many more over the next half-century, accelerated the migration of theaters, teahouses, and brothels to other sections of the city. After the great fire of 1911, in which several hundred Yoshiwara buildings burned down, the quarter was rebuilt with a more modern architectural character, and, along with much of Tokyo, it was leveled during World War II by American bombing campaigns. In addition to the lack of traditional Japanese architecture and waning demand for traditional arts, the Yoshiwara was dealt a final blow by legislation outlawing prostitution in 1956. Present-day Yoshiwara, officially Senzoku 4-chome, retains a notable density of unofficial brothels (called "soaplands"), but after significant shifts in the city's demographics and lifestyle, such as the rise of Kabukicho, Roppongi, and other entertainment districts, Yoshiwara's place as a vibrant pleasure quarter and center of culture has passed mostly into history and memory.

See also Appendix A, document 4.

Further Reading: De Becker, J. E. *The Nightless City, or, the History of the Yoshiwara Yukwaku*. New York: ICG Muse, 2003; Longstreet, Stephen, and Ethel Longstreet. *Yoshiwara: The Pleasure Quarters of Old Tokyo*. Tokyo: Yenbooks, 1970; Nishiyama, Matsunosuke. *Edo Culture: Daily Life and Diversions in Urban Japan, 1600–1868*, ed. and trans. Gerald Groemer. Honolulu: University of Hawaii Press, 1997; Screech, Timon. *Sex and the Floating World: Erotic Images in Japan, 1700–1820*. Honolulu: University of Hawaii Press, 1999; Seidensticker, Edward. *Low City, High City: Tokyo from Edo to the Earthquake*. New York: Knopf, 1983; Seigle, Cecilia Segawa. *Yoshiwara: The Glittering World of the Japanese Courtesan*. Honolulu: University of Hawaii Press, 1993; Swinton, Elizabeth de Sabato. *The Women of the Pleasure Quarter: Japanese Paintings and Prints of the Floating World*. New York: Hudson Hills Press, 1995.

Alex Feerst

Z

ZOLA, ÉMILE. Émile Edouard Charles Antoine Zola (1840–1902) was a French novelist and founder of the Naturalist movement in fiction. His series of 20 novels known under the generic title *Les Rougon-Macquart. Histoire naturelle et sociale d'une famille sous le Second Empire* (*The Rougon-Macquarts. The natural and social history of a family during the Second Empire*) included depictions of the lives of prostitutes, in particular the life of Nana in the novel of that name (published in 1880).

Zola researched in detail the lives of prostitutes and **courtesans** while preparing to write *Nana*, and his creation is a composite character, drawn both from his observations and from what he had been told about various courtesans. In particular, aspects of the historical characters of the Englishwoman **Cora Pearl** and

Émile Zola. Courtesy of the Library of Congress.

the French courtesan Blanche d'Antigny can be discerned in Zola's depiction of Nana. He was partly inspired to write the novel by Edouard Manet's painting, also called Nana (1877), which had in turn been inspired by Zola's earlier novel *L'Assommoir*, in which Nana makes her first appearance.

Zola was writing after the collapse of the Second Empire when attitudes toward prostitution were predominantly hostile and condemnatory; he was both influenced by and helped to perpetuate these attitudes. In one of his harshest diatribes in *Nana*, he likens a prostitute to a disease-carrying fly. He also reiterated the stereotypes catalogued by Dr. **Alexandre-Jean-Baptiste Parent-Duchâtelet** nearly half a century earlier, dwelling on the prostitute's so-called instability and talkativeness, her taste for **alcohol**, her love for food and passion for gambling, and her propensity toward laziness, lying, and anger. In a gruesome closing scene that came to symbolize the disgust felt by many contemporaries for the prostitute, he made Nana die a particularly unpleasant death from smallpox.

See also France, Second Empire; Les Grandes Horizontales.

Further Reading: Auriant. *La Véritable Histoire de 'Nana.'* Paris: Mercure de France, 1942.

Virginia Rounding

APPENDIX A: HISTORICAL ACCOUNTS

1. Prostitution in London (1862)

By Bracebridge Hemyng

Excerpts from Henry Philip Mayhew and Bracebridge Hemyng, *London Labour and the London Poor. Volume IV: Those That Will Not Work* (London: Griffin, Bohn, and Company, 1862).

Henry Mayhew is best known for his groundbreaking studies of urban workers and inhabitants of the street—including prostitutes—published in four volumes as London Labour and the London Poor in 1861 and 1862. Not only popular and influential in its day, London Labour and the London Poor also remains an important source for any study of Victorian prostitution.

The fourth volume of London Labour, titled Those That Will Not Work, contains a long discussion of prostitution, cowritten by Mayhew and Bracebridge Hemyng (1841–1901). Mayhew described prostitution around the world through the ages, and Hemyng provide groupings of prostitutes from "Sailor's Women" to "Clandestine Prostitutes" and "Cohabitant Prostitutes." Although Mayhew considered prostitution a type of theft, many of the fascinating interviews with prostitutes included in London Labour and the London Poor show a businesslike or professional attitude.

See also **Mayhew, Henry** *in this text.*

Many novelists, philanthropists, and newspaper writers have dwelt much upon the horrible character of a series of subterranean chambers or vaults in the vicinity of the Strand, called the Adelphi Arches. It is by no means even now understood that these arches are the most innocent and harmless places in London, whatever they might once have been. A policeman is on duty there at night, expressly to prevent persons who have no right or business there from descending into their recesses.

They were probably erected in order to form a foundation for the Adelphi Terrace. Let us suppose there were then no wharves, and no embankments, consequently the tide must have ascended and gone inland some distance, rendering the ground marshy, swampy, and next to useless. The main arch is a very fine pile of masonry, something like the Box tunnel on a small scale, while the other, running here and there like the intricacies of catacombs, looks extremely ghostly and suggestive of Jack Sheppards, Blueskins, Jonathan Wilds, and others of the same kind, notwithstanding they are so well lighted with gas. There is a doorway at the end of a vault leading up towards the Strand, that has a peculiar tradition attached to it. Not so very many years ago this door was a back exit from a notorious coffee and gambling house, where parties were decoyed by thieves, blacklegs, or prostitutes, and swindled, then drugged, and subsequently thrown from this door into the darkness of what must have seemed to them another world, and were left, when they came to themselves, to find their way out as best they could.

My attention was attracted, while in these arches, by the cries and exclamations of a woman near the river, and proceeding to the spot I saw a woman sitting on some steps, before what appeared to be a stable, engaged in a violent altercation with a man who was by profession a cab proprietor—several of his vehicles were lying about—and who, she vehemently asserted, was her husband. The man declared she was a common woman when he met her, and had since become the most drunken creature it was possible to meet with. The woman put her hand in her pocket and brandished something in his face, which she triumphantly said was her marriage-certificate. "That," she cried, turning to me, "that's what licks them. It don't matter whether I was one of Lot's daughters afore. I might have been awful, I don't say I wasn't, but I'm his wife, and this 'ere's what licks 'em."

I left them indulging in elegant invectives, and interlarding their conversation with those polite and admirable metaphors that have gained so wide-spread a reputation for the famous women who sell fish in Billingsgate; and I was afterwards informed by a sympathising bystander, in the shape of a stable-boy, that the inevitable result of this conjugal altercation would be the incarceration of the woman, by the husband, in a horse-box, where she might undisturbed sleep off the effects of her potations, and repent the next day at her leisure. "Neo dulces amores sperne puer."

Several showily-dressed, if not actually well-attired women, who are to be found walking about the Haymarket, live in St. Giles's and about Drury Lane. But the lowest class of women, who prostitute themselves for a shilling or less, are the most curious and remarkable class in this part. We have spoken of them before as growing grey in the exercise of their profession. One of them, a woman over forty, shabbily dressed, and with a disreputable, unprepossessing appearance, volunteered the following statement for a consideration of a spirituous nature.

"Times is altered, sir, since I come on the town. I can remember when all the swells used to come down here-away, instead of going to the Market; but those times is past, they is, worse luck, but, like myself, nothing lasts for ever, although I've stood my share of wear and tear, I have. Years ago Fleet Street and the Strand, and Catherine Street, and all round there was famous for women and houses. Ah! those were the times. Wish they might come again, but wishing's no use, it ain't. It only makes one miserable a thinking of it. I come up from the country when I was quite a gal, not above sixteen I dessay. I come from Dorsetshire, near Lyme Regis, to see a aunt of mine. Father was a farmer in Dorset, but only in a small way—tenant farmer, as you would say. I was mighty pleased, you may swear, with London, and liked being out at night when I could get the chance. One night I went up the area and stood looking through the railing, when a man passed by, but seeing me he returned and spoke to me something about the weather. I, like a child, answered him unsuspectingly enough, and he went on talking about town and country, asking me, among other things, if I had long been in London, or if I was born there. I not thinking told him all about myself; and he went away apparently very much pleased with me, saying before he went that he was very glad to have made such an agreeable acquaintance, and if I would say nothing about it he would call for me about the same time, or a little earlier, if I liked, the next night, and take me out for a walk. I was, as you may well suppose, delighted, and never said a word. The next evening I met him as he appointed, and two or three times subsequently. One night we walked longer than usual, and I pressed him to return, as I feared my aunt would find me out; but he said he was so fatigued with walking so far, he would like to rest a little before he went back again; but if I was very anxious he would put me in a cab. Frightened about him, for I thought he might be ill, I preferred risking being found out; and when he proposed that he should go into some house and sit down I agreed. He said all at once, as if he had just remembered something, that a very old friend of his lived near there, and we couldn't go to a better place, for she would give us everything we could wish. We found the door half open when we arrived. 'How careless,' said my friend, 'to leave the street-door open, any one might get in.' We entered without knocking, and seeing a door in the passage standing ajar we went in. My friend shook hands with an old lady who was talking to several girls dispersed over different parts of the room, who, she said, were her daughters. At this announcement some of them laughed, when she got very angry and ordered them out of the room. Somehow I didn't like the place, and not feeling all right I asked to be put in a cab and sent home. My friend made no objection and a cab was sent for. He, however, pressed me to have something to drink before I started. I refused to touch any wine, so I asked for some coffee, which I drank. It made me feel very sleepy, so sleepy indeed that I begged to be allowed to sit down on the sofa. They accordingly placed me on the sofa, and advised me to rest a little while, promising, in order to allay my anxiety, to send a messenger to my aunt. Of course I was drugged, and so heavily I did not regain my consciousness till the next morning. I was horrified to discover that I had been ruined, and for some days I was inconsolable, and cried like a child to be killed or sent back to my aunt.

"When I became quiet I received a visit from my seducer, in whom I had placed so much silly confidence. He talked very kindly to me, but I would not listen to him for some time. He came several times to see me, and at last said he would take me away if I liked, and give me a house of my own. Finally, finding how hopeless all was I agreed to his proposal, and he allowed me four pounds a week. This went on for some months, till he was tired of me, when he threw me over for some one else. There is always as good fish in the sea as ever came out of it, and this I soon discovered.

"Then for some years—ten years, till I was six-and-twenty,— I went through all the changes of a gay lady's life, and they're not a few, I can tell you. I don't leave off this sort of life because I'm in a manner used to it, and what could I do if I did? I've no character; I've never been used to do anything, and I don't see what employment I stand a chance of getting. Then if I had to sit hours and hours all day long, and part of the night too, sewing or anything like that, I should get tired. It would worrit me so; never having been accustomed, you see, I couldn't stand it. I lodge in Charles Street, Drury Lane, now. I did live in Nottingham Court once, and Earls Street. But, Lord, I've lived in a many places you wouldn't think, and I don't imagine you'd believe one half.

I'm always a-chopping and a-changing like the wind as you may say. I pay half-a-crown a week for my bed-room; it's clean and comfortable, good enough for such as me. I don't think much of my way of life. You folks as has honour, and character, and feelings, and such, can't understand how all that's been beaten out of people like me. I don't feel. *I'm used to it.* I did once, more especial when mother died. I heard on it through a friend of mine, who told me her last words was of me. I did cry and go on then ever so, but Lor', where's the good of fretting? I arn't happy either. It isn't happiness, but I get enough money to keep me in victuals and drink, and it's the drink mostly that keeps me going. You've no idea how I look forward to my drop of gin. It's everything to me. I don't suppose I'll live much longer, and that's another thing that pleases me. I don't want to live, and yet I don't care enough about dying to make away with myself. I arn't got that amount of feeling that some has, and that's where it is I'm kinder 'fraid of it."

This woman's tale is a condensation of the philosophy of sinning. The troubles she had gone through, and her experience of the world, had made her oblivious of the finer attributes of human nature, and she had become brutal.

I spoke to another who had been converted at a Social Evil Meeting, but from a variety of causes driven back to the old way of living.

The first part of her story offered nothing peculiar. She had been on the town for fifteen years, when a year or so ago she heard of the Midnight Meeting and Baptist Noel. She was induced from curiosity to attend; and her feelings being powerfully worked upon by the extraordinary scene, the surroundings, and the earnestness of the preacher, she accepted the offer held out to her, and was placed in a cab with some others, and conveyed to one of the numerous metropolitan homes, where she was taken care of for some weeks, and furnished with a small sum of money to return to her friends. When she arrived at her native village in Essex, she only found her father. Her mother was dead; her sister at service, and her two brothers had enlisted in the army. Her father was an old man, supported by the parish; so it was clear he could not support her. She had a few shillings left, with which she worked her way back to town, returned to her old haunts, renewed her acquaintance with her vicious companions, and resumed her old course of life.

I don't insert this recital as a reflection upon the refuges and homes, or mean to asperse the Midnight Meeting movement, which is worthy of all praise. On the contrary, I have much pleasure in alluding to the subject and acknowledging the success that has attended the efforts of the philanthropic gentlemen associated with the Rev. Mr. Baptist Noel.

PARK WOMEN, OR THOSE WHO FREQUENT THE PARKS AT NIGHT AND OTHER RETIRED PLACES

Park women, properly so called, are those degraded creatures, utterly lost to all sense of shame, who wander about the paths most frequented after nightfall in the Parks, and consent to any species of humiliation for the sake of acquiring a few shillings. You may meet them in Hyde Park, between the hours of five and ten (till the gates are closed) in winter. In the Green Park, in what is called the Mall, which is a nocturnal thoroughfare, you may see these low wretches walking about sometimes with men, more generally alone, often early in the morning. They are to be seen reclining on the benches placed under the trees, originally intended, no doubt, for a different purpose, occasionally with the head of a drunken man reposing in their lap. These women are well known to give themselves up to disgusting practices, that are alone gratifying to men of morbid and diseased imaginations. They are old, unsound, and by their appearance utterly incapacitated from practising their profession where the gas-lamps would expose the defects in their personal appearance, and the shabbiness of their ancient and dilapidated attire. I was told that an old woman, whose front teeth were absolutely wanting, was known to obtain a precarious livelihood by haunting the by-walks of Hyde Park, near Park Lane. The unfortunate women that form this despicable class have in some cases been well off, and have been reduced to their present condition by a variety of circumstances, among which are intemperance, and the vicissitudes natural to their vocation. I questioned one who was in the humour to be communicative, and she gave the subjoined replies to my questions:—

"I have not always been what I now am. Twenty years ago I was in a very different position. Then, although it may seem ludicrous to you, who see me as I now am, I was comparatively well off. If I were to tell you my history it would be so romantic you would not believe it. If I employ a little time in telling you, will you reward me for my trouble, as I shall be losing my time in talking to you? I am not actuated by mercenary motives exactly in making this request, but my time is my money, and I cannot afford to lose either one or the other. Well, then, I am the daughter of a curate in Gloucestershire. I was never at school, but my mother educated me at home. I had one brother who entered the Church. When I was old enough I saw that the limited resources of my parents would not allow them to maintain me at home without seriously impairing their resources, and I proposed that I should go out as a governess. At first they would not hear of it; but I persisted in my determination, and eventually obtained a situation in a family in town. Then I was very pretty. I may say so without vanity or ostentation, for I had many admirers, among whom I numbered the only son of the people in whose house I lived. I was engaged to teach his two sisters, and altogether I gave great satisfaction to the family. The girls were amiable and tractable, and I soon acquired an influence over their generous dispositions that afforded great facilities for getting them on in their studies. My life might have been very happy if an unfortunate attachment to me had not sprung up in the young man that I have before mentioned, which attachment I can never sufficiently regret was reciprocated by myself.

"I battled against the impulse that constrained me to love him, but all my efforts were of no avail. He promised to marry me, which in an evil hour I agreed to. He had a mock ceremony performed by his footman, and I went into lodgings that he had taken for me in Gower Street, Tottenham Court Road. He used to visit me very frequently for the ensuing six months, and we lived together as man and wife. At the expiration of that time he took me to the sea-side, and we subsequently travelled on the Continent. We were at Baden when we heard of his father's death. This didn't trouble him much. He did not even go to England to attend the funeral, for he had by his conduct offended his father, and estranged himself from the remainder of his family. Soon letters came from a solicitor informing him that the provisions of the will discontinued the allowance of five hundred a year hitherto made to him, and left him a small sum of money sufficient to buy himself a commission in the army, if he chose to do so. This course he was strongly advised to take, for it was urged that he might support himself on his pay if he volunteered for foreign service. He was transported with rage when this communication reached him, and he immediately wrote for the legacy he was entitled to, which arrived in due course. That evening he went to the gaming table, and lost every farthing he had in the world. The next morning he was a corpse. His remains were found in a secluded part of the town, he having in a fit of desperation blown his brains out with a pistol. He had evidently resolved to take this step before he left me, if he should happen to be unfortunate, for he left a letter in the hands of our landlady to be delivered to me in the event of his not returning in the morning. It was full of protestations of affection for me, and concluded with an avowal of the fraud he had practiced towards me when our acquaintance was first formed, which he endeavoured to excuse by stating his objections to be hampered or fettered by legal impediments.

"When I read this, I somewhat doubted the intensity of the affection he paraded in his letter. I had no doubt about the fervour of my own passion, and for some time I was inconsolable. At length I was roused to a sense of my desolate position, and to the necessity for action, by the solicitations and importunity of my landlady, and I sold the better part of my wardrobe to obtain sufficient money to pay my bills, and return to England. But fate ordered things in a different manner. Several of my husband's friends came to condole with me on his untimely decease; among whom was a young officer of considerable personal attractions, who I had often thought I should have liked to love, if I had not been married to my friend's husband. It was this man who caused me to take the second fatal step I have made in my life. If I had only gone home, my friends might have forgiven everything. I felt they would, and my pride did not stand in my way, for I would gladly have asked and obtained their forgiveness for a fault in reality very venial, when the circumstances under which it was committed are taken into consideration.

"Or I might have represented the facts to the family; and while the mother mourned the death of her son, she must have felt some commiseration for myself.

"The officer asked me to live with him, and made the prospect he held out to me so glittering and fascinating that I yielded. He declared he would marry me with pleasure on the spot, but he would forfeit a large sum of money, that he must inherit in a few years if he remained single, and it would be folly not to wait until then. I have forgotten to mention that I had not any children. My constitution being very delicate, my child was born dead, which was a sad blow to me, although it did not seem to affect the man I regarded as my husband. We soon left Baden and returned to London, where I lived for a month very happily with my paramour, who was not separated from me, as his leave of absence had not expired. When that event occurred he reluctantly left me to go to Limerick, where his regiment was quartered. There in all probability he formed a fresh acquaintance, for he wrote to me in about a fortnight, saying that a separation must take place between us, for reasons that he was not at liberty to apprise me of, and he enclosed a cheque for fifty pounds, which he hoped would pay my expenses. It was too late now to go home, and I was driven to a life of prostitution, not because I had a liking for it, but as a means of getting enough money to live upon. For ten years I lived first with one man then with another, until at last I was infected with a disease, of which I did not know the evil effects if neglected. The disastrous consequence of that neglect is only too apparent now. You will be disgusted, when I tell you that it attacked my face, and ruined my features to such an extent that I am hideous to look upon, and should be noticed by no one if I frequented those places where women of my class most congregate; indeed, I should be driven away with curses and execrations."

This recital is melancholy in the extreme. Here was a woman endowed with a very fair amount of education, speaking in a superior manner, making use of words that very few in her position would know how to employ, reduced by a variety of circumstances to the very bottom of a prostitute's career. In reply to my further questioning, she said she lived in a small place in Westminster called Perkins' Rents, where for one room she paid two shillings a week. The Rents were in Westminster, not far from Palace-yard. She was obliged to have recourse to her present way of living to exist ; for she would not go to the workhouse, and she could get no work to do. She could sew, and she could paint in water-colours, but she was afraid to be alone. She could not sit hours and hours by herself, her thoughts distracted her, and drove her mad. She added, she once thought of turning Roman Catholic, and getting admitted into a convent, where she might make atonement for her way of living by devoting the remainder of her life to penitence, but she was afraid she had gone too far to be forgiven. That was some time ago. Now she did not think she would live long, she had injured her constitution so greatly; she had some internal disease, she didn't know what it was, but a hospital surgeon told her it would kill her in time, and she had her moments, generally hours, of oblivion, when she was intoxicated, which she always was when she could get a chance. It she got ten shillings from a drunken man, either by persuasion or threats, and she was not scrupulous in the employment of the latter, she would not come to the Park for days, until all her money was spent ; on an average, she came three times a week, or perhaps twice; always on Sunday, which was a good day. She knew all about the Refuges. She had been in one once, but she didn't like the system; there wasn't enough liberty, and too much preaching, and that sort of thing; and then they couldn't keep her there always; so they didn't know what to do with her. No one would take her into their service, because they didn't like to look at her face, which presented so dreadful an appearance that it frightened people. She always wore a long thick veil, that concealed her features, and made her interesting to the unsuspicious and unwise. I gave her the money I promised her, and advised her again to enter a Refuge, which she refused to do, saying she could not live long, and she would rather die as she was. As I had no power to compel her to change her determination, I left her, lamenting her hardihood and obstinacy. I felt that she soon would be—

"One more unfortunate,
Weary of breath,
Rashly importunate,
Gone to her death."
[Thomas Hood, "The Bridge of Sighs"]

In the course of my peregrinations I met another woman, commonly dressed in old and worn-out clothes; her face was ugly and mature; she was perhaps on the shady side of forty. She was also perambulating the Mall. I knew she could only be there for one purpose, and I interrogated her, and I believe she answered my queries faithfully. She said:—

"I have a husband, and seven small children, the oldest not yet able to do much more than cadge a penny or so by cater-wheeling and tumbling in the street for the amusement of gents as rides outside 'busses. My husband's bedridden, and can't do nothing but give the babies a dose of 'Mother's Blessing' (that's laudanum, sir, or some sich stuff) to sleep 'em when they's squally. So I goes out begging all day, and I takes in general one of the kids in my arms and one as runs by me, and we sell hartifishal flowers, leastways 'olds 'em in our 'ands, and makes believe cos of the police, as is nasty so be as you 'as nothink soever, and I comes hout in the Parks, sir, at night sometimes when I've 'ad a bad day, and ain't made above a few pence, which ain't enough to keep us as we should be kep. I mean, sir, the children should have a bit of meat, and my ole man and me wants some blue ruin to keep our spirits up; so I'se druv to it, sir, by poverty, and nothink on the face of God's blessed earth, sir, shou'dn't have druv me but that for the poor babes must live, and who 'as they to look to but their 'ard-working but misfortunate mother, which she is now talking to your honour, and won't yer give a poor woman a hap'ny, sir? I've seven small children at home, and my 'usban's laid with the fever. You won't miss it, yer honour, only a 'apny for a poor woman as ain't 'ad a bit of bread between her teeth since yesty morning. I ax yer parding," she exclaimed, interrupting herself—"I forgot I was talking to yourself. I's so used to this way of speaking when I meant to ax you for summut I broke off into the old slang, but yer honour knows what I mean: ain't yer got even a little sixpence to rejoice the heart of the widow?"

"You call yourself a widow now," I said, "while before you said you were married and had seven children. Which are you?"

"Which am I? The first I tell you's the true. But Lor', I's up to so many dodges I gets what you may call confounded; sometimes I's a widder, and wants me 'art rejoiced with a copper, and then I's a hindustrious needle-woman thrown out of work and going to be druv into the streets if I don't get summut to do. Sometimes I makes a lot of money by being a poor old cripple as broke her arm in a factory, by being blowed hup when a steam-engine blowed herself hup, and I bandage my arm and swell it out hawful big, and when I gets home, we gets in some lush and 'as some frens, and goes in for a reglar blow-hout, and how as I have told yer honour hall about it, won't yer give us an 'apny as I observe before?"

It is very proper that the Parks should be closed at an early hour, when such creatures as I have been describing exist and practise their iniquities so unblushingly. One only gets at the depravity of mankind by searching below the surface of society; and for certain purposes such knowledge and information are useful and beneficial to the community. Therefore the philanthropist must overcome his repugnance to the task, and draw back the veil that is thinly spread over the skeleton.

CLANDESTINE PROSTITUTES

The next division of our subject is clandestine prostitution, whose ramifications are very extensive. In it we must include: 1. Female operatives; 2. Maid-servants, all of whom are amateurs, as opposed to professionals, or as we have had occasion to observe before, more commonly known as "Dollymops"; 3. Ladies of intrigue, who see men to gratify their passions; and 4. Keepers of houses of assignation, where the last-mentioned class may carry on their amours with secresy.

This in reality I regard as the most serious side of prostitution. This more clearly stamps the character of the nation. A thousand and one causes may lead to a woman's becoming a professional prostitute, but if a woman goes wrong without any very cogent reason for so doing, there must be something radically wrong in her composition, and inherently bad in her nature, to lead her to abandon her person to the other sex, who are at all times ready to take advantage of a woman's weakness and a woman's love.

There is a tone of morality throughout the rural districts of England, which is unhappily wanting in the large towns and the centres of particular manufactures. Commerce is incontestably demoralizing. Its effects are to be seen more and more every day. Why it should be so, it is not our province to discuss, but seduction and prostitution, in spite of the precepts of the Church, and the examples of her ministers, have made enormous strides in all our great towns within the last twenty years. Go through the large manufacturing districts, where factory-hands congregate, or more properly herd together, test them, examine them, talk to them, observe for yourself, and you will come away with the impression that there is room for much improvement. Then cast your eye over the statistics of births and the returns of the Registrar-General, and compare the number of legitimate with illegitimate births. Add up the number of infanticides and the number of death of infants of tender years—an item more alarming than any. Goldsmith has said that "honour sinks when commerce long prevails," and a truer remark was never made, although the animus of the poet was directed more against men than women.

Female Operatives. —When alluding casually to this subject before, I enumerated some of the trades that supplied women to swell the ranks of prostitution, amongst which are milliners, dress-makers, straw bonnet-makers, furriers, hat-binders, silk-winders, tambour-workers, shoe-binders, slop-women, or those who work for cheap tailors, those in pasty-cook, fancy and cigar-shops, bazaars, and ballet-girls.

I have heard it asserted in more than one quarter, although of course such assertions cannot be authenticated, or made reliable, for want of data, that one out of three of all the female operatives in London are unchaste, and in the habit of prostituting themselves when occasion offers, either for money, or more frequently for their own gratification.

I met a woman in Fleet Street, who told me that she came into the streets now and then to get money not to subsist upon, but to supply her with funds to meet the debts her extravagance caused her to contract. But I will put her narrative into a consecutive form.

"Ever since I was twelve," she said, "I have worked in a printing office where a celebrated London morning journal is put in type and goes to press. I get enough money to live upon comfortably; but then I am extravagant, and spend a great deal of money in eating and drinking, more than you would imagine. My appetite is very delicate, and my constitution not at all strong. I long for certain things like a woman in the family way, and I must have them by hook or by crook. The fact is the close confinement and the night air upset me and disorder my digestion. I have the most expensive things sometimes, and when I can, I live in a sumptuous manner, comparatively speaking. I am attached to a man in our office, to whom I shall be married some day. He does not suspect me, but on the contrary believes me to be true to him, and you do not suppose that I ever take the trouble to undeceive him. I am nineteen now, and have carried on with my 'typo' for nearly three years now. I sometimes go to the Haymarket, either early in the evening, or early in the morning, when I can get away from the printing; and sometimes I do a little in the day-time. This is not a frequent practice of mine; I only do it when I want money to pay anything. I am out now with the avowed intention of picking up a man, or making an appointment with some one for to-morrow or some time during the week. I always dress well, at least you mayn't think so, but I am always neat, and respectable, and clean, if the things I have on ain't worth the sight of money that some women's things cost them. I have good feet too, and as I find they attract attention, I always parade them. And I've hooked many a man by showing my ankle on a wet day. I shan't think anything of all this when I'm married. I believe my young man would marry me just as soon if he found out I went with others as he would now. I carry on with him now, and he likes me very much. I ain't of any particular family; to tell the truth. I was put in the workhouse when I was young, and they apprenticed me. I never knew my father or my mother, although 'my father was, as I've heard say, a well-known swell of capers gay, who cut his last fling with great applause;' or, if you must know, I heard that he was hung for killing a man who opposed him when committing a burglary. In other words, he was 'a macing-cove what robs,' and I'm his daughter, worse luck. I used to think at first, but what was the good of being wretched about it? I couldn't get over for some time, because I was envious, like a little fool, of other people, but I reasoned, and at last I did recover myself, and was rather glad that my position freed me from certain restrictions. I had no mother whose heart I shou'd break by my conduct, or no father who could threaten me with bringing his grey hairs with sorrow to the grave. I had a pretty good example to follow set before me, and I didn't scruple to argue that I was not to be blamed for what I did. Birth is the result of accident. It is the merest chance in the world whether you're born a countess or a washerwoman. I'm neither one nor t'other; I'm only a mot who does a little typographing by way of variety. Those who have had good nursing, and all that, and the advantages of a sound education, who have a position to lose, prospects to blight, and relations to dishonour, may be blamed for going on the loose, but I'll be hanged if I think that priest or moralist is to come down on me with the sledge-hammer of their denunciation. You look rather surprised at my talking so well. I know I talk well, but you must remember what a lot has passed through my hands for the last seven years, and what a lot of copy I've set up. There is very little I don't know, I can tell you. It's what old Robert Owen would call the spread of education."

I had to talk some time to this girl before she was so communicative; but it must be allowed my assiduity was amply repaid. The common sense she displayed was extraordinary for one in her position; but, as she said, she certainly had had superior opportunities, of which she had made the most. And her arguments, though based upon fallacy, were exceedingly clever and well put. So much for the spread of education amongst the masses. Who knows to what it will lead?

The next case that came under my notice was one of a very different description. I met a woman in Leadenhall Street, a little past the India House, going towards Whitechapel. She told me, without much solicitation on my part, that she was driven into the streets by want. Far from such a thing being her inclination, she recoiled from it with horror, and had there been no one else in the case, she would have preferred starvation to such a life. I thought of the motto Vergniaud the Girondist wrote on the wall of his dungeon in his blood, "Potius mori quam foedari," and I admired the woman whilst I pitied her. It is easy to condemn, but even vice takes the semblance of virtue when it has a certain end in view. Every crime ought to be examined into carefully in order that the motive that urged to the commission may be elicited, and that should be always thrown into the scale in mitigation or augmentation of punishment.

Her father was a dock labourer by trade, and had been ever since he came to London, which he did some years ago, when there was great distress in Rochdale, where he worked in a cotton factory; but being starved out there after working short time for some weeks, he tramped with his daughter, then about fourteen, up to town, and could get nothing to do but work in the docks, which requires no skill, only a good constitution, and the strength and endurance of a horse. This however, as every one knows, is a precarious sort of employment, very much sought after by strong, able-bodied men out of work. The docks are a refuge for all Spitalfields and the adjacent parishes for men out of work, or men whose trade is slack for a time. Some three weeks before I met her, the girl's father had the misfortune to break his arm and to injure his spine by a small keg of spirits slipping from a crane near to which he was standing. They took him to the hospital, where he then was. The girl herself worked as a hat-binder, for which she was very indifferently paid, and even that poor means of support she had lost lately through the failure of the house she worked for. She went to see her father every day, and always contrived to take him something, if it only cost twopence, as a mark of affection on her part, which he was not slow in appreciating, and no doubt found his daughter's kindness a great consolation to him in the midst of his troubles. She said, "I tried everywhere to get employment, and I couldn't. I ain't very good with my needle at fine needlework, and the slopsellers won't have me. I would have slaved for them though, I do assure you, sir; bad as they do pay you, and hard as you must work for them to get enough to live upon, and poor living, God knows, at that. I feel very miserable for what I've done, but I was driven to it; indeed I was, sir. I daren't tell father, for he'd curse me at first, though he might forgive me afterwards: for though he's poor, he's always been honest, and borne a good name; but now—I can't help crying a bit, sir. I ain't thoroughly hardened yet, and it's a hard case as ever was. I do wish I was dead and there was an end of everything, I am so awfully sad and heart-broken. If it don't kill me, I suppose I shall get used to it in time. The low rate of wages I received has often put it into my head to go wrong; but I have always withstood the temptation and nothing but so many misfortunes and trials coming together could ever have induced me to do it."

This, I have every reason to believe, was a genuine tale of distress told with all simplicity and truth, although everything that a woman of loose morals says must be received with caution, and believed under protest.

Ballet-girls have a bad reputation, which is in most cases well deserved. To begin with their remuneration—it is very poor. They get from nine to eighteen shillings. Columbine in the pantomime gets five pounds a week, but then hers is a prominent position. Out of these nine to eighteen shillings they have to find shoes and petticoats, silk stockings, etc., so that the pay is hardly adequate to their expenditure, and quite insufficient to fit them out and find them in food and lodging. Can it be wondered at, that while this state of things exists, ballet-girls should be compelled to seek a livelihood by resorting to prostitution?

Many causes may be enumerated to account for the lax morality of our female operatives. Among the chief of which we must class—

1. Low wages inadequate to their sustenance.
2. Natural levity and the example around them.
3. Love of dress and display, coupled with the desire for a sweetheart.
4. Sedentary employment, and want of proper exercise.
5. Low and cheap literature of an immoral tendency.
6. Absence of parental care and the inculcation of proper precepts. In short, bad bringing up.

Maid-Servants.—Maid-servants seldom have a chance of marrying, unless placed in a good family, where, after putting by a little money by pinching and careful saving, the housemaid may become an object of interest to the footman, who is looking out for a public-house, or when the housekeeper allies herself to the butler, and together they set up in business. In small families, the servants often give themselves up to the sons, or to the policeman on the beat, or to soldiers in the Parks; or else to shopmen, whom they may meet in the streets. Female servants are far from being a virtuous class. They are badly educated and are not well looked after by their mistresses as a rule, although every dereliction from the paths of propriety by them will be visited with the heaviest displeasure, and most frequently be followed by dismissal of the most summary description, without the usual month's warning, to which so much importance is usually attached by both employer and employed.

Marylebone was lately characterised by one of its vestrymen as being one of the seven black parishes in London. Half the women it is asserted who are sent from the workhouse, and have situations procured for them by the parochial authorities, turn out prostitutes. I have no means of corroborating the truth of this declaration, but it has been made and sent forth to the world through the medium of the public press, though I believe it has been partially contradicted by one of the workhouse authorities; however this may be, there can be no doubt that the tone of morality among servant-maids in the metropolis is low. I will not speak in the superlative—I merely characterise it as low. I had an opportunity of questioning a maid-of-all-work, a simple-minded, ignorant, uneducated, vain little body, as strong physically as a donkey, and thoroughly competent to perform her rather arduous duties, for the satisfactory performance of which she received the munificent remuneration of eight pounds annually, including her board and lodging.

She said: "I came from Berkshire, sir, near Windsor; father put me to service some years ago, and I've been in London ever since. I'm two and twenty now. I've lived in four or five different situations since then. Are followers allowed? No, sir, missus don't permit no followers. No, I ain't got no perleeceman. Have I got a young man? Well, I have; he's in the harmy, not a hoffisser, but a soldier. I goes out along of him on Sundays, leastways on Sunday afternoons, and missus she lets me go to see a aunt of mine, as I says lives at Camberwell, only between you and me, sir, there ain't no aunt, only a soldier, which he's my sweetheart, as I says to you before, sir."

Maid-servants in good families have an opportunity of copying their mistress's way of dressing, and making themselves, attractive to men of a higher class. It is a voluntary species of sacrifice on their part. A sort of suicidal decking with flowers, and making preparations for immolation on the part of the victim herself. Flattered by the attention of the eldest son, or some friend of his staying in the house, the pretty lady's maid will often yield to soft solicitation. Vanity is at the bottom of all this, and is one of the chief characteristics of a class not otherwise naturally vicious. The housemaids flirt with the footmen, the housekeeper with the butler, the cooks with the coachmen, and so on; and a flirtation often begun innocently enough ends in something serious, the result of which may be to blight the prospect of the unfortunate woman who has been led astray.

There are book-hawkers, who go about the country, having first filled their wallets from the filthy cellars of Holywell Street, sowing the seeds of immorality; servants in country houses will pay, without hesitation large prices for improper books. This denomination of evil, I am glad to say, is much on the decrease now, since the Immoral Publications Act has come into operation.

Maid-servants live well, have no care or anxiety, no character worth speaking about to lose, for the origin of most of them is obscure, are fond of dress, and under these circumstances it cannot be wondered that they are as a body immoral and unchaste.

Ladies of Intrigue and Houses of Assignation.—The reader will find more information about "ladies of intrigue" in the annals of the Divorce Court and the pages of the Causes Célèbres than it is in my power to furnish him with. By ladies of intrigue we must understand married women who have connection with other men than their husbands, and unmarried women who gratify their passion secretly.

There is a house in Regent Street, I am told, where ladies, both married and unmarried, go in order to meet with and be introduced to gentlemen, there to consummate their libidinous desires. This sort of clandestine prostitution is not nearly so common in England as in France and other parts of the Continent, where chastity and faithfulness among married women are remarkable for their absence rather than their presence. As this vice is by no means common or a national characteristic, but rather the exception than the rule, it can only expect a cursory notice at our hands.

An anecdote was told me illustrative of this sort of thing that may not be out of place here.

A lady of intrigue, belonging to the higher circles of society, married to a man of considerable property, found herself unhappy in his society, and after some time unwillingly came to the conclusion that she had formed an alliance that was destined to make her miserable. Her passions were naturally strong, and she one day resolved to visit a house that one of her female acquaintances had casually spoken about before her some little time before. Ordering a cab, she drove to the house in question, and went in. There was no necessity for her to explain the nature of her business, or the object with which she called. That was understood. She was shown into a handsome drawing-room, beautifully fitted up, for the house was situated in one of the best streets in May Fair, there to await the coming of her unknown paramour. After waiting some little time the door opened, and a gentleman entered. The curtains of the room were partially drawn round the windows, and the blinds were pulled down, which caused a "dim religious light" to pervade the apartment, preventing the lady from seeing distinctly the features of her visitor. He approached her, and in a low tone of voice commenced a conversation with her about some indifferent subject.

She listened to him for a moment, and then with a cry of astonishment, recognized her husband's voice. He, equally confused, discovered that he had accidentally met in a house of ill-fame the wife whom he had treated with unkindness and cruelty, and condemned to languish at home while he did as he chose abroad. This strange rencontre had a successful termination, for it ended in the reconciliation of husband and wife, who discovered that they were mutually to blame.

From the Divorce Court emanate strange revelations, to which the press gives publicity. It reveals a state of immorality amongst the upper and middle classes that is deplorable; but although this unveils the delinquencies of ladies of intrigue, they are not altogether the class we have under discussion. Those who engross our attention are ladies who, merely to satisfy their animal instincts, intrigue with men whom they do not truly love. But though we could multiply anecdotes and stories, it is not necessary to do more than say, they are a class far from numerous, and scarcely deserve to form a distinctive feature in the category of prostitution in London.

COHABITANT PROSTITUTES

The last head in our classification is "Cohabitant Prostitutes," which phrase must be understood to include—

1. Those whose paramours cannot afford to pay the marriage fees. This is a very small and almost infinitesimal portion of the community, as banns now cost so very little, that it is next to an absurdity to say "a man and woman" cannot get married because they have not money enough to pay the fees consequent upon publishing the banns, therefore this class is scarcely deserving of mention.

2. Those whose paramours do not believe in the sanctity of the ceremony.

There may be a few who make their religious convictions an object to marriage, but you may go a very long journey before you will be able to discover a man who will conscientiously refuse to marry a woman on this ground. Consequently we may dismiss these with a very brief allusion.

3. Those who have married a relative forbidden by law. We know that people will occasionally marry a deceased wife's sister, notwithstanding the anathemas of mother church are sure to be hurled at them. Yet ecclesiastical terrors may have weight with a man who has conceived an affection for a sister-in-law, for whom he will have to undergo so many penalties.

Perhaps parliamentary agitation may soon legitimatize these connections, and abolish this heading from our category of Cohabitant Prostitution.

4. Those who would forfeit their income by marrying,—as officers' widows in receipt of pensions and those who hold property only while unmarried.

This class is more numerous than any of those we have yet mentioned, but it offers nothing sufficiently striking or peculiar to induce us to dwell longer upon it, as it explains itself.

5. Those whose paramours object to marry them for pecuniary or family reasons. This is a subject upon which it has been necessary to dilate; for it includes all the lorettes in London, and the men by whom they are kept. By lorettes I mean those I have before touched upon as prima donnas, who are a class of women who do not call going to night-houses in Panton Street walking the Haymarket, and feel much insulted if you so characterize their nocturnal wanderings. The best women go to three or four houses in Panton Street, where the visitors are more select than in the other places, where the door porters are less discriminating. Sometimes women who are violent, and make a disturbance, are kept out of particular houses for months.

Of course, the visits of kept women are made by stealth, as the men who keep them would not countenance their going to such places. Perhaps their men are out of town, and they may then go with comparative safety.

Women who are well kept, and have always been accustomed to the society of gentlemen, have an intense horror of the Haymarket women, properly so called, who promenade the pavement in order to pick up men.

And in reality there is a greater distinction between the two classes than would at first appear. Even if a good sort of woman has been thrown over by her man, and is in want of money, she will not pick up any one at a night-house who may solicit her; on the contrary, she will select some fellow she has a liking for: while, on the other hand, the Haymarket women will pick up any low wretch who she thinks will pay her. She will not even object to a foreigner, though all the best women have a great dislike to low foreigners.

Were I to dwell longer upon this subject it is clear I should merely be recapitulating what I have already said in a former portion of this work.

The following narrative was given me by a girl I met in the Haymarket, when in search of information regarding the prostitution of the West-end of London. Her tale is the usual one of unsuspecting innocence and virtue, seduced by fraud and violence. The victim of passion became in time the mistress of lust, and sank from one stage to another, until she found herself compelled to solicit in the streets to obtain a livelihood. She was about twenty-one years of age, beneath the ordinary height, and with a very engaging countenance. She appeared to be a high-spirited intelligent girl, and gave her sad tale with unaffected candour and modesty.

Narrative of a Gay Woman at the West End of the Metropolis

"I was born in the county of—, in England, where my father was an extensive farmer, and had a great number of servants. I have three brothers and one younger sister. I was sent to a boarding school at B——, where I was receiving a superior education, and was learning drawing, music, and dancing. During the vacations, and once every quarter, I went home and lived with my parents, where one of my chief enjoyments was to ride out on a pony I had, over the fields, and in the neighbourhood, and occasionally to go to M——, a few miles distant. On these occasions we often had parties of ladies and gentlemen; when some of the best people in the district visited us. I had one of the happiest homes a girl could have.

"When I was out riding one day at M——, in passing through the town my pony took fright, and threatened to throw me off, when a young gentleman who was near rode up to my assistance. He rode by my side till we came to a hotel in town, when we both dismounted. Leaving the horses wit the hostlers, we had some refreshment. I took out my purse to pay the expenses, but he would not let me and paid for me. We both mounted and proceeded towards my home. On his coming to the door of the house, I invited him to come in, which he did. I introduced him to my papa and mamma, and mentioned the kind service he had done to me. His horse was put up in our stables, and he remained for some time, and had supper with us, when he returned to M——. He was very wealthy, resided in London, and only visited M—— occasionally with his servants.

"I was then attending a boarding-school at B——, and was about fifteen years of age. A few days after this I left home and returned to B——. We corresponded by letter for nearly twelve months.

"From the moment he rode up to me at M—— I was deeply interested in him, and the attachment increased by the correspondence. He also appeared to be very fond of me. He sometimes came and visited me at home during my school holidays for the next twelve months. One day in the month of May—in summer—he came to our house in his carriage, and we invited him to dinner. He remained with us for the night, and slept with one of my brothers. We were then engaged to each other, and were to be married, so soon as I was eighteen years of age.

"The next day he asked my parents if I might go out with him in his carriage. My mamma consented. She asked if any of our servants would go with us, but he thought there was no occasion for this, as his coachman and footman went along with us. We proceeded to B—— Railway Station. He left his carriage with the coachman and footman and pressed me to go with him to London. He pretended to my parents he was only going out for a short drive. I was very fond of him, and reluctantly consented to go with him to London.

"He first brought me to Simpson's hotel in the Strand, where we had dinner, then took me to the opera. We went to Scott's supper rooms in the Haymarket. On coming out we walked up and down the Haymarket. He then took me to several of the cafés, where we had wine and refreshments. About four o'clock in the morning he called a Hansom, and drove me to his house; and there seduced me by violence in spite of my resistance. I screamed out, but none of the servants in the house came to assist me. He told his servants I was his young wife he had just brought up from the country.

"I wanted to go home in the morning, and began to cry, but he would not let me go. He said I must remain in London with him. I still insisted on going home, and he promised to marry me. He then bought me a watch and chain, rings and bracelets, and presented me with several dresses. After this I lived with him in his house as though I had been his wife, and rode out with him in his brougham. I often insisted upon being married. He promised to do so, but delayed from time to time. He generally drove out every day over the finest streets, thoroughfares, and parks of the metropolis; and in the evenings he took me to the Argyle Rooms and to the Casino at Holborn. I generally went there very well dressed, and was much noticed on account of my youthful appearance. We also went to the fashionable theatres in the West-end, and several subscription balls.

"I often rode along Rotten Row with him, and along the drives in Hyde Park. We also went to the seaside, where we lived in the best hotels.

"This lasted for two years, when his conduct changed towards me.

"One evening I went with him to the Assembly Rooms at Holborn to a masked ball. I was dressed in the character of a fairy queen. My hair was in long curls hanging down my back.

"He left me in the supper-room for a short time, when a well-dressed man came up to me. When my paramour came in he saw the young sitting by my side speaking to me. He told him I was his wife, and inquired what he meant by it, to which he gave no reply. He then asked me if I knew him. I replied no. He asked the gentleman to rise, which he did, apologising for his seating himself beside me, and thereby giving offence. On the latter showing him his card, which I did not see, they sat down and had wine together.

"We came out of the supper-room, and we had a quarrel about the matter. We walked up and down the ball-room for some time, and at last drove home.

"When we got home he quarrelled again with me, struck me, and gave me two black eyes. I was also bruised on other parts of the body, and wanted to leave him that night, but he would not let me.

"In the morning we went out as usual after breakfast for a drive.

"Next evening we went to the Casino at Holborn. Many of the gentlemen were staring at me, and he did not like it. I had on a thick Maltese veil to conceal my blackened eyes.

"The gentleman who had accosted me the previous night came up and spoke to me and my paramour (whom we shall call S.), and had some wine with us. He asked the reason I did not raise my veil. S. said because I did not like to do it in this place. The gentleman caught sight of my eyes, and said they did not look so brilliant as the night before.

"S. was indignant, and told him he took great liberty in speaking of his wife in this manner. The other remarked that no one could help noticing such a girl, adding that I was too young to be his wife, and that he should not take me to such a place if he did not wish me to be looked at. He told him he ought to take better care of me than to bring me there.

"When we got home we had another quarrel, and he struck me severely on the side.

"We did not sleep in the same bed that night. On coming downstairs to breakfast next morning I was taken very ill, and a medical man was sent for. The doctor said I was in a fever, and must have had a severe blow or a heavy fall. I was ill and confined to my bed for three months. He went out every night and left me with a nurse and the servants, and seldom returned till three or four o'clock in the morning. He used to return home drunk; generally came into my bedroom and asked if I was better; kissed me and went downstairs to bed.

"When I got well he was kind to me, and said I looked more charming than ever. For three or four months after he took me out as usual.

"The same gentleman met me again in the Holborn one night while S. had gone out for a short time, leaving me alone. He came up and shook hands with me, said he was happy to see me, and wished me to meet him. I told him I could not. S. was meanwhile watching our movements. The gentleman asked me if I was married, when I said that I was. He admired my rings. Pointing to a diamond ring on his finger, he asked me if I would like it. I said no. He said your rings are not so pretty. I still refused it; but he took the ring off his finger and put it on one of mine, and said, 'See how well it looks,' adding, 'Keep it as a memento; it may make you think of me when I am far away.' He told me not to mention it to my husband.

"Meantime S. was watching me, and came up when the man had gone away, and asked what he had been saying to me. I told him the truth, that the same man had spoken to me again. He asked me what had passed between us, and I told him all, with the exception of the ring.

"He noticed the ring on my finger, and asked me where I had got it. I declined at first to answer. He then said I was not true to him, and if I would not tell him who gave me the ring he would leave me. I told him the man had insisted on my having it.

"He thereupon rushed along the room after him, but did not find him. On coming back he insisted on my going home without him.

"He took me outside to his brougham, handed me in it, and then left me. I went home and sat in the drawing-room till he returned, which was about three o'clock in the morning. He quarrelled with me again for not being true to him. I said I was and had never left his side for a moment from the time I rose in the morning till I lay down at night.

"I then told him I would go home and tell my friends all about it, and he was afraid.

"Soon after he said to me he was going out of town for a week, and wished me to stop at home. I did not like to remain in the house without a woman, and wished to go with him. He said he could not allow me, as he was to be engaged in family matters.

"He was absent for a week. I remained at home for three nights, and was very dull and wearied, having no one to speak to. I went to my bedroom, washed and dressed, ordered the carriage to be got ready, and went to the Holborn. Who should I see there but this gentleman again. He was astonished to see me there alone; came up and offered me his arm.

"I told him I was wearied at home in the absence of S., and came out for a little relaxation. He then asked to see me home, which I declined. I remained till the dancing was nearly over. He got into the brougham with me and drove to Sally's, where we had supper, after which he saw me home. He bade me 'good-bye,' and said he hoped to see me at the Holborn again some other night.

"Meantime S. had been keeping watch over me, it appears, and heard of this. When he came home he asked me about it. I told him. He swore the gentleman had connexion with me. I said he had not. He then hit me in the face and shook me, and threatened to lock me up. After breakfast he went out to walk, and I refused to go with him.

"When he had gone away I packed up all my things, told the servant to bring a cab, wrote a note and left it on the table. I asked the cabman if he knew any nice apartments a long way off from C——, where I was living. He drove me to Pimlico, and took me to apartments in—— where I have ever since resided.

"When I went there I had my purse full of gold, and my dresses and jewellery, which were worth about 300 £.

"One evening soon after I went to the Holborn and met my old friend again, and told him what had occurred. He was astonished, and said he would write to my relations, and have S. pulled up for it.

"After this he saw me occasionally at my lodgings, and made me presents.

"He met S. one day in the City, and threatened to write to my friends to let them know how I had been treated.

"I still went to the Holborn occasionally. One evening I met S., who wished me to go home with him again, but I refused, after the ill-usage he had given me.

"I generally spent the day in my apartments, and in the evening went to the Argyle, until my money was gone. I now and then got something from the man who had taken my part; but he did not give me so much as I had been accustomed to, and I used to have strange friends against my own wish.

"Before I received them I had spouted most of my jewellery, and some of my dresses. When I lived with S. he allowed me 10 £ a week, but when I went on the loose I did not get so much.

"After I had parted with my jewellery and most of my clothes I walked in the Haymarket, and went to the Turkish divans, 'Sally's,' and other cafés and restaurants.

"Soon after I became unfortunate and had to part with the remainder of my dresses. Since then I have been more shabby in appearance, and not so much noticed."

TRAFFIC IN FOREIGN WOMEN

One of the most disgraceful, horrible and revolting practices (not even eclipsed by the slave-trade), carried on by Europeans is the importation of girls into England from foreign countries to swell the ranks of prostitution. It is only very recently that the attention of Mr. Tyrrwhit, at the Marlborough Police Court, was drawn to the subject by Mr. Dalbert, agent to the "Society for the Protection of Women and Children."

It is asserted that women are imported from Belgium, and placed in houses of ill-fame, where they are compelled to support their keepers in luxury and idleness by the proceeds of their dishonour. One house in particular was mentioned in Marylebone; but the state of the law respecting brothels is so peculiar that great difficulty is experienced in extricating these unfortunate creatures from their dreadful position. If it were proved beyond the suspicion of a doubt, that they were detained against their will, the Habeas Corpus Act might be of service to their friends, but it appears they are so jealously guarded, that all attempts to get at them have hitherto proved futile, although there is every reason to believe that energetic measures will be taken by the above-mentioned Society to mitigate the evil and relieve the victims.

As this traffic is clandestine, and conducted with the greatest caution, it is impossible to form any correct idea of its extent. There are numbers of foreign women about, but it is probable that many of them have come over here of their own free-will, and not upon false pretences or compulsion. One meets with French, Spanish, Italian, Belgian, and other women.

The complaint made before the metropolitan magistrate a short while since was in favour of Belgian women. But the traffic is not confined to them alone. It would appear that the unfortunate creatures are deluded by all sorts of promises and cajolery, and when they arrive in this country are, in point of fact, imprisoned in certain houses of ill-fame, whose keepers derive considerable emolument from their durance. They are made to fetter themselves in some way or other to the trepanner, and they, in their simple-mindedness, consider their deed binding, and look upon themselves, until the delusion is dispelled, as thoroughly in the power of their keepers.

English women are also taken to foreign parts by designing speculators. The English are known to congregate at Boulogne, at Havre, at Dieppe, at Ostend, and other places. It is considered lucrative by the keepers of bawdy-houses at these towns to maintain an efficient supply of English women for their resident countrymen: and though the supply is inadequate to the demand, great numbers of girls are decoyed every year, and placed in the "Maisons de passé," or "Maisons de joie," as they are sometimes called, where they are made to prostitute themselves. And by the farm of their persons enable their procurers to derive considerable profit.

An Englishwoman told me how she was very nearly entrapped by a foreign woman. "I met an emissary of a French bawdy-house," she said, "one night in the Haymarket, and, after conversing with her upon various subjects, she opened the matter she had in hand, and, after a little mane-ouvring and bush-beating, she asked me if I would not like to go over to France. She specified a town, which was Havre. 'You will get lots of money,' she added, and further represented 'that I should have a very jolly time of it.' 'The money you make will be equally divided between yourself and the woman of the house, and when you have made as much as you want, you may come back to England and set up a café or night-house, where your old friends will be only too glad to come and see you. You will of course get lots of custom, and attain a better future than you can now possibly hope for. You ought to look upon me as the greatest friend you have, for I am putting a chance in your way that does not occur every day, I can tell you. If you value your own comfort, and think for a moment about your future, you cannot hesitate. I have an agreement in my pocket, duly drawn up by a solicitor, so you may rely upon its being all on the square, and if you sign this—'

"'To-night?' I asked.

"'Yes, immediately. If you sign this, I will supply you with some money to get what you want, and the day after to-morrow you shall sail for Havre. Madame—— is a very nice sort of person, and will do all in her power to make you happy and comfortable, and indeed she will allow you to do exactly as you please.'"

Fortunately for herself my informant refused to avail herself of the flattering prospect so alluringly held out to her. The bait was tempting enough, but the fish was too wary.

Now let us hear the recital of a girl who, at an early age, had been incarcerated in one of these "Maisons de passé." She is now in England, has been in a refuge, and by the authorities of the charity placed in an occupation which enables her to acquire a livelihood sufficient to allow her to live as she had, up to that time, been accustomed to. Her story I subjoin:—

"When I was sixteen years' old, my father, who kept a public-house in Bloomsbury, got into difficulties and became bankrupt. I had no mother, and my relations, such as they were, insisted upon my keeping myself in some way or other. This determination on their part thoroughly accorded with my own way of thinking, and I did not for an instant refuse to do so. It then became necessary to discover something by which I could support myself. Service suggested itself to me and my friends, and we set about finding out a situation that I could fill. They told me I was pretty, and as I had not been accustomed to do anything laborious, they thought I would make a very good lady's maid. I advertised in a morning paper, and received three answers to my advertisement. The first I went to did not answer my expectations, and the second was moderately good; but I resolved to go to the third, and see the nature of it before I came to any conclusion. Consequently I left the second open, and went to the third. It was addressed from a house in Bulstrode-street, near Welbeck-street. I was ushered into the house, and found a foreign lady waiting to receive me. She said she was going back to France, and wished for an English girl to accompany her as she infinitely preferred English to French women. She offered me a high salary, and told me my duties would be light; in fact by comparing her statement of what I should have to do with that of the others I had visited, I found that it was more to my advantage to live with her than with them. So after a little consultation with myself, I determined to accept her offer. No sooner had I told her so than she said in a soft tone of voice—

"'Then, my dear, just be good enough to sign this agreement between us. It is merely a matter of form—nothing more, *ma chère*.'

"I asked her what it was about, and why it was necessary for me to sign any paper at all?

"She replied, 'Only for our mutual satisfaction. I wish you to remain with me for one year, as I shall not return to England until then. And if you hadn't some agreement with me, to bind you as it were to stay with me, why, *mon Dieu!* you might leave me directly—oh! *c'est rien*. You may sign without fear or trembling.'

"Hearing this explanation of the transaction, without reading over the paper which was written on half a sheet of foolscap, (for I did not wish to insult or offend her by so doing.) I wrote my name.

"She instantly seized the paper, held it to the fire for a moment or two to dry, and folding it up placed it in her pocket.

"She then requested me to be ready to leave London with her on the following Thursday, which allowed me two days to make my preparations and to take leave of my friends, which I did in very good spirits, as I thought I had a very fair prospect before me. It remained for what ensued to disabuse me of that idea.

"We left the St. Katherine's Docks in the steamer for Boulogne, and instead of going to an hotel, as I expected, we proceeded to a private house in the Rue N—C—, near the Rue de l'Ecu. I have farther to tell you that three other young women accompanied us. One was a housemaid, one was a nursery governess, and the other a cook. I was introduced to them as people that I should have to associate with when we arrived at Madame's house. In fact they were represented to be part of the establishment; and they, poor things, fully believed they were, being as much deluded as myself. The house that Madame brought us to was roomy and commodious, and, as I afterwards discovered, well, if not elegantly, furnished. We were shown into very good bedrooms, much better than I expected would be allotted to servants; and when I mentioned this to Madame, and thanked her for her kindness and consideration, she replied with a smile:—

"'Did I not tell you how well you would be treated? we do these things better in France than they do in England.'

"I thanked her again as she was going away, but she said, '*Tais toi, Tais toi*,' and left me quite enchanted with her goodness."

I need not expatiate on what subsequently ensued. It is easy to imagine the horrors that the poor girl had to undergo. With some difficulty she was conquered and had to submit to her fate. She did not know a word of the language, and was ignorant of the only method she could adopt to insure redress. But this she happily discovered in a somewhat singular manner. When her way of living had become intolerable to her, she determined to throw herself on the generosity of a young Englishman who was in the habit of frequenting the house she lived in, and who seemed to possess some sort of affection for her.

She confessed her miserable position to him, and implored him to protect her or point out a means of safety. He at once replied, "The best thing you can do is to go to the British Consul and lay your case before him. He will in all probability send you back to your own country." It required little persuasion on her part to induce her friend to co-operate with her. The main thing to be managed was to escape from the house. This was next to impossible, as they were so carefully watched. But they were allowed occasionally, if they did not show any signs of discontent to go out for a walk in the town. The ramparts surrounding the "*Haute Ville*" were generally selected by this girl as her promenade, and when this privilege of walking out was allowed her, she was strictly enjoined not to neglect any opportunity that might offer itself. She arranged to meet her young friend there, and gave him notice of the day upon which she would be able to go out. If a girl who was so privileged chanced to meet a man known to the *Bonne* or attendant as a frequenter of the house, she retired to a convenient distance or went back altogether. The plot succeeded, the consul was appealed to and granted the girl a passport to return to England, also offering to supply her with money to pay her passage home. This necessity was obviated by the kindness of her young English friend, who generously gave her several pounds, and advised her to return at once to her friends.

Arrived in England, she found her friends reluctant to believe the tale she told them, and found herself thrown on her own resources. Without a character, and with a mind very much disturbed, she found it difficult to do anything respectable, and at last had recourse to prostitution;—so difficult is it to come back to the right path when we have once strayed from it.

Perhaps it is almost impossible to stop this traffic; but at any rate the infamous wretches who trade in it may be intimidated by publicity being given to their acts, and the indignation of the public being roused in consequence. What can we imagine more dreadful than kidnapping a confiding unsuspecting girl, in some cases we may say child, without exaggeration, for a girl of fifteen is not so very far removed from those who come within the provisions of the Bishop of Oxford's Act? I repeat, what can be more horrible than transporting a girl, as it were, by false representations from her native land to a country of strangers, and condemning her against her will to a life of the most revolting slavery and degradation, without her having been guilty of any offence against an individual or against the laws of the land?

It is difficult to believe that there can be many persons engaged in this white slave trade, but it is undeniably true.

It is not a question for the legislature; for what could Parliament do? The only way to decrease the iniquity is to widely disseminate the knowledge of the existence of such infamy, that those whom it most nearly concerns, may be put upon their guard, and thus be enabled to avoid falling into the trap so cunningly laid for them.

Much praise is due to those benevolent societies who interest themselves in these matters, and especially to that which we have alluded to more than once—"The Society for the Protection of Women and Children," over which Lord Raynham presides.

Much good may be done by this means, and much misery prevented. The mines of Siberia, with all their terrors, would be preferred—even with the knout in prospective—by these poor girls, were the alternative proffered them, to the wretched life they are decoyed into leading. For all their hopes are blasted, all their feelings crushed, their whole existence blighted, and their life rendered a misery to them instead of a blessing and a means of rational enjoyment.

The idea of slavery of any kind is repulsive to the English mind; but when that slavery includes incarceration, and mental as well as physical subjection to the dominant power by whom that durance is imposed, it becomes doubly and trebly repugnant. If it were simply the deprivation of air and exercise, or even the performance of the most menial offices, it might be borne with some degree of resignation by the sufferer, however unmerited the punishment. But here we have a totally different case: no offence is committed by the victim, but rather by nature, for what is her fault, but being pretty and a woman? For this caprice of the genius of form who presided over her birth she is condemned to a life of misery, degradation, and despair; compelled to receive caresses that are hateful to her, she is at one moment the toy of senile sensuality, and at others of impetuous juvenility, both alike loathsome, both alike detestable. If blandishments disgust her, words of endearment only make her state of desolation more palpable; while profusions of regard serve to aggravate the poignancy of her grief, all around her is hollow, all artificial except her wretchedness. When to this is added ostracism—banishment from one's native country— the condition of the unfortunate woman is indeed pitiable, for there is some slight consolation in hearing one's native language spoken by those around us, and more especially to the class from which these girls are for the most part taken. We must add *"pour comble d'injustice,"* that there is no future for the girl, no reprieve, no hope of mercy, every hope is gone from the moment the prison tawdry is assumed. The condemnation is severe enough, for it is for life. When her beauty and her charms no longer serve to attract the libidinous, she sinks into the condition of a servant to others who have been ensnared to fill her place. Happiness cannot be achieved by her at any period of her servitude; there must always be a restless longing for the end, which though comparatively quick in arriving is always too tardy.

The mind in time in many cases becomes depraved, and the hardness of heart that follows this depravity often prevents the girl from feeling as acutely as she did at first. To these religion is a dead letter, which is a greater and additional calamity. But to be brief, the victim's whole life from first to last is a series of disappointments, combined with a succession of woes that excite a shudder by their contemplation, and which may almost justify the invocation of Death:—

> "Death, Death, oh amiable lovely death!
> Thou odoriferous stench! sound rottenness!
> Arise forth from the couch of lasting night,
> Thou hate and terror to prosperity,
> And I will kiss thy detestable bones;
> And put my eyeballs in they vaulty brows;
> And ring these fingers with thy household worms;
> And stop this gap of breath with fulsome dust,
> And be a carrion monster like thyself;
> Come, grin on me; and I will think thou smil'st,
> And kiss thee as thy wife! Misery's love,
> O, come to me!
> SHAKESPERE. *King John*, Act iii. Scene 4.

2. "The Maiden Tribute of Modern Babylon" (1885)

By William Stead

"The Maiden Tribute of Modern Babylon, I: The Report of our Secret Commission." *The Pall Mall Gazette*, 6 July 1885, pp. 1–6.

> *Stead worked with Josephine Butler, William Coote, and other abolitionists in Victorian London. The following is the first of four installments published in London; by the time the fourth installment was published, riots had been incited.*
>
> *See also* **Butler, Josephine** *and* **"The Maiden Tribute of Modern Babylon"** *in this text.*

In ancient times, if we may believe the myths of Hellas, Athens, after a disastrous campaign, was compelled by her conqueror to send once every nine years a tribute to Crete of seven youths and seven maidens. The doomed fourteen, who were selected by lot amid the lamentations of the citizens, returned no more. The vessel that bore them to Crete unfurled black sails as the symbol of despair, and on arrival her passengers were flung into the famous Labyrinth of Daedalus, there to wander about blindly until such time as they were devoured by the Minotaur, a frightful monster, half man, half bull, the foul product of an unnatural lust. "The labyrinth was as large as a town and had countless courts and galleries. Those who entered it could never find their way out again. If they hurried from one to another of the numberless rooms looking for the entrance door, it was all in vain. They only became more hopelessly lost in the bewildering labyrinth, until at last they were devoured by the Minotaur." Twice at each ninth year the Athenians paid the maiden tribute to King Minos, lamenting sorely the dire necessity of bowing to his iron law. When the third tribute came to be exacted, the distress of the city of the Violet Crown was insupportable. From the King's palace to the peasant's hamlet, everywhere were heard cries and groans and the choking sob of despair, until the whole air seemed to vibrate with the sorrow of an unutterable anguish. Then it was that the hero Theseus volunteered to be offered up among those who drew the black balls from the brazen urn of destiny, and the story of his self-sacrifice, his victory, and his triumphant return, is among the most familiar of the tales which since the childhood of the world have kindled the imagination and fired the heart of the human race.

The labyrinth was cunningly wrought like a house, says Ovid, with many rooms and winding passages, that so the shameful creature of lust whose abode it was to be should be far removed from sight.

> Destinat hunc Minos thalamis removere pudorem,
> Multiplicique domo, caecisque includere tectis.
> Daedalus ingenio fabra celeberrimus artis
> Ponit opus: turbatque notas, et lumina flexura
> Ducit in errorera variarum ambage viarum.

And what happened to the victims—the young men and maidens—who were there interned, no one could surely tell. Some say that they were done to death; others that they lived in servile employments to old age. But in this alone do all the stories agree, that those who were once caught in the coils could never retrace their steps, so "inextricable" were the paths, so "blind" the footsteps, so "innumerable" the ways of wrong-doing. On the southern wall of the porch of the cathedral at Lucca there is a slightly traced piece of sculpture, representing the Cretan labyrinth, "out of which," says the legend written in straggling letters at the side, "nobody could get who was inside":—

> Hie quern credicus edit Dedalus est laberinthus
> De quo nullus vadere quirit qui fuit intus.

The fact that the Athenians should have taken so bitterly to heart the paltry maiden tribute that once in nine years they had to pay to the Minotaur seems incredible, almost inconceivable. This very night in London, and every night, year in and year out, not seven maidens only, but many times seven, selected almost as much by chance as those who in the Athenian market-place drew lots as to which should be flung into the Cretan labyrinth, will be offered up as the Maiden Tribute of Modern Babylon. Maidens they were when this morning dawned, but to-night their ruin will be accomplished, and to-morrow they will find themselves within the portals of the maze of London brotheldom. Within that labyrinth wander, like lost souls, the vast host of London prostitutes, whose numbers no man can compute, but who are probably not much below 50,000 strong. Many, no doubt, who venture but a little way within the maze make their escape.

But multitudes are swept irresistibly on and on to be destroyed in due season, to give place to others, who also will share their doom. The maw of the London Minotaur is insatiable, and none that go into the secret recesses of his lair return again. After some years' dolorous wandering in this palace of despair—for "hope of rest to solace there is none, nor e'en of milder pang," save the poisonous anodyne of drink—most of those ensnared to-night will perish, some of them in horrible torture. Yet, so far from this great city being convulsed with woe, London cares for none of these things, and the cultured man of the world, the heir of all the ages, the ultimate product of a long series of civilizations and religions, will shrug his shoulders in scorn at the folly of any one who ventures in public print to raise even the mildest protest against a horror a thousand times more horrible than that which, in the youth of the world, haunted like a nightmare the imagination of mankind. Nevertheless, I have not yet lost faith in the heart and conscience of the English folk, the sturdy innate chivalry and right thinking of our common people; and although I am no vain dreamer of Utopias peopled solely by Sir Galahads and vestal virgins, I am not without hope that there may be some check placed upon this vast tribute of maidens, unwitting or unwilling, which is nightly levied in London by the vices of the rich upon the necessities of the poor. London's lust annually uses up many thousands of women, who are literally killed and made away with—living sacrifices slain in the service of vice. That may be inevitable, and with that I have nothing to do. But I do ask that those doomed to the house of evil fame shall not be trapped into it unwillingly, and that none shall be beguiled into the chamber of death before they are of an age to read the inscription above the portal—"All hope abandon ye who enter here." If the daughters of the people must be served up as dainty morsels to minister to the passions of the rich, let them at least attain an age when they can understand the nature of the sacrifice which they are asked to make. And if we must cast maidens—not seven, but seven times seven—nightly into the jaws of vice, let us at least see to it that they assent to their own immolation, and are not unwilling sacrifices procured by force and fraud. That is surely not too much to ask from the dissolute rich. Even considerations of self-interest might lead our rulers to assent to so modest a demand. For the hour of Democracy has struck, and there is no wrong which a man resents like this. If it has not been resented hitherto, it is not because it was not felt. The Roman Republic was founded by the rape of Lucrece, but Lucrece was a member of one of the governing families. A similar offence placed Spain under the domination of the Moors, but there again the victim of Royal licence was the daughter of a Count. But the fathers and brothers whose daughters and sisters are purchased like slaves, not for labour, but for lust, are now at last enrolled among the governing classes—a circumstance full of hope for the nation, but by no means without menace for a class. Many of the French Revolutionists were dissolute enough, but nothing gave such an edge to the guillotine as the memory of the Pare aux Cerfs; and even in our time the horrors that attended the suppression of the Commune were largely due to the despair of the femme vengeresse. Hence, unless the levying of the maiden-tribute in London is shorn of its worst abuses—at present, as I shall show, flourishing unchecked—resentment, which might be appeased by reform, may hereafter be the virus of a social revolution. It is the one explosive which is strong enough to wreck the Throne.

LIBERTY FOR VICE, REPRESSION FOR CRIME

To avoid all misapprehension as to the object with which I propose to set forth the ghastly and criminal features of this infernal traffic, I wish to say emphatically at the outset that, however strongly I may feel as to the imperative importance of morality and chastity, I do not ask for any police interference with the liberty of vice. I ask only for the repression of crime. Sexual immorality, however evil it may be in itself or in its consequences, must be dealt with not by the policeman but by the teacher, so long as the persons contracting are of full age, are perfectly free agents, and in their sin are guilty of no outrage on public morals. Let us by all means apply the sacred principles of free trade to trade in vice, and regulate the relations of the sexes by the higgling of the market and the liberty of private contract. Whatever may be my belief as to the reality and the importance of a transcendental theory of purity in the relations between man and woman, that is an affair for the moralist, not for the legislator. So far from demanding any increased power for the police, I would rather incline to say to the police, "Hands off," when they interfere arbitrarily with the ordinary operations of the market of vice. But the more freely we permit to adults absolute liberty to dispose of their persons in accordance with the principles of private contract and free trade, the more stringent must be our precautions against the innumerable crimes which spring from vice, as vice itself springs from the impure imaginings of the heart of man. These crimes flourish on every side, unnoticed and unchecked—if, indeed, they are not absolutely encouraged by the law, as they are certainly practised by some legislators and winked at by many administrators of the law. To extirpate vice by Act of Parliament is impossible; but because we must leave vice free that is no reason why we should acquiesce helplessly in the perpetration of crime. And that crime of the most ruthless and abominable description is constantly and systematically practised in London without let or hindrance, I am in a position to prove from my own personal knowledge—a knowledge purchased at a cost of which I prefer not to speak. Those crimes may be roughly classified as follows:—

I.   The sale and purchase and violation of children.
II.   The procuration of virgins.
III. The entrapping and ruin of women.
IV.   The international slave trade in girls.
V.   Atrocities, brutalities, and unnatural crimes.

That is what I call sexual criminality, as opposed to sexual immorality. It flourishes in all its branches on every side to an extent of which even those specially engaged in rescue work have but little idea. Those who are constantly engaged in its practice naturally deny its existence. But I speak of that which I do know, not from hearsay or rumour, but of my own personal knowledge.

HOW THE FACTS WERE VERIFIED

When the Criminal Law Amendment Bill was talked out just before the defeat of the Ministry it became necessary to rouse public attention to the necessity for legislation on this painful subject. I undertook an investigation into the facts. The evidence taken before the House of Lords' Committee in 1882 was useful, but the facts were not up to date: members said things had changed since then, and the need for legislation had passed. It was necessary to bring the information up to date, and that duty—albeit with some reluctance—I resolutely undertook. For four weeks, aided by two or three coadjutors of whose devotion and self-sacrifice, combined with a rare instinct for investigation and a singular personal fearlessness, I cannot speak too highly, I have been exploring the London Inferno. It has been a strange and unexampled experience. For a month I have oscillated between the noblest and the meanest of mankind, the saviours and the destroyers of their race, spending hours alternately in brothels and hospitals, in the streets and in refuges, in the company of procuresses and of bishops. London beneath the gas glare of its innumerable lamps became, not like Paris in 1793—"a naphtha-lighted city of Dis"—but a resurrected and magnified City of the Plain, with all the vices of Gomorrah, daring the vengeance of long-suffering Heaven. It seemed a strange, inverted world, that in which I lived those terrible weeks—the world of the streets and of the brothel. It was the same, yet not the same, as the world of business and the world of politics. I heard of much the same people in the house of ill-fame as those of whom you hear in caucuses, in law courts, and on Change. But all were judged by a different standard, and their relative importance was altogether changed. It was as if the position of our world had suddenly been altered, and you saw most of the planets and fixed stars in different combinations, and of altogether different magnitudes, so that at first it was difficult to recognize them. For the house of evil fame has its own ethics, and the best man in the world—the first of Englishmen, in the estimation of the bawd—is often one of whom society knows nothing and cares less. To hear statesmen reckoned up from the standpoint of the brothel is at first almost as novel and perplexing an experience as it is to hear judges and Queen's Counsel praised or blamed, not for their judicial acumen and legal lore, but for their addiction to unnatural crimes or their familiarity with obscene literature.

After a time the eye grows familiar with the foul and poisonous air, but at the best you wander in a Circe's isle, where the victims of the foul enchantress's wand meet you at every turn. But with a difference, for whereas the enchanted in olden time had the heads and the voices and the bristles of swine, while the heart of a man was in them still, these have not put on in outward form "the inglorious likeness of a beast," but are in semblance as other men, while within there is only the heart of a beast—bestial, ferocious, and filthy beyond the imagination of decent men. For days and nights it is as if I had suffered the penalties inflicted upon the lost souls in the Moslem hell, for I seemed to have to drink of the purulent matter that flows from the bodies of the damned. But the sojourn in this hell has not been fruitless. The facts which I and my coadjutors have verified I now place on record at once as a revelation and a warning—a revelation of the system, and a warning to those who may be its victims. In the statement which follows I give no names and I omit addresses. My purpose was not to secure the punishment of criminals but to lay bare the working of a great organization of crime. But as a proof of good faith, and in order to substantiate the accuracy of every statement contained herein, I am prepared after an assurance has been given me that the information so afforded will not be made use of either for purposes of individual exposure or of criminal proceedings, to communicate the names, dates, localities referred to, together with full and detailed explanations of the way in which I secured the information, in confidence to any of the following persons:—

His Grace the Archbishop of Canterbury,
The Cardinal Archbishop of Westminster,
Mr. Samuel Morley, M.P.,
The Earl of Shaftesbury,
The Earl of Dalhousie, as the author of the Criminal Law Amendment Bill, and
Mr. Howard Vincent, ex-Director of the Criminal Investigation Department.

I do not propose to communicate this information to any member of the executive Government, as the responsibilities of their position might render it impossible for them to give the requisite assurance as to the confidential character of my communication. More than this I could not do unless I was prepared (1) to violate the confidence reposed in me in the course of my investigation, and (2) to spend the next six weeks of my life as a witness in the Criminal Court. This I absolutely refuse to do. I am an investigator; I am not an informer.

THE VIOLATION OF VIRGINS

This branch of the subject is one upon which even the coolest and most scientific observer may well find it difficult to speak dispassionately in a spirit of calm and philosophic investigation. The facts, however, as they have been elucidated in the course of a careful and painstaking inquiry are so startling, and the horror which they excite so overwhelming, that it is doubly necessary to approach the subject with a scepticism proof against all but the most overwhelming demonstration. It is, however, a fact that there is in full operation among us a system of which the violation of virgins is one of the ordinary incidents; that these virgins are mostly of tender age, being too young in fact to understand the nature of the crime of which they are the unwilling victims; that these outrages are constantly perpetrated with almost absolute impunity; and that the arrangements for procuring, certifying, violating, repairing, and disposing of these ruined victims of the lust of London are made with a simplicity and efficiency incredible to all who have not made actual demonstration of the facility with which the crime can be accomplished.

To avoid misapprehension, I admit that the vast majority of those who are on the streets in London have not come there by the road of organized rape. Most women fall either by the seduction of individuals or by the temptation which well-dressed vice can offer to the poor. But there is a minority which has been as much the victim of violence as were the Bulgarian maidens with whose wrongs Mr. Gladstone made the world ring some eight years ago. Some are simply snared, trapped and outraged either when under the influence of drugs or after a prolonged struggle in a locked room, in which the weaker succumbs to sheer downright force. Others are regularly procured; bought at so much per head in some cases, or enticed under various promises into the fatal chamber from which they are never allowed to emerge until they have lost what woman ought to value more than life. It is to this department of the subject that I now address myself.

Before beginning this inquiry I had a confidential interview with one of the most experienced officers who for many years was in a position to possess an intimate acquaintance with all phases of London crime. I asked him, "Is it or is it not a fact that, at this moment, if I were to go to the proper houses, well introduced, the keeper would, in return for money down, supply me in due time with a maid—a genuine article, I mean, not a mere prostitute tricked out as a virgin, but a girl who had never been seduced?" "Certainly," he replied without a moment's hesitation. "At what price?" I continued. "That is a difficult question," he said. "I remember one case which came under my official cognizance in Scotland-yard in which the price agreed upon was stated to be £20. Some parties in Lambeth undertook to deliver a maid for that sum——to a house of ill fame, and I have no doubt it is frequently done all over London." "But," I continued, "are these maids willing or unwilling parties to the transaction—that is, are they really maiden, not merely in being each a *virgo intacta* in the physical sense, but as being chaste girls who are not consenting parties to their seduction?" He looked surprised at my question, and then replied emphatically: "Of course they are rarely willing, and as a rule they do not know what they are coming for." "But," I said in amazement, "then do you mean to tell me that in very truth actual rapes, in the legal sense of the word, are constantly being perpetrated in London on unwilling virgins, purveyed and procured to rich men at so much a head by keepers of brothels?" "Certainly," said he, "there is not a doubt of it." "Why," I exclaimed, "the very thought is enough to raise hell." "It is true," he said; "and although it ought to raise hell, it does not even raise the neighbours." "But do the girls cry out?" "Of course they do. But what avails screaming in a quiet bedroom? Remember, the utmost limit of howling or excessively violent screaming, such as a man or woman would make if actual murder was being attempted, is only two minutes, and the limit of screaming of any kind is only five. Suppose a girl is being outraged in a room next to your house. You hear her screaming, just as you are dozing to sleep. Do you get up, dress, rush downstairs, and insist on admittance? Hardly. But suppose the screams continue and you get uneasy, you begin to think whether you should not do something? Before you have made up your mind and got dressed the screams cease, and you think you were a fool for your pains." "But the policeman on the beat?" "He has no right to interfere, even if he heard anything. Suppose that a constable had a right to force his way into any house where a woman screamed fearfully, policemen would be almost as regular attendants at childbed as doctors. Once a girl gets into such a house she is almost helpless, and may be ravished with comparative safety." "But surely rape is a felony punishable with penal servitude. Can she not prosecute?" "Whom is she to prosecute? She does not know her assailant's name. She might not even be able to recognize him if she met him outside. Even if she did, who would believe her? A woman who has lost her chastity is always a discredited witness. The fact of her being in a house of ill fame would possibly be held to be evidence of her consent. The keeper of the house and all the servants would swear she was a consenting party; they would swear that she had never screamed, and the woman would be condemned as an adventuress who wished to levy black mail." "And this is going on to-day?" "Certainly it is, and it will go on, and you cannot help it, as long as men have money, procuresses are skilful, and women are weak and inexperienced."

VIRGINS WILLING AND UNWILLING

So startling a declaration by so eminent an authority led me to turn my investigations in this direction. On discussing the matter with a well-known member of Parliament, he laughed and said: "I doubt the unwillingness of these virgins. That you can contract for maids at so much a head is true enough. I myself am quite ready to supply you with 100 maids at £25 each, but they will all know very well what they are about. There are plenty of people among us entirely devoid of moral scruples on the score of chastity, whose daughters are kept straight until they are sixteen or seventeen, not because they love virtue, but solely because their virginity is a realizable asset, with which they are taught they should never part except for value received. These are the girls who can be had at so much a head; but it is nonsense to say it is rape; it is merely the delivery as per contract of the asset virginity in return for cash down. Of course there may be some cases in which the girl is really unwilling, but the regular supply comes from those who take a strictly businesslike view of the saleable value of their maidenhead." My interlocutor referred me to a friend whom he described as the first expert on the subject, an evergreen old gentleman to whom the brothels of Europe were as familiar as Notre Dame and St. Paul's. This specialist, however, entirely denied that there was such a thing as the procuring of virgins, willing or unwilling, either here or on the Continent. Maidenheads, he maintained, were not assets that could be realized in the market, but he admitted that there were some few men whose taste led them to buy little girls from their mothers in order to abuse them. My respect for this "eminent authority" diminished, however, on receiving his assurance that all Parisian and Belgian brothels were managed so admirably that no minors could be harboured, and that no English girls were ever sent to the Continent for immoral purposes. Still even he admitted that little girls were bought and sold for vicious purposes, and this unnatural combination of slave trade, rape, and unnatural crime seemed to justify further inquiry.

I then put myself into direct and confidential communication with brothel-keepers in the West and East of London and in the provinces. Some of these were still carrying on their business, others had abandoned their profession in disgust, and were now living a better life. The information which I received from them was, of course, confidential. I am not a detective, and much of the information which I received was given only after the most solemn pledge that I would not violate their confidence, so as to involve them in a criminal prosecution. It was somewhat unfortunate that this inquiry was only set on foot after the prosecution of Mrs. Jefferies. The fine inflicted on her has struck momentary awe into the heart of the thriving community of "introducers." They could accommodate no one but their old customers.

A new face, suggested Mr. Minahan, and an inquiry for virgins or little girls by one who had not given his proofs, excited suspicion and alarm. But, aided by some trustworthy and experienced friends, I succeeded after a time in overcoming the preliminary obstacle so as to obtain sufficient evidence as to the reality of the crime.

THE CONFESSIONS OF A BROTHEL-KEEPER

Here, for instance, is a statement made to me by a brothel keeper, who formerly kept a noted House in the Mile-end road, but who is now endeavouring to start life afresh as an honest man. I saw both him and his wife, herself a notorious prostitute whom he had married off the streets, where she had earned her living since she was fourteen:—

"Maids, as you call them—fresh girls as we know them in the trade—are constantly in request, and a keeper who knows his business has his eyes open in all directions, his stock of girls is constantly getting used up, and needs replenishing, and he has to be on the alert for likely "marks" to keep up the reputation of his house. I have been in my time a good deal about the country on these errands. The getting of fresh girls takes time, but it is simple and easy enough when, once you are in it. I have gone and courted girls in the country under all kinds of disguises, occasionally assuming the dress of a parson, and made them believe that I intended to marry them, and so got them in my power to please a good customer. How is it done? Why, after courting my girl for a time, I propose to bring her to London to see the sights. I bring her up, take her here and there, giving her plenty to eat and drink—especially drink. I take her to the theatre, and then I contrive it so that she loses her last train. By this time she is very tired, a little dazed with the drink and excitement, and very frightened at being left in town with no friends. I offer her nice lodgings for the night: she goes to bed in my house, and then the affair is managed. My client gets his maid, I get my £10 or £20 commission, and in the morning the girl, who has lost her character, and dare not go home, in all probability will do as the others do, and become one of my "marks"—that is, she will make her living in the streets, to the advantage of my house. The brothel keeper's profit is, first, the commission down for the price of a maid, and secondly, the continuous profit of the addition of a newly seduced, attractive girl to his establishment. That is a fair sample case of the way in which we recruit. Another very simple mode of supplying maids is by breeding them. Many women who are on the streets have female children. They are worth keeping. When they get to be twelve or thirteen they become merchantable. For a very likely "mark" of this kind you may get as much as £20 or £40. I sent my own daughter out on the streets from my own brothel. I know a couple of very fine little girls now who will be sold before very long. They are bred and trained for the life. They must take the first step some time, and it is bad business not to make as much out of that as possible. Drunken parents often sell their children to brothel keepers. In the East-end, you can always pick up as many fresh girls as you want. In one street in Dalston you might buy a dozen. Sometimes the supply is in excess of the demand, and you have to seduce your maid yourself, or to employ some one else to do it, which is bad business in a double sense. There is a man called S—— whom a famous house used to employ to seduce young girls and make them fit for service when there was no demand for maids and there was a demand for girls who had been seduced. But as a rule the number seduced ready to hand is ample, especially among very young children. Did I ever do anything else in the way of recruiting? Yes. I remember one case very well. The girl, a likely "mark," was a simple country lass living at Horsham. I had heard of her, and I went down to Horsham to see what I could do. Her parents believed that I was in regular business in London, and they were very glad when I proposed to engage their daughter. I brought her to town and made her a servant in our house. We petted her and made a good deal of her, gradually initiated her into the kind of life it was; and then I sold her to a young gentleman for £15. When I say that I sold her, I mean that he gave me the gold and I gave him the girl, to do what he liked with. He took her away and seduced her. I believe he treated her rather well afterwards, but that was not my affair. She was his after he paid for her and took her away. If her parents had inquired, I would have said that she had been a bad girl and run away with a young man. How could I help that? I once sold a girl twelve years old for £20 to a clergyman, who used to come to my house professedly to distribute tracts. The East is the great market for the children who are imported into West-end houses, or taken abroad wholesale when trade is brisk. I know of no West-end houses, having always lived at Dalston or thereabouts, but agents pass to and fro in the course of business. They receive the goods, depart, and no questions are asked.

Mrs. S., a famous procuress, has a mansion at——, which is one of the worst centres of the trade, with four other houses in other districts, one at St. John's-wood. This lady, when she discovers ability, cultivates it—that is, if a comely young girl of fifteen falls into her net, with some intelligence, she is taught to read and write, and to play the piano."

THE LONDON SLAVE MARKET

This brothel-keeper was a smart fellow, and had been a commercial traveller once, but drink had brought him down. Anxious to test the truth of his statement, I asked him, through a trusty agent, if he would undertake to supply me in three days with a couple of fresh girls, maids, whose virginity would be attested by a doctor's certificate. At first he said that it would require a longer time. But on being pressed, and assured that money was no object, he said that he would make inquiries, and see what could be done. In two days I received from the same confidential source an intimation that for £10 commission he would undertake to deliver to my chambers, or to any other spot which I might choose to select, two young girls, each with a doctor's certificate of the fact that she was a virgo intacta. Hesitating to close with this offer, my agent received the following telegram:—"I think all right. I am with parties. Will tell you all to-morrow about twelve o'clock." On calling H—— said:—

"I will undertake to deliver at your rooms within two days two children at your chambers. Both are the daughters of brothel keepers whom I have known and dealt with, and the parents are willing to sell in both cases. I represented that they were intended for a rich old gentleman who had led a life of debauchery for years. I was suspected of baby-farming—that is, peaching, at first, and it required all my knowledge of the tricks of the trade to effect my purpose. However, after champagne and liquors, my old friend G——,M——lane, Hackney, agreed to hand over her own child, a pretty girl of eleven, for £5, if she could get no more. The child was *virgo intacta*, so far as her mother knew. I then went to Mrs. N——, of B—— street, Dalston, (B—— street is a street of brothels from end to end). Mrs. N—— required little persuasion, but her price was higher. She would not part with her daughter under £5 or £10, as she was pretty and attractive, and a virgin, aged thirteen, who would probably fetch more in the open market. These two children I could deliver up within two days if the money was right. I would, on the same conditions, undertake to deliver half a dozen girls, ages varying from ten to thirteen, within a week or ten days."

I did not deem it wise to carry the negotiations any further. The purchase price was to be paid on delivery, but it was to be returned if the girls were found to have been tampered with.

That was fairly confirmatory evidence of the existence of the traffic to which official authority has pointed; but I was not content. Making inquiries at the other end of the town, by good fortune I was brought into intimate and confidential communication with an ex-brothel keeper. When a mere girl she had been seduced by Colonel S——, when a maidservant at Petersfield, and had been thrown upon the streets by that officer at Manchester. She had subsequently kept a house of ill fame at a seaport town, and from thence had gravitated to the congenial neighbourhood of Regent's Park. There she had kept a brothel for several years. About a year ago, however, she was picked up, when in a drunken fit, by some earnest workers, and after a hard struggle was brought back to a decent and moral life. She was a woman who bore traces of the rigorous mill through which she had passed. Her health was impaired; she looked ten years older than her actual age, and it was with the greatest reluctance she could be prevailed upon to speak of the incidents of her previous life, the horror of which seemed to cling to her like a nightmare. By dint of patient questioning, however, and the assurance that I would not criminate either herself or any of her old companions, she became more communicative, and answered my inquiries. Her narrative was straightforward; and I am fully convinced it was entirely genuine. I have since made strict inquiries among those who see her daily and know her most intimately, and I am satisfied that the woman was speaking the truth. She had no motive to deceive, and she felt very deeply the shame of her awful confession, which was only wrung from her by the conviction that it might help to secure the prevention of similar crimes in the future.

HOW GIRLS ARE BOUGHT AND RUINED

Her story, or rather so much of it as is germane to the present inquiry, was somewhat as follows:—

"As a regular thing, the landlady of a bad house lets her rooms to gay women and lives on their rent and the profits on the drink which they compel their customers to buy for the good of the house. She may go out herself or she may not. If business is very heavy, she will have to do her own share, but us a rule she contents herself with keeping her girls up to the mark, and seeing that they at least earn enough to pay their rent, and bring home sufficient customers to consume liquor enough to make it pay. Girls often shrink from going out, and need almost to be driven into the streets. If it was not for gin and the landlady they could never carry it on. Some girls I used to have would come and sit and cry in my kitchen and declare that they could not go out, they could not stand the life. I had to give them a dram and take them out myself, and set them agoing again, for if they did not seek gentlemen where was I to get my rent? Did they begin willingly? Some; others had no choice. How had they no choice? Because they never knew anything about it till the gentleman was in their bedroom, and then it was too late. I or my girls would entice fresh girls in, and persuade them to stay out too late till they were locked out, and then a pinch of snuff in their beer would keep them snug until the gentleman had his way. Has that happened often? Lots of times. It is one of the ways by which you keep your house up. Every woman who has an eye to business is constantly on the lookout for likely girls. Pretty girls who are poor, and who have either no parents or are away from home, are easiest picked up, How is it done? You or your decoy find a likely girl, and then you track her down. I remember I once went a hundred miles and more to pick up a girl. I took a lodging close to the board school, where I could see the girls go backwards and forwards every day. I soon saw one that suited my fancy. She was a girl of about thirteen, tall and forward for her age, pretty, and likely to bring business. I found out she lived with her mother. I engaged her to be my little maid at the lodgings where I was staying. The very next day I took her off with me to London and her mother never saw her again. What became of her? A gentleman paid me £13 for the first of her, soon after she came to town. She was asleep when he did it—sound asleep. To tell the truth, she was drugged. It is often done. I gave her a drowse. It is a mixture of laudanum and something else. Sometimes chloroform is used, but I always used either snuff or laudanum. We call it drowse or black draught, and they lie almost as if dead, and the girl never knows what has happened till morning. And then? Oh! then she cries a great deal from pain, but she is 'mazed, and hardly knows what has happened except that she can hardly move from pain. Of course we tell her it is all right; all girls have to go through it some time, that she is through it now without knowing it, and that it is no use crying. It will never be undone for all the crying in the world. She must now do as the others do. She can live like a lady, do as she pleases, have the best of all that is going, and enjoy herself all day. If she objects, I scold her and tell her she has lost her character, no one will take her in; I will have to turn her out on the streets as a bad and ungrateful girl. The result is that in nine cases out of ten, or ninety-nine out of a hundred, the child, who is usually under fifteen, frightened and friendless, her head aching with the effect of the drowse and full of pain and horror, gives up all hope, and in a week she is one of the attractions of the house. Yon say that some men say this is never done. Don't believe them; if these people spoke the truth, it might be found that they had done it themselves. Landladies who wish to thrive must humour their customers. If they want a maid we must get them one, or they will go elsewhere. We cannot afford to lose their custom; besides, after the maid is seduced, she fills up vacancies caused by disease or drink. There are very few brothels which are not occasionally recruited in that way. That case which I mentioned was by no means exceptional; in about seven years I remember selling two maids for £20 each, one at £16, one at £15, one at £13 and others for less. Of course, where I bought I paid less than that. The difference represented my profit, commission, and payment for risk in procuring, drugging, &c."

BUYING GIRLS AT THE EAST-END

This experienced ex-procuress assured me that if she were to return to her old trade she would have no difficulty in laying her hands, through the agency of friends and relatives still in the trade, upon as many young girls as she needed. No house begins altogether with maids, but steps are at once taken to supply one or two young girls to train in. She did not think the alarm of the Jefferies trial had penetrated into the strata where she used to work. But said I, "Will these children be really maids, or will it merely be a plant to get off damaged articles under that guise?" Her reply was significant. "You do not know how it is done. Do you think I would buy a maid on her word? You can soon find out, if you are in the business, whether a child is really fresh or not. You have to trust the person who sells, no doubt, to some extent, but if you are in the trade they would not deceive you in a matter in which fraud can be so easily detected. If one house supplied another with girls who had been seduced, at the price of maids, it would get out, and their reputation would suffer. Besides you do not trust them very far. Half the commission is paid down on delivery, the other half is held over until the truth is proved." "How is that done?" "By a doctor or an experienced midwife. If you are dealing with a house you trust, you take their doctor's certificate. If they trust you they will accept the verdict of your doctor." "Does the girl know why you are taking her away?" "Very seldom. She thinks she is going to a situation. When she finds out, it is too late. If she knew what it meant she either would not come or her readiness would give rise to a suspicion that she was not the article you wanted—that, in fact, she was no better than she should be." "Who are these girls?" "Orphans, daughters of drunken parents, children of prostitutes, girls whose friends are far away." "And their price?" "In the trade from £3 to £5 is, I should think, a fair thing. But if you doubt it I will make inquiries, if you like, in my old haunts and tell you what can be done next week."

As there is nothing like inquiry on the spot, I commissioned her to inquire as to the maids then in stock or procurable at short notice by a single bad house in the East of London, whose keeper she knew. The reply was businesslike and direct. If she wanted a couple of maids for a house in the country three would be brought to Waterloo railway station next Saturday at three, from whom two could be selected at £5 per head. One girl, not very pretty, about thirteen, could be had at only at £3. Offer to be accepted or confirmed by letter—which of course never arrived.

A GIRL ESCAPES AFTER BEING SOLD

Being anxious to satisfy myself as to the reality of these transactions, I instructed a thoroughly trustworthy woman to proceed with this ex-keeper to the house in question, and see if she could see any of the children whose price was quoted like that of lambs at so much a head. The woman of the house was somewhat suspicious, owing to the presence of a stranger, but after some conversation she said that she had one fresh girl within reach, whom she would make over at once if they could come to terms. The girl was sent for, and duly appeared. She was told that she was to have a good situation in the country within a few miles of London. She said that she had been brought up at a home at Streatham, had been in service, but had been out of a place for three weeks. She was a pleasant, bright-looking girl, who seemed somewhat nervous when she heard so many inquiries and the talk about taking her into the country. The bargain, however, was struck. The keeper had to receive £2 down, and another sovereign when the girl was proved a maid. The money was paid, the girl handed over, but something said had alarmed her, and she solved the difficulty of disposing of her by making her escape. My friend who witnessed the whole transaction, and whose presence probably contributed something to the difficulty of the bargain, assures me that there was no doubt as to the sale and transfer of the girl. "Her escape," said the ex-keeper, "is one of the risks of the trade. If I had been really in for square business, I should never have agreed to take the girl from the house, partly in order to avoid such escape and partly for safety. It is almost invariably the rule that the seller must deliver the girl at some railway station. She is brought to you, placed in your cab or your railway carriage, and it is then your business, and an easy one, to see that she does not escape you. But the risks of delivery at a safe place are always taken by the seller."

A DREADFUL PROFESSION

When I was prosecuting these inquiries at the East-end, I was startled by a discovery made by a confidential agent at the other end of the town. This was nothing less than the unearthing of a house, kept apparently by a highly respectable midwife, where children were taken by procurers to be certified as virgins before violation, and where, after violation, they were taken to be "patched up," and where, if necessary, abortion could be procured. The existence of the house was no secret. It was well known in the trade, and my agent was directed thither without much ado by a gay woman with whom he had made a casual acquaintance. No doubt the respectable old lady has other business of a less doubtful character, but in the trade her repute is unrivalled, first as a certificator of virginity, and secondly for the adroitness and skill with which she can repair the laceration caused by the subsequent outrage.

That surely was sufficiently horrible. Yet there stood the house, imperturbably respectable in its outward appearance, apparently an indispensable adjunct of modern civilization, its experienced proprietress maintaining confidential relations with the "best houses" in the West-end. This repairer of damaged virgins is not a procuress. Her mission is remedial. Her premises are not used for purposes of violation. She knows where it is done, but she cannot prevent that. What she does is to minimize pain and repair as effectively as possible the ravages of the lust which she did not create, and which she cannot control. But she is a wise woman, whom great experience has taught many secrets, and if she would but speak! Not that she is above giving a hint to those who seek her advice as to where little children can best be procured. A short time ago, she says, there was no difficulty. "Any of these houses," mentioning several of the best known foreign and English houses in the West and North-west, "would, supply children, but at present they are timid. You need to be an old customer to be served. But, after all, it is expensive getting young girls for them. If you really have a fancy that way, why do you not do as Mr. —— does? It is cheaper, simpler, and safer." "And how does Mr. —— do, and who is Mr.——?" "Oh, Mr. —— is a gentleman who has a great penchant for little girls. I do not know how many I have had to repair after him. He goes down to the East-end and the City, and watches when the girls come out of shops and factories for lunch or at the end of the day. He sees his fancy and marks her down. It takes a little time, but he wins the child's confidence. One day he proposes a little excursion to the West. She consents. Next day I have another subject, and Mr. —— is off with another girl." "And what becomes of the subjects on which you display your skill?" "Some go home, others go back to their situations, others again are passed on to those who have a taste for second-hand articles," and the good lady intimated that if my agent had such a taste, she was not without hopes that she might be able to do a little trade.

WHY THE CRIES OF THE VICTIMS ARE NOT HEARD

At this point in the inquiry, the difficulty again occurred to me how was it possible for these outrages to take place without detection. The midwife, when questioned, said there was no danger. Some of the houses had an underground room, from which no sound could be heard, and that, as a matter of fact, no one ever had been detected. The truth about the underground chambers is difficult to ascertain. Padded rooms for the purpose of stifling the cries of tortured victims of lust and brutality are familiar enough on the Continent. "In my house," said a most respectable lady, who keeps a villa in the west of London, "you can enjoy the screams of the girl with the certainty that no one else hears them but yourself." But to enjoy to the full the exclusive luxury of revelling in the cries of the immature child, it is not necessary to have a padded room, a double chamber, or an underground room. "Here," said the keeper of a fashionable villa, where in days bygone a prince of the blood is said to have kept for some months one of his innumerable sultanas, as she showed her visitor over the well-appointed rooms, "Here is a room where you can be perfectly secure. The house stands in its own grounds. The walls are thick, there is a double carpet on the floor. The only window which fronts upon the back garden is doubly secured, first with shutters and then with heavy curtains. You lock the door and then you can do as you please. The girl may scream blue murder, but not a sound will be heard. The servants will be far away in the other end of the house. I only will be about seeing that all is snug." "But," remarked her visitor, "if you hear the cries of the child, you may yourself interfere, especially if, as may easily happen, I badly hurt and in fact all but kill the girl." "You will not kill her," she answered, "you have too much sense to kill the girl. Anything short of that, you can do as you please. As for me interfering, do you think I do not know my business?"

Flogging, both of men and women, goes on regularly in ordinary rooms, but the cry of the bleeding subject never attracts attention from the outside world. What chance is there, then, of the feeble, timid cry of the betrayed child penetrating the shuttered and curtained windows, or of moving the heart of the wily watcher—the woman whose business it is to secure absolute safety for her client. When means of stifling a cry—a pillow, a sheet, or even a pocket handkerchief—lie all around, there is practically no danger. To some men, however, the shriek of torture is the essence of their delight, and they would not silence by a single note the cry of agony over which they gloat.

NO ROOM FOR REPENTANCE

Whether the maids thus violated in the secret chambers of accommodation houses are willing or unwilling is a question on which a keeper shed a flood of light by a very pertinent and obvious remark: "I have never had a maid seduced in my house," he said, "unless she was willing. They are willing enough to come to my house to be seduced, but when the man comes they are never willing." And she proceeded to illustrate what she meant by descriptions of scenes which had taken place in her house when girls, who according to her story had implored her to allow them to be seduced in her rooms, had when the supreme moment arrived repented their willingness, and fought tooth and nail, when too late, for the protection of their chastity. To use her familiar phrase, they made "the devil's own row," and on at least one occasion it was evident that the girl's resistance had only been overcome after a prolonged and desperate fight, in which, what with screaming and violence, she was too exhausted to continue the struggle.

That was in the case of a full-grown woman. Children of twelve and thirteen cannot offer any serious resistance. They only dimly comprehend what it all means. Their mothers sometimes consent to their seduction for the sake of the price paid by their seducer. The child goes to the introducing house as a sheep to the shambles. Once there, she is compelled to go through with it. No matter how brutal the man may be, she cannot escape. "If she wanted to be seduced, and came here to be seduced," says the keeper, "I shall see that she does not play the fool. The gentleman has paid for her, and he can do with her what he likes." Neither Rhadamanthus nor Lord Bramwell could more sternly exact the rigorous fulfilment of the stipulations of the contract. "Once she is in my house," said a worthy landlady, "she does not go out till the job is done. She comes in willingly, but no matter how willing she may be to go out, she stays here till my gentleman has done with her. She repents too late when she repents after crossing my threshold."

STRAPPING GIRLS DOWN

In the course of my investigations I heard some strange tales concerning the precautions taken to render escape impossible for the girl whose ruin, with or without her consent, has been resolved upon. One fact, which is of quite recent occurrence in a fashionable London suburb, the accuracy of which I was able to verify, is an illustration of the extent to which those engaged in this traffic are willing to go to supply the caprices of their customers. To oblige a wealthy customer who by riot and excess had impaired his vitality to such an extent that nothing could minister to his jaded senses but very young maidens, an eminently respectable lady undertook that whenever the girl was fourteen or fifteen years of age she should be strapped down hand and foot to the four posts of the bedstead, so that all resistance save that of unavailing screaming would be impossible. Before the strapping down was finally agreed upon the lady of the house, a stalwart woman and experienced in the trade, had volunteered her services to hold the virgin down by force while her wealthy patron effected his purpose. That was too much even for him, and the alternative of fastening with straps padded on the under side was then agreed upon. Strapping down for violation used to be a common occurrence in Half-moon-street and in Anna Rosenberg's brothel at Liverpool. Anything can be done for money, if you only know where to take it.

HOW THE LAW ABETS THE CRIMINAL

The system of procuration, as I have already explained, is reduced to a science. The poorer brothel-keeper hunts up recruits herself, while the richer are supported by their agents. No prudent keeper of an introducing house will receive girls brought by other than her accredited and trusted agents. The devices of these agents are innumerable. They have been known to profess penitence in order to gain access to a home for fallen women, where they thought some Magdalens repenting of their penitence might be secured for their house. They go into work-houses, to see what likely girls are to be had. They use servants' registries. They haunt the doors of gaols when girls in for their first offence are turned adrift on the expiry of their sentences. There are no subterfuges too cunning or too daring for them to resort to in the pursuit of their game. Against their wiles the law offers the child over thirteen next to no protection. If a child of fourteen is cajoled or frightened, or overborne by anything short of direct force or the threat of immediate bodily harm, into however an unwilling acquiescence in an act the nature of which she most imperfectly apprehends, the law steps in to shield her violator. If permission is given, says "Stephen's Digest of the Criminal Law," " the fact that it was obtained by fraud, or that the woman did not understand the nature of the act is immaterial."

A CHILD OF THIRTEEN BOUGHT FOR £5

Let me conclude the chapter of horrors by one incident, and only one of those which are constantly occurring in those dread regions of subterranean vice in which sexual crime flourishes almost unchecked. I can personally vouch for the absolute accuracy of every fact in the narrative.

At the beginning of this Derby week, a woman, an old hand in the work of procuration, entered a brothel in —— st. M——, kept by an old acquaintance, and opened negotiations for the purchase of a maid. One of the women who lodged in the house had a sister as yet untouched. Her mother was far away, her father was dead. The child was living in the house, and in all probability would be seduced and follow the profession of her elder sister. The child was between thirteen and fourteen, and after some bargaining it was agreed that she should be handed over to the procuress for the sum of £5. The maid was wanted, it was said, to start a house with, and there was no disguise on either side that the sale was to be effected for immoral purposes. While the negotiations were going on, a drunken neighbour came into the house, and so little concealment was then used, that she speedily became aware of the nature of the transaction. So far from being horrified at the proposed sale of the girl, she whispered eagerly to the seller, "Don't you think she would take our Lily? I think she would suit." Lily was her own daughter, a bright, fresh-looking little girl, who was thirteen years old last Christmas. The bargain, however, was made for the other child, and Lily's mother felt she had lost her market.

The next day, Derby Day as it happened, was fixed for the delivery of this human chattel. But as luck would have it, another sister of the child who was to be made over to the procuress heard of the proposed sale. She was living respectably in a situation, and on hearing of the fate reserved for the little one she lost no time in persuading her dissolute sister to break off the bargain. When the woman came for her prey the bird had flown. Then came the chance of Lily's mother. The brothel-keeper sent for her, and offered her a sovereign for her daughter. The woman was poor, dissolute, and indifferent to everything but drink. The father, who was also a drunken man, was told his daughter was going to a situation. He received the news with indifference, without even inquiring where she was going to. The brothel-keeper having thus secured possession of the child, then sold her to the procuress in place of the child whose sister had rescued her from her destined doom for £5—£3 paid down and the remaining £2 after her virginity had been professionally certified. The little girl, all unsuspecting the purpose for which she was destined, was told that she must go with this strange woman to a situation. The procuress, who was well up to her work, took her away, washed her, dressed her up neatly, and sent her to bid her parents good-bye. The mother was so drunk she hardly recognized her daughter. The father was hardly less indifferent. The child left her home, and was taken to the woman's lodging in A——street.

The first step had thus been taken. But it was necessary to procure the certification of her virginity—a somewhat difficult task, as the child was absolutely ignorant of the nature of the transaction which had transferred her from home to the keeping of this strange, but apparently kind-hearted woman. Lily was a little cockney child, one of those who by the thousand annually develop into the servants of the poorer middle-class. She had been at school, could read and write, and although her spelling was extraordinary, she was able to express herself with much force and decision. Her experience of the world was limited to the London quarter in which she had been born. With the exception of two school trips to Richmond and one to Epping Forest, she had never been in the country in her life, nor had she ever even seen the Thames excepting at Richmond. She was an industrious, warm-hearted little thing, a hardy English child, slightly coarse in texture, with dark black eyes, and short, sturdy figure. Her education was slight. She spelled write "right," for instance, and her grammar was very shaky. But she was a loving, affectionate child, whose kindly feeling for the drunken mother who sold her into nameless infamy was very touching to behold. In a little letter of hers which I once saw, plentifully garlanded with kisses, there was the following ill-spelled childish verse:—

> As I was in bed
> Some little forths (thoughts) gave (came) in my head.
> I forth (thought) of one, I forth (thought) of two;
> But first of all I forth (thought) of you.

The poor child was full of delight at going to her new situation, and clung affectionately to the keeper who was taking her away—where, she knew not.

The first thing to be done after the child was fairly severed from home was to secure the certificate of virginity without which the rest of the purchase-money would not be forthcoming. In order to avoid trouble she was taken in a cab to the house of a midwife, whose skill in pronouncing upon the physical evidences of virginity is generally recognized in the profession. The examination was very brief and completely satisfactory. But the youth, the complete innocence of the girl, extorted pity even from the hardened heart of the old abortionist. "The poor little thing," she exclaimed. "She is so small, her pain will be extreme. I hope you will not be too cruel with her"—as if to lust when fully roused the very acme of agony on the part of the victim has not a fierce delight. To quiet the old lady the agent of the purchaser asked if she could supply anything to dull the pain. She produced a small phial of chloroform. "This," she said, "is the best. My clients find this much the most effective." The keeper took the bottle, but unaccustomed to anything but drugging by the administration of sleeping potions, she would infallibly have poisoned the child had she not discovered by experiment that the liquid burned the mouth when an attempt was made to swallow it. £1 1s. was paid for the certificate of virginity—which was verbal and not written—while £1 10s. more was charged for the chloroform, the net value of which was probably less than a shilling. An arrangement was made that if the child was badly injured Madame would patch it up to the best of her ability, and then the party left the house.

From the midwife's the innocent girl was taken to a house of ill fame, No.—, P——— street, Regent-street, where, notwithstanding her extreme youth, she was admitted without question. She was taken up stairs, undressed, and put to bed, the woman who bought her putting her to sleep. She was rather restless, but under the influence of chloroform she soon went over. Then the woman withdrew. All was quiet and still. A few moments later the door opened, and the purchaser entered the bedroom. He closed and locked the door. There was a brief silence. And then there rose a wild and piteous cry—not a loud shriek, but a helpless, startled scream like the bleat of a frightened lamb. And the child's voice was heard crying, in accents of terror, "There's a man in the room! Take me home; oh, take me home!"

And then all once more was still.

That was but one case among many, and by no means the worst. It only differs from the rest because I have been able to verify the facts. Many a similar cry will be raised this very night in the brothels of London, unheeded by man, but not unheard by the pitying ear of Heaven—

For the child's sob in the darkness curseth deeper
Than the strong man in his wrath.

3. "The Traffic in Women" (1910)

By Emma Goldman

From Emma Goldman's *Anarchism and Other Essays*, 2nd rev. ed. New York: Mother Earth Publishing Association, 1911, pp. 183–200.

> *"The Traffic in Women"* addressed the economic aspects of prostitution, then widely referred to as "trafficking."

OUR REFORMERS have suddenly made a great discovery—the white slave traffic. The papers are full of these "unheard of conditions," and lawmakers are already planning a new set of laws to check the horror.

It is significant that whenever the public mind is to be diverted from a great social wrong, a crusade is inaugurated against indecency, gambling, saloons, etc. And what is the result of such crusades? Gambling is increasing, saloons are doing a lively business through back entrances, prostitution is at its height, and the system of pimps and cadets is but aggravated.

How is it that an institution, known almost to every child, should have been discovered so suddenly? How is it that this evil, known to all sociologists, should now be made such an important issue?

To assume that the recent investigation of the white slave traffic (and, by the way, a very superficial investigation) has discovered anything new, is, to say the least, very foolish. Prostitution has been, and is, a widespread evil, yet mankind goes on its business, perfectly indifferent to the sufferings and distress of the victims of prostitution. As indifferent, indeed, as mankind has remained to our industrial system, or to economic prostitution.

Only when human sorrows are turned into a toy with glaring colors will baby people become interested—for a while at least. The people are a very fickle baby that must have new toys every day. The "righteous" cry against the white slave traffic is such a toy. It serves to amuse the people for a little while, and it will help to create a few more fat political jobs—parasites who stalk about the world as inspectors, investigators, detectives, and so forth.

What is really the cause of the trade in women? Not merely white women, but yellow and black women as well. Exploitation, of course; the merciless Moloch of capitalism that fattens on underpaid labor, thus driving thousands of women and girls into prostitution. With Mrs. Warren these girls feel, "Why waste your life working for a few shillings a week in a scullery, eighteen hours a day?"

Naturally our reformers say nothing about this cause. They know it well enough, but it doesn't pay to say anything about it. It is much more profitable to play the Pharisee, to pretend an outraged morality, than to go to the bottom of things.

However, there is one commendable exception among the young writers: Reginald Wright Kauffman, whose work *The House of Bondage* is the first earnest attempt to treat the social evil—not from a sentimental Philistine viewpoint. A journalist of wide experience, Mr. Kauffman proves that our industrial system leaves most women no alternative except prostitution. The women portrayed in *The House of Bondage* belong to the working class. Had the author portrayed the life of women in other spheres, he would have been confronted with the same state of affairs.

Nowhere is woman treated according to the merit of her work, but rather as a sex. It is therefore almost inevitable that she should pay for her right to exist, to keep a position in whatever line, with sex favors. Thus it is merely a question of degree whether she sells herself to one man, in or out of marriage, or to many men. Whether our reformers admit it or not, the economic and social inferiority of woman is responsible for prostitution.

Just at present our good people are shocked by the disclosures that in New York City alone one out of every ten women works in a factory, that the average wage received by women is six dollars per week for forty-eight to sixty hours of work, and that the majority of female wage workers face many months of idleness which leaves the average wage about $280 a year. In view of these economic horrors, is it to be wondered at that prostitution and the white slave trade have become such dominant factors?

Lest the preceding figures be considered an exaggeration, it is well to examine what some authorities on prostitution have to say:

"A prolific cause of female depravity can be found in the several tables, showing the description of the employment pursued, and the wages received, by the women previous to their fall, and it will be a question for the political economist to decide how far mere business consideration should be an apology on the part of employers for a reduction in their rates of remuneration, and whether the savings of a small percentage on wages is not more than counterbalanced by the enormous amount of taxation enforced on the public at large to defray the expenses incurred on account of a system of vice, *which is the direct result, in many cases, of insufficient compensation of honest labor*."[1]

Our present-day reformers would do well to look into Dr. Sanger's book. There they will find that out of 2,000 cases under his observation, but few came from the middle classes, from well-ordered conditions, or pleasant homes. By far the largest majority were working girls and working women; some driven into prostitution through sheer want, others because of a cruel, wretched life at home, others again because of thwarted and crippled physical natures (of which I shall speak later on). Also it will do the maintainers of purity and morality good to learn that out of two thousand cases, 490 were married women, women who lived with their husbands. Evidently there was not much of a guaranty for their "safety and purity" in the sanctity of marriage.[2]

Dr. Alfred Blaschko, in *Prostitution in the Nineteenth Century*, is even more emphatic in characterizing economic conditions as one of the most vital factors of prostitution.

"Although prostitution has existed in all ages, it was left to the nineteenth century to develop it into a gigantic social institution. The development of industry with vast masses of people in

---

1. Dr. Sanger, *The History of Prostitution*.
2. It is a significant fact that Dr. Sanger's book has been excluded from the U.S. mails. Evidently the authorities are not anxious that the public be informed as to the true cause of prostitution.

the competitive market, the growth and congestion of large cities, the insecurity and uncertainty of employment, has given prostitution an impetus never dreamed of at any period in human history."

And again Havelock Ellis, while not so absolute in dealing with the economic cause, is nevertheless compelled to admit that it is indirectly and directly the main cause. Thus he finds that a large percentage of prostitutes is recruited from the servant class, although the latter have less care and greater security. On the other hand, Mr. Ellis does not deny that the daily routine, the drudgery, the monotony of the servant girl's lot, and especially the fact that she may never partake of the companionship and joy of a home, is no mean factor in forcing her to seek recreation and forgetfulness in the gaiety and glimmer of prostitution. In other words, the servant girl, being treated as a drudge, never having the right to herself, and worn out by the caprices of her mistress, can find an outlet, like the factory or shopgirl, only in prostitution.

The most amusing side of the question now before the public is the indignation of our "good, respectable people," especially the various Christian gentlemen, who are always to be found in the front ranks of every crusade. Is it that they are absolutely ignorant of the history of religion, and especially of the Christian religion? Or is it that they hope to blind the present generation to the part played in the past by the Church in relation to prostitution? Whatever their reason, they should be the last to cry out against the unfortunate victims of today, since it is known to every intelligent student that prostitution is of religious origin, maintained and fostered for many centuries, not as a shame, but as a virtue, hailed as such by the Gods themselves.

"It would seem that the origin of prostitution is to be found primarily in a religious custom, religion, the great conserver of social tradition, preserving in a transformed shape a primitive freedom that was passing out of the general social life. The typical example is that recorded by Herodotus, in the fifth century before Christ, at the Temple of Mylitta, the Babylonian Venus, where every woman, once in her life, had to come and give herself to the first stranger, who threw a coin in her lap, to worship the goddess. Very similar customs existed in other parts of western Asia, in North Africa, in Cyprus, and other islands of the eastern Mediterranean, and also in Greece, where the temple of Aphrodite on the fort at Corinth possessed over a thousand hierodules, dedicated to the service of the goddess.

"The theory that religious prostitution developed, as a general rule, out of the belief that the generative activity of human beings possessed a mysterious and sacred influence in promoting the fertility of Nature, is maintained by all authoritative writers on the subject. Gradually, however, and when prostitution became an organized institution under priestly influence, religious prostitution developed utilitarian sides, thus helping to increase public revenue.

"The rise of Christianity to political power produced little change in policy. The leading fathers of the Church tolerated prostitution. Brothels under municipal protection are found in the thirteenth century. They constituted a sort of public service, the directors of them being considered almost as public servants."[3]

To this must be added the following from Dr. Sanger's work:

"Pope Clement II. issued a bull that prostitutes would be tolerated if they pay a certain amount of their earnings to the Church.

---

3. Havelock Ellis, *Sex and Society.*

"Pope Sixtus IV. was more practical; from one single brothel, which he himself had built, he received an income of 20,000 ducats."

In modern times the Church is a little more careful in that direction. At least she does not openly demand tribute from prostitutes. She finds it much more profitable to go in for real estate, like Trinity Church, for instance, to rent out death traps at an exorbitant price to those who live off and by prostitution.

Much as I should like to, my space will not admit speaking of prostitution in Egypt, Greece, Rome, and during the Middle Ages. The conditions in the latter period are particularly interesting, inasmuch as prostitution was organized into guilds, presided over by a brothel Queen. These guilds employed strikes as a medium of improving their condition and keeping a standard price. Certainly that is more practical a method than the one used by the modern wage-slave in society.

It would be one-sided and extremely superficial to maintain that the economic factor is the only cause of prostitution. There are others no less important and vital. That, too, our reformers know, but dare discuss even less than the institution that saps the very life out of both men and women. I refer to the sex question, the very mention of which causes most people moral spasms.

It is a conceded fact that woman is being reared as a sex commodity, and yet she is kept in absolute ignorance of the meaning and importance of sex. Everything dealing with that subject is suppressed, and persons who attempt to bring light into this terrible darkness are persecuted and thrown into prison. Yet it is nevertheless true that so long as a girl is not to know how to take care of herself, not to know the function of the most important part of her life, we need not be surprised if she becomes an easy prey to prostitution, or to any other form of a relationship which degrades her to the position of an object for mere sex gratification.

It is due to this ignorance that the entire life and nature of the girl is thwarted and crippled. We have long ago taken it as a self-evident fact that the boy may follow the call of the wild; that is to say, that the boy may, as soon as his sex nature asserts itself, satisfy that nature; but our moralists are scandalized at the very thought that the nature of a girl should assert itself. To the moralist prostitution does not consist so much in the fact that the woman sells her body, but rather that she sells it out of wedlock. That this is no mere statement is proved by the fact that marriage for monetary considerations is perfectly legitimate, sanctified by law and public opinion, while any other union is condemned and repudiated. Yet a prostitute, if properly defined, means nothing else than "any person for whom sexual relationships are subordinated to gain."[4]

"Those women are prostitutes who sell their bodies for the exercise of the sexual act and make of this a profession."[5]

In fact, Banger goes further; he maintains that the act of prostitution is "intrinsically equal to that of a man or woman who contracts a marriage for economic reasons."

Of course, marriage is the goal of every girl, but as thousands of girls cannot marry, our stupid social customs condemn them either to a life of celibacy or prostitution. Human nature asserts itself regardless of all laws, nor is there any plausible reason why nature should adapt itself to a perverted conception of morality.

4. Guyot, *La Prostitution.*
5. Bangert, *Criminalité et Condition Economique.*

Society considers the sex experiences of a man as attributes of his general development, while similar experiences in the life of a woman are looked upon as a terrible calamity, a loss of honor and of all that is good and noble in a human being. This double standard of morality has played no little part in the creation and perpetuation of prostitution. It involves the keeping of the young in absolute ignorance on sex matters, which alleged "innocence," together with an over-wrought and stifled sex nature, helps to bring about a state of affairs that our Puritans are so anxious to avoid or prevent.

Not that the gratification of sex must needs lead to prostitution; it is the cruel, heartless, criminal persecution of those who dare divert from the beaten track, which is responsible for it.

Girls, mere children, work in crowded, over-heated rooms ten to twelve hours daily at a machine, which tends to keep them in a constant over-excited sex state. Many of these girls have no home or comforts of any kind; therefore the street or some place of cheap amusement is the only means of forgetting their daily routine. This naturally brings them into close proximity with the other sex. It is hard to say which of the two factors brings the girl's over-sexed condition to a climax, but it is certainly the most natural thing that a climax should result. That is the first step toward prostitution. Nor is the girl to be held responsible for it. On the contrary, it is altogether the fault of society, the fault of our lack of understanding, of our lack of appreciation of life in the making; especially is it the criminal fault of our moralists, who condemn a girl for all eternity, because she has gone from the "path of virtue"; that is, because her first sex experience has taken place with out the sanction of the Church.

The girl feels herself a complete outcast, with the doors of home and society closed in her face. Her entire training and tradition is such that the girl herself feels depraved and fallen, and therefore has no ground to stand upon, or any hold that will lift her up, instead of dragging her down. Thus society creates the victims that it afterwards vainly attempts to get rid of. The meanest, most depraved and decrepit man still considers himself too good to take as his wife the woman whose grace he was quite willing to buy, even though he might thereby save her from a life of horror. Nor can she turn to her own sister for help. In her stupidity the latter deems herself too pure and chaste, not realizing that her own position is in many respects even more deplorable than her sister's of the street.

"The wife who married for money, compared with the prostitute," says Havelock Ellis, "is the true scab. She is paid less, gives much more in return in labor and care, and is absolutely bound to her master. The prostitute never signs away the right over her own person, she retains her freedom and personal rights, nor is she always compelled to submit to man's embrace."

Nor does the better-than-thou woman realize the apologist claim of Lecky that "though she may be the supreme type of vice, she is also the most efficient guardian of virtue. But for her, happy homes would be polluted, unnatural and harmful practice would abound."

Moralists are ever ready to sacrifice one-half of the human race for the sake of some miserable institution which they can not outgrow. As a matter of fact, prostitution is no more a safeguard for the purity of the home than rigid laws are a safeguard against prostitution. Fully fifty per cent. of married men are patrons of brothels. It is through this virtuous element that the married women—nay, even the children—are infected with venereal diseases. Yet society has not a word of condemnation for the man, while no law is too monstrous to be set in motion against the helpless victim. She is not only preyed upon by those who use her, but she is also absolutely at the mercy of every policeman and miserable detective on the beat, the officials at the station house, the authorities in every prison.

In a recent book by a woman who was for twelve years the mistress of a "house," are to be found the following figures: "The authorities compelled me to pay every month fines between $14.70 to $29.70, the girls would pay from $5.70 to $9.70 to the police." Considering that the writer did her business in a small city, that the amounts she gives do not include extra bribes and fines, one can readily see the tremendous revenue the police department derives from the blood money of its victims, whom it will not even protect. Woe to those who refuse to pay their toll; they would be rounded up like cattle, "if only to make a favorable impression upon the good citizens of the city, or if the powers needed extra money on the side. For the warped mind who believes that a fallen woman is incapable of human emotion it would be impossible to realize the grief, the disgrace, the tears, the wounded pride that was ours every time we were pulled in."

Strange, isn't it, that a woman who has kept a "house" should be able to feel that way? But stranger still that a good Christian world should bleed and fleece such women, and give them nothing in return except obloquy and persecution. Oh, for the charity of a Christian world!

Much stress is laid on white slaves being imported into America. How would America ever retain her virtue if Europe did not help her out? I will not deny that this may be the case in some instances, any more than I will deny that there are emissaries of Germany and other countries luring economic slaves into America; but I absolutely deny that prostitution is recruited to any appreciable extent from Europe. It may be true that the majority of prostitutes of New York City are foreigners, but that is because the majority of the population is foreign. The moment we go to any other American city, to Chicago or the Middle West, we shall find that the number of foreign prostitutes is by far a minority.

Equally exaggerated is the belief that the majority of street girls in this city were engaged in this business before they came to America. Most of the girls speak excellent English, are Americanized in habits and appearance,—a thing absolutely impossible unless they had lived in this country many years. That is, they were driven into prostitution by American conditions, by the thoroughly American custom for excessive display of finery and clothes, which, of course, necessitates money,—money that cannot be earned in shops or factories.

In other words, there is no reason to believe that any set of men would go to the risk and expense of getting foreign products, when American conditions are overflooding the market with thousands of girls. On the other hand, there is sufficient evidence to prove that the export of American girls for the purpose of prostitution is by no means a small factor.

Thus Clifford G. Roe, ex-Assistant State Attorney of Cook County, Ill., makes the open charge that New England girls are shipped to Panama for the express use of men in the employ of Uncle Sam. Mr. Roe adds that "there seems to be an underground railroad between Boston and Washington which many girls travel.'" Is it not significant that the railroad should lead to the very seat of Federal authority? That Mr. Roe said more than was desired in certain quarters is proved by the fact that he lost his position. It is not practical for men in office to tell tales from school.

The excuse given for the conditions in Panama is that there are no brothels in the Canal Zone. That is the usual avenue of escape for a hypocritical world that dares not face the truth. Not in the Canal Zone, not in the city limits,—therefore prostitution does not exist.

Next to Mr. Roe, there is James Bronson Reynolds, who has made a thorough study of the white slave traffic in Asia. As a staunch American citizen and friend of the future Napoleon of America, Theodore Roosevelt, he is surely the last to discredit the virtue of his country. Yet we are informed by him that in Hong Kong, Shanghai, and Yokohama, the Augean stables of American vice are located. There American prostitutes have made themselves so conspicuous that in the Orient "American girl" is synonymous with prostitute. Mr. Reynolds reminds his countrymen that while Americans in China are under the protection of our consular representatives, the Chinese in America have no protection at all. Every one who knows the brutal and barbarous persecution Chinese and Japanese endure on the Pacific Coast, will agree with Mr. Reynolds.

In view of the above facts it is rather absurd to point to Europe as the swamp whence come all the social diseases of America. Just as absurd is it to proclaim the myth that the Jews furnish the largest contingent of willing prey. I am sure that no one will accuse me of nationalistic tendencies. I am glad to say that I have developed out of them, as out of many other prejudices. If, therefore, I resent the statement that Jewish prostitutes are imported, it is not because of any Judaistic sympathies, but because of the facts inherent in the lives of these people. No one but the most superficial will claim that Jewish girls migrate to strange lands, unless they have some tie or relation that brings them there. The Jewish girl is not adventurous. Until recent years she had never left home, not even so far as the next village or town, except it were to visit some relative. Is it then credible that Jewish girls would leave their parents or families, travel thousands of miles to strange lands, through the influence and promises of strange forces? Go to any of the large incoming steamers and see for yourself if these girls do not come either with their parents, brothers, aunts, or other kinsfolk. There may be exceptions, of course, but to state that large numbers of Jewish girls are imported for prostitution, or any other purpose, is simply not to know Jewish psychology.

Those who sit in a glass house do wrong to throw stones about them; besides, the American glass house is rather thin, it will break easily, and the interior is anything but a gainly sight.

To ascribe the increase of prostitution to alleged importation, to the growth of the cadet system, or similar causes, is highly superficial. I have already referred to the former. As to the cadet system, abhorrent as it is, we must not ignore the fact that it is essentially a phase of modern prostitution,—a phase accentuated by suppression and graft, resulting from sporadic crusades against the social evil.

The procurer is no doubt a poor specimen of the human family, but in what manner is he more despicable than the policeman who takes the last cent from the street walker, and then locks her up in the station house? Why is the cadet more criminal, or a greater menace to society, than the owners of department stores and factories, who grow fat on the sweat of their victims, only to drive them to the streets? I make no plea for the cadet, but I fail to see why he should be mercilessly hounded, while the real perpetrators of all social iniquity enjoy immunity and respect. Then, too, it is well to remember that it is not the cadet who makes the prostitute. It is our sham and hypocrisy that create both the prostitute and the cadet.

Until 1894 very little was known in America of the procurer. Then we were attacked by an epidemic of virtue. Vice was to be abolished, the country purified at all cost. The social cancer was therefore driven out of sight, but deeper into the body. Keepers of brothels, as well as their unfortunate victims, were turned over to the tender mercies of the police. The inevitable consequence of exorbitant bribes, and the penitentiary, followed.

While comparatively protected in the brothels, where they represented a certain monetary value, the girls now found themselves on the street, absolutely at the mercy of the graft-greedy police. Desperate, needing protection and longing for affection, these girls naturally proved an easy prey for cadets, themselves the result of the spirit of our commercial age. Thus the cadet system was the direct outgrowth of police persecution, graft, and attempted suppression of prostitution. It were sheer folly to confound this modern phase of the social evil with the causes of the latter.

Mere suppression and barbaric enactments can serve but to embitter, and further degrade, the unfortunate victims of ignorance and stupidity. The latter has reached its highest expression in the proposed law to make humane treatment of prostitutes a crime, punishing any one sheltering a prostitute with five years' imprisonment and $10,000 fine. Such an attitude merely exposes the terrible lack of understanding of the true causes of prostitution, as a social factor, as well as manifesting the Puritanic spirit of the Scarlet Letter days.

There is not a single modern writer on the subject who does not refer to the utter futility of legislative methods in coping with the issue. Thus Dr. Blaschko finds that governmental suppression and moral crusades accomplish nothing save driving the evil into secret channels, multiplying its dangers to society. Havelock Ellis, the most thorough and humane student of prostitution, proves by a wealth of data that the more stringent the methods of persecution the worse the condition becomes. Among other data we learn that in France, "in 1560, Charles IX. abolished brothels through an edict, but the numbers of prostitutes were only increased, while many new brothels appeared in unsuspected shapes, and were more dangerous. In spite of all such legislation, *or because of it*, there has been no country in which prostitution has played a more conspicuous part."[6]

An educated public opinion, freed from the legal and moral hounding of the prostitute, can alone help to ameliorate present conditions. Wilful shutting of eyes and ignoring of the evil as a social factor of modern life, can but aggravate matters. We must rise above our foolish notions of "better than thou," and learn to recognize in the prostitute a product of social conditions. Such a realization will sweep away the attitude of hypocrisy, and insure a greater understanding and more humane treatment. As to a thorough eradication of prostitution, nothing can accomplish that save a complete transvaluation of all accepted values especially the moral ones—coupled with the abolition of industrial slavery.

4. "Hikite-jaya" ("Introducing Tea-Houses") (1899)[1]

By J. E. de BeckerDe Becker, J. E. "Hikite-jaya" ("Introducing Tea-houses"). In *The Nightless City or the History of the Yoshiwara Yukwaku*. Yokohama, Japan: Z. P. Maruya & Co., 1899.

> *Yoshiwara was an area of the old city of Edo (which became Tokyo), Japan. For three centuries, from the 1600s until the late 1800s, it was a center of prostitution, theater, and art. In the late 19th century, J. E. De Becker wrote a description of the brothel system of Edo Era Japan.*

The business of *hikite-jaya* is to act as a guide to the various brothels, and to negotiate introductions between guests and courtesans. There are seven of these introducing houses within the enclosure (*kuruwa*), fifty in Naka-naga-ya, Suidō-jiri, and outside of the O-mon (great gate).

Besides these there are many houses in Yedo-chō, Sumi-chō, Kyō-machi (It-chō-me and Ni-chō-me) Ageya-machi, etc. The first-mentioned seven houses are first-class, those in Nakanaga-

---

6. *Sex and Society.*

---

1. "Leading-by-the-hand tea-houses."

ya second-class, while those at Suidō-jiri and Gō-jik-ken are very inferior indeed. The reception of guests, and arranging affairs for them, is attended to by servant maids, three or four of whom are generally employed in each *hikite-jaya*. As, of course, the reputation of the house depends on these servant maids, their employers generally treat them very considerately, well knowing that if the girls attend to their duties satisfactorily the number of guests will continue to increase.

When a visitor arrives before the entrance of a *hikite-jaya*, the mistress of the house and her maid-servants run to welcome him with cries of "*irrasshai*" (you are very welcome!), and on entering the room to which he is conducted (in case of his being a stranger) the attendant will ask him the name of the brothel to which he desires to go, as well as that of the particular lady he wishes to meet. Then the attendant will guide him to the brothel selected, act as a go-between in negotiating for the courtesan's favours, and after all preliminaries have been settled will wait assiduously upon the guest throughout the banquet which inevitably follows, taking care to keep the *saké* bottles moving and the cups replenished. By and by, when the time comes for retiring, the attendant conducts the guest to his sleeping apartment, waits until his "lady friend" arrives, and then discreetly slips away and leaves the brothel. When one of these servant maids takes charge of a visitor she becomes, for the time being, the actual personal servant of such guest and attends to everything he requires. To perform the services rendered by her is professionally spoken of as "*mawasu*"(to turn round, to move round) because she goes bustling round in order to arrange a hundred and one matters for the guest she is in attendance upon. If the guest calls *geisha* (dancing and singing girls) the maid carries (supposing it to be night-time) the *geisha's samisen* (guitar) and the guest's night-dress in the left hand, and a "*Kamban chōchin*"[2] and a white porcelain *saké* bottle in the right[3]—a performance which requires considerable experience to achieve successfully.

With the exception of the guests, no persons are allowed to wear *zōri* (sandals) inside the brothels.

Of late it has become a rule that the office which manages all affairs in the Yoshiwara shall distribute to the various tea-houses registration books, of a uniform style, in which are to be minutely recorded the personal appearance of visitors, status and place of registration, profession, general figure and build, aspect, style of clothes, personal effects (i.e. rings, chains, watches, etc., etc.). The books are carefully off in columned blanks headed:—"Nose, Ears, Mouth, Status, Place of registration," etc., etc.; and the descriptions have to be written in under the respective headings. In short, these books (for which, by the way, a charge of 20/30 sen is made) are something like the usual Japanese hotel registers but more complex and detailed, and when the blanks are faithfully filled up an exceedingly good description of guests is secured. In all brothels similar books are kept, and the duty of comparing the entries in these with the entries in those of the *hikite-jaya* devolves on the staff of the Yoshiwara office. In addition to these duties there are a good many harassing and vexatious police regulations to be observed by the introducing

---

2. Literally a "sign-board lantern" so called because the lantern bears the name of the *hikite-jaya*. It is the custom for the maid to carry a lighted lantern (even inside the brothel) as far as the door of the room of the courtesan to whom the visitor is introduced. This lantern serves as a token to identify the *hikite-jaya* to which the maid belongs. On arriving before the door of the room the lantern is extinguished by shaking it, and not by blowing out the light in the usual way. A superstition exists against blowing out the light with one's lips:—it is supposed to be unlucky.

3. The *haku-chō* or white porcelain *saké* bottles used on these occasions hold about one *shō*, or say about 3 pints.

houses. Should any *hikite-jaya* keeper or employé secretly introduce a guest who is in possession of explosives, a sword, or poison, he is severely punished and caused no end of trouble. The payment of the guest's bill is made through the *hikite-jaya* on his return to the introducing house in the morning: the guest pays his total bill to the *hikite-jaya* and the latter squares up his accounts with the brothel. The rule is for the *hikite-jaya* to settle up these accounts daily with the brothels, but it has become a custom with the majority to balance accounts only twice a month—viz:—on the 14th and 30th day of each month. In case of a frequent visitor being without money, and unable to pay his bill, the *hikite-jaya* will not refuse him credit in consideration of the patronage he has extended to the house and in anticipation of future visits. Sometimes, however, it happens that a regular customer becomes heavily indebted to a certain house, and turning his back on this establishment he seeks for new pastures and fresh credit; but here the extraordinary secret intelligence system upsets his calculation. Among these tea-houses exists a kind of "honor among thieves" *esprit de corps*, and besides, self-protection has forced the houses to give secret information to each other where their mutual interests are threatened, so when a party is in debt to one of the *hikite-jaya* he will be boycotted by the others. A smart hand may successfully pretend to be a new arrival in the Yoshiwara once or twice, but his trick is sure to be discovered ere long. Faithful service of employés is ensured in Yoshiwara in a similar manner. In case of a servant-maid employed in one house being desirous to enter the service of another establishment, she must first obtain the consent of her employer, and the master of the house to which she wishes to go will certainly confer with the master of the establishment she wishes to leave. In ordering food from a *dai-ya* (a cook-house where food is cooked and sent out to order), or in making purchases from storekeepers in the Yoshiwara, a maid-servant belonging to any of the *hikite-jaya* requires no money with her because the dealers all place confidence in the house from which she has come, and this they know at once by the inscription on the lantern she carries. Immediately an order is given by a maid-servant the goods are handed over without the slightest hesitation, so under these circumstances an evil-minded woman might resort to fraud without any difficulty; but should she once be detected she would never again be able to get employment in the Yoshiwara.

The fifty tea-houses outside the *Oo-mon* (great gate) were in former times called "*Kitte-jaya*" (ticket tea-houses) or "*Kitte-mise*" (ticket shops); they were also colloquially termed in *Yedo* slang—"*Yoshiwara no go-ju-mai kitte*" (the fifty "tickets" of the Yoshiwara) because they had the monopoly of issuing tickets or passes for the Yoshiwara. In a book called the "*Hyōkwa Manroku*" is is recorded that in the 3rd year of *Keian* (1650) one of the tea-houses named "*Kikuya*" issued tickets—or rather passes—for the passage of women through the great gate. On one of these old passes was written:—

> I certify that these six ladies belong to the household of a gentleman who patronizes my establishment.
> January 26th—.
> Ticket-shop,
> (signed) Kikuya Hambei,
> To
> The keepers of the great gate.

It appears from this that every lady who wished to enter the precincts for the purpose of sightseeing, or for any other reason, had to obtain a pass from the tea-houses above-mentioned. Afterwards, the "*Midzu-chaya*" (rest houses) began to be built on the *Nihon-dsutsumi* (Dyke of Japan) and as they gradually increased and prospered they at length encroached on the *Naka-no-chō* where the tradesmen of the quarter were living. This continued until the street came to be monopolized by the *Midzu-chaya*, and from the latter the present *hikite-jaya* were finally evolved. It is recorded that since the era of *Genroku* (1688–1703) the keepers of *funa-yado* (a sort of tea-house where pleasure boats are kept and let out on hire for excursions and picnics) used to arrange for guests to go and come in their river-boats, "and among the sights of Yedo were the long lines of boats floating up and down the river with gaily-dressed courtesans and the *jeunesse dorée* of the city in them." During the 8th years of Kwambun (1668) all the unlicensed prostitutes in Yedo city were pounced upon by the authorities and placed in the Yoshiwara, and about this time the inconvenient custom of being obliged to visit brothels through an *ageya* was abolished. The tea-houses, which had their origin on the banks of the *Nihon-dsutsumi*, now acted as guides (*tebiki*) to intending visitors to brothels, the old custom of the place was broken, and the name of *hikite-jaya* come into existence. [The tea-houses belonging to the *Ageya* that were removed from the old Yoshiwara and the "*Amigasa-jaya*" (see this heading further on) that sprang into existence while the brothels were temporarily situated at Sanya, after the *Furisode-kwaji* (fire) of the era of Meireki, are separate establishments.] In this way the newly evolved tea-houses prospered greatly, and their influence grew apace until the older houses in Ageya-machi began to lose their trade. No doubt but the decadence of the older institutions is attributable to the superior facilities afforded to guests by the new houses. In the old days, the tea-houses in Ageya-machi were allowed to construct balconies on the second stories of their establishments for the convenience of those guests who desired to witness the processions of the courtesans (*Yuujo no dōchuu*) that formed one of the most interesting features in the life of the Yoshiwara. Prior to the fire of the Meiwa era (1764–1761) the second stories of all the tea-houses in *Naka –no- chō* were fitted with open lattice-work in front, but subsequent to that memorable conflagration this restriction was removed and the houses were built so as to render them convenient for sight-seeing from the upper floor. This freedom did not prove of much advantage to many of the houses, however, as it was decided that the processions should thenceforward be confined to the *Naka –no-chō*. In the 10th year of Hōreki (1760) the "*Ageya*" completely disappeared, and the receiving of and arranging matters for guests became the monopoly of the tea-houses. Taking advantage of the position attained, the tea-houses abused their prosperity and influence and allowed their establishments to be used by courtesans, geisha, taiko-mochi, and various guests, for the purpose of carrying on illicit intrigues and advancing amours between men and women of loose morals. Not only this, but the houses allowed their accounts with the brothels to fall into arrears, or made payment in an unpunctual and perfunctory manner, and for these reasons many were suspended from exercising their business. In the era of Tempō (1830–1843) all food served to the guests in *hikite-jaya* was prepared on the premises by professional cooks in the service of the houses.

At present, a first customer to a tea-house is called "*shōkwai*" (first meeting): the second time he comes "*ura*" (behind the scenes) and the third time "*najimi*" (on intimate terms). According to prevalent custom, guests have to pay a certain sum of money as "footing" on their second and third visits, and persons who are anxious to pass as "in the swim" are often willing to pay both these fees (*ura-najimi-kin* and *najimi-kin*) down at once. Ordinarily, the *najimi-kin* is fixed at from 2 1/2 yen or 3 *yen*, according to the brothels to which a visitor wishes to go, and the tea-houses do not guide visitors who do not patronize either a first (*ō-mise*) or second (*naka-mise*) class establishment. In addition to other small fees the visitor is expected to give a tip of 20 or 30 *sen* to the maid who acts as his guide, but if he does not hand it over voluntarily it is carefully included in his bill under the heading of "*o-tomo*" (your attendant). *Jinrikisha* fares advanced will also appear in the bill (*tsuké* = contraction of "*kakitsuke*" = an account, writing, or memo) under the title of "*o-tomo*" (your attendant). Experience of *hikite-jaya* will convince visitors that these establishments never fail to charge up every possible or impossible item in their accounts: when a man is returning home in the morning with a "swollen head" after a night's debauch his ideas of checking a bill are generally somewhat mixed up.

The expenses of planting flowers in the streets in Spring, setting up street lanterns (*tōrō*) in Autumn, and maintaining street dancing (*niwaka*) are defrayed by the tea-houses.

The profits of the *hikite-jaya* are chiefly derived from return commissions on the fees paid to courtesans and dancing girls, and percentages levied on the food and *saké* consumed by guests. (A large profit is made upon *saké*, as this is kept in stock by tea-houses themselves). Besides, they draw a handsome revenue from visitors in the shape of "*chadai*" (tea money) which rich prodigals bestow upon them in return for fulsome flattery and cringing servility. The guests will also often give a *sōbana* (present to all the inmates of the house) when they are well treated, and at special seasons of the year, festivals, and occasions of rejoicing, the liberality of visitors brings quite a shower of dollars, all nett [sic] profit into the coffers of the *chayai* proprietor.

It is one of the many curious customs of the Yoshiwara that the expression "*fukidasu*" (to blow out) is disliked, as also is the blowing out of the ground cherry (*hozuki*).[4]

I must not omit to state that there is a low class of tea-houses which resort to extortion and barefaced robbery in dealing with strangers to the Yoshiwara. These houses are known by the general term of "*bori-jaya*" and their *modus operandi* is to detail their rascally employés to prowl about outside the quarter and inveigle uninitiated visitors to the *kuruwa*. Under various pretexts, inexperienced persons are guided to *bori-jaya* by there touters, welcomed effusively, and pestered with the most fulsome flattery and attention. *Saké* and food is served to them, including a number of dishes never even ordered by the guest, and by and by *geisha* are called in to sing and dance, although the visitors have not requisitioned their services. Later on, when the guests are primed with liquor, they are urged to visit a brothel on the condition that the expenditure shall be kept as low as possible, but, one within the low stews to which they are taken, they are persuaded to squander money on *geisha* and other things. If meanwhile the visitor, fearing heavy expenses, should desire to settle his bill, the keeper of the house will put off the matter and invent various plausible excuses for delaying the making up of the account. Time flies and morning succeeds the night, but no bill is rendered, and every artifice and trick is employed to detain the guest, until the latter, overcome with *saké* and fatigue, rolls over on the floor in a drunken sleep. Meanwhile the pockets of the unfortunate victim are surveyed in order to discover the extent of his means, and as soon as it is evident that there is no more money left to be sucked he is allowed to depart. Sometimes however, the visitors prove too smart to be successfully swindled, but in these cases the houses afford them a very cold reception indeed. Sometimes it happens that the *bori-jaya* proprietors overestimate the pecuniary resources of guests who have fallen a prey to their wiles, and find that their purses are not lined sufficiently well to meet the bills run up against them. In such a case the proprietors will allow the guest to depart under the escort

----

4. As these places depend upon the custom of persons entering them, it is considered as unlucky to speak about blowing anything out. The *hozuki* is bitter or acid, and as a pregnant woman is supposed to like sour or acid things courtesans think that to blow the winter cherry is most ominous as it may presage pregnancy and injure their profession. The ordinary *geisha* (dancing girl) in Japan delights to sit making a squeaking noise by means of blowing and squeezing between her lower lip and teeth the dried and salted berry of the winter-cherry, from which the pulp has been deftly extracted at the stem. This practice seems as pleasant to the *geisha* as that of chewing gum does to some foreigners.

of one of the employés of the house. This man exercises strict surveillance over the guest, and follows him like grim death wherever he goes until the bill is settled. He is knowns [*sic*] as a *tsuki-uma* (an attendant—or "following"—horse) and if payment is not made he will inflict the disgrace of his presence upon the luckless wight he follows, tracking the latter home to his very doorstep and there making a noisy demand for the money owing. It is only fair to add, however, that such low tea-houses are not to be found in the *Naka-no-chō.*

APPENDIX B: POEMS AND LYRICS

Many poems feature references to or descriptions of prostitutes. Here is a small selection of some of the most famous poems and songs about prostitution.

5. *"Le Crépuscule du Soir"* ("Evening Twilight," 1861)

By Charles Baudelaire From *Les Fleurs du Mal*, 1857.

> *Baudelaire (1821–1867) wrote this evocative poem of a Paris neighborhood of vice and prostitution. The French original is followed by an English translation by Angus McIntyre.*

Voici le soir charmant, ami du criminel;
Il vient comme un complice, à pas de loup; le ciel
Se ferme lentement comme une grande alcôve,
Et l'homme impatient se change en bête fauve.
Ô soir, aimable soir, désiré par celui
Dont les bras, sans mentir, peuvent dire: Aujourd'hui
Nous avons travaillé!—C'est le soir qui soulage
Les esprits que dévore une douleur sauvage,
Le savant obstiné dont le front s'alourdit,
Et l'ouvrier courbé qui regagne son lit.
Cependant des démons malsains dans l'atmosphère
S'éveillent lourdement, comme des gens d'affaire,
Et cognent en volant les volets et l'auvent.
À travers les lueurs que tourmente le vent
La Prostitution s'allume dans les rues;
Comme une fourmilière elle ouvre ses issues;

Partout elle se fraye un occulte chemin,
Ainsi que l'ennemi qui tente un coup de main;
Elle remue au sein de la cité de fange
Comme un ver qui dérobe à l'Homme ce qu'il mange.
On entend çà et là les cuisines siffler,
Les théâtres glapir, les orchestres ronfler;
Les tables d'hôte, dont le jeu fait les délices,
S'emplissent de catins et d'escrocs, leurs complices,
Et les voleurs, qui n'ont ni trêve ni merci,
Vont bientôt commencer leur travail, eux aussi,
Et forcer doucement les portes et les caisses
Pour vivre quelques jours et vêtir leurs maîtresses.
Recueille-toi, mon âme, en ce grave moment,
Et ferme ton oreille à ce rugissement.
C'est l'heure où les douleurs des malades s'aigrissent!
La sombre Nuit les prend à la gorge; ils finissent
Leur destinée et vont vers le gouffre commun;
L'hôpital se remplit de leurs soupirs.—Plus d'un
Ne viendra plus chercher la soupe parfumée,
Au coin du feu, le soir, auprès d'une âme aimée.
Encore la plupart n'ont-ils jamais connu
La douceur du foyer et n'ont jamais vécu!

"Evening Twilight"

Behold the charming evening, friend of the criminal,
Come on with stealthy steps, like an accomplice;
The skycloses slowly like a huge alcove,
And the impatient man becomes a wild beast.
Evening, sweet evening, desired by he
Whose arms, in truth, can say: Today
We have worked! It is the evening that relieves
Those souls devoured by a savage pain
The stubborn scholar with his furrowed brow,
And the stooped worker who regains his bed.
But then unhealthy demons in the atmosphere
Wake heavily, like business men, take wing
And beat in passing on the shutters and the shades.
Prostitution kindles in the streets;
Like an anthill, opens up her gates
And everywhere she makes her secret way
Like an enemy who tries his master stroke;
Deep in the city's filth she writhes
Like a worm that steals from Man the food he eats.
Here and there you hear the kitchen's whistle,
The theatre's baying and the concert's drone;

The tables where gambling works its charm
Fill up with whores and con-men, their accomplices,
And thieves, who know no truce or pity,
Will soon begin their work as well
And softly force your doors and safes
To eat a few days more and clothe their mistresses.
Draw back, my soul, in this grave moment
And stop your ears against this roar.
It is the time when sick men's pains grow sharper!
Dark Night takes them by the throat; they end
Their destiny and go towards the common pit;
The hospital fills with their sighs.—More than one
Will come no more to seek the scented broth,
Beside the fire, next to a loved one.
And the greater part have never known
The sweetness of the hearth and never lived.

6. "Jenny" (1870)

By Dante Gabriel Rossetti

Rossetti (1828–1882) was a gifted English painter as well as poet and a founder of the Pre-Raphaelite movement in arts and literature in England. In the poem, a philosophical lover reflects for his prostitute lover.

"Vengeance of Jenny's case! Fie on her! Never name her, child!"

Lazy laughing languid Jenny,
Fond of a kiss and fond of a guinea,
Whose head upon my knee to-night
Rests for a while, as if grown light
With all our dances and the sound
To which the wild tunes spun you round:
Fair Jenny mine, the thoughtless queen
Of kisses which the blush between
Could hardly make much daintier;
Whose eyes are as blue skies, whose hair
Is countless gold incomparable:
Fresh flower, scarce touched with signs that tell
Of Love's exuberant hotbed:—Nay,
Poor flower left torn since yesterday
Until to-morrow leave you bare;
Poor handful of bright spring-water
Flung in the whirlpool's shrieking face;
Poor shameful Jenny, full of grace
Thus with your head upon my knee;—

Whose person or whose purse may be
The lodestar of your reverie?
This room of yours, my Jenny, looks
A change from mine so full of books,
Whose serried ranks hold fast, forsooth,
So many captive hours of youth,—
The hours they thieve from day and night
To make one's cherished work come right,
And leave it wrong for all their theft,
Even as to-night my work was left:
Until I vowed that since my brain
And eyes of dancing seemed so fain,
My feet should have some dancing too:—
And thus it was I met with you.
Well, I suppose 'twas hard to part,
For here I am. And now, sweetheart,
You seem too tired to get to bed.
It was a careless life I led
When rooms like this were scarce so strange
Not long ago. What breeds the change,—
The many aims or the few years?
Because to-night it all appears.
Something I do not know again.
The cloud's not danced out of my brain,—
The cloud that made it turn and swim
While hour by hour the books grew dim.
Why, Jenny, as I watch you there,—
For all your wealth of loosened hair,
Your silk ungirdled and unlac'd
And warm sweets open to the waist,
All golden in the lamplight's gleam,—
You know not what a book you seem,
Half-read by lightning in a dream!
How should you know, my Jenny? Nay,
And I should be ashamed to say:—
Poor beauty, so well worth a kiss!
But while my thought runs on like this
With wasteful whims more than enough,
I wonder what you're thinking of.

If of myself you think at all,
What is the thought?—conjectural
On sorry matters best unsolved?—
Or inly is each grace revolved
To fit me with a lure?—or (sad

To think!) perhaps you're merely glad
That I'm not drunk or ruffianly
And let you rest upon my knee.

For sometimes, were the truth confess'd,
you're thankful for a little rest,—
Glad from the crush to rest within,
Form the heart-sickness and the din
Where envy's voice at virtue's pitch
Mocks you because your gown is rich;
And from the pale girl's dumb rebuke,
Whose ill-clad grace and toil-worn look
Proclaim the strength that keeps her weak
And other nights than yours bespeak;
And from the wise unchildish elf,

To schoolmate lesser than himself
Pointing you out, what thing you are:—
Yes, from the daily jeer and jar,
From shame and shame's outbraving too,
Is rest not sometimes sweet to you?—
But most from the hatefulness of man
Who spares not to end what he began,
Whose acts are ill and his speech ill,
Who, having used you at his will,
Thrusts you aside, as when I dine
I serve the dishes and the wine.

Well, handsome Jenny mine, sit up,
I've filled our glasses, let us sup,
And do not let me think of you,
Lest shame of yours suffice for two.
What, still so tired? Well, well then, keep
Your head there, so you do not sleep;
But that the weariness may pass
And leave you merry, take this glass.
Ah! lazy lily hand, more bless'd
If ne'er in rings it had been dress'd
Nor ever by a glove conceal'd!
Behold the lilies of the field,
They toil not neither do they spin;
(So doth the ancient text begin,—
Not of such rest as one of these
Can share.) Another rest and ease
Along each summer-sated path
From its new lord the garden hath,

Than that whose spring in blessings ran
Which praised the bounteous husbandman,
Ere yet, in days of hankering breath,
The lilies sickened unto death.

What, Jenny, are your lilies dead?
Aye, and the snow-white leaves are spread
Like winter on the garden-bed.
But you had roses left in May,—

They were not gone too. Jenny, nay,
But must your roses die, and those
Their purfled buds that should unclose?
Even so; the leaves are curled apart,
Still red as from the broken heart,
And here's the naked stem of thorns.
Nay, nay, mere words. Here nothing warns
As yet of winter. Sickness here
Or want alone could waken fear,—
Nothing but passion wrings a tear.
Except when there may rise unsought
Haply at times a passing thought
Of the old days which seem to be
Much older than any history
That is written in any book;
When she would lie in fields and look
Along the ground through the blown grass,
And wonder where the city was,
Far out of sight, whose broil and bale
They told her then for a child's tale.

Jenny, you know the city now.
A child can tell the tale there, how
Some things which are not yet enroll'd
In market-lists are bought and sold
Even till the early Sunday light,
When Saturday night is market-night
Everywhere, be it dry or wet,
And market-night in the Haymarket.
Our learned London children know,
Poor Jenny, all your mirth and woe;
Have seen your lifted silken skirt
Advertize dainties through the dirt;
Have seen your coach-wheels splash rebuke
On virtue; and have learned your look
When, wealth and health slipped past, you stare

Along the streets alone, and there,
Round the long park, across the bridge,
The cold lamps at the pavement's edge
Wind on together and apart,
A fiery serpent for your heart.

Let the thoughts pass, an empty cloud!
Suppose I were to think aloud,—
What if to her all this were said?
Why, as a volume seldom read
Being opened halfway shuts again,
So might the pages of her brain
Be parted at such words, and thence
Close back upon the dusty sense.
For is there hue or shape defin'd
In Jenny's desecrated mind,
Where all contagious currents meet,
A lethe of the middle street?
Nay, it reflects not any face,
Nor sound is in its sluggish pace,
But as they coil those eddies clot,
And night and day remember not.

Why, Jenny, you're asleep at last!—
Asleep, poor Jenny, hard and fast,—
So young and soft and tired; so fair,
With chin thus nestled in your hair,
Mouth quiet, eyelids almost blue
As if some sky of dreams shone through!

Just as another woman sleeps!
Enough to throw one's thoughts in heaps
Of doubt and horror,—what to say
Or think,—this awful secret sway,
The potter's power over the clay!
Of the same lump (it has been said)
For honour and dishonour made,
Two sister vessels. Here is one.
My cousin Nell is fond of fun,
And fond of dress, and change, and praise,
So mere a woman in her ways:
And if her sweet eyes rich in youth
Are like her lips that tell the truth,
My cousin Nell is fond of love.
And she's the girl I'm proudest of.
Who does not prize her, guard her well?

The love of change, in cousin Nell,
Shall find the best and hold it dear:
The unconquered mirth turn quieter
Not through her own, through others' woe
The conscious pride of beauty glow
Beside another's pride in her,
One little part of all they share.
For Love himself shall ripen these
In a kind soil to just increase
Through years of fertilizing peace.

Of the same lump (as it is said)
For honour and dishonour made,
Two sister vessels. Here is one.
It makes a goblin of the sun.

So pure,—so fall'n! How dare to think
Of the first common kindred link?
Yet, Jenny, till the world shall burn
It seems that all things take their turn;
And who shall say but this fair tree
May need, in changes that may be,
Your children's children's charity?
Scorned then, no doubt, as you are scorn'd!
Shall no man hold his pride forewarn'd
Till in the end, the Day of Days,
At Judgment, one of his own race,
As frail and lost as you, shall rise,—
His daughter, with his mother's eyes?

How Jenny's clock ticks on the shelf!
Might not the dial scorn itself
That has such hours to register?
Yet as to me, even so to her
Are golden sun and silver moon,
In daily largesse of earth's boon,
Counted for life-coins to one tune.
And if, as blindfold fates are toss'd,
Through some one man this life be lost,
Shall soul not somehow pay for soul?

Fair shines the gilded aureole
In which our highest painters place
Some living woman's simple face.
And the stilled features thus descried
As Jenny's long throat droops aside,—
The shadows where the cheeks are thin,

And pure wide curve from ear to chin,—
With Raffael's or Da Vinci's hand
To show them to men's souls, might stand,
Whole ages long, the whole world through,
For preachings of what God can do.
What has man done here? How atone,
Great God, for this which man has done?
And for the body and soul which by
Man's pitiless doom must now comply
With lifelong hell, what lullaby
Of sweet forgetful second birth
Remains? All dark. No sign on earth
What measure of god's rest endows
The many mansions of his house.

If but a woman's heart might see
Such erring heart unerringly
For once! But that can never be.

Like a rose shut in a book
In which pure women may not look,
For its base pages claim control
To crush the flower within the soul;
Where through each dead rose-leaf that clings,
Pale as transparent psyche-wings,
To the vile text, are traced such things
As might make lady's cheek indeed
More than a living rose to read;
So nought save foolish foulness may
Watch with hard eyes the sure decay;
And so the life-blood of this rose,
Puddled with shameful knowledge, flows
Through leaves no chaste hand may unclose:
Yet still it keeps such faded show
Of when 'twas gathered long ago,
That the crushed petals' lovely grain,
The sweetness of the sanguine stain,
Seen of a woman's eyes, must make
Her pitiful heart, so prone to ache,
Love roses better for its sake:—
Only that this can never be:—
Even so unto her sex is she.

Yet, Jenny, looking long at you,
The woman almost fades from view.
A cipher of man's changeless sum
Of lust, past, present, and to come,

Is left. A riddle that one shrinks
To challenge from the scornful sphinx.
Like a toad within a stone
Seated while time crumbles on;
Which sits there since the earth was curs'd
For Man's transgression at the first;
Which, living through all centuries,
Not once has seen the sun arise;
Whose life, to its cold circle charmed,
The earth's whole summers have not warmed;
Which always—whitherso the stone
Be flung—sits there, deaf, blind, alone;—
Aye, and shall not be driven out
Till that which shuts him round about
Break at the very Master's stroke,
And the dust thereof vanish as smoke,
And the seed of Man vanish as dust:—
Even so within this world is Lust.

Come, come, what use in thoughts like this?
Poor little Jenny, good to kiss,—
You'd not believe by what strange roads
Thought travels, when your beauty goads
A man to-night to think of toads!
Jenny, wake up…. Why, there's the dawn!

And there's an early waggon drawn
To market, and some sheep that jog
Bleating before a barking dog;
And the old streets come peering through
Another night that London knew;
And all as ghostlike as the lamps.

So on the wings of day decamps
My last night's frolic. Glooms begin
To shiver off as lights creep in
Past the gauze curtains half drawn-to,
And the lamp's doubled shade grows blue,—
Your lamp, my Jenny, kept alight,
Like a wise virgin's, all one night!

And in the alcove coolly spread
Glimmers with dawn your empty bed;
And yonder your fair face I see
Reflected lying on my knee,
Where teems with first foreshadowings
Your pier-glass scrawled with diamond rings.

And now without, as if some word
Had called upon them that they heard,
The London sparrows far and nigh
Clamour together suddenly;
And Jenny's cage-bird grown awake
Here in their song his part must take,
Because here too the day doth break

And somehow in myself the dawn
Among stirred clouds and veils withdrawn
Strikes greyly on her. Let her sleep.
But will it wake her if I heap
These cushions thus beneath her head
Where my knee was? No,—there's your bed,
My Jenny, while you dream. And there
I lay among your golden hair
Perhaps the subject of your dreams,
These golden coins.
For still one deems

That Jenny's flattering sleep confers
New magic on the magic purse,—
Grim web, how clogged with shrivelled flies!
Between the threads fine fumes arise
And shape their pictures in the brain.
There roll no streets in glare and rain,
Nor flagrant man-swine whets his tusk;
But delicately sighs in musk
The homage of the dim boudoir;
Or like a palpitating star
Thrilled into song, the opera-night
Breathes faint in the quick pulse of light;
Or at the carriage-window shine
Rich wares for choice; or, free to dine,
Whirls through its hour of health (divine
For her) the concourse of the Park.
And though in the discounted dark
Her functions there and here are one,
Beneath the lamps and in the sun
There reigns at least the acknowledged belle
Apparelled beyond parallel.
Ah Jenny, yes, we know your dreams.

For even the Paphian Venus seems
A goddess o'er the realms of love,

When silver-shrined in shadowy grove:
Aye, or let offerings nicely placed
But hide Priapus to the waist,
And whoso looks on him shall see
An eligible deity.

Why, Jenny, waking here alone
May help you to remember one,
Though all the memory's long outworn
Of many a double-pillowed morn.
I think I see you when you wake,
And rub your eyes for me, and shake
My gold, in rising, from your hair,
A Danae for a moment there.

Jenny, my love rang true! for still
Love at first sight is vague, until
That tinkling makes him audible.
And must I mock you to the last,
Ashamed of my own shame,—aghast
Because some thoughts not born amiss
Rose at a poor fair face like this?

Well, of such thoughts so much I know:
In my life, as in hers, they show,
By a far gleam which I may near,
A dark path I can strive to clear.

Only one kiss. Goodbye, my dear.

7. "To a Common Prostitute" (1900)

By Walt Whitman

From *Leaves of Grass*. Philadelphia: D. McKay, 1900.

> *Whitman's (1819–1892) direct, natural, and figurative language addresses the prostitute in this poem.*

Be composed—be at ease with me—I am Walt Whitman, liberal and lusty as Nature;
Not till the sun excludes you, do I exclude you;
Not till the waters refuse to glisten for you, and the leaves to rustle for you, do my words refuse to glisten and rustle for you.
My girl, I appoint with you an appointment—and I charge you that you make preparation to be worthy to meet me,
And I charge you that you be patient and perfect till I come.
Till then, I salute you with a significant look, that you do not forget me.

8. "The Ruined Maid" (1901)

By Thomas Hardy

This poem by Hardy (1840–1928), who was also well known for his novels such as Jude the Obscure and Tess of the D'Urbervilles, is actually a satirical look at the concept of women being ruined by sexual experience. Here a young English woman who has become a city prostitute in fact appears to be better off than if she had stayed a poor girl at home in a rural area.

"O Melia, my dear, this does everything crown!
Who could have supposed I should meet you in Town?
And whence such fair garments, such prosperi-ty?"—
"O didn't you know I'd been ruined?" said she.

"You left us in tatters, without shoes or socks,
Tired of digging potatoes, and spudding up docks;
And now you've gay bracelets and bright feathers three!"—
"Yes: that's how we dress when we're ruined," said she.

—"At home in the barton you said 'thee' and 'thou,'
And 'thik oon,' and 'theäs oon,' and 't'other'; but now
Your talking quite fits 'ee for high compa-ny!"—
"Some polish is gained with one's ruin," said she.

—"Your hands were like paws then, your face blue and bleak
But now I'm bewitched by your delicate cheek,
And your little gloves fit as on any la-dy!"—
"We never do work when we're ruined," said she.

—"You used to call home-life a hag-ridden dream,
And you'd sigh, and you'd sock; but at present you seem
To know not of megrims or melancho-ly!"—
"True. One's pretty lively when ruined," said she.

—"I wish I had feathers, a fine sweeping gown,
And a delicate face, and could strut about Town!"—
"My dear—a raw country girl, such as you be,
Cannot quite expect that. You ain't ruined," said she.

9. "Frankie and Johnnie" (early 1900s)

This graphic and bawdy version of the folksong "Frankie and Johnnie" was printed in Immortalia: American Ballads, Sailors' Songs, Cowboy Songs, College Songs, Parodies, Limericks, and Other Humorous Verses and Doggerel, printed privately in 1927 by by "a gentleman about town" (From Thomas R. Smith [New York: Macy-Masius; later Jacob Baker, Vanguard Press], iii, 184 pp., 4to. Signatures gathered in eight leaves). It is most likely based on the story of the 1899 death of Albert Britt, a teenage piano player, who was shot and killed by Frankie Baker, a 23-year-old prostitute, in St. Louis.

Frankie and Johnnie were lovers;
Goodness, Oh God! How they'd love—
Swore to be true to each other,
True as the stars above.
For he was her man,
But he done her wrong!
Frankie was a good girl,
Most everybody knows,
She gave a hundred dollars
To Johnnie for a suit of clothes,
Cause he was her man,
But he done her wrong!

Frankie worked in a crib-joint,
A place that's got two doors;
Gave all her money to Johnnie;
Who spent it on parlor-house whores.
God-damn his soul,
He done her wrong!

Frankie was a fucky hussy—
That's what all the pimps said—
And they kept her so damn busy,
She never had time to get out of bed.
But he done her wrong,
God-damn his soul!

Frankie hung a sign on her door,
"No more fish for sale."
Then she went looking for Johnnie
To give him all her kale.
He was a-doin' her wrong,
God-damn his soul!

Frankie went down Fourth Street
To get a glass of steam-beer;
Said to the man called bartender,
"Has my lovin' Johnnie been here?
God-damn his soul,
He's a-doin' me wrong!"

"I couldn't tell you no story,
I couldn't tell you no lie,
I saw your Johnnie an hour ago
With a coon called Alice Bly.
God-damn his soul,
He was a-doin' you wrong!"

Frankie ran back to the crib-joint,
Took the oilcloth off the bed,
Took out a bindle of coke
And snuffed it right up her head;
God-damn his soul.
He was a-doin' her wrong!

Then she put on her red kimona, [*sic*]
This time it wasn't for fun;
Cause right underneath it
Was a great big forty-four gun.
She went huntin' her man,
Who was a-doin' her wrong!
She ran along Fish Alley,
And look in a window high,
And she saw her lovin' Johnnie
Finger-frigging Alice Bly.
He was a-doing' her wrong,
God-damn his soul!

Frankie went to the hop-joint,
Frankie rang the hop-joint bell:
"Stand back you pimps and whores,
Or I'll blow you straight to hell.
I'm huntin' my man,
Who's a-doin' me wrong!"

Frankie ran up the stairway—
Johnnie hollered, "Please don't shoot!"
But Frankie raised the forty-four
And went five times, root-ti-toot.
She shot her man,
'Cause he done her wrong!

"Turn me over Frankie,
Turn me over slow;
A bullet got me on my right side,
Oh Gawd! It hurts me so.
You've killed your man,
But I done you wrong!"

Then came the scene in the courthouse:
Frankie said, as bold as brass,
"Judge, I didn't shoot him in the third degree,
I shot him in his big fat ass;
'Cause he was my man,
An' he was a-doin' me wrong!"

Bring out your rubber-tired hearse.
Bring out your rubber-tired hacks.
Hearse to take Johnnie to the cemetery;
Hacks to bring all the whores back:
For he's dead and gone,
'Cause he done her wrong!

They brought a rubber-tired hearse,
And brought out rubber-tired hacks:
Thirteen pimps went to the cemetery
But only twelve came back.
He's dead and gone,
He was a-doin' her wrong!

The sergeant said to Frankie,
"It may all be for the best,
He always chased 'round parlor-house whores,
He sure was an awful pest; Now he's dead and gone,He was a-doin' her wrong!"
Three little pieces of crepe
Hanging on the crib-joint door,
Signifies that Johnnie
Will never be a pimp no more.
God-damn his soul,
He done her wrong!

10. "The House of the Rising Sun" (1937)

The music for "The House of the Rising Run" comes from a traditional English ballad of long ago, but these lyrics, by Georgia Turner and Bert Martin (both from Kentucky), were recorded by Alan Lomax in 1937.

There is a house in New Orleans
They call the Rising Sun.
It's been the ruin of many a poor girl,
and me, O God, for one.
If I had listened what Mamma said,
I'd 'a' been at home today.
Being so young and foolish, poor boy,
let a rambler lead me astray.

Go tell my baby sister
never do like I have done
to shun that house in New Orleans
they call the Rising Sun.

My mother she's a tailor;
she sold those new blue jeans.

My sweetheart, he's a drunkard, Lord, Lord,
drinks down in New Orleans.

The only thing a drunkard needs
is a suitcase and a trunk.
The only time he's satisfied
is when he's on a drunk.
Fills his glasses to the brim,
passes them around
only pleasure he gets out of life
is hoboin' from town to town.
One foot is on the platform
and the other one on the train.
I'm going back to New Orleans
to wear that ball and chain.
Going back to New Orleans,
my race is almost run.
Going back to spend the rest of my days
beneath that Rising Sun.

APPENDIX C: DOCUMENTS BY SEX WORKERS

11. World Charter for Prostitutes' Rights (1985)

The World Charter For Prostitutes' Rights was drafted in 1985 by sex workers from around the world at a meeting in Amsterdam.

From the International Committee for Prostitutes' Rights (ICPR), Amsterdam, 1985. Published in *A Vindication of the Rights of Whores*, ed. G. Pheterson. Seattle: Seal Press, 1989, p. 40.

LAWS

+ Decriminalize all aspects of adult prostitution resulting from individual decision.
+ Decriminalize prostitution and regulate third parties according to standard business codes. It must be noted that existing standard business codes allow abuse of prostitutes. Therefore special clauses must be included to prevent the abuse and stigmatization of prostitutes (self-employed and others).
+ Enforce criminal laws against fraud, coercion, violence, child sexual abuse, child labor, rape, racism everywhere and across national boundaries, whether or not in the context of prostitution.
+ Eradicate laws that can be interpreted to deny freedom of association, or freedom to travel, to prostitutes within and between countries. Prostitutes have rights to a private life.

HUMAN RIGHTS

+ Guarantee prostitutes all human rights and civil liberties, including the freedom of speech, travel, immigration, work, marriage, and motherhood and the right to unemployment insurance, health insurance and housing.

+ Grant asylum to anyone denied human rights on the basis of a "crime of status," be it prostitution or homosexuality.

WORKING CONDITIONS

+ There should be no law which implies systematic zoning of prostitution. Prostitutes should have the freedom to choose their place of work and residence. It is essential that prostitutes can provide their services under the conditions that are absolutely determined by themselves and no one else.
+ There should be a committee to insure the protection of the rights of the prostitutes and to whom prostitutes can address their complaints. This committee must be comprised of prostitutes and other professionals like lawyers and supporters.
+ There should be no law discriminating against prostitutes associating and working collectively in order to acquire a high degree of personal security.

HEALTH

+ All women and men should be educated to periodical health screening for sexually transmitted diseases. Since health checks have historically been used to control and stigmatize prostitutes, and since adult prostitutes are generally even more aware of sexual health than others, mandatory checks for prostitutes are unacceptable unless they are mandatory for all sexually active people.

SERVICES

+ Employment, counseling, legal, and housing services for runaway children should be funded in order to prevent child prostitution and to promote child well-being and opportunity.
+ Prostitutes must have the same social benefits as all other citizens according to the different regulations in different countries.
+ Shelters and services for working prostitutes and re-training programs for prostitutes wishing to leave the life should be funded.

TAXES

+ No special taxes should be levied on prostitutes or prostitute businesses.
+ Prostitutes should pay regular taxes on the same basis as other independent contractors and employees, and should receive the same benefits.

PUBLIC OPINION

+ Support educational programs to change social attitudes which stigmatize and discriminate against prostitutes and ex-prostitutes of any race, gender or nationality.
+ Develop educational programs which help the public to understand that the customer plays a crucial role in the prostitution phenomenon, this role being generally ignored. The customer, like the prostitute, should not, however, be criminalized or condemned on a moral basis.
+ We are in solidarity with workers in the sex industry.

ORGANIZATION

+ Organizations of prostitutes and ex-prostitutes should be supported to further implementation of the above charter.

12. Sex Workers' Manifesto (1997)

This Sex Workers' Manifesto was a product of the First National Conference of Sex Workers in India, which took place November 14–16, 1997, in Kolkata.

A new spectre seems to be haunting the society. Or maybe those phantom creatures who have been pushed into the shades for ages are taking on human form—and that is why there is so much fear. The sex workers' movement for last few years have made us confront many fundamental questions about social structures, life sexuality, moral rights and wrongs. We think an intrinsic component of our movement is to go on searching for the answers to these questions and raise newer ones.

WHAT IS THE SEX WORKERS' MOVEMENT ALL ABOUT?

We came together as a collective community through our active involvement as health workers, the Peer Educators, in a HIV/STD Control Project which has been running in Sonagachhi since 1992. The Project provided the initial space for building mutual support, facilitating reflection and initiating collective action among us, sex workers. Very early in the life of the Sonagachhi Project, we, with the empathetic support of those who had started the Project, clearly recognised that even to realise the very basic Project objectives of controlling transmission of HIV and STD it was crucial to view us in our totality—as complete persons with a range of emotional and material needs, living within a concrete and specific social, political and ideological context which determine the quality of our lives and our health, and not see us merely in terms of our sexual behaviour.

To give an example, while promoting the use of condoms, we soon realised that in order to change the sexual behaviour of sex workers it was not enough to enlighten them about the risks of unprotected sex or to improve their communication and negotiation skills. How will a sex worker who does not value herself at all think of taking steps to protect her health and her life? Even when fully aware of the necessity of using condoms to prevent disease transmission, may not an individual sex worker feel compelled to jeopardise her health in fear of losing her clients to other sex workers in the area unless it was ensured that all sex workers were able to persuade their clients to use condoms for every sexual act? Some sex workers may not even be in a position to try negotiate safer sex with a client as they may be too closely controlled by exploitative madams or pimps. If a sex worker is starving, either because she does not have enough custom or because most of her income goes towards maintaining a room or meeting the demands of madams, local power-brokers or the police, can she be really in a position to refuse a client who can not be persuaded to use condoms?

And what about the client? Is a man likely to be amenable to learn anything from a woman, particularly an uneducated 'fallen' woman? For him does not coming to a prostitute necessarily involve an inherent element of taking risk and behaving irresponsibly? In which case are not notions of responsibility and safety completely contradict his attitude towards his relationship with a prostitute? Does not a condom represent an unnecessary impediment in his way to 'total' pleasure?

In most case this male client himself may be a poor, displaced man. Is he in a position to value his own life or protect his health?

Then again why does not a sex worker who is ready to use condom with her client, would never have protected sex with her lover or husband? What fine balance between commercial transaction and love, caution and trust, safety and intimacy engender such behaviour? How do ideologies of love, family, motherhood influence our every sexual gesture?

Thus, thinking about such an apparently uncomplicated question—whether a sex worker can insist on having safe sex, made us realise that the issue is not at all simple. Sexuality and the lives and the movement of sex workers are intrinsically enmeshed in the social structure we live within and dominant ideology which shapes our values.

Like many other occupations, sex work is also an occupation, and it is probably one of the 'oldest profession' in the world because it meets an important social demand. But the term 'prostitute' is rarely used to refer to an occupational group who earn their livelihood through providing sexual services, rather it is deployed as a descriptive term denoting a homogenised category, usually of women, who poses threats to public health, sexual morality, social stability and civic order. Within this discursive boundary we systematically find ourselves to be targets of moralising impulses of dominant social groups, through missions of cleansing and sanitising, both materially and symbolically. If and when we figure in political or developmental agenda, we are enmeshed in discursive practices and practical projects which aim to rescue, rehabilitate, improve, discipline, control or police us. Charity organisations are prone to rescue us and put us in 'safe' homes, developmental organisations are likely to 'rehabilitate' us through meagre income generation activities, and the police seem bent upon to regularly raid our quarters in the name of controlling 'immoral' trafficking. Even when we are inscribed less negatively or even sympathetically within dominant discourses we are not exempt from stigmatisation or social exclusion. As powerless, abused victims with no resources, we are seen as objects of pity. Otherwise we appear as self-sacrificing and nurturing supporting cast of characters in popular literature and cinema, ceaselessly ready to give up our hard earned income, our clients, our 'sinful' ways and finally our lives to ensure the well-being of the hero or the society he represents. In either case we are refused enfranchisement as legitimate citizens or workers, and are banished to the margins of society and history.

The kind of oppression that can be meted out to a sex worker can never be perpetrated against a regular worker. The justification given is that sex work is not real work—it is morally sinful. As prostitution is kept hidden behind the facade of sexual morality and social order, unlike other professions there is no legitimacy or scope for any discussion about the demands and needs of the workers of the sex industry.

People who are interested in our welfare, and many are genuinely concerned, often can not think beyond rehabilitating us or abolishing prostitution altogether. However, we know that in reality it is perhaps impossible to 'rehabilitate' a sex worker because the society never allows to erase our identity as prostitutes. Is rehabilitation feasible or even desirable?

In a country where unemployment is in such gigantic proportions, where does the compulsion of displacing millions of women and men who are already engaged in an income earning occupation which supports themselves and their extended families, come from? If other workers in similarly exploitative occupations can work within the structures of their profession to improve their working conditions, why can not sex workers remain in the sex industry and demand a better deal in their life and work?

WHAT IS THE HISTORY OF SEXUAL MORALITY?

Like other human propensities and desires, sexuality and sexual need are fundamental and necessary to the human condition. Ethical and political ideas about sexuality and sexual practices are socially conditioned and historically and contexually specific. In the society as we know it now, ideologies about sexuality are deeply entrenched within structures of patriarchy and largely misogynist mores. The state and social structures only acknowledges a limited and narrow aspect of our sexuality. Pleasure, happiness, comfort and intimacy find expression through sexuality. On one hand we weave narratives around these in our literature and art. But on the other hand our societal norms and regulations allow for sexual expression only between men and women within the strict boundaries of marital relations within the institution of the family.

WHY HAVE WE CIRCUMSCRIBED SEXUALITY WITHIN SUCH A NARROW CONFINE, IGNORING ITS MANY OTHER EXPRESSIONS, EXPERIENCES AND MANIFESTATIONS?

Ownership of private property and maintenance of patriarchy necessitates a control over women's reproduction. Since property lines are maintained through legitimate heirs, and sexual intercourse between men and women alone carry the potential for procreation, capitalist patriarchy sanctions only such couplings. Sex is seen primarily, and almost exclusively, as an instrument for reproduction, negating all aspects of pleasure and desire intrinsic to it. Privileging heterosexuality, homosexuality is not only denied legitimacy, it is considered to be undesirable, unnatural, and deviant. Thus sex and sexuality are given no social sanction beyond their reproductive purpose.

Do we then not value motherhood? Just because our profession or our social situation does not allow for legitimate parenthood, are we trying to claim motherhood and bearing children is unworthy and unimportant for women? That is not the case. We feel that every woman has the right to bear children with if she so wishes. But we also think that through trying to establish motherhood as the only and primary goal for a woman the patriarchal structures try to control women's reproductive functions and curb their social and sexual autonomy. Many of us sex workers are mothers—our children are very precious to us. By social standards these children are illegitimate—bastards. But at least they are ours and not mere instruments for maintaining some man's property or continuing his genealogy. However, we too are not exempt from the ideologies of the society we live in. For many of us the impossible desire for family, home and togetherness is a permanent source of pain.

DO MEN AND WOMEN HAVE EQUAL CLAIMS TO SEXUALITY?

Societal norms about sex and sexuality do not apply similarly to men and women. If sexual needs are at all acknowledged beyond procreation, it is only for men. Even if there are minor variations from community to community and if in the name of modernity certain mores have changed in some place, it is largely men who have had enjoyed the right to be polygamous or seek multiple sexual partners. Women have always been expected to be faithful to a single man. Beyond scriptural prohibitions too, social practices severely restricts the expression of female sexuality. As soon as a girl reaches her puberty her behaviour is strictly controlled and monitored so as not to provoke the lust of men. In the name of 'decency' and 'tradition' a woman teacher is prohibited from wearing the clothes of her choice to the University. While selecting a bride for the son, the men of the family scrutinise the physical attributes of a potential bride. Pornographic representations of women satisfy the voyeuristic pleasures of millions of men. From shaving cream to bathroom fittings are sold through attracting men by advertisements depicting women as sex objects.

In this political economy of sexuality there is no space for expression of women's own sexuality and desires. Women have to cover up their bodies from men and at the same time bare themselves for male gratification. Even when women are granted some amount of subjecthood by being represented as consumers in commercial media, that role is defined by their ability to buy and normed by capitalist and patriarchal strictures.

IS OUR MOVEMENT ANTI-MEN?

Our movement is definitely against patriarchy, but not against all individual men. As it so happens, apart from the madams and landladies almost all people who profit from the sex trade are men. But what is more important is that their attitudes towards women and prostitution are biased with strong patriarchal values. They generally think of women as weak, dependent, immoral or irrational—who need to be directed and disciplined. Conditioned by patriarchal gender ideologies, both men and women in general approve of the control of sex trade and oppression of sex workers as necessary for maintaining social order. The power of this moral discourse is so strong that we prostitutes too tend to think of ourselves as morally corrupt and shameless. The men who come to us as clients are victims of the same ideology too. Sometimes the sense of sin adds to their thrill, sometimes it leads to perversion and almost always it creates a feeling of self loathing among them. Never does it allow for confident, honest sexual interchange.

It is important to remember that there is no uniform category as 'men'. Men, like women are differentiated by their class, caste, race and other social relations. For many men adherence to the dominant sexual norm is not only impracticable but also unreal. The young men who look for sexual initiation, the married men who seek the company of 'other' women, the migrant labourers separated from their wives who try to find warmth and companionship in the red light area can not all be dismissed as wicked and perverted. To do that will amount to dismissing a whole history of human search for desire, intimacy and need. Such dismissal creates an unfulfilled demand for sexual pleasure, the burden of which though shared by men and women alike, ultimately weighs more heavily on women. Sexuality—which can be a basis of an equal, healthy relationship between men and women, between people, becomes the source of further inequality and stringent control. This is what we oppose.

Next to any factory, truckers check points, market there has always been red light areas. The same system of productive relations and logic of profit maximisation, which drives men from their homes in villages to towns and cities, make women into sex workers for these men.

What is deplorable is that this patriarchal ideology is so deeply entrenched, and the interest of men as a group is so solidly vested in it, that women's question hardly ever find a place in mainstream political or social movements. The male workers who organise themselves against exploitation rarely address the issues of gender oppression, let alone the oppression of sex workers. Against the interest of women these radical men too defend the ideology of the family and patriarchy.

ARE WE AGAINST THE INSTITUTION OF FAMILY?

In the perception of society we sex workers and in fact all women outside the relation of conjugality are seen as threats to the institution of family. It is said that enticed by us, men stray from the straight and narrow, destroy the family. All institutions from religion to formal education reiterate and perpetuate this fear about us. Women and men too, are the victims of this all pervasive misogyny.

We would like to stress strongly that the sex workers movement is not against the institution of family. What we challenge is the inequity and oppression within the dominant notions of an 'ideal' family which support and justify unequal distribution of power and resources within the structures of the family. What our movement aims at is working towards a really humanitarian, just and equitable structure of the family which is perhaps yet to exist.

Like other social institutions the family too is situated within the material and ideological structures of the state and society. The basis of a normative ideal family is inheritance through legitimate heirs and therefore sexual fidelity. Historically, the structures of families in reality have gone through many changes. In our country, by and large joint families are being replaced by nuclear ones as a norm. In fact, in all societies people actually live their lives in many different ways, through various social and cultural relations—which deviate from this norm, but are still not recognised as the ideal by the dominant discourses.

If two persons love each other, want to be together, want to raise children together, relate to the social world it can be a happy, egalitarian, democratic arrangement. But does it really happen like that within families we see, between couple we know? Do not we know of many, many families where there is no love, but relations are based on inequality and oppression. Do not many legal wives virtually live the life of sex slaves in exchange for food and shelter? In most cases women do not have the power or the resources to opt out of such marriages and families. Sometimes men and women both remain trapped in empty relations by social pressure. Is this situation desirable? Is it healthy?

THE WHORE AND THE MADONNA—DIVIDE AND RULE

Within the oppressive family ideology it is women's sexuality that is identified as the main threat to conjugal relationship of a couple. Women are pitted against each other as wife against the prostitute, against the chaste and the immoral—both represented as fighting over the attention and lust of men. A chaste wife is granted no sexuality, only a de-sexed motherhood and domesticity. At the other end of the spectrum is the 'fallen' woman—a sex machine, unfettered by any domestic inclination or 'feminine' emotion. A woman's goodness is judged on the basis of her desire and ability to control and disguise her sexuality. The neighbourhood girl who dresses up can not be good, models and actresses are morally corrupt. In all cases female sexuality is controlled and shaped by patriarchy to reproduce the existing political economy of sexuality and safeguard the interest of men. A man has access to his docile home-maker wife, the mother of his children and the prostitute who sustain his wildest sexual fantasies. Women's sexual needs are not only considered to be important enough, in most cases its autonomy is denied or even its existence is erased.

Probably no one other than a prostitute really realises the extent of loneliness, alienation, desire and yearning for intimacy that brings men to us. The sexual need we meet for these men is not just about mechanical sexual act, not an momentary gratification of 'base' instincts. Beyond the sex act, we provide a much wider range of sexual pleasure which is to do with intimacy, touch and companiability—a service which we render without any social recognition of its significance. At least men can come to us for their sexual needs—however prurient or shameful the system of prostitution may be seen as. Women hardly have such recourse. The autonomy of women's sexuality is completely denied. The only option they have is to be prostitutes in the sex industry.

WHY DO WOMEN COME TO PROSTITUTION?

Women take up prostitution for the same reason as they may take up any other livelihood option available to them. Our stories are not fundamentally different from the labourer from Bihar who pulls a rickshaw in Calcutta, or the worker from Calcutta who works part time in a factory in Bombay. Some of us get sold into the industry. After being bonded to the madam who has bought us for some years we gain a degree of independence within the sex industry. A whole of us end up in the sex trade after going through many experiences in life,— often unwillingly, without understanding all the implications of being a prostitute fully.

But when do most of us women have access to choice within or outside the family? Do we become casual domestic labourer willingly? Do we have a choice about who we want to marry and when? The 'choice' is rarely real for most women, particularly poor women.

Why do we end up staying in prostitution? It is after all a very tough occupation. The physical labour involved in providing sexual services to multiple clients in a working day is no less intense or rigorous than ploughing or working in a factory. It is definitely not fun and frolic. Then there are occupational hazards like unwanted pregnancy, painful abortions, risk of sexually transmitted diseases. In almost all red light areas housing and sanitation facilities are abysmal, the localities are crowded, most sex workers quite poor, and on top of it there is police harassment and violence from local thugs. Moreover, to add to the material condition of deprivation and distress, we have to take on stigmatisation and marginalisation,— the social indignity of being 'sinful', being mothers of illegitimate children, being the target of those children's frustrations and anger.

DO WE ADVOCATE 'FREE SEX'?

What we advocate and desire is independent, democratic, non-coercive, mutually pleasurable and safe sex. Somehow 'free sex' seems to imply irresponsibility and lack of concern for other's well-being, which is not what we are working towards. Freedom of speech, expression or politics all come with obligations and need to acknowledge and accommodate other's freedom too. Freedom of sexuality should also come with responsibility and respect for other's needs and desires. We do want the freedom to explore and shape a healthy and mature attitude and practice about sex and sexuality—free from obscenity and vulgarity.

We do not yet know what this autonomous sexuality will be like in practice—we do not have the complete picture as yet. We are working people not soothsayers or prophets. When for the first time in history when workers agitated for class equity and freedom from capitalist exploitation, when the blacks protested against white hegemony, when feminist rejected the subordination of women they too did not know fully what the new system they were striving for would exactly be like. There is no exact picture of the 'ideal' future—it can only emerge and be shaped through the process of the movement.

All we can say in our imagination of autonomous sexuality men and women will have equal access, will participate equally, will have the right to say 'yes' or 'no', and there will be no space for guilt or oppression.

We do not live in an ideal social world today. We do not know when and if ever an idea social order will come into place. In our less than ideal world if we can accept the immorality of commercial transaction over food, or health why is sex for money so unethical and unacceptable. Maybe in an ideal world there will be no need for any such transactions—where material, emotional, intellectual and sexual needs of all will be met equitably and with pleasure and happiness. We do not know. All we can do now is to explore the current inequalities and injustices, question their basis and confront, challenge and change them.

WHICH WAY IS OUR MOVEMENT GOING?

The process of struggle that we, the members of Mahila Samanwaya Committee are currently engaged in has only just begun. We think our movement has two principal aspects. The first one is to debate, define and re-define the whole host of issues about gender, poverty, sexuality that are being thrown up within the process of the struggle itself. Our experience of Mahila Samanwaya Committee shows that for a marginalised group to achieve the smallest of gains, it becomes imperative to challenge an all encompassing material and symbolic order that not only shapes the dominant discourses outside but, and perhaps more importantly, historically conditions the way we negotiate our own locations as workers within the sex industry. This long term and complex process will have to continue.

Secondly, the daily oppression that is practised on us with the support of the dominant ideologies, have to be urgently and consistently confronted and resisted. We have to struggle to improve the conditions of our work and material quality of our lives, and that can happen through our efforts towards us, sex workers, gaining control over the sex industry itself. We have started the process—today in many red light areas in cities, towns and villages, we sex workers have come to organise our own forums to create solidarity and collective strength among a larger community of prostitutes, forge a positive identity for ourselves as prostitutes and mark out a space for acting on our own behalf.

MALE PROSTITUTES ARE WITH US TOO

The Durbar Mahila Samanwaya Committee was originally formed by women sex workers of Sonagachhi and neighbouring red light areas, and initially for women prostitutes. However, within two years of our coming into existence male sex workers have come and joined as at their own initiative. These male sex workers provide sexual services to homosexual men primarily. As our society is strongly homophobic, and in fact, penetrative sexual act even between con- senting adult men can still be legally penalised, the material and ideological status of male sex workers is even more precarious. We therefore had welcomed them in our midst as comrades in arms and strongly believe that their participation will make the sex workers' movement truly representative and robust.

Sex workers movement is going on—it has to go on. We believe the questions about sexuality that we are raising are relevant not only to us sex workers but to every men and women who question subordination of all kinds—within the society at large and also within themselves. This movement is for everyone who strives for an equal, just, equitable, oppression free and above all a happy social world. Sexuality, like class and gender after all makes us what we are. To deny its importance is to accept an incomplete existence as human beings. Sexual inequality and control of sexuality engender and perpetuate many other in- equalities and exploitation too. We're faced with situation to shake the roots of all such injustice through our movement. We have to win this battle and the war too—for a gender just, socially equitable, emotionally fulfilling, intellectually stimulating and exhilarating fu- ture for men, women and children.

13. Asia Pacific Network of Sex Workers Code of Practice for Working with Peer Educators (2004)

The Asia Pacific Network of Sex Workers developed this Code of Practice for Working with Peer Educators in December of 2004 in Cambodia. It is based on a similar document developed by Helping Individual Prostitutes Survive (HIPS), an organization in Washington, DC.

Preamble: Peer education programs utilise relationships between members of the sex work community to distribute health-related information and are a key strategy for HIV prevention. Peer educators perform activities ranging from the informal distribution of condoms amongst co-workers, to formal programs in which the sex worker acts as a representative of the host organisation to conduct a formal health education program.

Some peer education programs misuse the good will of sex workers and their desire to promote good health within the community. Amongst other things, these programs do not provide adequate training, place sex workers in dangerous situations and fail to provide decent working conditions.

This Code of Practice identifies core minimum standards for the engagement of sex workers as peer educators and is written with the intention of supporting NGOs to ensure that peer education programs are a success.

The Code of Practice outlined on the following pages is based on the notion of parity—that is, that peer educators should be given the same rights and working conditions as the staff of the organisations they work with.

WORK CONTRACTS:

+ Any organisation that works with peer educators must write a legal contract outlining the terms and conditions of the peer educators' relationship with the host organisation and details of the policies of the host organisation. These terms and conditions must meet the minimum employment standards of the relevant country, and must be comparable to the standards offered to the staff of the host organisation. This work contract must also include a job description that clearly states the roles and responsibilities of the peer educator and the exact requirements of the position. It must also specify grievance procedures as well as other workplace procedures and rights.

+ In order for this contract to be binding on the host organisation, it is not necessary for the peer educator to sign this contract or to be officially enrolled with the host organisation. It is sufficient that the peer educator is involved in a relationship with the host organisation and carries out the tasks of a peer educator on behalf of the host organisation.

+ The host organisation must offer a confidentiality agreement to all peer educators and respect their confidentiality at all times. Peer educators must not be required to make public any personal or professional information such as occupation, ethnicity, HIV status or immigration status.

WORKING CONDITIONS:

+ The host organisation must fully research the conditions in which the peer educators will be working and provide all peer educators with appropriate training and on-going support that suits these conditions. In particular, peer educators working in dangerous circumstances must be provided with additional training and support for example, a mobile phone, proof that they are working on behalf of an organisation in a format that is recognised by the police, and out of hours contact for host organisation.

- No peer educator should be expected to work in conditions that are below the conditions considered acceptable for the staff of the host organisation.
- The host organisation must ensure that peer educators are engaged under flexible working conditions, and that the host organisation builds an awareness of the personal and professional circumstances of peer educators into their program.

Remuneration: Peer educators must be provided with adequate remuneration. If the peer educator works set hours carrying out activities for the host organisation then they must be provided with remuneration in line with that received by paid staff of the host organisation. If the peer educator is a volunteer, then this remuneration can take the form of a stipend to cover expenses. Host organisations must also provide peer educators with training that provides skills, experiences and new opportunities both within and outside the host organisation.

Training: Peer educators must be provided with thorough training that covers all tasks that the peer educators are expected to perform and all circumstances in which they will work. This must include training on issues that are the subject of the peer education program. This must also include training necessary to ensure effective work by the peer educator such as, but not limited to, outreach strategies, counselling methods, conflict mediation, and personal safety. If peer educators require it, the host organisation must also provide basic literacy and/or numeracy training.

Information and Equipment: The host organisation must provide peer educators with all information and equipment necessary for the peer educator to meet the responsibilities of their role.

Assistance and Counselling: The host organisation must provide supervision to the peer educator as well as regular opportunities for the peer educator to provide feedback on their progress and to raise any problems that may have arisen. The host organisation must also provide peer educators with counselling services that recognise the conflicts that might occur between the identity of the peer educator as a health care professional, their identity as a professional sex worker, and their personal lives.

Decision-Making and Program Development: The host organisation must ensure that peer educators are meaningfully involved in the decision-making processes of the peer education program. This involvement should be tailored to the individual needs of the peer educators involved with the host organisation. The host organisation must also institute formal and informal mechanisms through which peer educators can comment on the peer education program and assist in program development. The host organisation must also provide peer educators with the opportunity for promotion, as well as methods to pursue a career path within the organisation and with other organisations.

Present Work: The host organisation will not place any restrictions on the other work peer educators engage in. In particular, the host organisation will respect the choice of peer educators to continue to work as sex workers, and not discourage this choice in any way.

Anti-Discrimination Policy: Any organisation that works with peer educators must have an anti-discrimination policy in place that ensures that the peer educators are not marginalised in the workplace or subject to discrimination in their dealings with host organisation staff. The host organisation must also ensure that all staff complete anti-discrimination training that deals specifically with working with peer educators.

Future Work: The host organisation must provide written and oral references for peer educators whenever required.

Insurance: The host organisation must provide health care and comprehensive worker or volunteer insurance including provision for loss of earnings.

14. Documents from the European Conference on Sex Work, Human Rights, Labour and Migration (2005)

> *Documents elaborated and endorsed by 120 sex workers from 26 countries at the European Conference on Sex Work, Human Rights, Labour and Migration, on October 15–17, 2005, in Brussels, Belgium, include the following:*
>
> • *Recommendations of the European Conference on Sex Work, Human Rights, Labour and Migration, Brussels, 2005*
> • *Sex Workers in Europe Manifesto*
> • *The Declaration of the Rights of Sex Workers in Europe*
>
> *Edited versions are included below. The original versions can be found online at http://www.sexworkeurope.org.*

RECOMMENDATIONS OF THE EUROPEAN CONFERENCE ON SEX WORK, HUMAN RIGHTS, LABOUR AND MIGRATION, BRUSSELS, 2005

The following is a summary of the main recommendations formulated by sex workers and their allies at the European Conference on Sex Work, Human Rights, Labour and Migration, hel 15 to 17 October in Brussels, Belgium. These relate to: state policies; human rights; labour rights; migration and trafficking; and violence. The full list of recommendations will be included in our report and used to advocate and lobby for sex workers' rights in Europe.

Prostitution policies

Policies that aim to make sex work invisible and that exclude sex workers from public places serve to add to the stigma associated with sex work, the social exclusion of sex workers, and sex workers' vulnerability.

We reject the double standard that allows prostitution only when it is hidden. All laws and measures that undermine the dignity and self-determination of sex workers should be abolished. Sex workers have the right to represent themselves. They should be part of any debate on laws, policies and measures that affect their lives. Self-organization of sex workers should be supported.

Sex Workers Rights are Human Rights

Governments should protect the basic human and social rights of all sex workers: female, male and transgender, migrant and domestic. These are common and accepted rights that apply to every citizen and that governments have already agreed to protect, yet they are denied to sex workers.

Sex Work is Work

Sex work is a profession. Sex workers are workers, and must be recognized as such.

Governments should protect sex workers' labour rights just as they do the rights of other workers. In particular, sex workers have the right to social security, health care and minimum wages.

Sex workers, including migrant workers, should be able to work legally.

Governments should ensure safe and healthy working conditions for sex workers, similar to those enjoyed by other workers. Mandatory medical checks and mandatory police registration-to which only sex workers are submitted- and other discriminatory measures should be abolished.

Migrants' rights are human rights

The EU should integrate a human rights impact assessment in all anti-trafficking and migration policies and programmes in order to protect and promote the rights of migrant sex workers and trafficked persons.

The EU should protect the human rights of migrant sex workers and trafficked persons, and in particular their right to a legal remedies and to effective access to justice. To this end, it should provide them with appropriate residency permits.

Migrant sex workers and trafficked persons, regardless of their immigration status, should have access to support services, including housing, education, vocational training, psychosocial counseling and legal assistance.

Violence against sex workers

Sex workers should have the right to unite and to work together to protect themselves from violence. Laws that prohibit sex workers to work together should be abolished.

Sex workers should have the right to support and protection when they are faced with violence, irrespective of their immigration status.

SEX WORKERS IN EUROPE MANIFESTO

Introduction

Although European sex workers come from many different countries and many different backgrounds, we have discovered that we face many of same problems in our work and in our lives.

In this document we explore the current inequalities and injustices in our lives and in the sex industry; we question their origin; we confront and challenge them; and we put forward our vision of the changes needed to create a more equitable society – one that acknowledges and values sex workers, our rights and our labour.

Background

In response to increasingly repressive legislations, policies and practices across Europe, a small group of sex workers and sex workers' allies in the Netherlands got together in 2002 to organise a conference to give sex workers a voice. They began by putting out a call across Europe, inviting sex workers, sex work projects and sex workers' organizations to join them. An Organising Committee (OC) was formed, composed mainly of se workers, and created the International Committee on the Rights of Sex Workers in Europe, with the purpose of raising funds for, and hosting, the conference.

The OC decided that the conference should not only give sex workers a voice, but also put in place tool for defending our rights across Europe and to creating alliances with human rights, labour and migrants' organisations. One of the toold the OC decided to develop was a Sex Workers'

Manifesto—created by sex workers, for sex workers - setting out a shared vision of an equitable society.

The committee undertook a year long consultation with sex workers across Europe, the results of which were then collated. It proceeded to create a draft manifesto, based on views shared by a majority of participants. The European Conference on Sex Work, Human Rights, Labour and Migration was held in Brussels, Belgium, 15 to 17 October 2005. There, 120 sex workers from 26 countries elaborated on the draft to create the Sex Workers in Europe Manifesto, which they then unanimously endorsed. On 17 October, they presented the Manifesto to the European Parliament, at the invitation of Monica Frassoni, Italian Member of European Parliament (Greens—European Free Alliance).

Beyond Tolerance and Compassion for the Recognition of Rights

We live in a society where services are bought and sold. The provision of sexual pleasure is one of these services. Sex work should not be criminalised.

Sacrificing sex workers' rights on the grounds of religious convictions or sexual mores is unacceptable. All people have the right to hold their own views on such matters, but these views should never be imposed on any individual, nor should they determine any political decision.

We wish to see a society in which sex workers are not denied social power.

We condemn the hypocrisy whereby our society uses our services while making our profession/businesses illegal. Legislation that criminalizes sex work results in abuse and in sex workers' lack of control over our work and lives.

We oppose the criminalisation of those identifying themselves as sex workers; their partners, clients, managers; and everyone else working in the sex industry. Such criminalisation denies sex workers of equal protection of the law.

Migration plays an important role in meeting the demands of the labour market. We demand our governments acknowledge and apply fundamental human, labour and civil rights for migrants.

The right to be free from discrimination

We demand an end to discrimination and abuse of power by the police and other public authorities. Offering sexual services is not an invitation to any kind of violence. The credibility of sex workers must be respected.

We demand that crimes against us and our testimonies be taken seriously by the justice system. Sex workers should, to the same extent as anyone else, be presumed innocent until guilt is proven.

Defamation of sex workers incites discrimination and hatred. We demand that sex workers be protected by anti-discrimination legislation.

The right to our bodies

Sex work is by definition consensual sex. Non consensual sex is not sex work; it is sexual violence or slavery.

We demand our right as human beings to use our bodies in any way that we do not find harmful be respected. This includes the right to establish consensual sexual relations, no matter the gender or ethnicity of our partners; regardless of whether they are paying.

The right to be heard

We assert our right to participate in public forums and policy debates where our working and living conditions are being discussed and determined.

We demand that our voices be heard, listened to and respected. Our experiences are diverse, but all are valid, and we condemn those who steal our voices and say that we do not have the capacity to make decisions or articulate our needs.

The right to associate and gather

We assert our right to associate with others of our choice. This includes the right to join and form professional associations and unions; formal and informal business partnerships; political parties; and social-reform and community projects.

We assert our right to be in any public space, and our right to demonstrate publicly.

Abuse in sex work

It is true that abuse happens in sex work. However, abuse does not *define* sex work.

Any discourse that defines sex work as violence is a simplistic one that denies our diversity and experience and reduces us to helpless victims. Such approaches undermine our autonomy and our right to self-determination.

Recognizing the rights of sex workers would allow us to report infringements of those rights.

We demand protection from those who threaten us and our families for exposing their abuse.

We demand that mechanisms be developed to allow us to remain anonymous when reporting grievances and crimes against us.

Young people in sex work

It is essential that education focus on empowering young people to have sexual autonomy. We demand that support, services and outreach be provided to young people, in order that they may have real choice in their lives, including the possibility of alternative work. Young people should have a voice in legislation and policies that affect them.

Our Lives

Being a sex worker

The 'identity' and 'social role' imposed on us by society defines us as intrinsically unworthy and a threat to moral, public, and social order. Labelling us sinners, criminals, or victims creates astigma that separates us from 'good' and 'decent' citizens – in fact, from the rest of society.

This stigma leads to an exclusively negative and stereotyped view of 'whores'. To protect ourselves, and to ensure we have a place within society, most sex workers hide means of our livelihood. Many absorb the societal stigma of shame and unworthiness, and live in fear of being exposed. For this reason, many sex workers accept abusive treatment. The social exclusion that results from the stigmatisation of sex workers leads to our being denied access to health, to housing, and to alternative work. It often enforces separation from our children and isolation from our families and communities.

Societal prejudices promote divisions within the sex industry, based on such factors as migrant status, race, ethnic origin, gender, age, sexuality, drug use, work sector, and services provided. This exacerbates the social exclusion and stigma experience by certain groups of sex workers.

We condemn such moralistic and prejudiced distinctions, and assert that *all* sex workers, and all forms of sex work, are equally valid and valuable.

We recognise stigma is the commonality that links all of us as sex workers, despite the enormous diversity in our realities at work and in our lives. We have come together to confront and challenge this stigma and the injustices it creates.

We assert that sex work is a sexual/economic activity, implying nothing about our identity, value, or participation in society.

Active citizenship

Sex workers should not be perceived as victims to be assisted, criminals to be arrested, or targets for public healthinterventions. We are members of society, with needs and aspirations, who have the potential to make real and valuable contributions to our communities.

We demand that existing mechanisms for representation and consultation be opened up to sex workers.

Privacy & family

We assert our right to establish personal relationships, and to have self-determination within those relationships, without judgement.

The labelling of our partners as pimps, exploiters, and/or abusers, simply because they are our partners, presupposes that we have no autonomy and implies we are not worthy of love or being in a relationship, thus denying us the possibility of a private life.

We demand an end to legislation that criminalises our partners, children and other family members for associating with us and living off our earnings.

The threat of losing our children We demand an end to the unjustifiable practice of social service agencies and courts removing our children simply because we provide sexual services.

Media and education

Our voices and experiences are often manipulated by the media; we are seldom given the right to reply; and our complaints in this regard are routinely dismissed.

The portrayal of sex workers in the mass media perpetuates the stereotypical image of us as unworthy, as victims, and/or as a threat to moral, public and social order. In particular, the xenophobic portrayal of migrant sex workers increases the stigma and vulnerability they already face. Such portrayals of sex workers give legitimacy to those within our society who seek to harm us and violate our rights.

Furthermore, our clients are represented in the media as being violent, perverted or psycologically disturbed. Paying for sexual services is not an intrinsically violent or problematic behaviour. Such stereotyping silences discussion about the reality of the sex industry. It perpetuates our isolation and obscures the violence perpetrated by people posing as clients. Moreover, it prevents us from addressing the behaviour of the small, but significant, number of clients who *do* cause problems.

Since mass media perpetuates stigma that does us harm, we require that our governments support us and our clients in educating and informing public officials and the general public, in order that we may participate fully in our society.

Combating violence against sex workers

Sex workers experience disproportionate levels of violence and crime. The stigmatisation of sex workers has led to society and public authorities condoning violence and crime against us, because such practices are seen as inherent to our work.

We demand that our governments recognise that violence against sex workers is a crime, whether perpetrated by local residents or other members of the public, by clients, by managers, by our partners, or by persons in positions of authority.

We require that our governments publicly condemn those who perpetrate actual violence against us. We demand that they take action in combating the actual violence we experience, rather than the perceived violence of prostitution, as put forward by abolitionists seeking to eradicate all forms of sex work.

Time and resources now spent arresting and prosecuting sex workers and non-violent clients should be redirected towards dealing with rape and other violent crimes against us.

Mechanisms must be developed to encourage and support sex workers in reporting crimes, including early warning systems amongst sex workers themselves about potentially violent clients.

Health and well being

No-one, least of all sex workers, denies there are health risks attached to sex work. However, it is a myth that we are 'dirty' or 'unclean'. In reality we are more knowledgeable about our sexual health, and practice safe sex more skillfully, than the general population. Moreover, most of us act as sexual health educators for our clients.

We call for the recognition of our role within society as a valuable resource for sexual well-being and health promotion.

Stigma remains a barrier to health care for sex workers. Prejudice and discrimination occur within healthcare settings: some health care workers subject sex workers to degrading and humiliating treatment. We demand that *all* health care workers treat us with respect and dignity, and that our complaints of discriminatory treatment are taken seriously.

In furtherance of the goal of the health and well-being of all sex workers, we demand our governments provide:

+ health services for *all* migrant sex workers
+ needle exchange and drug-treatment options for dependent drug users
+ transition treatment for people living with HIV, without which many may die unnecessarily
+ transitional treatment for transgender persons who desire it

Registration and mandatory testing

Registration and mandatory testing of sex workers are not effective measures for preventing disease, particularly when there is no requirement for clients to be tested. Where mandatory testing still exists, one of the consequences is that clients assume sex workers are 'healthy' and so resist the use of condoms, since they do not see themselves as threats to sex workers in this regard.

Registration and mandatory sexual health and HIV testing are a violation of sex workers' human rights. Such practices reinforce the stigmatisation of sex workers as a threat to public health, and promote the stereotypical view that only sex workers can transmit infections.

We demand an end to registration and mandatory testing.

Entitlement to travel, migration, asylum

The lack of opportunities to migrate can put our health, and indeed our very lives, in danger. We assert our right to travel and to work in any country. Information about working in the sex industry and its different sectors should be made available.

We assert the right of *all* people to move within and between countries for personal and financial reasons, including seeking gainful employment and residence in the area of their choice.

We demand that the education and qualifications of migrant workers in all fields be recognised on a basis of equality.

Violence, coercion and exploitation related to migration and sex work must be understood and tackled within a framework that recognises the worth, and the fundamental rights, of migrants.

Restrictive migration legislation and anti-prostitution policies must be identified as contributing factors to the violation of migrants' rights. Focussing discussion on 'trafficking' obscures the issues of migrants' rights.

Many trades are subject to the imposition of forced labour of practices resembling slavery. However, if a trade is legal and the labour of its workers recognised, there is far more potential for preventing abuse and for exposing and stopping the violation of workers' rights.

We demand our governments priories [sic] and protect the human rights of victims of forced labour and of practices resembling slavery, regardless of how they came to be in their situations, and regardless of their ability, or willingness, to cooperate, or testify, in criminal justice proceedings.

We demand the right to asylum for sex workers who are subjected to state and/or community violence because they sell sexual services.

We demand the right to asylum for anyone denied human rights on the basis of a 'crime of status', such as sex work, health status, gender or sexual orientation.

Our Labour

The body and mind are economic resources that people use in many different ways. We view all forms of sex work as equally valid. These include dancing, stripping, engaging in street or indoor prostitution, providing escort services, engaging in remunerated phone sex, and performing in pornography.

For some, the exchange of sex for money is part of their private lives. These individuals do not define remunerated sex as work.

For many others, sex becomes work. Some work independently, others work collectively. Many are 'employed' by third parties. For all of us, remunerated sex is an income generating activity and, as such, must be recognised as labour.

Alienation, exploitation, abuse and coercion do exist in the sex industry, as in any other industry, but they do not define us or our industry. It is possible to limit such problems when the workers within an industry are formally recognised, accepted by society at large, and supported by trade unions. The establishment of labour rights enables workers to use labour regulations to report abuses, and to organise against exploitation and unacceptable working conditions.

The lack of recognition of sex work as labour, and the criminalisation of activities within and around the sex industry, results in sex workers being treated like criminals, even when we do not break any laws. Many laws treat us as legal 'minors', as though we were unable to make informed decisions. Such treatment alienates us from the rest of society and, by preventing us from working collectively and safely, reduces our ability to control our work and our lives.

Treating sex workers like criminals creates greater possibilities for uncontrolled exploitation, abuse and coercion.Many of us are forced to tolerate unacceptable working hours, unsanitary working conditions, unfair division of income, and unreasonable restrictions on freedom of movement. Certain groups of sex workers, such as migrants, are disproportionately affected by unacceptable working conditions.

We demand that legislation ensuring just and favourable conditions of work, remuneration and protection against unemployment be extended to include sex workers.

We demand that sex work be recognised as gainful employment, enabling migrants to apply for work and residence permits, and that both documented and undocumented migrants be entitled to full labour rights.

We demand the creation of a European Commission Ombudsman to oversee national legislation on the sex industry. This can be a newly created post or can be added to the work of an existing ombudsman.

Professional and personal development

We assert our right to join and form unions.

As sex workers, we require the same possibilities for professional development as other workers. We assert our right to be able to develop vocational training and advice services, including offering support to those who wish to establish their own businesses.

We call for support to be provided to sex workers who wish to further their education or look for alternative employment.

We demand that anti-discrimination legislation be applied within the sex industry. We further demand that, given the specific difficulties sex workers face as a consequence of stigma, anti-discrimination legislation be applied to sex workers seeking alternative employment.

Taxes and welfare

We acknowledge every citizens' obligations to financially support the society in which they live. However, given that sex workers do not receive the same benefits as other citizens, and given that our right to equal protection under the law is denied, some sex workers do not feel this obligation.

We demand that we have access to social insurance, including the right to unemployment and sickness benefits, pensions and health care.

Sex workers should pay taxes on the same basis as other employees and independent contractors, and should receive the same benefits. Taxation schemes should not be used as a means to register sex workers, and should priorise [sic] efforts to remove stigma and protect confidentiality. Information on taxes must be accessible and easy to understand, and must be provided in many languages for migrant workers. Tax collection schemes should be transparent and easily understood by workers in order to avoid exploitation and abuse by employers.

The purchase of appropriate goods and services-including health services, where paid for-should be tax deductible.

Health and safety at work

Our bodies are our business. In order to maintain our health, we require free or affordable safe-sex products and access to health services.

We demand our governments prohibit the confiscation of condoms and other safe-sex products from sex workers and sex-work establishments.

We demand that our governments provide free or affordable access to sexual health care for *all* sex workers, including access to vaccinations for preventable diseases.

We demand that the health care needs of sex workers be included in all health insurance schemes and that, as with other occupations, sick pay be available for work-related illness.

Violence within any workplace is a health and safety issue. Our employers have an obligation to protect us and to take action against those who violate our safety while we're engaged in work.

We demand that our governments take our health and safety seriously. We demand that they promote safe working environments in which violence and abuse will not be tolerated. To this end, we urge governments to establish emergency telephone advice lines through which sex workers can anonymously seek advice and report abuses.

Working conditions

The fact that we engage in sexual activities for a living does not preclude our right to decide whom we have sex with, which sexual services we provide, and the conditions under which we provide those services.

We assert the right to engage in sex work without coercion; to move within the sex industry; and to leave it, if we choose.

No other person must be allowed to determine the nature of the services we provide or the conditions under which we provide them, whether we are employees or 'self-employed'. We reserve the right to refuse any client and to refuse to provide any service.

We demand the right to fair conditions of work, including entitlement to the minimum wage, to work breaks, to minimum rest periods, and to annual leave. Such conditions should also apply to those who are nominally 'self-employed' within a collective workplace.

We demand an end to unacceptable practices such as requiring sex workers to consume alcohol and/or drugs at work, to pay excessive costs for food, drink, services, and/or clothing in the workplace.

We demand that health and safety be prioritised in our workplaces and, for those who work independently in public places, that their health and safety also be protected. We demand that employers comply with data-protection legislation; that our personal information be treated confidentially; and that any abuse of sech personal information be taken seriously by relevant authorities.

Legislation regulating working hours and conditions is complex. It is important that clear and accurate information be provided to sex workers, and displayed within our workplaces, about our rights. Such information must be provided in many different languages to ensure that all migrants have access to it.

To improve our working conditions, it is important that we have opportunities to self organise, and advocate for our rights. We call upon trade unions to support us in our self-organizing efforts and in our struggle for fair working conditions.

We call for the establishment of designated areas for street prostitution. Such areas must be designated in consultation with, and agreement from, sex workers. This is necessary in order to enable those who work in public places to do so safely, without compromising any individual's choice of work venue. Such areas will enable us to work collectively and facilitate appropriate services. Within them, the police can ensure that we are free from the interference of criminals and other undesirables.

Decriminalisation of sex work

As we have already stated, the criminalization of activities related to sex work and the *de facto* criminalization of sex workers are unacceptable. We have also already specified a number of areas where law reform is required, including our rights to the use of our earnings to support our family and loved ones; to freedom of association, to freedom of movement within and between countries; and to designated public areas where sex workers and clients may meet one another (which designations must not infringe on individuals' rights to work where they choose). The following demands identify other specific areas where law reform is required: We demand to the repeal of all legislation that criminalises us; our clients; our families; those we work with; and any employer, organiser or managers who follows fair practices.

We demand that our right to work individually or collectively; as either independent workers or as employees, with the full protection of labour rights, be respected.

We demand the right to rent premises from which to work, to advertise our services, and to pay those who carry out services for us be respected.

We demand that sex-work businesses be regulated by standard business codes, and that, under such codes, businesses, rather than sex workers, be registered.

In order to make sex work safe for all, we demand that criminal laws be enforced against those who perpetrate fraud, coercion, child sexual abuse, child labour, violence, rape, or murder upon sex workers.

THE DECLARATION OF THE RIGHTS OF SEX WORKERS IN EUROPE

Why do we need a Declaration of the Rights of Sex Workers in Europe?

Europe has adopted a variety of approaches to the sex industry and to female, male and transgendered sex workers—including migrant sex workers. While some countries have accepted sex work as labour and even introduced labour rights for sex workers, others have criminalised a wide range of practices associated with sex work. In certain countries, sex workers' partners and/or clients have at times been criminalized, and being a sex worker has been made a 'status crime'.

The recent proliferation, at local, national and international levels, of legislative measures that restrict the fundamental rights and freedoms of sex workers, has been rationalised as a means of combating organised crime and promoting public health. However, UNAIDS and the World Health Organisation have explicitly stated that repressive legislation restricting the rights of sex workers actually undermines public health policies. It does so, they explain, by using practices central to safe sex (such as possession of condoms as evidence of criminal activity, and by driving the sex industry underground. Such measures fly in the face of the European Parliament's *1986 Resolution on Violence Against Women* [Document A2-44/86]. This Resolution called for the decriminalisation of prostitution; a guarantee of equal rights for prostitutes; and the protection of prostitutes' independence, health and safety. Moreover, many anti-prostitution measures violate the obligation of states, under international human rights legislation, to respect, promote and protect the human rights of all persons within their territories; without discrimination.

There is strong evidence that migrant workers in all sectors face ever-growing levels of abuse and exploitation. Yet European responses to increasing international migration have focussed on restrictive legislation, with little attention paid to protecting migrants' rights and freedoms. As of October 2005, Bosnia and Turkey are the only European countries to have ratified the *UN International Convention on the Protection of the Rights of All Migrant Workers and Members of Their Families*, which came into force 1 July 2003.

Sex workers' organisations—and projects providing services to sex workers—in Europe have accumulated substantial evidence that discriminatory legislation and behaviour occur throughout health and social care, housing, employment, education, administrative law and criminal justice systems. There is no country within Europe—regardless of the legal status of sex work—where sex workers have not reported discrimination and violations of their human rights.

Examples of discriminatory legislation

In Austria sex workers are subjected to mandatory sexual health controls, but other sexually active citizens are not. This discriminatory practice promotes the stereotyping of sex workers as 'unclean'.

In Finland, sex workers who work together for their mutual protection may be prosecuted for 'pimping' one another. This violates their rights to peaceful assembly and association and favourable conditions of work.

In France, a sex worker's child, upon reaching the age of majority, may be prosecuted with 'living off' the sex worker's earnings. This violates sex workers' right to respect for their private and family lives.

In Greece, where sex work is legal and sex workers are registered, sex workers who marry are not allowed to continue to work legally; their licenses are withdrawn. Sex workers are therefore forced to choose between the enjoyment of their right to marry and found a family, and their right to livelihood and to the practice of a profession. No person should be forced to make such a choice.

In Italy, police confiscate and throw away or burn sex workers' possessions with impunity. This violates sex workers' rights to property, to equal protection under the law, and to protection from discrimination.

In the Netherlands, where sex work is legal - unless one is a migrant sex worker. Such workers constitute the *only* category of employees excluded from getting legal work permits. All other non-nationals can obtain legal work permits, as long as they meet the conditions laid out in the *Law on Migrant Workers*.) This violates migrant sex workers' right to be free from discrimination.

In Portugal (and many other countries) sex workers may lose custody of their children in the absence of any specific evidence of harm or incapacity to parent. This violates their right to be free from arbitrary interference with their family life and non-discrimination.

In Romania, sex work is illegal. As a result of pressure from the Romanian government, the Austrian government has terminated the permits of Romanian sex workers. Thus women who have worked *legally* in Austria may face retribution on their return to Romania. This violates their right to seek gainful employment in a country other than their own.

In Russia, police have subjected sex workers to threats of being sold into slavery, and have forced them to have sex without payment. These practices violate sex workers' rights to security of the person and equal protection under the law.

In Slovakia, health care workers have discriminated against sex workers with impunity. They have refused medical care to sex workers, and have made discriminatory comments to pregnant sex workers, alleging that they are not fit to bear children. This violates sex workers' right to protection by the state of the highest attainable standard of physical and mental health care, as well as their right to found families.

In Spain, sex workers in brothels are not only required to undergo sexual health checks conducted by the brothel owners, but also to pay excessive fees for these checks. Moreover, test results are not kept confidential. In condoning these violations of medical codes, the state is failing to uphold sex workers' right to privacy and to the highest attainable standard of physical and mental health care.

In Sweden, politicians and policy makers have threatened to withdraw from public debates in which sex workers are permitted to participate. This violates sex workers' right to freedom of expression and opinion.

The United Kingdom, where street-based sex workers are criminalised, employs Anti-Social Behaviour Orders to restrict sex workers' freedom of movement. In some cities, posters bearing the names and photographs of sex workers have been printed and distributed. This violates sex workers' rights to privacy and to participation in public life, and exposes sex workers to discrimination and violence.

Under international law it is a fundamental human right that 'all persons are equal before the law and are entitled without any discrimination to the equal protection of the law'. Yet the examples above, and many other recorded violations, clearly demonstrate that sex workers in Europe are routinely denied equal access to legal protections. These workers have compelling reasons to avoid using the judicial system to challenge discrimination, violence and other abuses.

History of the Declaration

The process leading to the creation of this Declaration began with the formation of the Sexwork Initiative Group Netherlands (SIGN), a network of Dutch sex workers and sex workers' rights activists interested in organising a conference and advocating for the rights of sex workers in Europe. In June 2003 SIGN members solicited participation from sex workers and sex worker organisations across Europe to join them in planning a conference. In January 2004 an international Organisation Committee (OC) was established, consisting of 15 individuals. Most were current or former sex workers—including migrants—from several European countries. The OC, which is still in place, does not have representation from all countries or groups in Europe. However, it is supported by a large number of sex workers, sex workers' rights activists, and organisations working with sex workers across Europe and beyond.

The OC decided that a Declaration of the Rights of Sex Workers in Europe would provide a framework for organising the conference; would meet the ongoing need to raise awareness of sex workers' human rights; and would serve as a tool with which to examine and challenge the undermining and violation of these rights.

The OC established the International Committee on the Rights of Sex Workers in Europe (ICRSE) to both coordinate the conference and undertake future initiatives.

In addition to producing the Declaration, the ICRSE has committed itself to developing strategies for seeking public and political recognition and acceptance of the principles contained therein.

The Declaration outlines the rights to which all persons in Europe, including sex workers, are under international law. It thensets out measures for ensuring that sex workers in Europe be accorded these rights.

The Declaration is based on the following 17 documents:

+ *The United Nations (UN) International Covenant on Civil and Political Rights, 1966*
+ *The UN International Covenant on Economic, Social and Cultural Rights, 1966*
+ *The UN Convention on the Elimination of All Forms of Discrimination Against Women, 1979*
+ *The UN International Convention on the Protection of the Rights of All Migrant Workers and Members of Their Families, 1990*
+ *The UN Convention Relating to the Status of Refugees, 1951*
+ *The International Labour Organization (ILO) Convention concerning Forced or Compulsory Labour (no. 29), 1930 and the Abolition of Forced Labour Convention (no. 105), 1957*
+ *The ILO Freedom of Association and Protection of the Right to Organise Convention (no. 87), 1948*
+ *The ILO Migrant Workers (Supplementary Provisions) Convention (no. 143), 1975*[2]
+ *The European Convention for the Protection of Human Rights and Fundamental Freedoms, 1950*
+ *The UN Universal Declaration of Human Rights, 1948*
+ *The UN Declaration on the Right and Responsibility of Individuals, 1999*
+ *The UN Declaration on the Elimination of Violence against Women, 1993*
+ *The UN Declaration of Basic Principles of Justice for Victims of Crime and Abuse of Power, 1985*
+ *The ILO Declaration on Fundamental Principles and Rights at work, 1998*
+ *The ILO Recommendation Migrant Workers (no. 151), 1975*
+ *The European Social Charter, 1961 & 1996*
+ *The EU Charter of Fundamental Rights, 2000*

To reiterate: This Declaration is not a demand for special rights to be given to sex workers. Rather, it is based on the principle that the act of selling sexual services does not constitute grounds for the denial of the fundamental rights to which all human beings are entitled under international law.

Solidarity

This Declaration is based on an extensive consultation process conducted across Europe. The bringing together of individuals and groups with widely differing experiences and perspectives

---

1. NB: Art. 2 of the Migrant Workers Convention, 1990, defines a migrant worker as any person *'who is to be engaged, is engaged or has been engaged in a remunerated activity in a State of which he or she is not a national'*.

has has served to emphasise the many factors common to sex workers and other marginalised groups whose rights are not always respected. Furthermore, the Declaration assists sex workers in Europe to make connections in other parts of the world. Although specific to Europe, the Declaration, furnishes a shared language—the language of rights—comprehensible to the peoples of all countries.

Use of the Declaration

Information is a powerful force. Knowing one's rights is the first step in being able to stand up for them. By stating existing rights, the Declaration can serve as a tool for empowering sex workers to defend themselves from abuses, with authority and justice on their side.

Beyond this, the Declaration aims to act as a benchmark by which sex workers can judge what has been achieved so far, what progress is currently being made, and where to direct future efforts. It provides a basis for organisations and groups to lobby for the upholding of universally accepted rights, and to advocate for sex workers in particular cases where their rights might be in dispute.

Moreover, the Declaration offers guidance to organisations and institutions seeking to achieve equitable, non-discriminatory policies and practices.

Finally, it is hoped that this Declaration will help in the long-term aim of winning public recognition that respect for the human rights of *all persons* is integral to a healthy society.

If you wish to be included as a supporter or if you are able to provide evidence of successes or failures in promoting human rights for sex workers, please contact the International Committee on the Rights of Sex Workers in Europe at declaration@sexworkeurope.org

THE DECLARATION OF THE RIGHTS OF SEX WORKERS IN EUROPE

All individuals within Europe, including sex workers, are entitled to certain rights under international human rights law. All European Governments are obliged to respect, protect and fulfil [*sic*]:

They include

- The right to life, liberty and security of the person
- The right to be free from slavery, forced labour and servitude
- The rights to be free from torture and from inhumane or degrading treatment
- The right to be protected against violence, physical injury, threats and intimidation
- The right to privacy and protection of family life, including the right to marry and found a family, and the right to be free from arbitrary or unlawful interference with privacy, family, home, or correspondence
- The right to be free from attacks on honour and reputation
- The right to marry and found a family
- The right to liberty of movement and residence
- The right to leave any country, including one's own, and to return to one's own country.
- The right to seek asylum and not to be returned to a dangerous or otherwise unacceptable situation.
- The right to equal protection of the law, including the right to a fair trial
- The right to protection from discrimination and from any incitement to discrimination
- The right to freedom of opinion and expression

- The right to work, to free choice of employment, to just and favourable conditions of work, and protection against unemployment
- The right to the highest attainable standard of physical and mental health
- The right to peaceful assembly and to freedom of association
- The right to organise and, in particular, the right to form and join a union
- The right of documented and undocumented migrants to information
- The right to effective remedies against injustice
- The right to participate in the cultural and public life of the society
- The right to benefit from states' obligation to combat prejudices and practices, customary or otherwise, based on the idea of the inferiority or superiority of either of the sexes, or on stereotyped gender roles

These human rights are established in international treaties that European Governments have agreed to uphold. Moreover, most treaties contain a clause stipulating that these rights should be upheld without discrimination on. Specifically, there must be no discrimination based on a person's as [sic] race, colour, sex, language, religion, political or other opinion, national or social origin, association with a national minority, property, birth, *or other status.* Moreover, the United Nations Human Rights Committee has stated [in General comment 15] that *'each one of the rights of the Covenant must be guaranteed without discrimination between citizens and aliens'.*

Although these rights apply to all human beings, the experience of sex workers all over Europe is that states do not respect, protect, fulfil and promote their rights on a basis of equality with other nationals.

Thi signatories of this declaration hereby declare the rights of sex workers in Europe, and urge European Governments to enforce these rights.

I. Life, Liberty and Security

Sex workers have the right to life, to liberty, and to security of the person, including the right to determine their own sexuality. In respect of this right:

1 No person should be forced to provide sexual services against her or his will, or under conditions to which she or he does not consent.
2 Condoms are vital for the protection of life and security. Therefore, the confiscation of condoms from sex workers should be prohibited.
3 The governments of all countries should investigate murders of sex workers and other violent crimes against sex workers, and should punish all perpetrators of such crimes, including law enforcement officials who commit such crimes.

II. Privacy & family life

Sex workers have the right to be free from arbitrary interference with respect to their private and family lives, their homes and their correspondence, and from attacks on their honour and reputation. In respect of this right:

4   No person should be denied the right to establish and develop relationships.[2] The labelling of sex workers' partners and adult children as 'pimps' is discriminatory and implies that it is not appropriate for sex workers to have a private and family life and for other persons to establish or develop relationships. [sic]

5   Sex workers have the right to determine the number and spacing of their children. Current or former engagement in sex work should not be considered grounds for challenging a person's fitness to be a parent or have custody of his or her children.

III. Health

Sex workers, regardless of immigration status, have the right to the highest attainable standard of physical and mental health, including sexual and reproductive health. In respect of this right:

6   No person should be subjected to mandatory sexual health and HIV screening. All health tests should be conducted with the primary goal of promoting the health and rights of the person affected.

7   Information about sexual health and HIV status should be kept confidential.

IV. Freedom of Movement

Sex workers have the right to freedom of movement and residence. In respect of this right,

8   No restrictions should be placed on the free movement of individuals between states on the grounds of their engagement in sex work .

9   No restrictions should be placed on the freedom of movement of individuals within states, or within their own communities. All regulation, at any level, that seeks to control sex workers must not infringe upon their rights to freedom of movement, including the freedom to leave and return to one's residence, visit family or access services.

V. Freedom from Slavery and Forced Labour

Sex workers have the right to be free from slavery, forced labour and servitude. In respect of this right

10   Measures should be taken to ensure that sex workers enjoy full labour rights, are fully informed of such rights, and have access to the full range of measures and standards intended to end exploitive working conditions.

11   Measures should be taken to provide appropriate assistance and protection to victims of trafficking, forced labour, and any practice resembling slavery, with full respect for

---

2. In accordance with a judement of the European Court of Human Rights, the right to privacy includes the right 'to establish and develop relationships with other human beings, especially in the emotional sphere, for the development and fulfilment of one's own personality.' *Dudgeon v. United Kingdom*, Judgement of the European Court of Human RIghts (1981) 4 EHRR 149.

the protection of these persons' human rights. Residency permits should be provided to ensure effective access to justice and legal remedies, including compensation, irrespective of willingness to collaborate with law enforcement. Trafficked persons must not be returned to situations that will result in further harms.

VI. Equal Protection of the Law, and Protection from Discrimination

Sex workers have the right to equal protection under the law, including access to effective remedies. They also have the right to protection from discrimination and from any incitement to discrimination. In respect of this right,

12 Where a sex worker has not committed an offence and the selling of sexual services is not illegal, law enforcement officers must be prohibited from abusing their authority by interfering with or harassing this worker. When engaged in criminal investigation or arrest, officers must respect the rights of all accused and defendants, regardless of their status as sex workers.

13 States are responsible for investigating, prosecuting and adjudicating crimes committed against persons, regardless of involvement in sex work and of immigration status. Measures should be taken to ensure that the criminal justice system are able and willing to properly respond to crimes reported by sex workers. Law enforcement officers, prosecutors and judiciary must be adequately trained, and their work must be overseen in an appropriate manner. Moreover, evidence submitted by sex workers in the course of criminal proceedings should not be dismissed on the basis of their profession.

14 No person should have her or his legal belongings arbitrarily confiscated or destroyed by law enforcement agencies.

In respect to the right to protection from discrimination,

15 No person should be discredited in civil and family courts because of her or his current or former engagement in sex work.

16 Measures should be taken to protect sex workers and their dependents from discrimination in the areas of employment; housing; legal services; childcare; and the provision of medical, social and welfare services; and services provided by private insurance companies.

17 There should be public and professional education whose specific objective is the elimination of discrimination against sex workers.

VII. Marriage and Family

Sex workers have the right to marry and to found a family. iIn respect of this right,

18 Current or former engagement in sex work should not restrict or prohibit sex workers from marrying the partner of her or his choice, pr from founding a family and raising children.

19 Governments should ensure that current or former engagement in sex work does not prevent any person, or her or his families, from accessing health care. Governments should ensure that public authorities and health services do not discriminate

against sex workers and their families, and that they respect sex workers' rights to privacy and to family life.

VIII. Work and Working Conditions

Sex workers have the right to work; to free choice of employment; to just and favourable conditions of work; and to protection from unemployment. In respect of this right,

20 Governments should recognize sex work as work. The lack of acknowledgement of sex work as labour, or as a profession, has adverse consequences on the working conditions of sex workers, and denies them access to protection provided by national and European labour legislation.

21 Sex workers should be able to determine, without interference or pressure from others, the nature and conditions of the sexual services they provide.

22 Sex workers are entitled to safe and healthy workplaces. Accurate and up-to-date information about health and safety should be available to sex workers, whether self-employed or employed by others. No sex worker should be required to consume alcohol or other drugs as a condition of employment.

23 All persons are entitled to be treated respectfully within their workplaces, and to be free from sexual harassment. Sex industry workplaces, like all other workplaces, should promote respectful treatment, and freedom from abuse and harassment.

24 Sex workers should be entitled to equitable employment and social security benefits, including paid sick leave; paid pregnancy and parental leave; holidays; and the right to unemployment benefits in the event that their employment is terminated or they decide to leave sex work.

25 Sex workers should not have to pay inflated rates for rentals or for essential items-such as food or services - within the workplace on the grounds of its being a sex work venue.

26 No person should be barred from employment or dismissed from alternative forms of employment on the grounds of having previously engaged in sex work.

IX. Peaceful Assembly & Association

Sex workers have the right to peaceful assembly and association. In respect of this right,

27 Engagement in sex work should not be considered grounds for limiting sex workers' ability to cooperate, unite and create associations to express their opinions; engage in collective bargaining; and advocate for their rights.

X. Freedom of Movement

Sex workers have the right to leave any country, including their own, and to return to their own country. In respect of this right,

28 Engagement in sex work should not be considered grounds for limiting any person's right to leave or return to her or his own country, and any return must be conducted with full regard for her or his safety and security.

XI. Asylum

Sex workers have the right to seek asylum and cannot be returned to situations of inhuman and degrading treatment or torture. In respect of this right,

29 Governments should take measures to ensure that participation in sex work does not create barriers to the right to seek asylum, and not to be returned to situations entailing unacceptable treat.ment.

XII. Public Participation

Sex workers have the right to participate in the cultural and public life of their society. In respect of this right,

30 Sex workers should have the right to participate in the formulation of the laws and policies affecting their working and living environments.

15. Occupational Health and Safety in the Australian Sex Industry (2000)

Excerpts from *A Guide to Best Practice: Occupational Health and Safety in the Australian Sex Industry.* Produced by the Scarlet Alliance and the Australian Federation of AIDS Organizations, 2000. http://www.scarletalliance.org.au/pub/

> *Australia was the first nation to develop occupational safety and health standards for the sex industry. These standards were produced by the Scarlet Alliance and the Australian Federation of AIDS Organizations in 2000.*

8. PUBLIC HEALTH LAWS

In NSW, public health laws make it an offence to sell or buy sex when you are aware you have a sexually transmissible medical condition. It is also an offence for a person who has a sexually transmissible condition to have sex without revealing the fact to their potential partner. SWOP the local sex worker organization will be able to provide more detailed information on legislation in NSW. In other states and territories these offences fall under prostitution laws and other areas of the criminal code. Some state and territory laws provide for penalties against an employer who allows an employee to work with a sexually transmissible medical condition.

10. SEXUAL HEALTH ASSESSMENT FOR EMPLOYEES IN THE SEX INDUSTRY

Sex workers should attend a sexual health centre, Family Planning Association clinic or private doctor for regular sexual health assessment, counselling and education appropriate to the individual's needs. Sexual health screening should adhere to the guidelines for sexual health of sex workers developed by the National Venereology Council of Australia. Frequency of assessment is a matter for determination by the individual sex worker in consultation with his/her clinician and must be voluntary.

Sexual health certificates do not guarantee freedom from sexually transmitted infections (STIs), and must not be presented to clients as such. Nor can they be used as an alternative to strict adherence to safe sex practices.

Employers should encourage employees to monitor their own sexual health. They may request that employees present a certificate which indicates attendance for regular sexual health assessment but which does not disclose results of this assessment. These certificates are the property of the employee and must not be displayed anywhere in the sex industry establishment.

It is recommended that sex workers be immunised against Hepatitis B and in areas of high prevalence Hepatitis A, following consultation with their medical practitioner or sexual health service.

Examination of all clients for visible signs of STIs before service should be enforced as standard practice (see fact sheet 5). Local sex worker organizations can recommend information in printed and video format to assist in training employees on carrying out client examinations.

10.3. Sex work and lifetime sexually transmissible conditions

Some sex workers (and indeed their clients) have lifelong conditions such as HIV infection, Hepatitis and Herpes. There is no reason for excluding sex workers with these conditions from working in the sex industry. Workplace health and safety should emphasise maintaining the health and well being of the person with a lifelong condition in the workplace, as well as undertaking all necessary measures to avoid transmitting the condition to others. Further information about these conditions can be obtained from sex worker organizations and sexual health clinics in each state and territory. See section 8 regarding public health laws concerning sex work and sexually transmissible medical conditions.

14. SECURITY AND SAFETY FROM VIOLENCE

14.1 Violence in the workplace is never acceptable.

Violence can take many forms. It can be abusive communication, intimidation or bullying, as well as physical abuse, sexual harassment or stalking. Abusive or violent situations may arise through working with clients, and in some cases from co-workers or management.

Being on the receiving end of any form of abuse can affect different people in different ways. Physical and emotional reactions to violence or abuse may appear some time after the actual event. Additionally, other employees may be adversely affected by the abuse of one of their co-workers.

Employees performing escort work have particular issues in relation to security and safety from violence (see fact sheet 8 for security and safety guidelines for escort workers and their employers).

14.2 Responsibilities of employer

Employers, owners or managers are responsible for eliminating potentially abusive situations, violence or intimidation from their workplace whatever the source. Employers carry out this responsibility by:

- identifying tasks or circumstances where employees may possibly be exposed to some form of abuse or violence;

- communication skills training as part of employee induction;
- working with employees to develop strategies to eliminate risks;
- developing and documenting procedures to be followed at times when potentially dangerous situations arise. (see example below of steps to include in development of a procedure);
- ensuring all existing and new employees are made aware of these procedures;
- organising training for employees on how to identify potentially dangerous situations and how to protect themselves;
- installing safety devices such as accessible alarm buttons in all rooms, and ensuring that everyone is aware of the procedure to follow if the alarm sounds;
- enforcing a strict policy of ejecting and not readmitting clients who are behaving unacceptably, for example clients who are verbally or physically threatening or abusive;
- providing appropriate training and procedures for employees taking bookings, staffing phones or reception areas;
- supporting and encouraging employees to report all incidents of violence to the employer and/or the police; this may be done with the assistance of the local sex worker organization.
- ensuring an employee who has experienced a violent or abusive work situation receives any medical, legal, support and counselling services that they require;
- acknowledging that employees have the right to refuse particular clients on the basis of prior violent, abusive or threatening behaviour by that client.
- provide secure lockable facilities in which employees may leave their clothes, valuables etc while they are working.

Example

A procedure to follow when an employee is with a client, and the client begins to threaten the employee, should include:

a. How the employee should extricate himself or herself safely from the client's presence.
b. What measures to take to alert others to the situation.
c. Instructions as to how the receptionist is expected to act in the situation.
d. Advice as to how other staff should respond.
e. Advice on the circumstances in which the police must be called.
f. What follow up needs to be done to ensure that the client is not admitted or booked again.
g. Ensuring the local sex worker organization is given information about the client for inclusion in their "ugly mug" publication.
h. Identifying what support mechanisms are provided for the worker.

In some states and territories, particularly where law reform has yet to occur, contacting the police, who in many cases may have previously prosecuted sex work businesses and harassed sex work employees, may not be a useful thing to do.

Some state and territory police forces, both in places where law reform has occurred and where it has not, have appointed sex worker liaison officers to assist sex workers in accessing the protection of the law, and in prosecuting those who commit crimes against sex workers.

Your local sex worker organization can advise you about any contact you may have, or consider having, with the police.

FACT SHEET 5: EXAMINATION OF CLIENTS PRIOR TO PROVISION OF SERVICE

Regardless of the service to be provided all clients should first be examined to detect any visible signs of Sexually Transmitted Infections (STIs)

As a client may have an STI and not be displaying any visible signs checking of clients should not be seen as an alternative to or lessening the need for workers to undergo regular Sexual Health monitoring and maintenance of safe sex practice.

Ideally the client should be checked before he has a shower/wash or urinates as this can remove discharge from the penis that would indicate an STI.

Before providing any service the worker should, using a strong direct light source, such as a lamp with a 100-watt globe, examine the client for

+ any sores, ulcers, lumps, warts or blisters on the genitals or surrounding area.
+ pubic lice (crabs) or their eggs in the pubic hair
+ any signs of itching or rashes in the genital or anal area
+ cold sores on the mouth
+ any discharges from the genital or anal area
+ unpleasant odours

After visually inspecting the client gently squeeze along the shaft of the client's penis to see if a discharge emerges. A thick discharge yellow or grey in colour, which may have an odour, is a sign of a possible STI. A clear sticky discharge would be pre-cum and nothing to be concerned about. If unsure about a possible STI ask another experienced worker to have a look.

Workers doing outcalls should carry a small torch to be used in the event of there being unsatisfactory lighting for a thorough examination of a client in the clients home, hotel room, car etc. The sex worker has the right to refuse to engage in any sexual practice with a client

+ whom the worker suspects of having an STI
+ who will not allow an examination
+ who will not agree to safe sexual practice

Any client who displays signs of a possible STI should be referred for medical consultation at a Sexual Health clinic or private General Practitioner.

For further information or advice on checking clients for STIs contact the sex worker organization in your state or territory.

FACT SHEET 8: SAFETY AND SECURITY GUIDELINES FOR ESCORT WORKERS

Introduction:

Sex Industry workers performing escort work have issues of safety and security particular to this form of sex work. Employers in an escort service also have added responsibilities to ensure the safety of their employees whilst working.

Having an established Escort Work Safety Procedure is essential; as is adhering to it. The following guidelines are designed to assist escort workers maximise their health, safety and wellbeing.

Bookings:

Whoever is taking bookings for escort work, either the receptionist or the escort themselves should follow the following steps:

- When a client calls, take their name, address and phone number and tell the client you will call them back to take the booking. Call (013) and verify the name matches the name and address given.
- Keep the Ugly Mug Reports from your local sex worker organization on hand to check the client is not on record.
- When calling the client back, the caller should ascertain whether the client is alone. The caller should explain that the escort will not stay if the client has misrepresented how many people are there.
- Establish clearly with the client that the escort will only provide services that conform to safer sex practices.
- Receptionists should keep all potentially necessary emergency phone numbers up to date and close to the phone.

Getting To The Job:

- Drivers must be provided with training in their role by the employer and be clear as to their responsibilities.
- On arrival, the escort should note whether the house is well lit and listen as (s)he approaches the front door for voices that may indicate more than one person. If the client is not alone, then the escort may require the driver to accompany her inside. The escort should try and ascertain whether the client is too intoxicated. If the escort feels uncomfortable or endangered at any stage, (s)he should leave immediately.
- The escort should always get the payment first. (S)he should give it to the driver or put it straight into a discreet pocket or bag. The money/bag should be kept within sight at all times, even when the escort goes to the bathroom.
- The escort should phone in on arrival. Repeating the address, the booking in and out time and having a pre-arranged code word or phrase that represents a dangerous situation is strongly advised.
- If the escort is working alone, (s)he should still make the phone call to a friend. Even calling his/her own number is better than nothing, so that the client believes that someone is aware of her/his location at all times.

Doing The Job:

- The escort should always carry a 'work kit' containing condoms, lubricant, dams, gloves and any other tools of the trade with them at all times.
- Checking the client for visible signs of sexually transmitted infections is strongly advised. A lamp with a 100-watt globe or a strong pocket torch should be used for the check.

Employers' Responsibility For Escort Workers' Safety:

+ Employers must ensure that escorts are aware of, understand and follow any safety guidelines and policies.

+ Escort service employers should provide employees with a mobile phone and personal alarm while working, at no cost to the escort.

+ Employers provide training in procedures and responsibilities to all employees carrying out escort work, reception staff and drivers.

+ Employers must ensure that drivers have adequate driving skills, do not indulge in intoxicating substances whilst working and interact with escorts in a respectful and supportive manner.

+ Employers must provide training to new employees on all aspects of escort work including safer sex practices. Local sex work organizations can assist with training provision.

+ Employers must provide secure lockable facilities for use by escorts to store clothing, valuables etc.

APPENDIX D:
LEGAL DOCUMENTS
AND COMMENTARY

16. The Mann Act (1910)

> *The Mann Act of 1910, the U.S. federal law also called the White Slave Traffic Act, was selectively enforced until it was limited by the Meese Commission in 1986. Here is the original text with the limitations. The act was passed in 1910 during a white slavery panic. It is a federal law, meaning that it is in force throughout the United States and its territory. This Act initially prohibited women and girls, but not men and boys, from traveling across state lines for unspecified "immoral purposes" and for prostitution, debauchery, or inducement to become a prostitute or debauched. The Mann Act was passed in the name of protecting women from "white slavery," but the people prosecuted under the Mann Act were overwhelmingly women, many of whom were arrested for traveling to meet boyfriends and fiancés. This is the full text of the WhiteSlave Traffic Act, as passed by the Sixty-First U.S. Congress on June 25, 1910, with 1986 Limitations.*

CHAP. 395—An Act to further regulate interstate commerce and foreign commerce by prohibiting the transportation therein for immoral purposes of women and girls, and for other purposes.

Be it enacted by the Senate and House of Representatives of the United States of America in Congress assembled, That the term "interstate commerce," as used in this Act, shall include transportation from any State or Territory or the District of Columbia, and the term "foreign commerce," as used in this Act, shall include transportation from any State or Territory or the District of Columbia to any foreign country and from any foreign country to any State or Territory or the District of Columbia.

SEC. 2. That any person who shall knowingly transport or cause to be transported, or aid or assist in obtaining transportation for, or in transporting, in interstate or foreign commerce, or in any Territory or in the District of Columbia, any woman or girl for the purpose of prostitution or debauchery, or for any other immoral purpose, or with the intent and purpose to induce, entice, or compel such woman or girl to become a prostitute or to give herself up to debauchery, or to engage in any other immoral practice; or who shall knowingly procure or obtain, or cause to be procured or obtained, or aid or assist in procuring or obtaining, any ticket or tickets, or any form of transportation or evidence of the right thereto, to be used by any woman or girl in interstate or foreign commerce, or in any Territory or the District of Columbia, in going to any place for the purpose of prostitution or debauchery, or for any other immoral purpose, or with the intent or purpose on the part of such person to induce, entice, or compel her to give herself up to the practice of prostitution, or to give herself up to the practice of debauchery, or any other immoral practice, whereby any such woman or girl shall be transported in interstate or foreign commerce, or in any Territory or the District of Columbia, shall be deemed guilty of a felony, and upon conviction thereof shall be punished by a fine not exceeding five thousand dollars, or by imprisonment of not more than five years, or by both such fine and imprisonment, in the discretion of the court.

SEC. 3. That any person who shall knowingly persuade, induce, entice, or coerce, or cause to be persuaded, induced, enticed, or coerced, or aid or assist in persuading, inducing, enticing or coercing any woman or girl to go from one place to another in interstate or foreign commerce, or in any Territory or the District of Columbia, for the purpose of prostitution or debauchery, or for any other immoral purpose, or with the intent and purpose on the part of such person that such woman or girl shall engage in the practice of prostitution or debauchery, or any other immoral practice, whether with or without her consent, and who shall thereby knowingly cause or aid or assist in causing such woman or girl to go and be carried or transported as a passenger upon the line or route of any common carrier or carriers in interstate or foreign commerce, or any Territory or the District of Columbia, shall be deemed guilty of a felony and on conviction thereof shall be punished by a fine of not more than five thousand dollars, or by imprisonment for a term not exceeding five years, or by both fine and imprisonment, in the discretion of the court.

SEC. 4. That any person who shall knowingly persuade, induce, entice or coerce any woman or girl under the age of eighteen years from any State or Territory or the District of Columbia to any other State or Territory or the District of Columbia, with the purpose and intent to induce or coerce her, or that she shall be induced or coerced to engage in prostitution or debauchery, or any other immoral practice, and shall in furtherance of such purpose knowingly induce or cause her to go and to be carried or transported as a passenger in interstate commerce upon the line or route of any common carrier or carriers, shall be deemed guilty of a felony, and in conviction there of shall be punished by a fine of not more than ten thousand dollars, or by imprisonment for a term not exceeding ten years, or by both such fine and imprisonment, in the discretion of the court.

SEC. 5. That any violation of any of the above sections two, three, and four shall be prosecuted in any court having jurisdiction of crimes within the district in which said violation was committed, or from, through, or into which any such woman or girl may have been carried or transported as a passenger in interstate or foreign commerce, or in any Territory or the District of Columbia, contrary to the provisions of any of said sections.

SEC. 6. That for the purpose of regulating and preventing the transportation in foreign commerce of alien women and girls for purposes of prostitution and debauchery, and in pursuance of and for the purpose of carrying out the terms of the agreement of project of arrangement for the suppression of the white-slave traffic, adopted July twenty-fifth, nineteen hundred and two, for submission to their respective governments by the delegates of various powers represented at the Paris conference and confirmed by a formal agreement signed at Paris on May eighteenth, nineteen hundred and four, and adhered to by the United States on June sixth, nineteen hundred and eight, as shown by the proclamation of the President of the United States, dated June fifteenth, nineteen hundred and eight, the Commissioner-General of Immigration is hereby designated as the authority of the United States to receive and centralize information concerning the procuration of alien women and girls with a view to their debauchery, and to exercise supervision over such alien women and girls, receive their declarations, establish their identity, and ascertain from them who induced them to leave their native countries, respectively; and it shall be the duty of said Commissioner-General of Immigration to receive and keep on file in his office the statements and declarations which may be made by such alien women and girls, and those which are hereinafter required pertaining to such alien women and girls engaged in prostitution and debauchery in this country, and to furnish receipts for such statements and declarations provided for in this act to the persons, respectively, making and filing them.

Every person who shall keep, maintain, control, support or harbor in any house or place for the purpose of prostitution, or for any other immoral purpose, any alien woman or girl within three years after she shall have entered the United States from any country, party to the said arrangement for the suppression of the white-slave traffic, shall file with the Commissioner-General of Immigration a statement in writing setting forth the name of such alien woman or girl, the place at which she is kept, and all facts as to the date of her entry into the United States, the port through which she entered, her age, nationality, and parentage, and concerning her procuration to come to this country within the knowledge of such person, and any person who shall fail within thirty days after such person shall commence to keep, maintain, control, support, or harbor in any house or place for the purpose of prostitution, or for any other immoral purpose, any alien woman or girl within three years after she shall have entered the United States from any of the countries, party to the said arrangement for the suppression of the white-slave traffic, to file such statement concerning such alien woman or girl with the Commissioner-General of Immigration, or who shall knowingly and willfully state falsely or fail to disclose in such statement any fact within his knowledge or belief with reference, to the age, nationality, or parentage of any such alien woman or girl, or concerning her procuration to come to this country, shall be deemed guilty of a misdemeanor, and on conviction shall be punished by a fine of not more than two thousand dollars, or by imprisonment for a term not exceeding two years, or by both such fine and imprisonment, in the discretion of the court.

In any prosecution brought under this section, if it appear that any such statement required is not on file in the office of the Commissioner-General of Immigration, the person whose duty it shall be to file such statement shall be presumed to have failed to file said statement, as herein required, unless such person or persons shall prove otherwise. No person shall be excused from furnishing the statement, as required by this section, on the ground or for the reason that the statement so required by him, or the information therein contained, might tend to criminate him or subject him to a penalty or forfeiture, but no person shall be prosecuted or subjected to any penalty or forfeiture under any law of the United States for or on account of any transaction, matter, or thing, concerning which he may truthfully report in such statement, as required by the provisions of this section.

SEC. 7. That the term "Territory," as used in this Act, shall include the district of Alaska, the insular possessions of the United States, and the Canal Zone. The word "person," as used in this Act, shall be construed to import both the plural and the singular, as the case demands, and shall include corporations, companies, societies, and associations. When construing and enforcing the provisions of this Act, the act, omission, or failure of any officer, agent, or other person, acting for or employed by any other person or by any corporation, company, society, or association, within the scope of his employment or office, shall in every case be also deemed to be the act, omission, or failure of such other person, or of such company, society, or association as well of that of the person himself.

SEC. 8. That this Act shall be known and referred to as the "White-slave traffic Act."

Approved, Sixty-First Congress, June 25, 1910.

The Mann Act was amended to apply only to acts that are criminal in the location in which they were committed:

18 USCS @ 2421 (1994) @ 2421.

*** THIS SECTION IS CURRENT THROUGH P.L. 103–321, APPROVED 8/26/94 ***

TITLE 18. CRIMES AND CRIMINAL PROCEDURE PART I. CRIMES CHAPTER 117. TRANSPORTATION FOR ILLEGAL SEXUAL ACTIVITY AND RELATED CRIMES @ 2421.

Transportation generally

Whoever knowingly transports any individual in interstate or foreign commerce, or in any Territory or Possession of the United States, with intent that such individual engage in prostitution, or in any sexual activity for which any person can be charged with a criminal offense, shall be fined under this title or imprisoned not more than five years, or both

17. The 1949 Convention for the Suppression of the Traffic in Persons and of the Exploitation of the Prostitution of Others

United Nations Document
Resolution 317(IV) of 2 December 1949

> *The 1949 Convention for the Suppression of the Traffic in Persons and of the Exploitation of the Prostitution of Others at the United Nations was really not about trafficking but instead only about prostitution. This convention document never defines trafficking. Nations that signed and ratified the 1949 Convention were obligated to reform their national laws to be in accord with this document. This law was part of the motivation for the closure of brothels in Venice and elsewhere, given that managing a brothel would be defined under this resolution as exploitation of the prostitution of others.*

Approved by General Assembly resolution 317(IV) of 2 December 1949 entry into force 25 July 1951, in accordance with article 24 status of ratifications, reservations and declarations.

PREAMBLE

Whereas prostitution and the accompanying evil of the traffic in persons for the purpose of prostitution are incompatible with the dignity and worth of the human person and endanger the welfare of the individual, the family and the community, Whereas, with respect to the suppression of the traffic in women and children, the following international instruments are in force:

(1) International Agreement of 18 May 1904 for the Suppression of the White Slave Traffic, as amended by the Protocol approved by the General Assembly of the United Nations on 3 December 1948,

(2) International Convention of 4 May 1910 for the Suppression of the White Slave Traffic, as amended by the above-mentioned Protocol,

(3) International Convention of 30 September 1921 for the Suppression of the Traffic in Women and Children, as amended by the Protocol approved by the General Assembly of the United Nations on 20 October 1947,

(4) International Convention of 11 October 1933 for the Suppression of the Traffic in Women of Full Age, as amended by the aforesaid Protocol,

Whereas the League of Nations in 1937 prepared a draft Convention extending the scope of the above-mentioned instruments, and

Whereas developments since 1937 make feasible the conclusion of a convention consolidating the above-mentioned instruments and embodying the substance of the 1937 draft Convention as well as desirable alterations therein:

Now therefore

The Contracting parties

Hereby agree as hereinafter provided:

ARTICLE 1

The Parties to the present Convention agree to punish any person who, to gratify the passions of another:

(1) Procures, entices or leads away, for purposes of prostitution, another person, even with the consent of that person;

(2) Exploits the prostitution of another person, even with the consent of that person.

ARTICLE 2

The Parties to the present Convention further agree to punish any person who:

(1) Keeps or manages, or knowingly finances or takes part in the financing of a brothel;

(2) Knowingly lets or rents a building or other place or any part thereof for the purpose of the prostitution of others.

ARTICLE 3

To the extent permitted by domestic law, attempts to commit any of the offences referred to in articles 1 and 2, and acts preparatory to the commission thereof, shall also be punished.

ARTICLE 4

To the extent permitted by domestic law, intentional participation in the acts referred to in articles 1 and 2 above shall also be punishable.

To the extent permitted by domestic law, acts of participation shall be treated as separate offences whenever this is necessary to prevent impunity.

ARTICLE 5

In cases where injured persons are entitled under domestic law to be parties to proceedings in respect of any of the offences referred to in the present Convention, aliens shall be so entitled upon the same terms as nationals.

ARTICLE 6

Each Party to the present Convention agrees to take all the necessary measures to repeal or abolish any existing law, regulation or administrative provision by virtue of which persons who engage in or are suspected of engaging in prostitution are subject either to special registration or to the possession of a special document or to any exceptional requirements for supervision or notification.

ARTICLE 7

Previous convictions pronounced in foreign States for offences referred to in the present Convention shall, to the extent permitted by domestic law, be taken into account for the purposes of:

(1) Establishing recidivism;
(2) Disqualifying the offender from the exercise of civil rights.

ARTICLE 8

The offences referred to in articles 1 and 2 of the present Convention shall be regarded as extraditable offences in any extradition treaty which has been or may hereafter be concluded between any of the Parties to this Convention.

The Parties to the present Convention which do not make extradition conditional on the existence of a treaty shall henceforward recognize the offences referred to in articles 1 and 2 of the present Convention as cases for extradition between themselves.

Extradition shall be granted in accordance with the law of the State to which the request is made.

ARTICLE 9

In States where the extradition of nationals is not permitted by law, nationals who have returned to their own State after the commission abroad of any of the offences referred to in articles 1 and 2 of the present Convention shall be prosecuted in and punished by the courts of their own State.

This provision shall not apply if, in a similar case between the Parties to the present Convention, the extradition of an alien cannot be granted.

ARTICLE 10

The provisions of article 9 shall not apply when the person charged with the offence has been tried in a foreign State and, if convicted, has served his sentence or had it remitted or reduced in conformity with the laws of that foreign State.

ARTICLE 11

Nothing in the present Convention shall be interpreted as determining the attitude of a Party towards the general question of the limits of criminal jurisdiction under international law.

ARTICLE 12

The present Convention does not affect the principle that the offences to which it refers shall in each State be defined, prosecuted and punished in conformity with its domestic law.

ARTICLE 13

The Parties to the present Convention shall be bound to execute letters of request relating to offences referred to in the Convention in accordance with their domestic law and practice.

The transmission of letters of request shall be effected:

(1) By direct communication between the judicial authorities; or

(2) By direct communication between the Ministers of Justice of the two States, or by direct communication from another competent authority of the State making the request to the Minister of Justice of the State to which the request is made; or

(3) Through the diplomatic or consular representative of the State making the request in the State to which the request is made; this representative shall send the letters of request direct to the competent judicial authority or to the authority indicated by the Government of the State to which the request is made, and shall receive direct from such authority the papers constituting the execution of the letters of request.

In cases 1 and 3 a copy of the letters of request shall always be sent to the superior authority of the State to which application is made.

Unless otherwise agreed, the letters of request shall be drawn up in the language of the authority making the request, provided always that the State to which the request is made may require a translation in its own language, certified correct by the authority making the request.

Each Party to the present Convention shall notify to each of the other Parties to the Convention the method or methods of transmission mentioned above which it will recognize for the letters of request of the latter State.

Until such notification is made by a State, its existing procedure in regard to letters of request shall remain in force.

Execution of letters of request shall not give rise to a claim for reimbursement of charges or expenses of any nature whatever other than expenses of experts.

Nothing in the present article shall be construed as an undertaking on the part of the Parties to the present Convention to adopt in criminal matters any form or methods of proof contrary to their own domestic laws.

ARTICLE 14

Each Party to the present Convention shall establish or maintain a service charged with the co-ordination and centralization of the results of the investigation of offences referred to in the present Convention.

Such services should compile all information calculated to facilitate the prevention and punishment of the offences referred to in the present Convention and should be in close contact with the corresponding services in other States.

ARTICLE 15

To the extent permitted by domestic law and to the extent to which the authorities responsible for the services referred to in article 14 may judge desirable, they shall furnish to the authorities responsible for the corresponding services in other States the following information:

(1) Particulars of any offence referred to in the present Convention or any attempt to commit such offence;

(2) Particulars of any search for any prosecution, arrest, conviction, refusal of admission or expulsion of persons guilty of any of the offences referred to in the present Convention, the movements of such persons and any other useful information with regard to them.

The information so furnished shall include descriptions of the offenders, their fingerprints, photographs, methods of operation, police records and records of conviction.

ARTICLE 16

The Parties to the present Convention agree to take or to encourage, through their public and private educational, health, social, economic and other related services, measures for the prevention of prostitution and for the rehabilitation and social adjustment of the victims of prostitution and of the offences referred to in the present Convention.

ARTICLE 17

The Parties to the present Convention undertake, in connection with immigration and emigration, to adopt or maintain such measures as are required, in terms of their obligations under the present Convention, to check the traffic in persons of either sex for the purpose of prostitution.

In particular they undertake:

(1) To make such regulations as are necessary for the protection of immigrants or emigrants, and in particular, women and children, both at the place of arrival and departure and while en route;

(2) To arrange for appropriate publicity warning the public of the dangers of the aforesaid traffic;

(3) To take appropriate measures to ensure supervision of railway stations, airports, seaports and en route, and of other public places, in order to prevent international traffic in persons for the purpose of prostitution;

(4) To take appropriate measures in order that the appropriate authorities be informed of the arrival of persons who appear, prima facie, to be the principals and accomplices in or victims of such traffic.

ARTICLE 18

The Parties to the present Convention undertake, in accordance with the conditions laid down by domestic law, to have declarations taken from aliens who are prostitutes, in order to establish their identity and civil status and to discover who has caused them to leave their State. The information obtained shall be communicated to the authorities of the State of origin of the said persons with a view to their eventual repatriation.

ARTICLE 19

The Parties to the present Convention undertake, in accordance with the conditions laid down by domestic law and without prejudice to prosecution or other action for violations thereunder and so far as possible:

(1) Pending the completion of arrangements for the repatriation of destitute victims of international traffic in persons for the purpose of prostitution, to make suitable provisions for their temporary care and maintenance;

(2) To repatriate persons referred to in article 18 who desire to be repatriated or who may be claimed by persons exercising authority over them or whose expulsion is ordered in conformity with the law. Repatriation shall take place only after agreement is reached with the State of destination as to identity and nationality as well as to the place and date of arrival at frontiers. Each Party to the present Convention shall facilitate the passage of such persons through its territory.

Where the persons referred to in the preceding paragraph cannot themselves repay the cost of repatriation and have neither spouse, relatives nor guardian to pay for them, the cost of repatriation as far as the nearest frontier or port of embarkation or airport in the direction of the State of origin shall be borne by the State where they are in residence, and the cost of the remainder of the journey shall be borne by the State of origin.

ARTICLE 20

The Parties to the present Convention shall, if they have not already done so, take the necessary measures for the supervision of employment agencies in order to prevent persons seeking employment, in particular women and children, from being exposed to the danger of prostitution.

ARTICLE 21

The Parties to the present Convention shall communicate to the Secretary-General of the United Nations such laws and regulations as have already been promulgated in their States, and thereafter annually such laws and regulations as may be promulgated, relating to the subjects of the present Convention, as well as all measures taken by them concerning the application of the Convention. The information received shall be published periodically by the Secretary-General and sent to all Members of the United Nations and to non-member States to which the present Convention is officially communicated in accordance with article 23.

ARTICLE 22

If any dispute shall arise between the Parties to the present Convention relating to its interpretation or application and if such dispute cannot be settled by other means, the dispute shall, at the request of any one of the Parties to the dispute, be referred to the International Court of Justice.

ARTICLE 23

The present Convention shall be open for signature on behalf of any Member of the United Nations and also on behalf of any other State to which an invitation has been addressed by the Economic and Social Council.

The present Convention shall be ratified and the instruments of ratification shall be deposited with the Secretary-General of the United Nations.

The States mentioned in the first paragraph which have not signed the Convention may accede to it.

Accession shall be effected by deposit of an instrument of accession with the Secretary-General of the United Nations.

For the purposes of the present Convention the word "State" shall include all the colonies and Trust Territories of a State signatory or acceding to the Convention and all territories for which such State is internationally responsible.

ARTICLE 24

The present Convention shall come into force on the ninetieth day following the date of deposit of the second instrument of ratification or accession.

For each State ratifying or acceding to the Convention after the deposit of the second instrument of ratification or accession, the Convention shall enter into force ninety days after the deposit by such State of its instrument of ratification or accession.

ARTICLE 25

After the expiration of five years from the entry into force of the present Convention, any Party to the Convention may denounce it by a written notification addressed to the Secretary-General of the United Nations.

Such denunciation shall take effect for the Party making it one year from the date upon which it is received by the Secretary-General of the United Nations.

ARTICLE 26

The Secretary-General of the United Nations shall inform all Members of the United Nations and non-member States referred to in article 23:

(a) Of signatures, ratifications and accessions received in accordance with article 23;
(b) Of the date on which the present Convention will come into force in accordance with article 24;
(c) Of denunciations received in accordance with article 25.

ARTICLE 27

Each Party to the present Convention undertakes to adopt, in accordance with its Constitution, the legislative or other measures necessary to ensure the application of the Convention.

ARTICLE 28

The provisions of the present Convention shall supersede in the relations between the Parties thereto the provisions of the international instruments referred to in subparagraphs 1, 2, 3 and 4 of the second paragraph of the Preamble, each of which shall be deemed to be terminated when all the Parties thereto shall have become Parties to the present Convention.

FINAL PROTOCOL

Nothing in the present Convention shall be deemed to prejudice any legislation which ensures, for the enforcement of the provisions for securing the suppression of the traffic in persons and of the exploitation of others for purposes of prostitution, stricter conditions than those provided by the present Convention.

The provisions of articles 23 to 26 inclusive of the Convention shall apply to the present Protocol.

18. International Human Rights Standards and the Rights of Sex Workers (2005)

**Sex Workers Project
Urban Justice Center
New York, New York
http://www.sexworkersproject.org
June 2005**

> *International Human Rights Standards and the Rights of Sex Workers describes how specific international documents address prostitution.*

INTRODUCTION

The body of international human rights law is useful in advocating on behalf of the human rights of sex workers (even though it may not carry the force of local and federal law). A number of United Nations Conventions and other relevant documents can be used to identify violations of sex workers' rights and the duties of government, including local, state, and federal, in preventing and addressing these violations.[1]

---

1. In looking for international law applicable to sex workers' rights, it is helpful to keep in mind that sex workers are not defined by one single trait—there is no U.N. Convention on the Rights of Sex Workers. Instead, a more appropriate framework is to understand a sex worker as an intersection of many different traits; his or her rights are more effectively and holistically addressed at this intersection. For example, sex workers are not simply "women," or "trafficking victims," or "a minority race", but often possess several such variables that simultaneously implicate different international laws and standards. A useful discussion of a "framework of intersectionality" is found in Margaret L. Satterthwaite, *Crossing Borders, Claiming Rights: Using Human Rights Law to Empower Women Migrant Workers*, 8 Yale Human Rights and Development Law Journal 1 (2005).

International human rights treaties, such as United Nations Conventions or other formal instruments, impose a duty on states to follow and ensure respect for human rights law, including a duty to prevent and investigate violations, take appropriate action against violators and afford remedies and reparation to those who have been injured as a consequence of violations. Specifically, United Nations Treaties, Conventions, and Covenants[2] are binding on the countries that ratify them.[3] A state that only signs, but does not ratify, a Treaty is bound to refrain from doing something that proactively violates the document. States that have ratified the Treaty have the positive obligation to *prevent* and *provide remedy* for human rights violations committed not only by the state, but also by private actors. As the International Committee for Human Rights notes, "An act by a private individual and therefore not directly imputable to a State can generate international responsibility of the State, not because of the act itself, but because of the lack of due diligence to prevent the violation or for not taking the necessary steps to provide the victims with reparation."[4]

In addition to Treaties, U.N. General Comments and Recommendations are authoritative interpretations of international agreements. U.N. Resolutions may be understood as documents of political consensus. U.N. Standards and other such rules are often developed by experts but are less authoritative. Finally, certain practices can become binding law (customary international law) where there is evidence of uniform and consistent usage among the states based on recognition that a legal norm exists.[5]

A Note about Case Studies in this Document:

Throughout this document, case studies are used to highlight the real-life relevance of international human rights for sex workers. Some specific details and all names in these case studies have been changed to protect the privacy of the people involved.

U.N. DECLARATION OF HUMAN RIGHTS

The U.N. Declaration of Human Rights, the ICCPR and the ICESCR (see below) are together known as the International Bill of Rights. The Declaration is the foundation for international human rights law, and it "marked the first time that the rights and freedoms of individuals were set forth in such detail." Articles 3–21 set out civil and political rights for all, including the right to life, liberty, and personal security. Articles 22–27 touch on economic, social, and cultural rights. "The cornerstone of these rights is Article 22, acknowledging that, as a member of society, everyone has the right to social security and is therefore entitled to the realization of the economic, social and cultural rights 'indispensable' for his or her dignity and free and full personal development."[6]

---

2. Treaties, Conventions, and Covenants all refer to the same thing and hold the same status.

3. Though further action may be necessary to make them part of national law, this does not change the fact that these Treaties are binding international law nor does it give a country an excuse to ignore or violate Treaty obligations.

4. International Committee for Human Rights, *Non State Actors and Corporate Responsibility* (visited October 15, 2004) <http://www.ichr-law.org/english/expertise/areas/non_state.htm>.

5. National Law Center on Homelessness and Poverty, Homelessness in the United States and the Human Right to Housing, at 25 (2004).

6. United Nations, *A United Nations Priority* (visited October 8, 2004) <http://www.un.org/rights/HRToday/declar.htm>.

INTERNATIONAL COVENANT ON CIVIL AND POLITICAL RIGHTS (ICCPR)

The ICCPR expands upon many civil and political rights originally laid out in the U.N. Declaration of Human Rights. The United States has ratified this Covenant, but with some reservations, because the United States asserts that some of the substantive standards delineated in the ICCPR are equivalent to our own constitutional standards.[7] Despite these reservations, the ICCPR remains quite useful in understanding the rights of sex workers and is binding on the U.S. as a matter of international law.

Article 7 sets out the right to be free of cruel, inhuman or degrading treatment or punishment, whether by the government or individuals.[8] Related to this, Article 9 states that everyone is entitled to the right to liberty and security of person, and that a person shall not be arbitrarily arrested.[9] Article 10 builds upon this, guaranteeing those who are detained the right to humane treatment.[10] Article 14 guarantees that everyone is equal before the court, and, in addition, provides for adequate understanding of criminal charges and access to legal assistance.[11] These Articles are useful in addressing sex workers' experience with police violence, the lack of police response to violence, and the overall criminal justice system.

- *Samantha deals with police harassment and threats of violence on a regular basis. Because she sometimes works from the streets and other times works out of a local massage parlor, local police officers know who she is and often threaten her with arrest (and several times have arrested her) even when she is not engaging in sex work—for example, when she goes*

7. For example, governmental distinctions based on race, birth, etc., prohibited by the ICCPR in Articles 2 and 26 are understood by the U.S. to be acceptable distinctions if they are "at minimum, rationally related to a legitimate governmental objective ... "

8. International Covenant on Civil and Political Rights (hereinafter ICCPR), G.A. res. 2200A (XXI), 21 U.N. GAOR Supp. (No. 16) at 52, U.N. Doc. A/6316 (1966), 999 U.N.T.S. 171, *entered into force* Mar. 23, 1976, article 7. General Comment No. 28 states, "To assess compliance with article 7 of the Covenant ... the Committee needs to be provided information on national laws and practice with regard to domestic and other types of violence against women, including rape ... The information provided by States parties on all these issues should include measures of protection, including legal remedies, for women whose rights under article 7 have been violated." *General Comment 28, Equality of Rights between Men and Women*, U.N. Human Rights Committee, 68th Sess. (2000), para. 11.

9. ICCPR, article 9. General Comment No. 8 interprets the applicability of this right broadly, applying much of the article to deprivations of liberty for reasons other than criminal cases, such as "mental illness, vagrancy, drug addiction, educational purposes, immigration control, etc." *General Comment 8, Compilation of General Comments and General Recommendations Adopted by Human Rights Treaty Bodies*, U.N. Human Rights Committee, 16th Sess. (1982), U.N. Doc. HRI/GEN/1/Rev.6 at 130 (2003), para. 1.

10. ICCPR, article 10. General Comment No. 21 states that, "Treating all persons deprived of their liberty with humanity and with respect for their dignity is a fundamental and universally *applicable* rule. Consequently, the application of this rule, as a minimum, cannot be dependent on the material resources available in the State party. This rule must be applied without distinction of any kind, such as race, colour, sex, language, religion, political or other opinion, national or social origin, property, birth or other status." The Comment also invites states to utilize the Standard Minimum Rules for the Treatment of Prisoners when officially reporting on how they treat prisoners, and states that the role of the penitentiary system should never be only retributory, but "should essentially seek the reformation and social rehabilitation of the prisoner." *General Comment 21, Compilation of General Comments and General Recommendations Adopted by Human Rights Treaty Bodies*, U.N. Human Rights Committee, 44th Sess. (1992), U.N. Doc. HRI/GEN/1/Rev.6 at 153 (2003), paras. 4 and 10.

11. ICCPR, article 14.

to the local store or to visit a friend. Officers have physically abused her or threatened her with physical abuse on several occasions. Twice, an officer has demanded a sexual act in exchange for letting her go. Samantha has not reported these incidents to the police because she is frightened of them and is worried that it will get back to the officers who committed the crimes, with whom she deals on an almost daily basis. When she experiences violence or robbery at the hands of customers or in her own personal life, she also does not bother reporting this to the police. The one time she attempted to report a beating and robbery, officers told her that she should expect as much in her line of work and that she was lucky that they did not arrest her. Her experiences with the criminal justice system have left her confused as to what her criminal record is and what her legal rights are. She is usually told by her public defense attorney to plead guilty in order to be released quickly, but is often unsure what the ultimate conviction is for and if she has any outstanding warrants for missed community service sentences.

INTERNATIONAL COVENANT ON ECONOMIC, SOCIAL AND CULTURAL RIGHTS (ICESCR)

Like the ICCPR, the ICESCR spells out in more detail the economic, social, and cultural rights originally recognized in the U.N. Declaration of Human Rights. The United States has signed, but not ratified, the ICESCR. The Covenant is useful in exploring the connection between specific problems facing sex workers and their right under the ICESCR to enjoy a standard of living that provides for food, housing, health, and education. Whether it is in accessing the services that sex workers need while engaged in sex work, or those services necessary to successfully leave sex work, the ICESCR highlights the failures of our social service system in providing a safety net for sex workers.

Article 6 recognizes the right to work, elaborating that states should take steps that "include technical and vocational guidance and training programmes, policies and techniques to achieve steady economic, social and cultural development and full and productive employment under conditions safeguarding fundamental political and economic freedoms to the individual."[12] Article 11 guarantees "the right of everyone to an adequate standard of living for himself and his family, including adequate food, clothing and housing, and to the continuous improvement of living conditions."[13] These Articles relate to the frustration that many sex workers express with respect to difficulty in finding a job that pays them a living wage.

---

12. International Covenant on Economic, Social and Cultural Rights (hereinafter ICESCR), G.A. res. 2200A (XXI), 21 U.N. GAOR Supp. (No. 16) at 49, U.N. Doc. A/6316 (1966), 993 U.N.T.S. 3, *entered into force* Jan. 3, 1976, article 6.

13. ICESCR, article 11. General Comment No. 4 states that the human right to adequate housing is imperative for the "enjoyment of all economic, social and cultural rights." It is not simply a right to basic shelter, but a right to live in "security, peace and dignity." Particularly of importance for sex workers and their need for stable and secure housing, the Comment highlights the right to be free of "forced eviction, harassment and other threats" that "endanger the legal security of tenure." *General Comment 4, The right to adequate housing,* Committee on Economic, Social and Cultural Rights, 16th Sess. (1997), para. 1, 7, and 8(a).

Article 12 sets out the right to the "highest attainable standard of physical and mental health" including "the creation of conditions which would assure to all medical service and medical attention in the event of sickness."[14] Finally, Article 13 describes the right to education.[15]

- *Maria grew up in a poor neighborhood and did not complete high school. She worked numerous jobs in the service industries, ranging from waiting tables to clerical work, but was unable to make a living wage. She has suffered from severe depression for most of adulthood and has recently been battling diabetes, but has not had health insurance to access treatment. Since the depression and diabetes has worsened, she has started using drugs and alcohol quite seriously. Maria had been living doubled-up with a friend, but become homeless when the friend was evicted. She began engaging in sex work when she realized she could not get by on service industry salaries, though she wanted to go to school to become a medical assistant. She has since become increasingly involved in street-based sex work and her drug and alcohol problems have worsened. She has not been able to access treatment programs because subsidized programs are in short supply and she does not know who to talk to about finding a program. She stays in Single Room Occupancy hotels some nights, but often sleeps on the streets.*

- *Lydia lives in a working class neighborhood and began working in a massage business (where she occasionally engages in sex work) when she could not afford rent and money to feed and support her children on her secretary's salary. She occasionally works for a local escort service. Lydia has a chronic disease that is exacerbated by her lack of health insurance and regular health care. Last month she visited the emergency room and was given emergency surgery to save her life. Lydia now owes the hospital more than eighty thousand dollars. She is afraid to apply for Medicaid, due to her illegal sources of income. She also assumes correctly that she will not qualify, given that the income eligibility for Medicaid is very low, and her unlawful income is higher than this Medicaid threshold. After her landlord found out about Lydia's recent arrest for practicing massage without a license, she is at risk of losing her housing.*

CONVENTION AGAINST TORTURE AND OTHER CRUEL, INHUMAN OR DEGRADING TREATMENT OR PUNISHMENT (CAT)[16]

The Convention against Torture (CAT), ratified by the United States in 1994, is concerned with torture by government agents or agents acting with government sanction; importantly, it interprets state agents engaged in misconduct (e.g., physical abuse by the police, including sexual

---

14. ICESCR, article 12. This right is subject to its own lengthy General Comment that interprets the right to health broadly and in connection to the needs of particularly vulnerable groups. *General Comment 14, The right to the highest attainable standard of health*, Committee on Economic, Social and Cultural Rights, 22nd Sess. (2000).

15. ICESCR, article 13. General Comment No. 13 recognizes this right as "an indispensable means of realizing other human rights. As an empowerment right, education is the primary vehicle by which economically and socially marginalized adults and children can lift themselves out of poverty and obtain the means to participate fully in their communities." Education, the Comment notes, is key to empowering women and to helping prevent sexual exploitation of children. *General Comment 13, The right to education*, Committee on Economic, Social and Cultural Rights, 21st Sess. (1999), para. 1.

16. Convention against Torture and Other Cruel, Inhuman or Degrading Treatment or Punishment (hereinafter CAT), G.A. res. 39/46, annex, 39 U.N. GAOR Supp. (No. 51) at 197, U.N. Doc. A/39/51 (1984), *entered into force* June 26, 1987, article 1.

assault)[17] to be subject to the CAT. Article 10 of the CAT ensures that states correctly educate state agents, such as law enforcement personnel, as to the prohibition against torture.[18]

The U.N. Committee against Torture addressed some of the issues relevant to sex workers' experience with police abuse in an official reaction to a United States' report on its CAT progress. The Committee expressed ongoing concern for "the number of cases of police ill-treatment of civilians," and "alleged cases of sexual assault upon female detainees and prisoners by law enforcement officers and prison personnel." It continued, "Female detainees are also very often held in humiliating and degrading circumstances," and recommended that the U.S. "take such steps as are necessary to ensure that those who violate the Convention are investigated, prosecuted and punished, especially those who are motivated by discriminatory purposes or sexual gratification."[19]

- *Jamie was raped by a police officer while in custody for a prostitution arrest. None of the few officers to whom she reported the rape took the situation seriously or reported the incident. Jamie still sees the officer working in her neighborhood regularly.*

- *Satoko, who is a transgender male-to-female sex worker, was recently arrested. When she was brought into the police station for processing, officers argued over who would be forced to search Satoko's person, complaining that the "she-male" was disgusting. Officers placed Satoko in the male holding cell, even though Satoko identifies and dresses as a female and is designated a female on her driver's license. She was harassed by other incarcerated males and police officers; one officer grabbed Satoko's genitals and made degrading remarks about her transgender status.*

CONVENTION ON THE ELIMINATION OF ALL FORMS OF DISCRIMINATION AGAINST WOMEN (CEDAW)[20]

As stated by Human Rights Watch, "CEDAW defines what constitutes discrimination against women and sets a framework for national action to end such discrimination."[21] The United States has signed, but failed to ratify, CEDAW, to the great chagrin of many human rights and women's rights organizations.[22] Some cities, including San Francisco, have enacted

---

17. Conclusions and Recommendations of the Committee against Torture, United States of America, U.N. Doc. A/55/44, paras. 175–80, (2000).

18. CAT, article 10.

19. *Supra*, note 18.

20. Convention on the Elimination of All Forms of Discrimination against Women (hereinafter CEDAW), G.A. res. 34/180, 34 U.N. GAOR Supp. (No. 46) at 193, U.N. Doc. A/34/46, *entered into force* Sept. 3, 1981.

21. Human Rights Watch, *CEDAW: The Women's Treaty*, (last modified on Oct. 1, 2003) <http://www.hrw.org/campaigns/cedaw/>. It also is important to note that discrimination against women under the CEDAW includes discriminatory impact without intent, which runs counter to the current legal treatment of discrimination against women in the United States.

22. The United States and Monaco are the only countries in Europe and North America who have not ratified CEDAW. Human Rights Watch writes, "Although the United States has long claimed to be at the forefront of the women's rights movement, failing to ratify CEDAW hurts women in the U.S. and diminishes the U.S.'s credibility when it critiques other countries' records on women's rights. By ratifying CEDAW, the U.S. would send a strong message that it is serious about the protection of women's human rights around the world. Ratification would also enable the U.S. to nominate experts to the CEDAW Committee, and thereby be in a position to take part in interpreting CEDAW." *Id.*

local ordinances to enact CEDAW. In New York City, the New York City Human Rights Initiative has proposed legislation that draws from broad human rights principles as well as from the two key international treaties addressing gender and race discrimination—CEDAW and CERD (the Convention on the Elimination of All Forms of Racial Discrimination), respectively.[23]

The U.N. Committee on the Elimination of All Forms of Discrimination Against Women, a committee of experts that oversees the progress of women in countries that are the States Parties to the CEDAW, authored General Recommendation No.19 in regards to violence against women. This Recommendation interprets discrimination under CEDAW to include gender-based violence[24], which is defined as "violence that is directed against a woman because she is a woman or that affects women disproportionately. It includes acts that inflict physical, mental or sexual harm or suffering, threats of such acts, coercion and other deprivations of liberty."

Article 6 of the CEDAW requires states to take measures to suppress all forms of traffic in women and exploitation of the prostitution of women.[25] General Recommendation No. 19 elaborates on the specific dangers of prostitution and the impetus behind it.[26]

The CEDAW Committee's Conclusions and Recommendations in response to a report by Germany on its progress under CEDAW highlights the CEDAW's relevance for sex workers. Specifically, in response to Germany's Act Regulating the Legal Situation of Prostitutes, which gave prostitutes in Germany more access to social insurance and the actionable right to an agreed wage, the Committee was concerned that, "although they are legally obliged to pay taxes, prostitutes still do not enjoy the protection of labour and social law. The Committee recommends that the Government improve the legislative situation affecting these women so as to render them less vulnerable to exploitation and increase their social protection."

To help effectuate implementation of the CEDAW and further define violence against women, the U.N. General Assembly adopted the Declaration on the Elimination of Violence

---

23. The New York City Human Rights Initiative is a coalition coordinated by the Human Rights Project at the Urban Justice Center, Legal Momentum, ACLU Women's Rights Project, Amnesty International USA Women's Human Rights Program, and the Women of Color Policy Network/Roundtable of Institutions of People of Color. The legislation would give the city practical tools to better assess how its policies affect New Yorkers, promote equality by stopping discrimination before it happens, and give city residents a greater say in solving the problems facing their communities. The legislation was introduced in New York City Council on December 7, 2004 as Intro 512. The New York City Human Rights Initiative is a citywide coalition of community-based organizations, legal advocacy groups, policymakers and human rights activists and educators, working to address systemic problems of inequality in New York City using the vision and tools of the human rights system.

24. General Recommendation 19, Violence against Women, Committee on the Elimination of all forms of Discrimination against Women, 11th Sess. (1992), paras. 6 and 7. The Recommendation notes that gender-based violence is discriminatory under Article 1 of CEDAW if it impairs or nullifies the women's enjoyment of human rights and fundamental freedoms under international law or human rights conventions that include the right to life, the right not to be subject to torture or cruel, inhuman or degrading treatment or punishment, the right to liberty and security of person, the right to equal protection, the right to highest standard attainable of phys and mental health, and the right to just and favorable conditions of work.

25. CEDAW, article 6.

26. General Recommendation No. 19 states, "Poverty and unemployment force many women, including young girls, into prostitution. Prostitutes are especially vulnerable to violence because their status, which may be unlawful, tends to marginalize them. They need the equal protection of laws against rape and other forms of violence." *Supra,* note 25, para. 14.

against Women. This Declaration states that violence against women encompasses physical, sexual, and psychological violence like rape or intimidation, and also "trafficking in women and forced prostitution."[27] Also relevant to sex workers is the Declaration's recommendation that states ensure that law enforcement officers and public officials who are responsible for preventing, investigating, and punishing violence against women "receive training to sensitize them to the needs of women,"[28] and that states focus in general on eliminating "violence against women who are especially vulnerable to violence."[29]

INTERNATIONAL CONVENTION ON THE ELIMINATION OF ALL FORMS OF RACIAL DISCRIMINATION (ICERD)

The ICERD, which was ratified by the United States in 1994, requires that States Parties to the Convention condemn racial discrimination and pursue policies that would eliminate all forms of racial discrimination based on race, color, descent, or national or ethnic origin. Many sex workers are of minority race or ethnicity or foreign birth; roughly half of the sex workers in this study are non-white and roughly one-third were not born in the United States. Article 5 guarantees that all are equal in their rights before the law, and specifically guarantees equality in regards to the civil, political, economic and social rights discussed in above sections.[30] In addition, while ICERD allows states to draw distinctions between citizens and non-citizens, this is not meant as a tool to restrict the rights of aliens protected under other treaties, such as the International Covenant on Civil and Political Rights and the Migrant Worker's Convention.[31]

U.N. PROTOCOL TO PREVENT, SUPPRESS AND PUNISH TRAFFICKING IN PERSONS, ESPECIALLY WOMEN AND CHILDREN (TRAFFICKING PROTOCOL)

Some people who engage in sex work have been the victims of trafficking.[32] The Trafficking Protocol is a supplement to the U.N. Convention against Transnational Organized Crime, which the United States has signed, but not ratified. Together these two documents include standards relevant to people who are trafficked.[33]

---

27 Declaration on the Elimination of Violence Against Women, G.A. res. 48/104, 48 U.N. GAOR Supp. (No. 49) at 217, U.N. Doc. A/48/49 (1993), article 2.

28. *Id*, article 4(i).

29. *Id*, article 4(l).

30. International Convention on the Elimination of All Forms of Racial Discrimination (hereinafter ICERD), 660 U.N.T.S. 195, *entered into force* Jan. 4, 1969, article 5.

31. Satterthwaite, *supra* note 1, at 36.

32. Whether they knew that they were being trafficked for the purpose of sex work and were subject to treatment or conditions they did not expect, or whether they were totally misled as to the type of work for which they were being trafficked—both cases fall under the Trafficking Protocol.

33. Protocol to Prevent, Suppress and Punish Trafficking in Persons, Especially Women and Children, supplementing the United Nations Convention against Transnational Organized Crime, G.A. res. 55/25, annex II, 55 U.N. GAOR Supp. (No. 49) at 60, U.N. Doc. A/45/49 (Vol.I) (2001). For more information on the Trafficking Protocol, see Global Rights (formerly the Human Rights International Law Group), *Annotated Guide to the Complete U.N. Trafficking Protocol*, (visited Oct. 8, 2004) <http://www.globalrights.org/site/DocServer/Traff_AnnoProtocol.pdf?docID = 203>.

While the U.S. has created its own specific domestic trafficking legislation (the TVPA), the main emphasis of both the U.S. legislation and the U.N. Trafficking Protocol is as a law enforcement instrument focused on combating perpetrators, and less as a guarantee of the human rights of trafficking victims.[34] However, the *Recommended Principles and Guidelines on Human Rights and Human Trafficking*,[35] promulgated by the U.N. High Commissioner on Human Rights emphasize that "the human rights of trafficked persons shall be at the centre of all efforts to prevent and combat trafficking and to protect, assist and provide redress to victims." These Principles and Guidelines give important context to a reading of the Trafficking Protocol. Generally, the Guidelines state that a government should not adopt measures that violate the human rights of trafficking victims in its efforts to combat trafficking.[36]

> • *Alicia came to the United States from Mexico two years ago. Through her boyfriend, Carlos, she found work in a brothel, where she earns $30 for every customer. However, instead of keeping her half of these earnings, Carlos takes all of the money and "holds it" for her. Whenever Alicia demands her share of the money or threatens to leave him and go off on her own, Carlos reminds her that if she disobeys him, she will not be allowed to see her son, who lives with Carlos' mother in Mexico. One day, the brothel is raided by immigration agents, and Alicia is held in an immigration detention center while the government interviews her to decide whether she has been trafficked, or whether she is working on a voluntary basis. This detention center houses people who have been convicted of violent crimes and Alicia is scared. Alicia is afraid to tell the immigration agents that she may never see her son again if she gives them any information. She is held in the federal detention center for a month before she is deported by the government because she is not a cooperative witness and will not admit to being trafficked.*

U.N. INTERNATIONAL CONVENTION ON THE PROTECTION OF THE RIGHTS OF ALL MIGRANT WORKERS AND MEMBERS OF THEIR FAMILIES (MIGRANT WORKERS CONVENTION, OR MWC)

The Migrant Workers Convention is also useful in addressing the rights of non-citizens engaging in sex work in the United States. It recognizes the right to leave any state, the right of the individual to return to his or her state of origin, and the right to move freely within a state when he or she is there legally.[37] The Migrant Workers Convention notes the vulnerability of these workers and recognizes, among other rights, their right to liberty and security of person and their right to "effective protection by the State against violence, physical injury, threat and intimidation, whether by public officials or by private individuals, groups or institutions."[38]

---

34. However, Section II, Articles 6–8, deal specifically with *Protection of victims of trafficking in persons. Id.* articles 6–8.

35. United Nations High Commissioner for Human Rights, Principles and Guidelines on Human Rights and Trafficking, E/2002/68/Add.1 (2002). Guideline No. 6 concentrates on the specific protection and support for trafficking victims that states must ensure.

36. The Principles and Guidelines notably state that "States shall ensure that trafficked persons are protected from further exploitation and harm and have access to adequate physical and psychological care. Such protection and care shall not be made condition upon the capacity or willingness of the trafficked person to cooperate in legal proceedings." *Id*, para. 8.

37. International Convention on the Protection of the Rights of All Migrant Workers and Members of Their Families, G.A. res. 45/158, annex, 45 U.N. GAOR Supp. (No. 49A) at 262, U.N. Doc. A/45/49 (1990), *entered into force* July 1, 2003, article 8.

38. *Id*, article 16, para. 2.

- *Sara came to the United States from Russia on a student visa ten years ago, which has long since expired. Because she is now here illegally and lacks proper working papers, Sara took an under-the-table housecleaning job, where she is subject to long hours and consistent under-payment. One of her bosses recently threatened to fire her and report her to INS if she did not begin providing entertainment at his parties for a little extra cash; this has included sex acts. Sara feels that she cannot risk deportation by reporting or refusing his demands.*

STANDARD MINIMUM RULES FOR THE TREATMENT OF PRISONERS

These Standards address states' treatment of people deprived of their liberty in both a criminal or a civil context.[39] While these standards are not binding, U.N. Committees have looked to them for guidance in interpreting U.N. treaties. Thus, these Standards are seen as persuasive, and may be considered a source of international customary law.[40] Many sex workers experience multiple arrests and some experience longer-term incarceration.

The Standards note that the "purpose and justification of a sentence of imprisonment ... is to protect society against crime. This can only be achieved if the period of imprisonment is used to ensure, so far as possible, that upon his return to society the offender is not only willing but able to lead a law-abiding and self-supporting life." Thus, the institution should utilize all the "remedial, educational, moral, spiritual and other forces and forms of assistance which are appropriate and available, and should seek to apply them according to the individual treatment needs of prisoners." In order for treatment to "encourage self-respect and develop a sense of responsibility ... all appropriate means shall be used ... including education, vocational guidance and training, social casework, employment counseling, physical development and strengthening of moral character," which should be tailored to individual needs of the prisoner. In addition, special attention should be paid to a prisoner's future after release, e.g. maintaining a relationship with family and establishing relationships with agencies outside of the institution that might provide the best help for family and social rehabilitation.

- *Renee has been arrested multiple times for different offenses relating to sex work. Most recently, she was arrested in a raid on the strip club in which she worked. Renee appeared before the New York Midtown Community Court, which is supposed to use arrest as a gateway to services for people like Renee. She suffers from substance dependency, homelessness, racial discrimination, and a lack of education and marketable job skills. She has been funneled through the Midtown court several times and released back onto the streets, where she is often arrested shortly thereafter for another sex work-related offense. The only service Renee has ever been offered by the Midtown Court system was a two-hour health class focusing on sexual health and STD prevention.*

---

39. Standard Minimum Rules for the Treatment of Prisoners, adopted Aug. 30, 1955, by the First United Nations Congress on the Prevention of Crime and the Treatment of Offenders, U.N. Doc. A/CONF/611, annex I, E.S.C. res. 663C, 24 U.N. ESCOR Supp. (No. 1) at 11, U.N. Doc. E/3048 (1957), amended E.S.C. res. 2076, 62 U.N. ESCOR Supp. (No. 1) at 35, U.N. Doc. E/5988 (1977), para. 4.

40. "In subsequent resolutions in 1971 and 1973, the United Nations urged its members to adopt and incorporate these rules into their national legislation and 'to make all possible efforts to implement the Standards.' These standards, while non-binding, are a source of international customary law." Taken from Martin A. Greer, *Human Rights and Wrongs in Our Own Backyard: Incorporating International Human Rights Protections Under Domestic Civil Rights Law—A Case Study of Women in United States Prisons*, 13 Harvard Human Rights Journal 71 (2000). Some U.S. Courts have looked to the Standard Rules as instructive in evaluating treatment of prisoners. *See, e.g., Lareau v. Manson*, 651 F.2d 96, 106–107 (2nd Cir. 1981).

· *Paula received a longer jail sentence after her most recent arrest for prostitution. While incarcerated, she lost custody of her daughter and has fallen out with her family. She has not received any job training or counseling that addresses a possible transition out of sex work. Paula has no plans regarding where to go or what to do once she is released.*

INTERNATIONAL HUMAN RIGHTS STANDARDS

Convention against Torture and Other Cruel, Inhuman or Degrading Treatment or Punishment, G.A. res. 39/46, annex, 39 U.N. GAOR Supp. (No. 51) at 197, U.N. Doc. A/39/51 (1984), *entered into force* June 26, 1987.

Convention on the Elimination of All Forms of Discrimination against Women, G.A. res. 34/180, 34 U.N. GAOR Supp. (No. 46) at 193, U.N. Doc. A/34/46, *entered into force* Sept. 3, 1981.

International Convention on the Elimination of All Forms of Racial Discrimination, 660 U.N.T.S. 195, *entered into force* Jan. 4, 1969.

International Convention on the Protection of the Rights of All Migrant Workers and Members of Their Families, G.A. res. 45/158, annex, 45 U.N. GAOR Supp. (No. 49A) at 262, U.N. Doc. A/45/49 (1990), *entered into force* July 1, 2003.

International Covenant on Civil and Political Rights, G.A. res. 2200A (XXI), 21 U.N. GAOR Supp. (No. 16) at 52, U.N. Doc. A/6316 (1966), 999 U.N.T.S. 171, *entered into force* Mar. 23, 1976.

International Covenant on Economic, Social and Cultural Rights, G.A. res. 2200A (XXI), 21 U.N. GAOR Supp. (No. 16) at 49, U.N. Doc. A/6316 (1966), 993 U.N.T.S. 3, *entered into force* Jan. 3, 1976.

Protocol to Prevent, Suppress and Punish Trafficking in Persons, Especially Women and Children, supplementing the United Nations Convention against Transnational Organized Crime, G.A. res. 55/25, annex II, 55 U.N. GAOR Supp. (No. 49) at 60, U.N. Doc. A/45/49 (Vol. I) (2001).

Standard Minimum Rules for the Treatment of Prisoners, adopted Aug. 30, 1955, by the First United Nations Congress on the Prevention of Crime and the Treatment of Offenders, U.N. Doc. A/CONF/611, annex I, E.S.C. res. 663C, 24 U.N. ESCOR Supp. (No. 1) at 11, U.N. Doc. E/3048 (1957), amended E.S.C. res. 2076, 62 U.N. ESCOR Supp. (No. 1) at 35, U.N. Doc. E/5988 (1977).

Universal Declaration of Human Rights, G.A. res. 217A (III), U.N. Doc A/810 at 71 (1948).

19. On Laws Affecting Sex Workers (2003, 2005)

International Human Rights Standards and the Rights of Sex Workers is a legal resource from the Sex Workers Project in New York City. This is accompanied by excerpts from Melissa Ditmore, "Trafficking and Prostitution: A Problematic Conflation." PhD dissertation, Graduate Center of the City University of New York, 2003 and Juhu Thukral, Melissa Ditmore, and Alexandra Murphy, *Behind Closed Doors* (New York: Sex Workers Project, 2005).

*These items address the **Victims of Trafficking and Violence Protection Act of 2000** and New York State laws pertaining to prostitution.*

INTERNATIONAL HUMAN RIGHTS STANDARDS AND THE RIGHTS OF SEX WORKERS

The body of international human rights law is useful in advocating on behalf of the human rights of sex workers (even though it may not carry the force of local and federal law.) A number of United Nations Conventions and other relevant documents can be used to identify violations of sex workers' rights and the duties of government, including local, state, and federal, in preventing and addressing these violations.[1]

For further analysis of specific international standards that are applicable to the human rights of sex workers, please see Appendix documents 16-18, which discuss: the U.N. Declaration of Human Rights; the International Covenant on Civil and Political Rights (ICCPR); the International Covenant on Economic, Social and Cultural Rights (ICESCR); the Convention against Torture and Other Cruel, Inhuman or Degrading Treatment or Punishment (CAT); the Convention on the Elimination of all forms of Discrimination Against Women (CEDAW); the International Convention on the Elimination of all forms of Racial Discrimination (ICERD); the U.N. Protocol to Prevent, Suppress and Punish Trafficking in Persons, Especially Women and Children (Trafficking Protocol); the U.N. International Convention on the Protection of the Rights of All Migrant Workers and Members of Their Families (Migrant Workers Convention, or MWC); and the Standard Minimum Rules for the Treatment of Prisoners....

U.S. Anti-Trafficking Law

In recent years, the United States government has turned its attention to the issue of human trafficking with renewed vigor. This focus has culminated in national legislation, the Trafficking Victims Protect Act (TVPA) of 2000.[2] The TVPA aims to "combat trafficking in persons, a contemporary manifestation of slavery whose victims are predominantly women and children, to ensure just and effective punishment of traffickers, and to protect their victims."[3] The law offers strong but flawed protections for trafficked persons, including the possibility of obtaining a nonimmigrant visa; access to healthcare; and services such as mental health counseling, job training, and English as a Second Language classes.

---

1. In looking for international law applicable to sex workers' rights, it is helpful to keep in mind that sex workers are not defined by one single trait—there is no U.N. Convention on the Rights of Sex Workers. Instead, a more appropriate framework is to understand a sex worker as an intersection of many different traits; his or her rights are more effectively and holistically addressed at this intersection. For example, sex workers are not simply "women," or "trafficking victims," or "a minority race", but often possess several such variables that simultaneously implicate different international laws and standards. A useful discussion of a "framework of intersectionality" is found in Margaret L. Satterthwaite, *Crossing Borders, Claiming Rights: Using Human Rights Law to Empower Women Migrant Workers*, 8 Yale Human Rights and Development Law Journal (2005).

2. Trafficking Victims Protection Act of 2000, Pub. L. No. 106–386 Division A, 114 Stat. 1464 (2000) (codified as amended in scattered sections of the U.S.C.) [*hereinafter* TVPA]. The TVPA was amended and reauthorized in December 2003 by the Trafficking Victims Protection Reauthorization Act of 2003, Pub. L. No. 108–193, 117 Stat. 2875 (2003) (codified as amended in scattered sections of the U.S.C.) [*hereinafter* TVPA Reauthorization].

3. TVPA § 102(a). The legislation does not explain its source or methodology in asserting that victims of human trafficking are predominantly women and children.

The TVPA requires that trafficked persons over the age of 18 who seek legal status or government-sponsored benefits be willing to cooperate with reasonable requests from law enforcement in the investigation or prosecution of acts of trafficking.[4] This requirement applies to persons who have been trafficked into the sex industry, and who have been the focus of much of the legal response to trafficking in persons. While this legislation has helped a number of formerly trafficked prostitutes, it is still very difficult for many people who have been trafficked into the sex industry to benefit from the new law, especially in cases involving people who do not fit the stereotype of an innocent girl forced into prostitution. The difficulty stems from the fact that this cooperation requirement necessarily includes contact with law enforcement and questioning by police and immigration authorities.

However, immigrant sex workers are often afraid to come forward and trust that law enforcement will assist them. Many people who have been trafficked are afraid of police and immigration agencies because they have engaged in unlawful behavior (for example, they may be in the U.S. unlawfully); they have been arrested in the past; or they have been told that they will be deported if they come forward with their complaints. These difficulties are compounded for people in the sex industry, even those who are involved against their will, for the fact that prostitution is unlawful and not all trafficked persons are duped into prostitution. Additionally, law enforcement officers do not always recognize trafficked persons as victims of crime. With continued education in both immigrant communities and among law enforcement about the reality of human trafficking, it is possible that the TVPA will be utilized to its fullest potential to protect such victims.

FROM "TRAFFICKING AND PROSTITUTION: A PROBLEMATIC CONFLATION"

Victims Trafficking and Violence Protection Act (VTVPA)

Section 103 (3) says "The term 'commercial sex act' means any sex act on account of which anything of value is given to or received by any person." Section 103 (8) defines severe forms of trafficking in persons as

(A) sex trafficking in which a commercial sex act is induced by force, fraud, or coercion, or in which the person induced to perform such act has not attained 18 years of age; or

(B) the recruitment, harboring, transportation, provision, or obtaining of a person for labor or services, through the use of force, fraud, or coercion for the purpose of subjection to involuntary servitude, peonage, debt bondage, or slavery.

Section 103 (9) defines sex trafficking as "the recruitment, harboring, transportation, provision, or obtaining of a person for a commercial sex act."

Section 112 strengthens laws addressing prosecution and punishment of traffickers, in some cases by amending existing laws. This includes adding separate sections, numbered 1589–1594, to Chapter 77 of title 18, U.S. Code. Section 1592 (a) (3), "Unlawful conduct with respect to documents in furtherance of trafficking, peonage, slavery, involuntary servitude, or forced labor" makes it a crime punishable by up to five years imprisonment or a fine to confiscate, destroy or otherwise deprive a person of their travel documents "to prevent or restrict or to attempt to prevent or restrict, without

---

4. TVPA § 107(e)(1)(C); TVPA Reauthorization § 4(b)(1)(A).

lawful authority, the person's liberty to move or travel, in order to maintain the labor or services of that person...." This makes it a crime to withhold or destroy a person's passport or other documents. This is an aggravated form of theft and should be so treated. However this statute specifically refers to situations in which a person is not allowed to leave, situations in which a person's mobility is intentionally restricted. In some cases this would be akin to kidnapping. The statute goes further and links this restriction to the purpose of servitude and forced labor—in other words, slavery. This language, including "purpose" means that the "mens rea" or intent to force labor must be proven in court as well as the acts themselves.

Such action is more than appropriate to the crime of trafficking, which is often reported to involve the attempt to gain control over another by limiting their movements including theft or destruction of travel papers. It is the single most important aspect of this anti-trafficking legislation, as the serious forms of trafficking are already defined by other crimes, i.e. kidnapping, fraud and slavery.

Section 1593, "Mandatory restitutions," provides restitution to trafficked persons by payment of wages or losses incurred. This is an extremely important provision, but by specifying wages this excludes prostitutes, which is ironic in the light of the Act's focus on the sex industry. As previously discussed, prostitution is not recognized as labor and therefore not subject to payment of wages under the law. The Department of Justice has sought damages for trafficked prostitutes in the Northern Mariana Islands.[5] It remains to be seen whether this will still be possible in light of this new legislation.

FROM "LAWS AFFECTING SEX WORKERS" IN *BEHIND CLOSED DOORS*

Prostitution Laws in New York State

New York, like the overwhelming majority of the rest of the United States, uses a prohibitionist model in relation to prostitution. This is not the case with other aspects of the sex industry, including stripping, pornography and its production, and internet-based adult-oriented businesses.

Criminal Law

In New York State, the five main subcategories of prostitution-related offenses are: prostitution, New York State Penal Law (NYPL) Section 230.00; patronizing a prostitute (1st, 2nd, 3rd or 4th degree) NYPL Sections 230.03–230.07; promoting prostitution (1st, 2nd, 3rd or 4th degree) NYPL Sections 230.15, 230.20, 230.20, 230.32, 230.35; permitting prostitution, NYPL Section 230.40; and loitering for the purpose of engaging in a prostitution offense, NYPL Section 240.37.

Prostitution as defined in the New York statute occurs when a "person engages or agrees or offers to engage in sexual conduct with another person in return for a fee." Sexual conduct is not defined within the statute. This essentially grants courts the discretion to decide what amounts to sexual conduct on a case-by-case basis. Most recent court decisions cite *People v. Costello*,[6] where the court found that the purpose of NYPL Section 230.00 was to "prohibit commercial exploitation of sexual gratification." The court in *Costello* reasoned that the "common understanding of prostitution" comprises three specific prongs: sexual intercourse, deviate

---

5. Human Rights Caucus meeting with the Department of Justice, 2000.

6. *People v. Costello*, 90 Misc. 2d 431, 395 N.Y.S.2d 139 (N.Y. Sup. Ct., N.Y. Co. 1977).

sexual intercourse and masturbation. Although the ruling in *Costello* has not been overturned, other courts, as in *People v. Hinzman*,[7] have expanded its definition to include "conduct done to satisfy a sexual desire." A more recent decision in *People v. Medina*[8] opted for a less restrictive definition: "inasmuch as the *Costello* court derived its definition of 'sexual conduct' not from the statute but from 'common understanding' which is subject to change, this court is not persuaded that it should accept the categories of sexual activity offered there." The court based its decision on a present-day "common understanding" of sexual conduct, again allowing for case-specific determinations of what constitutes sexual conduct for the purpose of prostitution.

Patronizing a prostitute involves: providing payment in compensation for having engaged in sexual conduct with another person; providing payment with the understanding that such person or a third party will later engage in sexual conduct with the purchaser; or soliciting or requesting that another person engage in sexual conduct with the purchaser for a fee (NYPL Section 230.02). There are varying degrees of this offense based on the ages of both the person patronizing and the person providing the sexual service. The most severe of these can be found in Section 230.06 where it is a Class D felony to patronize a prostitute who is less than 11 years old.

Promoting prostitution is defined both as "advancing prostitution" and "profiting from prostitution" (NYPL Section 230.15). It too has varying degrees of severity depending in large part on the age of the prostitutes involved and the methods used to advance prostitution, such as force or coercion. When the owner of property that is being used for the purposes of prostitution does not make a reasonable effort to "halt or abate such use," he or she can be charged with permitting prostitution under NYPL Section 230.40.

Loitering for the purposes of engaging in prostitution is a separate offense defined in NYPL Section 240.37 of the New York Penal Code. This statute prohibits remaining in and/or wandering about a public place in order to engage in prostitution. Beckoning to cars and pedestrians, conversing or trying to converse with people walking by or blocking the sidewalk for the purpose of engaging in prostitution is a criminal offense separate from the crime of prostitution itself. It applies to those acting as prostitutes, those patronizing prostitutes and those who promote prostitution. Loitering for the purposes of prostitution is a violation at the first offense and thereafter, a misdemeanor offense.

Although not specific to prostitution, criminal solicitation in the fifth degree defined in NYPL Section 100.00 occurs when "with intent that another person engage in conduct constituting a crime, he solicits, requests, commands, importunes or otherwise attempts to cause such other person to engage in such conduct," and may additionally be used to charge those accused of engaging in prostitution.

Civil Law

Housing Law

Prostitution-related offenses may also be found in the civil (non-criminal) law of New York. Sections 2320–2334 of the New York Public Health Law, for instance, define "houses of prostitution" as a public nuisance and detail legal action that may be taken against the owners of such houses as well as the penalties that will result from conviction. A "house of prostitution" is

---

7. *People v. Hinzman*, 177 Misc. 2d 531, 534, 677 N.Y.S.2d 440, 442 (N.Y. Crim. Ct., Bx. Co. 1998).
8. *People v. Medina*, 179 Misc. 2d 617, 621, 685 N.Y.S.2d 599, 602 (N.Y. Crim. Ct., N.Y. Co. 1999).

formally defined in the statute as "any building, erection, or place used for the purpose of lewd-ness, assignation, or prostitution" and qualifies as a "nuisance." Anyone who "erect(s), establish(s), continue(s), maintain(s), use(s), own(s), or lease(s)" a house of prostitution may be charged under the statute.

There are also regulations that entitle the landlord of a multiple dwelling to terminate the lease or the owner of a multiple dwelling to repossess such dwelling if it is being used as a house of prostitution in any way (New York Multiple Dwelling Law Sections 352–360). These laws would be particularly applicable to those who engage in sex work in their homes or on properties that they share with others and are currently leasing.

For those persons not necessarily living in a multiple dwelling but who are party to a lease or occupancy agreement, New York Real Property Law Section 231 stipulates that the lease or occupancy agreement made with any person or persons convicted two or more times in one year for prostitution-related offenses that occurred on the premises, will be void. This then grants the owner or lessor of the premises the right to re-enter the property. For procedure regulations and the grounds for repossessing property "illegally used," see New York Real Property Actions and Proceedings Law Section 715.

Education Law

New York Education Law addresses legal "massage therapy." Section 7801 of New York Education Law defines the practice of massage therapy as "engaging in applying a scientific system of activity to the muscular structure of the human body by means of stroking, kneading, tapping and vibrating with the hands or vibrators for the purpose of improving muscle tone and circulation." In order to legally advertise and practice massage therapy, and legally use the title "masseur," "masseuse," or "massage therapist," a person must be licensed and authorized by the State (Section 7802).

To become licensed and authorized (Section 7804), an individual must be a high school graduate of at least eighteen years of age, and must have graduated from a "school or institute of massage therapy" with a registered program (or its substantial equivalent). The individual must also be a U.S. citizen or a lawful alien admitted for permanent residence in the U.S. He or she must file an application with the appropriate department, pass an examination, and pay a series of fees. Finally, an individual must be of good moral character, as determined by the State.

Violation of New York Education Law, Sections 7801–04, is a Class A misdemeanor. How-ever, there is also a broader statute regulating the practice of any profession for which a license is prerequisite (New York Education Law, Section 6512). Violation of this law is a Class E Felony and it has been applied to those who offer to practice, hold themselves out as able to practice, or practice "massage therapy" without a license.

Sex Workers as Victims of Sex Offenses

Although not directly related to the criminal prosecution of prostitution-related offenses, the New York Criminal Procedure Law (NYCPL) poses a particular challenge to sex workers who have been the victims of a sex offense, including rape. NYCPL Section 60.42(2) states that evi-dence of a victim's sexual conduct is not admissible in a prosecution unless it "proves or tends to prove that the victim has been convicted of an offense under section 230.00 (Prostitution) of the penal law within three years prior to the sex offense which is the subject of the prosecution."

20. "Crime, Sex, Money and Migration: The Negotiations on the United Nations Protocol on Trafficking in Persons" (2003)

Melissa Ditmore and Marjan Wijers

During its meeting of 15 November 2000 the General Assembly of the United Nations adopted a new Convention Against Transnational Organized Crime. The purpose of this new international instrument is to prevent and combat criminal offences of a transnational nature committed by organized criminal groups. The Convention is supplemented by two Optional Protocols, one of which addresses smuggling of persons and the other trafficking in persons.[1] The Convention and the Protocols were negotiated at a series of eleven meetings of a special intergovernmental Ad-hoc Committee under the auspices of the UN Crime Commission, which were held in Vienna from January 1999 until October 2000 and in which more than 100 countries took part. They were opened for signature in December 2000 at a high level meeting in Palermo, Italy. While all countries, without exception, signed the Convention, eighty countries, among which the Netherlands, also signed the Trafficking Protocol.[2]

This article focuses on the Trafficking Protocol—in full: United Nations Protocol to Prevent, Suppress and Punish Trafficking in Persons, Especially Women and Children, supplementing the United Nations Convention Against Transnational Organized Crime—and in particular on the NGO-lobby and the dynamics of the negotiations at the UN International Crime Commission. Both authors attended (part of) these negotiations as members of the Human Rights Caucus, an alliance of NGOs working in the field of human rights, trafficking and prostitutes' rights.[3] One author has an anti-trafficking background, the other is a sex workers' rights activist.

One of the most controversial and hotly debated issues during the negotiations concerned the first major lobbying goal of the participating NGOs, namely the definition of trafficking. This is not surprising, as one of the fundamental problems in combating trafficking until then had been the lack of international consensus on a definition and thus on precisely which practices should be combated. Underlying this lack of consensus are two diametrically opposed views on sex work. The depth of this controversy was reflected in the presence of two opposed NGO-lobbying blocs, representing two types of feminist response to sex work and, consequently, the issue of how to define trafficking in persons. One sees all sex work as trafficking *per se*. The other view holds that conditions of (forced) labour in all industries, including the sex industry, should be addressed.

The debate whether prostitution *per se* is slavery and therefore equivalent to trafficking in persons was related most directly and vehemently to the definition of trafficking in the Protocol, but

---

1. A third protocol, dealing with the trade in firearms and weapons, was adopted the year after at the General Assembly meeting 8 June 2001 (Res. 55/255).

2. The Convention, the Protocols and the countries that signed them can be found at the UN website http://www.unodc.org/unodc/en/crime_cicp_convention_.html. The Travaux Preparatoires can be found at http://www.unodc.org/unodc/crime_cicp_convention_documents.html.

3. For this article use has been made of the many documents that the Caucus produced during the negotiations, a.o. *Recommendations and Commentary on the draft Protocol* (July 1999), *Commentary on proposals made by States* (October 1999), *Recommendations and Commentary Articles 1–3, 5–7, 8,10 and 13* (January 2000), *UN Trafficking Protocol: lost opportunity to protect the rights of trafficked persons* (October 23, 2000), and of the *Annotated Guide to the complete UN Trafficking Protocol*, made by the International Human Rights Law Group (May 2002, updated August 2002). These documents can be find on the following websites: http://www.hrlawgroup.org, http://www.stoptraffic.org/news.html, http://www.thai.net/gaatw, http://www.nswp.org.

permeated the whole negotiating process. In order to understand why this was so, it is important to have some insight in the dynamics of the negotiation process.

THE POWER DYNAMICS OF THE INTERNATIONAL NEGOTIATION PROCESS

The negotiations that led to the formulation of the Protocol were carried out by government representatives, the vast majority of whom were male, and NGO lobbyists, who were almost uniformly female. This stereotypical divide between the male embodiment of political authority and the female embodiment of day-to-day experience was complicated by the necessity to discuss prostitution. This introduced a moral element in the debate, whereby the women taking part were in a position of 'moral authority', while the men were morally on the defensive. One might say the male political authority was nagged by a female conscience. This factor was most evidently present in the debates on addressing 'the demand side of prostitution', but more generally acted as an undercurrent during all debates. However, while one might assume that the female lobbyists' moral edge would have given them an advantage at the negotiating table, in actual fact it made any difference of opinion among themselves concerning the nature of prostitution highly painful and emotionally charged.

On the level of the general negotiations, preoccupation with the morality of prostitution deflected from the more general issue of human rights and migrant labour. Migration is actually the heart of international traffic in persons, as trafficked persons are (usually undocumented) migrants seeking work elsewhere who find themselves in untenable working conditions. It is these conditions, achieved by deception or outright enslavement, that distinguish between trafficked and smuggled persons. A smuggled person, like many (but not all) trafficked person, has clandestinely crossed a border or been transported, but unlike trafficking, smuggling is not linked to work. Whereas the illegal crossing of borders is the aim of smuggling, the aim of trafficking is the exploitation of one's labour. In other words, the issue of smuggling concerns the protection of the state against illegal migrants, while the issue of trafficking concerns the protection of individual persons against violence and abuse.

At the NGO level, the debate concerning the role that prostitution should play in the definition of trafficking became so highly charged that cooperation appeared to be impossible even on the issue on which both factions could in principle have been in agreement, notably the need to include adequate protection and assistance provisions for trafficked persons in the Protocol. As a result the NGOs were ill-equipped to counter the natural tendency of government representatives to focus on repressive measures against illegal migration and organized crime, rather than on strengthening migrants' human rights.

After an introduction of the two NGO lobbying blocs who attended the negotiations, we will discuss how their distinct approaches to sex work were reflected in the more general debates on the definition of trafficking. Subsequently we will show how, through lack of a concerted lobbying strategy to promote the inclusion of human rights protections, the Protocol in the end mostly provided Western states with a broader scope for repressive measures. Improvements in the protection of migrant workers against exploitation were marginal at best.

THE TWO NGO LOBBYING BLOCS

At the beginning of the negotiations, only one of the two NGO lobbying blocs—operating under the name of Human Rights Caucus—was engaged in the lobbying process. The Human

Rights Caucus consisted of an alliance of human rights, anti-trafficking and sex workers' rights organisations and activists, with a leading role for the International Human Rights Law Group (IHRLG) and the Global Alliance Against Trafficking in Women (GAATW).[4] The very composition of this alliance was significant, in that for the first time these three distinct movements worked together in a joint lobby. In particular, the combination of anti-trafficking and pro sex workers' rights groups can be considered radical, bridging an historical gap between these two movements caused by the traditional and persistent conflation of 'trafficking' and 'prostitution'.[5] Historically, anti-trafficking measures have been more concerned with protecting women's 'purity' than with ensuring the human rights of those working in the sex industry.[6] This has led—and still leads—to a history of abuse of anti-trafficking measures to police and punish female (migrant) sex workers and to restrict their freedom of movement rather than protect them. Examples are the confiscation of passports of 'alleged' female prostitutes in order to prevent them from crossing borders 'so that they cannot become victims of trafficking' and the singling out of young female migrants as 'possible' prostitutes at the border to refuse them entry.[7]

Lobbying efforts by the Human Rights Caucus focused on the definition of trafficking in persons, advocating a broad and inclusive definition to cover all trafficking into forced labour, slavery and servitude, irrespective of the nature of the work or services provided or the sex of the trafficked person, and clearly excluding voluntary, non-coercive prostitution or other sex work. This would mean that sex work and trafficking are different issues, whereby trafficking is defined by the presence of coercion, deception, debt bondage, abuse of authority or any other form of abuse in relation to the conditions of recruitment and/or the conditions of work. It also means that a distinction is made between adults and children, whereby, to qualify as trafficking, an element of coercion is not required in the case of children as their legal status is different from that of adults. Additionally, the Caucus worked to include human rights protections for trafficked persons, regardless of their willingness to act as witnesses for the prosecution and including the right to a safe shelter, social, medical and legal assistance, the ability to sue for back wages and damages, as well as residency

---

4. During the first part of the negotiations GAATW was represented by the Dutch Foundation Against Trafficking in Women, for which one of the authors then worked. The following organisations were part of the Human Rights Caucus: International Human Rights Law Group (IHRLG, US), Global Alliance Against Trafficking in Women (GAATW, Thailand), Foundation Against Trafficking in Women (STV, the Netherlands), Asian Women's Human Rights Council (AWHRC, Philippines, India), La Strada (Poland, Ukraine, Czech Republic), Fundacion Esperanza (Colombia, Netherlands, Spain), Ban-Ying (Germany), Foundation for Women (Thailand), KOK-NGO Network Against Trafficking in Women (Germany), Women's Consortium of Nigeria, Women, Law and Development in Africa (Nigeria).

5. The Netherlands have always formed an exception in that from its start in 1987 the Dutch Foundation Against Trafficking in Women has worked together with the Red Thread, the Dutch prostitutes' rights organisation, based on the view that anti-violence and pro-rights strategies were two sides of the same coin.

6. See *Commentary on the Draft Protocol To Combat International Trafficking in Women and Children*, Network of Sex Work Projects, January 1999 (available at http://www. nswp.org/mobility/untoc-comment.html). See for a historical description of how efforts to combat trafficking have ended up justifying repressive measures against prostitutes themselves in the name of protection for women and children also Jo Doezema (2002).

7. These examples stem from contemporary anti-trafficking measures of respectively Hungary and Great Britain. They are, however, not 'new': already in 1912 Greece fought 'white slavery' by passing legislation forbidding women under 21 to travel abroad without a special permit (Doezema 2002).

and working permits during judicial proceedings. Finally, an important goal was the inclusion of an anti-discrimination clause to ensure that trafficked persons are not subjected to discriminatory treatment in law or in practice.[8]

Having discovered the relevance of what happened in Vienna, the second bloc, led by the originally American based Coalition Against Trafficking in Persons (CATW), stepped in after the first meeting of the Crime Commission. Contrary to the Caucus, the Coalition and its partners, among which the European Women's Lobby (EWL) and the International Abolitionist Federation (IAF),[9] regard the institution of prostitution itself as a violation of human rights, akin to slavery. While the Caucus took a sex workers' rights stance, that sex work is a form of labour and should be addressed as such, outside criminality and deviance, the CATW-led Network took a victim's stance, that sex work is inherently a human rights violation and should be abolished and punished, without punishing prostitutes themselves as this would constitute blaming and punishing the victim. Within their view any distinction which refers to the will or consent of the women concerned is meaningless, as no person, not even an adult, is believed to be able to give genuine consent to engage in prostitution. Neither do the conditions of recruitment or work bear any relevance as a criterion of 'force'. Any distinction between 'forced' and 'free' prostitution is considered to be a false one as prostitution is by definition 'forced'.[10] For the same reasons, the term 'sex work' is rejected as legitimating the sex industry. Consequently the Network sought to include all prostitution as well as other sex work in the definition of trafficking in the Protocol, irrespective of conditions of consent or force. As negotiations progressed, both groups brought larger numbers of representatives in order to have greater impact.

In this context, it is imperative to note that sex workers' rights advocates acknowledge that sex work is hard work and that conditions in the sex industry vary from relatively good to extremely exploitative and abusive, the latter often facilitated by the exclusion of (migrant) sex workers from the rights and legal protection granted to others as citizens and workers.[11] Consequently, they seek to correct these abuses by improving conditions and affording legal recognition to the sex industry, in contrast to the 'abolitionists' who seek to make the sex industry more illegal than it currently is and to prosecute and punish men involved as clients or otherwise.

---

8. For an extensive discussion of the definition of trafficking and human rights protections for trafficked persons as advocated by the Caucus, see also the *Human Rights Standards for the treatment of trafficked persons*, drafted by the Foundation Against Trafficking in Women (STV), the International Human Rights Law Group and the Global Alliance Against Traffic in Women (1999). The standards are found in several languages on the GAATW website: http://www.thai.net/gaatw.

9. Abolition here stands for the abolition of prostitution. Other members of the CATW-faction were Soroptimist International, the International Human Rights Federation and Equality Now. Documents explaining their position can be found at the CATW website http://www.catwinternational.org

10. In fact the terms 'forced' vs. 'free' prostitution are misleading, because they suggest that force refers only to the conditions of recruitment, i.e. to force somebody into prostitution. 'Forced' in this interpretation does not address coercive working conditions but only the way a woman came to be a prostitute: as a result of her own decision or forced by others, thus reinforcing the distinction between 'innocent' women who are deserving of protection and 'guilty' ones who can be abused with impunity because it is their own fault. From this perspective, once a woman works as a prostitute, the conditions under which she is working are of no importance. Therefore, it would be preferable to speak of abusive or coerced conditions of recruitment and work vs. conditions based on mutual agreement.

11. See e.g. Sprinkle and Leigh, both in Nagle (1997). See also 'Addressing Sex Work as Labour', presented by one of the authors to the UN Working Group on Contemporary Forms of Slavery during the June 1999 NGO Consultation (available at www.swimw.org).

THE DEBATES SURROUNDING THE DEFINITION OF TRAFFICKING IN THE PROTOCOL

Art. 3 of the Protocol defines trafficking in persons. Given the fundamental differences in the approaches taken, consensus was extremely difficult to achieve. The definition was discussed at all eleven sessions and was hotly contested every step of the way. Informal meetings and specially scheduled lunchtime meetings were held almost daily by a (closed) working group of governmental delegates devoted to discussing proposed definitions and trying to find middle ground after no headway was made during the plenary meetings. The frequency of special meetings not only demanded much time from the delegates concerned but also demonstrated the difficulty of achieving consensus. New definitions with slight but significant changes were circulated regularly. Central issues in the debate concerned women's agency—i.e. whether or not women can actually choose to work in the sex industry—and, in relation to this, the question if trafficking should be defined by the nature of the work involved or by the use of deceit and coercion. To provide more insight in the dynamics of the negotiations, we will describe two of the more contentious points of debate in more detail: the concept of agency and the issue of consent.

Men, women and children: the concept of agency

The two Optional Protocols, on smuggling and trafficking in persons, each address movement of persons, but with different levels of agency. Trafficking in persons defines a victim of crime rather than an agent, while smuggling necessarily implicates the person who has engaged the services of a smuggler: a smuggled person is not a victim but a criminal, an illegal immigrant, an undocumented alien, while a trafficked person is assumed to be an innocent victim.

This conception of agency divides in the imagination if not in reality along gender lines, as reflected in the title of the Trafficking Protocol: 'Optional Protocol to Prevent, Suppress and Punish Trafficking in Persons, *Especially Women and Children*' (emphasis added). This language was explicitly sought by the CATW-led Network, which initially argued in favour of the original title 'Trafficking in Women and Children', leaving men out of the equation entirely. The Smuggling Protocol has no such coda and no specific emphasis on gender. Smuggled migrants are assumed to be men seeking work elsewhere without proper documentation, while trafficked persons are assumed to be duped victims, usually women. In these documents trafficking is something that happens to women while smuggling is the province of men. This gendered distinction follows longstanding stereotypes of women as victims and men as less able to be victimised.

Contrary to the CATW-Network, the Caucus advocated the protocol to address trafficking in all persons, women and men, and the use of the term 'trafficked persons' rather than 'victims of trafficking'. Apart from the evident fact that men can be trafficked as well,[12] the historical linkage of 'women and children' has proven problematic in many ways. Often this linkage entails the treatment of women as if they were children and denies women the rights attached to adulthood, such as the right to have control over one's own body and life. When laws target typically 'female' occupations, they tend to be overly protective and prevent women from making the same type of decisions that adult men are able

---

12. Although trafficking in women in the context of the sex industry has received most attention, women, men and children are trafficked for a variety of work and services, including domestic labour, marriage, sweatshop labour and agriculture.

to make. This is reflected in the position that prostitution is 'forced' by definition, which effectively places women on the same level as children and denies them the agency to make their own decision to engage in sex work among the options available to them. Examples of corresponding strategies are 'anti-trafficking measures' which aim to prohibit or prevent women from migrating for (sex) work[13] and the type of 'prevention campaigns' which predominantly aim to scare women from going abroad by 'warning them about the dangers of being trafficked', up to the use of (semi-pornographic) illustrations of women held in cages or hung up on meat hooks.[14] Moreover, the linkage of women with children emphasises a single role for women as caretakers of children and obscures women's increasing role as the sole supporter of dependent family members and, consequently, as economic migrants in search of work.

For similar reasons the Caucus advocated the term 'trafficked person' rather than 'victim' because of its lack of gender ideology and the agency reflected in this term. Consistent use of the term 'victim' in the context of trafficking often results in policies and laws aimed more at 'protection' than at 'empowering'. Moreover, it tends to reduce the identity of, in particular, women to that of passive victim, rather than recognising that someone is only a victim in relation to a particular crime and for a particular period of time, and that trafficked persons are not only victims of a crime, but also, and more importantly, persons having rights under international human rights law.

Another objection to the term 'victim' is that is does not reflect the complexity of the issue or the experiences of all people who have undertaken to leave their homes and families to pursue a better future via economic migration (Finkel 2001b, Human Rights Watch 2000, Skrobanek et al 1997). Trafficked persons are often the go-getters of their home communities. It is ironic that the ambitious and industrial poor who undertake migration are unrewarded in this legislation, while 'innocent victims' garner greater sympathy. The insistence on the title of 'victim' from an anti-sexual feminist camp has historic precedent. Dubois and Gordon (1984) write that feminists of earlier eras 'consistently exaggerated the coerciveness of prostitution. In their eagerness to identify the social structural forces encouraging prostitution, they denied the prostitute any role other than that of passive victim. They insisted that the women involved were sexual innocents, women who 'fell' into illicit sex. They assumed that prostitution was so degraded that no woman could freely choose it, not even with the relative degree of freedom with which she could choose to be a wife or a wage earner' (p. 33).

The issue of consent

A second recurring issue regarded the inclusion in the definition of language like 'irrespective of the consent of the person' or 'with or without her consent'. An argument put forward by the CATW-led network was that without this phrase the consent of the victim could be used as a defence by traffickers to escape punishment. This argument in turn was used to defend the position that all sex work should be defined as trafficking without regard to the means used. The Caucus took the position that trafficking should not be defined by the nature of the work but by the use of deceptive or coercive means and/or purposes,

---

13. In 1996, the Indonesian government e.g. announced that its citizens would no longer be allowed to work overseas as maids by the year 2000 after reports of maltreatment of Indonesian domestic workers (Asian Migrant Bulletin, Vol. IV, nr. 2, April–June 1996).

14. See e.g. the IOM 'prevention campaign' for the Baltic states (http://www.focus-on-trafficking. net/index.php?ln = en). Of course this is also inspired by increasingly repressive immigration policies, especially by the rich Western states.

that is, the conditions of recruitment and work. Moreover, it argued that while people can consent to migrate or to work in prostitution, they cannot consent to forced labour, slavery or servitude:

> 'Obviously, by definition, no one consents to abduction or forced labour, but an adult woman is able to consent to engage in an illicit activity (such as prostitution, where this is illegal or illegal for migrants). If no one is forcing her to engage in such an activity, then trafficking does not exist. (…) The Protocol should distinguish between adults, especially women, and children. It should also avoid adopting a patronising stance that reduces women to the level of children, in the name of 'protecting' women. Such a stance historically has 'protected' women from the ability to exercise their human rights' (Human Rights Caucus 1999).

In fact the issue of consent is more a matter of evidence and not of definition. Once the existence of forced labour, slavery or servitude is established, 'consent' actually is irrelevant. The fact that force or deception is not always easy to prove is not solved by penalising a specific type of labour or services. If that were so, the Protocol should penalise all work or services to be effective, as it addresses trafficking and forced labour in all industries and not just the sex industry.[15] Ultimately, agreement was reached on art. 3 (b), stating that

> 'The consent of a victim of trafficking in persons to the intended exploitation set forth in subparagraph (a) shall be irrelevant where any of the means set forth in subparagraph (a) have been used'.[16]

Art. 3 (a) defines as the means that determine the occurrence of trafficking

> ' … the threat or use of force or other forms of coercion, of abduction, of fraud, of deception, of the abuse of power or of a position of vulnerability[17] or of the giving or receiving of payments or benefits to achieve the consent of a person having control over another person….'.

These means essentially require the use of force and/or deception. The elimination of this clause would define all sex work as trafficking in persons, while the inclusion of this clause still enables signatory states to address sex work as they see fit in their domestic law, including further reaching criminalisation than the Protocol requires. The fact that so much discussion revolved around whether or not the use of coercive or deceptive means was a nec-

---

15. In fact this argument was successfully used in the Netherlands by the then minister of Justice to include in the article on trafficking in the Penal Code a subsection criminalising any recruitment for prostitution across borders, irrespective of the use of deception or coercion. See Roelof Haveman & Marjan Wijers (1992) and Eke Gerritsma & Marjan Wijers (2003).

16. UN interpretative note: 'The *Travaux Preparatoires* should indicate that subparagraph (b) should not be interpreted as imposing any restriction on the right of accused persons to a full defence and to the presumption of innocence. The *Travaux Preparatoires* should also indicate that it should not be interpreted as imposing on the victim the burden of proof. As in any criminal case, the burden of proof is on the State or public prosecutor, in accordance with domestic law. Further, the *Travaux Preparatoires* will refer to article 11, paragraph 6, of the Convention, which preserves applicable legal defences and other related principles of the domestic laws of States parties'.

17. UN interpretative note: 'The *Travaux Preparatoires* should indicate that the reference to the abuse of a position of vulnerability is understood to refer to any situation in which the person involved has no real and acceptable alternative but to submit to the abuse involved'

essary constituent of the crime of trafficking, reflected the exclusive focus on trafficking for prostitution, as nobody would want to argue that any recruitment *per se* for e.g. domestic or agricultural labour is trafficking, irrespective of the means used. States that were so focused included the Philippines, the Holy See and South Africa, while Belgium changed position more than once during the discussion. South Africa led one bloc of African nations. Others such as the Netherlands, Germany and Australia were adamantly opposed to a formulation of trafficking that would essentially define all prostitution or any sex work as trafficking in persons, because it would require them to alter their national domestic law upon ratification of the Protocol.

A similar problem arose over the description of the purposes of trafficking, in particular the use of the terms 'exploitation of the prostitution of others' and 'sexual exploitation'. Arguments against the inclusion of 'sexual exploitation' were that this term is undefined, imprecise and emotive when used in connection with adults and would undermine consensus, as countries that have laws decriminalising or regulating prostitution would be unable or unwilling to sign the Protocol if it forced them to change their prostitution policies. This position was supported by the High Commissioner for Human Rights,[18] the Special Rapporteur on Violence Against Women[19] and the International Labour Organisation,[20] which all proposed a definition concentrating on forced and/or bonded labour and servitude. A similar position was taken by the Netherlands, which submitted a written proposal to this aim.

For the same reasons, the inclusion of the term 'exploitation of the prostitution of others' was problematic as this is defined as all prostitution, with or without the consent of the person, in the 1949 Convention for the Suppression of the Traffic on Persons and of the exploitation of the prostitution of others, the only international instrument dealing with trafficking and prostitution until the adoption of the Protocol.[21] Ultimately, on the suggestion of the Caucus, a compromise was reached in the final stages of the negotiations to retain these two terms, but to leave them undefined, thus allowing individual governments to interpret these phrases according to their domestic legal regime. The final text of the Protocol reads:

> 'Trafficking in persons shall mean […] for the purpose of exploitation. Exploitation shall
> include, at a minimum, the exploitation of the prostitution of others or other forms of sexual

---

18. See Informal note by the United Nations High Commissioner for Human Rights (A/AC.254/16), Fourth session, 28 June–9 July 1999, available at http://www.uncjin.org/Documents/Conventions/dcatoc/4session/16e.pdf.

19. A/AC.254/CRP.13. This document is not available anymore on the website of the Crime Commission, but can be asked for through the contact address of the Centre for International Crime Prevention: http://www.unodc.org/unodc/contact_us.html.

20. A/AC.254/CRP.14. Ibid.

21. The 1949 Convention defines prostitution as 'incompatible with the dignity and worth of the human person' and obliges states to penalise all recruitment for and exploitation of prostitution, even with the consent of that person. Although this convention is ratified by very few states, prostitution policies of the majority of countries are based on an abolitionist view. In practice, prohibitions often not only aim at the 'profit making third parties' but also at prostitutes—like those that prohibit soliciting, loitering or advertising -, and/or their non-profit making associates—like partners and adult children of sex workers-, thus severely limiting not only the space for a professional life but also for a private life. For a discussion of the various legal regimes regarding prostitution and trafficking see Marjan Wijers & Lin Lap-Chew 1999.

exploitation, forced labour or services, slavery or practices similar to slavery, servitude or the removal of organs[22]

with an UN interpretative note, reading:

'The *Travaux Preparatoires* should indicate that the Protocol addresses the exploitation of the prostitution of others and other forms of sexual exploitation only in the context of trafficking in persons. The terms 'exploitation of the prostitution of others' or 'other forms of sexual exploitation' are not defined in the Protocol, which is therefore without prejudice to how States Parties address prostitution in their respective domestic laws.'

Irreconcilable differences

The issues addressed in the Protocol were serious and have strong emotional appeal. This fact led to great tension and argument between the NGO blocs. This is significant because it demonstrates the bitterness between ideologies both in such fora and in feminism more generally. Examples of bad behaviour, bitter arguing and accusations demonstrated both how emotionally charged these issues are and the rancour and bad blood between the feminist factions addressing trafficking in persons. Especially the issue whether to define prostitution as trafficking *per se* evoked extremely emotional responses.

This malice was neither new nor unique to the Crime Commission meetings. For example, earlier CATW-publications referred to a number of members of the Caucus (among whom the authors of this article) as 'pro-prostitution' advocates 'paid by pimps'. This language is akin to the use of the term 'pro-abortion' rather than 'pro-choice' by activists who seek to ban abortion. Alice Echols, in her article about the sexuality debates in the larger feminist movement, described similar discrediting and silencing tactics when she wrote:

'Anti-pornography feminists have tried to silence their intra-movement critics with the same red-baiting tactics of feminist capitalism. Recently, Kathy Barry characterised the feminist opposition to the anti-pornography movement as a cabal of leftist lesbian and heterosexual women who want to destroy the movement so that 'male leftists can continue their sexual abuse of women without fear of censure.' (Echols 1984, p. 54)

In the same way, rumour had it—as reported to a Caucus lobbyist by a government delegate—that the Human Rights Caucus was funded by the 'European prostitution mafia'. When confronting the CATW-bloc with this accusation, it was asserted that the positions put forward by the Caucus were those which traffickers wanted and therefore the Caucus was essentially advocating for traffickers, to which was added that the Caucus could not deny working with traffickers. Other examples included the taking away of Caucus documents from the desks of government delegates and the CATW-block dubbing their coalition the Human Rights Network and duplicating the format and font of the Caucus documents distributed earlier in a move seemingly intended to confuse government delegates.

One of the most detrimental effects, however, was that on the issue of human rights protections, cooperation became well-nigh impossible.

---

22. The inclusion of 'the removal of organs' seems incongruous, but numerous delegates repeatedly requested to include the trade in organs and the issue evoked relatively little debate. See for more information on the trade in organs Finkel (2001a) and Donovan (2001).

HUMAN RIGHTS PROTECTIONS FOR TRAFFICKED PERSONS

The second important lobbying goal was the inclusion of strong human rights protections for trafficked persons in the Protocol, separate and distinct from their value as witnesses for the prosecution. At a minimum, assistance and protection provisions should meet basic international human rights standards, which clearly provide that victims of human rights violations, such as trafficking, should be provided with access to adequate and appropriate remedies. Core issues were the access to adequate housing, health care, legal assistance and other necessary support facilities; protection of trafficked persons against immediate deportation and/or detention or prosecution for offences related to their status of being trafficked (including violation of immigration law, prostitution, etc.); respect for the right to privacy, including confidentiality of legal proceedings; the right to information with regard to court and administrative proceedings; access to a temporary and, if needed, permanent residence; guarantees on safe and voluntary return; and access to appropriate and adequate remedies, including compensation for damages. The inclusion of such protections would not only be in the interest of trafficked persons and in line with international human rights law, but would also be in the interest of prosecution as it would encourage trafficked persons to co-operate with the authorities and thereby contribute to achieving the law enforcement goals of the Protocol.

However, while the Caucus succeeded in its goal to achieve a broad definition, covering all forms of trafficking into slavery, forced labour and servitude and leaving out voluntary, non-coerced (migrant) sex work, it did not accomplish this second goal. Whereas the Protocol contains strong law enforcement provisions, its few protection and assistance provisions are all discretionary.

Delegates were not keen to commit their countries to protecting the rights of non-nationals and managed to avoid a serious debate on the need for mandatory protections due to lack of time created by the protracted debate on the definition. In discussing the need for mandatory protections, there was a clear division between countries which perceived themselves as 'sending states', those countries whose nationals were expected to be trafficked and who were interested in protecting the rights of their nationals in other states, and countries which perceived themselves as receiving states, who expected trafficked persons to arrive, perhaps illegally, within their jurisdiction and whom they expected to prosecute or deport or offer protections as required. This division is not obvious as many state[s] are both sending and receiving countries, as well as 'transit' countries where people pass through and may work to earn money to continue moving. Working while in transit is not unusual in long-distance migration and has long precedent in history, both in migration and nomadic movement and even pilgrimage.

Moreover, many delegates came from a law enforcement background and were not trained in human rights issues, which meant that especially in the beginning of the negotiations, a great number of them did not even see the connection between combating the crime of trafficking and the need to provide assistance to trafficked persons and protect their rights. Insofar as the need for assistance of trafficked persons was recognised in the course of the negotiations, this was viewed as a prosecution tool rather than a state obligation. Numerous delegates expressed the view that trafficked persons were valuable as witnesses and, therefore, deserving of protections during trials but that they should be deported immediately after the trial. One delegate even wanted assurances that the Protocol would not prevent his government from 'prosecuting the victims'. Whereas the developed countries were mostly concerned with according rights to 'illegal migrants', the developing countries

APPENDIX D

were especially concerned about the financial costs of taking up obligations to provide such protections and assistance. This meant that both types of countries had their own—be it different—interests in keeping such provisions discretionary.

A serious additional problem was the lack of co-operation between the NGO-blocs. Although the issue of human rights protections was not related to the definition of trafficking and therefore not in dispute between NGO factions, the Network refused to make any efforts to address anything but the definition of trafficking or even to support the protection language proposed by the Caucus. A concerted lobby could—and probably would—have made a difference here, but appeared to be impossible to achieve.

Support, however, did come from e.g. the Office of the High Commissioner on Human Rights[23], UNICEF and the International Organisation for Migration (IOM)[24] which stated their objection to the discretionary nature of the provisions as unnecessarily restrictive and not in accordance with international human rights law. Although this helped to include at least a number of human rights inspired provisions, it did not succeed in making these protections mandatory. Almost all provisions contained in art. 6–8 regarding assistance and protection, the status of trafficked persons in receiving states and repatriation are phrased in terms as 'in appropriate cases', 'to the extent possible under its domestic law', 'shall consider', 'shall take into account', 'shall give appropriate consideration' etc. rather than in terms of 'shall' or 'shall ensure', meaning that basically there is no obligation for states to implement these provisions. In this sense the Protocol represents a regression in international human rights law and undermines commitments in other international human rights instruments, because it transforms rights into privileges that can be conferred or withheld by governments for any reason. Moreover, under the present Protocol trafficked persons appear to gain very little from co-operating with national authorities.

INTERNATIONAL EFFORTS AT PREVENTION AND CO-OPERATION

Specific law enforcement measures such as border control, control of documents and sharing of information internationally as well as preventive efforts are delineated in art. 9–13. These issues include information sharing among law enforcement, immigration or other relevant authorities—a.o. to determine whether individuals illegally (attempting to) cross an international border are 'perpetrators or victims'-, legal paperwork including actual documents and who may receive them, as well as the socio-economic roots of trafficking in persons.

Measures intended to 'prevent and combat trafficking in persons' and to protect trafficked persons, 'especially women and children' from re-victimisation are listed in art. 9. Significant is para. 5 of art. 9, which encourages states to take measures 'to discourage the demand that fosters all forms of exploitation of persons, especially women and children, that leads to trafficking'. Apart from its focus on prostitution, this ambiguous 'demand' language is mostly strategic, not to enable multiple efforts, but illustrates the appeal to shame for men that visit prostitutes that permeated the debate. This 'demand' essentially defines all sex work as trafficking and as immoral. In this lexicon, the reference to sex allows one to condemn trafficking as immoral rather than condemning slave-like conditions. This language would allow states to prosecute clients of prostitutes as traffickers. Most clients certainly do not merit such treatment, especially when they are

---

23. Informal Note of the UNHCHR.

24. Note of the OHCHR, UNICEF and IOM (A/AC.254/27), available at http://www.uncjin.org/ Documents/Conventions/dcatoc/8session/27e.pdf.

the people most likely to bring prostitutes in coercive situations to the attention of those who can help them.

Another risk of 'preventive' anti-trafficking measures is that they, as formulated by the High Commissioner on Human Rights, can be and have been used to discriminate against women and other groups in a manner that amounts to a denial of their basic right to leave a country and to migrate legally.[25] Therefore, the inclusion of a provision was advocated to the effect that actions aimed at preventing trafficking should not have discriminatory effects or infringe upon the right of an individual to leave her or his country or legally migrate to another. This proposal failed, but a reminiscence of it is found in the article dealing with 'border measures' (art. 11), which states that measures to strengthen border control to prevent and detect trafficking, should be 'without prejudice to international commitments in relation to the free movement of people'. Additionally a savings clause was included in art. 14 (1), which reads 'Nothing is this Protocol shall affect the rights, obligations and responsibilities of States and individuals under international law, including international humanitarian law and international human rights law and, in particular, where applicable, the 1951 Convention and the 1967 Protocol relating to the Status of Refugees and the principle of non-refoulement as contained therein'.

NON-DISCRIMINATION CLAUSE

For similar reasons the inclusion of a broad non-discrimination clause was advocated. Not only is this a fundamental principle of international human rights law, it is also particularly relevant in this framework given the vulnerable and often marginalised situation of the groups the Protocol deals with. As a model the non-discrimination clause of the Rome Statute of the International Criminal Court of Justice was proposed, which prohibits discrimination on a wide number of grounds, such as gender, age, race, colour, language, religion or belief, political or other opinion, national, ethnic or social origin, wealth, birth or other status.[26] Again, however, delegates appeared not to be willing to include strong human rights protections. The final clause in art. 14 (2) of the Trafficking Protocol is a pale shadow of the ICC provision:

'The measures set forth in this Protocol shall be interpreted and applied in a way that is not discriminatory to persons on the ground that they are victims of trafficking in persons. The interpretation and application of those measures shall be consistent with internationally recognised principles of non-discrimination'.

CONCLUSIONS

Negotiations in international law occur between government delegates, not non-governmental organisations. This was especially true in this case because contact between the two blocs of NGOs was almost entirely hostile and accompanied by covert malicious behaviour. The rancour resembled interactions between pro-choice and anti-abortion advocates. Even common ground was unable to

---

25. See the Informal Note of the UNHCHR.

26. Art. 21 (3) of the Rome Statute reads 'The application and interpretation of law pursuant to this article must be consistent with internationally recognised human rights, and be without any adverse distinction founded on grounds such as gender as defined in article 7, paragraph 3, age, race, colour, language, religion or belief, political or other opinion, national, ethnic or social origin, wealth, birth or other status'.

be pursued. This schism is seen whenever trafficking is discussed[27] and mirrored the delegates deliberations over the definition of trafficking. The debates reflected two opposing positions. One position is that sex work is work and that trafficking is a grievous violation of human rights. The other position views prostitution itself as a human rights violation and trafficking a vehicle to use to address this violation. A third view, neatly summarised by Meillón (2001, p. 156–157), describes the realisation by many at the United Nations Beijing + 5 conference that this debate will not be resolved in the near future and that therefore these conferences are not the place to come to conclusions about whether sex work is *per se* trafficking. This third view has emerged in other discussions of trafficking, including the Crime Commission negotiations, and led to the compromise in the final definition, in which each nation legislates its own view of prostitution. The Protocol thus recognises the existence of both coerced and non-coerced participation in sex work and takes no position on the legal treatment of adult, non-coerced sex work.

The division between NGOs, however, had serious consequences, the most disturbing of which that it effectively blocked a concerted advocacy to protect the rights of trafficked persons. The preoccupation with the morality of prostitution and the unwillingness to compromise made cooperation even on the issue upon which both factions could be supposed to agree—the need for more and stronger protections for trafficked persons—impossible. This enabled government delegates to avoid any serious debate on the human rights dimensions of trafficking and turned the Protocol into a lost opportunity to strengthen migrants' human rights. For local NGOs it means that they will keep encountering enormous obstacles in advocating for mandatory protections in their domestic trafficking laws since the Protocol fails to contain any obligation for governments to treat trafficked persons differently from undocumented migrants. Ultimately, however, not NGOs but the migrants concerned will suffer the consequences of this inability to overcome an exclusive focus on prostitution in the interest of a common goal. This seems to be too high a price and underlines the need to find more sensible and productive ways of dealing with differences of views, if only in the interest of a more effective human rights advocacy in international decision making processes.

The fact that trafficking is a complex issue is demonstrated both by its long definition and the specific views of trafficking described above. Although lobbying literature addresses difficult issues and includes complex recommendations, simpler analysis is tempting. Some delegates may have preferred shorter documents with less analysis, even at the expense of specificity and accuracy. While simplifying issues may help some people understand them, this is to the detriment of complex problems—an overly simplistic solution is not a solution but a seed for new problems. The anti-prostitution stance also represents an overly simple and inefficient analysis that claims moral high ground while eclipsing not only the plight of many trafficked people in other industries and trafficked men, but also the potentially harmful consequences for a group that already find themselves in a marginalised position. An additional concern is that policies that restrict travel, and especially women's travel, actually encourage the practice of trafficking in persons by closing legal avenues of migration, which promotes the use of the services of traffickers and smugglers by would-be migrants (Meillón 2001, Kwong 1997).

The definition finally agreed upon necessarily allows a certain interpretative leeway for its enforcement by signatory nations in order to achieve consensus in such a large meeting. While

27. This has been the case at other meetings, such as Beijing + 5 (Mitchell 2000) and the United Nations Working group on Contemporary Forms of Slavery.

the Protocol leaves governments free to treat sex work as legitimate work, it also does not prevent them from further criminalisation of sex work and sex workers in the name of combating trafficking. In addition, the Protocol does little to protect the rights of trafficked persons, leaving it to the discretion of the signatory countries whether to arrest, prosecute and deport them or provide them with protection and assistance. However, despite these comments, there are reasons for optimism in light of this document. As Radhika Coomaraswamy, UN Special Rapporteur on Violence Against Women, has rightly stated, this definition of trafficking is a 'breakthrough'[28] because of its establishment of trafficking as a crime that extends beyond the realm of prostitution and of which both women and men are possible victims. The inclusion of force or deception as an essential element of trafficking signifies an important departure from the abolitionist perspective of the 1949 Convention and has an emancipatory potential. This was enabled by the move to actual conditions and crimes against persons as opposed to sexuality and morality.

REFERENCES

Ditmore, Melissa, *Addressing Sex Work as Labor*, 1999, http://www.swimw.org.

Ditmore, Melissa (forthcoming), 'Feminists and Sex Workers: Working Together', in: *Feminist Visions for the Twenty-first Century*, Amy Elaine Wakeland (ed.), New York: Rowman and Littlefield.

Doezema, Jo, *Who gets to choose? Coercion, consent and the UN Trafficking Protocol*, available at www.walnet.org/csis/papers/doezema-choose.html. A later version of this paper was published in *Gender and Development*, Volume 10, Number 1, March 2000.

Donovan, Pamela, *Crime Legends in Old and New Media* (dissertation), New York: Graduate Center of the City University of New York 2001.

DuBois, Ellen Carol and Linda Gordon, 'Seeking Ecstasy on the Battlefield: Danger and Pleasure in Nineteenth-century Feminist Sexual Thought', in: *Pleasure and Danger*, Carole Vance (ed.), Boston: Routledge & Kegan Paul 1984, p. 31–49.

Echols, Alice (1984). "The Taming of the Id," in Vance, Carole, editor (1984). Pleasure and Danger (Boston: Routledge & Kegan Paul), 50–72.

Finkel, Michael (2001a), 'For Sale, Used Kidneys: Buyer Beware', *The New York Times Magazine*, May 27, 2001, reproduced May 31, 2001 at http://www.iht.com/articles/21515.htm.

Finkel, Michael (2001b), 'Is Youssef Male a Slave?', *The New York Times Magazine*, November 18, 2001, p. 43–47, 62.

Foundation Against Trafficking in Women, International Human Rights Law Group, Global Alliance Against Traffic in Women, *Human Rights Standards for the treatment of trafficked persons*, Bangkok 1999 (available at http://www.thai.net/gaatw).

Gerritsma, Eke & Marjan Wijers, 'Vrijwillige werving van prostituees over de grens. Economische activiteit of misdrijf?', *Nemesis* 2003 nr. 3.

Haveman, Roelof & Marjan Wijers, 'Vrouwenhandel als politiek spel', *Nemesis* 1992 nr. 5.

Human Rights Caucus, *Recommendations and Commentary on the draft Protocol to Prevent, Suppress and Punish Trafficking in Persons, especially Women and Children, supplementing the United Nations Convention against International organized Crime*, July 1999 (A/AC.254/4/Add.3/Rev.2).

Human Rights Watch, *Owed Justice: Thai Women Trafficked into Debt Bondage in Japan*, New York: Human Rights Watch 2000.

---

28. Talk delivered at Columbia University Law School, April 2001.

Jordan, Ann D., *Annotated Guide to the complete UN Trafficking Protocol*, Washington: International Human Rights Law Group May 2002, updated August 2002 (available at http://www.hrlawgroup.org).

Kwong, Peter, *Forbidden Workers*, New York: New Press 1997.

Meillón, Cynthia (ed.) in collaboration with Charlotte Bunch, *Holding on to the Promise: Women's Human Rights and the Beijing + 5 Review*, New Brunswick: Rutgers 2001.

Mitchell, Grace, *Disputed Subjects in the Global Movement for Sex Workers' Rights*, unpublished paper 2000.

Nagle, Jill (ed.), *Whores and Other Feminists*, New York: Routledge 1997.

Rubin, Gayle, 'Thinking Sex', in: *Pleasure and Danger*, Carole Vance (ed.), Boston: Routledge & Kegan Paul 1984, p. 267–319.

Skrobanek, Siriporn, Nattaya Boonpakdi, Chutima Janthakeero, *The Traffic in Women*, London and New York: Zed Books 1997.

Wijers, Marjan & Lin Lap-Chew, *Trafficking in Women, Forced Labour and Slavery-like Practices in Marriage, Domestic Labour and Prostitution*, Utrecht/ Bangkok: Foundation Against Trafficking in Women/ Global Alliance Against Trafficking in Women 1997/1999 (revised edition).

21. What Is "Demand" in the Context of Trafficking in Persons?

Sex Workers Project at the Urban Justice Center, Network of Sex Work Projects, and Prostitutes of New York, March 2005, for Beijing + 10.

"Demand" is a current buzzword among some anti-trafficking activists, in which they argue that demand for sex work drives trafficking in persons, and that arresting clients who patronize sex workers will reduce the problem. However, demand for sex work is not a predominant driving factor for trafficking, which is driven by poverty, race, and gender inequities.

The term "demand" can, in one sense, refer to the legitimate concerns raised by migrants and labor rights advocates who address the issues relating to the need in the global north for exploitable labor and services. However, this new narrow focus of the term represents a dangerous slippage into an anti-sex work, anti-male and homophobic mindset which, under the guise of protecting sex workers, is another way of undermining sex workers' autonomy and causing more harm to them. To trivialize this issue by sexualizing it in voyeuristic ways by appealing to male shame and female chastity is a travesty.

How can anti-trafficking policy effectively address "demand"?

- Anti-trafficking policies must focus on the full scope of the problem. The Special Rapporteur on Trafficking in Persons, Especially Women and Children ("Special Rapporteur"), has recently affirmed that "significant numbers of human beings are trafficked for labour exploitation."[1]
- A recent IOM report suggests that "the notion of 'demand' for the labour/services of a 'trafficked' person … can refer to an employer's need for cheap and docile labour, or to consumer demand for cheap goods and/or services, or for household labour or

---

1. Report of the Special Rapporteur on Trafficking in Persons, Especially Women and Children, E/CN.4/2005/71 (22 December 2004) at 2.

subsistence labour, or to any or all of these."[2] Proponents addressing "demand" focus on sex workers' clients as perpetrators of violence against women. However, there are a number of flaws with this approach:

+ Sex workers around the world point not to their clients but to the state and its agents as the prime violators of their human rights. Extending the powers of law enforcement into yet another sphere of the lives of sex workers presents a great threat to the human rights of sex workers.

+ Sex workers are most vulnerable to violence in situations where sex work is criminalized or stigmatized and they are treated as outsiders or are not encouraged to avail themselves of legal protections.

+ The Special Rapporteur has expressed concerns that "trafficking continues to be treated as mainly a 'law and order' problem" and expresses her intent to focus on human rights protections.[3]

+ The IOM has pointed out that increased border security exacerbates markets for trafficking and smuggling of migrants.[4] "Victims of cross-border trafficking are criminalized and prosecuted as illegal aliens, undocumented workers or irregular migrants, rather than as victims of a crime."[5] Efforts to address trafficking will be ineffective with a narrow focus on demand for sex work. Instead, anti-trafficking efforts must address effective labor and migration policies that recall the basic principle set forth by the Special Rapporteur: "that the human rights of trafficked persons shall be at the centre of all efforts to combat trafficking and to protect, assist and provide redress to those affected by trafficking."[6]

---

2. International Organization for Migration, Is Trafficking in Human Beings Demand Driven? A Multi-Country Pilot Study (2003) at 10.

3. Report of the Special Rapporteur, E/CN.4/2005/71 at 56.

4. International Organization for Migration, Is Trafficking in Human Beings Demand Driven? at 7-8.

5. Report of the Special Rapporteur, E/CN.4/2005/71 at ¶ 10.

6. Report of the Special Rapporteur, E/CN.4/2005/71 at ¶ 11.

SELECTED BIBLIOGRAPHY

Abramovich, E. "Childhood Sexual Abuse as a Risk Factor for Subsequent Involvement in Sex Work: A Review of Empirical Findings." *Journal of Psychology and Human Sexuality* 17 (2005): 131–46.

Abrams, Kathryn. "Sex Wars Redux: Agency and Coercion in Feminist Legal Theory." *Columbia Law Review* 95 (1995): 304–76.

Achebe, Nwando. "The Road to Italy: Nigerian Sex Workers at Home and Abroad." *Women's Labors*, Special Issue of *Journal of Women's History* 15 (2004): 177–84.

Ackerly, J. R. *My Father and Myself*. New York: Coward-McCann, 1968.

Adams, J. N. "Words for 'Prostitute' in Latin." *Rheinisches Museum für Philologie* 126 (1983): 321–58.

Adams, Simon, and Raelene Frances. "Lifting the Veil: The Sex Industry, Museums and Galleries." *Labour History* 85 (2003): 36 pars. http://www.historycooperative.org/journals/lab/85/adams.html.

Addams, Jane. *A New Conscience and an Ancient Evil*. Champaign: University of Illinois Press, 2002.

Addams, Jane. "Twenty Years at Hull-House." In *Written by Herself*, ed. Jill Ker Conway. New York: Vintage Books, 1992.

Aderinto, Saheed. "Demobilization and Repatriation of Undesirables: Prostitutes, Crime, Law and Reformers in Colonial Nigeria" and "Prostitution: A Social Legacy of Colonialism in Nigeria." In *Urban History of Nigeria: Past and Present*, ed. Hakeem Tijani. Lanham, MD: University Press of America, 2005.

Adler, Polly. *A House Is Not a Home*. New York: Rinehart & Company, 1950.

Aggleton, Peter, ed. *Men Who Sell Sex: International Perspectives on Male Prostitution and HIV/AIDS*. Philadelphia: Temple University Press, 1999.

Aguiar, Sarah Appleton. *The Bitch Is Back: Wicked Women in Literature*. Carbondale: Southern Illinois University Press, 2001.

Agustín, Laura. "The Disappearing of a Migration Category: Migrants Who Sell Sex." *Journal of Ethnic and Migration Studies* 32 (2006). http://www.rhizomes.net/issue10/agustin.htm.

———.*La Industria del Sexo y "Las Migrantes."* http://www.geocities.com/litertulia/0041)_agustin.htm.

———. "A Migrant World of Services." *Social Politics* 10 (2003): 377–96.

———. "The Plight of Migrant Women: They Speak, but Who's Listening?" In *Women@Internet: Creating New Cultures in Cyberspace,* ed. Wendy Harcourt. London: Zed Books, 1999.

———. *Sex Work and Migrations/Trabajo Sexual y Migraciones.* http://www.swimw.org/agustin.html.

———. "Trabajar en la industria del sexo." *OFRIM/Suplementos,* Madrid, June 2000. http://www.nodo50.org/mujeresred/laura)agustin-1.html.

Agustín, Laura, and Jo Weldon. "The Sex Sector: A Victory for Diversity." *Global Reproductive Rights Newsletter* 66/67 (2003): 31–34. http://www.nswp.org/mobility/agustin-sector.html.

Ahmed, Julia. "Health Impacts of Prostitution: Experience of Bangladesh Women's Health Coalition." *Research for Sex Work* 4 (2001): 8–9. http://www.med.vu.nl/hcc/artikelen/ahmed.htm.

Aihara, Kyoko. *Geisha.* London: Carlton Books, 1999.

Albert, Alexa E. *Brothel.* New York: Random House, 2001.

Alegría, M., M. Vera, D. H. Freeman, R. Robles, M. C. Santos, and C. L. Rivera. "HIV Infection, Risk Behaviors, and Depressive Symptoms among Puerto Rican Sex Workers." *American Journal of Public Health* 84, no. 12 (1994): 2000–2002.

Alexander, M. Jacqui. "Imperial Desire/Sexual Utopias: White Gay Capital and Transnational Tourism." In *Talking Visions: Multicultural Feminism in a Transnational Age,* ed. Ella Shohat. Cambridge, MA: MIT Press, 1998, pp. 281–305.

Alexander, Priscilla. "Bathhouses and Brothels: Symbolic Sites in Discourse and Practice." In *Policing Public Sex,* ed. Ephen Glenn Colter, Wayne Hoffman, Eva Pendleton, Alison Redick, and David Serlin. Boston: South End Press, 1996.

———. "A Chronology, of Sorts: Scapegoating Sex Workers for the Epidemic." In *AIDS: The Women,* ed. Ines Rieder and Patricia Ruppelt. San Francisco: Cleis Press, 1988, pp. 169–72.

———. "Feminism, Sex Workers, and Human Rights." In *Whores and Other Feminists,* ed. Jill Nagle. New York: Routledge, 1997, pp. 83–97.

———. "Health Care for Sex Workers Should Go Beyond STD Care." *Research for Sex Work* 2 (1999): 14–15.

———. "(In)visible Workers: Sex Workers." Unpublished paper, 2001. http://www.swimw.org/isw.html.

———. "Making a Living: Women Who Go Out." In *Women's Experiences with AIDS,* ed. E. Maxine Ankrah and Lynel Long. New York: Columbia University Press, 1997.

———. "Prostitution: Still a Difficult Issue for Feminists." In *Sex Work: Writings by Women in the Sex Industry,* ed. Frederique Delacoste and Priscilla Alexander. San Francisco: Cleis Press, 1987, 1998.

———. "Sex Industry." In *Encyclopedia of Occupational Health and Safety,* ed. Jeanne Mager Stellman. Geneva: International Labour Office, 1997.

———. "Sex Work and Health: A Question of Safety in the Workplace." *Journal of the American Medical Woman's Association* 53 (1998): 77–82.

———. "Sex Workers Fight against AIDS: An International Perspective." In *Women Resisting AIDS: Strategies of Empowerment,* ed. Beth E. Schneider and Nancy Stoller. Philadelphia: Temple University Press, 1995.

Allen, Robert C. *Horrible Prettiness: Burlesque and American Culture.* Chapel Hill: University of North Carolina Press, 1991.

Allison, Anne. *Nightwork: Sexuality, Pleasure, and Corporate Masculinity in a Tokyo Hostess Club.* Chicago: University of Chicago Press, 1994.

Almodovar, Norma Jean. *Cop to Call Girl: Why I Left the LAPD to Make an Honest Living as a Beverly Hills Prostitute.* New York: Simon and Schuster, 1993.

Altink, Sietske. *Stolen Lives: Trading Women into Sex and Slavery.* London: Scarlet Press; New York: Harrington Park Press, 1995.

Altink, Sietske, Martine Groen, and Ine Vanwesenbeeck. *Sekswerk: Ervaringen van Vrouwen in de Prostitutie.* Amsterdam: Sua Amsterdam, 1991.

Anarfi, John K. *Female Migration and Prostitution in West Africa: The Case of Ghanaian Women in Côte d'Ivoire.* Accra, Ghana: GTZ Regional AIDS Programme for West and Central Africa, 1995.

Anbinder, Tyler. *Five Points: The 19th-Century New York City Neighborhood That Invented Tap Dance, Stole Elections, and Became the World's Most Notorious Slum.* New York: Plume, 2002.

Andaya, Barbara Watson. "From Temporary Wife to Prostitute: Sexuality and Economic Change in Early Modern Southeast Asia." *Journal of Women's History* 9 (1998): 11–35.

Anderson, Amanda. *Tainted Souls and Painted Faces: The Rhetoric of Fallenness in Victorian Culture.* Ithaca, NY: Cornell University Press, 1993.

Anderson, Leslie. *Restavek: Child Domestic Labor in Haiti.* Minneapolis: Minnesota Lawyers International Human Rights Committee, 1990.

Andros, Phil. *My Brother, the Hustler.* San Francisco: Gay Parisian Press, 1970.

———. *San Francisco Hustler.* San Francisco: Gay Parisian Press, 1970.

Andrushchak, L. I., and L. N. Khodakhevich. "The Reduction of the HIV Vulnerability of Women Involved in the Sex Business in Ukraine through Social Mobilization and the Creation of Self Support Networks." *Zhurnal Mikrobiologii, Epidemiologii i Immunobiologii* 4 (2000): 118–19.

Anonymous. *The Pretty Women of Paris.* Hertfordshire, UK: Wordsworth Editions, 1996.

———. *Sins of the Cities of the Plain; or Confessions of a Mary-Anne.* 1881. Reprint, New York: Masquerade Books, 1992.

———. *Teleny: The Reverse of the Medal.* Edited by H. Montgomery Hyde. 1893. Reprint, London: Icon, 1966.

Anthony, Jane. "Prostitution as 'Choice.'" *Ms.* magazine, January/February 1992, pp. 86–87.

Arceneaux, Pamela. "Guidebooks to Sin: The Blue Books of Storyville." *Louisiana History* 28 (1987): 397–405.

Armstrong, Carol. *Odd Man Out: Readings of the Work and Reputation of Edgar Degas.* Chicago: University of Chicago Press, 1991.

Asbury, Herbert. *The Gangs of New York: An Informal History of the Underworld.* New York: Thunder's Mouth Press, 2001.

———. *Gem of the Prairie.* New York: Knopf, 1940.

Asia Foundation East West. "Summary Report of Baseline Characteristics of NGO Counterparts in Uzbekistan, Tajikistan, and Kyrgyzstan." Prepared under the Drug Demand Reduction Programme in Central Asia. Moscow: AFEW, 2003.

Asia Watch Women's Rights Project. *Contemporary Forms of Slavery in Pakistan.* New York: Human Rights Watch, 1997.

———. *A Modern Form of Slavery Trafficking of Burmese Women and Girls into Brothels in Thailand.* New York: Human Rights Watch, 1993.

———. *Rape for Profit.* New York: Human Rights Watch, 1997.

Asociacion de Trabajadora Autónomas "22 de Junio" de El ORO en Fundación Quimera. "Trabajadoras del sexo. Memorias Vivas." Machala, Ecuador: MamaCash, 2002.

Assante, Julia. "The *kar.kid/harimtu*, Prostitute or Single Woman?" *Ugarit Forschungen* 30 (1998): 5–96.

Atchison, Chris, Laura Fraser, and John Lowman. "Men Who Buy Sex: Preliminary Findings of an Exploratory Study." In *Prostitution: On Whores, Hustlers, and Johns*, ed. James E. Elias, Vern L. Bullough, Veronica Elias, and Gwen Brewer. New York: Prometheus Books, 1998.

Auerbach, Nina. *Woman and the Demon: The Life of a Victorian Myth.* Cambridge, MA: Harvard University Press, 1982.

Auriant. *La Véritable Histoire de "Nana."* Paris: Mercure de France, 1942.

Bailey, Beth, and David Farber. *The First Strange Place: The Alchemy of Race and Sex in World War Two Hawaii.* New York: Free Press, 1992.

Bakwesegha, Christopher J. *Profiles of Urban Prostitution: A Case Study from Uganda.* Nairobi: East African Literature Bureau, 1982.

Banach, Linda, and Sue Metzenrath. *Model Principles for Sex Industry Law Reform.* Sydney, Australia: Scarlet Alliance/AFAO, 2000.

Barabas, SuzAnne, and Gabor Barabas. *Gunsmoke: A Complete History and Analysis of the Legendary Broadcast Series.* Jefferson, NC: McFarland, 1990.

"Barbara." "It's a Pleasure Doing Business with You." *Social Text* 37 (1993): 11–22.

Barlow, Caroline. "A Brothel Owner's View." In *Sex Work and Sex Workers in Australia*, ed. Roberta Perkins. Sydney, Australia: UNSW Press, 1991.

Barmé, Scot. *Woman, Man, Bangkok Love, Sex and Popular Culture in Thailand.* Lanham, MD: Rowman and Littlefield, 2002.

Barnard, Marina A. "Violence and Vulnerability: Conditions of Work for Streetworking Prostitutes." *Sociology of Health and Illness* 15 (1993): 683–705.

Barnhart, Jacqueline Baker. *The Fair but Frail: Prostitution in San Francisco 1849–1900.* Reno: University of Nevada Press, 1986.

Barrett, Gregory. *Archetypes in Japanese Film: The Sociopolitical and Religious Significance of the Principal Heroes and Heroines.* Toronto: Associate Universities Press, 1989.

Barrows, Sydney B., and William Novak. *Mayflower Madam.* New York: Ballantine Books, 1986.

Barry, Kathleen. *Female Sexual Slavery.* New York: New York University Press, 1979.

———. *The Prostitution of Sexuality: The Global Exploitation of Women.* New York: New York University Press, 1995.

———, Charlotte Bunch, and Shirley Castley. "International Feminism: Networking against Female Sexual Slavery." Report presented at the Global Feminist Workshop to Organize against Traffic in Women, Rotterdam, Netherlands, 6–15 April 1983.

Bartley, Paula. *Prostitution: Prevention and Reform in England, 1860–1914.* New York: Routledge, 2000.

Barzaghi, Antonio. *Donne o Cortigiane? La Prostituzione a Venezia. Documenti di Costume dal XVK al XVIII secolo.* Verona: Bertani Editore, 1980.

Basch, Francoise. *Relative Creatures: Victorian Women in Society and the Novel.* New York: Schocken, 1974.

Basham, A. L. *The Wonder That Was India.* London: 1954. Reprint, Calcutta: Rupa, 1981.

Basinger, Jeanine. *A Woman's View: How Hollywood Spoke to Women, 1930–1960.* New York: Alfred A. Knopf, 1993.

Bassermann, Lujo. *The Oldest Profession: A History of Prostitution.* New York: Dorset Press, 1965, 1967.

Baston, Lewis. *Sleaze: The State of Britain.* London: Macmillan, 2000.

Bastow, Karen. "Prostitution and HIV/AIDS." *HIV/AIDS Policy and Law Newsletter* 2 (1995). http://www.walnet.org/csis/papers/bastow-aidslaw.html.

Baumeister, Roy F., and Kathleen D. Vohs. "Sexual Economics: Sex as Female Resource for Social Exchange in Heterosexual Interactions." *Personality and Social Psychology Review* 8, no. 4 (2004): 339–63.

Beard, Mary, and John Henderson. "With This Body I Thee Worship: Sacred Prostitution in Antiquity." In *Gender and the Body in the Ancient Mediterranean*, ed. M. Wyke. Oxford: Blackwell Publishers, 1998.

Beck, Stephen V. "Syphilis: The Great Pox." In *Plague, Pox and Pestilence: Disease in History*, ed. Kenneth F. Kiple. New York: Barnes and Noble, 1997.

Becker, Charles, Jean-Pierre Dozon, Christine Obbo, and Mouriba Touré, eds., *Experiencing and Understanding AIDS in Africa*. Paris: Codesria, 1998.

Begg, Paul, Martin Fido, and Keith Skinner. *The Jack the Ripper A-Z*. Terra Alta, WV: Headline, 1996.

Beith-Halahmi, Esther Yael. *Angell Fayre or Strumpet Lewd: Jane Shore as an Example of Erring Beauty in Sixteenth-Century Literature*. 2 vols. Salzburg: Universität Salzburg, 1974.

Bell, Laurie, ed., *Good Girls/Bad Girls: Feminists and Sex Trade Workers Face to Face*. Seattle: Seal Press, 1987.

Bell, Shannon. *Reading, Writing, and Rewriting the Prostitute Body*. Bloomington: Indiana University Press, 1994.

———. *Whore Carnival*. Brooklyn, NY: Autonomedia, 1995.

Bellanger, Marguerite. *Confessions: Mémoires anecdotiques*. Paris: Librairie Populaire, 1882.

Belle, Jennifer. *Going Down: A Novel*. New York: Riverhead Books, 1996.

Benotsch, E., A. M. Somlai, S. D. Pinkerton, J. A. Kelly, D. Ostrovski, C. Gore-Felton, and A. P. Kozlov. "Drug Use and Sexual Risk Behaviors among Female Russian IDUs Who Exchange Sex for Money or Drugs." *International Journal of STD & AIDS* t15 (2004): 343–47.

Berer, Marge, with Sunanda Ray. *Women and HIV/AIDS*. London: Pandora, 1993.

Bericht der Österreichischen Liga zur Bekämpfung des Mädchenhandels über das Vereinsjahr. Vienna: Privately printed, 1908.

Berlin, Jennifer V. "Bahnhof Boys: Policing Male Prostitution in Post-Nazi Berlin." *Journal of the History of Sexuality* 12 (2003): 605–37.

Bernheimer, Charles. *Figures of Ill Repute: Representing Prostitution in Nineteenth-Century France*. Cambridge, MA: Harvard University Press, 1989.

Bernstein, Elizabeth. *Temporarily Yours: Sexual Commerce in Post-Industrial Culture*. Chicago: University of Chicago Press, in press.

———. "The Meaning of the Purchase: Desire, Demand and the Commerce of Sex." *Ethnography* 2, no. 3 (2001): 389–420.

———. "What's Wrong with Prostitution? What's Right with Sex Work? Comparing Markets in Female Sexual Labor." *Hastings Women's Law Journal* 10, no. 1 (1999): 91–117.

Bernstein, Laurie. *Sonia's Daughters: Prostitutes and Their Regulation in Imperial Russia*. Berkeley: University of California Press, 1995.

Bignamini, Ilaria, and Martin Postle. *The Artist's Model: Its Role in British Art from Lely to Etty*. Exh. Cat. Nottingham, England: Nottingham University Art Gallery, 1991.

Bindman, Jo, and Jo Doezema. "Redefining Prostitution as Sex Work on the International Agenda." London: Anti-Slavery International, 1997. http://www.walnet.org/csis/papers/redefining.html.

Bird, Kristina D. "The Use of Spermicide Containing Nonoxynol-9 in the Prevention of HIV Infection." *AIDS* 5 (1991): 791–96.

Bird, Phyllis. *Missing Persons and Mistaken Identities*. Minneapolis: Fortress Press, 1997.

———. "'To Play the Harlot': An Inquiry into an Old Testament Metaphor." In *Gender and Difference in Ancient Israel*, ed. Peggy Day. Minneapolis: Fortress Press, 1989.

Bishop, Ryan, and Lillian S. Robinson. *Night Market: Sexual Cultures and the Thai Economic Miracle*. New York: Routledge, 1998.

Blain, Roxy. "A Female Sex Worker's View." In *Sex Work and Sex Workers in Australia*, ed. Roberta Perkins. Sydney, Australia: UNSW Press, 1991.

Bland, Lucy. 1992. "'Purifying' the Public World: Feminist Vigilantes in Late Victorian England." *Women's History Review* 1 (1992): 397–412.

Bleuel, Hans Peter. *Sex and Society in Nazi Germany.* New York: J. P. Lippincott, 1973.

Bock, Gisela. "Keine Arbeitskräfte in diesem Sinne: Prostituierte im Nazi-Staat." In *"Wir sind Frauen wie andere auch!": Prostitutierte und ihre Kämpfe,* ed. Pieke Biermann. Hamburg: Reinbek, 1980.

Boles, Jacqueline, and Kirk Elifson. "Out of CASH: The Rise and Demise of a Male Prostitutes' Rights Organization." In *Prostitution: On Whores, Hustlers, and Johns,* ed. James E. Elias, Vern L. Bullough, Veronica Elias, and Gwen Brewer. New York: Prometheus Books, 1998.

Bolt, Christine. *The Women's Movements in the United States and Britain from the 1790s to the 1920s.* Amherst: University of Massachusetts Press, 1993.

Bond, Katherine C., David D. Celentano, and Chayan Vaddhanaphuti. "'I'm Not Afraid of Life or Death': Women in Brothels in Northern Thailand." In *Women's Experiences with AIDS: An International Perspective,* ed. Lynellyn Long and Maxine E. Ankrah. New York: Columbia University Press, 1996.

Booth, Karen M. "Technical Difficulties: Experts, Women and the State in Kenya's AIDS Crisis." Ph.D. diss., University of Wisconsin-Madison, 1995.

Bornoff, Nicholas. *Pink Samurai: Love, Marriage, and Sex in Contemporary Japan.* New York: Pocket Books, 1991.

Borzello, Frances. *The Artist's Model.* London: Junction Books, 1982.

Bourgois, P. *In Search of Respect: Selling Crack in El Barrio.* Cambridge MA: Harvard University Press, 1995.

Bowers, Jane, and Judith Tick, eds. *Women Making Music: The Western Art Tradition, 1150–1950.* Urbana: University of Illinois Press, 1987.

Boyle F. M., M. P. Dunne, J. M. Najman, J. S. Western, C. Wod Turrell, and S. Glennon. "Psychological Distress among Female Sex Workers." *Australian and New Zealand Journal of Public Health* 21 (1997): 643–46.

Brame, William, Gloria Brame, and Jon Jacobs. *Different Loving: The World of Sexual Domination and Submission.* New York: Random House, 1993.

Brandt, Allan M. "AIDS: From Social History to Social Policy." In *AIDS: The Burdens of History,* ed. Elizabeth Fee and Daniel M. Fox. Berkeley: University of California Press, 1988.

———. "A Historical Perspective." In *AIDS and the Law: A Guide for the Public,* ed. Harlon L. Dalton and Scott Burris. New Haven, CT: Yale University Press, 1987.

———. *No Magic Bullet: A Social History of Venereal Disease in the United States since 1880.* New York: Oxford University Press, 1985.

Brants, Chrisje. "The Fine Art of Regulated Tolerance: Prostitution in Amsterdam." *Journal of Law and Society* 25, no. 4 (1998): 621–35.

Brennan, Denise. "Selling Sex for Visas: Sex Tourism as a Stepping-Stone to International Migration." In *Global Woman: Nannies, Maids and Sex Workers in the New Economy,* ed. Barbara Ehrenreich and Arlie Russell Rochschild. New York: Metropolitan/Owl Books, 2002.

———. *What's Love Got to Do with It?: Transnational Desires and Sex Tourism in the Dominican Republic.* Durham, NC: Duke University Press, 2004.

Brents, Barbara G., and Kathryn Hausbeck. "State-Sanctioned Sex: Negotiating Formal and Informal Regulatory Practices in Nevada Brothels." *Sociological Perspectives* 44 (2001): 307–32.

———. "Violence and Legalized Brothel Prostitution in Nevada: Examining Safety, Risk, and Prostitution Policy." *Journal of Interpersonal Violence* 20, no. 3 (2005): 270–95.

Brewer, T. H., J. Hasbun, C. A. Ryan, S. E. Hawes, S. Martinez, J. Sanchez, M. Butler De Lister, J. Castanzo, J. Lopez, and K. K. Holmes. "Migration, Ethnicity and Environment: HIV Risk Factors for Women on the Sugar Cane Plantations of the Dominican Republic." *AIDS* 12 (1998): 1879–87.

Bristow, Edward J. *Prostitution and Prejudice: The Jewish Fight against White Slavery 1870–1939.* Oxford: Clarendon Press, 1982.

———. *Vice and Vigilance: Purity Movements in Britain since 1700.* Totowa, NJ: Rowman and Littlefield, 1977.

Broberg, G., and N. Roll-Hansen, eds. *Eugenics and the Welfare State: Sterilization Policy in Denmark, Sweden, Norway and Finland.* East Lansing: Michigan State University Press, 1996.

Brock, Debi. *Making Work, Making Trouble: Prostitution as a Social Problem.* Toronto: University of Toronto Press, 1998.

———. "Prostitutes Are Scapegoats in the AIDS Panic." *Resources for Feminist Research* 18 (1989): 13–17.

Bromberg, Sara. "Feminist Issues in Prostitution." In *Prostitution: On Whores, Hustlers, and Johns,* ed. James Elias, Vern L. Bullough, Veronica Elias and Gwen Brewer. New York: Prometheus Books, 1998.

Broude, Norma. "Degas's Misogyny." In *Feminism and Art History: Questioning the Litany,* ed. Norma Broude and Mary D. Garrard. Boulder, CO: Westview Press, 1982.

———, and Mary D. Garrard. *The Expanding Discourse: Feminism and Art History.* New York: HarperCollins, 1992.

Broun, Heywood. *Anthony Comstock, Roundsman of the Lord.* New York: Boni, 1927. Reprint, Whitefish, MT: Kessinger Publishing, 2004.

Brown, Larry K. *The Hog Ranches of Wyoming: Liquor, Lust and Lies under Sagebrush Skies.* Glendo, WY: High Plains Press, 1995.

Browne, Jan, and Victor Minichiello. "Promoting Safer Sex in the Male Sex Work Industry: A Professional Responsibility." *AIDS Patient Care* 11 (1997): 353–58.

———. "The Social and Work Context of Commercial Sex between Men: A Research Note." *Australian and New England Journal of Sociology* 32 (1996): 86–92.

Bruckert, Chris, Colette Parent, and Pascale Robitaille. "Erotic Service/Erotic Dance Establishments: Two Types of Marginalized Labour." Ottawa: Law Commission of Canada, 2003. http://www.lcc.gc.ca/research_project/03_erotic_1-en.asp?lang_update=1.

Brundage, James A. *Law, Sex, and Christian Society in Medieval Europe.* Chicago: University of Chicago Press, 1987.

———. "Prostitution in the Medieval Canon Law." *Signs: Journal of Women in Culture and Society* 1 (1975): 825–45.

Brussa, Licia, ed. *Health, Migration and Sex Work: The Experience of TAMPEP.* Amsterdam: TAMPEP International, 1999.

Buchwald, Emilie, Pamela R. Fletcher, and Martha Roth, eds. *Transforming a Rape Culture.* Minneapolis, MN: Milkweed Editions, 1993.

Buckner, Margaret. "Village Women as Town Prostitutes: Cultural Factors Relevant to Prostitution and HIV Epidemiology in Guinea Bissau." In *Social Sciences and AIDS in Africa: Review and Prospects; Experiencing and Understanding AIDS in Africa.* Paris: Karthala, 1999.

Budin, Stephanie L. "*Pallakai,* Prostitutes, and Prophetesses." *Classical Philology* 98 (2003): 148–59.

———. "Sacred Prostitution in the First Person." In *Prostitutes and Courtesans in the Ancient World,* ed. Laura McClure and Christopher Faraone. Madison: University of Wisconsin Press, 2006.

Bujra, J. M. "Production, Property, Prostitution—Sexual Politics in Atu." *Cahiers d' Etudes Africanes* 17 (1977): 13–39.

———. "Proleterianization and the 'Informal Economy': A Case Study from Nairobi." *African Urban Studies* 3 (1978–79): 47–66.

Bullough, Vern L. *The History of Prostitution.* New York: University Books, 1954.

———, and Bonnie Bullough. *Sexual Attitudes: Myths and Realities.* New York: Prometheus Books, 1995.

———, and Bonnie Bullough. *Sin, Sickness, and Sanity: A History of Sexual Attitudes.* New York: New American Library, 1977.

————, and Bonnie Bullough. *Women and Prostitution: A Social History*. New York: Crown Books, 1987.

Burris S., and D. Villena. "Adapting to the Reality of Difficult HIV Policy Choices in Russia, China, and India." *Human Rights* (Winter 2002). http://www.abanet.org/irr/hr/fall04/reality.htm.

Burtt, Shelley. "The Societies for the Reformation of Manners: Between John Locke and the Devil in Augustan England." In *The Margins of Orthodoxy: Heterodox Writing and Cultural Response, 1660–1750*, ed. Roger D. Lund. Cambridge: Cambridge University Press, 1995.

Butcher, Kate. "Feminists, Prostitutes and HIV." In *AIDS: Setting a Feminist Agenda*, ed. Lesley Doyal, Jennie Naidoo, and Tamsin Wilton. London: Taylor and Francis, 1994.

Butler, Anne M. *Daughters of Joy, Sisters of Misery: Prostitutes in the American West 1865–1890*. Champaign: University of Illinois Press, 1985.

Butler, Anne. "Military Myopia: Prostitution on the Frontier." *Prologue: Journal of the National Archives* 13, no. 4 (1981): 233–50.

Butler, Josephine. "The Double-Standard of Morality." *Philanthropist*, October 1886.

Cabezas, Amalia. "Discourses of Prostitution: The Case of Cuba." In *Global Sex Workers: Rights, Resistance, and Redefinition*, ed. Kamala Kempadoo and Jo Doezema. New York: Routledge, 1998.

Calandruccio, Giuseppe. "A Review of Recent Research on Human Trafficking in the Middle East." *International Migration* 43, nos. 1/2 (2005): 267–99.

Califia, Pat. *Public Sex: The Culture of Radical Sex*. San Francisco: Cleis Press, 1994.

Callen, Anthea. *The Spectacular Body: Science, Method and Meaning in the Work of Degas*. New Haven, CT: Yale University Press, 1995.

Cameron, Liz. "Research: Empowering or Exploitative?" In *Partnership for Prevention: A Report of a Meeting between Women's Health Advocates, Program Planners, and Scientists*. Washington, DC: Program Council for Women's Health and the International Women's Health Coalition, 1994. www.popcouncil.org/pdfs/ebert/partprev.pdf.

Campbell, Carole A. "Prostitution, AIDS, and Preventive Health Behavior." *Social Science Medicine* 32 (1991):1367–78.

Campbell, Maria. *Halfbreed*. Toronto: McClelland and Stewart, 1973.

Campbell, Rosie. "Invisible Men: Making Visible Male Clients of Female Prostitutes in Merseyside." In *Prostitution: On Whores, Hustlers, and Johns*, ed. James E. Elias, Vern L. Bullough, Veronica Elias, and Gwen Brewer. New York: Prometheus Books, 1998.

Campbell, Russell. "'Fallen Woman' Prostitute Narratives in Cinema." http://www.latrobe.edu.au/screeningthepast/firstrelease/fr1199/rcfr8b.htm.

Canosa, Romano, and Isabella Colonnello. *Storia della prostituzione in Italia dal quattrocento alla fine del settecento*. Rome: Sapere 2000.

Carby, Hazel. "It Just Be's Dat Way Sometime: The Sexual Politics of Women's Blues." *Radical America* 20 (1986): 9–22.

Carlton, Charles. *Royal Mistresses*. London: Routledge, 1990.

Carmen, Arlene, and Howard Moody. *Working Women: The Subterranean World of Street Prostitution*. New York: Harper and Row, 1985.

Casillo, Charles. *Outlaw: The Lives and Careers of John Rechy*. Los Angeles: Advocate Books, 2002.

Castillo, D. A., M.G.R. Gomez, and B. Delgado. "Border Lives: Prostitute Women in Tijuana." *Signs* 24 (1999): 387–422.

Caukins, S., and N. Coombs. "The Psychodynamics of Male Prostitution." *American Journal of Psychotherapy* 30 (1975): 441–52.

Cavan, Sherri. *Liquor License: An Ethnography of Bar Behavior*. Chicago: Aldine, 1966.

Centers for Disease Control. "The CDC Tuskegee Syphilis Study Page." http://www.cdc.gov/nchstp/od/tuskegee/index.html.

Central and Eastern Europe Harm Reduction Network. *Sex Work, HIV/AIDS and Human Rights in Central and Eastern Europe and Central Asia*. Vilnius, Lithuania: CEEHRN, 2005.

Chancer, L. "Prostitution, Feminist Theory, and Ambivalence: Notes from the Sociological Underground." *Social Text* 37 (1993):143–72.

Chancer, Lynn. *Reconcilable Differences*. Berkeley: University of California Press, 1998.

Chang, Kang-i Sun, and Haun Saussy, eds. *Women Writers of Traditional China*. Stanford, CA: Stanford University Press, 1999.

Chapkis, Wendy. *Live Sex Acts: Women Performing Erotic Labor*. New York: Routledge, 1997.

———. "Power and Control in the Commercial Sex Trade." In *Sex for Sale: Prostitution, Pornography, and the Sex Industry*, ed. Ronald John Weitzer. New York: Routledge, 2000.

———. "Trafficking, Migration, and the Law: Protecting Innocents, Punishing Immigrants." *Gender and Society* 17, no. 6 (2003): 923–37.

Chapman, H. Perry. *Jan Steen: Painter and Storyteller*. Washington, DC: National Gallery of Art, 1996.

Chaudhuri, Nirad C. *The Continent of Circe: An Essay on the Peoples of India*. London: Chatto and Windus, 1975.

Chauncey, George. *Gay New York: Gender, Urban Culture, and the Making of the Gay World, 1890–1940*. New York: Basic Books, 1994.

Cheng, Weikun. "The Challenge of the Actresses: Female Performers and Cultural Alternatives in Early Twentieth Century Beijing and Tianjin." *Modern China* 22, no. 2 (April 1996): 197–233.

———. "The Use of 'Public' Women: Commercialized Performance, Nation-Building, and Actresses' Strategies in Early Twentieth-Century Beijing." *Working Papers on Women and International Development* 275. East Lansing, MI: Michigan State University, June 2002.

Chesler, Ellen. *Woman of Valor: Margaret Sanger and the Birth Control Movement in America*. New York: Anchor Books, 1992.

Christian, Laurent, Karim Seke, Ndeye Coumba, Toune Kane et al. "Prevalence of HIV and Other Sexually Transmitted Infections, and Risk Behaviors in Unregistered Sex Workers in Dakar, Senegal." *AIDS* 17 (2002): 1811–16.

Christiansen, Rupert. *Tales of the New Babylon: Paris 1869–1875*. London: Sinclair-Stevenson, 1994.

Clancy-Smith, Julia. "Islam, Gender, and Identities in the Making of French Algeria." *Domesticating the Empire: Race, Gender and Family Life in French and Dutch Colonialism, 1830–1962*. Charlottesville: University Press of Virginia, 1998.

———. "Marginality and Migration: Europe's Social Outcasts in Pre-colonial Tunisia, 1830–81." In *Outside In: On the Margins of the Modern Middle East*, ed. Eugene Rogan. New York: I. B. Tauris, 2002.

———, and Frances Gouda. Introduction to *Domesticating the Empire: Race, Gender and Family Life in French and Dutch Colonialism, 1830–1962*. Charlottesville: University Press of Virginia, 1998.

Clark, Timothy J. "A Bar at the Folies Bergère." In *The Painting of Modern Life: Manet and His Contemporaries*, ed. Bradford Collins. Princeton, NJ: Princeton University Press, 1996.

Clayson, Hollis. *Painted Love: Prostitution in French Art of the Impressionist Era*. New Haven, CT: Yale University Press, 1991.

Cleland, John. *Memoirs of a Woman of Pleasure*, ed. Peter Sabor. New York: Oxford University Press, 1985.

Clement, Elizabeth. "Prostitution and Community in Turn-of-the-Century New York City." In *Prostitution: On Whores, Hustlers, and Johns*, ed. James E. Elias, Vern L. Bullough, Veronica Elias, and Gwen Brewer. New York: Prometheus Books, 1998.

Clements, Tracy M. "Prostitution and the American Health Care System: Denying Access to a Group of Women in Need." *Berkeley Women's Law Journal* 11 (1996):49–98.

Cleugh, James. *The Marquis and the Chevalier.* New York: Duell, Sloan and Pearce, 1952.

Cloke, Gillian. *"This Female Man of God": Women and Spiritual Power in the Patristic Age,* A.D. *350–450.* New York: Routledge, 1995.

Coalition against Trafficking in Women. "CATW Debates Pro-Prostitution NGOS." *Coalition Report* 5–6 (1998–2000): 8–9.

Cobb, Jodi. *Geisha: The Life, the Voices, the Art.* New York: Alfred A. Knopf, 1995.

Cohen, Bernard. *Deviant Street Networks: Prostitution in New York City.* Lexington, MA: Lexington Books, 1980.

Cohen, Edward E. "An Economic Analysis of Athenian Prostitution." In *Courtesans and Prostitutes in the Ancient World,* ed. Laura McClure and Christopher Faraone. Madison: University of Wisconsin Press, 2006.

Cohen, Judith B., and Priscilla Alexander. "Female Sex Workers: Scapegoats in the AIDS Epidemic." In *Women at Risk: Issues in the Primary Prevention of AIDS,* ed. A. O'Leary and L. S. Jemmott. New York: Plenum, 1995.

———, and Constance Wofsy. "Prostitutes and AIDS: Public Policy Issues." *AIDS and Public Policy Journal* 3 (1988): 16–22.

Cohen, Patricia Cline. *The Murder of Helen Jewett.* New York: Random House, 1998.

Cohen, Sherrill. *The Evolution of Women's Asylums since 1500: From Refuges for Ex-prostitutes to Shelters for Battered Women.* New York: Oxford University Press, 1992.

Cohen, Stanley. *Folk Devils and Moral Panics: The Creation of the The Mods and Rockers.* London: Martin Robinson, 1972.

Cohen, Yehudi. "The Sociology of Commercialized Prostitution in Okinawa." *Social Forces* 37, no. 2 (1958): 160–68.

Colette. *Seven by Colette.* New York: Farrar, Strauss, and Cudahy, 1955.

Collins, Bradford, ed. *Twelve Views of Manet's Bar.* Princeton, NJ: Princeton University Press, 1996.

Colombier, Marie. *Mémoires: Fin d'Empire.* Paris: Flammarion, 1898.

Colton, John, and Clemence Randolph. *Rain: A Play in Three Acts.* New York: Boni and Liveright, 1925.

Commonwealth Department of Health and Aging. "5th National HIV Strategy; Revitalising Australia's Response." Canberra, Australia: Commonwealth of Australia, 2005.

Connelly, Mark Thomas. *The Response to Prostitution in the Progressive Era.* Chapel Hill: University of North Carolina Press, 1980.

Cook, Richard I. "'The Great Leviathan of Leachery': Mandeville's *Modest Defence of Publick Stews* (1724)." In *Mandeville Studies: New Explorations in the Art and Thought of Dr. Bernard Mandeville 1670–1733,* ed. I. Primer. The Hague: Martinus Nijhoff, 1975.

Cooke, Thomas Darlington. *The Old French and Chaucerian Fabliaux: A Study of Their Comic Climax.* Columbia: University of Georgia Press, 1978.

Cooper, Douglas. *Masters of Art: Toulouse-Lautrec.* New York: Harry N. Abrams, 1983.

Corbin, Alain. *Women for Hire: Prostitution and Sexuality in France after 1850.* Translated by Alan Sheridan. Cambridge, MA: Harvard University Press, 1990.

Cordasco, Francesco, and Thomas Monroe Pitkin. *The White Slave Trade and the Immigrants: A Chapter in American Social History.* Detroit: Blaine Ethridge, 1981.

Corley, Kathleen. *Private Women, Public Meals.* Peabody, MA: Hendrickson Publishers, 1993.

Corso, Carla, and Sandra Landi. *Ritratto a Tinte Forti.* Florence: Giunti Gruppo Editoriale, 1991.

Cott, Nancy. "Passionlessness: An Interpretation of Victorian Sexual Ideology, 1790–1850." *Signs* 4 (Winter 1978): 219–36.

Cotton, Ann, Melissa Farley, and Robert Baron. "Attitudes toward Prostitution and Acceptance of Rape Myths." *Journal of Applied Social Psychology* 32, no. 9 (2002): 1790–96.

Crago, Anna Louise. "Unholy Alliance." www.alternet.org.

Craig, Alec. *The Banned Books of England.* London: Allen and Unwin, 1962.

Cressey, Paul, *The Taxi Hall Dance.* Chicago: University of Chicago Press, 1932.

Crosby, Sarah. "Health Care Provision for Prostitute Women: A Holistic Approach." In *Prostitution: On Whores, Hustlers, and Johns,* ed. James E. Elias, Vern L. Bullough, Veronica Elias, and Gwen Brewer. New York: Prometheus Books, 1998.

Crouch, Emma Elizabeth. *The Memoirs of Cora Pearl.* London: George Vickers, 1886.

Curtis, T. C., and W. A. Speck. "The Societies for the Reformation of Manners: A Case Study of the Theory and Practice of Moral Reform." *Literature and History* 3 (1976): 45–64.

Cusick, L. "Non-use of Condoms by Prostitute Women." *AIDS Care* 10 (1998): 133–46.

D'Costa, Lourdes J., Francis A. Plummer, Ian Bowmer, Lieve Fransen, Peter Piot, Allen R. Ronald, and Herbert Nsanze. "Prostitutes Are a Major Reservoir of Sexually Transmitted Diseases in Nairobi, Kenya." *Sexually Transmitted Diseases* 12 (1985): 64–67.

D'Emilio, John D., and Estelle B. Freedman. *Intimate Matters: A History of Sexuality in America.* New York: Harper and Row, 1988.

Dalby, Liza Crihfield. *Geisha.* Berkeley: University of California Press, 1983.

Dalla, Rochelle. "Exposing the 'Pretty Woman' Myth: A Qualitative Examination of the Lives of Female Streetwalking Prostitutes." *Journal of Sex Research* 37, no. 4 (2000): 344–53.

Dally, Ann. *Women under the Knife.* London: Routledge. 1992.

Damodaragupta. *Kuttani-mata.* Edited by T. M. Tripathi. Calcutta: Asiatic Society of Bengal, 1944.

Dangerous Bedfellows, ed. *Policing Public Sex.* Boston: South End Press, 1996.

Danville, Eric. *The Complete Linda Lovelace.* New York: Power Process Publishing, 2001.

Darrow, William W. "Assessing Targeted AIDS Prevention in Male and Female Prostitutes and Their Clients." In *Assessing AIDS Prevention,* ed. F. Paccaud, J .P. Vader, and F. Gutzwiller. Basel: Birkhäuser Verlag, 1992.

———. "Prostitution, Intravenous Drug Use, and HIV-1 in the United States." In *AIDS, Drugs, and Prostitution,* ed. Martin Plant. London: Tavistock/Routledge, 1990.

———. "Prostitution and Sexually Transmitted Diseases." In *Sexually Transmitted Diseases,* ed. King K. Holmes. New York: McGraw-Hill, 1984.

Dauphin, Claudine. *Brothels, Baths, and Babes: Prostitution in the Byzantine Holy Land.* Vol. 3. Dublin, Ireland: University College, 1996.

Davanzo Poli, Doretta, et al. *Il gioco dell'amore: Le Cortegiane di Venezia dal Trecento al Settecento.* Milan: Berenice, 1990.

Davenport-Hines, Richard. *Sex, Death and Punishment: Attitudes to Sex and Sexuality in Britain since the Renaissance.* London: Fontana Press/HarperCollins, 1990.

Davidson, James N. *Courtesans and Fishcakes: The Consuming Passions of Classical Athens.* New York: St. Martin's Press, 1998.

Davidson, Julia O. *Children in the Global Sex Trade.* London: Polity Press, 2005.

Davies, John Booth. *The Myth of Addiction.* Amsterdam: Harwood Academic Publishers, 1998.

Davis, Angela Y. *Blues Legacies and Black Feminism: Gertrude "Ma" Rainey, Bessie Smith, and Billie Holiday.* New York: Pantheon Books, 1998.

Davis, Kingsley. "The Sociology of Prostitution." *American Sociological Review* 2 (October 1937): 746–55.

Davis, Sylvia, with Martha Shaffer. "Prostitution in Canada: Invisible Menace or the Menace of Invisibility?" 1994. http://www.walnet.org/csis/papers/sdavis.html.

Day, Sophie. "Editorial Review: Prostitute Women and AIDS: Anthropology." *AIDS* 2 (1988): 421–28.

De Becker, J. E. *The Nightless City, or, the History of the Yoshiwara Yukwaku*. 1899. Reprint, New York: ICG Muse, 2003.

Decker, John F. "Prostitution as a Public Health Issue." In *AIDS and the Law: A Guide for the Public*, ed. Harlon L. Dalton, Scott Burris, and the Yale AIDS Law Project. New Haven, CT: Yale University Press, 1987.

Decker, John R. *Prostitution: Regulation and Control*. Littleton, CO: Fred B. Rothman, 1979.

De Graaf, Lawrence B. "Race, Sex, and Region: Black Women in the American West, 1850–1920." *Pacific Historical Review* 49 (May 1980): 285–313.

De Graaf, Ron. *Prostitutes and Their Clients: Sexual Networks and Determinants of Condom Use*. Den Haag: CIP-Gegevens Koninklijke Bibliotheek, 1995.

Delacoste, Frederique, and Priscilla Alexander, eds. *Sex Work: Writings by Women in the Sex Industry*. San Francisco: Cleis Press, 1998.

Dell'Orso, Claudio. *Venezia erotica*. Florence: Glittering Images, 1995.

———. *Venezia Libertina: I Luoghi della Memoria Erotica*. Venice: Arsenale, 1999.

Demaere, Kate. "Decriminalisation as Partnership: An Overview of Australia's Sex Industry Law Reform Model." *Research for Sex Work* 8 (2005): 14–15. http://www.researchforsexwork.org.

Demand, Nancy. *Birth, Death, and Motherhood in Classical Greece*. Baltimore: Johns Hopkins University Press, 1994.

De Marco, J. "The World of Gay Strippers." *Gay and Lesbian Review* (March/April 2002): 12–14.

Dembrowski, P. F. *La Vie de Ste. Marie Egyptienne*. Geneva: Droz, 1977.

Denisova, Tatyana A. "Trafficking in Women and Children for Purposes of Sexual Exploitation: The Criminological Aspect." *Trends in Organized Crime* 6 (2001): 30–36.

Denning, Lord Alfred. *John Profumo and Christine Keeler 1963*. London: H. M. Stationery Office, 1963.

Deren S., M. Shedlin, W. Davis Rees, M. C. Clatts, S. Balcorta, M. M. Beardsley, J. Sanchez, and D. Des Jarlais. "Dominican, Mexican, and Puerto Rican Prostitutes: Drug Use and Sexual Behaviors." *Hispanic Journal of Behavioral Science* 19 (1997): 202–13.

Desquitado, Marivic R. *Behind the Shadows: Towards a Better Understanding of Prostituted Women*. Davao City, The Philippines: Talikala, Inc., 1992.

Devereux, Cicely. "'The Maiden Tribute' and the Rise of the White Slave in the Ninteenth Century: The Making of an Imperial Construct." *Victorian Review* 26 (2001): 1–23.

Diana, Lewis. *The Prostitute and Her Clients: Your Pleasure Is Her Business*. Springfield, IL: Charles C. Thomas, 1985.

Dickie, Phil. "Civilising the Sex Trade." Brisbane Institute, 25 July 2001. http://www.brisinst.org.au/resources/dickie_phil_prostitution.html.

Dickinson, Peter. *Here Is Queer: Nationalisms, Sexualities and the Literatures of Canada*. Toronto: University of Toronto Press, 1999.

"Dime Novels and Penny Dreadfuls." http://www-sul.stanford.edu/depts/dp/pennies/home.html.

Dinan, Kinsey Alden. "Establishing an International Standard for States' Treatment of Trafficked Persons: The UN Anti-Trafficking Protocol and the UN Convention against Transnational Organized Crime." In *"To Prevent, Suppress and Punish": Ideology, Globalization and the Politics of Human Trafficking*, ed. Nancie Caraway. New York: Routledge, forthcoming.

Ditmore, Melissa. "Addressing Sex Work as Labor." http://www.swimw.org/aslabor.html.

———. "Contemporary Anti-trafficking Legislation in the United States." http://www.nswp.org/mobility/legislation.html.

———. "How Immigration Status Affects Sex Workers' Health and Vulnerability to Abuse: A Comparison of Two Countries." *Research for Sex Work* 5, 2002. http://www.med.vu.nl/hcc/artikelen/ditmore5.htm.

———. "Hysterical Policy: Morality in New Laws Addressing Trafficking and Sex Work." Paper presented at the annual conference of the Institute for Women's Policy Research, Washington, DC, June 23, 2003. http://www.iwpr.org/pdf/Ditmore_Melissa.pdf.

———. "L'ethique dans les Essays Incluant des Travailleuses du Sexe." *Action* 98 Paris: Act Up Paris, 2005.

———. "New U.S. Funding Policies on Trafficking Affect Sex Work HIV-Prevention Efforts World Wide." *SIECUS Report* 33 (2005): 26–29.

———. "Reaching Out to Sex Workers." *Reaching the Hardly Reached (Program for Appropriate Technology and Health).* 2002. http://www.path.org/files/RHR-Article-3.pdf.

———. "Report from the USA: Do Prohibitory Laws Promote Risk?" *Research for Sex Work* 4, 2001. http://www.med.vu.nl/hcc/artikelen/ditmore.htm.

———. "Sex Workers Are Organizing in Kolkata." In *New Sociologies,* ed. Patricia Clough and Jean Halley. Chapel Hill, NC: Duke University Press, forthcoming.

———. "Trafficking in Lives: The Impact of New International Anti-Trafficking Law in Asia." In *Trafficking and Prostitution Reconsidered: New Perspectives on Migration, Sex Work and Human Rights,* ed. Kamala Kempadoo, Bandana Pattanaik, and Jyothi Sanghera. Boulder, CO: Paradigm Press, 2005.

———, and Catherine Poulcallec-Gordon. "Human Rights Violations: The Acceptance of Violence against Sex Workers." *Research for Sex Work* 6 (2003): 20–21.

———, and Marjan Wijers. "The Negotiations on the UN Protocol on Trafficking in Persons: Moving the Focus from Morality to Actual Conditions." *Nemesis,* no. 4 (2003). Network of Sex Work Projects Web site http://www.nswp.org/pdf/NEMESIS.PDF.

———, and Penelope Saunders. "Sex Work and Sex Trafficking." *Sexual Health Exchange* 1 (1998). http://www.kit.nl/information_services/exchange_content/html/1998_1_sex_work.asp.

Do Espirito Santo, Maria Eugeñia G., and Gina Etheredge. "And Then I Became a Prostitute … Some Aspects of Prostitution and Brothel Prostitutes in Dakar, Senegal." *Social Science Journal* 41 (2004): 137–46.

Doezema, Jo. "Forced to Choose: Beyond the Voluntary v. Forced Prostitution Dichotomy." In *Global Sex Workers: Rights, Resistance, and Redefinition,* ed. Kamala Kempadoo and Jo Doezema. New York: Routledge, 1998, pp. 34–50.

———. "Loose Women or Lost Women? The Re-emergence of the Myth of 'White Slavery' in Contemporary Discourses of 'Trafficking in Women.'" *Gender Issues* 18 (2000): 23–50. http://www.walnet.org/csis/papers/doezema-loose.html.

———. "Ouch! Western Feminists' 'Wounded Attachment' to the Third-World Prostitute." *Feminist Review* 67 (2001): 16–38.

Dollimore, Jonathan. "Shakespeare Understudies: The Sodomite, the Prostitute, the Transvestite and Their Critics." In *Essays in Cultural Materialism.* 2nd ed., ed. Jonathan Dollimore and Alan Sinfield. Ithaca, NY: Cornell University Press, 1994.

Donaldson, Stephen. *A Million Jockers, Punks, and Queens: Sex among American Male Prisoners and Its Implications for Concepts of Sexual Orientation.* New York: Stop Prisoner Rape, 1993. http://www.spr.org.

Donovan, Pamela. *No Way of Knowing: Crime, Urban Legends, and the Internet.* New York: Routledge, 2003.

Downer, Lesley. *Women of the Pleasure Quarters: The Secret History of the Geisha.* New York: Broadway Books, 2001.

Drachman, Virginia. "The Loomis Trial: Social Mores and Obstetrics in the Mid-Nineteenth Century." In *Women and Health in America,* ed. Judith Waltzer Leavitt. Madison: University of Wisconsin Press, 1984.

Dreizin, A. "Work with 'Street' Prostitutes in the Framework of a Harm Reduction Project in Kaliningrad." *Russian Journal of HIV/AIDS and Related Issues* 4, no. 1 (2000): 134.

Drew, William M. *D. W. Griffith's Intolerance: Its Genesis and Its Vision.* Jefferson, NC: McFarland, 1986.

DuBois, Ellen Carol, and Linda Gordon. "Seeking Ecstasy on the Battlefield: Danger and Pleasure in Nineteenth-Century Feminist Sexual Thought." In *Pleasure and Danger*, ed. Carole Vance. Boston: Routledge and Kegan Paul, 1984.

Duggan, Lisa, and Nan Hunter. *Sex Wars: Sexual Dissent and Political Culture.* New York: Routledge, 1995.

Dunae, Patrick. "Penny Dreadfuls: Late Nineteenth-Century Boys' Literature and Crime." *Victorian Studies* 22 (1979):133–50.

Durbar Mahila Samanwaya Committee. "Manifesto for Sex Workers' Rights." 1997. BAYSWAN Web site http://www.bayswan.org/manifest.html.

Duval, Jean. *A Study of Prostitution in Shanghai at the End of the Qing Dynasty as It Appears in the "Shanghai" Novels.* Paris: VERLCA, 1972.

Dworkin, Andrea. *Intercourse.* New York: Free Press, 1987.

———. *Pornography: Men Possessing Women.* New York: Perigee, 1981.

———. *Woman Hating.* New York: Dutton, 1974.

———, and Catharine MacKinnon, eds. *In Harm's Way: The Pornography Civil Rights Hearings.* Cambridge, MA: Harvard University Press, 1997.

Eadie, Jo, ed. *Sexuality: The Essential Glossary.* London: Hodder Arnold Publishers, 2004.

Echols, Alice. "The Taming of the Id." In *Pleasure and Danger*, ed. Carole Vance. Boston: Routledge and Kegan Paul, 1984.

Edlin, Brian R., Kathleen L. Irwin, Sairus Faruque, Clyde B. McCoy, Carl Word, Yolanda Serrano, James A. Inciardi, Benjamin P. Bowser, Robert F. Schilling, and Scott D. Holmberg for the Multicenter Crack Cocaine and HIV Infection Study Team. "Intersecting Epidemics—Crack Cocaine Use and HIV Infection among Inner-City Young Adults." *New England Journal of Medicine* 331, no. 21 (1994): 1422–27.

Egger, Steven A. *The Need to Kill: Inside the World of the Serial Killer.* Upper Saddle River, NJ: Prentice Hall, 2003.

Ehrenreich, Barbara, and Arlie Russell Hochschild, eds. *Global Woman: Nannies, Maids, and Sex Workers in the New Economy.* New York: Henry Holt, 2002.

El-Bassel N., and S. Witte. "Designing Effective HIV Prevention Strategies for Female Street Sex Workers." *AIDS Patient Care and STDs* 12 (1998): 599–603.

———, Robert F. Schilling, Kathleen L. Irwin, Sairus Faruque, L. Gilbert, J. Von Bargen, Yolanda Serrano, and Brian R. Edlin. "Sex Trading and Psychological Distress among Women Recruited from the Streets of Harlem." *American Journal of Public Health* 87 (1997): 66–70.

Elias, James E., Vern L. Bullough, Veronica Elias, and Gwen Brewer, eds. *Prostitution: On Whores, Hustlers, and Johns.* New York: Prometheus Books, 1998, pp. 91–106.

Elliot, Robert C., ed. *Twentieth Century Interpretations of* Moll Flanders: *A Collection of Critical Essays.* Englewood Cliffs, NJ: Prentice Hill, 1970.

Ellman, Richard. *Oscar Wilde.* New York: Alfred A. Knopf, 1984, 1987.

Emeljanow, Victor. "Lola Montez." In *American National Biography.* Vol. XV. New York: Oxford University Press, 1999.

English, Dierdre. "The Fear That Feminism Will Free Men First." In *Powers of Desire*, ed. Ann Snitow, Christine Stansell, and Sharon Thompson. New York: Monthly Review Press, 1983.

Enloe, Cynthia. *Bananas, Beaches and Bases: Making Feminist Sense of International Politics.* London: Pandora Press, 1989.

———. *Does Khaki Become You?: The Militarisation of Women's Lives.* Boston: South End Press, 1983.

Ennew, Judith. *The Sexual Exploitation of Children*. Cambridge: Polity Press, 1986.

———, Kusum Gopal, Janet Heeran, and Heather Montgomery. *Children and Prostitution. How Can We Measure and Monitor the Commercial Sexual Exploitation of Children? Literature Review and Annotated Bibliography*. 1996. Oslo, Childwatch International Web site http://childabuse.com/childhouse/childwatch/cwi/projects/indicators/prostitution/.

Erenberg, Lewis A. *Steppin' Out: New York Nightlife and the Transformation of American Culture*. Westport, CT: Greenwood Press, 1984.

Erickson, P., D. Riley, Y. Cheung, and P. O'Hare, eds. *Harm Reduction: A New Direction for Policies and Programs*. Toronto: University of Toronto Press, 1997.

Escoffier, Jeffrey. "Porn Star/Stripper/Escort: Economic and Sexual Dynamics in a Sex Work Career." In *Male Sex Workers*, ed. Todd Morrison. Binghampton, NY: Haworth Press, forthcoming.

Estébanez, P., and J. C. Grant. "The Value of Workplace versus Income in Determining HIV Status and Other STDs among a Sample of Spanish Sex Workers." *STDs* 25 (1998): 194–95.

———, K. Fitch, and R. Nájera. "HIV and Female Sex Workers." *Bulletin of the World Health Organization* 71 (1993): 397–412.

Fabian, Cosi. "The Holy Whore: A Woman's Gateway to Power." In *Whores and Other Feminists*, ed. Jill Nagle. New York: Routledge, 1997.

Fagbohungbe, Tunde, ed. *The Rape of the Innocents: Evolving an African Initiative against Human Trafficking*. Proceedings of the First Pan African Conference on Human Trafficking, Abuja, Nigeria, 19–23 February 2001.

Fahmy, Khaled. "Prostitution in Egypt in the Nineteenth Century." In *Outside In: On the Margins of the Modern Middle East*, ed. Eugene Rogan. New York: I. B. Tauris, 2002.

Fairstein, Linda. *Sexual Violence: Our War against Rape*. New York: William Morrow, 1993.

Family Health International. "Microbicide Products Enter Human Trials." http://www.FHI.org/en/RH/Pubs/Network/v20_2/Nwvol20–2microbicides.htm.

Farley, Melissa, Isin Baral, Merab Kiremire and Ufuk Sezgin. "Prostitution in Five Countries: Violence and Posttraumatic Stress Disorder." *Feminism and Psychology* 8, no. 4 (1998): 405–26.

———, and Barkan, H. "Prostitution, Violence against Women, and Posttraumatic Stress Disorder." *Women and Health* 27 (1998): 37–49.

———, A. Cotton, J. Lynne et al. "Prostitution and Trafficking in Nine Countries: An Update on Violence and Posttraumatic Stress Disorder." In *Prostitution, Trafficking and Traumatic Stress*, ed. M. Farley. Binghamton, NY: Haworth Press, 2003.

FaSanto, Maria Eugenia, G. Do Espirito, and Gina D. Etheredge. "And Then I Became a Prostitute … Some Aspects of Prostitution and Brothel Prostitutes in Dakar, Senegal." *Social Science Journal* 41 (2004): 137–46.

Feder, Sid. *The Luciano Story*. New York: D. McKay, 1954.

Fee, Elizabeth. "Sin vs. Science: Venereal Disease in Baltimore in the Twentieth Century." *Journal of the History of Medicine and Allied Sciences* 43 (1988): 141–64.

Fellner, Jamie, and Marc Mauer. *Losing the Vote: The Impact of Felony Disenfranchisement Laws in the United States*. New York: Human Rights Watch, the Sentencing Project, 1998.

Fessenden, Tracy, Nicholas F. Radel, and Magdalena J. Zabrorwska. *The Puritan Origins of Sex: Religion, Sexuality, and National Identity in American Literature*. New York: Routledge, 2001.

Fine, Bob. "Labelling Theory: An Investigation into the Sociological Critique of Deviance." *Economy and Society* 6 (1977): 166–93.

Finger, Ernest, and A[nton] Baumgarten. *Sammlung der für die Bekämpfung des Mädchenhandels in etracht kommenden österreichischen Gesetze, Verordnungen und Erlässe*. Vienna: Privately printed, 1909.

Finnegan, Frances. *Do Penance or Perish: Magdalen Asylums in Ireland*. Oxford: Oxford University Press, 2004.

————. *Poverty and Prostitution: A Study of Victorian Prostitutes in York*. Cambridge: Cambridge University Press, 1979.

Fiorenza, Elisabeth Schuessler. *In Memory of Her*. New York: Crossroad, 1985.

Fischer, B., S. Wortley, C. Webster, and M. Kirst. "The Socio-Legal Dynamics and Implications of Diversion: The Case Study of the Toronto 'John School' for Prostitution Offenders." *Criminal Justice* 2 (2003): 385–410.

Fisher, Trevor. *Prostitution and the Victorians*. New York: St. Martin's, 1997.

Fisk, Robert. "A Nation's Best-Kept Secret: The Women Lured to Lebanon with a One-Way Ticket into Slavery." *Independent*, 6 July 2002.

Fissell, Mary E. "Speculations on the Speculum." *Women's Health in Primary Care* 3 (2000): 298.

Fleiss, Heidi. *Pandering*. Los Angeles: One Hour Entertainment, 2003.

Flemming, Rebecca. "*Quae Corpore Quaestum Facit*: The Sexual Economy of Female Prostitution in the Roman Empire." *Journal of Roman Studies* 89 (1999): 38–61.

Flexner, Abraham. *Prostitution in Europe*. New York: Century Co., 1914.

Flowers, Amy. *The Fantasy Factory: An Insider's View of the Phone Sex Industry*. Philadelphia: University of Pennsylvania Press, 1998.

Foa, Anna. "The New and the Old: The Spread of Syphilis (1494–1530)." In *Sex and Gender in Historical Perspective*, ed. Edward Muir and Guido Ruggiero. Baltimore: Johns Hopkins University Press, 1990.

Foat, Ginny. *Never Guilty, Never Free*. New York: Random House, 1985.

Foley, Brenda. "Naked Politics: *Erie, PA v. the Kandyland Club*." *NWSA Journal* 14 (2002): 1–17.

Ford, Kimberly-Anne. "Evaluating Prostitution as a Human Service Occupation." In *Prostitution: On Whores, Hustlers, and Johns*, ed. James E. Elias, Vern L. Bullough, Veronica Elias, and Gwen Brewer. New York: Prometheus Books, 1998.

Forrai, Judit. "Prostitution at the Turn of the Century in Budapest." In *Civilization, Sexuality and Social Life in Historical Context: The Hidden Face of Urban Life*. Budapest: Uj-aranydíd Kft, 1996.

Frank, Katherine. *G-Strings and Sympathy: Strip Club Regulars and Male Desire*. Durham, NC: Duke University Press, 2002.

————. "The Production of Identity and the Negotiation of Intimacy in a Gentleman's Club." *Sexualities* 1, no. 2 (1998): 175–201.

Free the Slaves and Human Rights Law Center. *Hidden Slaves: Forced Labor in the United States*. Washington, DC: Free the Slaves and Human Rights Law Center, 2004. http://www. hrcberkeley.org/download/hiddenslaves_report.pdf.

Freedom House Country Reports. Freedom House website http://www.freedomhouse.org/research/ index.htm/.

French, Dolores, and Linda Lee. *Working: My Life as a Prostitute*. New York: E. P. Dutton, 1988.

Frey, Julia. *Toulouse-Lautrec: A Life*. New York: Viking Penguin, 1994.

Friedman, Mack. *Strapped for Cash: A History of American Hustler Culture*. Los Angeles: Alyson Books, 2003.

Fusco, Coco. "Hustling for Dollars: Jineterismo in Cuba." In *Global Sex Workers*, ed. Kamala Kempadoo and Jo Doezema. New York: Routledge, 1998.

Fysh, Geoffrey. "Sex Work, HIV and Money." MA thesis, Nepean University, Western Sydney, Australia, 1995.

Gallagher, John. *Geisha: A Unique World of Tradition, Elegance and Art*. New York: PRC Publishing, 2003.

Gansinghe, Mallika. "No Stray Dogs: Sex Worker Empowerment in Sri Lanka." *Research for Sex Work* 3 (2000): 21–22, http://www.nswp.org/r4sw.

Gateley, Edwina. *I Hear a Seed Growing*. Trabuco Canyon, CA: Source Books, 1990.

Gendron, Bernard. *From Montmarte to the Mudd Club*. Chicago: University of Chicago Press, 2002.

Gentry, Curt. *The Madams of San Francisco: An Irrelevant History of the City by the Golden Gate*. New York: Doubleday, 1964.

George, Andrew. *The Epic of Gilgamesh: The Babylonian Epic Poem and Other Texts in Akkadian and Sumerian*. London: Penguin Books, 1999.

Gerassi, John. *The Boys of Boise: The True Story of a Homosexual Scandal Exploited for Political Purposes*. New York: MacMillan, 1966.

Gibson, Barbara. *Male Order: Life Stories from Boys Who Sell Sex*. London: Cassell, 1995.

Gibson, Ian. *The Erotomaniac. The Secret Life of Henry Spencer Ashbee*. London: Faber and Faber, 2001.

Gibson, Mary. *Prostitution and the State in Italy, 1860–1915*. New Brunswick, NJ: Rutgers University Press, 1986.

Giddis, Diane. "The Divided Woman: Bree Daniels in *Klute*." *Women and Film* 3–4, no. 1 (1973): 57.

Gilfoyle, Timothy J. *City of Eros: New York City, Prostitution, and the Commercialization of Sex, 1790–1920*. New York: W. W. Norton, 1992.

———. "From Soubrette Row to Show World: The Contested Sexualities of Times Square, 1880–1995." In *Policing Public Sex: Queer Politics and the Future of AIDS Activism*, ed. E. G. Colter, W. Hoffman, E. Pendleton, A. Redick, and D. Serlin. Boston: South End Press, 1996.

Giobbe, Evalina. "Prostitution: Buying the Right to Rape." In *Rape and Sexual Assault III: A Research Handbook*, ed. Ann Wolbert Burgess. New York: Garland Press, 1991.

Glancy, Jennifer. *Slavery in Early Christianity*. New York: Oxford University Press, 2002.

Gledhill, Christine. "*Klute* 1: A Contemporary Film Noir and Feminist Criticism" and "*Klute* 2: Feminism and *Klute*." In *Women in Film Noir*, ed. E. Ann Kaplan. London: British Film Institute, 1998.

Gleß, Sabine. *Die Reglementierung von Prostitution in Deutschland*. Berlin: Duncker and Humblot, 1999.

Global Coalition on Women and AIDS and the World Health Organization. "Sexual violence in conflict settings and the risk of HIV." Information Bulletin Series, no. 2, http://www.who.int/entity/gender/en/infobulletinconflict.pdf.

"'Gold Digging' Ban Signed by Olson: Breach of Promise Suits Barred by Law." *San Francisco Examiner*, 3 May 1939, pp. 1–2.

Goldberg, P.J.P. "Pigs and Prostitutes: Streetwalking in Comparative Perspective." In *Young Medieval Women*, ed. Katherine Lewis, James Menuge, and Kim M. Phillips. Stroud, UK: Sutton Publishing, 1999.

Goldman, Emma. "Marriage and Love." http://www.radio4all.org/redblack/books/marriageandlove.html.

———. "The Traffic in Women." In *Anarchism and Other Essays*. New York: Dover, 1969.

Goldman, Marion S. *Gold Diggers and Silver Miners: Prostitution and Social Life on the Comstock Lode*. Ann Arbor: University of Michgan Press, 1981.

Goldsmith, Barbara. *Other Powers: The Age of Suffrage, Spiritualism and the Scandalous Victoria Woodhull*. New York: Alfred A. Knopf, 1998.

Goldstein, Paul J. *Prostitution and Drugs*. Lexington, MA: Lexington Books, 1979.

Goldstone, Bobbie. "*Klute*, Again." *Off Our Backs*, 31 October 1971.

Gomezjara, Francisco, and Estanislao Barrera. *Sociologia de la Prostitucion*. Mexico, DF: Fontamara, S.A., 1978.

Goncourt, Edmond de. "Utamaro: The Painter of Pleasure Quarters." In *Outamaro—le Peintre des Maisons Vertes*. Paris: Biblioteque-Charpentier, 1891.

Goode, Erich, and Nachman Ben-Yehuda. *Moral Panics: The Social Construction of Deviance*. Cambridge, MA: Blackwell, 1994.

Goodwin, Sarah Webster. "Wordsworth and Romantic Voice: The Poet's Song and the Prostitute's Cry." In *Embodied Voices: Representing Female Vocality in Western Culture*, ed. Leslie C. Dunn and Nancy A. Jones. Cambridge: Cambridge University Press, 1994.

Gorna, Robin. *Vamps, Virgins and Victims: How Can Women Fight AIDS?* London: Cassell, 1996.

Goss, D., and D. Adam-Smith. *Organizing AIDS: Workplace and Organizational Responses to the HIV/AIDS Epidemic.* New York: Taylor and Francis, 1995.

Gould, Stephen Jay. "Syphilis and the Shepherd of Atlantis (Renaissance Poem about Syphilis Attempts to Explain Its Origins; Genetic Map Revealed in 1998)." *Natural History* 109 (2000): 38–42 and 74–82.

Grant, Emma, and Gretchen Soderlund. "Girls (Forced to) Dance Naked! The Politics and Presumptions of Anti-trafficking Laws." *Bad Subjects* 40 (October 1998). http://bad.eserver.org/issues/1998/40/soderlund-grant.html.

Grant, W. R. *Post-Soul Black Cinema: Discontinuities, Innovations, and Breakpoints, 1970–1995.* New York: Routledge, 2004.

Grayzel, Susan. *Women's Identities at War.* Chapel Hill: University of North Carolina Press, 1999.

Green, Bill. *The Dancing Was Lively: Fort Concho Texas: A Social History, 1867 to 1882.* San Angelo, TX: Privately printed, 1974.

Grittner, Frederick K. *White Slavery Myth, Ideology, and American Law.* New York: Garland, 1990.

Groneman, Carol. "Nymphomania: The Historical Construction of Female Sexuality." *Signs* 19 (1994): 337–67.

Gronewold, Sue. "Beautiful Merchandise." *Women and History* 4 (1982): 3–102.

———. *Beautiful Merchandise: Prostitution in China 1860–1936.* New York: Harrington Park Press, 1985.

Grossmann, Atina. *Reforming Sex: The German Movement for Birth Control and Abortion Reform.* New York: Oxford University Press, 1995.

Grosz-Ngaté, Maria, and Omari H. Kokole, eds. *Gendered Encounters: Challenging Cultural Boundaries and Social Hierarchies in Africa.* New York: Routledge, 1997.

Guan, Hanqing. "A Sister Courtesan Comes to the Rescue." *Renditions* 49 (1998): 7–41.

"A Guide to Best Practice: Occupational Health and Safety in the Australian Sex Industry." 2000. Australian Federation of AIDS Organizations Web site http://www.afao.org.au/view_articles.asp?pxa = veandpxs = 100andpxsc = andpxsgc = andid = 204.

"A Guide to Occupational Health and Safety in the New Zealand Sex Industry." 2004. Department of Occupational Safety and Health of New Zealand Web site http://www.osh.dol.govt.nz/order/catalogue/235.shtml.

Guider, Margaret Eletta. *Daughters of Rahab: Prostitution and the Church of Liberation in Brazil.* Minneapolis: Fortress Press, 1995.

Gusfield, Joseph. *Symbolic Crusade: Status Politics and the American Temperance Movement.* Champaign: University of Illinois Press, 1963.

Guy, Donna. *Sex and Danger in Buenos Aires: Prostitution, Family, and Nation in Argentina.* Lincoln: University of Nebraska Press, 1990.

———. "'White Slavery,' Citizenship and Nationality in Argentina." In *Nationalisms and Sexualities*, ed. Andrew Parker, Mary Russo, Doris Sommer, and Patricia Yaeger. New York: Routledge, 1992.

———. "White Slavery, Public Health, and the Socialist Position on Legalized Prostitution in Argentina, 1913–1936." *Latin American Research Review* 23 (1988): 60–80.

Gysels, M., et al. "Truck Drivers, Middlemen and Commercial Sex Workers: AIDS and the Mediation of Sex in South West Uganda." *AIDS Care* 13, no. 3 (June 2001): 373–85.

Haeri, Shahla. *Law of Desire: Temporary Marriage in Shi'i Iran.* Syracuse, NY: Syracuse University Press, 1989.

————. "Temporary Marriage and the State in Iran: An Islamic Discourse on Female Sexuality." *Social Research* 59 (Spring 1992): 201–24.

Hai, Wan Yan. "Sex Work and Public Policies in China." In *Prostitution: On Whores, Hustlers, and Johns*, ed. James E. Elias, Vern L. Bullough, Veronica Elias, and Gwen Brewer. New York: Prometheus Books, 1998.

Haidt, Jonathan, and Matthew A. Hersh. "Sexual Morality: The Cultures and Emotions of Conservatives and Liberals." *Journal of Applied Social Psychology* 31, no. 1 (2001): 191–221.

Haine, Scott W. *The World of the Paris Café: Sociability among the French Working Class, 1789–1914*. Baltimore, MD: Johns Hopkins University Press, 1996.

Hall, Laurel Meredith. "'Night Life' in Kenya." In *A Vindication of the Rights of Whores*, ed. Gail Pheterson. Seattle: Seal Press, 1989.

Hall, Stuart, Chas Critcher, Tony Jefferson, John Clarke, and Brian Roberts. *Policing the Crisis: Mugging, the State, and Law and Order*. New York: Holmes and Meier Publishers, 1978.

Hammar, Lawrence. "Caught between Structure and Agency: Gendered Violence and Prostitution in Papua New Guinea." *Transforming Anthropology* 8 (1998): 77–96.

Hanna, Judith Lynne. *Dance, Sex and Gender: Signs of Identity, Dominance, Defiance, and Desire*. Chicago: University of Chicago Press, 1988.

————. "Toying with the Striptease Dancer and the First Amendment." In *Play and Culture Studies*. Vol. 2, edited by S. Reifel. Westport, CT: Ablex, 1999.

————. "Undressing the First Amendment and Corsetting the Striptease Dancer." *Drama Review* 42, no. 2 (1998): 38–69.

Hapke, Laura. *Girls Who Went Wrong: Prostitutes in American Fiction, 1885–1917*. Bowling Green, OH: Bowling Green University Popular Press, 1989.

Harsin, Jill. *Policing Prostitution in Nineteenth-Century Paris*. Princeton, NJ: Princeton University Press, 1985.

Haskell, Molly. *From Reverence to Rape: The Treatment of Women in the Movies*. 2nd ed. Chicago: University of Chicago Press, 1987.

Hausbeck, Kathryn, and Barbara G. Brents. "Inside Nevada's Brothel Industry." In *Sex for Sale: Prostitution, Pornography and the Sex Industry*, ed. Ronald Weitz. New York: Routledge, 2000.

Hawkes, Ellen. *Feminism on Trial: The Ginny Foat Case and the Future of the Women's Movement*. New York: William Morrow, 1986.

Hayes, Anne. *Female Prostitution in Costa Rica: Historical Perspectives, 1880–1930*. New York; Routledge, 2006.

Heather, N., A. Wodak, E. Nadelmann, and P. O'Hare eds. *Psychoactive Drugs and Harm Reduction: From Faith to Science*. London: Whurr, 1993.

Heimann, Jim. *Sins of the City: The Real Los Angeles Noir*. San Francisco: Chronicle Books, 1999.

Held, David et al. *Global Transformations*. Cambridge: Polity Press, 1999.

Heller, Reinhold. *Toulouse-Lautrec: The Soul of Montmartre*. New York: Prestel, 1997.

Henriot, Christian. *Prostitution and Sexuality in Shanghai: A Social History, 1849–1949*. Cambridge: University of Cambridge Press, 1997.

Henriques, Fernando. *Prostitution in Europe and the Americas*. Vol. II of *Prostitution and Society*. New York: Citadel Press, 1965.

Henry, Maleleine M. *Prisoner of History: Aspasia of Miletus and Her Biographical Tradition*. New York: Oxford University Press, 1995.

Herausgegeben vom Prostituiertenprojekt Hydra. *Beruf: Hure*. Hamburg, Galgenberg, 1988.

Herausgegeben vom Prostituiertenprojekt Hydra. Helga Bilitewski, Maya Czajka, Claudia Fischer, Stephanie Klee, and Claudia Repetto. *Freier: Das Heimliche Treiben der Männer*. Hamburg: Galgenberg, 1991.

Herbert, Robert L. *Impressionism: Art, Leisure and Parisian Society.* New Haven, CT: Yale University Press, 1988.

Herek, Gregory M. "Facts about Homosexuality and Mental Health." Sexual Orientation, Science, Education and Policy Web site http://psychology.ucdavis.edu/rainbow/html/facts_mental_health.html.

Herlihy, James Leo. *Midnight Cowboy: A Novel.* New York: Simon and Schuster, 1965.

Herman, J. L. *Trauma and Recovery.* New York: Basic Books, 1997.

Hershatter, Gail, *Dangerous Pleasures: Prostitution and Modernity in Twentieth-Century Shanghai.* Berkeley: University of California Press, 1997.

Herstory: Lesbians in the Arts: Colette. Herstory Web site http://www.geocities.com/SoHo/Suite/9048/COLETTEbio.htm.

Herzog, Dagmar. "Hubris and Hypocrisy, Incitement and Disavowal: Sexuality and German Fascism." *Journal of the History of Sexuality* 11, nos. 1/2 (January/April 2002): 3–21.

Hess, Marcy A. "Discursive Decontamination: Domesticating the Great Social Evil in Early Victorian Novels." Ph.D. diss., University of Alabama, 2001.

Heyl, Barbara Sherman. *The Madam as Entrepreneur: Career Management in House Prostitution.* New Brunswick, NJ: Transaction Publishers, 1979.

———. "The Madam as Teacher: The Training of House Prostitutes." *Social Problems* 24 (1977): 535–45.

Hickey, Gary. *Beauty and Desire in Edo Period Japan.* Canberra: National Gallery of Australia, 1998.

Hicks, George. *The Comfort Women.* St. Leonards, New South Wales: Allen and Unwin, 1995.

Hicks, R. "Women in Tourism: A Case Study of Bukit Lawang." Honors thesis, Murdoch University, Perth, Australia, 1994.

Hill, Marilynn Wood. *Their Sisters' Keepers: Prostitution in New York City, 1830–1870.* Berkeley: University of California Press, 1993.

Hines, John. *The Fabliau in English.* London: Longman, 1993.

Hirschfeld, Magnus. *The Homosexuality of Men and Women.* Translated by Michael Lombardi-Nash. 1913. Reprint, Amherst, NY: Promethius Books, 2000.

Ho, Elaine Yee Lin. "Connecting Cultures: Hong Kong Literature in English, the 1950s." *New Zealand Journal of Asian Studies* 5, no. 2 (2003): 5–25.

Hobson, Barbara Meil. *Uneasy Virtue: The Politics of Prostitution and the American Reform Tradition.* New York: Basic Books, 1987.

Hodgson, Dorothy L., and Sheryl A. McCurdy, eds. *"Wicked" Women and the Reconfiguration of Gender in Africa.* Portsmouth, NH: Heinemann, 2001.

Hohmann, Marti. "Whore Stories: Prostitution and Sex-Positive Feminism." In *Prostitution: On Whores, Hustlers, and Johns,* ed. James E. Elias, Vern L. Bullough, Veronica Elias, and Gwen Brewer. New York: Prometheus Books, 1998.

Hoigard, Cecilie, and Liv Finstad. *Backstreets: Prostitution, Money and Love.* University Park: Pennsylvania State University Press, 1986.

Holland, Merlin. *The Real Trial of Oscar Wilde.* New York: Fourth Estate/HarperCollins, 2003.

Hollander, Elizabeth. "Artists' Models in Nineteenth Century America: A Study of Professional Identity." *Annals of Scholarship* 10, nos. 3–4 (1993): 281–303.

Hollis, Patricia. *Women in Public, 1850–1900: Documents of the Victorian Women's Movement.* London: Allen and Unwin, 1979.

Holmes, Ronald M., and Stephen T. Holmes, eds. *Current Perspectives on Sex Crimes.* Thousand Oaks, CA: Sage Publications, 2002.

Honour, Hugh. "Black Models and White Myths." In *The Image of the Black in Western Art,* ed. Karen C. C. Dalton. Vol. 4. Cambridge, MA: Harvard University Press, 1989.

Hooks, Stephen M. *Sacred Prostitution in Israel and the Ancient Near East.* Ph.D. diss., Hebrew Union College, 1985.

Horn, Pierre L., and Mary Beth Pringle. *The Image of the Prostitute in Modern Literature.* New York: Frederick Ungar, 1984.

Horowitz, Helen, L. *Rereading Sex: Battles over Sexual Knowledge and Suppression in Nineteenth Century America.* New York: Alfred A. Knopf, 2002.

Howard, Keith. *True Stories of the Korean Comfort Women.* London: Cassell, 1995.

Hucker, Stephen. "Paraphilias." PsychDirect Web site http://www.psychdirect.com/forensic/Criminology/para/paraphilia.htm.

Hügel, Franz Seraph. *Zur Geschichte, Statistik und Regelung der Prostitution Sozial-medizinische Studien in ihrer praktischen Behandlung und Anwendung auf Wien und andere Grossstädte.* Vienna: Zamarski u. Dittmarsch, 1865.

Hughes, Donna. "The 2002 Trafficking in Persons Report: Lost Opportunity for Progress: 'Foreign Government Complicity in Human Trafficking: A Review of the State Department's 2002 Trafficking in Persons Report.'" Oral presentation to the House Committee on International Relations, Washington, DC, 19 June 2002.

Human Rights Watch. "Ignorance Only: HIV/AIDS, Human Rights and Federally Funded Abstinence-Only Programs in the United States; Texas: A Case Study." September 2002. http://hrw.org/reports/2002/usa0902/.

———. "The Less They Know, the Better: Abstinence-Only and HIV/AIDS Programs in Uganda." March 2005. http://hrw.org/reports/2005/uganda0305/.

———. *Making Their Own Rules: Police Beatings, Rape, and Torture of Children in Papua New Guinea.* New York: Human Rights Watch, 2004. http://hrw.org/reports/2005/png0905/.

———. *Owed Justice: Thai Women Trafficked into Debt Bondage in Japan.* New York: Human Rights Watch, 2000.

———. *Policy Paralysis: A Call for Action on HIV/AIDS-Related Human Rights Abuses against Women and Girls in Africa.* New York: Human Rights Watch, 2003. http://www.hrw.org/reports/2003/africa1203.

———. *Ravaging the Vulnerable: Abuses against Persons at High Risk of HIV in Bangladesh.* New York: Human Rights Watch, 2003. http://www.hrw.org/reports/2003/bangladesh0803/.

Humphreys, Laud. "New Styles in Homosexual Manliness." In *The Homosexual Dialectic*, ed. Joseph McCaffrey. Englewood Cliffs, NJ: Prentice-Hall, 1972. Originally published in *Transaction* 8 (March-April 1971): 38ff.

———. *Tearoom Trade: Impersonal Sex in Public Places: Enlarged Edition with a Retrospect on Ethical Issues.* Chicago: Aldine Publishing, 1982.

Hunt, Alan. *Governance of the Consuming Passions: A History of Sumptuary Law.* New York: St. Martin's Press, 1996.

Hunt, Morton. *Gay: What You Should Know about Homosexuality.* New York: Simon and Schuster, 1977.

Hunter, Richard. *The New Comedy of Greece and Rome.* Oxford: Oxford University Press, 1985.

Hurtado, Albert L. *Intimate Frontiers: Sex, Gender, and Culture in Old California.* Albuquerque: University of New Mexico Press, 1999.

Huysmans, Joris-Karl. *À Rebours.* 1884. Reprint, London: Oxford University Press, 1998.

Hyam, Ronald, *Empire and Sexuality: The British Experience.* Manchester: Manchester University Press, 1990, 1991, 1992.

Hyde, H. Montgomery. *The Cleveland Street Scandal.* New York: Coward, McGann and Geoghegan, 1976.

I Love India Web site "Odissi Dance Form." http://www.dances.iloveindia.com/classical-dances/odissi.html.

Idem, Semper. *The Blue Book, a Bibliographical Attempt to Describe the Guide Books to the Houses of Ill Fame*. New Orleans: Privately printed, 1936.

Igbinivia, P. E. "Prostitution in Black Africa." *International Journal of Women's Studies* 7 (November-December 1984): 430–49.

Images Asia. "Burmese Women Sex Workers in Thailand." Oral presentation for NGO Forum on Women, Beijing, China, 30 August–8 September 1995. Chiang Mai, Thailand: Images Asia, 1995.

International Council for Women of African Descent. "Trafficking of African Women Fact Sheet." http://www.npcbw.org/newweb/icwad_04_trafficking_facts.htm.

Internet Medieval Source Book. "Aquinas on Sex." http://www.fordham.edu/halsall/source/aquinas-sex.html.

Irwin, Mary Ann. "'White Slavery' as Metaphor: Anatomy of a Moral Panic." *Ex Post Facto: The History Journal* 5 (1996). http://www.walnet.org/csis/papers/irwin-wslavery.html.

Isaacs, Tina. "The Anglican Hierarchy and the Reformation of Manners, 1688–1738." *Journal of Ecclesiastical History* 33, no. 3 (1982): 391–411.

Iwasaki, Mineko. *Geisha: A Life*. New York: Simon and Schuster, 2002.

Jaget, Claude, ed. *Prostitutes, Our Life*. Translated by Anne Furse, Suzie Fleming, and Ruth Hall. London: Falling Wall Press, 1980.

James, Jennifer. "Prostitution and Addiction—Interdisciplinary Approach." *Addictive Diseases* 2, no. 4 (1976): 601–18.

———. "Prostitutes and Prostitution." In *Deviants: Voluntary Actors in a Hostile World*, ed. Edward Sagarin and Fred Montanino. New York: General Learning Press, Scott, Foresman, 1977.

———, and Jane Meyerding. "Early Sexual Experience and Prostitution." *American Journal of Psychiatry* 234 (1977): 12.

James, Louis. *Fiction for the Working Man 1830–50*. London: Oxford University Press, 1963.

Jana, Smarajit, Nandinee Bandyopadhyay, Amitrajit Saha, and Mrinal Kanti Dutta. "Creating an Enabling Environment: Lessons Learnt from the Sonagachi Project, India." *Sex Work and Research* (1999): 22–24.

Jancovich, Mark et al., eds. *Defining Cult Movies: The Cultural Politics of Oppositional Taste*. Manchester, UK: Manchester University Press, 2003.

Järvinen, Margaretha. "Prostitution in Helsinki: A Disappearing Social Problem?" *Journal of the History of Sexuality* 3 (1999): 608–30.

Jaschok, Maria. *Concubines and Bondservants: The Social History of a Chinese Custom*. London: Zed Books, 1988.

Jeffers, H. Paul. *Diamond Jim Brady: Prince of the Gilded Age*. New York: John Wiley, 2001.

Jeffrey, Leslie Ann. *Sex and Borders: Gender, National Identity, and Prostitution Policy in Thailand*. Chiang Mai, Thailand: Silkworm Books, 2002.

Jenkins, Carol. "Cambodian Sex Workers Conduct Their Own Research." *Research for Sex Work* 8, 2005: 3-4. http://www.researchforsexwork.org.

———. "Final Report to UNAIDS: Police and Sex Workers in Papua New Guinea, 1997." http://www.walnet.org/csis/papers/jenkins_papua.html.

Jenness, Valerie. "From Sex as Sin to Sex as Work: Coyote and the Reorganization of Prostitution as a Social Problem." *Social Problems* 37 (1990): 403–17.

———. *Making It Work: The Prostitutes' Rights Movement in Perspective*. New York: Aldine de Gruyter, 1993.

Jezic, Diane Peacock, and Elizabeth Wood, eds. *Women Composers: The Lost Tradition Found*. 2nd ed. New York: Feminist Press, 1993.

Jiminez, Jill, ed. *Dictionary of Artist's Models*. London: Fitzroy-Dearborn, 2001.

Joesoef, M. R., L. A. Valleroy, T. M. Kuntjoro, A. Kamboji, M. Linnan, Y. Barakbah, A. Bajadi, and M. E. St. Louis. "Risk Profile of Female Sex Workers Who Participate in a Routine Penicillin Prophylaxis Program in Surabaya, Indonesia." *Internation Journal of STD and AIDS* 9 (1998): 756–60.

Johnson, Edgar. *Charles Dickens: His Tragedy and Triumph.* New York: Simon and Schuster, 1952.

Jolin, A. "On the Backs of Working Prostitutes: Feminist Theory and Prostitution Policy." *Crime and Delinquency* 40, no. 1 (January 1994): 69–83.

Jones, Ann Rosalind, and Margaret Rosenthal, eds. and trans. *Veronica Franco: Poems and Selected Letters.* Chicago: University of Chicago Press, 1999.

Jones, D. L., K. L. Irwin, J. Inciardi, B. Bowser, R. Schilling, C. Word, P. Evans, S. Faruque, H. V. McCoy, and B. R. Edlin. "The High-Risk Sexual Practices of Crack-Smoking Sex Workers Recruited from the Streets of Three American Cities." The Multicenter Crack Cocaine and HIV Infection Study Team. *Journal of Sexually Transmitted Diseases* 25, no. 4 (1998):187–93.

Jones, James H. *Bad Blood: The Tuskegee Syphilis Experiment.* New York: Free Press, 1981.

Jones, Victor Pierce. *Saint or Sensationalist: The Story of W. T. Stead.* Chichester: Gooday, 1988.

Jordan, Ann D. *The Annotated Guide to the Complete UN Trafficking Protocol.* Washington, DC: International Human Rights Law Group, 2002. http://www.globalrights.org/site/PageServer?pagename = wwd_index_49.

Jordan, Jane. *Josephine Butler.* London: John Murray, 2001.

Joselit, Jenna Weissman. *A Perfect Fit: Clothes, Character, and the Promise of America.* New York: Henry Holt, 2001.

Jušik, Karin J. *Auf der suche nach der Verlorenen. Die Prostitutionsdebatten im Wien der Jahrhundertwende.* Vienna: Löcker Verlag, 1994.

Justice Policy Institute. *Cellblocks or Classrooms?* Washington, DC: JPI, 2002.

Kail B. L., D. D. Watson, and S. Ray. "Needle-Using Practices within the Sex Industry." *American Journal of Drug and Alcohol Abuse* 21 (1995): 241–55.

Kanouse D., S. H. Berry, N. Duan, J. Lever, S. Carson, J. F. Perlman, and B. Levitan. "Drawing a Probability Sample of Female Street Prostitutes in Los Angeles County." *Journal of Sex Research* 36 (1999): 45–51.

Kao Tha, Chuon Srey Net, Sou Sotheavy, Pick Sokchea, and Chan Sopheak. "The Tenofovir Trial Controversy in Cambodia." *Research for Sex Work* 7 (2004): 10–11.

Kapur, Promilla. *The Indian Call Girls.* New Delhi: Orient Paperbacks, 1979.

Karras, Ruth Mazo. *Common Women: Prostitution and Sexuality in Medieval England.* New York: Oxford University Press, 1996.

———. "Holy Harlots: Prostitute Saints in Medieval Legend." *Journal of the History of Sexuality* 1, no. 1 (1990): 3–32.

Kaye, Kerwin. "Male Prostitution in the Twentieth Century: Pseudohomosexuals, Hoodlum Homosexuals, and Exploited Teens." *Journal of Homosexuality* 46, no. 1/2 (2003): 1–77.

Kaye, Kerwin. "Sex and the Unspoken in Male Street Prostitution." *Journal of Homosexuality.*

Kearney, Patrick J. *A History of Erotic Literature.* London: Macmillan, 1983.

Keefe, Tim. *Some of My Best Friends Are Naked: Interviews with Seven Erotic Dancers.* San Francisco: Barbary Coast, 1993.

Keeler, Christine, with Douglas Thompson. *The Truth at Last: My Story.* London: Sidgwick and Jackson, 2001.

Kempadoo, Kamala. *Sexing the Caribbean: Gender, Race, and Sexual Labor.* New York: Routledge, 2004.

———, ed. *Sun, Sex, and Gold: Tourism and Sex Work in the Caribbean.* Lanham, MD: Rowman and Littlefield, 1999.

————, and Jo Doezema, eds., *Global Sex Workers: Rights, Resistance, and Redefinition*. New York: Routledge, 1998.

————, ed., with Bandana Pattanaik, and Jyothi Sanghera. *Trafficking and Prostitution Reconsidered: New Perspectives on Migration, Sex Work and Human Rights*. Boulder, CO: Paradigm, 2005.

Kendall, Richard, and Griselda Pollock, eds. *Dealing with Degas: Representations of Women and the Politics of Vision*. London: Pandora, 1992.

Kennedy, Dolores, with Robert Nolin. *On a Killing Day: The Bizarre Story of Convicted Murderer Aileen "Lee" Wuornos*. Chicago: Bonus Books, 1992.

Kennedy, Ludovic. *The Trial of Stephen Ward*. London: Victor Gollancz, 1964.

Kersenboom-Story, Saskia. *Nityasumangali: Devadasi Tradition in South India*. New Delhi: Motilal Banarisidass, 1987.

Kessler, Ronald. *The Bureau: The Secret History of the FBI*. New York: St. Martin's Press, 2002.

Kettle, Ann J. "Ruined Maids: Prostitutes and Servant Girls in Later Medieval England." In *Matrons and Marginal Women in Medieval Society*, ed. Robert R. Edwards and Vickie Ziegler. Rochester, NY: Boydell Press, 1995.

Kevles, Daniel J. "Eugenics and Human Rights: Statistical Data Included." *British Medical Journal* (1999): 319, 435–38.

Kimball, Nell. *Nell Kimball: Her Life as an American Madam*, ed. Stephen Longstreet. New York: Macmillan, 1970.

Kim-Gibson, Dal Sil. *Silence Broken: Korean Comfort Women*. Parkersburg, IA: Mid-Prairie Books.

Kincaid, James, ed. *My Secret Life: An Erotic Diary of Victorian London*. New York: Signet Classics, 1996.

King, John. *Magical Reels: A History of Cinema in Latin America*. New York: Verso, 1990.

Kinnell, Hilary. "Murder Made Easy: The Final Solution to Prostitution?" In *Prostitution Now*, ed. Rosie Campbell and Maggie O'Neill. Devon, UK: Willan Publishers, 2006.

Kinyamba, Shomba. *La Prostitution son Vrai Visage au Zaïre*. Lubumbashi: Editions Africa, 1987.

Kippen, Cameron. *The History of Footwear*. Curtin University Department of Podiatry Web site http://podiatry.curtin.edu.au/history.html.

Klap, Marieke, Yvonne Clerk, and Jacqueline Smith. *Combatting Traffic in Persons*. Utrecht, Netherlands: Institute of Human Rights, 1995.

Kobayashi, Tadashi. *Utamaro*. New York: Kodansha International, 1993.

Kohn, George Childs, ed. *Encyclopedia of Plague and Pestilence*. New York: Checkmark Books, 2001.

Koken, Juline A., David S. Bimbi, Jeffrey T. Parsons, and Perry N. Halkitis. "The Experience of Stigma in the Lives of Male Internet Escorts." *Journal of Psychology and Human Sexuality* 16 (2004): 13–32.

Korn, Jim, "My Sexual Encounters with Sex Workers: The Effects on a Consumer." In *Prostitution: On Whores, Hustlers, and Johns*, ed. James E. Elias, Vern L. Bullough, Veronica Elias, and Gwen Brewer. New York: Prometheus Books, 1998.

Kraus, Karl. "Die Prozeß Riehl." *Die Fackel*, 13 November 1906, p. 8.

Kreiss, Joan, Elisabeth Ngugi, King Holmes, Jeckoniah Ndinya-Achola, Peter Waiyaki, Pacita L. Roberts, Irene Ruminjo, Rose Sajabi, Joyce Kimata, Thomas R. Fleming, Aggrey Anzala, Donna Holton, and Francis Plummer. "Efficacy of Nonoxynol 9 Contraceptive Sponge Use in Preventing Heterosexual Acquisition of HIV in Nairobi Prostitutes." *Journal of the American Medical Association* 268 (1992): 477–82.

Kreiss, Joan, Irene Ruminjo, Elisabeth Ngugi et al. "Efficacy of Nonoxynol-9 in Preventing HIV Transmission." *International Conference on AIDS*, Abstract no. M.A.O.36, 1989.

Kukla, Karel Ladislav. *Konec bahna Prahy*. Prague: Václav Svec, 1927.

Kunzel, Regina. *Fallen Women, Problem Girls: Unmarried Mothers and the Professionalization of Social Work*. New Haven, CT: Yale University Press, 1993.

Kuo, Lenore. *Prostitution Policy: Revolutionizing Practice through a Gendered Perspective.* New York: New York University Press, 2002.

Kurke, Leslie. *Coins, Bodies, Games and Gold: The Politics of Meaning in Archaic Greece.* Princeton, NJ: Princeton University Press, 1999.

Kurova, T, S. M. Malceva, and P. A. Mardh. "Prostitution in Riga, Latvia—A Socio-medical Matter of Concern." *Acta Obstetricia Gunecologia, Scandinavia* 77, no. 1 (1998): 83–86.

Kwong, Peter. *Forbidden Workers.* New York: New Press, 1997.

La-Fountain-Stokes, Lawrence. "*De un Pájaro las dos Alas:* Travel Notes of a Queer Puerto Rican in Habana." *GLQ* 3, nos. 1–2 (2002): 7–33.

Lakhumalani, V. "The Prostitution Situation in a Number of Cities of Russia, Ukraine and Belarus." *Zhurnal Mikrobiologii, Epidemiologii i Immunobiologii* 1(1997): 102–4.

Lamphear, Trisha L. "Milestones in Microbicide Research and Development." *Microbicide Quarterly* (December 2004): 6–8.

Landau, Emily Epstein. "'Spectacular Wickedness': New Orleans, Prostitution, and the Politics of Sex, 1897–1917." Ph.D. diss., Yale University, 2005.

Langley, Erika. *The Lusty Lady: Photographs and Texts.* Zurich: Scalo, 1997.

Langum, David J. *Crossing over the Line: Legislating Morality and the Mann Act.* Chicago: University of Chicago Press, 1994.

Larsen, Jeanne, trans. *Brocade River Poems: Selected Works of the Tang Dynasty Courtesan Xue Tao.* Princeton, NJ: Princeton University Press, 1987.

LaSalle, Mick. *Complicated Women: Sex and Power in Pre-Code Hollywood.* New York: St. Martin's Press, 2000.

Lathers, Marie. *Bodies of Art: French Literary Realism and the Artist's Model.* Lincoln: University of Nebraska Press, 2001.

Laughran, Michelle A. "In the Body: Public Health and Social Control in Sixteenth-Century Venice." Ph.D. diss., University of Connecticut, 1998.

Law, Lisa. "A Matter of 'Choice': Discourses on Prostitution in the Philippines." In *Sites of Desire, Economies of Pleasure,* ed. Lenore Manderson and Margaret Jolly. Chicago: University of Chicago Press, 1997.

Leaton, Anne. *Pearl.* New York: Alfred A. Knopf, 1985.

Lee, Danny. "Street Fight." *New York Times,* 31 March 2002, p. C1.

Lefkowitz, Mary R., and Maureen B. Fant. *Women's Life in Greece and Rome: A Source Book in Translation.* 2nd ed. Baltimore: Johns Hopkins University Press, 1992.

Leigh, Carol, ed. In Defense of Prostitution: Prostitutes Debate Their 'Choice' of Profession." *Gauntlet* 1, no. 7(1993).

———. "P.I.M.P. (Prostitutes in Municipal Politics)." In *Policing Public Sex: Queer Politics and the Future of AIDS Activism,* ed. E. G. Colter, W. Hoffman, E. Pendleton, A. Redick, and D. Serlin. Boston: South End Press, 1996.

———. "Prostitution in the United States: The Statistics." *Gauntlet* 1, no. 7 (1994): 17–18.

Leigh, Carol, a.k.a. Scarlot Harlot. "Inventing Sex Work." In *Whores and Other Feminists,* ed. Jill Nagle. New York: Routledge, 1997.

———. *Unrepentant Whore.* San Francisco: Last Gasp, 2004.

Lemire, Michel. *Artistes et Mortels.* Paris: Chadaud, 1990.

Lenderová, Milena. *Chtyla Patrola aneb Prostituce za Rakouska i Republiky.* Prague: Karolinum, 2002.

Leonard, Terri L. "Male Clients of Female Street Prostitutes: Unseen Partners in Sexual Disease Transmission." *Medical Anthropology Quarterly* 4 (1990): 41–55.

Leonard, Zoe, and Polly Thistlethwaite. "Prostitution and HIV Infection." In *Women, AIDS and Activism,* ed. Act Up/NY Women and AIDS Book Group. Boston: South End Press, 1990.

Lerner, Gerda. *The Creation of Patriarchy.* New York: Oxford University Press, 1986.

Lerum, Kari. "Sexuality, Power, and Camaraderie in Service Work." *Gender and Society* 18, no. 6 (2004): 756–76.

Lever, Janet, David E. Kanouse, "Offstreet Prostitution in Los Angeles County." In *Prostitution: On Whores, Hustlers, and Johns*, ed. James E. Elias, Vern L. Bullough, Veronica Elias, and Gwen Brewer. New York: Prometheus Books, 1998.

Levine, Harry. "The Discovery of Addiction: Changing Conceptions of Habitual Drunkenness in America." *Journal of Studies on Alcohol* 15 (1978): 493–506.

Levine, Philippa. "Consistent Contradictions: Prostitution and Protective Labour Legislation in Nineteenth Century England." *Social History* 19 (1994):17–35.

———. "Public and Private Paradox: Prostitution and the State." *Arena* 1 (1993): 131–44.

———. "Rereading the 1890s: Venereal Disease as 'Constitutional Crisis' in Britain and British India." *Journal of Asian Studies* 55 (1996): 585–612.

———. "Rough Usage: Prostitution, Law and the Social Historian." In *Rethinking Social History, English Society 1570–1920 and Its Interpretation*, ed. Adrian Wilson. Manchester, UK: Manchester University Press, 1993.

———. "Venereal Disease, Prostitution and the Politics of Empire: The Case of British India." *Journal of the History of Sexuality* 4 (1994): 579–602.

———. "Walking the Streets in a Way No Decent Woman Should: Women Police in World War One." *Journal of Modern History* 66 (1994): 34–78.

———. "Women and Prostitution: Metaphor, Reality, History." *Canadian Journal of History* 28 (1993): 479–94.

Lewis, J., and E. Maticka-Tyndale. "Methodological Challenges Conducting Research Related to Sex Work." In *Escort Services in a Border Town: Transmission Dynamics of STDs within and between Communities*. Report issued by Division of STD Prevention and Control, Laboratory Centres for Disease Control, Health Canada. Ottawa, 2000.

Lewis, J., E. Maticka-Tyndale, F. Shaver, and H. Schramm. "Managing Risk and Safety on the Job: The Experiences of Canadian Sex Workers." *Journal of Psychology and Human Sexuality* 17 (2005): 147–67.

Lewis, James C. et al. "Beer Halls as a Focus for HIV Prevention Activities in Rural Zimbabwe." *Sexually Transmitted Diseases* 32, no. 6 (2005): 364–70.

Leyton, Elliott. *Hunting Humans: The Rise of the Modern Multiple Murderer*. New York: Carroll and Graf, 2003.

Liedtke, Walter A. *Vermeer and the Delft School*. New York: Metropolitan Museum of Art, 2001.

Liepe-Levinson, Katherine. *Strip Show: Performances of Gender and Desire*. New York: Routledge, 2002.

Lim, Lin Lean, ed. *The Sex Sector: The Economic and Social Bases of Prostitution in Southeast Asia*. Geneva: International Labour Organization, 1998.

Linehan, Mary. "Vicious Circle: Prostitution, Reform, and Public Policy in Chicago, 1830–1930." Ph.D. diss., University of Notre Dame, 1991.

Linz, D., K. C. Land, J. R. Williams, B. Paul, and M. E. Ezel. "An Examination of the Assumption That Adult Businesses Are Associated with Crime in Surrounding Areas: A Secondary Effects Study in Charlotte, North Carolina." *Law and Society Review* 38 (2004): 69–104.

Lipking, Lawrence. *Abandoned Women and Poetic Tradition*. Chicago: University of Chicago Press, 1988.

Liu, Ts'un-yan, and John Minford, eds. *Chinese Middlebrow Fiction*. Seattle: University of Washington Press, 1984.

Lloyd, Sarah. "Pleasure's 'Golden Bait': Prostitution, Poverty and the Magdalen Hospital in Eighteenth-Century London." *History Workshop Journal* 41 (1996): 50–70.

Loconto, Allison. "The Trafficking of Nigerian Women into Italy." *TED Case Studies* 656 (January 2002): 1–15. http://www.american.edu/TED/italian-trafficking.htm.

Loebner, Hugh Gene. "Being a John." In *Prostitution: On Whores, Hustlers, and Johns*, ed. James E. Elias, Vern L. Bullough, Veronica Elias, and Gwen Brewer. New York: Prometheus Books, 1998.

Loff, Bebe, Carol Jenkins, Melissa Ditmore, Cheryl Overs, and Rosanna Barbero. "Unethical Clinical Trials in Thailand: A Community Response." *Lancet* 6 (May 2005): 1618–19.

Long, Alecia P. *The Great Southern Babylon: Sex, Race, and Respectability in New Orleans, 1865–1920.* Baton Rouge: Louisiana State University Press, 2004.

Long, F., M. Horsburgh, M. Rodgers, and R. Roberts. *Pleasure in Paradise?: Sex Tourism in Asia.* Sydney, Australia: General Synod Office, 1993.

Longo, Paulo. "From Subjects to Partners: Experience of a Project in Rio de Janeiro, Brazil." *Research for Sex Work* 7 (2004). http://www.nswp.org/r4sw/.

———, and Melissa Ditmore. "100% Condom Use Programs: Empowerment or Abuse?" *Research for Sex Work* 6 (2003): 3–5.

Longstreet, Stephen, ed. *Nell Kimball: Her Life as an American Madam by Herself.* New York: Macmillan, 1970.

———, and Ethel Longstreet. *Yoshiwara: The Pleasure Quarters of Old Tokyo.* Tokyo: Yenbooks, 1970.

Loomis, William T. "Prostitutes and Pimps." In *Wages, Welfare Costs and Inflation in Classical Athens*, ed. William T. Loomis. Ann Arbor: University of Michigan Press, 1998.

Lopez, Ana. "A Short History of Latin American Film History." *Journal of Film and Video* 37, no. 1 (Winter 1985): 55–69.

Loseva, O., and M. Nashkhoev. "Sex Workers: Social Origins, Sexual Behavior, Potential for Spreading STIs." *Dermatology and Venerology Bulletin* 3 (1999): 16–22.

Lotchin, Roger W. *San Francisco, 1846–1856: From Hamlet to City.* New York: Oxford University Press, 1974.

Louis, Lisa. *Butterflies of the Night: Mama-sans, Geisha, Strippers, and the Japanese Men They Serve.* New York: Tengu Books, 1992.

Lovelace, Linda. *Ordeal.* Secaucus, NJ: Citadel Press, 1980.

Lowman, John. "Prostitution Law in Canada." *Comparative Law Review* 23 (1989): 13–48.

———. "Street Prostitution Control: Some Canadian Reflections on the Finsbury Park Experience." *British Journal of Criminology* 32 (Winter 1992): 1–17.

———. "Violence and the Outlaw Status of (Street) Prostitution in Canada." *Violence against Women* 6 (September 2000): 987–1011.

Luckenbill, D. "Deviant Career Mobility: The Case of Male Prostitutes." *Social Problems* 33 (1986): 283–96.

Luddy, Maria. *Women and Philanthropy in Nineteenth Century Ireland.* Cambridge: Cambridge University Press, 1995.

Lukas, Karli. "*Klute.*" Senses of Cinema Web site http://www.sensesofcinema.com/contents/cteq/01/13/klute.html.

Mackay, Thomas C. *Red Lights Out: A Legal History of Prostitution, Disorderly Houses, and Vice Districts, 1870–1917.* New York: Garland Publishing, 1987.

Mackerras, Colin. *Chinese Theater: From Its Origins to the Present Day.* Honolulu: University of Hawaii Press, 1989.

———. "Peking Opera before the Twentieth Century." *Comparative Drama* 28, no. 1 (Spring 1994): 19–42.

MacKinnon, Catharine. *Feminism Unmodified: Discourses on Life and Law.* Cambridge, MA: Harvard University Press, 1987.

MacKinnon, Catharine A. *Only Words.* Cambridge, MA: Harvard University Press, 1993.

———. *Women's Lives, Men's Laws.* Cambridge, MA: Belknap Press/Harvard University Press, 2005.

MacQueen, Kathleen M., and Jeremy Sugarman. "Back to the Rough Ground: Working in International HIV Prevention as Ethical Debates Continue." *IRB: Ethics and Human Research* (March-April 2003): 11–13.

Madeleine: An Autobiography. New York: Persea Books, 1986.

Madigan, Timothy J. "The Discarded Lemon: Kant, Prostitution, and Respect for Persons." In *Prostitution: On Whores, Hustlers, and Johns,* ed. James E. Elias, Vern L. Bullough, Veronica Elias, and Gwen Brewer. New York: Prometheus Books, 1998.

Maggie's and the Prostitutes' Safe Sex Project. www.walnet.org/csis/groups/maggies/.

Magner, C. *Barbara Strozzi: la Virtuosissima Cantatrice.* http://www.home.earthlink.net/~barbarastrozzi/index.htm.

Maher, Lisa, and Kathleen Daly. "Women in the Street-Level Economy: Continuity or Change?" *Criminology* 34 (1996): 4.

Maher, Lisa et al. "Gender, Power, and Alternative Living Arrangements in the Inner-City Crack Culture." *Journal of Research in Crime and Delinquency* 33 (1996): 2.

Maher, Lynne, and Ric Curtis. "Women on the Edge of Crime: Crack Cocaine and the Changing Contexts of Street-Level Sex Work in New York City." *Crime, Law and Social Change* 18 (1992): 221–58.

Mahipati's *Bhakativijaya,* trans. Justin E. Abbott and N. R. Godbole as *Stories of Indian Saints. Vol II.* Pune, India, 1933, reprint Delhi: Motilal Banarsidass, 1982. Mahood, Linda. *The Magdalenes: Prostitution in the Nineteenth Century.* London: Routledge, 1990.

Maisch, Ingrid. *Mary Magdalene: The Image of a Woman through the Centuries.* Translated by Linda Malony. Collegeville, MN: Liturgical Press, 1998.

Mallstad, John E. "Bathouses, Hustlers, and a Sex Club: The Reception of Mikhail Kuzmin's *Wings.*" *Journal of the History of Sexuality* 9 (2000): 85–104.

Mandell, Laura. "Bawds and Merchants: Engendering Capitalist Desires." *English Literary History* 59, no. 1 (1992): 107–23.

Manderson, L. "Public Sex Performances in Patpong and Explorations of the Edges of Imagination." *Journal of Sex Research* 29, no. 4 (1992): 451–75.

Mandeville, Bernard (attributed author). *A Modest Defence of Publick Stews.* London, 1724. Facsimile reprint no. 162, Los Angeles: Augustan Reprint Society, 1973.

Mandeville, Bernard. *The Fable of the Bees: or, Private Vices, Publick Benefits,* 2 vols., ed. F. B. Kaye. Oxford: Clarendon Press, 1924. Reprint, Indianapolis, IN: Liberty Fund, 1988.

Mann, Jonathan, Daniel J. M. Tarantola, and Thomas W. Netter, eds. *AIDS in the World: A Global Report.* Cambridge, MA: Harvard University Press, 1992.

Mann, William J. *Edge of Midnight: The Life of John Schlesinger.* London: Hutchinson, 2004.

Manzo Rodas, R., M. Briones Velasteguí, and T. Cordero Velásquez. "Nosotras, Las Señoras Alegres." Quito: Abrapalabra Ediciones, 1991.

Marcus, Steven. *The Other Victorians.* New York: Basic Books, 1966.

Marechera, Dambudzo. *The House of Hunger.* Oxford: Heinemann, 1978.

Marlatt, Allan, ed. *Harm Reduction: Pragmatic Strategies for Managing High Risk Behaviors.* New York: Guilford Press, 1998.

Martin, Jay. *Always Merry and Bright: The Life of Henry Miller.* Santa Barbara, CA: Capra, 1978.

Masoch, Leopold von Sacher. *Venus in Furs.* Translated by Joachim Neugroschel. New York, 2000. http://www.gutenberg.org/etext/6852 .

Mason, Richard. *The World of Suzie Wong*. London: Collins, 1957.

Massey, Doreen. "Imagining Globalization: Power-Geometries of Time-Space." In *Global Futures: Migration, Environment and Globalization*, ed. A. Brah, M. Hickman, and M. Mac an Ghaill. London: Macmillan, 1999.

Massey, Douglas et al. "Theories of International Migration: A Review and Appraisal." *Population and Development Review* 19 (1993): 431–66.

Massood, Paula J. *Black City Cinema: African American Urban Experiences in Film*. Philadelphia: Temple University Press, 2003.

Masuda, Sayo. Trans. *Autobiography of a Geisha*. Translated by G. G. Rowley. New York: Columbia University Press, 2003.

Matlock, Jann. *Scenes of Seduction: Prostitution, Hysteria, and Reading Difference in Nineteenth-Century France*. New York: Columbia University Press, 1994.

Mattias, Arnold. *Henri de Toulouse-Lautrec: 1964–1901, The Theatre of Life (Basic Art)*. Munich: Taschen, 2000.

May, Glenn. "Jail Assaults Described." *Pittsburgh Tribune-Review*, 25 March 2004.

Mayhew, Henry. *Those That Will Not Work*. Vol. 4 of *London Labour and the London Poor*. New York: A. M. Kelley, 1967.

———. *Selections from 'London Labour and the London Poor.' chosen and with an introduction by John L. Bradley.*. London: Oxford University Press, 1965.

Maynard, Steven. "'Horrible Temptations': Sex, Men, and Working-Class Male Youth in Urban Ontario, 1890–1935." *Canadian Historical Review* 78, no. 2 (June 1997): 191–235.

Mayreder, Rosa. "Die Frauen und der Prozess Riehl." 18/11 *Neues Frauenleben* (1906).

McCall, Andrew. *The Medieval Underworld*. London: A. M. Heath, 1979.

McClintock, Anne. *Imperial Leather: Race, Gender and Sexuality in the Colonial Contest*. New York: Routledge, 1995.

———. "Maid to Order: Commercial Fetishism and Gender Power." *Social Text* 37 (1993b): 87–116.

———. "Sex Workers and Sex Work: Introduction." *Social Text* 37 (1993a): 1–10.

McClure, Laura. *Courtesans at Table: Gender and the Greek Literary Tradition in Athenaeus*. New York: Routledge, 2003.

———, and Christopher Faraone, eds. *Prostitutes and Courtesans in the Ancient World*. Madison: University of Wisconsin Press, 2005.

McCoy, Clyde B., and James A. Inciardi. *Sex, Drugs, and the Continuing Spread of AIDS*. Los Angeles: Roxbury Publishing Company, 1995.

McDonald, Keiko. *Mizoguchi*. Boston: Twayne Publishers, 1984.

McElroy, Wendy. *XXX: A Woman's Right to Pornography*. New York: St. Martin's Press, 1995.

———. "Prostitutes, Anti-Pro Feminists and the Economic Associates of Whores." In *Prostitution: On Whores, Hustlers, and Johns*, ed. James E. Elias, Vern L. Bullough, Veronica Elias, and Gwen Brewer. New York: Prometheus Books, 1998.

McGinn, Thomas A. J. *The Economy of Prostitution in the Roman World: A Study of Social History and the Brothel*. Ann Arbor: University of Michigan Press, 2004.

———. *Prostitution, Sexuality, and the Law in Ancient Rome*. New York: Oxford University Press, 1998.

McIntosh, Mary. "Feminist Debates on Prostitution." In *Sexualizing the Social: Power and the Organization of Sexuality*, ed. Lisa Adkins and Vicki Merchant. New York: St. Martin's Press, 1996.

McKeganey, N. P. "Prostitution and HIV: What Do We Know and Where Might Research Be Targeted in the Future?" *AIDS* 8, no. 9 (September 1994): 1215–26.

————. "Why Do Men Buy Sex and What Are Their Assessments of the HIV Related Risks When They Do?" *AIDS Care* no. 3 (1994).

McKeganey, Neil, and Marina Barnard. *Working the Streets: Sex Workers and Their Clients*. London: Open University Press, 1996.

————, and Michael Bloor. "A Comparison of HIV-Related Risk Behaviour and Risk Reduction between Female Street Working Prostitutes and Male Rent Boys in Glasgow." *Sociology of Health and Illness* 12 (1992): 247–92.

McKewon, Elaine. *The Scarlet Mile: A Social History of Prostitution in Kalgoorlie, 1894–2004*. Nedlands: University of Western Australia Press, 2005.

McKinley, Edward H. *Marching to Glory: The History of the Salvation Army in the United States, 1880–1992*. Grand Rapids, MI: William B. Eerdmans, 1995.

McLaren, John, and Lowman, John. "Enforcing Canada's Prostitution Laws, 1892–1920: Rhetoric and Practice." In *Securing Compliance: Seven Case Studies*, ed. M. L. Friedland. Toronto: University of Toronto Press, 1990.

McLary, Susan. *Feminine Endings: Music, Gender and Sexuality*. Minneapolis: University of Minnesota Press, 1991.

McLeon, Eileen. *Women Working: Prostitution Now*. London: Croom Helm, 1982.

McNamara, Robert. *The Times Square Hustler: Male Prostitution in New York City*. Westwood, CT: Praeger, 1994.

Mead, Margaret. *Coming of Age in Samoa: A Psychological Study of Primitive Youth for Western Civilisation*. New York: Harper Collins, 2001.

Meigs, Cornelia. *Jane Addams: Pioneer for Social Justice*. Boston: Little, Brown, 1970.

Mellor, Anne K. *Romanticism and Feminism*. Bloomington: Indiana University Press, 1988.

Mendes, Peter. *Clandestine Erotic Fiction in English 1800–1930. A Bibliographical Study*. Aldershot, UK: Scolar Press, 1993.

Mendik, Xavier, and Graham Harper. *Unruly Pleasures: The Cult Film and Its Critics*. San Francisco: Last Gasp, 2000.

Metzenrath, Sue. "To Test or Not To Test." Scarlet Alliance Web site http://www.scarletalliance.org.au/library/metrenrath-testdonttest/file_view.

Meyer, Marvin, with Esther A. de Boer. *The Gospels of Mary: The Secret Tradition of Mary Magdalene, the Companion of Jesus*. San Francisco: HarperCollins, 2004.

Miles, Christopher, and John Julius Norwich. *Love in the Ancient World*. London: Seven Dials, 1997.

Miller, E. M. *Street Woman*. Philadelphia: Temple University Press, 1986.

Miller, Heather G., Charles F. Turner, and Lincoln Moses, eds. *AIDS: The Second Decade*. Washington, DC: National Academy Press, 1990.

Miller, Nancy K. *The Heroine's Text: Readings in the French and English Novel, 1722–1782*. New York: Columbia University Press, 1980.

Min, Pyong Gap. "Korean 'Comfort Women': The Intersection of Colonial Power, Gender, and Class." *Gender and Society* 17, no. 6 (2003): 938–57.

Minta, Stephen. *García Márquez: Writer of Colombia*. New York: Harper and Row, 1987.

Moch, Leslie Page. *Moving Europeans: Migration in Western Europe since 1650*. Bloomington: Indiana University Press, 1992.

Mokashi-Punekar, Rohini. *On the Threshold: Songs of Chokhamela*. Lanham, MD: AltaMira Press, 2005.

Molina, Fanny Polanía, and Marie-Louise Janssen. *I Never Thought This Would Happen to Me: Prostitution and Traffic in Latin American Women in the Netherlands*. Rotterdam: Foundation Esperanzo, 1998.

Monahan, Sherry. *The Wicked West*. Tucson, AZ: Rio Nuevo Publishers, 2005.

Montgomery, Heather. "Children, Identity and Child Prostitution in a Tourist Resort in Thailand." In *Global Sex Workers: Rights, Resistance and Redefinition*, ed. Kamala Kempadoo and Jo Doezema. London: Routledge, 1998.

Moodie, T. Dunbar, with Vivienne Ndatshe and British Sibuyi. "Migrancy and Male Sexuality on the South African Gold Mines." In *Hidden from History: Reclaiming the Gay and Lesbian Past*, ed. Martin Duberman, Martha Vicinius, and George Chauncey, Jr. New York: New American Library, 1989.

Moon, Katherine. *Sex among Allies: Military Prostitution in U.S.–Korea Relations*. New York: Columbia University Press, 1997.

Moore, Lisa Jean. "The Variability of Safer Sex Messages: What Do the Centers for Disease Control, Sex Manuals, and Sex Workers Do When They Produce Safer Sex?" In *Prostitution: On Whores, Hustlers, and Johns*, ed. James E. Elias, Vern L. Bullough, Veronica Elias, and Gwen Brewer. Amherst, NY: Prometheus Books, 1998.

Morgan, Thomas R. "HIV and the Sex Industry." In *Working with Women and AIDS: Medical, Social, and Counseling Issues*, ed. Judy Bury, Val Morrison, and Sheena McLachlan. London: Tavistock/Routledge, 1992.

———. "AIDS Risks, Alcohol, Drugs, and the Sex Industry: A Scottish Study." In *AIDS, Drugs, and Prostitution*, ed. Martin Plant. London: Tavistock/Routledge, 1990.

Morisky, D. E., T. V. Tiglao, C. D. Sneed, S. B. Tampongko, J. C. Baltazar, R. Detels, and J. A. Stein. "The Effects of Establishment Practices, Knowledge and Attitudes on Condom Use among Filipina Sex Workers." *AIDS Care* 10 (1998): 213–20.

Morris, Sylvia Jukes. *Rage for Fame: The Ascent of Clare Boothe Luce*. New York: Random House, 1997.

Morrison, T. G., and B. W. Whitehead. "Strategies of Stigma Resistance among Canadian Gay-Identified Sex Workers. *Journal of Psychology and Human Sexuality* 17 (2005): 169–79.

Morse, E. V., P. M. Simon, H. J. Osofsky, P. M. Balson, and H. R. Gaumer. "The Male Street Prostitute: A Vector for Transmission of HIV Infection into the Heterosexual World." *Social Science and Medicine* 32 (1991): 535–39.

Mort, Frank. *Dangerous Sexualities: Medico-Moral Politics in England since 1830*. London: Routledge and Kegan Paul, 1987.

Morton, James. "Legalising Brothels." *Journal of Criminal Law* 68 (2004): 87–89.

Moser, Charles, and Peggy Kleinplatz. "DSM-IV-TR and the Paraphilias: An Argument for Removal." Paper presented at the annual meeting of the American Psychiatric Association, San Francisco, CA, May 2004.

Mudge, Bradford K. *The Whore's Story: Women, Pornography, and the British Novel, 1684–1830*. New York: Oxford University Press, 2000.

Muga, Erasto, ed. *Studies in Prostitution (East, West and South Africa, Zaire and Nevada)*. Nairobi: Kenya Literature Bureau, 1980.

Murdoch, Norman H. *Origins of the Salvation Army*. Knoxville: University of Tennessee Press, 1994.

Murname, M., and Kay Daniels. "Prostitution and 'Purveyors of Disease': Venereal Disease Legislation in Tanzania, 1886–1945." *Hecate* 5 (1979): 5–21.

Murphy, Mary. "The Private Lives of Public Women: Prostitution in Butte, Montana, 1878–1917." In *The Women's West*, ed. Susan Armitage and Elizabeth Jameson. Norman: University of Oklahoma Press, 1987.

Murray, Alison. "Debt Bondage and Trafficking: Don't Believe the Hype." In *Global Sex Workers: Rights, Resistance, and Redefinition*, ed. Kamala Kempadoo and Jo Doezema. New York: Routledge, 1998, pp. 51–64.

———. "Femme on the Streets, Butch in the Sheets (a Play on Whores)." In *Mapping Desire: Geographies of Sexualities*, ed. David Bell and Gill Valentine. London: Routledge, 1995.

———. *No Money, No Honey: A Study of Street Traders and Prostitutes in Jakarta*. Singapore: Oxford University Press, 1991.

———. *Pink Fits: Sex, Subcultures and Discourses in the Asia-Pacific*. Clayton, Australia: Monash Asia Institute, Monash University Press, 2001. http://www.arts.monash.edu.au/mai/cseas/monsea.html.

Myers, Ted et al. "Gay and Bisexual Men's Sexual Partnerships and Variations in Risk Behavior." *Canadian Journal of Human Sexuality* 8, no. 2 (Summer 1999): 115–27.

N.B. [William T. Stead], "The Maiden Tribute of Modern Babylon." *Pall Mall Gazette*, July 1885.

Nagar, Richa. "Religion, Race, and the Debate over *Mut'a* in Dar es Salaam." *Feminist Studies* 26 (Fall 2000): 661–90.

Nagel, Joane. *Race, Ethnicity, and Sexuality: Intimate Intersections, Forbidden Frontiers*. New York: Oxford University Press, 2003.

Nagle, Jill, ed. *Whores and Other Feminists*. New York: Routledge, 1997.

Nanda, Serena. *Neither Man nor Woman: The Hijras of India*. Belmont, CA: Wadsworth, 1990.

Nashkhoev, M. R. "Social-Psychological and Behavioral Characteristics of Sex Workers and the Prevention of Sexually Transmitted Infection in This Group." Moscow: Central Academic Research Institute of Dermatovenerology, Ministry of Health, Russian Federation. Russian University of Friendship of the People, 2002.

National Library of Medicine. "Visual Culture and Public Health Posters: Veneral Disease" http://www.nlm.nih.gov/exhibition/visualculture/venereal.html.

Ndibe, Okey. *Arrows of Rain*. Portsmouth, NH: Heinemann, 2000.

Neequaye, Alfred. "Prostitution in Accra." In *AIDS, Drugs, and Prostitution*, ed. Martin Plant. London: Tavistock Publications, 1987.

Nelson, Nici. "'Selling Her Kiosk': Kikuyu Notions of Sexuality and Sex for Sale in Mathare Valley, Kenya." In *The Cultural Construction of Sexuality*, ed. Pat Kaplan. London: Tavistock Publications, 1987.

Nencel, Lorraine. *Ethnography and Prostitution in Peru*. London: Pluto Press, 2001.

Nettleton, Sarah. *The Sociology of Health and Illness*. Cambridge: Polity Press, 1995.

Nichols, Jeffrey. *Prostitution, Polygamy, and Power: Salt Lake City, 1847–1918*. Urbana: University of Illinois Press, 2002.

Nishiyama, Matsunosuke. *Edo Culture: Daily Life and Diversions in Urban Japan, 1600–1868*. Edited and Translated by Gerald Groemer. Honolulu: University of Hawai'i Press, 1997.

Nochlin, Linda. "A House Is Not a Home: Degas and the Subversion of the Family." In *Dealing with Degas: Representations of Women and the Politics of Vision*, ed. Richard Kendall and Griselda Pollock. London: Pandora, 1992.

Nord, Deborah Epstein. *Walking the Victorian Streets: Women, Representation, and the City*. Ithaca, NY: Cornell University Press, 1995.

Norton, Richard. "The Vere Street Coterie." *Queer Culture* Web site http://www.infopt.demon.co.uk/vere.htm.

NSW Rape Crisis Center. "I Am a Sex Worker." http://www.nswrapecrisis.com.au/Information%20Sheets/I-am-a-sex-worker.htm.

Nuffield, J. *User Report: Diversion Programs for Adults*. Ottawa: Ministry of the Solicitor General of Canada, 1997.

Nzioka, Charles. "AIDS Policies in Kenya: A Critical Perspective on Prevention." In *AIDS: Foundation for the Future*, ed. Peter Aggleton, Peter Davies, and Graham Hart. London: Taylor and Francis, 1994.

O'Connell-Davidson, Julia. *Children in the Global Sex Trade*. Cambridge: Polity Press, 2005.

———. "Prostitution and the Contours of Control." In *Sexual Cultures: Communities, Values and Intimacy*, ed. Jeffrey Weeks and Janet Holland. New York: St. Martin's Press, 1996.

Oden, Robert A., Jr. *The Bible without Theology.* Urbana: University of Illinois Press, 2000.

Odzer, Cleo. *Patpong Sisters: An American Woman's View of the Bangkok Sex World.* New York: Blue Moon Books/Arcade Publishing, 1994.

Öhlschläger, Claudia. *Unsägliche Lust des Schauens. Die Konstruktion der Geschlechter im Voyeuristischen Text.* Freiburg: Rombach, 1996.

O'Leary, Claudine, and Olivia Howard. *The Prostitution of Women and Girls in Metropolitan Chicago: A Preliminary Prevalence Report.* Chicago: Center for Impact Research, 2001.

Oleru, U. G. "Prostitution in Lagos: A Sociomedical Study." *Journal of Epidemiology and Community Health* 34 (December 1980): 312–15.

Olson, Thomas Grant. "Reading and Righting *Moll Flanders.*" *Studies in English Literature 1500–1900* 41 (2001): 467–81.

O'Neill, Maggie, and Rosemary Barberet. "Victimization and the Social Organization of Prostitution in England and Spain." In *Sex for Sale: Prostitution, Pornography, and the Sex Industry,* ed. Ronald John Weitzer. New York: Routledge, 2000.

Oostenk, Annemiek, "A Visit to Burkina Faso." In *A Vindication of the Rights of Whores,* ed. Gail Pheterson. Seattle: Seal Press, 1989.

Oostvogels, R. "Assessment of Commercial Sex Circuits in Bishkek, Kyrgyzstan." Bishkek, Kyrgyzstan: UNAIDS, 1997.

———. "Assessment of Commercial Sex Circuits in Karaganda, Kazahkstan." Karaganda, Kazakhstan: UNDP, 1999.

Otis, Leah Lydia. *Prostitution and Medieval Society: The History of an Urban Institution in Languedoc.* Chicago: University of Chicago Press, 1985.

Overall, Christine. "What's Wrong with Prostitution? Evaluating Sex Work." *Signs: Journal of Women in Culture and Society* 17 (1992): 705–24.

Overs, Cheryl. "Sex work, HIV and the state: an interview with Nel Druce." *Feminist Review* 48 (1994): 114–21.

———, and Paulo Longo. *Making Sex Work Safe.* London: Russell, 1997.

PSI. "Sweetheart Relationships in Cambodia: Love, Sex and Condoms in the Time of HIV." December 2002. www.psi.org/resources/pubs/cambodia.

Padian, Nancy S. "Editorial Review: Prostitute Women and AIDS: Epidemiology." *AIDS* 2 (1988): 413–19.

Padilla, Mark. "Looking for Life: Male Sex Work, HIV/AIDS, and the Political Economy of Gay Sex Tourism in the Dominican Republic." Ph.D. diss., Emory University, 2003.

Pajalich, Armando. "Come nelle Fiabe. Per Adele, l'ultima 'battona' Veneziana." *Insula Quaderni: Stranieri e Foresti a Venezia* 6 (2004): 101–2.

Pal, Minu, Sadhana Mukherji, Madhabi Jaiswal, and Bacchu Dutta. "The Winds of Change Are Whispering at Your Door." In *Global Sex Workers: Rights, Resistance and Redefinition,* ed. Kamala Kempadoo and Jo Doezema. New York: Routledge, 1998.

Panicker, K. Ayyappa, ed. *Kamasuthra of Vatsyayana* (Malayalam). Kottayam, India: DC Books, 1998.

Paone, D., H. Cooper, J. Alperen, Q. Shi, and D.C. Des Jarlais. "HIV Risk Behaviours of Current Sex Workers Attending Syringe Exchange: The Experience of Women in Five U.S. Cities." *AIDS Care* 11 (1999): 269–80.

Parent-Duchâtelet, A.J.B. *De la Prostitution dans la Ville de Paris, Considérée sous le Rapport de l'Hygiène Publique, de la Morale et de l'Administration.* Paris: J. B. Baillière, 1836.

Paris, M., E. Gotuzzo, G. Goyzueta, J. Aramburu, C. F. Caceres, T. Castellano, N. N. Jordan, S. H. Vermund, and E. W. Hook. "Prevalence of Gonoccoccal and Chlamydial Infections in Commercial Sex Workers in a Peruvian Amazon City." *STD* (February 1999): 103–7.

Parish, James Robert. *Prostitution in Hollywood Films: Plots, Critiques, Casts, and Credits for 389 Theatrical and Made-for-Television Releases.* Jefferson, NC: McFarland, 1992.

Parish, Lawrence Charles, Gretchen Worden, Joseph A. Witkowski, Albrecht Scholz, and Daniel H. Parish. "Wax Models in Dermatology." *Studies of the College of Philadelphia* 13, no. 1 (1991): 29–74.

Parke, Derek. *Nell Gwyn.* Thurpp, Stroud: Sutton, 2000.

Parsons, Jeffrey, Juline Koken, David Bimbi, and Perry Halkitis. "Looking beyond HIV: Eliciting Community and Individual Needs of Male Escorts." *Journal of Psychology and Human Sexuality.* In press.

———. "The Use of the Internet by Gay and Bisexual Male Escorts: Sex Workers as Sex Educators." *AIDS Care* 16 (2004): 1–15.

Passet, Joan. *Sex Radicals and the Quest for Woman's Equality.* Urbana: University of Illinois. 2003.

Patton, Cindy. *Last Served? Gendering the HIV Pandemic.* London: Taylor and Francis, 1994.

Paul, Christa. *Zwangsprostitution: Staatlich errichtete Bordelle im Nationalsozialismus.* Berlin: Edition Hentrich, 1994.

Pavlovskis, Zoja. "The Life of St. Pelagia the Harlot: Hagiographic Adaptation of Pagan Romance." *Classical Folio* 30 (1976): 138–49.

Payton, Lewis. "Strip Tease." *Genre* (July 2003): 50–54.

Peace, Richard. *Dostoyevsky: An Examination of the Major Novels.* Cambridge: Cambridge University Press, 1971.

Pearl, Julie. "The Highest Paying Customers: America's Cities and the Costs of Prostitution Control." *Hastings Law Journal* 38 (April 1987): 769–800.

Pearson, Michael. *The £5 Virgins.* New York: Saturday Review Press, 1972.

Peary, Danny. *Cult Movies.* New York: Gramercy, 1998.

Pechter, Edward. "Why Should We Call Her Whore? Bianca in *Othello.*" In *Shakespeare and the Twentieth Century: The Selected Proceedings of the International Shakespeare Association World Congress Los Angeles, 1996,* ed. Jonathan Bate, Jill L. Levenson, and Dieter Mehl. Newark: University of Delaware Press, 1998.

Pedraza, Silvia. "Women and Migration: The Social Consequences of Gender." *Annual Review of Sociology* 17 (1991): 303–25.

Peele, Stanton. *The Meaning of Addiction.* San Francisco: Jossey-Bass, 1998.

Peffer, George Anthony. *If They Don't Bring Their Women Here: Chinese Female Immigration before Exclusion.* Urbana: University of Illinois Press, 1999.

Peiss, Kathy, "'Charity Girls' and City Pleasures: Historical Notes on Working-Class Sexuality, 1880–1920." In *Powers of Desire,* ed. Ann Snitow, Christine Stansell, and Sharon Thompson. New York: Monthly Review Press, 1983.

Pendleton, Eva. "Love for Sale: Queering Heterosexuality." In *Whores and Other Feminists,* ed. Jill Nagle. New York: Routledge, 1997.

"People and Events: Anthony Comstock's 'Chastity' Laws." http://www.pbs.org/wgbh/amex/pill/peopleevents/e_comstock.html.

People's Union for Civil Liberties. "Human Rights Violations against the Transgender Community." http://www.pucl.org/Topics/Gender/2003/transgender.htm.

Peracca, S., J. Knodel, and C. Saengtienchai. "Can Prostitutes Marry? Thai Attitudes toward Female Sex Workers." *Social Science Medicine* 47 (1998): 255–67.

Perkins, Roberta, ed. *Sex Work and Sex Workers in Australia.* Sydney, Australia: University of New South Wales Press, 1991, pp. 133–39.

———. "Sexual Health and Safety among a Group of Prostitutes." In *Sex Industry and Public Policy: Proceedings of a Conference Held 6–8 May 1991,* ed. Sally-Anne Gerull and Boronia Halstead. Canberra: Australian Institute of Criminology, 1992, pp. 147–53.

———. *Working Girls: Prostitutes, Their Life and Social Control.* Canberra: Australian Institute of Criminology, 1991.

———, and G. Bennett. *Being a Prostitute: Prostitute Women and Prostitute Men.* 2nd ed. Sydney: George Allen and Unwin, 1997.

Perry, Mary Elizabeth. *Crime and Society in Early Modern Seville.* Hanover, NH: University Press of New England, 1980.

Petrie, Glen. *A Singular Iniquity: The Campaigns of Josephine Butler.* New York: Viking Press, 1971.

Petrik, Paula. *No Step Backward: Women and Family on the Rocky Mountain Mining Frontier, Helena, Montana 1865–1900.* Helena: Montana Historical Society Press, 1987.

Pettiway, Leon. *Honey, Honey, Miss Thang: Being Black, Gay, and on the Streets.* Philadelphia: Temple University Press, 1996.

Pheterson, Gail. "The Category 'Prostitute' in Social Scientific Inquiry." *Journal of Sex Research* 27 (August 1990): 397–407.

———. *The Prostitution Prism.* Amsterdam: University of Amsterdam Press, 1996.

———. "Right to Asylum, Migration and Prostitution." In *The Prostitution Prism*, ed. Gail Pheterson. *The Prostitution Prism.* Amsterdam: Amsterdam University Press, 1996.

———. *Vindication of the Rights of Whores.* Seattle: Seal Press, 1989.

———. "The Whore Stigma: Female Dishonor and Male Unworthiness." *Social Text* 37 (1993): 39–64.

Phongpaichit, Pasuk. *From Peasant Girls to Bangkok Masseuses.* Geneva: International Labour Office, 1982.

Pickering, Helen. "Social Science Methods Used in a Study of Prostitutes in the Gambia." In *Challenge and Innovation: Methodological Advances in Social Research on HIV/AIDS*, ed. Mary Boulton. London: Taylor and Francis, 1994.

Pickering, Helen et al. "Prostitutes and Their Clients: A Gambian Survey." *Social Science Medicine* 34 (1992): 75–88.

———. "Sexual Networks in Uganda: Casual and Commercial Sex in a Trading Town." *AIDS Care* 9, no. 2 (1997): 199–208.

Pinzer, Maimie. *The Maimie Papers: Letters from an Ex-Prostitute*, ed. Ruth Rosen and Sue Davidson. New York: Feminist Press, 1977.

Pitt, Leonard. *Los Angeles A to Z: An Encyclopedia of the City and the County.* Berkeley: University of California Press, 1997.

Pivar, David J. *Purity Crusade: Sexual Morality and Social Control, 1868–1900.* Westport, CT: Greenwood Press, 1973.

Plachy, Sylvia, and James Ridgeway. *Red Light: Inside the Sex Industry.* New York: Powerhouse Books, 1996.

Planned Parenthood Federation of America. "Birth Control." Web site http://www.plannedparenthood.org/pp2/portal/medicalinfo/birthcontrol/pub-condom.xml.

———. "A History of Contraceptive Methods." Web site http://www.plannedparenthood.org/pp2/portal/medicalinfo/birthcontrol/.

Plant, Martin, ed. *AIDS, Drugs, and Prostitution.* London: Tavistock/Routledge, 1990.

Platt, L., T. Rhodes, C. M. Lowndes, P. Madden, A. Sarang, L. Mikhailova, A. Renton, Y. Pevzner, K. Sullivan, and M. Khutorskoy. "The Impact of Gender and Sex Work on Sexual and Injecting Risk Behaviors and Their Association with HIV Positivity amongst Injecting Drug Users in an HIV Epidemic in Togliatti City, Russian Federation." *Sexually Transmitted Diseases* 32, no. 10 (2005): 605–12.

Plummer, Francis A., and Elizabeth N. Ngugi. "Prostitutes and Their Clients in the Epidemiology and Control of Sexually Transmitted Diseases." In *Sexually Transmitted Diseases*, 2nd ed., ed. King K. Holmes, Per-Anders Mårdh, and P. Frederick Sparling et al. New York: McGraw-Hill, 1990.

Pollard, Tanya, ed. *Shakespeare's Theater: A Sourcebook.* Oxford: Blackwell, 2004.

Pomeroy, Sarah B. *Goddesses, Whores, Wives and Slaves: Women in Classical Antiquity.* New York: Schocken Books, 1995.

Porter, D. "A Plague on the Borders: HIV, Development and Traveling Identities in the Golden Triangle." In *Sites of Desire, Economies of Pleasure: Sexualities in Asia and the Pacific,* ed. L. Manderson and M. Jolly. Chicago: University of Chicago Press, 1997.

Porter, Judith, and Louis Bonilla. "Drug Use, HIV, and the Ecology of Street Prostitution." In *Sex for Sale: Prostitution, Pornography, and the Sex Industry,* ed. Ronald John Weitzer. New York: Routledge, 2000.

Portes, Alejandro, Luís Guarnizo, and Patricia Landolt. "The Study of Transnationalism: Pitfalls and Promise of an Emergent Research Field." *Ethnic and Racial Studies* 22 (1999): 217–37.

Posner, Richard, and Katharine Silbaugh. *A Guide to America's Sex Laws.* Chicago: University of Chicago Press, 1996.

Postle, Martin, and William Vaughan. *The Artist's Model from Etty to Spencer.* Exh. Cat. London: Merrell Holberton, 1999.

Potterat, J. J., D. D. Brewer et al. "Mortality in a Long-Term Open Cohort of Prostitute Women." *American Journal of Epidemiology* 159 (April 2004): 778–85.

Potterat J. J., R. B. Rothenberg, S. Q. Muth, W. W. Darrow, and L. Phillips-Plummer. "Pathways to Prostitution: The Chronology of Sexual and Drug Abuse Milestones." *Journal of Sex Research* 35 (November 1998): 333–40.

Powers, Richard G. *Secrecy and Power: The Life of J. Edgar Hoover.* Glencoe, IL: Free Press, 1987.

Prasad, Monica. "The Morality of Market Exchange: Love, Money, and Contractual Justice." *Sociological Perspectives* 42, no. 2 (1999): 181–214.

Price, Roger D. *Napoleon III and the Second Empire.* New York: Routledge, 1997.

Primov, George, and Carolynne Kieffer. "The Peruvian Brothel as Sexual Dispensary and Social Arena." *Archives of Sexual Behavior* 6 (1977): 245–53.

Prioleau, Betsy. *Seductress: Women Who Ravished the World and Their Lost Art of Love.* New York: Penguin Group, 2003.

Prostitutes Education Network. "Prostitution Law Reform: Defining Terms." http://www.bayswan.org/defining.html.

The Protection Project. "Human Rights Report of North Africa and the Middle East." http://www.protectionproject.org/main1.htm.

Public Health Agency of Canada. *What You Need to Know about Sexually Transmitted Infections.* Minister of Public Works and Government Services Canada, 2002. Public Health Agency of Canada Web site http://www.phac-aspc.gc.ca/publicat/std-mts/.

Pullen, Kirsten. *Actresses and Whores: On Stage and in Society.* Cambridge: Cambridge University Press, 2005.

Pyett, Priscilla M. "Researching with Sex Workers: A Privilege and a Challenge." In *Prostitution: On Whores, Hustlers, and Johns,* ed. James E. Elias, Vern L. Bullough, Veronica Elias, and Gwen Brewer. New York: Prometheus Books, 1998.

Pyett, P. M., and D. J. Warr. "Vulnerability on the Streets: Female Sex Workers and HIV Risk." *AIDS Care* 9 (1997): 539–47.

Pyle, Jean L. "Sex, Maids, and Export Processing: Risks and Reasons for Gendered Global Production Networks." *International Journal of Politics, Culture and Society* 15 (2001): 55–76.

Queeley, Andrea. "Hip Hop and the Aesthetics of Criminalization." *Souls: A Critical Journal of Black Politics, Culture, and Society* 5, no. 1 (2003): 1–14.

Queen, Carol. *Real Live Nude Girl: Chronicles of Sex-Positive Culture.* Seattle: Cleis, 1997.

Quétel, Claude. *The History of Syphilis.* Baltimore: Johns Hopkins University Press, 1990.

Raghuramaiah, K. Lakshmi. *Night Birds: Indian Prostitutes from Devadasis to Call Girls.* Delhi: Chankya Publications, 1991.

Ramjee G., A. E. Weber, and N. S. Morar. "Recording Sexual Behavior: Comparison of Recall Questionnaires with a Coital Diary." *Sexually Transmitted Diseases* 26, no. 7 (August 1999): 374–80.

Raphael, Jody. *Listening to Olivia: Violence, Poverty, and Prostitution.* Boston: Northeastern University Press, 2004.

Ratner, Mitchell, ed. *Crack Pipe as Pimp: An Eight City Ethnographic Study of the Sex-for-Crack Phenomenon.* Lexington, MA: Lexington Books, 1992.

Réal, Grisélidis. *La Passe Imaginaire.* Levallois-Perret, France: Éditions Manya, 1992.

Rechy, John. *City of Night.* New York: Grove Press, 1963.

Reilly, Philip R. *The Surgical Solution: A History of Involuntary Sterilization in the United States.* Baltimore: Johns Hopkins University Press, 1991.

Reinarman, C., and H. Levine. "The Crack Attack: Politics and Media in the Crack Scare." In *Crack in America,* ed. C. Reinarman and H. Levine. Berkeley: University of California Press, 1997.

Reinarman, C., D. Waldorf, S. Murphy, and H. Levine. "The Contingent Call of the Pipe: Bingeing and Addiction among Heavy Cocaine Smokers." In *Crack in America,* ed. C. Reinarman and H. Levine. Berkeley: University of California Press, 1997.

Reiss, Albert, Jr. "The Social Integration of Queers and Peers." In *Deviance: The Interactionist Perspective,* 5th ed., ed. Earl Rubington and Martin Weinberg. New York: Macmillan, 1987.

Renton, A. M., K. Borisenko, A. Meheus, and A. E. Gromyko. "Epidemics of Syphilis in the Newly Independent States of the Former Soviet Union." *Sexually Transmitted Infections* 74 (1998): 165–66.

Reppetto, Thomas A. *American Mafia: A History of Its Rise to Power.* New York: Henry Holt, 2004.

Reuben, David. *Everything You Always Wanted to Know about Sex (But Were Afraid to Ask).* New York: HarperCollins, 1969, 1999.

Reynolds, Helen. *The Economics of Prostitution.* Springfield, IL: Charles Thomas Publishers, 1985.

Reys, Jeff. "LA Outlaw." *Blue* 46 (September 2003): 40–43.

Rhoades, Michelle K. "'No Safe Women': Prostitution, Masculinity, and Disease in France during the Great War." Ph.D. diss., University of Iowa, 2001.

———. "'There Are No Safe Women': Prostitution in France during the Great War." *Proceedings of the Western Society for French History* 27 (2001): 43–50.

Richard, Amy O'Neil. "CIA Report on Trafficking, 2000." http://www.cia.gov/csi/index.html.

Richard, Marthe. *Appel des Sexes.* Paris: Editions du Scorpion, 1951.

Richards, David A. J. "Commercial Sex in the American Struggle for the Rights of the Person." In *Prostitution: On Whores, Hustlers, and Johns,* ed. James E. Elias, Vern L. Bullough, Veronica Elias, and Gwen Brewer. New York: Prometheus Books, 1998.

Richards, Jeffrey. *Sex, Dissidence and Damnation: Minority Groups in the Middle Ages.* London: Routledge, 1990.

Richardson, Joanna. *The Courtesans: The Demi-monde in Nineteenth-Century France.* London: Phoenix Press, 2000.

———. *La Vie Parisienne 1852–1870.* London: Hamish Hamilton, 1971.

Riley, Glenda. "American Daughters: Black Women in the West." *Montana: The Magazine of Western History* 38 (Spring 1988): 14–27.

Ringdal, Nils Johan. *Love for Sale: A World History of Prostitution.* Translated by Richard Daly. New York: Grove Press, 2004.

Roach, Joseph. *Cities of the Dead: Circum-Atlantic Performance.* New York: Columbia University Press, 1996.

Robb, Graham. *Strangers: Homosexual Love in the Nineteenth Century.* New York: W. W. Norton, 2004.

Robbins, Brent Dean. *Mythos and Logos.* www.mythosandlogos.com/Dostoyevsky.html.

Roberts, Nickie. *The Front Line: Women in the Sex Industry Speak.* London: Grafton, 1986.

———. *Whores in History: Prostitution in Western Society.* London: Grafton, 1992.

Robinson, Portia. *The Women of Botany Bay: A Reinterpretation of the Role of Women in the Origins of Australian Society.* Sydney: Macquarie Library, 1988.

Rocke, Michael. *Forbidden Friendships: Homosexuality and Male Culture in Renaissance Florence.* New York: Oxford University Press, 1994.

Roddy, R. E., M. Cordero, C. Cordero, and J. A. Fortney. "A Dosing Study of Nonoxynol-9 and Genital Irritation." *International Journal of STD and AIDS* 4 (1993): 165–70.

Roddy, R. E., L. Zekeng, K. A. Ryan, U. Tamoufé, S. S. Weir, and E. L. Wong. "A Controlled Trial of Nonoxynol-9 Film to Reduce Male-to-Female Transmission of Sexually Transmitted Diseases." *New England Journal of Medicine* 339 (1998): 504–10.

Rofes, Eric. *Dry Bones Breathe: Gay Men Creating Post-AIDS Identities and Subcultures.* Binghamton, NY: Harrington Park Press, 1998.

Rogal, Samuel J. "The Selling of Sex: Mandeville's *Modest Defence of Publick Stews.*" *Studies in Eighteenth-Century Culture* 5 (1976): 141–50.

Rollo-Koster, Joëlle. "From Prostitutes to Brides of Christ: The Avignonese *Repenties* in the Late Middle Ages." *Journal of Medieval and Early Modern Studies* 32, no. 1 (2002): 109–44.

Roos, Julia. "Backlash against Prostitutes' Rights: Origins and Dynamics of Nazi Prostitution Policies." *Journal of the History of Sexuality* 11, nos. 1/2 (January/April 2002): 67–94.

Roper, Lyndal. *Holy Household: Women and Morals in Reformation Augsburg.* Oxford: Oxford University Press, 1991.

Rose, Al. *Storyville, New Orleans: Being an Authentic, Illustrated Account of the Notorious Red Light District.* Tuscaloosa, AL: University of Alabama Press, 1974.

Rose, Jacqueline. *Sexuality in the Field of Vision.* New York: Verso, 1986.

Rose, Rex. "The Last Days of Ernest J. Bellocq." *Exquisite Corpse: A Journal of Letters and Life,* no. 10 (1999). http://www.corpse.com/issue_10/gallery/bellocq.

Rosen, Ruth. *The Lost Sisterhood: Prostitution in America, 1900–1918.* Baltimore: Johns Hopkins University Press, 1982.

———, and Sue Davidson. *The Maimie Papers.* Old Westbury, NY: Feminist Press, 1977.

Rosenberg, Charles and Carroll Smith Rosenberg, ed. *The Prostitute and the Social Reformer: Commercial Vice in the Progressive Era.* New York: Arno Press, 1974.

Rosenberg, Michael J., "Prostitutes and AIDS: A Health Department Priority?" *American Journal of Public Health* 78 (April 1988): 418–23.

Rosenblum, Constance. *Gold Digger: The Outrageous Life and Times of Peggy Hopkins Joyce.* New York: Metropolitan Books, 2000.

Rosenthal, Margaret F. *The Honest Courtesan: Veronica Franco, Citizen and Writer in Sixteenth-Century Venice.* Chicago: University of Chicago Press, 1992.

Ross, Ishbel. *The Uncrowned Queen: Life of Lola Montez.* New York: Harper and Row, 1972.

Rossiaud, Jacques. *Medieval Prostitution.* Translated by Lydia G. Cochrane. Oxford: Basil Blackwell, 1988.

Rounding, Virginia. *Grandes Horizontales: The Lives and Legends of Four Nineteenth-Century Courtesans.* New York: Bloomsbury, 2003.

Rubin, Gayle. "Thinking Sex: Notes for a Radical Theory of the Politics of Sexuality" In *Social Perspectives in Lesbian and Gay Studies; A Reader,* ed. Peter M. Nardi and Beth E. Schneider. New York: Routledge, 1984.

Ruggiero, Guido. *Binding Passions: Tales of Magic, Marriage and Power at the End of the Renaissance.* New York: Oxford University Press, 1993.

———, ed. *Storia dossier: La Storia della Prostituzione.* Florence: Giunti, 1988.

Ruggles, Steven. "Fallen Women: The Inmates of the Magdalen Society Asylum of Philadelphia, 1836–1908." *Journal of Social History* 16, no. 3 (Spring 1983): 65–82.

Russell, Robert P., trans. *Divine Providence and the Problem of Evil: A Translation of Saint Augustine's De ordine.* New York: Cosmopolitan Science and Art Service, 1942.

Russell, Sabin. "The Role of Prostitution in South Asia's Epidemic: Push for Safe Sex in Red Light Districts." *San Francisco Chronicle,* 5 July 2004.

Russell, Sue. *Lethal Intent.* New York: Pinnacle Books, 2002.

Ryan, M. *Prostitution in London, with a Comparative View of That of Paris and New York.* London: H. Baillière, 1839.

Sagarin, E., and R. J. Jolly. "Prostitution: Profession and Pathology." In *Sexual Dynamics of Anti-Social Behavior,* 2nd ed., ed. L. B. Schlesinger and E. R. Revitch. Springfield, IL: Charles C. Thomas, 1997.

Sanchez, J., E. Gotuzzo, J. Escamilla, C. Carrillo, L. Moreyra, W. Stamm, R. Ashle, P. Swenson, and K. K. Holmes. "Sexually Transmitted Infections in Female Sex Workers: Reduced by Condom Use But Not by a Limited Periodic Examination Program." *Sexually Transmitted Diseases* (February 1998): 82–89.

Sancho, N., and M. Layador, eds. *Traffic in Women: Violation of Women's Dignity and Fundamental Human Rights.* Manila: Asian Women's Human Rights Council, 1993.

Sanders, Teela. "It's Just Acting: Sex Workers' Strategies for Capitalizing on Sexuality." *Gender, Work and Organization* 12 (2005): 319–42.

Sandos, James. "Prostitution and Drugs: The United States Army on the Mexican-American Border, 1916–1917." *Pacific Historical Review* 49, no. 4 (1980): 621–45.

Sanger, Margaret. "Plan for Peace." *Birth Control Review* (1932): 107–8.

Sanger, William W. *The History of Prostitution: Its Extent, Causes and Effects throughout the World.* New York: Medical Publishing, 1910.

Sante, Luc. *Low Life: Lures and Snares of Old New York.* New York: Vintage, 1992.

Sassen, Saskia. *Guests and Aliens.* New York: New Press, 1999.

Sauertig, Lutz D. H. "Sex, Medicine and Morality during the First World War." In *War, Medicine and Modernity,* ed. Roger Cooter, Mark Harris, and Steve Sturdy. Phoenix Mill, Stroud, UK: Sutton, 1998.

Savage, Philip. "A Practice of Medicine in San Bernardino in the 1930s." San Bernardino Historical and Pioneer Society *Heritage Tales* (1984): 1–25.

Scambler, Graham, and Annette Scambler. *Rethinking Prostitution: Purchasing Sex in the 1990s.* London: Routledge, 1997.

Scambler, Graham, and Rebecca Graham-Smith. "Female Prostitution and AIDS: The Realities of Social Exclusion." In *AIDS: Rights, Risk and Reason,* ed. Peter Aggleton, Peter Davies, and Graham Hart. London: Falmer Press, 1992.

Schaberg, Jane. *The Resurrection of Mary Magdalene.* New York: Continuum, 2003.

Schaefer, Eric. *"Bold! Daring! Shocking! True!": A History of Exploitation Films, 1919–1959.* Durham, NC: Duke University Press, 1999.

Schank, Josef. *Die Amtlichen Vorschriften, Betreffend die Prostitution in Wien, in ihrer Administrativen, Sanitären und Strafgerichtlichen Anwendung.* Vienna: Josef Safar, 1899.

Schifter, Jacobo. *Latino Truck Driver Trade: Sex and HIV in Central America.* New York: Haworth Hispanic/Latino Press, 2001.

———. *Lila's House: Male Prostitution in Latin America.* New York: Harrington Press, 1998.

Schikorra, Christa. "Prostitution weiblicher KZ-Häftlinge als Zwangsarbeit." *Dachauer Hefte* no. 16 (November 2000): 112–24.

Schloenhardt, Andreas. "Organized Crime and the Business of Migrant Trafficking." *Crime, Law and Social Change* 32 (1999): 203–33.

Schnalke, Thomas. *Diseases in Wax: The History of the Medical Moulage*. Chicago: Quintessence Publishing, 1995.

Schreiber, Mark, ed. *Tabloid Tokyo*. Tokyo: Kodansha, 2005.

———. *Tokyo Confidential: Titillating Tales from Japan's Wild Weeklies*. Tokyo: East Publications, 2001.

Schwarzenbach, Sibyl. "On Owning the Body." In *Prostitution: On Whores, Hustlers and Johns*, ed. James E. Elias, Vern L. Bullough, Veronica Elias, and Gwen Brewer. New York: Prometheus Books, 1998.

Scott, George Riley. *The History of Prostitution*. London: Senate, 1996. Previously published as *Ladies of Vice*. London: Tallis Press, 1968.

Scott, John. *How Modern Governments Made Prostitution a Social Problem: Creating a Responsible Prostitute Population*. New York: Edwin Mellen Press, 2005.

Scott, Maria M. *Re-presenting Jane Shore: Harlot and Heroine*. Aldershot, UK: Ashgate, 2005.

Scranton, Philip, ed. *Beauty and Business: Commerce, Gender, and Culture in Modern America*. New York: Routledge, 2001.

Screech, Timon. *Sex and the Floating World: Erotic Images in Japan, 1700–1820*. Honolulu: University of Hawai'i Press, 1999.

Seagraves, Anne. *Soiled Doves: Prostitution in the Early West*. Hayden, ID: Wesanne Publications, 1994.

Seidensticker, Edward. *Low City, High City: Tokyo from Edo to the Earthquake*. New York: Alfred A. Knopf, 1983.

Seigle, Cecilia Segawa. *Yoshiwara: The Glittering World of the Japanese Courtesan*. Honolulu: University of Hawai'i Press, 1993.

Self, Helen J. *Prostitution, Women and Misuse of the Law: The Fallen Daughters of Eve*. London: Frank Cass, 2003.

Seligman, Edwin R. A., ed. *The Social Evil: With Special Reference to Conditions Existing in the City of New York*. New York: G. P. Putnam's Sons, 1912.

Senkoro, Fikeni. *The Prostitute in African Literature*. Dar es Salaam: Dar es Salaam University Press, 1982.

Sesonske, Alexander. *Jean Renoir: The French Films, 1924–1939*. Cambridge, MA: Harvard University Press, 1980.

Severs, J. B., and A. E. Hartung. *A Manual of the Writings in Middle English 1050–1400*. 8 Vols. New Haven: Connecticut Academy of Arts and Sciences, 1967–2004.

"Sexual Behaviour of Young People." *Progress in Reproductive Health Research* 41 (1997). World Health Organization Web site http://www.who.int/reproductivehealth/hrp/progress/41/news41_1.en.html.

Seymour, Bruce. *Lola Montez: A Life*. New Haven, CT: Yale University Press, 1996.

Shaner, Lora. *Madam: Inside a Nevada Brothel*. Bloomington, IN: Authorhouse, 2001.

Shanley, Mary Lyndon. *Feminism, Marriage, and the Law in Victorian England*. Princeton, NJ: Princeton University Press, 1989.

Shapiro, Nat, and Nat Hentoff, comps. *Hear Me Talkin' to Ya*. New York: Rhinehart, 1955. Reprint, New York: Dover, 1966.

Shapiro, Nina. "The New Abolitionists." *Seattle Weekly*, 24–31 August 2004.

Sharrar, Jack F. *Avery Hopwood: His Life and Plays*. Ann Arbor: University of Michigan Press, 1989.

Shastri, Ajaya Mitra. *India as Seen in the Kuttani-mata of Damodarragupta*. Delhi: Motilal Banarsidas, 1975.

Shaver, Frances M. "A Critique of the Feminist Charges against Prostitution." *Atlantis* 14 (Fall 1988): 82.

———. "Demystifying Sex Work." Paper presented at When Sex Works: International Conference on Prostitution and Other Sex Work, Montreal, 27–29 September 1996. http://www.walnet. org/csis/papers/shaver-distort.html.

———. "Prostitution: A Critical Analysis of Three Policy Approaches." *Canadian Public Policy* 9 (1985): 493–503.

———. "Prostitution: A Female Crime?" In *In Conflict with the Law: Women and the Canadian Justice System*, ed. Ellen Adelberg and Claudia Currie. Vancouver: Press Gang Publishers, 1993.

———. "Prostitution: On the Dark Side of the Service Industry." In *Post Critical Criminology*, ed. Tom Fleming. Scarborough, Ontario: Prentice Hall, 1995.

———. "The Regulation of Prostitution: Avoiding the Morality Traps." *Canadian Journal of Law and Society* 9 (Spring 1994): 123–45.

———. "Sex Work Research: Methodological and Ethical Challenges." *Journal of Interpersonal Violence* 20 (2005): 296–319.

Sheldon, Michael. *The Enemy Within*. London: William Heinemann, 1994.

Sheller, Mimi. *Consuming the Caribbean: From Arawaks to Zombies*. New York: Routledge, 2003.

Shepard, Benjamin. "Culture Jamming a SexPanic!" In *From ACT UP to the WTO: Urban Protest and Community-Building in the Era of Globalization*, ed. Benjamin Shepard and Ron Hayduk. New York: Verso Press, 2002.

Shoemaker, Robert B. "Reforming the City: The Reformation of Manners Campaign in London, 1690–1738." In *Stilling the Grumbling Hive*, ed. Lee Davison et al. New York: St. Martin's Press, 1992.

Shrage, Laurie. *Moral Dilemmas of Feminism: Prostitution, Adultery, and Abortion*. New York: Routledge, 1994.

Shumsky, Neil Larry, and Larry M. Springer. "San Francisco's Zone of Prostitution, 1880–1934." *Journal of Historical Geography* 7, no. 1 (1981): 71–89.

Sidwell, Keith. *Chattering Courtesans and Other Sardonic Sketches*. New York: Penguin, 2005.

Silbert, Mimi, and A. M. Pines. "Child Sexual Abuse and Adolescent Prostitution: A Comparative Analysis." *Social Work* 28 (1983): 285–89.

Silverstein, Charles and Felice Picano. *The Joy of Gay Sex*. New York: HarperCollins, 2003.

Simon, Patricia M., Edward V. Morse, Howard J. Osofsky, Paul M. Balson, and H. Richard Gaumier. "Psychological Characteristics of Male Street Prostitutes." *Archives of Sexual Behavior* 21, no. 1, (1992): 33–44.

Simmons, Sherwin. "Ernst Kirchner's Streetwalkers: Art, Luxury, and Immorality in Berlin, 1913–1916." *Art Bulletin* 82, no. 1 (March 2000): 117–48.

Simons, R. L., and L. B. Whitbeck. "Sexual Abuse as a Precursor to Prostitution and Victimization among Adolescent and Adult Homeless Women." *Journal of Family Issues* 12 (1991): 361–79.

Simpson, Colin, Lewis Chester, and David Leitch. *The Cleveland Street Affair*. Boston: Little, Brown, 1976.

Singleton, Ann, and Paolo Barbesino. "The Production and Reproduction of Knowledge on International Migration in Europe: The Social Embeddedness of Social Knowledge." In *Into the Margins: Migration and Exclusion in Southern Europe*, ed. F. Anthias and G. Lazaridis. Aldershot, UK: Ashgate, 1999.

Skrobanek, Siriporn, Nattaya Boonpakdi, and Chutima Janthakeero, eds. *The Traffic in Women*. New York: Zed Books, 1997.

Sleightholme, Carolyn, and Indrani Sinha. *Guilty without Trial: Women in the Sex Trade in Calcutta*. New Brunswick, NJ: Rutgers University Press, 1996.

Slim, Iceberg. *Pimp: The Story of My Life*. Los Angeles: Holloway House, 1987.

Sölle, Dorothée. *Great Women of the Bible in Art and Literature*. Macon, GA: Mercer University Press, 1994.

"The Sonagachi Project: A Global Model for Community Development." *Horizons Report* May 2002: 7.

Spongberg, Mary. *Feminizing Venereal Disease: The Body of the Prostitute in Nineteenth-Century Medical Discourse.* New York: New York University Press, 1997.

Springhall, John. "'A Life Story for the People'? Edwin J. Brett and the London 'Low-Life' Penny Dreadfuls of the 1860s." *Victorian Studies* 33, no. 2 (1990): 223–46.

Sprinkle, Annie. *Post Porn Modernist: My 25 Years as a Multi-Media Whore.* San Francisco: Cleis, 1998.

———. "We've Come A Long Way—And We're Exhausted!" In *Whores and Other Feminists,* ed. Jill Nagle. New York: Routledge, 1997.

Spurlock, John. *Free Love: Marriage and Middle-Class Radicalism in America, 1825–1860.* New York: New York University Press, 1988.

St. James, Margo. "The Reclamation of Whores." In *Good Girls/Bad Girls: Feminists and Sex Trade Workers Face to Face,* ed. Laurie Bell. Seattle: Seal Press, 1987.

"St. Mary of Egypt." In *Women Saints' Lives in Old English Prose,* ed. and trans. Leslie Donovan. Cambridge, UK: D. S. Brewer, 1999.

Stamp, Shelley Lindsey. "Is Any Girl Safe? Female Spectators at the White Slave Films." *Screen* 37, no. 1 (1996): 1–15.

Stansell, Christine. *City of Women: Sex and Class in New York, 1789–1860.* Urbana: University of Illinois Press, 1987.

Stanton, Kay. "Made to Write 'Whore' Upon: Male and Female Use of the Word 'Whore' in Shakespeare's Canon." In *A Feminist Companion to Shakespeare,* ed. Dympna Callaghan. Oxford: Blackwell, 2000.

Stead, William T. *If Christ Came to Chicago: A Plea for the Union of All Who Love in the Service of All Who Suffer.* Chicago: Laird and Lee, 1894.

Steinfatt, T. M. *Measuring the Number of Trafficked Women and Children in Cambodia. Part I of a Series.* Phnom Penh, Cambodia: USAID, Embassy of the United States of America, 13 November 2002. http://slate.msn.com/Features/pdf/Trfcamf3.pdf.

———. *Measuring the Number of Trafficked Women and Children in Cambodia: A Direct Observation Field Study. Part III of a Series.* Phnom Penh, Cambodia: USAID, Embassy of the United States of America, 6 October 2003. http://slate.msn.com/Features/pdf/Trfciif.pdf.

———. *Working at the Bar: Sex Work and Health Communication in Thailand.* Westport, CT: Greenwood Press, 2002.

———, and J. Mielke. "Communicating Danger: The Politics of AIDS in the Mekong Region." In *Power in the Blood: A Handbook on AIDS, Politics, and Communication,* ed. William N. Elwood. Mahwah, NJ: Lawrence Earlbaum Associates, 1999.

Sterk, Claire E. *Tricking and Tripping: Prostitution in the Era of AIDS.* Putnam Valley, NY: Social Change Press, 2000.

Stern, L. S. *Tricks of the Trade.* Harm Reduction Coalition Web site http://www.harmreduction.org/.

Sterry, David Henry. *Chicken: Self-Portrait of a Young Man for Rent.* New York: Regan Books, 2003.

Steward, Samuel (as Phil Andros). *$tud.* Boston: Alyson Publications, 1966.

Steward, Samuel. *Understanding the Male Hustler.* New York: Harrington Park Press, 1991.

Stoller, Robert J. *Pain and Passion: A Psychoanalyst Explores the World of S&M.* New York: Plenum, 1991.

Stone, Katherine M., and Herbert B. Peterson. "Spermicides, HIV, and the Vaginal Sponge." *Journal of the American Medical Association* 268 (July 1992): 521–23.

Stoneking, Mark. "Women on the Move." *Nature Genetics* 20 (1998): 219–20.

Stubbes, Philip. *The Anatomie of Abuses*. Edited by Margaret Jane Kidnie. Tempe: Arizona Center for Medieval and Renaissance Studies in conjunction with Renaissance English Text Society, 2002.

Stubbs, Kenneth K. *Women of the Light: The New Sacred Prostitute*. Tucson, AZ: Secret Garden Publishing, 1995.

Stubbs, Liz. *Documentary Filmmakers Speak*. New York: Allworth Press, 2002.

Sturdevant, Saundra Pollack, and Brenda Stoltzfus. *Let the Good Times Roll: Prostitution and the U.S. Military in Asia*. New York: New Press, 1992.

Sugden, Philip. *The Complete History of Jack the Ripper*. London: Constable and Robinson, 1995.

Sullivan, Elroy, and William Simon. "The Client: A Social, Psychological, and Behavioral Look at the Unseen Patron of Prostitution." In *Prostitution: On Whores, Hustlers, and Johns*, ed. James E. Elias, Vern L. Bullough, Veronica Elias, and Gwen Brewer. New York: Prometheus Books, 1998.

Sullivan, Steve. *Va Va Voom!: Bombshells, Pin-ups, Sexpots, and Glamour Girls*. Los Angeles: General Publishing Group, 1995.

Surratt, H. L., S. P. Kurtz, J. C. Weaver, and J. A. Inciardi. "The Connections of Mental Health Problems, Violent Life Experiences, and the Social Milieu of the 'Stroll' with the HIV Risk Behaviors of Female Street Sex Workers." *Journal of Psychology and Human Sexuality* 17 (2005): 23–44.

Swan, Laura. *The Forgotten Desert Mothers: Sayings, Lives, and Stories of Early Christian Women*. New York: Paulist Press, 2001.

Swinton, Elizabeth de Sabato, ed. *The Women of the Pleasure Quarter: Japanese Paintings and Prints of the Floating World*. New York: Hudson Hill Press, in association with the Worcester Art Museum, 1996.

Sycamore, Matt Bernstein, ed. *Tricks and Treats: Sex Workers Write about Their Clients*. Binghamton, New York: Harrington Park Press, 2000.

Sykora, Katharina. *Weiblichkeit, Grossstadt, Moderne: Ernst Ludwig Kirchners Berliner Strassenszenen 1913–1915*. Berlin: Museumspädagogischer Dienst Berlin, 1996.

Symanski, Richard. *The Immoral Landscape: Female Prostitution in Western Societies*. Toronto: Butterworths, 1981.

Tabet, Paola. "I'm the Meat, I'm the Knife: Sexual Service, Migration, and Repression in Some African Societies." In *A Vindication of the Rights of Whores*, ed. Gail Pheterson. Seattle: Seal Press, 1989.

Tambe, Ashwini. "The Elusive Ingénue: A Transnational Feminist Analysis of European Prostitution in Colonial Bombay." *Gender and Society* 19, no. 2 (2005): 160–79.

Tambiah, Yasmin. "Turncoat Bodies: Sexuality and Sex Work under Militarization in Sri Lanka." *Gender and Society* 19, no. 2 (2005): 243–61.

Tanaka, Yuki. *Japan's Comfort Women: Sexual Slavery and Prostitution during World War II and the U.S. Occupation*. New York: Routledge, 1995.

Tao, Muning. *Qinglou wénxué yú Zhongguó wénhuà*. Beijing: Dongfang chubânshè, 1993.

Tatar, Maria. "'Das war ein Stuck Arbeit!': Jack the Ripper and Wedekind's Lulu Plays." In *Themes and Structures: Studies in German Literature from Goethe to the Present*, ed. Alexander Stephan. Columbia, SC: Camden House, 1997.

Taylor, Allegra. *Prostitution: What's Love Got to Do with It?* London: Optima, Macdonald, 1991.

Teo, Stephen. "Seijun Suzuki: Authority in Minority." Senses of Cinema Web site http://www.sensesofcinema.com/contents/00/8/miff/suzuki.html.

Tetlock, Philip. E. Orie Kristel, Beth Elson, Melanie Green, and Jennifer Lerner. "The Psychology of the Unthinkable: Taboo Trade-offs, Forbidden Base Rates, and Heretical Counterfactuals." *Journal of Personality and Social Psychology* 78 (2000): 853–70.

Thanh-Dam Truong. *Sex, Money and Morality: Prostitution and Tourism in Southeast Asia*. London: Zed Books, 1990.

Thapar, Romila. *A History of India*. Vol. 1. London: Penguin, 1966.

———, ed. "State and Economy: South India circa A.D. 400–1300." In *Recent Perspectives of Early Indian History*. Bombay, India: Popular Prakashan, 1995.

Theoharis, Athen G. *The FBI and American Democracy: A Brief Critical History*. Lawrence: University Press of Kansas, 2004.

Theroux, Paul. *Nurse Wolf and Dr. Sacks*. London: Faber and Faber, 2001.

Thomas, Donald. *The Marquis de Sade: A New Biography*. Secaucus, NJ: Citadel Press, 1992.

Thompson, E. P., and Elaine Yeo. *The Unknown Mayhew*. London: Pantheon Books, 1971.

Thorbek, Suzanne, *Voices from the City: Women of Bangkok*. London: Zed Books, 1987.

Thormalen, Marianne. *Rochester: The Poems in Context*. New York: Cambridge University Press, 1993.

Thukral, Juhu, and Melissa Ditmore. "Revolving Door: An Analysis of Street-based Prostitution in New York City." New York: Urban Justice Center, 2003. http://www.sexworkersproject.org/ reports/ RevolvingDoor.html.

———, Melissa Ditmore, and Alexandra Murphy. *Behind Closed Doors: An Analysis of Indoor Sex Work in New York City*. New York: Urban Justice Center, 2005. http://www.sexworkersproject. org/reports/BehindClosedDoors.html.

Tian, Min. "Male Dan: The Paradox of Sex, Acting, and Perception of Female Impersonation in Traditional Chinese Theatre." *Asian Theatre Journal* 17, no. 1 (Spring 2000): 78–97.

Ting, Jan C. "'Other Than a Chinaman' : How U.S. Immigration Law Resulted from and Still Reflects a Policy of Excluding and Restricting Asian Immigration." *Temple Political and Civil Rights Law Review* (Spring 1995): 301–15.

Tisdale, Sallie. *Talk Dirty to Me: An Intimate Philosophy of Sex*. New York: Doubleday, 1994.

Tone, Andrea. *Devices and Desires: A History of Contraceptives in America*. New York: Hill and Wang, 2001.

Tong, Benson. *Unsubmissive Women: Chinese Prostitutes in Nineteenth-Century San Francisco*. Norman: University of Oklahoma Press, 1994.

Trafficked Persons Rights Project. "Introduction to the VTVPA." http://www.tprp.org/resources/ index.html.

Trask, Michael. *Cruising Modernism: Class and Sexuality in American Literature and Social Thought*. Ithaca, NY: Cornell University Press, 2003.

Traywick, Ben T. *Hell's Bells of Tombstone*. Tombstone, AZ: Red Marie's, 1993.

Trujillo, L., D. Muñoz, E. Gotuzzo, A. Yi, and D. M. Watts. "Sexual Practices and Prevalence of HIV, HTLV-I/II, and Treponema Pallidum among Clandestine Female Sex Workers in Lima, Peru." *Sexually Transmitted Diseases* (February 1999): 115–18.

Truong, Thanh-Dam. "Gender, International Migration and Social Reproduction: Implications for Theory, Policy, Research and Networking." *Asian and Pacific Migration Journal* 5 (1996):27–52.

———. *Sex, Money and Morality: Prostitution and Tourism in South-east Asia*. London: Zed Books, 1990.

———. *Virtue, Order, Health and Money: Towards a Comprehensive Perspective on Female Prostitution in Asia*. Bangkok: United Nations Economic and Social Commission for Asia and the Pacific, 1986.

Turner, James Grantham. *Libertines and Radicals in Early Modern London: Sexuality, Politics, and Literary Culture, 1630–1685*. New York: Cambridge University Press, 2002.

Udoh, I., and C. Dillard Smith. "The Harm Reduction Model: Effective HIV Prevention Interventions for Prostitutes and Other High Risk Populations in Urban Settings." International Conference on AIDS, Durban, South Africa, July 2000, Abstract ThPeB5180.

Underhill, Lois B. *The Woman Who Ran for President: The Many Lives of Victoria Woodhull.* Bridgehampton, NY: Bridge Works, 1995.

United Nations Consultation with UN/IGOs on Trafficking in Persons, Prostitution and the Global Sex Industry. "Trafficking in Persons and the Global Sex Industry: Need for Human Rights Framework." 1999. http://www.imadr.org/project/petw/seminarPETW.pdf.

United Nations Office on Drugs and Crime. "The United Nations Convention against Transnational Organized Crime and Its Protocols." United Nations Office on Drugs and Crime Web site http://www.unodc.org/unodc/index.html.

"United Nations Universal Declaration of Human Rights." United Nations Web site http://www.un.org/Overview/rights.html.

United States Victims of Trafficking and Violence Protection Act of 2000: Trafficking in Persons Report. http://www.state.gov/g/tip/rls/tiprpt/2004/

van Damme, L. "Advances in Topical Microbicides." Paper presented at the XIII International AIDS Conference, Durban, South Africa, 9–14 July 2000.

Van Damme, Lut, Gita Ramjee, Michel Alary, Bea Vuylsteke, Verapol Chandeying, Helen Rees, Pachara Sirivongrangson, Lonard Mukenge-Tshibaka, Virginie Ettigne-Traore, Charn Uaheowitchai, Salim S. Abdool Karim, Benot Msse, Jos Perrins, and Marie Laga on behalf of the COL-1492 Study Group. "Effectiveness of COL-1492, a Nonoxynol-9 Vaginal Gel, on HIV-1 Transmission in Female Sex Workers: A Randomised Controlled Trial." *Lancet* 360 (September 2002): 971–77.

van de Pol, Lotte C. "Beeld en Werkelijkheid van de Prostitutie in de Zeventiende Eeuw." In *Soete Minne en Helsche Boosheit. Seksuele Voorstellingen in Nederland, 1300–1850,* ed. G. Hekma and H. Roodenburg. Nijmegen: SUN, 1988.

———. *Het Amsterdams Hoerdom. Prostitutie in de zeventiende en achttiende eeuw.* Amsterdam: Wereldbibliotheek, 1996.

———. "The History of Policing Prostitution in Amsterdam." In *Regulating Morality: A Comparison of the Role of the State in Mastering the Mores in the Netherlands and the United States,* ed. Hans Krabbendam and Hans-Martien ten Napel. Antwerp, Belgium: Apeldoorn, 2000.

———. *La puta y el ciudadano. La prostitución en Amsterdam en los siglos XVII y XVIII.* Madrid: Siglo XXI, 2005.

van der kolk, B. A., A. C. McFarlan. and L. Weisaeith, eds. *Traumatic Stress: The Effects of Overwhelming Experience on Mind, Body, and Society.* New York: Guilford Press, 1996.

Van Gennep, Arnold. *The Rites of Passage.* Chicago: University of Chicago Press. 1960.

Vance, Carole, ed. *Pleasure and Danger: Exploring Female Sexuality.* Boston: Routledge, 1984.

Vanwesenbeeck, Ine. "Another Decade of Social Scientific Work on Sex Work: A Review of Research 1990–2000." *Annual Review of Sex Research* 12 (2001): 242–89.

———. *Prostitutes' Well-Being and Risk.* Amsterdam: VU University Press, 1994.

———, R. van Zessen, C. J. de Graaf, and S. Straver. "Contextual and Interactional Factors Influencing Condom Use in Heterosexual Prostitution Contacts." *Patient Education and Counseling* 24 (1994): 307–22.

Vice Commission of Chicago. *The Social Evil in Chicago: A Study of Existing Conditions.* Chicago: Gunthorp-Warren Printing Company, 1911.

Vijaisri, Priyadarshini. *Recasting the Devadasi: Patterns of Sacred Prostitution in Colonial South India.* New Delhi: Kanishka Publishers, 2004.

Visano, Livy. *This Idle Trade.* Concord, Ontario: VitaSana Books, 1987.

Visness, C. M., P. Ulin, S. Pfannenschmidt, and L. Zekeng. "Views of Cameroonian Sex Workers on a Woman-Controlled Method of Contraception and Disease Protection." *International Journal of STD and AIDS* 9 (1998): 695–99.

Vitiello, Giovanni. "The Forgotten Tears of the Lord of Longyang: Late Ming Stories of Male Prostitution and Connoisseurship." In *Linked Faiths*, ed. Jan A. M. de Meyer and Peter M. Engelfriet. Leiden: Brill, 2000.

Voragine, Jacobus de. *The Golden Legend: Readings on the Saints*. Translated by William Granger Ryan. Princeton, NJ: Princeton University Press, 1993.

Wagner, D. "The Universalization of Social Problems." *Critical Sociology* 23 (1997): 3–23.

Wahab, Stéphanie. "Evaluating the Usefulness of a Prostitution Diversion Project." *Qualitative Social Work* 5, no. 1 (2006): 67–92.

———. "Navigating Mixed Theory Projects: Lessons from a Qualitative Evaluation of Salt Lake City's Prostitution Diversion Project." *Affilia*, 20, no. 2 (2005): 203–21.

———, and R. Davis. "An Evaluation of Salt Lake City's Prostitution Diversion Project." Unpublished report. Salt Lake City: University of Utah, College of Social Work, 2004.

Walgrave, L. "Diversion? It Depends on What We Divert To: Some Comments on Diversion and the Restorative Alternatives." In *Diversion and Informal Social Control*, ed. G. Albrecht and W. Ludwig-Mayerhofer. Berlin: Walter de Gruyter, 1995.

Walkowitz, Judith R. *City of Dreadful Delight: Narratives of Sexual Danger in Late-Victorian London*. Chicago: University of Chicago Press, 1992.

———. "Male Vice and Female Virtue: Feminism and the Politics of Prostitution in 19th Century Britain." In *Powers of Desire: The Politics of Sexuality*, ed. Ann Snitow, Christine Stansell, and Sharon Thompson. New York: Monthly Review Press, 1983.

———. *Prostitution and Victorian Society: Women, Class, and the State*. Cambridge: Cambridge University Press, 1980.

Wallis, Brian, curator. "The Mysterious Monsieur Bellocq." International Center of Photography Web site http://www.icp.org/exhibitions/bellocq/ICP_brochure_bellocq.pdf.

Wan, Xianchu. *Famous Prostitutes of Ancient China (Zhong Guo Ming Ji)*. Taipei: Xiapu Press, 1994.

Wang, Shunu. *Zhongguo changji shi ("A History of Entertainer-Prostitutes in China")*. Shanghai: Shanghai shudian, 1995.

Ward, Benedicta. *Harlots of the Desert: A Study of Repentance in Early Monastic Sources*. Kalamazoo, MI: Cistercian Publications, 1987.

Ward, Prescilla. "Cultures and Carriers: 'Typhoid Mary' and the Social Science of Control." *Social Text* 52–53 (1997): 181–214.

Washburn, Josie. *The Underworld Sewer: A Prostitute Reflects on Life in the Trade*. Lincoln: University of Nebraska Press, 1909, 1997.

Wasserman, Joanne. "Prison Rapes 'Routine.'" *New York Daily News*, 28 January 2003.

Watkins, S. Craig. *Hip Hop Matters: Politics, Popular Culture, and the Struggle for the Soul of a Movement*. Boston: Beacon Press, 2005.

Watkinson, Mike, Pete Anderson, and Scott Walker. *A Deep Shade of Blue*. London: Virgin Books, 1995.

Watt, George. *The Fallen Woman in the Nineteenth-Century English Novel*. London: Croom Helm, 1984.

Watts, Sheldon. "The Secret Plague: Syphilis in West Europe and East Asia, 1492–1965." In *Epidemics and History: Disease, Power and Imperialism*, ed. Sheldon Watts. New Haven, CT: Yale University Press, 1997.

Wedekind, Frank. *Lulu*. Translated by Nicholas Wright. London: Nick Hern Books, 2001.

———. *The Lulu Plays and Other Sex Tragedies*. Translated by Stephen Spender. London: John Calder, 1972.

Weeks, Jeffrey. *Coming Out: Homosexual Politics in Britain, from the Nineteenth Century to the Present*. London: Quartet Books, 1977.

———. "Inverts, Perverts, and Mary-Annes: Male Prostitution and the Regulation of Homosexuality in England in the Nineteenth and Early Twentieth Centuries." In *The Gay Past: A Collection of Historical Essays*, ed. Salatore Licata and Robert Peterson. New York: Haworth Press, 1985.

Weir, S. S., R. E. Roddy, L. Zekeng, K. A. Ryan, and E. L. Wong. "Measuring Condom Use: Asking 'Do You or Don't You' Isn't Enough." *AIDS Education and Prevention* 10 (1998): 293–302.

Weisner-Hanks, Mary. *Convents Confront the Reformation: Catholic and Protestant Nuns in Germany*. Milwaukee, WI: Marquette University Press, 1996.

Weitzer, Ronald John, ed. *Sex for Sale: Prostitution, Pornography, and the Sex Industry*. New York: Routledge, 2000.

Weldon, Jo. "Shut Up, I Can't Hear You: What Happened at NYU March 2, 2001." http://gstringsforever.com/march2.html.

Wells, Jess. *A Herstory of Prostitution in Western Europe*. Berkeley, CA: Shameless Hussy Press, 1982.

Werbner, Richard, and Terence Ranger, eds. *Postcolonial Identities in Africa*. London: Zed Books, 1997.

Werther, Ralph, a.k.a. Jennie June. *The Female Impersonators*. New York: Medico-Legal Journal, 1922.

Wertz, Robert, and Dorothy Wertz. *Brought to Bed*. New Haven, CT: Yale, 1989.

West, Donald J., in association with Buz de Villiers. *Male Prostitution*. Binghamton, NY: Haworth Press, 1993.

West Australian Police. "Police Re-open Shirley Finn Murder File." 23 June 2005. www.police.wa.gov.au/MediaAndPublicAffairs/MediaReleases/3232.pdf.

Westenholz, Joan G. "Tamar, Qedeša, Qadištu, and Sacred Prostitution in Mesopotamia." *Harvard Theological Review* 82 (1989): 245–65.

Westermann, Mariët. *The Amusements of Jan Steen: Comic Painting in the Seventeenth Century*. Zwolle: Waanders, 1997.

White, Luise. *The Comforts of Home: Prostitution in Colonial Nairobi*. Chicago: University of Chicago Press, 1990.

———. "Prostitution, Differentiation and the World Economy: Nairobi, 1899–1939." In *Connecting Spheres: Women in the Western World, 1500 to the Present*, ed. Marilyn J. Boxer and Jean H. Quataert. New York: Oxford University Press, 1986, pp. 223–31.

———. "Prostitution, Identity, and Class Consciousness during World War II." *Signs: Journal of Women in Culture and Society* 11 (1986): 255–73.

———. "Prostitution, Reformers and Historians." *Criminal Justice History* 6 (1985): 201–17.

———. "Vice and Vagrant: Prostitution, Housing and Casual Labour in Nairobi the Mid 1930s." In *Labour, Law and Crime: An Historical Perspective*, ed. Francis Snyder and Douglas Hay. London: Tavistock, 1987.

———. "Women's Domestic Labor in a Colonial City: Prostitution in Nairobi, 1900–1950." In *Patriarchy and Class: African Women at Home and in the Workplace*, ed. Jane Parpart and Sharon Stichter. Boulder, CO: Westview Press, 1988.

White, Susan M. *The Cinema of Max Ophuls: Magisterial Vision and the Figure of Woman*. New York: Columbia University Press. 1995.

Whiteaker, Larry. *Seduction, Prostitution, and Moral Reform in New York, 1830–1860*. New York: Garland, 1997.

Whitehead, Judy. "Community Honor/Sexual Boundaries: A Discursive Analysis of *Devadasi* Criminalization in Madras, India, 1920–1947." In *Prostitution: On Whores, Hustlers, and Johns*, ed. James E. Elias, Vern L. Bullough, Veronica Elias, and Gwen Brewer. New York: Prometheus Books, 1998, pp. 91–106.Widmer, Ellen, and Kang-i Sun Chang, eds. *Writing Women in Late Imperial China*. Stanford, CA: Stanford University Press, 1997.

Wijers, Marjan, and Lin Lap Chew. *Trafficking in Women: Forced Labour and Slavery-like Practices in Marriage, Domestic Labour and Prostitution*. Utrecht, Netherlands: Foundation against Trafficking in Women (STV), 1997.

Wikholm, Andrew. "Scandal in Cleveland Street." 1999. http://www.gayhistory.com/rev2/events/1889.htm.

Wilkinson, David, and Gillian Fletcher. *Sex Talk—Peer Ethnographic Research with Male Students and Waitresses in Phnom Penh*. Phnom Penh: PSI, 2002.

Williams, T. *The Cocaine Kids*. Reading, MA: Addison-Wesley, 1989.

Willis, Ellen. "Feminism, Moralism, and Pornography." In *Powers of Desire: The Politics of Sexuality*, ed. Ann Snitow, Christine Stansell, and Sharon Thompson. New York: Monthly Review Press, 1983.

Wilmot, John, Earl of Rochester. *The Complete Poems*. Edited by David M. Vieth. New Haven, CT: Yale University Press, 1968.

Wilson, David, et al. "A Pilot Study for an HIV Prevention Programme among Commercial Sex Workers in Bulawayo, Zimbabwe." *Social Science Medicine* 31 (1990): 609–18.

Wilson, John H. *Nell Gwyn, Royal Mistress*. New York: Pellegrini and Cudahy, 1952.

Winick, Charles, and Paul Kinsie. *The Lively Commerce*. Chicago: Quadrangle, 1971.

Winnifrith, Tom. *Fallen Women in the Nineteenth-Century Novel*. New York: St. Martin's Press, 1994.

"Winston Leyland Interviews John Rechy." In *Gay Sunshine Interviews*, ed. Winston Leyland. San Francisco: Gay Sunshine Press, 1978. Originally published in *Gay Sunshine* 23 (1974).

Wisdom, Mark. *The Trokosi System*. Accra-North, Ghana: Mercury Press, 2001.

Wistrom, Brent. "Elusive Evidence in Rape Cases; Allred Investigation Not Accurate, ACLU Says." *Times Record News*, 27 February 2004.

Wockner, Rex. "Sex-lib Activists Confront 'SexPanic!'" *Gaywave*, 2 December 1997. http://gaytoday.badpuppy.com/garchive/events/111797ev.htm/.

Wojcicki, J. M. "'She Drank His Money': Survival Sex and the Problem of Violence in Taverns in Gauteng Province, South Africa." *Medical Anthropology Quarterly* 16, no. 3 (2002): 267–93.

Wolfenden, John. *Turning Points: The Memoirs of Lord Wolfenden*. London: Bodley, 1976.

Wolffers, Ivan. "Empowerment of Sex Workers and HIV Prevention." *Research for Sex Work* 3 (2000): 1–3.

Woodward, Charrlotte, and Jane Fischer. "Regulating the World's Oldest Profession: Queensland's Experience with a Regulated Sex Industry." *Research for Sex Work* 8 (2005): 16–18. http://www.researchforsexwork.org.

Wooster, Robert. *Soldiers, Sutlers, and Settlers: Garrison Life on the Texas Frontier*. College Station Texas A & M University Press, 1987.

Worth, Robert. "Tolerance in Village Wears Thin: Drug Dealing and Prostitution Are Becoming a Hazard in a Normally Quiet West Village Area." *New York Times*, 19 January 2002.

Wortley, S., B. Fischer, and C. Webster. "Vice Lessons: A Survey of Prostitution Offenders Enrolled in the Toronto John School Diversion Program." *Canadian Journal of Criminology* 3 (2002): 227–48.

Wotton, Rachel. "The Relationship between Street-based Sex Workers and the Police in the Effectiveness of HIV Prevention Strategies." *Research for Sex Work* 8 (2005): 11–13. http://www.researchforsexwork.org.

Wright, Raymond. *Who Stole the Mace?* Melbourne, Australia: Victorian Parliament Library, 1991.

Wu, Cuncun. *Homoerotic Sensibilities in Late Imperial China*. London: RoutledgeCurzon, 2004.

Wynter, Sarah, a.k.a. Evelina Giobbe. "Whisper: Women Hurt in Systems of Prostitution Engaged in Revolt." In *Sex Work: Writings by Women in the Sex Industry*, ed. Frederique Delacoste and Priscilla Alexander. San Francisco: Cleis Press, 1987.

Yaffe, David. *Fascinating Rhythm*. Princeton, NJ: Princeton University Press, 2006.

Yao, Ping. "The Status of Pleasure: Courtesan and Literati Connections in T'ang China, 618–907." *Journal of Women's History* 14, no. 2 (2002): 26–53.

Yehuda, R., ed. *Psychological Trauma*. Washington, DC: American Psychiatric Press, 1998.

Zausner, Michael. *The Streets: A Factual Portrait of Six Prostitutes as Told in Their Own Words*. New York: St. Martin's Press, 1986.

Zekeng, L., P. J. Feldblum, R. M. Oliver, and L. Kaptue. "Barrier Contraceptive Use and HIV Infection among High-risk Women in Cameroon." *AIDS* 7 (1992): 725–31.

Zelliot, Eleanor, and Rohini Mokashi-Punekar. *Untouchable Saints: An Indian Phenomenon*. New Delhi: Manohar, 2005.

Zimmerman, Susan. "'Making a Living from Disgrace': The Politics of Prostitution, Female Poverty and Urban Gender Codes in Budapest and Vienna, 1860–1920." In *The City in Central Europe: Culture and Society from 1800 to the Present*, ed. Malcolm Gee et al. Aldershot, UK: Ashgate, 1999.

Zinberg, Norman. *Drug, Set, and Setting: The Basis for Controlled Intoxicant Use*. New Haven, CT: Yale University Press, 1984.

Zola, Émile. *Nana*. Translated by George Holden. Harmondsworth, UK: Penguin Books, 1972.

Zürn, Gaby. "Von der Herbertstraße nach Auschwitz." In *Frauenbiographien des Nationalsozialismus*, ed. Angelika Ebbinghaus. Nördlingen: Greno-Verlag, 1987.

Web Sites

Adult Industry Medical Health Care Foundation Web site http:///www.aim-med.org.

Annie Sprinkle's Web site http://www.anniesprinkle.org.

Coalition against Trafficking in Women (CATW) Web site www.catw.org.

Complete Linda Lovelace Web site http://www.completelindalovelace.com/.

Foundation Napoleon Web site http://www.napoleonica.org/us/na/na_fondation.html.

Global Alliance against Trafficking in Women Web site http://www.gaatw.org/.

Global Campaign for Microbicides. http://www.global-campaign.org.

Hardy, Valérie. *Sidonie-Gabrielle Colette*. Colette Web site http://www.colette.org/.

Harm Reduction Coalition Web site http://www.harmreduction.org/.

International Sex Worker Foundation for Art, Culture and Education Web site http://www.iswface.org.

International Union of Sex Workers Web site http://www.iusw.org/.

PsychNet-UK Web site http://www.psychnet-uk.com/dsm_iv/voyerism_disorder.htm.

Research for Sex Work Web site http://www.researchforsexwork.org.

Rode Draad Web site http://www.rodedraad.nl.

Scarlet Alliance Web Site http://www.scarletalliance.org.au.

Sex Education Links Web site. http://www.bigeye.com/sexeducation/voyeurism.html.

Touching Base Web site http://www.touchingbase.org.

Victoria Woodhull and Company W eb site http://www.victoria-woodhull.com.

Films

Festival of Pleasure. [Documentary]. Produced by Sex Workers Forum Kerala, 2003.

Funari, Vicky and Julia Query. *Live Nude Girls Unite!* [Documentary]. 2000.

Noriko, Sekiguchi. *Senso Daughters*. Distributed by First Run/Icarus Films. 1989.

Sex in a Cold Climate. [Documentary]. Directed by Stephen Humphries. Testimony Films for Channel Four Television Corporation, 1997.

INDEX

Note: Pages in **boldface** refer to the main entry on the subject

Faulkner, William, 20

Fawcett, Edgar, 20

Female boarding house, **154**

Female Moral Reform Society, 375

Feminism, **154–60**; forced prostitution and, 168, 317; literature of, 48, 77; misogyny and, 317; patriarchy theories and, 348–49; prostitutes right's movement and, 208; prostitution terminology and, 476; rape theories and, 142; *Sex Work* (Delacoste), 433–34

Feminists: abolitionism philosophy of, 6; Barry, Kathleen, 156; Chancer, Lynn, 157; Dworkin, Andrea, 154; Kipnis, Laura, 157; Longo, Paulo, 158; MacKinnon, Catharine, 154; neo-abolitionist feminists, 6; Pendleton, Eva, 157; Vance, Carole, 157

Ferrer, Jose, 487

Festival of Pleasure, 302–3

Fetishes (Broomfield), 164, 423

Fiction, speculative, goals of, 151

Films, **160–62**; blaxploitation, 165–66; pimpmobiles depicted in, 358; transgender sex workers in, 505; voyeurism in, 529

Films, cult, **162–64**

Films, documentary, **164–65**

Films, exploitation, **165–66**

Finn, Shirley, 53

First Amendment (U.S. Constitution), 155, 185

First National Meeting of Prostitutes, 251

First Offenders of Prostitution Program (FOPP), 137–38

Five Points, New York City, **166–67**, 330, 379

Flaubert, Gustav, 44, 416

Fleiss, Heidi, 267–68

A Flower in a Sea of Sins (Zeng Pu), 106

Foat, Ginny, **167–68**

Folies Bergère, 17

Fonda, Jane, 241

Fontane, Anne, 176

FOPP. *See* First Offenders of Prostitution Program

Forced prostitution, **168–70**, 349, 375, 540; child prostitution and, 170; human rights and, 168, 218; MacKinnon, Catharine, and, 168; misogyny as factor in, 317; patriarchy and, 349; trafficking and, 170, 490; transgender sex workers and, 168; WHISPER and, 169

Ford, John, 66

Fortune (magazine), 64

Foster, Alan Dean, 152

Found (Rossetti), 149

Foxy Brown (Hill), 166

France: cinema of, 175–76; courtesans of, 349, 416; literature of, 177–81, 554–55; Marthe, Richard, 402; Parent-Duchâtelet, Alexandre-Jean-Baptiste,

343; prostitution in, 65; Sabatier, Appolonie, 416–17; sexual offense legislation of, 100

France, Anatole, 479

France, Second Empire, **171–72**, 190

France, Hector, 45

Francesco, Albino, 244

Franco, Veronica, **172–73**, 516

Franco-Prussian War, 172

Frederic, Harold, 20

Free Enquirer, 173

Free Love, **173–75**

French Cinema, **175–77**

The French Disease, 468–69

French literature, **177–81**, 554–55

Friedkin, William, 163

From Here to Eternity (Zimmerman), 160

Funny money. *See* Brothel tokens

"Furniture Man" (blues), 62

Gaiety Theater (New York City), 283

Gallegos, Rómulo, 246

Gallet, Louis, 479

García Márquez, Gabriel, **182**, 246

Gaskell, Elizabeth, 67, 150

Gate of Flesh (Suzuki), 233

Gautierr, Théophile, 416

Gay bars, 343

Gay Nineties era, 64

Geisha, 10, 17, **182–85**; portraits of, 514; Yoshiwara and, 552

Genderqueer movement, 500

Gentlemen Prefer Blondes (Loos), 187

Gentlemen's Clubs, **185–86**

Germany: Expressionist artist group of, 240; imprisonment of prostitutes in, 147; *Lulu* of, 263–64; sexual offense legislation of, 100; Society for Combating Venereal Diseases, 327; Weimar Republic of, 325, 327, 530–32. *See also* Nazi Germany

GFE. *See* Girlfriend experience

Ghana: prostitutes of, 111, 112; *trokosi* (religious slavery) of, 102–3

Gibson, William, 153

Gigi (Colette), 110

Gilbert, Marie Dolores Rosanna. *See* Montez, Lola

Gilded Age era, 64

Girlfriend experience (GFE), 240

Global Fund for Women (U.S.), 48

Global Health Council, 158

Global Programme on AIDS (GPA), 209

Globalization, **186–87**; ports and, 364; of sex, 82; transgender sex workers and, 505

Godard, Jean-Luc, 161, 176

God's Bits of Wood (Sembene Ousmane), 14

ABOUT THE EDITOR, ADVISORS AND CONTRIBUTORS

EDITOR

Melissa Hope Ditmore is the editor of *Research for Sex Work* and Coordinator of the Network of Sex Work Projects. She is also a research consultant and was the principal investigator for "Revolving Door," the first report released by the Sex Workers Project. Ditmore has written about trafficking and the sex industry in various books and journals. She has spoken about sex work at varied venues including the United Nations, universities, academic and political conferences, and community events.

ADVISORS

Laura Agustín is a lecturer at the School of Sociology and Social Policy, University of Liverpool, United Kingdom. She has focused her research and publications on the connections between migrations of non-European women to Europe, where they sell domestic, caring and sexual services, and the large social sector that proposes to help them. She has worked in *educación popular* both in Latin America and with migrants in various parts of the West and has been an evaluator of social programming for the International Labour Organization (ILO) and the European Commission. She moderates a romance-language email list for sex workers and their allies.

Priscilla Alexander is co-editor of *Sex Work Writings by Women in the Sex Industry*.

Elizabeth Bernstein is an associate professor of sociology and women's studies at Barnard College, Columbia University. She is the co-editor, with Laurie Schaffner, of *Regulating Sex: The politics of intimacy and identity*.

Andrew Hunter is a co-coordinator of the Asia Pacific Network of Sex Workers.

Kamala Kempadoo, an associate professor in social science at York University, Canada, is the author of *Sexing the Caribbean: Gender, Race, and Sexual Labor* (2004) and editor of *Trafficking and Prostitution Reconsidered: New Perspectives on Migration, Sex Work and Human Rights* (2005).

Helen J. Self is the author of *Prostitution, Women and Misuse of the Law: The Fallen Daughters of Eve*. She has conducted an extensive study of prostitution both historically and in its contemporary setting.

Nancy M. Wingfield is an associate professor of history at Northern Illinois University. Her recent publications include *Gender and World War in Twentieth-Century Eastern Europe*, co-edited with Maria Bucur.

CONTRIBUTORS

Nwando Achebe is an associate professor of history at Michigan State University. She is the author of *Farmers, Traders, Warriors and Kings: Female Power and Authority in Northern Igboland, 1900–1960.*

Saheed Aderinto is a research assistant at the French Institute for Research in Africa (IFRA), University of Ibadan. He specializes in the social and urban history of Africa with an interest in the history of prostitution and human trafficking.

Jennifer Adler is an adjunct professor for the City University of New York system. Her academic focus is environmental psychology and design research.

Rachel Aimeé has written about gender, sexuality, sex work, and popular culture for the feminist webzine *The F Word* and is co-editor of *$pread Magazine*, a sex workers' advocacy publication.

Dan Allman is a research associate at the HIV Social Behavioural and Epidemiological Studies Unit, University of Toronto, and a postgraduate at the Centre for Research on Families and Relationships at the University of Edinburgh. He has written on sexuality, sex work, substance use, harm reduction, social inclusion, and community-based research.

Clinton P.E. Atchley is an associate professor of English at Henderson State University in Arkadelphia, Arkansas.

Melynda Barnhart directs the Anti-Trafficking Initiative at the International Rescue Committee.

Pierre Marc Bellemare teaches classics and philosophy at Saint Paul University in Ottawa, Canada.

Laurie Bernstein is the author of *Sonia's Daughters: Prostitutes and Their Regulation in Imperial Russia*. She is an associate professor in the History Department of Rutgers University–Camden as well as director of Women's Studies.

Elizabeth Bishop teaches modern Arab history at the University of Texas at Austin.

Lee Y. Blouin (MA, University of Arizona, 2004) is a doctoral candidate in English literature at the University of Arizona, where she teaches English literature and composition. Her research explores the intersection between literature and reproductive medicine in the early modern period.

Bruce E. Brandt is a professor of English at South Dakota State University.

Malin Lidström Brock is a doctoral candidate of the English faculty at Oxford University, United Kingdom.

Siobhan Brooks is a doctoral candidate at the New School. She was a union organizer at the Lusty Lady Theater in San Francisco, and is featured in Julia Query's documentary, *Live, Nude, Girls, Unite!*

Stephanie Lynn Budin is a professor of intellectual heritage at Temple University in Philadelphia. Her main scholarly interests are ancient Greece and the Near East, sex and gender, and myth and religion.

Rachel Epp Buller teaches at Bethel College in North Newton, Kansas. Her research examines German art of the 1920s, American art of the 1960s, and feminist art.

Diane Cady is an assistant professor in the Department of English at St. John's University in New York City. Her research and teaching interests include Chaucer, gender, and new economic criticism.

Michael Carden is a research coordinator at the Center for the Study of Hepatitis C at Weill Medical College of Cornell University.

Central and Eastern Europe Harm Reduction Network is a regional network with a mission to support, develop, and advocate for harm reduction approaches in the field of drugs, HIV/AIDS, public health, and social exclusion by following the principles of humanism, tolerance, partnership, and respect for human rights and freedoms.

Melinda Chateauvert teaches African American studies and public policy at the University of Maryland. She is also a founder of the Woodhull Freedom Foundation, a nonprofit human rights advocacy organization working for sexual freedom, and a writer whose work first appeared in the landmark volume, *Sex Work: Writings by Women in the Sex Industry* (1986).

Sora Chung is a graduate student at New York University's Wagner School of Public Service.

Jim Daems is a sessional instructor in the English Department at Simon Fraser University.

Eric Danville is the author of *The Complete Linda Lovelace*.

Catherine Davis is copy chief at *Spin* magazine.

Kevin De Ornellas is a lecturer at the University of Ulster in Northern Ireland.

Karen De Riso is writing an ethnography of brothels.

Carlos Ulises Decena is an assistant professor in the departments of Women's and Gender Studies and Puerto Rican and Hispanic Caribbean Studies at Rutgers University.

Cecily Devereux is an associate professor in the Department of English at the University of Alberta and specializes in issues of gender and imperialism from the late 1880s to World War II and in Canadian women's writing.

Kinsey Alden Dinan is an independent researcher and consultant on the issue of trafficking in women, and particularly migrant women's experiences in Asia and related international human rights standards. As a researcher for Human Rights Watch, she wrote *Owed Justice: Thai Women Trafficked into Debt Bondage in Japan* and has participated in a range of advocacy efforts, including lobbying delegates at the negotiations for the United Nations Protocol on Trafficking.

Jo Doezema first became active in the sex workers' rights movement through her work with the Red Thread in Amsterdam. She is a former sex worker and holds a doctorate from the Institute for Development Studies. She was an inaugural board member of the Network of Sex Work Projects and a co-editor of *Global Sex Workers*.

Pamela Donovan is an assistant professor of sociology and criminal justice at Bloomsburg University, Pennsylvania. She is the author of *No Way of Knowing: Crime, Urban Legends, and the Internet* (2004).

Robert P. Dunn, a professor of English at La Sierra University in Riverside, California, teaches the English Bible as literature.

Jeffrey Escoffier writes on sexuality, lesbian and gay politics, and dance. His most recent book is *Sexual Revolution*, an anthology of writings from the 1960s and 70s on the sexual revolution. He is also the author of *American Homo: Perversity and Community* (1998).

Janelle Fawkes is a former president of the Scarlet Alliance, the Australian sex workers' organization.

Alex Feerst is a visiting assistant professor in the English Department at Macalester College.

Kathryn Ferguson is a doctoral candidate in history and English at LaTrobe University.

Shawna Ferris is a doctoral candidate in Canadian literature and cultural studies at McMaster University.

LaSara Firefox's first book, *Sexy Witch*, was published in 2005.

Gisela Fosado works at the Margaret Mead Film and Video Festival in New York City.

Anne Marie Fowler is an online adjunct professor for Keiser College, where she teaches English and American literature.

Katherine Frank is a Social Science Research Council Sexuality Research Postdoctoral Fellow in the Department of Sociology at the University of Wisconsin, Madison, and a faculty associate at the College of the Atlantic in Bar Harbor, Maine. She has written on the sex industry, masculinity, pornography, feminism, eating disorders, and swinging and is the author of *G-Strings and Sympathy: Strip Club Regulars and Male Desire* (2002).

John J. Gaines is a Ph.D. student at Texas Tech University in Lubbock. His primary research interests are the American Civil War, 19th-century America, and gender issues.

Tom Garretson is a writer, music producer, and music-industry professional.

Alexandra Gerber is a graduate student in the Sociology Department at the University of Michigan. Her research interests include social movements and political activism among sex workers in both the United States and Eastern Europe.

Kate Gilhuly is an assistant professor of classical studies at Wellesley College. She has written articles about Lucian's *Dialogues of the Courtesans*.

Roger Giner-Sorolla is a lecturer in the Department of Psychology at the University of Kent in Canterbury, England. His research covers the role of emotions in attitudes, self-control, and moral judgment. He is a member of the Centre for Study of Group Processes and the AHRC Research Centre for Law, Gender and Sexuality.

Esther Godfrey is completing her Ph.D. at the University of Tennessee.

Angela Gosetti-Murrayjohn is an assistant professor of classics at the University of Mary Washington.

Heike Grundmann is a lecturer in English and comparative literature at the University of Munich.

Jennifer Gutbezahl works at Lesley University providing support to those developing educational programs in math and science.

W. Scott Haine teaches at the University of Maryland University College and in the San Mateo County Community College District. He is the author of *The World of the Paris Cafe: Sociability among the French Working Class, 1789–1914* (Johns Hopkins University Press, 1996), *The History of France* (Greenwood Press, 2000), and the forthcoming *The Culture and Customs of France* (Greenwood Press, 2006). He is the author of *The World of the Paris Cafe: Sociability among the French Working Class, 1789–1914*.

Geoff Hamilton is a Killam Postdoctoral Fellow at the University of British Columbia.

Lawrence Hammar is a senior research fellow at the Papua New Guinea Institute of Medical Research, where he conducts research on issues of reproductive health and sexual behavior.

Anne Hayes, a former documentary film editor, received a Ph.D. in Latin American History from City University of New York in 2004.

Marcy A. Hess is an assistant professor of Victorian studies at Valdosta State University. She has written on contagion theory, representations of prostitution in Victorian print culture, and early Victorian novels.

Jose A. Hidalgo is a psychiatrist at the Trauma Center at Justice Resource Institute, specializing in traumatic stress disorders. He is the director of Project REACH, providing crisis mental health services for victims of human trafficking.

Nels P. Highberg is an assistant professor of rhetoric, language, and culture at the University of Hartford, where he teaches courses in composition, argumentation, and gender studies.

John Holmstrom founded PUNK magazine in 1975, which was instrumental in the success of many New York City punk bands. Holmstrom has also produced work for bands The Ramones, Blondie, The Dandy Warhols, Murphy's Law, Meat Depressed, and Mykel Board and publications from Scholastic, *The Village Voice, High Times, Heavy Metal, Video Games* and many other magazines.

Karen Humphreys teaches French literature at Trinity College in Hartford, Connecticut. She has published articles on Barbey d'Aurevilly, Robert Desnos, and Valentine Penrose's *La Comtesse sanglante (The Bloody Countess).*

Jennifer Hunter is a freelance writer and editor and the author of *Rites of Pleasure: Sexuality in Wicca and NeoPaganism* (2004).

Avaren Ipsen is a Ph.D. candidate in biblical studies at the Graduate Theological Union in Berkeley.

Saul Isbister is a private sex worker and activist for sex workers' rights based in Sydney, Australia. He is a co-initiator of the Touching Base project as well as the project's media spokesperson and Webmaster.

Deborah Israel is an assistant professor of English at the University of Central Oklahoma.

Lisa Hartsell Jackson is a lecturer in the English Department at the University of North Texas.

Elizabeth K. Hopper, Ph.D. is a clinical psychologist at the Trauma Center at Justice Resource Institute in Boston and at Boston University School of Medicine. She is the associate director of Project REACH, a program that provides consultation and crisis mental health services for victims of human trafficking in the eastern United States.

Trudy Jacobsen is a research fellow at the Key Centre for Ethics, Law, Justice and Governance at Griffith University, Brisbane, and the author of *Beyond Apsara: Women, Time and Power in Cambodia* (2005).

H. Paul Jeffers is the author of *Diamond Jim Brady: Prince of the Gilded Age* and other biographies.

Elena Jeffreys is a sex-worker activist based in Australia.

Joe E. Jeffreys teaches courses in lesbian and gay performance studies at New York University.

Kerwin Kaye is the editor of *Male Lust: Pleasure, Power, and Transformation.*

Patrick J. Kearney is the author of *A History of Erotic Literatures* (1983) and several other works on erotic literature.

Eva Kernbauer is an art historian and critic living in Vienna, with research interests in contemporary and early modern art.

Hilary Kinnell is the coordinator of the United Kingdom Network of Sex Work Projects.

Cameron Kippen is a freelance writer and broadcaster.

Juline A. Koken is a Ph.D. student in social–personality psychology at the CUNY Graduate Center. Her research interests center around how sexually marginalized individuals, particularly sex workers and gay, lesbian, bisexual, and transgender persons, manage and resist the impact of stigma on their lives.

Kate Kramer is the deputy directory of the Center for 21st Century Studies at the University of Wisconsin at Milwaukee.

Lenore Kuo holds the Nancy's Chair in Women's Studies at Mt. St. Vincent University in Halifax, Nova Scotia, and is a professor at California State University at Fresno.

Emily Epstein Landau wrote her Yale Ph.D. dissertation, "'Spectacular Wickedness': New Orleans, Prostitution, and the Politics of Sex, 1897–1917," about Storyville, New Orleans' famous red light district.

Marie Lathers is Treuhaft Professor of Humanities and French at Case Western Reserve University. She specializes in 19th-century French literature and art.

Michelle A. Laughran is an associate professor of history at Saint Joseph's College of Maine.

Nomi Levenkron works at the Hotline for Migrant Workers in Tel Aviv, Israel.

Antonia Levy is an adjunct lecturer in sociology and labor studies at Queens College, New York. Her work focuses on social movements, political sociology, gender and society, sexuality, and urban sociology.

Dina A. Ligaga is a doctoral candidate in the Department of African Literature at the University of the Witwatersrand, South Africa.

Mary Linehan is a visiting associate professor at the College of Wooster and teaches courses on gender, sexuality, politics, and prostitution.

Bebe Loff is head of Human Rights and Bioethics in the Department of Epidemiology and Preventive Medicine at Monash University in Australia.

Paulo Henrique Longo, who died in 2004, was a cofounder of the Network of Sex Work Projects and coauthor of *Making Sex Work Safe* with Cheryl Overs.

Ana Lopes is the founder of the International Union of Sex Workers and a key figure in the process of official unionization of sex workers in the United Kingdom.

Tonette B. Lopez is a staunch advocate against discrimination against sexual minorities in the Philippines and founder of the first human rights nongovernmental organization in Asia, GAHUM-Philippines and Advocates of Sexuality's Discrimination.

Alexandra Lutnick is a sex worker, research coordinator for St. James Infirmary, and staff research associate for the University of California–San Francisco. She coordinates the St. SWEAT project, a multilevel study that aims to identify the ways in which social capital impacts the health of female sex workers in San Francisco.

Jaimy M. Mann is a doctoral fellow at the University of Florida Department of English.

Maria Markantonatou is RTN Fellow on the faculty of sociology at Humboldt University in Berlin.

Melissa Ellis Martin is a doctoral candidate at the University of Washington. She is researching the prostitution and the traffic in women and children in fin-de-siécle Austria-Hungary.

Shelley Martin is a Ph.D. student in the Department of English, specializing in women's studies, at the University of Louisiana at Lafayette.

Laura McClure is the Jane Ellen Harrison Professor of Classics at the University of Wisconsin–Madison. Her most recent book is *Courtesans at Table: Gender and Literary Culture in Athenaeus* (2003).

Jill McCracken is a doctoral candidate in rhetoric at the University of Arizona.

Thomas A. J. McGinn teaches Classics at Vanderbilt University.

Angus McIntyre is a writer, translator and photographer who lives in New York City.

Maria Mikolchak is an associate professor at St. Cloud State University.

Mireille Miller-Young is a postdoctoral researcher at the University of California Santa Barbara. Her work concerns women of color, sex workers in the pornography industry, and issues of race and sexuality in visual media.

Rohini Mokashi-Punekar is an assistant professor in the Department of Humanities and Social Sciences at the Indian Institute of Technology, Guwahati, India.

Sherry Monahan is the author of *The Wicked West, Taste of Tombstone,* and *Pikes Peak: Adventurers, Communities & Lifestyles.*

Heather Montgomery is a lecturer in childhood studies at the Open University. She has written extensively about child prostitution in Thailand and is the author of *Modern Babylon?: Prostituting Children in Thailand* (2001).

Ananya Mukherjea is an assistant professor in women's studies and sociology at the City University of New York, College of Staten Island. Her research compares social organizing done in response to HIV/AIDS in Kolkata, India, and New York City.

Alison Murray is the author of *Pink Fits: Sex, Subcultures and Discourses in the Asia-Pacific* and *No Money, No Honey: A Study of Street Traders and Prostitutes in Jakarta.* She is currently working as Scarlet Alliance's Papua New Guinea project officer.

Lorraine Nencel is an anthropologist in the Department of Social Research Methodology at the Vrije Universiteit in Amsterdam. Her research interests involve issues of sexuality, gender, and identity.

Thomas Nesbit is a visiting professor in the Department of English and American Studies at Charles University in Prague, Czech Republic.

Caryn E. Neumann is a lecturer and doctoral candidate in U.S. women's history at Ohio State University. She is a former managing editor of the *Journal of Women's History.*

Kathryn Norberg is an associate professor of history at the University of California at Los Angeles.

Jesse Norris is a Ph.D student in the Department of Sociology at the University of Wisconsin–Madison.

Hannington Ochwada is a doctoral student in the Department of History at Indiana University, Bloomington.

Jaime Ramon Olivares is a professor of American history at Houston Community College–Central.

Debbie Clare Olson is a doctoral student in film and critical theory at Oklahoma State University.

David L. Orvis is a doctoral candidate in English literature at the University of Arizona.

Cheryl Overs cofounded the Australian sex workers organization the Scarlet Alliance in the mid-1980s. In 1991 she cofounded the International Network of Sex Work Projects with her late husband Paulo Longo and was coordinator of the NSWP from 1992 to 2000. She is Senior Programme Officer for Focused Prevention at the International HIV/AIDS Alliance based in the United Kingdom.

Kathryn Parker is a graduate student studying 18th-century Gothic romanticism, erotica, and feminist psychoanalytic theory in the English and Comparative Literature departments at Washington University, St. Louis.

Gail Pheterson is the author of *The Prostitution Prism* (1996) and the editor of *A Vindication of the Rights of Whores* (1989).

Chloé Pirson is an art historian and researcher at Université libre de Bruxelles, Belgium, and also works for the Medicine Museum of Brussels.

Randall Platt writes fiction for adults and young adults. Several of Platt's books have been nationally recognized, won awards and/or have been optioned for film. Platt has created *Slangmaster,* an interactive and searchable dictionary of slang.

Richard Porton has taught at New York University, Hunter College, and the College of Staten Island (CUNY) and is an editor at *Cineaste* magazine.

Victoria E. Price is a lecturer in the Department of Theatre, Film and Television Studies at the University of Glasgow.

Irwin Primer is retired from the English Department of Rutgers University's Newark campus. His most recent work is a new edition of Bernard Mandeville's 1720 *A Modest Defence of Publick Stews*.

Kirsten Pullen is an assistant professor of English at the University of Calgary. She has published essays on online fan activity, burlesque history, Zsa Zsa Gabor, and many prostitutes and performers.

Tracy Quan is the author of *Diary of a Married Call Girl: A Nancy Chan Novel* and *Diary of a Manhattan Call Girl.*

Michelle K. Rhoades teaches history at Wabash College.

Althea E. Rhodes is an assistant professor of English/rhetoric at the University of Arkansas, Ft. Smith.

Anita R. Rose teaches English at Converse College in Spartanburg, South Carolina.

Tracey S. Rosenberg is completing doctoral work at the University of Edinburgh.

Virginia Rounding is a sexual and social historian based in London and the author of *Grandes Horizontales: The Lives and Legends of Four Nineteenth-century Courtesans* (2003).

Carrie Runstedler is a Ph.D. candidate at the University of Saskatchewan.

Joelle Ruby Ryan is a doctoral candidate in the American Culture Studies Program at Bowling Green State University.

Margaret Sankey is an assistant professor of history at Minnesota State University at Moorhead.

Michelle M. Sauer is an associate professor of English and Coordinator of Gender Studies at Minot State University (ND) and the managing editor of *Medieval Feminist Forum.*

Eden C. Savino currently lives and works in Washington, DC. She has worked on the issue of female street prostitution at Hydra, e.V., a meeting place and counseling center for prostitutes in Berlin, Germany.

Scarlet Alliance is the national organization of sex workers in Australia.

Shannon Schedlich-Day is a doctoral candidate in the History Department of Flinders University in Australia. She has written on women's history and art history.

Rebecca Schleifer is a researcher in the HIV/AIDS and Human Rights Program at Human Rights Watch.

John Scott is a lecturer in sociology at the University of New England, NSW, Australia. He has written extensively on female and male sex workers.

Meena Saraswati Seshu is the General Secretary of SANGRAM, Sangli, in India.

Jeff Shantz teaches in the Department of Sociology at York University in Toronto, Canada.

Benjamin Shepard is the author/co-editor of two books: *White Nights and Ascending Shadows: An Oral History of the San Francisco AIDS Epidemic* (1997) and *From ACT UP to the WTO: Urban Protest and Community Building in the Era of Globalilzation* (2002).

Lisa Shahriari is a doctoral candidate in Literature at the University of Essex. Her doctoral thesis "'In Her Nature or in Her Sex:' Virginia Woolf and the Politics of Difference" considers prostitution in Woolf's writing. Her research interests include feminist theory and modernism.

Laurie Shrage is a professor of philosophy at California Polytechnic University, Pomona.

Clarence R. Slavens teaches English and Drama at Indian Hills Community College in Ottumwa, Iowa.

Evgeny Steiner has taught art and cultural history in universities in Russia, Japan, Israel, and New York.

Thomas M. Steinfatt is a professor of communication at the University of Miami.

Karen K. Swope is a historical archaeologist.

Gulshan R. Taneja is a professor in the Department of English at R.L.A. College, University of Delhi, India.

Janet Tanke is the assistant director of the Feminist Press and is an adjunct instructor at Queensborough Community College.

Gayle Thomas has more 20 years of experience developing multiple social service programs for disenfranchised populations, with a primary focus on women. Her expertise is in program development, harm reduction, domestic violence, chemical health, sexual violence, prostitution, and work with dually diagnosed populations.

Lana Thompson is the author of *The Wandering Womb: A Cultural History of Outrageous Beliefs about Women*.

Subhash Thottiparambil works as a consultant for CARE in India. He has translated into Malayalam the Human Rights Watch report *Future Forsaken: Abuses Against Children Affected by HIV/AIDS in India* and Tracy Quan's *Diary of Manhattan Call Girl*.

Juhu Thukral is the director of the Sex Workers Project in New York City.

C. Tinker is a lecturer in French at Heriot-Watt University, Edinburgh.

Claudette L. Tolson is a doctoral candidate at Loyola University.

Benson Tong is an associate professor of History at Gallaudet University. He is the author of *Unsubmissive Women: Chinese Prostitutes in Nineteenth Century San Francisco*.

Shun-Chang Kevin Tsai is a doctoral candidate in the Department of Comparative Literature at Princeton University. He has written on gender, medieval Chinese fiction, Roman poetry, and translation studies.

Michael Uebel has taught at the University of Virginia and Georgetown University. He is the author of *Ecstatic Transformation* (2005).

Sharmain van Blommestein is a Ph.D. student at the University of Florida, Gainesville.

L. C. van de Pol is at the Free University of Berlin, Germany, and is affiliated with the Research Institute for History and Culture of the University of Utrecht, the Netherlands. She has written two books on early modern Dutch Prostitution.

Emily van der Meulen is a Ph.D. student in women's studies at York University in Toronto and is researching how prostitute organizing and activism affect policy development and legal reform.

Marieke van Doorninck is a lobbyist with La Strada International, a network to prevent trafficking in persons, in Central and Eastern Europe. She is a member of the board of the International Committee on the Rights of Sex workers in Europe.

T. J. Vaughan is a doctoral student in U.S. history at Northern Illinois University in DeKalb. His work focuses on the relationship between sex, race, and law in 19th-century Louisiana.

Salvador Vidal-Ortiz is an assistant professor of sociology at American University in Washington, DC.

Stéphanie Wahab is an associate professor of social work at Portland State University.

E. Alyn Warren III is an assistant professor in the Department of Media in the School of Media and Communication at National University.

Jo Weldon maintains the Web site www.gstringsforever.com.

Kip Wheeler is an assistant professor of English at Carson-Newman College.

Rachel Hays Williams is a Ph.D. candidate at the University of Washington,.

Laura Madeline Wiseman teaches in the Southwest.

Nathaniel D. Wood is a postdoctoral scholar of modern European history at the University of Nevada, Reno.

Cuncun Wu lectures in Chinese language and culture in the School of Languages, Cultures and Linguistics at the University of New England, Australia. She has written extensively on sexuality, eroticism, and literature in Chinese history.

Yusheng Yao teaches history at Rollins College.

David Yost is a graduate student in English at the University of Louisiana at Lafayette.

Wenxian Zhang is an associate professor and college archivist at Rollins College in Winter Park, Florida.

Zi Teng is a sex workers-concern organization in Hong Kong that promotes the human rights, labor rights and fair and equal treatment in the legal and judicial system for women in the sex industry.